Family in Transition

Family in Transition

**Rethinking Marriage,
Sexuality,
Child Rearing,
and Family Organization**

Third Edition

Arlene Skolnick
Jerome H. Skolnick
University of California, Berkeley

Little, Brown and Company
Boston Toronto

Library of Congress Catalog Card No. 79–89893

First Printing

Published simultaneously in Canada
by Little, Brown & Company (Canada) Limited

Printed in the United States of America

For the third time, for Michael and Alexander

Preface to Third Edition

The family has genuinely been in transition since the early 1970s, when we began work on the first edition of this book. This third edition contains a new and expanded introduction in which we review changes in the family over the last decade as well as controversies about how to interpret these changes. We have included a major section on couples, with new articles on love, divorce, divorce law, and remarriage. Where appropriate, we have reprinted new articles on old subjects and also kept some old favorites. Altogether, more than 70 percent of the articles are entirely new, reflecting a significant growth in quantity and quality of family scholarship. Our introductions have also been expanded and updated to reflect this growth. In addition, a complimentary test blank with test items for each selection is available to instructors who request it on their school letterhead.

Since the first edition of this book appeared, we have had many helpful conversations with colleagues, by now too numerous to single out. We have become increasingly indebted to the students and faculty who have used this book and helped shape its contents with their feedback and comments. As always, the Center for the Study of Law and Society and its staff—headed by Rod Watanabe—provided able and critical assistance when needed. We are especially grateful to Mary Lou Martin, whose professional library skills proved invaluable in surveying what has become a vast and nearly unmanageable field of scholarship. Tina Miller, Ingrid Barclay, and Diana Dupree pitched in and cheerfully typed sometimes illegible drafts. We are grateful, really.

Arlene Skolnick
Jerome H. Skolnick
Berkeley, May 15, 1979

A Note on the Photographs

The photographs on the cover of this book are by Helen Nestor, a photographer who lives in Berkeley. They are from a series entitled "New American Families," which portrays the wide range of family types in contemporary America, including traditional nuclear families, single parent families, families with stepparents, and other alternative family forms. These photographs are not only aesthetically evocative, but, in capturing a particular family at a particular time and place, they reveal an essential truth about families: there is no such reality as "The Family."

Contents

Family in Transition

Introduction:
Family in Transition

It is now almost a decade since we began work on the first edition of this book. Since that time, many aspects of family behavior and attitudes have changed dramatically. There is a major debate about whether the changes are for good or ill: Is the family dying, or alive and well, or alive and not well? All sides agree that a profound historical transformation is taking place. Even those who assert that the family is here to stay (Bane, 1976) describe today's family as quite different from what it was in the recent past.

Demographic patterns over the past decade and a half provide the most impressive evidence of change (Glick and Norton, 1977). A strong decline in the birth rate suggests that Americans now want and are having fewer children than at any time in our history. The 1960s and 1970s witnessed a remarkable rise in the divorce rate. The rate has levelled off but remains at the highest point in history. Approximately 40 percent of all marriages of young adults will end in divorce. Since 1975 over a million divorces a year have involved over 3 million men, women, and children annually. Since 1965 the annual number of first marriages has been declining.

The number of unmarried couples living together has also risen. Between 1960 and 1970, the number doubled, with most change occurring since 1977. By March 1977 about 2 million people were involved in such living arrangements (Glick and Norton, 1977). Although the proportion of unmarried adults in such arrangements is small, the younger generation is approaching the level of Sweden, where 12 percent of all couples live together informally (Trost, 1976). Attitudes towards unmarried cohabitation have changed also. No longer considered living in sin or confined to the very poor, it has become a socially acceptable way of life in middle-class circles, especially among educated and professional persons.

Change has taken place even within the traditional family structure: the conventional nuclear family consisting of the housewife-mother, breadwinner-father, and their children is now a statistical minority. Both married partners are apt to have outside jobs, even when young children are in the home.

The rise of the single person household marks another significant departure

1

from the past, when the unattached individual was likely to live with relatives or with an unrelated family. Recent census data reveal that almost 20 percent of American households now contain only one person. This population consists mainly of two age groups: young people who have not yet married, and the formerly married, mostly older people who have lost a spouse. Not only are unattached individuals more likely to live in nonfamily households, but there has been a marked increase in the population of young singles. Whether these young men and women will marry later or never remains to be seen.

In addition to census data, a variety of surveys also indicates important changes in attitudes. The avant-garde ideas of the 1960s concerning such matters as premarital sexuality, women's equality, and the value of self-realization have spread to the mainstream of the American population. For example, between 1964 and 1974, surveys of women's attitudes revealed a consistent trend away from tradition and towards greater similarity between men's and women's roles inside and outside the home (Mason, et al., 1976). In 1957, four-fifths of the respondents in one national survey thought that a man or woman who did not want to marry was sick, immoral, and selfish. By 1967, only one-fourth of respondents thought that choice was bad. Two-thirds were neutral, and 14 percent viewed the choice as good (ISR Newsletter, 1979).

The legal system provides another set of indicators of change in family life and values. Although the law has in the past lagged behind social reality and sometimes still does, some recent legal changes have advanced popular opinion. The 1973 Supreme Court decision that abortion is a woman's personal right and the recent decisions stating that women are entitled to abortions without the consent of their parents or spouses are the most dramatic—and controversial—examples.

Although abortion is the most publicized legal issue, other significant changes have occurred in family law. The new trend towards no-fault divorce is changing the legal rules concerning the legal dissolution of marriage. It is also, as Weitzman and Dixon observe in their article in chapter 7, bringing about fundamental changes in the definition of marriage and the relationships and responsibilities of husbands and wives to one another. Although it is still too early to judge the ultimate effects the new laws will have on marriage as an institution, it is clear that the laws codify a very different conception of marriage and divorce than had formerly existed.

Illegitimacy is still another area of family law showing marked change. The age-old distinction between babies born of married and unmarried parents is becoming blurred. The courts have greatly expanded inheritance rights of illegitimate children, and state governments are becoming increasingly unwilling to stigmatize children as bastards by requiring that birth certificates tell whether a child is legitimate or not. In 1979, the United States Supreme Court struck down a New York law that blocked fathers of children born out of wedlock from contesting their children's adoption. Thus, the ties between fathers and their children are increasingly recognized, regardless of whether a marriage has occurred.

Along the same lines, there is a growing trend for unwed mothers to keep their babies. While most of these mothers are teenagers and other women who "accidently" become pregnant, some represent a new social type: the well-educated, middle-class woman in her twenties or thirties, who may or may not want to marry but who does want to have a child. For this woman, unwed motherhood is not an accident but the result of conscious choice (Eiduson, 1979).

Finally, the decision of the American Psychiatric Association that homosexuality is not a mental illness, while not a legal change, is another indicator of shifting definitions of deviance and normality in sex and family matters. Homosexuality illustrates another important point: the increasing politicization of sex and family conduct. In the past, those who deviated from the mainstream rules of sex and family behavior tended to agree with, or at least not openly challenge, the prevailing definitions of their behavior as sick or immoral. The new politics of the family—with organized groups taking opposed positions on such subjects as abortion, women's roles, and homosexuality—also demonstrates a marked break with tradition.

Looking Backward

Taken alone, none of the particular changes we have described would amount to a transformation of the family. But taken together, the changes are striking. The intellectual climate was markedly different when we put together the first edition of *Family in Transition*. The title itself was something of a gamble. We felt that something was happening to family life, but our main companions in that view were the mass media, the counterculture dissidents of the sixties—the commune movement and others trying out alternative life styles—and the first waves of feminism and gay liberation. The professional literature of 1969 and 1970 (the writings of sociologists, psychologists, and other social scientists) showed little awareness that changes in sexuality, marriage, and parenthood were happening. More importantly, it seemed to deny that change was possible in family structure, the relations between the sexes, and parenthood. Along with the concept of the family, the male as the sole breadwinner, the dependent housewife, and premarital virginity were thought to be here to stay.

Most social scientists shared a particular set of assumptions about the nature of the family and its relation to society. One assumption was that human beings were equipped with a fixed set of psychological needs and tendencies, which were expressed in the family. An extreme version of this view was the statement by an anthropologist that the nuclear family (mother, father, and children) "is a biological phenomenon . . . as rooted in organs and physiological structures as insect societies" (La Barre, 1954, p. 104). Another assumption was that family stability was the basis of social order. Any changes in the basic structure of the family roles or in child rearing were assumed to be unworkable if not unthinkable.

The family in modern industrial society was portrayed as a streamlined, more highly evolved version of the universal family. The traditional or preindustrial family carried out many tasks. It was a workplace, a school, a hospital. According to Talcott Parsons and his followers, the family in modern society underwent structural differentiation or specialization. It transferred work and educational roles to other agencies and specialized in child rearing and emotional support. The modern family thus was no less important for having relinquished certain tasks; it was indispensable because it was now the only part of society to carry out such functions.

These ideas about the family have lost their credibility. As Glenn Elder recently observed, the study of the family and its relation to social change during the postwar era was "shaped more by simplistic abstract theory and ideological preferences" than by the detailed study of the realities of family life in particular times, places, and circumstances (Elder, 1978).

The family theories of the postwar era were descriptively correct insofar as they portrayed the ideal middle-class family patterns of a particular society at a particular historical period. But they went astray in elevating the status quo to the level of a timeless necessity. In addition, the theories could not embrace variations in family lives or stylistic change. Such family life styles as, for example, that of the working mother or the single parent family, could be seen only as deviant behavior. Similarly, social change in family life on a large scale, as in the rise of women's employment or of divorce, could be interpreted only as social disorder and the disintegration of the social system.

Still another flaw in the dominant sociological view was its neglect of major internal strains within the family, even when the family was presumably functioning as it was supposed to do. Paradoxically, these strains were devastatingly described by the very theorists who idealized the role of the family in modern society. Parsons, for example, noted that when home no longer functioned as an economic unit, women, children, and old people were placed in an ambiguous position. They became dependent on the male breadwinner and were cut off from society's major source of achievement and status.

Parsons saw women's roles as particularly difficult; being a housewife was not a real occupation. It was vaguely defined, highly demanding, yet not considered real work in a society which measures achievement by the size of one's paycheck. The combination of existing strains and the demystifying effects of the challenges to the family status quo seem to have provided, as Judith Blake points out, a classic set of conditions for social change (Blake, 1978, p. 11).

A Time of Troubles

The recent transformation would have been unsettling even if other social conditions had remained stable. But everything else was also changing quickly. Despite assassinations and turmoil in the streets, the sixties were an optimistic period. Both the dissident movements and the establishment agreed that progress was possible, that problems could be solved, and that today's children would live in a better world. Both sides believed in limitless economic growth.

No one foresaw that the late 1970s would dramatically reverse this optimism and the social and economic conditions which had sustained it. The seventies were a time of deepening malaise. Rather than hearing of limitless abundance and an end to scarcity and poverty, we heard of lowered expectations, survival, and lifeboat ethics. For the first time in history, Americans had to confront the possibility that their children and children's children might not lead better lives.

This malaise, arising from sources outside the family, seems to be mingling in strange and contradictory ways with the attitudinal and behavioral changes set in motion during the sixties. There is some evidence that people are turning inward toward home, family, and private life. Many of the dissident young people of the sixties are forming committed relationships, getting married, having children. College students of the 1970s, to a greater extent than those of the previous decade, expect family life and individual needs to take priority over careers as a way of retaining a feeling of self-worth, self-determination, and self-fulfillment (Gottlieb, 1974). People who think of themselves as critics of society no longer necessarily assume that they must also be critics of the family or of monogamy.

One of the surprising themes of the decade is in fact the celebration of family in the name of social criticism. A new domesticity of the left has emerged on the intellectual scene. For some, the defense of the family is a new way of fighting an old enemy—corporate capitalism. For others, marching under the banner of the family seems to be a means of advancing social policies that can no longer be justified in the name of the poor. Kenneth Keniston and the Carnegie Council on Children, for example, in their report *All Our Children* reflect this familistic trend. Their liberal policy analysis would increase government spending for families. Meanwhile, conservatives fall back on the family as a way of reducing the state's budgetary problems: If families would take care of the very young, the very old, the sick, and the mentally ill, there would be less need for day care, hospitals, and Social Security and public resources and agencies.

Some radical attacks on the modern world and its ways seem consonant with traditional conservative arguments. Historian Christopher Lasch (1978) argues that while the family once provided a haven of love and decency in a heartless world, it no longer does so. The family has been invaded by outside forces—advertising, the media, experts, and family professionals—and stripped of its functions and authority. Corporate capitalism, with its need for limitless consumption, has created a "culture of narcissism," in which nobody cares about anybody else.

While Lasch laments the passing of the strong, authoritarian father, Alice Rossi (1978) denounces the intrusion of technological society into the natural biological processes of motherhood. In a startling reversal of her earlier feminist writings, Rossi revives the idea of biologically based maternal instincts.

All of this ferment has made our task here more complicated. In the past we had to argue against the overly optimistic assumptions of the 1950s view that all was for the best in the best of all possible family and social worlds. Now, in the 1980s, it is necessary to deal with pessimism of the 1970s. In its most extreme form this pessimism turns the notion of progress upside down and replaces it with a fierce nostalgia. The past is portrayed as a time of strong and stable families, while the present is interpreted as a nightmarish wasteland with hardly a single redeeming virtue. Reality of course lies somewhere in between; change does not always mean progress, but it does not always mean social disorganization either.

The State of the Contemporary Family

What sense *can* be made of the current changes in family life? The various statistics we quoted earlier can and are being interpreted to show that the family is either thriving or falling apart. Falling birthrates can be taken to mean that people are too selfish to want to have any or many children. Or they can mean that people are no longer having children by accident, without thought, or because of social pressure but because they truly want children. High divorce rates can signify that marriage is an institution on the rocks or is considered so important that people will no longer put up with the kinds of dissatisfactions and empty-shell marriages previous generations tolerated. High rates of remarriage could mean that people are giving up not on marriage but on unsatisfactory relationships. Or they can be thought to mean that the strain of living in a capitalistic society drives people into marriage but makes marriage difficult to sustain.

Is the rise in illegitimacy a sign of moral breakdown? Or does it simply reflect a different, more enlightened set of moral norms, reflecting a society no longer eager to punish unmarried mothers or to damage a child's life chances because of the circumstances of its birth?

One's conclusions about the current state of the family often derive from deeper values and assumptions one holds in the first place about the definition and role of the family in society. We noted earlier that the family theories of the postwar era were largely discredited within sociology itself (Blake, 1978; Elder, 1978). Yet many of the assumptions of those theories continue to influence discussions of the family in both popular and scholarly writings. Let us look in more detail at these persistent assumptions.

1. The Assumption of the Universal Nuclear Family

To say that the family is the same everywhere is in some sense true. But the differences are more interesting, just as a portrait of an individual is interesting because of the person's uniqueness rather than because faces usually have eyes, ears, and a mouth. Families possess even more dissimilar traits than do faces. They vary in organization, membership, life cycles, emotional environments, ideologies, social and kin networks, and economic and other functions. Although anthropologists have tried to come up with a single definition of family that would hold across time and place, they generally have concluded that doing so is not useful (Geertz, 1965; Stephens, 1963).

The idea of the universal nuclear family is based on biology: A woman and a man must unite sexually to produce a child. But no social kinship ties or living arrangements flow inevitably from biological union. Indeed, the definition of marriage is not the same across cultures. Although some cultures have weddings and notions of monogamy and permanence, many cultures lack one or more of these attributes. In some cultures, the majority of people mate and have children without legal marriage and often without living together. In other societies, husbands, wives, and children do not live together under the same roof.

The husband is by no means a universal family breadwinner. Wives raise their own crops in many cultures and are partially or wholly self-supporting (Stephens, 1963, p. 15). In the United States a father is culturally defined as the biological creator of a child, its provider and legal guardian, and the husband of the child's mother. Among some peoples, however, the identity of the biological father is irrelevant; the child belongs to the husband of its mother who is said to experience all the emotions of fatherhood. Our concept of fatherhood thus is not universal.

In our own society, the assumption of universality has usually defined what is normal and natural both for research and therapy and has subtly influenced our thinking to regard deviations from the nuclear family as sick or perverse or immoral. As Suzanne Keller points out in chapter 10:

> The fallacy of universality has done students of behavior a great disservice. By leading us to seek and hence to find a single pattern, it has blinded us to historical precedents for multiple legitimate family arrangements. (Keller, 1971)

An example of this disservice is the treatment of illegitimacy. For decades. the so-called principle of legitimacy, set forth by Malinowski (1930), was taken as evidence for the universality of the nuclear family. The principle stated that in every society a child must have a socially recognized father to give the child a status in the community. Malinowski's principle naturally leads to the assumption that illegitimacy is a sign of social breakdown.

Although the principle has been usually treated by social scientists as if it were a natural law, in fact it is based on certain prior assumptions about society (Goode, 1960; Blake, 1978). Chiefly, it assumes that children inherit their status from their father or from family origin rather than achieve it themselves. The traditional societies that anthropologists study are of course societies that do ascribe status in this way. Modern, democratic societies, such as the United States, are based, in theory at least, on achievement; a child's future is not supposed to be determined solely by who its father happens to be. The Malinowski principle, however compelling in understanding traditional societies, hence has decreasing relevance for modern ones. Current legal changes which blur the distinction between legitimate and illegitimate births may be seen as a way of bringing social practice in line with national ideals.

2. The Assumption of Family Harmony

Every marriage, as Jessie Bernard has pointed out, contains two marriages: the husband's and the wife's. Similarly, every family contains as many families as family members. Family members with differing perspectives may find themselves in conflict, occasionally in bitter conflict. Outside intervention is sometimes necessary to protect the weaker from the stronger. Those who romanticize the family as a haven of nurture are curiously silent on the problem of child abuse or other kinds of family violence.

To question the idea of the happy family is not to say that love and joy are not found in family life or that many people do not find their deepest satisfactions in their families. Rather, the happy family assumption omits important, if unpleasant, aspects of family life. Western society has not always assumed such a sentimental model of the family. From the Bible to the fairy tale, from Sophocles to Shakespeare to Eugene O'Neill to the soap opera, there is a tragic tradition portraying the family as a high-voltage, emotional setting, charged with love and hate, tenderness and spite, even incest and murder.

There is also a low comedy tradition. George Orwell once pointed out that the world of henpecked husbands and tyrannical mothers-in-law is as much a part of the Western cultural heritage as Greek drama. Although the comic tradition tends to portray men's discontents rather than women's, it scarcely views the family as a setting for ideal happiness.

Nor have social theorists always portrayed the family as harmoniously fulfilling the needs of its members and society. Around the turn of the century, the founders of sociology took for granted that conflict was a basic part of social life and that individuals, classes, and social institutions would struggle to promote their own interests and values. Freud and Simmel were among the leading conflict theorists of the family. They argued that intimate relations inevitably involve antagonism as well as love. This mixture of strong positive and negative feelings sets close relationships apart from less intimate ones.

In recent years, family scholars in a number of areas have been reviving these older ideas about the family. Some scholars have even been studying such family violence as child abuse and wife beating to understand better the realistic strains of family life. Long-known facts about family violence have not until recently been incorporated into a general analysis of the family. More policemen are killed and injured dealing with family fights than those dealing with any other kind of situation; of all the relationships between murderers and their victims the family relationship is most common (Steinmetz and Straus, 1974). Recent studies of family violence reveal that it is much more widespread than had been assumed, cannot easily be attributed to mental illness, and is not confined to the lower classes. Family violence seems to be a product of psychological tensions and external stresses which can affect all families at all social levels.

The study of family interaction has also undermined the traditional image of the happy, harmonious family. About two decades ago, researchers and therapists began to bring mental patients and their families together to watch how they behaved with one another. Was there something about family interaction that could explain the behavior of disturbed offspring? Oddly, whole family groups had not been systematically studied before.

At first, the family interactions were interpreted as pathogenic: a parent expressing affection in words but showing nonverbal hostility, alliances being made between different family members, family having secrets, one family member being singled out as a scapegoat to be blamed for the family's troubles, parents caring for children only as reflections of themselves, parents making belittling and sarcastic statements to children. As more and more families began to be studied, such patterns were found in many families, not just in those families with a schizophrenic child. As comparisons were made, it became harder to perceive differences between normal families and those with mentally ill offspring. Although family processes discovered by this line of research did not teach us much about the causes of mental illness, they made an important discovery about family life: So-called normal families can often be, in the words of one study, "difficult environments for interaction."

3. The Assumption of Parental Determinism

Throughout American history the family has been seen as the basis of social order and stability. Through reproduction and socialization, the family presumably guarantees the continuation of society through time. Traditionally, theories of socialization have taken either of two perspectives. In the first—social molding—the child is likened to a blank slate or lump of clay, waiting to be shaped by the environment. In the second—animal taming—the infant is a wild beast, whose antisocial instincts need to be tamed by parents.

Despite their differences, both views of socialization have much in common. Both consider children as passive objects and assign an all-powerful, Pygmalion-like role to parents. Both view the child's later life as a reenactment of early experience. Both view conformity to social norms as the outcome of successful socialization. Both tend to blame deviance of any kind (mental illness, crime, drug use) on the family. Finally, both share a view of socialization as a precarious enterprise, with failure and unhappiness the likely result of any parental mistake.

Although the belief that early family experience is the most powerful influence in a child's life is widely shared by social scientists and the public, it is not well supported by evidence and theory. There are serious flaws in two of its underlying assumptions: the assumption of the passive child and the assumption that parents independently exert influence in a virtual vacuum.

The model of the passive child is no longer tenable. Recent empirical work in human development shows that children come into the world with unique temperamental and other characteristics, and children shape parents as much as parents shape children. Further, thanks to the monumental work of Piaget in intellectual development and of Chomsky in language development, we know that the child's mind is not an empty vessel or a blank state to be filled by parental instruction. Children are active agents in the construction of knowledge about the world. Even behavioristic—stimulus-response—psychologists recognize the importance of cognitive factors and the child's own activity in the learning process.

The assumption of parental determinism is also not well founded. Parents are not simply independent agents who train children free of outside influence. An employed parent may behave quite differently than an unemployed one. Parents indirectly communicate to their children what to worry about—job loss, prejudice, and discrimination. The stresses or supports parents find in the neighborhood, the workplace, the economy, the political climate all influence child rearing.

Children also learn from the world around them. The parental determinism model has encouraged the peculiar belief that children know nothing about the world except what parents teach. Poor black children therefore are said to do badly in school because their parents fail to use the right techniques. It is easier to blame the parents than to change the neighborhood, school, or the economy or to assume that ghetto children's correct perception of their life chances has something to do with school performance.

Finally, other kinds of research show that early experience is not the all-powerful, irreversible kind of influence it has been thought to be. An unfortunate childhood does not necessarily lead to a despairing adulthood. Nor does a happy childhood guarantee a similarly sunny adulthood (McFarlane, 1964).

4. The Assumption of a Stable, Harmonious Past

Laments about the current decay of the family imply some earlier era when the family was more stable and harmonious than it is now. But unless we can agree what earlier time should be chosen as a baseline and what characteristics of the family should be selected for, it makes little sense to speak of family decline. Historians have not, in fact, located a golden age of the family gleaming at us from the depths of history (Demos, 1976).

Recent historical studies of family life also cast doubt on the reality of family tranquility. Historians have found that premarital sexuality, illegitimacy, generational conflict, and even infanticide can best be studied as a part of family life itself rather than as separate categories of deviation.

The division of families into a normal type and a pathological type is simply not borne out by historical evidence. For example, William Kessen, in his history of the field of child study, observes:

> Perhaps the most persistent single note in the history of the child is the reluctance of mothers to suckle their babies. The running war between the mother, who does not want to nurse, and the philosopher-psychologists, who insist she must, stretches over two thousand years. (Kessen, 1965, pp. 1–2)

The most shocking finding of the new historical studies is the prevalence of infanticide throughout European history. Infanticide has long been attributed to primitive peoples or assumed to be the desperate act of an unwed mother. It now appears that infanticide provided a major means of population control in all societies lacking reliable contraception, Europe included, and that it was practiced by families on legitimate children. Historians now believe that rises and falls in recorded birthrates may actually reflect variations in infanticide rates (Shorter, 1973).

David Hunt's (1970) study of child-rearing practices in early modern France found what would be considered by today's standards widespread mistreatment of children or, as he puts it, a "breakdown in parental care," although his study was limited to upper-class families. Rather than being an instinctive trait, having tender feelings toward infants—the sense that a baby is a precious individual—seems to emerge only when infants have a decent chance of surviving and adults experience enough security to avoid feeling that children are competing with them in a struggle for survival. Throughout many centuries of European history, both of these conditions were lacking. In the allocation of scarce resources, European society, as one historian put it, preferred adults to children (Trexler, 1973, p. 110).

Even during more recent and prosperous historical times, the nostalgic image of a more stable and placid family turns out to be a myth. Death and birth, essentially uncontrollable and unpredictable, hovered constantly over every household, only about seventy years ago. It is hard to comprehend how profoundly family life has been affected by the reduction in mortality and spread of contraception during the past six or seven decades. Although infant and child mortality rates had begun to decline a century earlier, the average family could not assume it would see all its infants survive to middle or old age. Death struck most often at children. But adults with an average life expectancy of about fifty years (Ridley, 1972) would often die in the prime of their productive years. The widow and widower with young children were more familiar figures on the social landscape than the divorced person is today.

To put it another way, it has been only during the twentieth century that a majority of people could expect to live out a normal family cycle: leaving home, marrying, having children, and surviving to age fifty with one's spouse still alive. Before 1900, only forty percent of the female population experienced this life cycle. The majority either died before they got married, never married, died before childbirth, or were widowed while their children were still young (Uhlenberg, 1974).

Contrary to the myth of the three generation family in past time, grandparents are also a twentieth century phenomenon (Hareven, 1978). In the past, when people lived shorter lives, they married later. The lives of parents and children thus had fewer years in which to overlap. As a result of these trends, there is for the first time in history a significant number of families with four generations alive at the same time.

A Heritage of Family Crisis

Our ancestors not only experienced family instability, they worried about the shakiness of the family as an institution. The idea that the family is falling apart is not really new. In fact, if we use a deep enough historical perspective, we see that the postwar era with its optimistic view of family life was the exception rather than the rule in American life. It was part of what one historian calls "the long amnesia" (Filene, 1975): the decades between the 1920s and the 1960s during which concerns were muted about family crises, women's roles, child rearing, and declining morals which had so agitated earlier generations. Anxiety about the family is an American tradition. Some historians trace it to the 1820s and the beginnings of industrialism. Others would date the sense of crisis even earlier, from the time the first settlers set foot on American soil. Immigration, the frontier, geographic and social mobility—the basic ingredients of the American experience—were all disruptive of parental authority and familial bonds.

Although concern about the family may have begun earlier, anxiety increased during the second quarter of the nineteenth century, and discussions took on an entirely new tone. There began to be a widespread sense of alarm about the decline of the family and of parental authority. A new self-consciousness about family life emerged; writings about the family dealt anxiously with the proper methods of child rearing and with women's special roles.

In contrast to earlier periods, people began to experience a split between public and private life: the world outside the home came to be seen as cold, ugly, and threatening, while the home became a cozy retreat. The home was idealized as a place of perfect love and harmony, while at the same time it was blamed as the cause of juvenile delinquency, crime, and mental illness. These conflicting themes have a decidedly contemporary ring.

The Rise of the Modern Family

These anxieties about the family that began in the 1820s were in response to the changed circumstances brought about by modernization, a shorthand way of referring to the massive growth of industrial capitalism that occurred in the nineteenth century. Modernization created dilemmas for family life which have not been resolved to this day. Although the changes and dilemmas to be discussed in the following paragraphs exist to some extent in all urbanized, advanced technological societies (i.e., in the Soviet Union and Eastern Europe as well as the United States), they may be found in their purest and most acute form under advanced capitalism, particularly in America.

Modernization implies not merely economic or technological change but also profound social and psychological change. It affects all aspects of life: the physical environment, the types of communities people live in, the way they view the world, the way they organize their daily lives, the meaning of work, the emotional quality of family relationships, plus the most private aspects of individual experience.

It is, of course, a great oversimplification to talk about the effects of modernization on what is known as the family. Living in an industrial economy has had a different impact on people in different social classes and ethnic groups. Poor and working-class families were and still are confronted with survival issues: the need for steady incomes, decent housing, and health care, the tensions that result from not being sure basic needs will be met. In order to ensure survival and because their values tend to be familistic rather than individualistic, working-class, immigrant, and poor families have usually depended on strong networks of kin and kinlike friendships. Middle-class, affluent families, freed from worries about basic subsistence, confront in more acute ways the social and psychological dilemmas brought on by modernization. They more often fit the model of the inwardly turned, emotionally intense, relatively isolated nuclear family.

Since the nineteenth century, when the effects of industrialism and urbanization began really to be felt, scholars have debated the impact of industrialization on the family. Many scholars and laymen were convinced that the family had outlived its usefulness. For the first time in history, men and women could find work and satisfy basic needs outside the bonds of blood or marriage. They felt, therefore, that the family would disintegrate.

The functional sociologists of the postwar era scoffed at predictions of family disintegration, As we saw earlier, they judged it to be more important than ever. The family nurtured and raised children and provided refuge for adults from the impersonality and competition of public and industrial life.

It now appears that both views were right and wrong. Those who thought that life in a mass society would undermine family life were correct. But they were wrong in assuming that most people would want to spend their lives as isolated individuals. Those who argued that the conditions of urban-industrial society create exceptional needs for nurturant, intimate relationships were also correct. But they never understood that those same conditions would make it hard for the family to fulfill such needs. Family ties have become more intense than they were in the past, and yet at the same time they have become more fragile.

Although most Western Europeans never lived in large extended-family households (Laslett and Wall, 1972), kinship ties exerted much stronger constraints over the individual before the modern era. Work and marriage were not matters of individual choice. A person's economic and marital destiny was determined by hereditary status, tradition, and economic necessity. Continuity of marriages and conformity to prescribed behavior, both within the family and outside it, were enforced by severe economic, familial, and community sanctions.

Another extremely important aspect of family life in past times was its embeddedness in the community. The home was not set off as a private place, a refuge to make up for deprivations in the world of work. There was no world of work outside the home, family members were fellow workers. Nor did the world outside one's front door consist of strangers or half-strangers, such as neighbors often are today. Rather, most people lived in a community of people known since childhood and with whom one would expect to have dealings for the rest of one's life. These outsiders could enter the household freely and were entitled, and even obligated, to intervene if relations between parents and children and husbands and wives were not as they should be. The most vivid example of community control over family life in preindustrial times was the practice known as *charivari:* community festivals in which people who violated family norms would be mocked and shamed (Shorter, 1975).

Modernization involves political as well as economic and social change. In English and American history, striking parallels exist between political ideals and the family, with the family being seen as a small version of the state—a little commonwealth. When the divine right of kings prevailed, the family ideal was likewise hierarchy and authority, with children and wives owing unquestioning obedience. When ideas about democracy and individual rights challenged the rule of kings, family ideologies also became more democratic (Stone, 1977). An ideology of liberation still accompanies replacement of the traditional pattern of work and family by the modern one. Modernization promises freedom of opportunity to find work that suits one's talents, freedom to marry for love and dissolve the marriage if it fails to provide happiness, and greater equality in the family between husband and wife and between parents and children (Goode, 1963).

In addition to promoting an ideology of individualism, modern technological societies change the inner experience of the self. The person living in an unchanging, traditional social world does not have to construct an identity to discover who he or she really is. "I am the son of this man, I came from that village, I work at that trade" would be enough to tell a man who he was.

There is still another source of the modern preoccupation with self. Much of daily life in modern society is spent in such roles as student, worker, customer, client. People begin to experience themselves as replaceable role players (Berger, Berger, and Kellner, 1973; Davis, 1973). As we become aware of a discrepancy between the role we are playing and our real and whole selves, we come to have a need for a private world, a set of relationships where we can express those aspects of ourselves that must be repressed in role demands of work and public behavior. Individualization and intimacy are, as Howard Gadlin puts it, "the Siamese twins of modernization" (1977).

Although the need for intimacy increases, the very conditions creating that need make it more difficult to satisfy. For example, affluence may buy privacy, but, like King Midas' touch, family privacy is a dream that turns up unexpected costs when fulfilled. The family's "major burden," writes Napier, "is its rootlessness, its aloneness with its tasks. Parents are somewhwere else; the business you can't trust; the neighbors you never see; and friends are a help, when you see them, but never enough. Sometimes, late at night, the parent wakes up and on a sea of silence hears the ship creak, feels it drift, fragile and solitary, with its cargo of lives" (1972, p. 540).

Family privacy needs illustrate only one example of how contradictory cultural instructions clash in the modern family. There is also the contradiction between a newer morality of enjoyment and self-fulfillment and an older morality of duty, responsibility, work, and self-denial. Fun morality is expressed by the advertising industry, credit cards, the buy-now-pay-later philosophy. The new morality can reunite families in activities that everyone can enjoy, but it also pulls family members apart in its emphasis on individual pursuit of enjoyment. Also, fun morality imposes a paradoxical demand: In the past, one could live up to demands of marriage and parenthood by doing one's duty. Today duty is not enough; we are also obliged to enjoy family life (Wolfenstein, 1954). As a result, pleasurable activities, including sex itself, become matters for evaluation and therefore of discontent.

Ironically, then, many of the difficulties besetting family life today are the consequences of some very positive changes: the decline of infant mortality and death rates in general, the fact that people are living longer, the use of birth control, the spread of mass education, the increasing control of the individual over basic life decisions (whether to marry, when to marry, whom to marry, whether or not to have children, and how many to have).

This very voluntariness can be disturbing. Freedom in modern family life is bought at the price of fragility and instability. Now the whole structure of family life comes to rest on a tenuous basis: the mutual feelings of two individuals. As Georg Simmel (1950, pp. 118–144) has shown, the couple or dyad is not only the most intimate of social relationships, it is also the most unstable. In traditional family systems, the inevitable tensions of marriage are contained by kin and community pressures, as well as by low expectations concerning the romance or happiness to be found in marriage.

Demographic and economic change has had a profound effect on women's roles. When death rates fall, as they do with modernization, women no longer have to have five or seven or nine children to make sure that two or three will survive to adulthood. Women today are living longer and having fewer children. After having children, the average woman can look forward to three or four decades without maternal responsibilities. Since traditional assumptions about women are based on the notion that women are constantly involved with pregnancy, child rearing, and related domestic concerns, the current ferment about women's roles may be seen as a way of bringing cultural attitudes in line with existing social realities.

As people live longer, they can stay married longer. Actually, the biggest change in twentieth century marriage is not the proportion of marriages disrupted through divorce, but the potential length of marriage and the number of years spent without children in the home. Census data suggest that the statistically average couple marrying now will spend only 18 percent of their married lives raising young children, compared with 54 percent a century ago (Bane, 1976). As a result, marriage is becoming less of a union between parents raising a brood of children and more of a personal relationship between two people.

To sum it up then, a knowledge of family history reveals that the solution to contemporary problems will not be found in some lost golden age. Families have always struggled with outside circumstances and inner conflict. Our current troubles inside and outside the family are genuine, but we should never forget that many of the most vexing issues confronting us as men and women, parents and children, derive from the very benefits of modernization—benefits too easily taken for granted or forgotten in the lately fashionable denunciation of modern times. There was no problem of the aged in the past, because most people never aged; they died before they got old. Nor was adolescence a difficult stage of the life cycle when children worked and education was a privilege of the rich. And when most people were hungry illiterates, only aristocrats could worry about sexual satisfaction and self-fulfillment. Modernization surely brings trouble in its wake, but how many would, on balance, really want to trade the troubles of our own era for the ills of earlier times?

References

Bane, M. J. 1976. *Here to Stay*. New York: Basic Books.

Berger, P.; Berger, B.; and Kellner, H. 1973. *The Homeless Mind: Modernization and Consciousness*. New York: Random House.

Blake, J. "Structural Differentation and the Family: A Quiet Revolution." Presentation at American Sociology Association, San Francisco, 1978.

Davis, M. S. 1973. *Intimate Relations*. New York: The Free Press.

Eiduson, B. "Single Motherhood as an Alternative Life Style." Paper presented at Society for Research in Child Development, San Francisco, 1979.

Elder, G. 1978. "Approaches to Social Change and the Family." In *Turning Points*, edited by J. Demos and S. S. Boocock, pp. 1–38. Supplement to *American Journal of Sociology*, vol. 84, 1978.

Filene, P. 1975. *Him, Her, Self: Sex Roles in Modern America*. New York: Mentor.

Gadlin, H. 1977. "Private Lives and Public Order." In *Close Relationships: Perspectives in the Meaning of Intimacy*. Amherst: University of Massachusetts Press, pp. 73–86.

Geertz, G. 1965. "The Impact of the Concept of Culture on the Concept of Man." *In New Views of the Nature of Man*, edited by J. R. Platt, pp. 93–118. Chicago: University of Chicago Press.

Glick, P. C.; Norton, A. J. 1977. "Marrying, Divorcing and Living Together in the United States Today." *Population Bulletin*, vol. 32, October, 1977.

Goode, W. J. 1960. "A Deviant Case: Illegitimacy in the Caribbean." *American Sociological Review,* vol. 25, pp. 21–30.

Goode, W. J. 1963. *World Revolution and Family Patterns.* New York: The Free Press.

Gottlieb, E. 1974. *Youth and the Meaning of Work.* U.S. Department of Labor. Washington, D. C.: Government Printing Office.

Hareven, T. K. 1978. "Family Time and Historical Time." In *The Family,* edited by A. S. Rasse, J. Kagan, and T. K. Hareven. New York: W. W. Norton and Company, pp. 57–70. (Reprint of *Daedalus.* Spring 1977.)

Hunt, D. 1970. *Parents and Children in History: The Psychology of Family Life in Early Modern France.* New York: Basic Books.

ISR Newsletter. 1979. Institute for Social Research. The University of Michigan. Winter 1979.

Kessen, E. W. 1965. *The Child.* New York: John Wiley.

LaBarre, W. 1954. *The Human Animal.* Chicago: University of Chicago Press.

Lasch, C. 1978. *Haven in a Heartless World.* New York: Basic Books.

Laslett, P., and Ware, R. (eds.). 1972. *Household and Family in Past Time.* Cambridge: Cambridge University Press.

Macfarlane, J. W. 1964. "Perspectives on Personality Consistency and Change from the Guidance Study." *Vita Humana,* vol. 7, pp. 115–126.

Malinowski, B. 1930. "Parenthood, the Basis of the Social Order." In *The New Generation,* Calverton and Schmalhousen. New York: Macauley Company, pp. 113–168.

Mason, K. O.; Czajka, J.; and Aiker, S. 1976. "Change in U.S. Women's Sex Role Attitudes, 1964–1974." *American Sociological Review,* 41, pp. 573–596.

Napier, A. 1972. Introduction to section four in *The Book of Family Therapy,* edited by A. Farber, M. Mendelsohn, and A. Napier. New York: Science House.

Rassi, A. S. 1978. "A Biosocial Perspective on Parenting." In *The Family,* edited by A. S. Rassi, J. Kagan, and T. K. Hareven. New York: W. W. Norton and Company. (Reprinted of *Daedalus,* Spring 1977.)

Ridley, J. C. 1972. "The Effects of Population Change on the Roles and Status of Women." In *Toward a Sociology of Women,* edited by S. Safillios-Rothschild. Lexington, Mass.: Xerox College Publishing, pp. 372–386.

Ryder, N. B. 1974. "The Family in Developed Countries." *Scientific American,* September, pp. 123–132.

Shorter, E. 1973. "Infanticide in the Past." *History of Childhood Quarterly,* Summer, pp. 178–180.

Simmel. G. 1950. *The Sociology of George Simmel,* edited by K. Wolff. New York: Free Press.

Steinmetz, D., and Straus, M. A. (eds.). 1974. *Violence in the Family.* New York: Dodd, Mead Co.

Stephens, W. N. 1963. *The Family in Cross-Cultural Perspective.* New York: World.

Stone, L. 1977. *The Family, Sex and Marriage in England, 1500–1800.* New York: Harper and Row.

Trost, J. 1976. "Married and Unmarried Cohabitation: The Case of Sweden with Some Comparison." In *Beyond the Nuclear Family Model,* edited by L. Lenew-Obew. Beverly Hills: California Sage.

Trexler, R. C. 1973. "Infanticide in Florence: New Sources and First Results." *History of Childhood Quarterly,* Summer, pp. 98–116.

Uhlenberg, P. 1974. "Cohort Variations in Family Life Cycle Experiences of U.S. Females." *J. Marriage and the Family,* pp. 284–292.

Wolfenstein, M. 1954. "Fun Morality: An Analysis of Recent American Child Training Literature." In *Childhood in Contemporary Cultures,* edited by M. Mead and M. Wolfenstein. Chicago: University of Chicago Press, pp. 168–178.

1

The Evolving Family

Introduction

Introduction

The study of the family does not fit neatly within the boundaries of any single scholarly field; genetics, physiology, archeology, history, anthropology, sociology, and psychology all touch upon it. Religious and ethical authorities claim a stake in the family. Also, troubled individuals and families generate therapeutic demands on family scholarship. In short, the study of the family is interdisciplinary, controversial, and necessary for the formulation of social policy and practices. Interdisciplinary subjects demand competence in more than one field. At a time when competent scholars find it difficult to master even one corner of a field—say the terminology of kinship, or the history of feminism, or the physiology of sexual arousal—intellectual demands on students of the family become vast. Although writers on the family confront many issues, their professional competence is usually limited. Thus a biologist may cite articles in psychology to support a position, without comprehending the tentativeness with which psychologists regard the researcher and his work. Similarly, a psychologist or sociologist may draw upon controversial biological studies. Professional competence means more than the ability to read technical journals; it includes informal knowledge—being "tuned in" to verbal understandings and evaluations of research validity. Usually a major theory or line of research is viewed more critically in its own field than outsiders realize.

Interdisciplinary subjects present other characteristic problems. Each discipline has its own assumptions and views of the world, which may not directly transfer into another field. For example, some biologists and physically oriented anthropologists analyze human affairs in terms of individual motives and instincts; for them, society is a shadowy presence, serving mainly as the setting for biologically motivated individual action. Many sociologists and cultural anthropologists, in contrast, perceive the individual as an actor playing a role written by culture and society; according to this view, the individual has no wholly autonomous thoughts and impulses. An important school of psychologists sees people neither as passive recipients of social pressures nor as creatures driven by powerful lusts, but as information processors trying to make sense of their environment. There is no easy way to reconcile such perspectives. Scientific paradigms—characteristic ways of looking at the world

—determine not only what answers will be found, but what questions will be asked. This fact has perhaps created special confusion in the study of the family.

"We speak of families," R. D. Laing has observed, "as though we know what families are. We identify, as families, networks of people who live together over time, who have ties of marriage or kinship to one another" (Laing 1971, p. 3). Yet as Laing observes further, the more one studies the emotional dynamics of groups presently called "families," the less clear it becomes how these differ from groups not designated "families." Further, contemporary family patterns and emotional dynamics may not appear in other places and times.

As an object of study, the family is thus plagued with a unique set of problems. There is the assumption that family life, so familiar a part of everyday experience, is easily understood. But familiarity may breed a sense of destiny—what we experience is transformed into the "natural":

> One difficulty in the psychological sciences lies in the familiarity of the phenomena with which they deal. A certain intellectual effort is required to see how such phenomena can pose serious problems or call for intricate explanatory theories. One is inclined to take them for granted as necessary or somehow "natural." (Chomsky 1968, p.21)

Only in the past decade or so have family scholars come to recognize how problematic a subject "the family" is and how hard it is to answer basic questions: Is there a definition of family that can apply to all places and times? What is the relationship between the family as an abstraction and particular families with their own idiosyncrasies and differences from each other? What "test" can we apply to distinguish between a family and a group that is not a family?

The selections in part 1 discuss both the concept of the family and the development of the family from prehistoric times through the contemporary United States. As one reads the selections, one observes the enormous variation that is possible in family structure and family organization through time and its accompanying economic and social conditions. Moreover, a careful examination of every family system reveals deeply embedded notions of propriety, health, legality, sex, and age role assignments. Only one thing seems constant through time and place with respect to relations among men, women, and children—everyone feels strongly about these. Moreover, prevailing family forms and norms tend to be idealized as the right and proper ones. Perhaps that is because, although the family is scarcely the building block of society claimed by early functional sociologists, it is without doubt the institution possessing the most emotional significance in society. If you believe in a woman's right to medical abortion, or if you don't, and if you have an egalitarian or subordinate vision of the roles of men, women, and children, you probably feel strongly about these—even more strongly than you feel about inflation and unemployment. The family grabs us where we live. Not only do we become excited about it, but is seems more than any other institution to generate controversy and moral indignation.

References

Chomsky, N. 1968. *Language and Mind.* New York: Harcourt, Brace and World.
Laing, R. D. 1971. *The Politics of the Family.* New York: Random House.

Chapter 1

Family Origins and Future

The Origin of the Family
Kathleen Gough

The trouble with the origin of the family is that no one really knows. Since Engels wrote *The Origin of the Family, Private Property and the State* in 1884, a great deal of new evidence has come in. Yet the gaps are still enormous. It is known *when* the family originated, although it was probably between 2 million and 100,000 years ago. It is not known whether it developed once or in separate times and places. It is not known whether some kind of embryonic family came before, with, or after the origin of language. Since language is the accepted criterion of humanness, this means that we do not even know whether our ancestors acquired the basics of family life before or after they were human. The chances are that language and the family developed together over a long period, but the evidence is sketchy.

Although the origin of the family is speculative, it is better to speculate with than without evidence. The evidence comes from three sources. One is the social and physical lives of nonhuman primates—especially the New and Old World monkeys and, still more, the great apes, humanity's closest relatives. The second source is the tools and home lives of hunters and gatherers of wild provender who have been studied in modern times.

Each of these sources is imperfect: monkeys and apes, because they are *not* prehuman ancestors, although they are our cousins; fossil hominids, because they left so little vestige of their social life; hunters and gatherers, because none of them has, in historic times, possessed a technology and society as primitive as those of early humans. All show the results of long endeavor in specialized, marginal environments. But together, these sources give valuable clues.

Defining the Family

To discuss the origin of something we must first decide what it is. I shall define the family as "a married couple or other group of adult kinsfolk who

From the *Journal of Marriage and the Family* (November 1971), pp. 760–770. Copyrighted 1971 by the National Council on Family Relations. Reprinted by permission.

cooperate economically and in the upbringing of children, and all or most of whom share a common dwelling."

This includes all forms of kin-based household. Some are extended families containing three generations of married brothers or sisters. Some are "grand-families" descended from a single pair of grandparents. Some are matrilineage households, in which brothers and sisters share a house with the sisters' children, and men merely visit their wives in other homes. Some are compound families, in which one man has several wives, or one woman, several husbands. Others are nuclear families composed of a father, mother, and children.

Some kind of family exists in all known human societies, although it is not found in every segment or class of all stratified, state societies. Greek and American slaves, for example, were prevented from forming legal families, and their social families were often disrupted by sale, forced labor, or sexual exploitation. Even so, the family was an ideal which all classes and most people attained when they could.

The family implies several other universals. (1) Rules forbid sexual relations and marriage between close relatives. Which relatives are forbidden varies, but all societies forbid mother-son mating, and most, father-daughter and brother-sister. Some societies allow sex relations but forbid marriage between certain degrees of kin. (2) The men and women of a family cooperate through a division of labor based on gender. Again, the sexual division of labor varies in rigidity and in the tasks performed. But in no human society to date is it wholly absent. Child care, household tasks, and crafts closely connected with the household tend to be done by women; war, hunting, and government, by men. (3) Marriage exists as a socially recognized, durable, although not neces-sarily lifelong relationship between individual men and women. From it springs social fatherhood, some kind of special bond between a man and the child of his wife, whether or not they are his own children physiologically. Even in polyandrous societies, where women have several husbands, or in matrilineal societies, where group membership and property pass through women, each child has one or more designated "fathers" with whom he has a special social, and often religious, relationship. This bond of *social* father-hood is recognized among people who do not know about the male role in procreation or where, for various reasons, it is not clear who the physiological father of a particular infant is. Social fatherhood seems to come from the division and interdependence of male and female tasks, especially in relation to children, rather than directly from physiological fatherhood, although in most societies, the social father of a child is usually presumed to be its physio-logical father as well. Contrary to the beliefs of some feminists, however, I think that in no human society do men, as a whole category, have *only* the role of insemination and *no* other social or economic role in relation to women and children. (4) Men in general have higher status and authority over the women of their families, although older women may have influence, even some authority, over junior men. The omnipresence of male authority, too, goes contrary to the belief of some feminists that in "matriarchal" societies, women were either completely equal to or had paramount authority over men, either in the home or in society at large.

It is true that in some matrilineal societies, such as the Hopi of Arizona or the Ashanti of Ghana, men exert little authority over their wives. In some, such as the Nayars of South India or the Minangkabau of Sumatra, men may even live separately from their wives and children, that is, in different families. In such societies, however, the fact is that women and children fall under greater or lesser authority from the women's kinsmen—their eldest brothers, mothers' brothers, or even their grown-up sons.

In matrilineal societies, where property, rank, office, and group membership are inherited through the female line, it is true that women tend to have greater independence than in patrilineal societies. This is especially so in matrilineal tribal societies where residence is matrilocal—that is, men come to live in the homes or villages of their wives. Even so, in all matrilineal societies for which adequate descriptions are available, the ultimate headship of households, lineages, and local groups is usually with men. (See Schneider and Gough, 1961, for common and variant features of matrilineal systems.)

There is in fact no true "matriarchal," as distinct from "matrilineal," society in existence or known from literature, and the chances are there never has been.* This does not mean that women and men have never had relations that were dignified and creative for both sexes, appropriate to the knowledge, skills, and technology of their times. Nor does it mean that the sexes cannot be equal in the future or that the sexual division of labor cannot be abolished. I believe that it can and must be. But it is not necessary to believe myths of a feminist Golden Age in order to plan for parity in the future.

Primate Societies

Within the primate order, humans are most closely related to the anthropoid apes (the African chimpanzee and gorilla and the Southeast Asian orang-utan and gibbon), and of these, to the chimpanzee and the gorilla. More distantly related are the Old, and then the New, World monkeys, and finally, the lemurs, tarsiers, and tree shrews.

All primates share characteristics without which the family could not have developed. The young are born relatively helpless. They suckle for several months or years and need prolonged care afterwards. Childhood is longer, the

*The Iroquois are often quoted as a "matriarchal" society, but in fact Morgan himself refers to "the absence of equality between the sexes" and notes that women were subordinate to men, ate after men, and that women (not men) were publicly whipped as punishment for adultery. Warleaders, tribal chiefs, and *sachems* (heads of matrilineal lineages) were men. Women did, however, have a large say in the government of the long-house or home of the matrilocal extended family, and women figured as tribal counsellors and religious officials, as well as in arranging marriages. (Lewis H. Morgan: The League of the *Ho-de-ne Sau-nee or Iroquois,* Human Relations Area Files, 1954) closer the species is to humans. Most monkeys reach puberty at about four to five and mature socially between about five and ten. Chimpanzees, by contrast, suckle for up to three years. Females reach puberty at seven to ten; males enter mature social and sexual relations as late as thirteen. The long childhood and maternal care produce close relations between children of the same mother who play together and help tend their juniors until they grow up.

Monkeys and apes, like humans, mate in all months of the year instead of in a rutting season. Unlike humans, however, female apes experience unusually strong sexual desire for a few days shortly before and during ovulation (the oestrus period) and have intensive sexual relations at that time. The males are attracted to the females by their scent or by brightly colored swellings in the sexual region. Oestrus mating appears to be especially pronounced in primate species more remote from humans. The apes and some monkeys carry on less intensive, month-round sexuality in addition to oestrus mating, approaching human patterns more closely. In humans, sexual desires and relations are regulated less by hormonal changes and more by mental images, emotions, cultural rules, and individual preferences.

Year-round (if not always month-round) sexuality means that males and females socialize more continuously among primates than among most other mammals. All primates form bands or troops composed of both sexes plus children. The numbers and proportions of the sexes vary, and in some species an individual, a mother with her young, or a subsidiary troop of male juveniles may travel temporarily alone. But in general, males and females socialize continually through mutual grooming* and playing as well as through frequent sex relations. Keeping close to the females, primate males play with their children and tend to protect both females and young from predators. A "division of labor" based on gender is thus already found in primate society between a female role of prolonged child care and a male role of defense. Males may also carry or take care of children briefly, and nonnursing females may fight. But a kind of generalized "fatherliness" appears in the protective role of adult males towards young, even in species where the sexes do not form long-term individual attachments.

Sexual Bonds Among Primates

Some nonhuman primates do have enduring sexual bonds and restrictions, superficially similar to those in some human societies. Among gibbons a single male and female live together with their young. The male drives off other males and the female, other females. When a juvenile reaches puberty it is thought to leave or be expelled by the parent of the same sex, and he eventually finds a mate elsewhere. Similar *de facto,* rudimentary "incest prohibitions" may have been passed on to humans from their prehuman ancestors and later

*Combing the hair and removing parasites with hands or teeth.

codified and elaborated through language, moral custom, and law. Whether this is so may become clearer when we know more about the mating patterns of the other great apes, especially of our closest relatives, the chimpanzees. Present evidence suggests that male chimpanzees do not mate with their mothers.

Orang-utans live in small, tree-dwelling groups like gibbons, but their forms are less regular. One or two mothers may wander alone with their young, mating at intervals with a male; or a male-female pair or several juvenile males may travel together.

Among mountain gorillas of Uganda, South Indian langurs, and hamadryas baboons of Ethiopia, a single, fully mature male mates with several females, especially in their oestrus periods. If younger adult males are present, the females may have occasional relations with them if the leader is tired or not looking.

Among East and South African baboons, rhesus macaques, and South American woolly monkeys, the troop is bigger, numbering up to two hundred. It contains a number of adult males and a much larger number of females. The males are strictly ranked in terms of dominance based on both physical strength and intelligence. The more dominant males copulate intensively with the females during the latter's oestrus periods. Toward the end of oestrus a female may briefly attach herself to a single dominant male. At other times she may have relations with any male of higher or lower rank provided that those of higher rank permit it.

Among some baboons and macaques the young males travel on the outskirts of the group and have little access to females. Some macaques expel from the troop a proportion of the young males, who then form "bachelor troops." Bachelors may later form new troops with young females.

Other primates are more thoroughly promiscuous, or rather indiscriminate, in mating. Chimpanzees and also South American howler monkeys live in loosely structured groups, again (as in most monkey and ape societies) with a preponderance of females. The mother-child unit is the only stable group. The sexes copulate almost at random and most intensively and indiscriminately during oestrus.

A number of well-known anthropologists have argued that various attitudes and customs often found in human societies are instinctual rather than culturally learned and come from our primate heritage. They include hierarchies of ranking among men, male political power over women, and the greater tendency of men to form friendships with one another, as opposed to women's tendencies to cling to a man. (See, for example, Morris, 1967; Fox, 1967).

I cannot accept these conclusions and think that they stem from the male chauvinism of our own society. A "scientific" argument which states that all such features of female inferiority are instinctive is obviously a powerful weapon in maintaining the traditional family with male dominance. But in fact, these features are *not* universal among nonhuman primates, including some of those most closely related to humans. Chimpanzees have a low degree of male dominance and male hierarchy and are sexually virtually indiscriminate. Gibbons have a kind of fidelity for both sexes and almost no male dominance or hierarchy. Howler monkeys are sexually indiscriminate and lack male hierarchies or dominance.

The fact is that among nonhuman primates male dominance and male hierarchies seem to be adaptations to particular environments, some of which did become genetically established through natural selection. Among humans, however, these features are present in variable degrees and are almost certainly learned, not inherited at all. Among nonhuman primates there are fairly general differences between those that live mainly in trees and those that live largely on the ground. The tree dwellers (for example gibbons, orang-utans, South American howler, and woolly monkeys) tend to have to defend themselves less against predators than do the ground dwellers (such as baboons, macaques, or gorillas). Where defense is important, males are much larger and stronger than females, exert dominance over females, and are strictly hierarchized and organized in relation to one another. Where defense is less important there is much less sexual dimorphism (difference in size between male and female), less or no male dominance, a less pronounced male hierarchy, and greater sexual indiscriminacy.

Comparatively speaking, humans have a rather small degree of sexual dimorphism, similar to chimpanzees. Chimpanzees live much in trees but also partly on the ground, in forest or semiforest habitats. They build individual nests to sleep in, sometimes on the ground but usually in trees. They flee into trees from danger. Chimpanzees go mainly on all fours, but sometimes on two feet, and can use and make simple tools. Males are dominant, but not very dominant, over females. The rank hierarchy among males is unstable, and males often move between groups, which vary in size from two to fifty individuals. Food is vegetarian, supplemented with worms, grubs, or occasional small animals. A mother and her young form the only stable unit. Sexual relations are largely indiscriminate, but nearby males defend young animals from danger. The chances are that our prehuman ancestors had a similar social life. Morgan and Engels were probably right in concluding that we came from a state of "original promiscuity" before we were fully human.

Human Evolution

Judging from the fossil record, apes ancestral to humans, gorillas, and chimpanzees roamed widely in Asia, Europe, and Africa some 12 to 28 million years ago. Toward the end of that period (the Miocene) one appears in North India and East Africa, Ramapithecus, who may be ancestral both to later hominids and to modern humans. His species were small like gibbons, walked upright on two feet, had human rather than ape cornerteeth, and therefore probably used hands rather than teeth to tear their food. From that time evolution toward humanness must have proceeded through various phases until the emergence of modern homo sapiens, about 70,000 years ago.

In the Miocene period before Ramapithecus appeared, there were several time spans in which, over large areas, the climate became dryer and subtropical forests dwindled or disappeared. A standard reconstruction of events, which I accept, is that groups of apes, probably in Africa, had to come down from the trees and adapt to terrestrial life. Through natural selection, probably over millions of years, they developed specialized feet for walking. Thus freed, the hands came to be used not only (as among apes) for grasping and tearing, but for regular carrying of objects such as weapons (which had hitherto been sporadic) or of infants (which had hitherto clung to their mothers' body hair).

The spread of indigestible grasses on the open savannahs may have encouraged, if it did not compel, the early ground dwellers to become active hunters rather than simply to forage for small, sick, or dead animals that came their way. Collective hunting and tool use involved group cooperation and helped foster the growth of language out of the call systems of apes. Language meant the use of symbols to refer to events not present. It allowed greatly increased foresight, memory, planning, and division of tasks—in short, the capacity for human thought.

With the change to hunting, group territories became much larger. Apes range only a few thousand feet daily; hunters, several miles. But because their infants were helpless, nursing women could hunt only small game close to home. This then produced the sexual division of labor on which the human family has since been founded. Women elaborated upon ape methods of child care and greatly expanded foraging, which in most areas remained the primary and most stable source of food. Men improved upon ape methods of fighting off other animals and of group protection in general. They adapted these methods to hunting, using weapons which for millennia remained the same for the chase as for human warfare.

Out of the sexual division of labor came, for the first time, home life as well as group cooperation. Female apes nest with and provide foraged food for their infants. But adult apes do not cooperate in food getting or nest building. They build new nests each night wherever they may happen to be. With the development of a hunting-gathering complex, it became necessary to have a G.H.Q., or home. Men could bring meat to this place for several days' supply. Women and children could meet men there after the day's hunting and could bring their vegetable produce for general consumption. Men, women, and children could build joint shelters, butcher meat, and treat skins for clothing.

Later, fire came into use for protection against wild animals, for lighting, and eventually for cooking. The hearth then provided the focus and symbol of home. With the development of cookery, some humans—chiefly women and perhaps some children and old men—came to spend more time preparing nutrition so that all people need spend less time in chewing and tearing their food. Meals—already less frequent because of the change to a carnivorous diet

—now became brief, periodic events instead of the long feeding sessions of apes.

The change to humanness brought two bodily changes that affected birth and child care. These were head size and width of the pelvis. Walking upright produced a narrower pelvis to hold the guts in position. Yet as language developed, brains and hence heads grew much bigger relative to body size. To compensate, humans are born at an earlier stage of growth than apes. They are helpless longer and require longer and more total care. This in turn caused early women to concentrate more on child care and less on defense than do female apes.

Language made possible not only a division and cooperation in labor but also all forms of tradition, rules, morality, and cultural learning. Rules banning sex relations among close kinfolk must have come very early. Precisely how or why they developed is unknown, but they had at least two useful functions. They helped to preserve order in the family as a cooperative unit by outlawing competition for mates. They also created bonds *between* families, or even between separate bands, and so provided a basis for wider cooperation in the struggle for livelihood and the expansion of knowledge.

It is not clear when all these changes took place. Climatic change with increased drought began regionally up to 28 million years ago. The divergence between prehuman and gorilla-chimpanzee stems had occurred in both Africa and India at least 12 million years ago. The prehuman stem led to the Australopithecenes of East and South Africa, about 1,750,000 years ago. These were pygmylike, two-footed, upright hominids with larger than ape brains, who made tools and probably hunted in savannah regions. It is unlikely that they knew the use of fire.

The first known use of fire is that of cave-dwelling hominids (Sinanthropus, a branch of the Pithecanthropines) at Choukoutien near Peking, some half a million years ago during the second ice age. Fire was used regularly in hearths, suggesting cookery, by the time of the Acheulean and Mousterian cultures of Neanderthal man in Europe, Africa, and Asia before, during, and after the third ice age, some 150,000 to 100,000 years ago. These people, too, were often cave dwellers and buried their dead ceremonially in caves. Cave dwelling by night as well as by day was probably, in fact, not safe for humans until fire came into use to drive away predators.

Most anthropologists conclude that home life, the family and language had developed by the time of Neanderthal man, who was closely similar and may have been ancestral to modern homo sapiens. At least two anthropologists, however, believe that the Australopithecenes already had language nearly 2 million years ago, while another thinks that language and incest prohibitions did not evolve until the time of homo sapiens some 70,000 to 50,000 years ago. (For the former view, see Hockett and Ascher, 1968; for the latter, Livingstone, 1969). I am myself inclined to think that family life built around tool use, the use of language, cookery, and a sexual division of labor must have been established sometime between about 500,000 and 200,000 years ago.

Hunters and Gatherers

Most of the hunting and gathering societies studied in the eighteenth to twentieth centuries had technologies similar to those that were widespread in the Mesolithic period, which occurred about 15,000 to 10,000 years ago, after the ice ages ended but before cultivation was invented and animals domesticated.

Modern hunters live in marginal forest, mountain, arctic, or desert environments where cultivation is impracticable. Although by no means "primeval," the hunters of recent times do offer clues to the types of family found during that 99 percent of human history before the agricultural revolution. They include the Eskimo, many Canadian and South American Indian groups, the forest BaMbuti (Pygmies) and the desert Bushmen of Southern Africa, the Kadar of South India, the Veddah of Ceylon, and the Andaman Islanders of the Indian Ocean. About 175 hunting and gathering cultures in Oceania, Asia, Africa, and America have been described in fair detail.

In spite of their varied environments, hunters share certain features of social life. They live in bands of about 20 to 200 people, the majority of bands having fewer than 50. Bands are divided into families, which may forage alone in some seasons. Hunters have simple but ingenious technologies. Bows and arrows, spears, needles, skin clothing, and temporary leaf or wood shelters are common. Most hunters do some fishing. The band forages and hunts in a large territory and usually moves camp often.

Social life is egalitarian. There is of course no state no organized government. Apart from religious shamans or magicians, the division of labor is based only on sex and age. Resources are owned communally; tools and personal possessions are freely exchanged. Everyone works who can. Band leadership goes to whichever man has the intelligence, courage, and foresight to command the respect of his fellows. Intelligent older women are also looked up to.

The household is the main unit of economic cooperation, with the men, women, and children dividing the labor and pooling their produce. In 97 percent of the 175 societies classified by G. P. Murdock, hunting is confined to men; in the other 3 percent it is chiefly a male pursuit. Gathering of wild plants, fruits, and nuts is women's work. In 60 percent of societies, only women gather, while in another 32 percent gathering is mainly feminine. Fishing is solely or mainly men's work in 93 percent of the hunting societies where it occurs.

For the rest, men monopolize fighting, although interband warfare is rare. Women tend children and shelters and usually do most of the cooking, processing, and storage of food. Women tend, also, to be foremost in the early household crafts such as basketry, leather work, the making of skin or bark clothing, and, in the more advanced hunting societies, pottery. (Considering that women probably *invented* all of these crafts, in addition to cookery, food storage, and preservation, agriculture, spinning, weaving, and perhaps even house construction, it is clear that women played quite as important roles as men in early cultural development.) Building dwellings and making tools and ornaments are variously divided between the sexes, while boat building is largely done by men. Girls help the women, and boys play at hunting or hunt small game until they reach puberty, when both take on the roles of adults. Where the environment makes it desirable, the men of a whole band or of some smaller cluster of households cooperate in hunting or fishing and divide their spoils. Women of nearby families often go gathering together.

Family composition varies among hunters as it does in other kinds of societies. About half or more of known hunting societies have nuclear families (father, mother, and children), with polygynous households (a man, two or more wives, and children) as occasional variants. Clearly, nuclear families are the most common among hunters, although hunters have a slightly higher proportion of polygynous families than do nonhunting societies.

About a third of hunting societies contain some stem-family households— that is, older parents live in together with one married child and grandchildren, while the other married children live in independent dwellings. A still smaller proportion live in large extended families containing several married brothers (or several married sisters), their spouses, and children. (For exact figures, see Murdock, 1957; Coult, 1965; and Murdock, 1967. In the last-named survey, out of 175 hunting societies, 47 percent had nuclear family households, 38 percent had stem families, and 14 percent had extended families.) Hunters have fewer extended and stem families than do nonhunting societies. These larger households become common with the rise of agriculture. They are especially found in large, preindustrial agrarian states such as ancient Greece, Rome, India, the Islamic empires, and China.

Hunting societies also have few households composed of a widow or divorcee and her children. This is understandable, for neither men nor women can survive long without the work and produce of the other sex, and marriage is the way to obtain them. That is why so often young men must show proof of hunting prowess and girls of cooking before they are allowed to marry.

The family, together with territorial grouping, provides the framework of society among hunters. Indeed, as Morgan and Engels clearly saw, kinship and territory are the foundations of all societies before the rise of the state. Not only hunting and gathering bands, but the larger and more complex tribes and chiefdoms of primitive cultivators and herders organize people through descent from common ancestors or through marriage ties between groups. Among hunters, things are simple. There is only the family, and beyond it the band. With the domestication of plants and animals, the economy becomes more productive. More people can live together. Tribes form, containing several thousand people loosely organized into large kin groups such as clans and lineages, each composed of a number of related families. With still further development of the productive forces the society throws up a central political leadership, together with craft specialization and trade, and so the chiefdom emerges. But this, too, is structured through ranked allegiances and marriage ties between kin groups.

Only with the rise of the state does class, independently of kinship, provide the basis for relations of production, distribution, and power. Even then, kin groups remain large in the agrarian state and kinship persists as the prime organizing principle within each class until the rise of capitalism. The reduction in significance of the family that we see today is the outgrowth of a decline in the importance of "familism" relative to other institutions, that began with the rise of the state but became speeded up with the development of capitalism and machine industry. In most modern socialist societies, the family is even less significant as an organizing principle. It is reasonable to suppose that in the future it will become minimal or may disappear, at least as a legally constituted unit for exclusive forms of sexual and economic cooperation and of child care.

Morgan and Engels (1942) thought that from a state of original promiscuity, early humans at first banned sex relations between the generations of parents and children but continued to allow them indiscriminately between brothers, sisters, and all kinds of cousins within the band. They called this the "consanguineal family." They thought that later, all mating within the family or some larger kin group became forbidden, but that there was a stage (the "punaluan") in which a group of sisters or other close kinswomen from one band were married jointly to a group of brothers or other close kinsmen from another. They thought that only later still, and especially with the domestication of plants and animals, did the "pairing family" develop in which each man was married to one or two women individually.

These writers drew their conclusions not from evidence of actual group-marriage among primitive peoples but from the kinship terms found today in certain tribal and chiefly societies. Some of these equate all kin of the same sex in the parents' generation, suggesting brother-sister marriage. Others equate the father's brothers with the father and the mother's sisters with the mother, suggesting the marriage of a group of brothers with a group of sisters.

Modern evidence does not bear out these conclusions about early society. All known hunters and gatherers live in families, not in communal sexual arrangements. Most hunters even live in nuclear families rather than in large extended kin groups. Mating is individualized, although one man may occasionally have two wives, or (very rarely) a woman may have two husbands. Economic life is built primarily around the division of labor and partnership between individual men and women. The hearths, caves, and other remains of Upper Palaeolithic hunters suggest that this was probably an early arrangement. We cannot say that Engels's sequences are completely ruled out for very early hominids—the evidence is simply not available. But it is hard to see what economic arrangements among hunters would give rise to group, rather than individual or pairing marriage arrangements, and this Engels does not explain.

Soviet anthropologists continued to believe in Morgan and Engels's early "stages" longer than did anthropologists in the West. Today, most Russian anthropologists admit the lack of evidence for "consanguineal" and "punal-uan" arrangements, but some still believe that a different kind of group marriage intervened between indiscriminate mating and the pairing family. Semyonov, for example, argues that in the stage of group marriage, mating was forbidden within the hunting band, but that the men of two neighboring bands had multiple, visiting sex relations with women of the opposite band (Semyonov, 1967).

While such an arrangement cannot be ruled out, it seems unlikely because many of the customs which Semyonov regards as "survivals" of such group marriage (for example, visiting husbands, matrilineage dwelling groups, widespread clans, multiple spouses for both sexes, men's and women's communal houses, and prohibitions of sexual intercourse inside the huts of the village) are actually found not so much among hunters as among horticultural tribes and even quite complex agricultural states. Whether or not such a stage of group marriage occurred in the earliest societies, there seems little doubt that pairing marriage (involving family households) came about with the development of elaborate methods of hunting, cooking, and the preparation of clothing and shelters—that is, with a fully fledged division of labor.

Even so, there *are* some senses in which mating among hunters has more of a group character than in archaic agrarian states or in capitalist society. Murdock's sample shows that sex relations before marriage are strictly prohibited in only 26 percent of hunting societies. In the rest, marriage is either arranged so early that premarital sex is unlikely, or (more usually) sex relations are permitted more or less freely before marriage.

With marriage, monogamy is the normal *practice* at any given time for most hunters, but it is not the normal *rule*. Only 19 percent in Murdock's survey prohibit plural unions. Where polygyny is found (79 percent) the most common type is for a man to marry two sisters or other closely related women of the same kin group—for example, the daughters of two sisters or of two brothers. When a woman dies it is common for a sister to replace her in the marriage, and when a man dies, for a brother to replace him.

Similarly, many hunting societies hold that the wives of brothers or other close kinsmen are in some senses wives of the group. They can be called on in emergencies or if one of them is ill. Again, many hunting societies have special times for sexual license between men and women of a local group who are not married to each other, such as the "lights out" games of Eskimo sharing a communal snow house. In other situations, an Eskimo wife will spend the night with a chance guest of her husband's. All parties expect this as normal hospitality. Finally, adultery, although often punished, tends to be common in hunting societies, and few if any of them forbid divorce or the remarriage of divorcees and widows.

The reason for all this seems to be that marriage and sexual restrictions are practical arrangements among hunters designed mainly to serve economic and survival needs. In these societies, some kind of rather stable pairing best accomplishes the division of labor and cooperation of men and women and the care of children. Beyond the immediate family, either a larger family group or the whole band has other, less intensive but important kinds of cooperative activities. Therefore, the husbands and wives of individuals within that group can be summoned to stand in for each other if need arises. In the case of Eskimo wife lending, the extreme climate and the need for lone wandering in search of game dictate high standards of hospitality. This evidently becomes extended to sexual sharing.

In the case of sororal polygyny or marriage to the dead wife's sister, it is natural that when two women fill the same role—either together or in sequence —they should be sisters, for sisters are more alike than other women. They are likely to care more for each other's children. The replacement of a dead spouse by a sister or a brother also preserves existing intergroup relations. For the rest, where the economic and survival bonds of marriage are not at stake, people can afford to be freely companionate and tolerant. Hence, premarital sexual freedom, seasonal group license, and a pragmatic approach to adultery.

Marriages among hunters are usually arranged by elders when a young couple are ready for adult responsibilities. But the couple know each other and usually have some choice. If the first marriage does not work, the second mate will almost certainly be self-selected. Both sexual and companionate love between individual men and women are known and are deeply experienced. With comparative freedom of mating, love is less often separated from or opposed to marriage than in archaic states or even than in some modern nations.

The Position of Women

Even in hunting societies it seems that women are always in some sense the "second sex," with greater or less subordination to men. This varies. Eskimo and Australian aboriginal women are far more subordinate than women among the Kadar, the Andamanese, or the Congo Pygmies—all forest people.

I suggest that women have greater power and independence among hunters when they are important food obtainers than when they are mainly processors of meat or other supplies provided by men. The former situation is likelier to exist in societies where hunting is small-scale and intensive than where it is extensive over a large terrain, and in societies where gathering is important by comparison with hunting.

In general in hunting societies, however, women are less subordinated in certain crucial respects than they are in most, if not all, of the archaic states, or even in some capitalist nations. These respects include men's ability to deny women sexuality or to force it upon them, to command or exploit their labor or to control their produce, to control or rob them of their children, to confine them physically and prevent their movement, to use them as objects in male transactions, to cramp their creativeness, or to withhold from them large areas of the society's knowledge and cultural attainments.

Especially lacking in hunting societies is the kind of male possessiveness and exclusiveness regarding women that leads to such situations as savage punishments or death for female adultery, the jealous guarding of female chastity and virginity, the denial of divorce to women, or the ban on a woman's remarriage after her husband's death.

For these reasons, I do not think we can speak, as some writers do, of a class division between men and women in hunting societies. True, men are more mobile than women and they lead in public affairs. But class society requires that one class control the means of production, dictate its use by the other classes, and expropriate the surplus. These conditions do not exist among hunters. Land and other resources are held communally, although women may monopolize certain gathering areas, and men, their hunting grounds. There is rank difference, role difference, and some difference respecting degrees of authority between the sexes, but there is reciprocity rather than domination or exploitation.

As Engels saw, the power of men to exploit women systematically springs from the existence of surplus wealth and, more directly, from the state, social stratification, and the control of property by men. With the rise of the state, because of their monopoly over weapons, and because freedom from child care allows them to enter specialized economic and political roles, some men—especially ruling-class men—acquire power over other men and over women. Almost all men acquire it over women of their own or lower classes, especially within their own kinship groups. These kinds of male power are shadowy among hunters.

To the extent that men *have* power over women in hunting societies, this seems to spring from the male monopoly of heavy weapons, from the particular division of labor between the sexes, or from both. Although men seldom use weapons against women, they *possess* them (or possess superior weapons) in addition to their physical strength. This does give men an ultimate control of force. When old people or babies must be killed to ensure band or family survival, it is usually men who kill them. Infanticide—rather common among hunters, who must limit the mouths to feed—is more often female infanticide than male.

The hunting of men seems more often to require them to organize in groups than does the work of women. Perhaps because of this, about 60 percent of hunting societies have predominantly virilocal residence. That is, men choose which band to live in (often, their fathers'), and women move with their husbands. This gives a man advantages over his wife in terms of familiarity and loyalties, for the wife is often a stranger. Sixteen to 17 percent of hunting societies are, however, uxorilocal, with men moving to the households of their wives, while 15 to 17 percent are bilocal—that is, either sex may move in with the other on marriage.

Probably because of male cooperation in defense and hunting, men are more prominent in band councils and leadership, in medicine and magic, and in public rituals designed to increase game, to ward off sickness, or to initiate boys into manhood. Women do, however, often take part in band councils; they are not excluded from law and government as in many agrarian states. Some women are respected as wise leaders, story tellers, doctors, or magicians or are feared as witches. Women have their own ceremonies of fertility, birth, and healing, from which men are often excluded.

In some societies, although men control the most sacred objects, women are believed to have discovered them. Among the Congo Pygmies, religion centers about a beneficent spirit, the Animal of the Forest. It is represented by wooden trumpets that are owned and played by men. Their possession and use are hidden from the women and they are played at night when hunting is bad, someone falls ill, or death occurs. During the playing men dance in the public campfire, which is sacred and is associated with the forest. Yet the men believe that women originally owned the trumpet and that it was a woman who stole fire from the chimpanzees or from the forest spirit. When a woman has failed to bear children for several years, a special ceremony is held. Women lead in the songs that usually accompany the trumpets, and an old woman kicks apart the campfire. Temporary female dominance seems to be thought necessary to restore fertility.

In some hunting societies women are exchanged between local groups, which are thus knit together through marriages. Sometimes, men of different bands directly exchange their sisters. More often there is a generalized exchange of women between two or more groups or a one-way movement of women within a circle of groups. Sometimes the husband's family pays weapons, tools, or ornaments to the wife's in return for the wife's services and, later, her children.

In such societies, although they may be well treated and their consent sought, women are clearly the moveable partners in an arrangement controlled by men. Male anthropologists have seized on this as evidence of original male dominance and patrilocal residence. Fox and others, for example, have argued that until recently, *all* hunting societies formed outmarrying patrilocal bands, linked together politically by the exchange of women. The fact that fewer than two-thirds of hunting societies are patrilocal today and only 41 percent have band-exogamy is explained in terms of modern conquest, economic change, and depopulation.

I cannot accept this formula. It is true that modern hunting societies have been severely changed, deculturated, and often depopulated by capitalist imperialism. I can see little evidence, however, that the ones that are patrilocal today have undergone less change than those that are not. It is hard to believe that in spite of enormous environmental diversity and the passage of thousands, perhaps millions, of years, hunting societies all had band exogamy with patrilocal residence until they were disturbed by western imperialism. It is more likely that early band societies, like later agricultural tribes, developed variety in family life and the status of women as they spread over the earth.

There is also some likelihood that the earliest hunters had matrilocal rather than patrilocal families. Among apes and monkeys, it is almost always males who leave the troop or are driven out. Females stay closer to their mothers and their original site; males move about, attaching themselves to females where availability and competition permit. Removal of the wife to the husband's home or band may have been a relatively late development in societies where male cooperation in hunting assumed overwhelming importance.* Conversely, after the development of horticulture (which was probably invented and is mainly carried out by women), those tribes in which horticulture predominated over stock raising were most likely to be or to remain matrilocal and to develop matrilineal descent groups with a relatively high status of women. But where extensive hunting of large animals or, later, the herding of large domesticates, predominated, patrilocal residence flourished and women were used to form alliances between male-centered groups. With the invention of metallurgy and of agriculture as distinct from horticulture after 4000 B.C., men came to control agriculture and many crafts, and most of the great agrarian states had patrilocal residence with patriarchal, male-dominant families.

Conclusions

The family is a human institution, not found in its totality in any prehuman species. It required language, planning, cooperation, self-control, foresight, and cultural learning and probably developed along with these.

The family was made desirable by the early human combination of prolonged child care with the need for hunting with weapons over large terrains. The sexual division of labor on which it was based grew out of a rudimentary prehuman division between male defense and female child care. But among humans this sexual division of functions for the first time became crucial for food production and so laid the basis for future economic specialization and cooperation.

Morgan and Engels were probably right in thinking that the human family was preceded by sexual indiscriminacy. They were also right in seeing an egalitarian group quality about early economic and marriage arrangements.

*Upper Palaeolithic hunters produced female figurines that were obvious emblems of fertility. The cult continued through the Mesolithic and into the Neolithic period. Goddesses and spirits of fertility are found in some patrilineal as well as matrilineal societies, but they tend to be more prominent in the latter. It is thus possible that in many areas even late Stone Age hunters had matrilocal residence and perhaps matrilineal descent, and that in some regions this pattern continued through the age of horticulture and even—as in the case of the Nayars of Kerala and the Minangkabau of Sumatra—into the age of plow agriculture, of writing, and of the small-scale state.

They were without evidence, however, in believing that the earliest mating and economic patterns were entirely group relations.

Together with tool use and language, the family was no doubt the most significant invention of the human revolution. All three required reflective thought, which above all accounts for the vast superiority in consciousness that separates humans from apes.

The family provided the framework for all prestate society and the fount of its creativeness. In groping for survival and for knowledge, human beings learned to control their sexual desires and to suppress their individual selfishness, aggression, and competition. The other side of this self-control was increased capacity for love—not only love of a mother for her child, which is seen among apes, but of male for female in enduring relationships and of each sex for ever-widening groups of humans. Civilization would have been impossible without this initial self-control, seen in incest prohibitions and in the generosity and moral orderliness of primitive family life.

From the start, women have been subordinate to men in certain key areas of status, mobility, and public leadership. But before the agricultural revolution, and even for several thousands of years thereafter, the inequality was based chiefly on the unalterable fact of long child care combined with the exigencies of primitive technology. The extent of inequality varied according to the ecology and the resulting sexual division of tasks. But in any case it was largely a matter of survival rather than of man-made cultural impositions. Hence the impressions we receive of dignity, freedom, and mutual respect between men and women in primitive hunting and horticultural societies. This is true whether these societies are patrilocal, bilocal, or matrilocal, although matrilocal societies, with matrilineal inheritance, offer greater freedom to women than do patrilocal and patrilineal societies of the same level of productivity and political development.

A distinct change occurred with the growth of individual and family property in herds, in durable craft objects and trade objects, and in stable, irrigated farmsites or other forms of heritable wealth. This crystallized in the rise of the state, about 4000 B.C. With the growth of class society and of male dominance in the ruling class of the state, women's subordination increased and eventually reached its depths in the patriarchal families of the great agrarian states. Knowledge of how the family arose is interesting to women because it tells us how we differ from prehumans, what our past has been, and what have been the biological and cultural limitations from which we are emerging. It shows us how generations of male scholars have distorted or overinterpreted the evidence to bolster beliefs in the inferiority of women's mental processes—for which there is no foundation in fact. Knowing about early families is also important to correct a reverse bias among some feminist writers, who hold that in "matriarchal" societies women were completely equal with or were even dominant over men. For this, too, there seems to be no basis in evidence.

The past of the family does not limit its future. Although the family probably emerged with humanity, neither the family itself nor particular family forms are genetically determined. The sexual division of labor—until recently, universal—need not, and in my opinion should not, survive in industrial society. Prolonged child care ceases to be a basis for female subordination when artificial birth control, spaced births, small families, patent feeding, and communal nurseries allow it to be shared by men. Automation and cybernation remove most of the heavy work for which women are less well equipped than men. The exploitation of women that came with the rise of the state and of class society will presumably disappear in poststate classless society—for which the technological and scientific basis already exists.

The family was essential to the dawn of civilization, allowing a vast qualitative leap forward in cooperation, purposive knowledge, love, and creativeness. But today, rather than enhancing them, the confinement of women in homes and small families—like their subordination in work—artificially limits these human capacities. It may be that the human gift for personal love will make some form of voluntary, long-term mating and of individual devotion between parents and children continue indefinitely, side by side with public responsibility for domestic tasks and for the care and upbringing of children. There is no need to legislate personal relations out of existence. But neither need we fear a social life in which the family is no more.

References

Coult, Allen D. *Cross Tabulations of Murdock's World Ethnographic Sample.* Columbia: University of Missouri Press, 1965.

Fox, Robin. *Kinship and Marriage.* London: Pelican Books, 1967.

Hockett, Charles F., and Robert Ascher. "The Human Revolution." In *Man in Adaptation: The Biosocial Background,* edited by Yehudi A. Cohen. Chicago: Aldine, 1968.

Livingstone, Frank B. "Genetics, Ecology and the Origin of Incest and Exogamy." *Current Anthropology,* February 1969.

Morris, Desmond. *The Naked Ape.* Jonathan Cape, 1967.

Murdock, G. P. "World Ethnographic Sample." *American Anthropologist,* 1957.

Murdock, G. P. *Ethnographic Atlas.* Pittsburgh: University of Pittsburgh, 1967.

Schneider, David M., and Kathleen Gough. *Matrilineal Kinship.* Berkeley and Los Angeles: University of California Press, 1961.

Semyonov, Y. I. "Group Marriage, Its Nature and Role in the Evolution of Marriage and Family Relations." In *Seventh International Congress of Anthropological and Ethnological Sciences,* Vol. IV. Moscow, 1967.

World Revolution and Family Patterns

William J. Goode

Idealization of the Recent Past: The United States

In order to weigh the extent and type of changes now taking place in family systems in various parts of the world, it is necessary to examine the recent past; otherwise no trends can be seen. We then usually discover only idealized or stereotyped descriptions of family systems of a generation ago. We must correct such stereotypes in order to measure present-day trends.

In another context, I labeled this stereotype of the United States family of the past, when *praised,* "the classical family of Western nostalgia." It is a pretty picture of life down on grandma's farm. There are lots of happy children, and many kinfolk live together in a large rambling house. Everyone works hard. Most of the food to be eaten during the winter is grown, preserved, and stored on the farm. The family members repair their own equipment, and in general the household is economically self-sufficient. The family has many functions; it is the source of economic stability and religious, educational, and vocational training. Father is stern and reserved and has the final decision in all important matters. Life is difficult but harmonious, because everyone knows his task and carries it out. All boys and girls marry, and marry young. Young people, especially the girls, are likely to be virginal at marriage and faithful afterward. Though the parents do not arrange their children's marriages, the elders do have the right to reject a suitor and have a strong hand in the final decision. After marriage, the couple lives harmoniously, either near the boy's parents or with them, for the couple is slated to inherit the farm. No one divorces.

Those who believe we are seeing progress rather than retrogression often accept the same stereotype but describe the past in words of different emotional effect. We have progressed, they say, from the arbitrary power of elders toward personal freedom for the young, from cold marriages based on economic arrangements to unions based on the youngsters' right of choice, from rigidly maintained class barriers between children to an open class system, from the subjugation of the wife to equalitarianism and companionship in marriage, and from the repression of children's emotions to permissiveness.

Like most stereotypes, that of the classical family of Western nostalgia leads us astray. When we penetrate the confusing mists of recent history we find few examples of this "classical" family. Grandma's farm was not economically self-sufficient. Few families stayed together as large aggregations of kinfolk. Most houses were small, not large. We now *see* more large old houses than

From *The Journal of Marriage and the Family* (November 1971), pp. 624–635. Copyright © 1971 by William J. Goode. Reprinted by permission.

small ones; they survived longer because they were likely to have been better constructed. The one-room cabins rotted away. True enough, divorce was rare, but we have no evidence that families were generally happy. Indeed, we find, as in so many other pictures of the glowing past, that in each past generation people write of a period *still* more remote, *their* grandparents, generation, when things really were much better.

If, then, the stereotype of the United States and Western family is partially incorrect, we may suppose stereotypes of other past family systems to be similarly in error. We shall, therefore, describe current changes in family patterns while ascertaining, where possible, what the patterns of the recent past were.

The Conjugal Family as an Ideal Type

As now used by family analysts, the term *conjugal family* is technically an *ideal type;* it also represents an ideal. The concept was not developed from a summary or from the empirical study of actual United States urban family behavior; it is a *theoretical* construction, derived from intuition and observation, in which several crucial variables have been combined to form a hypothetical structural harmony. Such a conceptual structure may be used as a measure and model in examining real time trends or contemporary patterns. In the ensuing discussion, we shall try to separate the fundamental from the more derivative variables in this construction.

As a concept, the conjugal family is also an *ideal* in that when analysts refer to its spread they mean that an increasing number of people view some of its characteristics as *proper* and legitimate, no matter how reality may run counter to the ideal. Thus, although parents in the United States agree that they *should* not play an important role in their children's choice of spouse, they actually do. Relatives *should* not interfere in each other's family affairs, but in a large (if unknown) percentage of cases they do. Since, however, this ideal aspect of the conjugal family is also part of the total reality, significant for changes in family patterns, we shall comment on it later as an ideology.

The most important characteristic of the ideal typical construction of the conjugal family is the relative exclusion of a wide range of affinal and blood relatives from its everyday affairs: There is no great extension of the kin network. Many other traits may be derived theoretically from this one variable. Thus, the couple cannot count on a large number of kinfolk for help, just as these kin cannot call upon the couple for services. Neither couple nor kinfolk have many *rights* with respect to the other, and so the reciprocal *obligations* are few. In turn, by an obvious sociological principle, the couple has few moral controls over their extended kin, and these have few controls over the couple.

The locality of the couple's household will no longer be greatly determined by their kin since kinship ties are weak. The couple will have a "neolocal" residence; that is, they will establish a new household when they marry. This in turn reinforces their relative independence, because it lowers the frequency of social interaction with their kin.

The choice of mate is freer than in other systems, because the bases upon which marriage is built are different: The kin have no strong rights or financial interest in the matter. Adjustment is primarily between husband and wife, not between the incoming spouse and his or her in-law group. The courtship system is therefore ideally based, and, at the final decision stage, empirically as well, on the mutual attraction between the two youngsters.

All courtship systems are market or exchange systems. They differ from one another with respect to who does the buying and selling, which characteristics are more or less valuable in that market, and how open or explicit the bargaining is. In a conjugal family system mutual attraction in both courtship and marriage acquires a higher value. Nevertheless, the elders do not entirely lose control. Youngsters are likely to marry only those with whom they fall in love, and they fall in love only with the people they meet. Thus, the focus of parental controls is on who is allowed to meet whom at parties, in the school and neighborhood, and so on.

When such a system begins to emerge in a society, the age at marriage is likely to change because the goals of marriage change, but whether it will rise or fall cannot be predicted from the characteristics mentioned so far. In a conjugal system, the youngsters must now be old enough to take care of themselves; that is, they must be as old as the economic system forces them to be in order to be independent at marriage. (Alternative solutions also arise: Some middle-class youngsters may marry upon the promise of support from their parents, while they complete their education.) Thus, if the economic system changes its base, for example, from agriculture to industry, the age at marriage may change. The couple decides the number of children they will have on the basis of their own needs, not those of a large kin group; and contraception, abortion, or infanticide may be used to control this number. Whether fertility will be high or low cannot, however, be deduced from these conjugal traits. Under some economic systems, for example, frontier agriculture, the couple may actually need a large number of children.

This system is bilineal or, to use Max Gluckman's term, multilineal: The two kin lines are of nearly equal importance, because neither has great weight. Neolocality and the relative freedom from control by an extended kin network prevent the maintenance or formation of a powerful lineage system, which is necessary if one line is to be dominant over the other.

Since the larger kin group can no longer be counted on for emotional sustenance, and since the marriage is based on mutual attraction, the small marital unit is the main place where the emotional input-output balance of the individual husband and wife is maintained, where their psychic wounds can be salved or healed. At least there is no other place where they can go. Thus, the emotions within this unit are likely to be intense, and the relationship between husband and wife may well be intrinsically unstable, depending as it does on affection. Consequently, the divorce rate is likely to be high. Remarriage is likely because there is no larger kin unit to absorb the children and no unit to prevent the spouses from reentering the free marriage market.

Finally, the couple and children do recognize some extended kin, but the husband recognizes a somewhat different set of kindred than does his wife, since they began in different families. And the children view as important a somewhat different set of kindred than do their parents: The parents look back a generation greater in depth than do the children and perhaps a greater distance outward, because they have had an adult lifetime in which to come to know more kin. That is, each individual takes into account a somewhat different set of kindred, though most of them are the same for all within the same nuclear unit.

The foregoing sketch is an ideal typical construction and thus must be compared with the reality of both behavior *and* ideal in those societies which are thought to have conjugal family patterns. To my knowledge, no such test has been made. Very likely, the *ideals* of a large proportion of United States families fit this construction very well. Some parts of the construction also fit the *behavior* of a considerable but unknown fraction of United States families, for example, the emphasis on emotionality within the family; the free choice of spouse; and neolocality, bilineality, and instability of the individual family. On the other hand, data from both England and the United States indicate that even in lower-class urban families, where the extension of kin ties might be thought to be shorter (following the ideal type), many kin ties are active. . . . No one has measured the intensity and extensiveness of kin ties in a range of societies in order to ascertain how Western family patterns compare in these respects. It is quite possible that those countries thought to be closest to the conjugal pattern do in fact have a less extended kin network.

Nevertheless, the ideal type conflicts sharply with reality *and* theory in one important respect. Theoretical considerations suggest that, without the application of political pressure, the family *cannot* be as limited in its kin network as the ideal typical construction suggests. Both common observation and theory coincide to suggest that (1) grandparent-grandchild ties are still relatively intense and (2) emotional ties among siblings are also strong. Consequently, (3) parents-in-law interact relatively frequently with their children-in-law, and (4) married people have frequent contacts with their brothers- or sisters-in-law. It follows, then, that (5) children maintain contacts, at least during their earlier years, with their uncles and aunts, as well as with their first cousins. Without question, of all types of "visiting" and "social occasions," the most common, even in the urban United States, is "visiting with relatives."

If no active ties are maintained with the categories of kin mentioned above, the family feels that some explanation is called for and pleads some excuse ("They live too far away" or "We've never gotten along well").

In addition, perhaps most families have *some* tie with one or more relatives still further away in the kin network. Those noted above seem to be linked to the nuclear family in an inescapable way; it is difficult to ignore or reject any of them without simultaneously rejecting a fellow member of *one's own* nuclear family. The child cannot ignore his uncle without hurting one of his own parents, and reciprocally. A girl may not neglect her sister-in-law without impairing her relationship with her brother. Of course, brother and sister may combine against their own spouses, and social interaction may continue even under an impaired relationship. Cousins are dragged along by their parents, who are siblings and siblings-in-law to one another. The extension of the family network to this point, then, seems determined by the emotional ties within the nuclear family unit itself. To reduce the unit to the nuclear family would require coercive restriction of these ties between siblings or between parents, as the Chinese commune has attempted to do.

The "Fit" Between the Conjugal Family and the Modern Industrial System

The argument as to whether political and economic variables, or the reverse, generally determine family patterns seems theoretically empty. Rather, we must establish any determinate relations (whichever direction the causal effect) among any particular family variables and the variables of other institutional orders—not a simple task. Even the relation between the conjugal family and industrialization is not yet entirely clear. The common hypothesis—that the conjugal form of the family emerges when a culture is invaded by industrialization and urbanization—is an undeveloped observation which neglects three issues: (1) the theoretical harmony or "fit" between this ideal typical form of the family and industrialization; (2) the empirical harmony or fit between industrialization and any actual system; and (3) the effects upon the family of the modern (or recent past) organizational and industrial system, that is, how the factors in the system influence the family.

At present, only the first of these can be treated adequately. The second has been dealt with primarily by researchers who have analyzed a peasant or primitive culture with reference to the problem of labor supply and who suggest that family systems *other* than the conjugal one do not adequately answer the demands of an expanding industrial system. Malinowski asserted, for example, that although young Trobriander men could earn more by working on plantations than by growing yams, they preferred to grow yams because this activity was defined as required for their family roles. Similarly, a head tax was necessary to force young men to leave their families to work in the South African mines. Men's objections to women's leaving the home for outside jobs have limited the labor supply in various parts of the world, especially in Islamic areas. On the other hand, within conjugal or quasi-conjugal systems such as those in the West, the strains between family patterns and industrial requirements have only rarely been charted empirically.

This last task would require far more ingenious research designs than have been so far utilized. It requires that the exact points of impact between family and industrial organization be located and the degree of impact measured. Succeeding chapters will devote some attention to this problem. Specific decisions or choices need to be analyzed in which both family and industrial variables are involved.

Nevertheless, if we are to achieve a better understanding of world changes in family systems, it may help if we can correct the theoretical analyses of the first problem, the fit between the ideal typical form of the conjugal family and industrialization. It seems possible to do this through some reference to common observations about both United States and European family patterns.

Let us consider first the demands of industrialization, which is the crucial element in the complex types of change now occurring in even remote parts of the world. Although bureaucratization may occur without industrialization (witness China), and so may urbanization (for example, Dahomey, Tokugawa Japan), neither occurs without some rise in a society's technological level, and certainly the modern system of industry never occurs without *both* urbanization and bureaucratization.

The prime social characteristic of modern industrial enterprise is that the individual is ideally given a job on the basis of his ability to fulfill its demands, and that this achievement is evaluated universalistically; the same standards apply *to all who hold the same job.* His link with the job is functionally specific; in other words, the enterprise cannot require behavior of him which is not relevant to getting the job done.

Being achievement-based, an industrial society is necessarily open-class, requiring both geographical and social mobility. Men must be permitted to rise or fall depending on their performance. Moreover, in the industrial system, jobs based on ownership and exploitation of land (and thus on inheritance) become numerically less significant, again permitting considerable geographical mobility to that individuals are free to move about in the labor market. The neolocality of the conjugal system correspondingly frees the individual from ties to the specific geographical location where his parental family lives.

The conjugal family's relationship to class mobility is rather complex. Current formulations, based on ancient wisdom, assert that by limiting the extensiveness of the kin network, the individual is less hampered by his family in rising upward in the job structure. Presumably, this means that he owes less to his kin and so can allocate his resources of money and time solely to further his career; perhaps he may also more freely change his style of life, his mode of dress, and speech, in order to adjust to a new class position without criticism from his kin. On the other hand, an industrial system pays less attention to what the individual does off the job, so that family and job are structurally somewhat more separated than in other systems. Consequently, one might reason that differential social or occupational mobility (as among siblings or cousins) would not affect kin ties. Yet the emotional ties within the conjugal system are intense, compared to other systems, so that even though there are fewer relatives, the weight of kin relationships to be carried upward by the mobile individual might be equivalent to that in a system with more, but less intense, ties.

An alternative view must also be considered. Under some circumstances the kin network actually contributes greatly to the individual's mobility, and "social capillarity" as a process (that is, that individual rises highest who is burdened with least kin) moves fewer people upward than does a well-integrated kin network. A brief theoretical sketch of this alternative view also throws light on the supposed "adjustment" between the needs of the small conjugal family and those of a modern industrial system.

First, in the modern industrial system, the middle and upper strata are by definition more "successful" in the obvious sense that they own it, dominate it, occupy its highest positions, and direct its future. One must concede that they are "well adjusted" to the modern industrial society. Paradoxically, their kin pattern is in fact *less* close to the ideal typical form of the conjugal family than is the family behavior of the lower strata. The upper strata recognize the widest extension of kin, maintain most control to give and receive help from one another.

Consequently, the lower strata's freedom from kin is like their "freedom" to sell their labor in an open market. They are less encumbered by the weight of kin when they are able to move upward, but they also get less help from their kin. Like English peasants, who from the sixteenth to eighteenth centuries were gradually "freed" from the land by the enclosure movement, or nineteenth-century workers, who were "freed" from their tools by the development of machinery, the lower strata have fewer family ties, less family stability, and enjoy less family-based economic and material security. The lower-class family pattern is indeed most "integrated" with the industrial system but mainly in the sense that the individual is forced to enter its labor market with far less family support—his family *does not prevent industry from using him for its own goals.* He may move where the system needs him, hopefully where his best opportunity lies, but he *must* also fit the demands of the system, since no extended kin network will interest itself greatly in his fate. The job demands of the industrial system move the individual about, making it difficult for him to keep his kin ties active; and because his kin are also in the lower strata he has little to lose by relinquishing those ties. In short, lower-strata families are most likely to be "conjugal" and to serve the needs of the industrial system; this system may not, however, serve the needs of that family pattern. This means that when industrialization begins, it is the lower-class family that loses least by participating in it and that lower-class family patterns are the first to change in the society. We might speculatively infer further that *now,* a century after the first great impact of industrialization of the lower-class family in the Western urban world, family patterns of Western middle and upper classes may be changing more rapidly than those of the lower. (Whether rural changes

may not be occurring equally rapidly cannot be deduced from these inferences.) However, although this inference may be empirically correct, the available data demand a more cautious inference: Whether or not the middle and
upper strata *are* now changing more rapidly in the Western world, they *do*
have more resources with which to resist certain of the industrial system's
undermining pressures (e.g., capital with which to support their youngsters
through a long professional training) and a considerable interest in resisting
them because their existing kin network is more active and useful. We would
suppose, then, that in an industrializing process both the peasants and primi-
tives are forced to adjust their family patterns to the demands of industrial
enterprise more swiftly and see less to lose in the adjustment. By contrast, the
middle and upper strata are better able to utilize the new opportunities of
industrialization by relinquishing their kin ties more slowly, so that these
changes will occur only in a later phase of industrialization, such as the United
States is now undergoing.

Continuing now with our analysis of the "fit" of the conjugal family to
industrial needs, the more limited conjugal kin network opens mobility channels somewhat by limiting the "closure" of class strata. In general, rigid class
boundaries can be maintained partly by the integration of kin bonds against
the "outsider" through family controls. When the network of each family is
smaller, the families of an upper stratum are less integrated, the web of kin
less tightly woven, and entrance into the stratum easier. Since the industrial
system requires relatively free mobility, this characteristic of the conjugal
pattern fits the needs of that system. This general principle also holds for
classical China, where an empirically different system prevailed. A successful
family would normally expand over generations but thereby have insufficient
resources to maintain so many at a high social rank. That is, the reciprocal
exchange necessary for tightness and closure of the kin system could be kept
up only by a few individual families in the total network. If all the families in
the network shared alike as kinsmen (which did not happen), the entire network would lose social rank. If the few well-to-do families helped their kin only
minimally and maintained ties with other upper stratum families, the integration of the stratum was kept intact and the stratification system was not
threatened.

The modern technological system is psychologically burdensome on the
individual because it demands an unremitting discipline. To the extent that
evaluation is based on achievement and universalism, the individual gets little
emotional security from his work. Some individuals, of course, obtain considerable pleasure from it, and every study of job satisfaction shows that in
positions offering higher prestige and salaries a higher proportion of people are
satisfied with their work and would choose that job if they had to do it again.
Lower level jobs give little pleasure to most people. However, in higher level
professional, managerial, and creative positions the standards of performance

are not only high but are often without clearly stated limits. The individual is under considerable pressure to perform better than he is able.

The conjugal family again integrates with such a system by its emphasis on emotionality, especially in the relationship of husband and wife. It has the task of restoring the input-output emotional balance of individualism in such a job structure. This is so even for lower strata jobs where the demands for performance are kept within limits by an understood quota but where, by contrast with upper strata jobs, there is less intrinsic job satisfaction. Of course, the family cannot fully succeed in this task, but at least the technological system has no moral responsibility for it and can generally ignore the problem in its work demands.

Bilateral in pattern, this family system does not maintain a lineage. It does not concentrate family land or wealth in the hands of one son through whom the property would descend, or even in the hands of one sex. Dispersal of inheritance keeps the class system fluid. Daughters as well as sons will share as heirs, and a common legal change in the West is toward equal inheritance by all children (as is already the situation generally in the United States). Relatively equal advantages are given to all the sons, and although even United States families do not invest so heavily in daughters as in sons (more boys than girls complete college), the differences in training the two sexes are much less than in other family systems. Consequently, a greater proportion of all children are given the opportunity to develop their talents to fit the manifold opportunities of a complex technological and bureaucratic structure.

The conjugal system also specifies the status obligations of each member in much less *detail* than does an extended family system, in which entrepreneurial, leadership, or production tasks are assigned by family position. Consequently, wider individual variations in family role performance are permitted, to enable members to fit the range of possible demands by the industrial system as well as by other members of the family.

Since the young adult is ideally expected to make his own choice of spouse and the young couple is expected to be economically independent, the conjugal system, by extending the adolescent phase of development, permits a long period of tutelage. For example, it is expected that the individual should be grown up before marrying. Note, however, that it is not the family itself that gives this extended tutelage, but public, impersonal agencies, such as schools, military units, and corporations, which ideally ignore family origin and measure the individual by his achievement and talent. This pattern permits the individual to obtain a longer period of training, to make a freer choice of his career, and to avoid the economic encumbrance of marriage until he has fitted himself into the industrial system. Thus, the needs of the industrial system are once more served by the conjugal family pattern.

The *different* adjustment of families in *different* classes to the industrial system emphasizes the *independence* of the two sets of variables, the familial and the industrial, as well as the presence of some "disharmonies" between the two. Further points where the two do not adjust fully may be noted here. The modern woman is given little relief from child care, which is typically handed over to one person, the wife, rather than to several women, some of them elders, who are part of the family unit in more extended systems. Adjustments in modes of child care, which seem to accompany industrialization, are in part a result of the decline of a family tradition handed down from older women to the younger. With the weakening of ties with the older generation younger women depend increasingly on the published opinions of experts as a guide for child-rearing practices.

Even the substantial development of labor-saving devices and technology has not lightened labor in the modern United States home, contrary to both advertising in women's magazines and the stereotyped notions of Europeans. Most of these devices merely raise the standards for cleanliness and repairs, and allow the housewife to turn out more "domestic production" each day. Every study of the time allocation of mothers shows that housewives work extremely long hours. For those who have assumed otherwise, let me remind them that the washing machine brings back into the home a job that an earlier generation delegated to lower-class labor or the laundry; that the vacuum cleaner merely raises standards without substantially speeding up work; that the electric sewing machine is exactly analogous to the washing machine. On the other hand, the organized activities of children have become so complex, and the number of objects in the house so numerous, that even the middle-class housewife must spend much of her time in essentially administrative activities when she is not laboring with her hands. Marx, commenting on John Stuart Mill's doubt that mechanical inventions had lightened man's toil, asserted that lightened toil was not the *aim* of the capitalist use (for the modern scene, read "industrial use") of machinery. While one might quarrel with Marx's concept of *deliberate* aim, it remains true that it is difficult to release even well-trained women from their household tasks and especially from their emotional tasks; there is no one to substitute for that labor, unless new agencies such as communal nurseries are created. In addition, since the amount of work is great and there is presumptive equality of husband and wife, the husband generally has to step in to help after work, which in turn diverts some of his energy from his occupation.

Ignoring the question of feasibility of additional time, it also remains true that for women, the roles of wife and mother are their central obligations. For this reason, and because there is no one else who can be given the care of house and children, over the past half-century in the United States, women have not become much more "career-minded" than they were, and polling evidence suggests that a similar conclusion may be applied to Europe. Even though an increasing percentage of women in the United States are in the labor force, as in some countries of Europe, there has been over the past few decades (in the United States) only a very slight increase in the proportion of mothers of small children who are in the labor force, and these are predominantly in the lower income groups, where the economic pressure to work is great. Much of the recent great increase in female participation in the United States labor force has been concentrated in the older age groups. Toward the higher economic strata, generally a lower proportion of women work.

Unlike men, women do not as yet think of job holding as a *career*, as a necessary and intrinsic part of their destiny. From 1910 to 1950 in the United States, while the conjugal family was spreading beyond the city, the proportion of women in the established professions did not change greatly. The number of women physicians increased from 6 percent to 6.1 percent. In dentistry, the proportion decreased slightly. In law, engineering, architecture, and the ministry, the increase was substantial, but in none did the proportion rise above 4.1 percent. In college teaching there was a slight increase, so that women constituted 23.2 percent of the total in 1958, as compared with 19.8 percent in 1899–1900. The proportion of college-educated women who have gone into the established professions has dropped during the past half-century, although of course the percentage of women has increased substantially within a range of technical or semiprofessional jobs in the natural sciences. Clearly, the "needs" of industrialization are not in easy adjustment with the role obligations of women.

The Future of American Fertility   *Norman B. Ryder*

Some thirty years ago, just after the end of the second world war, the contributors to population literature seemed obsessed with the long-standing decline of fertility. In the United States, the total fertility rate—a measure of the number of children born per woman over the course of her life-time—had slid steadily downward from more than seven at the beginning of the nineteenth century to somewhere in the neighborhood of two. The accepted explanation was the complex changes summed up under the rubric of "modernization." Since nothing was perceived to stand in the way of that juggernaut, the prognosis was still further reproductive retrenchment, perhaps even to extinction. To be sure, the postwar birth rate was up a bit, but everyone wrote that off as only a momentary interruption of our demographic version of the Decline of the West (Population Index, 1948). The only problem was that the forecast proved to be very wrong.

From *Social Problems,* 26:3 (February 1979), pp. 359–370. Copyright © 1979 by the Society for the Study of Social Problems. Reprinted by permission.

In the late 1970s, most demographers are again predicting a cessation of growth in the United States, and on essentially the same theoretical premises (Current Population Reports, 1975). But, given the previous forecasting debacle, why should anyone pay attention to a demographer who presumes to talk about the future of fertility?

To find out what went wrong before and try not to make the same mistakes again, consider the situation a generation ago. Demographers had available a rather brief history of American fertility, utilizing unsophisticated measures, along with impressions of the nineteenth century, and that added onto a large amount of presumably comparable European experience. The history was straightforward—decline all the way—and the obvious correlates were the various aspects of the modernization process. The latter continued but the former did not.

As the years after World War II passed, fertility stayed high. With each annual addition to the evidence, a bit more of the confidence of demographers in their ideas disappeared, their morale was shattered by the baby boom, and their general response was to abandon theoretical pretensions and retreat into the empty safety of empiricism. In my judgment, they were victims of a failure of nerve: they should have stuck to their theoretical guns.

The contemporary history of American fertility, dated conveniently in terms of how long we have had the kinds of statistics necessary for refined measurement, extends over about sixty years. Within this same time span, the dominant feature is a single massive fluctuation, with a trough in the mid-1930s, a peak in the mid-1950s, and a further collapse in the past decade. What explanation of this fluctuation can we find to give us a basis for an informed guess as to what happens next?

In his presidential address to the Population Association of America, Richard Easterlin (1978) proposed an alternative to the conventional wisdom which he claimed had led us astray. He said that the fertility prediction went wrong because it ignored a major demographic influence tending to turn fertility around—the growing scarcity of young adults and the resulting rise in their relative affluence.

His theory is that young people decide on their eventual number of children by comparing their opportunities (which depend on their numbers) with their aspirations (which depend on their family of orientation). Thus those who belong to a small cohort (such as persons born in the 1930s) fare well in the labor market and convert their good fortune into more babies; those who belong to a large cohort (such as persons born in the 1950s) do poorly in the labor market and respond by having fewer babies. The thesis is essentially a cyclical one. Bad times mean fewer children, whose economic opportunities are better because there are fewer of them coming on the labor market, and those opportunities look better because they were raised in bad times. They in turn experience good times, and have more children, whose economic opportunities look worse because they were raised in good times. It would follow that, as the small birth crops of the past decade come of economic age, fertility will rise, *ceteris paribus.*

There are problems with the cohort size theory. In the first place, the empirical support is suggestive rather than definitive. A relationship would be found based solely on the fact that the length of time between the early 1930s (a time of low fertility) and the late 1950s (a time of high fertility) was about one generation and that fertility has been declining since. The hypothesis concerns the direction and timing of swings about what would otherwise have been happening. To use it alone is to assume that there is no underlying trend. Admittedly, fluctuation does dominate trend in this century. But it would be a mistake, having been betrayed by a trend theory which ignored fluctuation, to shift to a fluctuation theory which ignored trend.

Moreover, the labor market prospects for males can be affected by short-run economic disturbances quite apart from cohort size. The major short-term swings in the birth rate over the past sixty years have been occasioned by participation in three wars. The theory links labor market prospects of young males to their numbers, on the assumption of a traditional division of labor. (Females are regarded as only casually involved in the labor force because their primary responsibilities are domestic.) Yet currently, in addition to 57 million men in the labor force, there are 40 million women (Miller, 1978). A smaller cohort size for males implies the same for females, and that makes labor force participation easier for females as well as for males. Would that not work against rather than for fertility?

One fundamental difficulty of theories like this one, which link completed family size with economic circumstances, is that the evidence is equivocal. Despite the dogma of economists that children can be thought of as a consumer durable good, the demand for which tends to rise and fall with income, there is a dearth of data to support that proposition. That there is a strong relationship between economic circumstances and reproductive behavior I would not deny, but I would prefer to cast it in a different light. In my view, the relative ease or difficulty of entry into the labor force, dependent in large part on the size of the cohort relative to its predecessors, is directly translated into a relatively earlier or later age of entry into parenthood. While that may have some consequences for the eventual size of a family, it certainly does modify the time pattern of fertility. We now know that such modifications are central to the understanding of contemporary movements of the birth rate.

Prior to the modern era, most observations of fertility referred to behavior within a particular period rather than to the behavior of a cohort of women aging with each passing year. Period measures are notoriously unstable relative to cohort measures, in part because all cohorts tend to be affected in the same way be period-specific influences, but in part because the changing tempo of cohort fertility (swinging from later to earlier, and back again) has a distorting effect on the quantity of births occurring in particular years. When the tempo is decelerating, period fertility is depressed; when the tempo is accelerating, period fertility is elevated. Because an acceleration of tempo ordinarily accompanies a rise in fertility, period fertility tends to rise more than cohort fertility; the converse proposition holds for fertility decline.

Here we have the principal explanation of the baby boom. Most of that explosion in period fertility was caused not by a change in the amount of cohort fertility but by a change in its tempo. Fifty-eight percent of the rise in fertility and 55 percent of the subsequent decline would have occurred even if the numbers of babies borne by women throughout their lives had remained fixed. The principal source of that change in tempo was variation in the mean age at entry into parenthood, and that seems to be closely linked with cohort size (Ryder, 1978a).

Although most of the upward movement in period fertility in the early postwar years, and most of the downward movement since then, are attributable to shifts in the time pattern of cohort fertility, there remains a substantial component associated with changes in the amount of reproduction per woman. Detailed examination of the successive phases of reproductive life reveals a discontinuity between the time series for the proportion of women ending up with at least two children, and that for the average number of births to those with at least two children. This empirical dichotomy has theoretical justification. Social norms in the United States, at least until recently, have pressed people into a preference for marriage over nonmarriage, parenthood over nonparenthood, and at least two children rather than an only child—with the proviso that one should be in a position to fulfill one's parental obligations. Beyond the second child, the progression is primarily a matter of individual preference, although friends, neighbors, and relatives may look askance if the number goes beyond four.

During the postwar era, 90 percent of the increase in the quantity of cohort fertility derived from a rise in the proportion of women having at least two children—from 55 to 82 percent (Ryder, 1978a). Postwar conditions permitted almost universal adherence to the norm; both economic improvement and parenthood were feasible.

What made the idea of having a family so popular? In my opinion, one need not infer that new goals became established. What happened was that the wherewithal to accomplish an old ideal finally became available to most people for the first time. There is a constant temptation, which sociologists are not always sufficiently resolute to resist, to observe a change in behavior and then explain it by reference to changing values. Yet it is unwise to have recourse to such a blockbuster argument until one has exhausted alternatives, because such hypotheses tend to be irrefutable and therefore scientifically impotent. Two decades ago, no such explanation was required. The steady rise in real income, together with increasing governmental intervention which effectively transferred resources away from nonparents and towards parents, made feasible the almost universal adherence to a long-standing norm of proper behavior.

In the past fifteen years, the proportion of women ending up with fewer than two births has doubled (from 18 percent to 36 percent). This accounts for about one-third of the quantitative decline in cohort fertility. It is difficult to assess the import of this change. From the end of the war until 1970, real income per family rose steadily; it has not risen since 1970, but it has not declined either (Danziger and Lampman, 1978). Perhaps we must consider the possibility that the norms themselves may be changing—that motherhood is becoming less a matter of obligation and more a matter of preference.

The average number of births to those with at least two children played a minuscule role in the baby boom, no more than a temporary halt in a very long-standing decline (going back at least to the beginning of the nineteenth century). The consensus of demographic opinion about the baby boom was that it was a rise in the number of children wanted, from two to three or four, without much change (and perhaps even some improvement) in the extent and effectiveness of fertility regulation, associated with growing sophistication and openness of discussion, and specifically as a side-effect of military service. From our National Fertility Studies—the best available evidence—we now know that the small rise in the higher-parity component was predominantly an increase in unintended births. The number of children wanted (by women with at least two) did not change, but the extent and effectiveness of fertility regulation worsened (Ryder, 1978b).

There are two reasons behind the worsening of fertility regulation in the early postwar period, and they are of approximately equal import. First, there was increased exposure to risk of an unintended child, because there was a more rapid tempo of reproduction—the last intended child arrived sooner—and military separations no longer played a role. Second, there was an increased rate of unintended childbearing, partly because the additional exposure was in the high risk (prime-time) ages, and a decline in diligence because the gravity of the consequences of a termination failure was perceived to be less than before. Ineffective regulation arises from weak motivation, where the intent represents exercise of an option rather than the force of necessity, in a context in which effectiveness depends greatly on motivation because of the kinds of contraception available.

In the past fifteen years, the probability that a woman with at least two children will have another in any year plummeted by about 50 percent. This continues a trend of perhaps two centuries' duration. It is further evidence of the incompatibility of modernization and the large family. This time it is occurring at an accelerated pace because of the extraordinary recent improvement in fertility regulation. There has been a souring of the economic situation, and there has been a shortening of the period of exposure to risk, because of a rise in the age at which the second child comes along. But the predominant explanation is the contraceptive revolution (Westoff and Ryder, 1977). Three-quarters of those now using a method are either sterilized, or on the pill, or using the IUD. Moreover, many failures are being cancelled by abortion. These methods were either nonexistent or negligible during the baby boom. They are highly effective primarily because they separate the control of fertility from the act of copulation and thus reduce the level of motivation required for effective prevention. The plague of unwanted births is now essentially over. The small residuum of families with more than two children is found disproportionately among minority groups, that is, among those whom we still seem reluctant to admit to full membership in the modern society.

On the basis of this assessment of postwar fertility, we may not be in a substantially better position to make a forecast, although we are undoubtedly wiser about the obstacles which stand in the way of such an accomplishment. The task is twofold: to identify the reproductive pattern toward which we appear to be moving over the long run and to anticipate sources or irregularity which are likely to be superimposed on the trend from now to then. The beginning point is the lowest annual fertility ever recorded. Because family income has not been rising in real terms since 1970, many analysts have voiced the suspicion that couples are postponing their fertility, that is, that the current level is abnormally low and there will soon be a rebound. Although there is undoubtedly some truth to this proposition, the configuration of recent changes at the most refined level does not correspond to a postponement model. The government now asks married women each year not only how many babies they have had so far, but how many more they expect to have (U.S. Bureau of the Census, 1978). Granted the responses should be regarded with skepticism, but what these wives say is that they intend to call a halt, reproductively speaking, with the smallest birth crop in history, even if all the births they now consider as postponed eventually occur.

Short-term irregularities aside, the current level of cohort fertility is 10 percent below what would be required to replace the population and is declining. In order to make a guess about the long-term direction, it is helpful to decompose overall fertility into the proportion having at least two children and the average number of births these women end up with. The latter (much the smaller component quantitatively) shows a very long secular decline, still continuing, to a current record low, with one brief small departure from the negative trend, occasioned by the ineffectuality of premodern fertility regulation. It requires no particular courage to project still further decline, although probably at a slackening rate.

The former component, that is, the proportion of women having at least two children, has swung back and forth over the past six decades. Some observers respond to an oscillation like this with the opinion that since fertility is a matter of fashion, the index may well go up again soon. Having babies was the thing to do in the 1950s; parenthood has for the time being gone out of style, but it will come back. Such an explanation is fail-safe: The evidence for the change in fashion is the behavior it is invoked to explain. It is probably true that once a new behavior pattern is established, deviants from that pattern can be disseminated through the populace. It provides no guide to the future because it gives no clue to the origin or character of the change of style.

It is hard to take seriously the idea that people could be whimsical about the number of their children in the same way as they are, for example, about how far a hemline is above the floor. I doubt that any behavior pattern which is paramount to the survival of society—and reproductivity certainly is— would be left to individual caprice and happenstance. The fashion hypothesis is only a short remove from the prejudice that what causes human beings to behave the way they do is essentially unknowable—human nature being what it is—and moreover that is probably a good thing. For anyone concerned with the employment of social scientists this must be labeled as heresy.

Perhaps the lower proportion of women with at least two children indicates that alternatives to motherhood are now respectable, even attractive. There certainly seems to be a secular rise in the labor force participation of women. In a subtle way also, the accessibility of good fertility regulation may enhance the disposition to think of maternity in terms of the costs and benefits of children much more than before. Yet if the proportion with at least two children is as likely to continue declining as to rise again, and if the other component of overall fertility continues its long-standing decline, then the prospect is for fertility to fall even further below replacement than it is now.

The central projection in the most recent forecasts of the Bureau of the Census is keyed to the assumption that fertility is destined to move into equilibrium with mortality (Census, 1975). That may be based less on reason than on faith—a belief in some kind of automatic corrective which comes into play as a population approaches the replacement level, impelling young couples to make the necessary actuarial calculations each night as they get into bed and then proceed to fulfill their probabilistic duty. Attachment to such a view may be reinforced by the elegant simplicity of the demographic transition theory, the underpinning for so much of our thinking about population questions. One begins with fertility and mortality in equilibrium at a high level. The nature of the forces operating to ensure equilibration at that level is clear. Fertility is considered fixed, reflecting the characteristics of our species. Improvement in resources brings a decline of mortality, followed by a rise in population size, followed by a rise of mortality, so that we are once again in balance with our ecological niche. The transition occurs when modernization breaks out of that niche, first propelling mortality downward and then fertility as well. The theory is compelling in its description of the forces prescribing a negative slope for fertility but says nothing about what might stop the decline in fertility. At the terminal low stage, mortality is considered fixed—again reflecting the characteristics of our species—but there is no specification of the feedback system which would bring fertility into alignment with mortality.

If we were to construct a fertility projection (say over the next thirty years) the thrust of the preceding arguments would be that the level of cohort fertility is more likely to continue declining from its present value (some 10 percent below replacement) than to rise again. Superimposed on this trend we should expect to find short-term swings in the birth rate. On the basis of postwar experience, the most worthwhile clue would seem to be the link between the size of a cohort (relative to its immediate predecessors) and the age of mothers at the birth of their first child. Simply stated, the larger a cohort, the more difficulty it has becoming established occupationally and the longer the delay of entry into parenthood; the converse holds for a smaller cohort. The empirical support for this relationship is strong. We have reasonable estimates of the mean age of mothers at the birth of their first child (M) for the cohorts born in each year from 1891 through 1950. For 1891–1914, the size of the cohort was increasing and M rose; for 1914–1939, the size of the cohort was not increasing (and frequently declining) and M declined appreciably; for 1939–1950, the size of the cohort was increasing (considerably, if irregularly) and M rose appreciably. The two time series are remarkably synchronized in their turning points.

Knowing this relationship between cohort size and age of mothers at the birth of their first child would be a distinct advantage in attempting projections, because we already know the relevant cohort size for the next several decades. On the assumption that the regression persists, we would expect M (the mean age of mothers at birth of their first child) to continue rising for perhaps another five years and then decline substantially to the end of the century. The implicit change in the tempo of cohort fertility would yield (against a backdrop of a constant level of cohort fertility) a rise in the period total fertility rate over the next fifteen years (from 1.8 to 2.2) and then a decline in the same rate over the following fifteen years (from 2.2 to 1.7). Beyond that distortion of the annual record, occasioned by the link between cohort size and the tempo of cohort childbearing, there is the direct arithmetical impact of cohort size on the numbers of births themselves. When this too is taken into account, the prognosis becomes a rise in the birth rate from a current fifteen per thousand per annum to about twenty in the early years of the next decade, followed by a precipitous decline to a level of about twelve by the end of the century. To repeat, the assumptions underlying this projection are an unchanging long-run pattern of cohort fertility (with respect to quantum and tempo) and a persistence of the relationship between cohort size and cohort tempo in the short run. Realistically, there will be more or less departure from these assumptions, together with unforeseeable shocks to the system of societal reproduction as political and economic conditions change and as the relevant norms take new form.

If this prognosis has approximate validity, the key analytic question is the source of dwindling reproductivity, and the answer in my judgment lies in what is happening to the family institution itself (Ryder, 1974). In every society, the family is the institution charged with responsibility for replacement of the population. In premodern times, high mortality made that a very large responsibility indeed, but our survival as a species shows that the traditional family proved adequate to its assignment. It is beginning to look as if the modern family is not.

I want now to suggest some characteristics of change in the family during the course of modernization which may be the source of the problem. In premodern times, the family was the basic unit in the economy. The head of the family was by virtue of that fact the owner and the employer. To the individual member, the family represented the source of technical education, the avenue of employment, the channel of credit and Social Security, and the source of protection and defense. The gravity of the responsibilities of the traditional family were manifest in its authoritarian structure, specifically the power of parent over child and male over female. In the community at large, the most important piece of information about a person was his or her family name. The family indeed has been the foundation of all systems of ascribing status on the basis of characteristics fixed at birth, and thus of stratification systems, whether they are oriented to caste or class or race.

How different it is with the modern family. One by one its functions have been shifted to the specialized institutions characteristic of the developed society. The father is no longer the source of land or other capital or the person under whom one could serve an appropriate apprenticeship. The head of the family can no longer act as if he owned his wife and children. The intrusion into the family structure of an ideology emphasizing the individual has diluted respect and gratitude alike. The parents can no longer control the marriage of their child, nor indeed is it important to them that they do so. The new calculus of production emphasizes not who a person is but what he or she can do, and that in turn depends more one one's individual accreditation in educational institutions, controlled not by the family but by society.

Fertility was once high for a simple reason—the productivity of the child accrued to the benefit of the parent. But then the fundamental direction of obligation in the intergenerational contract shifted from what the child owed the parent to what the parent owed the child. As the benefits of children to parents approached the zero point, the costs of children to parents rose, without an apparent ceiling to date. Is it any wonder that fertility fell? Indeed a more interesting question is what might stop it from falling.

Those who view with alarm the modern family are apt to emphasize its conjugal aspects. For example, there is great concern about the prevalence of divorce, and indeed this has grown to disconcerting proportions. Yet it seems to me that frequent divorce is the understandable consequence of making the satisfaction of the individual the test of a good marriage. The burden of proof has shifted from what the individual can do for the family to what the family can do for the individual. Yet I doubt that the frequency of divorce is a distinctive signal of the disintegration of the marital institution. As the family was stripped of its economic and political responsibilities, it too became a specialized institution, specialized in the development and maintenance of the individual self. In a modern society, the individual has greater need for emotional support, and the conjugal family is more exclusively the source of that support. The family provides an emotional haven to comfort individuals on

their return from exposure to the frequently damaging consequences of participation in the impersonal competitive modern economy. One testament to the
continuing importance of marriage as an institution is the alacrity with which
most divorced choose to remarry, as a vote of confidence in the institution
which has failed them only in particular.

A second example of concern with conjugal aspects of the family is the
growing practice of young people living togther without taking vows, a practice my generation views with antipathy or at least unease, as well as a covert
admixture of envy. I think the young are making a mistake if they consider
sex to be an appetite which can be adequately satisfied without a sense of
commitment—they are denying themselves the fullness of the experience—but
I seriously doubt that their experimentation is a threat to the idea of marriage.
As a companionate institution, marriage will survive, if only because the
individual has such a need for it. The risks and loneliness of an uncommitted
life are too evident and too large.

What concerns me most about the modern family are not these conjugal
aspects—for such problems, no matter how perplexing, are essentially irrelevant to the reproductive issue—but its generational aspects, the other dimension of the family. To be explicit, I think the child has come to mean rather
little to the parent today, and the parent rather little to the child. The generations were once bound together by concern of the parent for the child and
respect of the child for the parent, a concern and respect that were solidly
embedded in the importance of each for the future of the other. But now almost
the only bond is love, and that tends to be fragile and brittle.

There was a time when parents assumed total responsibility for the socialization of the child, but now the traditional functions of the family are passing
out of the home and into the hands of professional providers. Perhaps the most
important institutional encroachment was the compulsory public school, but
parents have also been displaced by doctors and nurses, community workers,
playground leaders, probation officers, and psychiatrists. As responsibility for
the child is shifted from the parents to the agencies, the ties between parent
and child are weakened. It is almost as if the child is too important to the
society to be left to the parents. Society has a large stake in a healthy, educated,
and socially conforming child, and inept parents cannot be allowed to stand
in the way.

Perhaps the principal reason for the recent decline in fertility is the possibility now gradually opening for women to derive legitimate rewards in the
pursuit of activities other than motherhood. At considerable risk of oversimplification, I would assert that our past success at population replacement,
throughout all of human history, has been conditional on the discriminatory
treatment of women. If we are now prepared to consider this as fundamentally
inequitable and are ready to respect the woman who chooses a nonmaternal
way of life, we may be pulling out the prop that has all along made possible
our survival as a species. Although I am apprehensive about the consequences,

I believe we must accept them, because it is meet and right and proper for women as well as men to be self-determining persons.

Despite the evident inferior positions to which we still assign women in the occupational sphere, the labor force now has only one-third fewer women than men. Although some may be propelled into a job by family financial problems, others are unwilling to remain trapped at home with the children and the housework. The word is out that the satisfactions of raising children require more personal sacrifices by women than by men. Women are now entering the marketplace with greater confidence, expanding their social circles beyond that of their husbands' friends, and experiencing more independence. Those who remain housewives now feel obliged to apologize. Being a wife and a mother is no longer an occupation sufficient unto itself. And the plain fact is that working and mothering are competing activities. As women gain access to the full range of educational and professional opportunities—and they still have far to go—the alternative opportunity cost of reproduction will rise and press fertility further downward. This is the final frontier of modernization—the elimination of discrimination by gender.

In summary of this account of the present family, I believe that there is less satisfaction from parenthood today, and there are alternative modes of living which appear preferable to a significant proportion of young women. This is not to predict that many will decide against parenthood, but rather that enough will exercise a legitimate option to keep fertility low. Simply speaking, we should be prepared for population size to decline.

Imperceptibly but inexorably the population of the future will come to differ in many important respects from anything we have known (Ryder, 1975). Before touting what I think some of those differences will be, two points need to be made clear. First, the propositions to be advanced do not depend on complete acceptance of what I have so far been saying—they hold within a rather broad range of fertility forecasts. Second, the problems to be advertised are not new—they are all with us now. The point of the exercise is not that new problems will be created by prospective demographic change but that old problems will be exacerbated by it.

The first fact about the new world ahead is that our population will be much older than it is now. In particular, the proportion of people who are above age sixty-five will approximately double. This prospect has already aroused considerable concern about the financing of Social Security, for example. When the problem of supporting a dependent population is raised, it is not always recognized that while elder dependents will increase, younger dependents will decrease: the total quantitative burden (to use the ugly jargon word) on those of working age will not change. Still, the transformation of the family institution has long since produced a more evident and perplexing quandary: What is the most fitting and humane social setting for old people? I wish I could provide an answer.

An associated fact about the world to come is that the working population itself will be older. What does that signify? The typical commentary asserts, with little solid evidence, that an older work force will be a less productive one. Younger workers are considered superior in strength, speed and energy, whereas older workers are given the edge in skill, dependability, and wisdom. Such trade-offs seem more reasonable, of course, to each cohort as it gets older. More worrisome than such cross-sectional considerations, in my view, is the fact that age signifies time of birth and thus the historical location of one's training. Perhaps the most sensible way to solve that problem would be for us to shake off the shibboleth that all education must precede all labor force participation. Why should we not contemplate opening the doors between the world of work and the world of education throughout the entire life span?

The problems of the productivity of an older work force have their parallel in the question of the willingness of older entrepreneurs to take risks. Just as older workers tend to be less flexible and less mobile, because they have more to lose from change—they have paid off more of their mortgage—so older entrepreneurs may tend to err on the safe side, to the detriment of initiative and innovation. Maybe that is a valid generalization about the attributes of age, but maybe it just reflects the sociological truism that the older persons, like everyone else in an ascribed system, tend to behave in the ways they are expected to behave. Until more and better research is done on the subject, we should withhold judgement. Moreover, organizations need not be intimidated by the seniority principle. Surely we can find ways of transferring leadership and power from the older to the younger members of organizations without sacrificing altogether the assets those older members represent, perhaps by putting a strict time limit on tenure in high office. The one proposed answer to the problem of the older work force with which I am least in sympathy is the Procrustean solution of lowering the retirement age. In my opinion, retirement is a major cause of death.

Furthermore, there is reason to doubt that the principal issue for the future is whether we will be sufficiently productive. Indeed in a sense we are already overproductive. We no longer need the work of youth, any more than we need the work of the old, or of women, or of the depressed minorities. Yet to say that our society can afford the luxury of idleness does not mean that the individuals themselves can. In a society in which work gives meaning to life, obligatory idleness is less a privilege than a curse. The challenge of our future is much less to increase productivity than to find meaningful roles for all of our citizens.

It seems to me that the most important socioeconomic implications for the future lie in what may be called the processual rather than the structural characteristics of the population. There are only two ways in which a population can be transformed—by some process in which its constituent members assume different characteristics and by the replacement of individuals of one kind by individuals of another kind. The latter mode of transformation I have termed "demographic metabolism" (Ryder, 1975). The evidence is strong that the technological evolution of developed societies has been accomplished mainly by the recruitment of members of new cohorts, that is, by metabolism rather than by the retraining of the members of old cohorts. Of course personnel turnover in itself is not important. What matters is the opportunity that turnover provides for modification of the system of role allocation and the socialization of entrants. Just like any other population, the working population has a kind of birth rate, that is, rate of entry into it. With the shift from a growing to a declining population, the birth rate of the labor force will decline by some 40 percent. The problem, in principle, applies to all organizations—political, cultural, social, and educational. One of the ways we try to keep our research institutions alive is by linking them with graduate education in the belief that the continual infusion of fresh young minds will invigorate the enterprise. If comparable possibilities become substantially more scarce, it is incumbent upon us to devote much more attention than now to recruitment, selection, and training so that we may maximize the efficacy of demographic metabolism as well as enlarge the opportunities for those already within the system to improve their credentials and refresh their education, to help compensate for more sluggish turnover.

The final point concerning the implications of low fertility is the most obvious one—the population will be smaller than it would otherwise have been. There has been a large amount of literature, some of it credible, concerning the relationship between population size on the one hand and resources and the environment on the other (Ryder, 1973). I would be more cheered by the prospect were I not convinced that the problems of most concern are rooted elsewhere than in the sheer numbers of people. But rather than alienate the considerable numbers of zealots on such questions, let me concede that the task of solution by whatever means will be easier if there is less population growth.

I have been presenting an assessment that population decline is a likely prospect and that it will highlight institutional flaws for which we must find institutional rather than demographic remedies. Is there an acceptable demographic solution to the problems posed by population decline? One logical option would be to restrict access to the means of fertility regulation, for example by passing legislation against sterilization and abortion and banning the production of the oral contraceptive. In my view, such actions, even if they could be enforced, would be politically and morally regressive. The issue is not survival willy-nilly but survival of what we believe in. Would it not be tragic if, in an attempt to preserve our population size, we so departed from our ideals that what persisted was not worthy of preservation? Similarly, if my diagnosis is correct that the crucial source of low fertility is the newfound women's freedom, then, in theory, men could save the day demographically by ordering women back to the kitchen. Would we really prefer to live in such a world? Measures which improve the quality of life of individuals—such as freedom of fertility regulation and freedom from discrimination on the basis of gender—should surely be pursued even if they exacerbate prevailing population trends.

Because the society has such a large stake in the production of sufficient numbers of new members, it would seem appropriate that the society assume a larger share in the cost of bearing and rearing children. Efforts in this direction have been tried, and they have been to little avail so far as the birth rate is concerned. I see no evidence from the research to date that suggests that if people only had higher incomes they would surely have more children. In brief, I don't think we can buy babies. One encourages fertility with family benefits, geared to birth orders above two, and help to mothers in combining a job with family responsibilities. One cannot easily combine working and mothering under the rules of full days and full weeks of work; perhaps we need new ways of working. The price for sustaining a replacement level would undoubtedly be high and the magnitude of the income transfer sufficient to inspire a taxpayers' revolt. The problem is that one occupation, that of housewife and mother, is now very low-paid, and the nonmaterial rewards are apparently insufficient to compensate for the low pay. Is the government prepared to guarantee an annual wage to the housewife-mother?

The public authorities may not be able to exert an appreciable influence on the level of fertility. Although economic hardship may balk a few people in their desires for more children, others have different reasons they consider overriding and decisive. If a program of income transfer would suffice to raise fertility, it would seem to follow that a general rise in income would have the same effect. But there is no historical evidence that this is true except in the short run.

It is possible to counteract population decline by immigration, but nearly all countries cherish the idea of a one-culture nation-state. Although this was the way America was populated, we have not yet learned, nor have most comparable countries, how to manage decently a multicultural society. With large income differences between wealthy and poor nations, there will be a strong migratory pull on the developing countries, so that we could set high qualifications on entry. But that would make high the cost to the sending country. The populations of labor-exporting countries are disadvantaged if they are deprived of their more vigorous and qualified elements. Immigration can offset main structural rigidities of the labor force in the short term, at the lower levels of the economic hierarchy deserted by the domestic work force, but it entails serious social tensions. I have a long-run vision of a world in which national boundaries become progressively permeable, to the point of erosion of the very concept of a nation-state, so that someday every child born into the world is looked on as our child—but I recognize that to be a utopian contribution to a realistic policy discussion.

It does seem unlikely that any nation would long tolerate a negative rate of natural increase. I read recently in the *New York Times* a warning by the President of France to his countrymen that no nation with a middle-sized population could realistically aspire to grandeur. The article continued with what I take to be their operational definition of grandeur—it was observed that, in the Napoleonic era, France had three times as many people as Britain.

Population stimulants are associated with raising armies and the Nazi era. Thus, although France may dare to call for subsidization of larger families by appeal to French nationalism and the nation's military credibility, there is squeamishness about such exhortations in West Germany. The apprehensions go beyond national boundaries—similar thinking produces the warning that the West may soon be hopelessly outnumbered by the Third World, and such a disparity in size will create a dangerous political imbalance. This is a primitive logic, but it is a prevalent political reality, which probably plays an implicit part in the demographic philosophy of many national leaders.

Past population policy pressed the cause of what were perceived to be collective interests over what individuals were clearly signalling was in their interest. In my view, the burden of proof is squarely on the government to make an unequivocal case for such collective interests relative to individual well-being. Governments are ambivalent about population size and the rate of growth. They know the case that can be made for reduction of growth as an aid in solving the problems of resource depletion and environmental pollution. For all the apprehension about the negative consequences of a stationary or declining population, there are positive consequences as well; and I have been arguing at many points here that the negative ones are more likely to respond to institutional than to demographic remedies.

The past history of governmental action in the field of fertility has been pronatalist—especially through inhibiting individual access to satisfactory fertility regulation—but individuals and families proceeded in an antinatalist direction nevertheless. What is happening to our fertility now is mostly based on the choices people are making about how they can best achieve an optimum quality of life in the prevailing circumstances. I propose that governments treat such choices with the respect they deserve.

In conclusion, then, I think we are for a considerable demographic transformation, but not one to be feared. I doubt that governments are able to modify the trend of fertility more than marginally, provided they can be restrained from regressive measures. And I doubt that they should even if they could—because the people know what they are doing.

Danziger, Sheldon H. and Robert J. Lampman
    1978   "Getting and spending." *The Annals* 435:23-39.
Easterlin, Richard A.
    1978   "What will 1984 be like? Socioeconomic implications of recent twists in age structure." Presidential address, Population Association of America, Atlanta, Georgia (Mimeo).
Editors of *Population Index*
    1948   "The population forecasts of the Scripps Foundation." *Population Index* 4(3):188-195.
Miller, Ann R.
    1978   "Changing work life patterns: A twenty-five year review." *The Annals* 435:83-101.
Ryder, N. B.
    1973   "Two cheers for ZPG." *Daedalus* 102(4):45-62.
    1974   "The family in developed countries." *Scientific American* 231(2):122-132.
    1975   "Notes on stationary populations." *Population Index* 41(1):3-28.

1978a "Components of temporal variations in American fertility." Symposium on Recent
        Changes in Demographic Patterns in Developed Societies, Society for the Study of
        Human Biology, London, England.
1978b "A model of fertility by planning status." *Demography* 15(4).
U.S. Bureau of the Census
    1975   "Projections of the population of the United States: 1975 to 2050." *Current Population
            Reports,* Series P-25, No. 601. Washington, D.C.: U.S. Government Printing Office.
    1978   "Fertility of American women." *Current Population Reports,* Series P-20, No. 325,
            Washington, D.C.: USGPO.
Westoff, Charles F. and Norman B. Ryder
    1977   *The Contraceptive Revolution.* Princeton University Press.

Does the Family Have a Future?

Suzanne Keller

Some thirty-five years ago, two venerable students of human behavior en-gaged in a six-session debate on marriage and the family over the B.B.C. Their names were Bronislaw Malinowski and Robert Briffault, the one a world-famous anthropologist best known for his studies of the Trobriand Islands, the other a social historian devoted to resurrecting the matriarchies of prehistory. Of the two, paradoxically, it was Briffault, the self-trained historian, who turned out to be the cultural relativist, whereas Malinowski, a pioneer in cross-cultural research, exhibited the very ethnocentrism his studies were designed to dispel.

Both men noted that the family was in trouble in their day. Both were distressed by this and sought to discover remedies if not solutions. Despite their common concern, however, they were soon embroiled in vivid and vocif-erous controversy about the nature of the crisis and its cure (*Marriage: Past and Present,* ed. M. F. Ashley-Montagu, Boston, Porter Sargent, 1956).

Briffault concluded from this reading of the evidence that the family rests on sentiments rooted in culture and social tradition rather than in human nature. Unless one grasps these social and cultural essentials, one cannot hope to understand, much less cure, what ails it. No recourse to natural instinct or to the "dictatorship of tradition or moral coercion" could save the modern family from its destined decline.

Malinowski disagreed. The family, he admitted, might be passing through a grave crisis, but the illness was not fatal. Marriage and the family, "the foundation of human society" and a key source of spiritual and material progress, were here to stay, though not without some needed improvements. Among these were the establishment of a single standard of morality, greater

From the *Journal of Comparative Family Studies* (Spring 1971). Reprinted by permission.

legal and economic equality between husband and wife, and greater freedom in parent-child relations.

The disagreement of these two men stemmed, as it so often does, not from different diagnoses but from different definitions of the phenomenon. Malinowski defined the family as a legal union of one man and one woman, together with their offspring, bound by reciprocal rights and duties and cooperating for the sake of economic and moral survival. Briffault defined the family much more broadly as an association involving economic production and sexual procreation. In his sense, the clan was a family.

The two agreed on only one point: parenthood and, above all, maternity are the pivots in the anatomy of marriage and the family. If these change so must the familial organization that contained them. Thus if one can identify such pivotal changes their difficulties are overcome while ours may be said to be just beginning.

There is good reason to suppose that such changes are now upon us. The malaise of our time reflects not simply a temporary disenchantment with an ancient institution but a profound convulsion of the social order. The family is indeed suffering a sea change.

It is curious to note how much more quickly the popular press, including the so-called women's magazines, have caught on to changing marital, sexual, and parental styles. While many of the experts are still serving up conventional and tradition-bound idols—the hard-working, responsible, breadwinner husband-father; the self-effacing, ministering wife-mother; the grateful, respectful children—these magazines tempt the contemporary reader with less standard and more challenging fare. Whether in New York or in Athens, the newsstands flaunt their provocative titles—"Is This the Last Marrying Generation?", "Alimony for Ex-Husbands," "Why We Don't Want to Have Children," "Are Husbands Superfluous?"—in nonchalant profusion. These and other assaults on our sexual and moral codes in the shape of the new theater, the new woman, the new youth, and TV soap operas akin to a psychiatrist's case files, persuade us that something seems to be afoot in the whole sphere of marriage and family relations which many had thought immune to change. In point of fact the question is not *whether* the family is changing but how and how much; how important are these changes, how permanent, how salutary? The answers depend largely on the way we ask our questions and define our terms.

The family means many things to many people, but in its essence it refers to those socially patterned ideals and practices concerned with biological and cultural survival of the species. When we speak of the family we are using a kind of shorthand, a label for a social invention not very different, in essence, from other social inventions, let us say the corporation or the university, and no more permanent than these. This label designates a particular set of social practices concerned with procreation and child rearing, with the heterosexual partnership that makes this possible and the parent-child relations that make it enduring. As is true of all collective habits, once established, such practices

are exceedingly resistant to change, in part because they evoke strong sentiments and in part because no acceptable alternatives are offered. Since most
individuals are unable to step outside of their cultures, they are unable to note
the arbitrary and variable nature of their conventions. Accordingly, they
ascribe to their folkways and creeds an antiquity, an inevitability, and a universality these do not possess.

The idea that the family is universal is highly misleading despite its popularity. All surviving societies have indeed found ways to stabilize the processes
of reproduction and child care else they would not have survived to tell their
tale. But since they differ greatly in how they arrange these matters (and since
they are willing to engage in hot and cold wars to defend such differences), the
generalization does not help us explain the phenomenon but more nearly
explains it away.

In truth there are as many forms of the family as there are forms of society,
some so different from ours that we consider them unnatural and incomprehensible. There are, for example, societies in which couples do not share a
household and do not have sole responsibility for their offspring; others in
which our domestic unit of husband and wife is divided into two separate units,
a conjugal one of biological parents and a brother-sister unit for economic
sustenance. There are societies in which children virtually rear each other and
societies in which the wise father does not know his own child. All of these
are clearly very different from our twentieth century, industrial-urban conception of the family as a legally united couple, sharing bed and board, jointly
responsible for bearing and rearing their children and formally isolated from
their next of kin in all but a sentimental sense. This product of a long and
complicated evolutionary development from prehistoric times is no simple
replica of the ancient productive and reproductive institutions from which it
derives its name and some of its characteristic features. The contemporary
family really has little in common with its historic Hebrew, Greek, and Roman
ancestors.

The family of these great civilizations of the West was a household community of hundreds, and sometimes thousands, of members (*familia* is the Latin
term for household). Only some of the members were related by blood, and
by far the larger part were servants and slaves, artisans, friends, and distant
relations. In its patriarchal form (again culturally variable), this large community was formally held together by the role of eldest male, who more nearly
resembled the general of an army than a modern husband-father. In its prime,
this household community constituted a miniature society, a decentralized
version of a social organization that had grown too large and unwieldly for
effective management. In this it resembles the giant bureaucracies of our own
day and their proposed decentralization into locally based, locally staffed
subsystems, designed to offset the evils of remote control while nevertheless
maintaining their connection with it. Far from having been universal, this
ancient family type, with its gods and shrines, schools and handicrafts, was not

even widely prevalent within its own social borders. Confined to the landed and propertied upper classes, it remained an unattainable ideal for the bulk of common men who made up the society.

The fallacy of universality has done students of human behavior a great disservice. By leading us to seek and hence to find a single pattern, it has blinded us to historical precedents for multiple legitimate family arrangements. As a result we have been rather impoverished in our speculations and proposals about alternative future arrangements in the family sphere.

A second common fallacy asserts that the family is *the* basic institution of society, hereby revealing a misunderstanding of how a society works. For as a social institution, the family is by definition a specialized element which provides society with certain needed services and depends on it for others. This means that you cannot tamper with a society without expecting the family to be affected in some way and vice versa. In the comtemporary jargon, we are in the presence of a feedback system. Whatever social changes we anticipate, therefore, the family cannot be kept immune from them.

A final fallacy concerns the presumed naturalness of the family in proof of which a motley and ill-assorted grab bag of anecdotal evidence from the animal kingdom is adduced. But careful perusal of ethological accounts suggests that animals vary as greatly as we do, their mating and parental groupings including such novelties as the love death, males who bear children, total and guilt-free "promiscuity," and other "abnormal" features. The range of variation is so wide, in fact, that virtually any human arrangement can be justified by recourse to the habits of some animal species.

In sum, if we wish to understand what is happening to the family—to our family—in our own day, we must examine and observe it in the here and now. In so doing it would be well to keep in mind that the family is an abstraction at best, serving as guide and image of what a particular society considers desirable and appropriate in family relations, not what takes place in actual fact. In reality there are always a number of empirical family types at variance with this, though they usually pay lip service to the overarching cultural ideal.

Challenges to the Contemporary Industrial Family

In the United States, as in other industrial societies, the ideal family consists of a legally constituted husband-wife team, their young, dependent children, living in a household of their own, provided for by the husband's earnings as main breadwinner, and emotionally united by the wife's exclusive concentration on the home. Probably no more than one-third of all families at a particular moment in time, and chiefly in the middle and would-be middle classes, actually live up to this image. The remaining majority all lack one or more of the essential attributes—in lacking a natural parent, or in not being economically self-sufficient, or in having made other necessary modifications.

One contrasting form is the extended family in which the couple share household arrangements and expenses with parents, siblings, or other close relatives. The children are then reared by several generations and have a choice of models on which to pattern their behavior. This type, frequent in working class and immigrant milieus, may be as cohesive and effective as the ideal type; but it lacks the cultural legitimacy and desirability of the latter.

A third family type, prevalent among the poor of all ethnic and racial backgrounds, is the mother-child family. Contrary to our prejudices this need not be a deviant or distorted family form, for it may be the only viable and appropriate one in its particular setting. Its defects may stem more from adverse social judgments than from intrinsic failings. Deficient in cultural resources and status, it may nevertheless provide a humane and spirited setting for its members, particularly if some sense of stability and continuity has been achieved. Less fortunate are the numerous non-families, ex-families, and non-intact families such as the divorced, the widowed, the unmarriageables, and many other fragmented social forms who have no recognized social place. None of these, however, threaten the existing order, since they are seen and see themselves as involuntarily different, imperfect, or unfortunate. As such they do not challenge the ideals of family and marital relations but simply suggest how difficult it is to live up to them. When we talk of family change or decline, however, it is precisely the ideal standards which we have in mind. A challenge to them cannot be met by simple reaffirmations of old truths, disapproval, shock, or ridicule of the challengers, or feigned indifference. Such challenges must be met head on.

Today the family and its social and psychological underpinnings are being fundamentally challenged from at least three sources: (1) from accumulated failures and contradictions in marriage; (2) from pervasive occupational and educational trends including the changing relations between the sexes, the spread of birth control, and the changing nature of work; and (3) from novel developments in biology. Let me briefly examine each.

It is generally agreed that even in its ideal form, the industrial-urban family makes great, some would say excessive, demands on its members. For one thing it rests on the dyadic principle or pair relationship which, as Georg Simmel observed long ago, is inherently tragic and unstable. Whether in chess, tennis, or marriage, two are required to start and continue the game but only one can destroy it. In this instance, moreover, the two are expected to retain their separate identities as male and female and yet be one in flesh and spirit. No wonder that the image of the couple, a major source of fusion and of schism in our society, is highly contradictory according to whether we think of the sexes as locked in love or in combat. Nor do children, the symbols of their union, necessarily unify them. Their own growing pains and cultural demands force them into mutually exclusive socio-sexual identities, thereby increasing the intimate polarity. In fact, children arouse parental ambivalence in a number of ways, not the least of which is that they demand all but give back all too little. And yet their upbringing and sustenance, the moral and emotional climate, as well as the accumulation of economic and educational resources needed for survival, all rest on this small, fragile, essential but very limited unit. Held together by sentimental rather than by corporate bonds, the happiness of the partners is a primary goal, although no one is very sure what happiness means nor how it may be achieved and sustained.

To these potentials for stress and strain must be added the loss of many erstwhile functions to school, state, and society, and with it something of the glamour and challenge of family commitments. Few today expect the family to be employment agency, welfare state, old-age insurance, or school for life. Yet once upon a time, however, with fewer resources, some new burdens have been added stemming from rising standards of child health, education, and welfare. This makes parents even more crucially responsible for the potential fate of their children over whom they have increasingly less exclusive control.

Like most social institutions in the throes of change, moreover, the modern family is also beset by numerous internal contradictions engendered by the conflict between traditional patterns of authority and a new egalitarianism between husbands and wives and parents and children. The equality of the spouses, for example, collides with the continuing greater economic responsibilities, hence authority, of the husband. The voluntary harness of love chafes under the constraint of numerous obligations and duties imposed by marriage; and dominance patterns by sex or age clash with new demands for mutuality, reciprocity, equity, and individualism. These, together with some unavoidable disillusionments and disappointments in marriage, set the stage for the influence of broader and less subjective social trends.

One such trend, demographic in nature but bound to have profound social implications, concerns the lengthened life expectancy and the shortened reproductive span for women. Earlier ages at marriage, fewer children per couple, and closer spacing of children means: the girl who marries at 20 will have all her children by age 26, have all her children in school by her early thirties, have the first child leave home for job, schooling, or marriage in her late thirties, and have all her children out of the home by her early forties. This leaves some thirty to forty years to do with as personal pleasure or social need dictate. The contrast with her grandmother is striking: later marriage and more children spaced farther apart meant all the children in school no earlier than her middle or late thirties and the last to leave home (if he or she ever did) not before her early fifties At which time grandmother was probably a widow and close to the end of her own life span. The empty nest thus not only occurs earlier today, but it lasts longer, affecting not this or that unfortunate individual woman but many, if not most, women. Hence what may in the past have been an individual misfortune has turned into a social emergency of major proportions. More unexpected free time, more time without a socially recognized or appreciated function, more premature retirements surely puts the conventional modern wife, geared to the domestic welfare of husband, home, and children, at a singular disadvantage relative to the never-married career woman. Destined to outlive her husband, stripped of major domestic responsibilities in her prime years, what is she to do with this windfall of extra hours and years? Surely we must expect and prepare for a major cultural shift in the education and upbringing of female children. If women cannot afford to make motherhood and domestic concerns the sole foci of their identities, they must be encouraged, early in life, to prepare themselves for some occupation or profession not as an adjunct or as a last resort in case of economic need but as an equally legitimate pursuit. The child rearing of girls must increasingly be geared to developing a feminine identity that stresses autonomy, non-dependency, and self-assertion in work and in life.

Some adjunct trends are indirectly stimulating just such a reorientation. When women are compelled, as they often are, to earn their own living or to supplement inadequate family resources necessitated by the high emphasis on personal consumption and the high cost of services increasingly deemed essential as national standards rise, conventional work-dependency patterns are shattered. For, since the male breadwinner is already fully occupied, often with two jobs, or if he cannot or will not work, his wife is forced to step in. Thus there is generated internal family pressure—arising from a concern for family welfare but ultimately not confined to it—for wives to bearing gainfully employed outside of the home. And fully three-fourths in the post-childbearing ages already are, albeit under far from ideal conditions. Torn between home and job, between the precepts of early childhood with its promise of permanent security at the side of a strong male and the pressures of a later reality, unaided by a society unaware or indifferent to her problems, the double-duty wife must manage as best she can.

That this need not be so is demonstrated by a number of modern societies whose public policies are far better meshed with changing social realities. Surely one of our more neglected institutions—the single-family household which, despite all the appliances, remains essentially backward and primitive in its conditions of work—will need some revamping and modernizing. More household appliances, more and more attractive alternatives to the individually run household, more nursery schools, and a total overhaul of work schedules not now geared to a woman's life and interests cannot be long in coming. While these will help women in all of their multiple tasks, they may also of course further challenge the presumed joys of exclusive domesticity.

All in all, it would appear that the social importance of the family relative to other significant social arenas will, as Briffault, among others, correctly anticipated, decline. Even today when the family still exerts a strong emotional and sentimental hold, its social weight is not what it once was. All of us ideally are still born in intact families but not all of us need to establish families to survive. Marriage and children continue to be extolled as supreme social and personal goals but they are no longer—especially for men—indispensable for a meaningful existence. As individual self-sufficiency, fed by economic affluence or economic self-restraint, increases, so does one's exemption from unwanted economic as well as kinship responsibilities. Today the important frontiers seem to lie elsewhere, in science, politics, and outer space. This must affect the attractions of family life for both men and women. For men, because they will see less and less reason to assume full economic and social responsibilities for four to five human beings in addition to themselves as it becomes more difficult and less necessary to do so. This, together with the continued decline of patriarchal authority and male dominance—even in the illusory forms in which they have managed to hang on—will remove some of the psychic rewards which prompted many men to marry, while the disappearance of lineage as mainstays of the social and class order will deprive paternity of its social justification. For women, the household may soon prove too small for the scope of their ambitions and power drives. Until recently these were directed first of all to their children, secondarily to their mates. But with the decline of parental control over children, a major erstwhile source of challenge and creativity is removed from the family sphere. This must weaken the motherwife complex, historically sustained by the necessity and exaltation of motherhood and the taboo on illegitimacy.

Above all, the move towards worldwide population and birth control must affect the salience of parenthood for men and women, as a shift of cultural emphasis and individual priorities deflates maternity as woman's chief social purpose and paternity as the prod to male exertions in the world of work. Very soon, I suspect, the cultural presses of the world will slant their messages against the bearing and rearing of children. Maternity, far from being a duty, not even a right, will then become a rare privilege to be granted to a select and qualified few. Perhaps the day is not far off when reproduction will be confined to a fraction of the population, and what was once inescapable necessity may become voluntary, planned choice. Just as agricultural societies in which everyone had to produce food were once superseded by industrial societies in which a scant 6 percent now produce food for all, so one day the few may produce children for the many.

This, along with changing attitudes towards sex, abortion, adoption, illegitimacy, the spread of the pill, better knowledge of human behavior, and a growing scepticism that the family is the only proper crucible for childrearing, creates a powerful recipe for change. Worldwide demands for greater and better opportunities for self-development and a growing awareness that these opportunities are inextricably enhanced or curtailed by the family as a prime determinant of life-chances will play a major role in this change. Equal opportunity, it is now clear, cannot stop at the crib but must start there. "It is idle," commented Dr. Robert S. Morrison, a Cornell biologist, "to talk of a society of equal opportunity as long as that society abandons its newcomers solely to their families for their most impressionable years" (*New York Times,* October 30, 1966). One of the great, still largely unchallenged injustices may well be that one cannot choose one's parents.

The trends that I have sketched would affect marriage, male-female, and parent-child relations even if no other developments were on the horizon. But there are. As yet barely discernible and still far from being applicable to human beings, recent breakthroughs in biology—with their promise of a greatly extended life span, novel modes of reproduction, and dramatic possibilities for genetic intervention—cannot be ignored in a discussion devoted to the future of the family.

Revolution in Biology

If the early part of this century belonged to physics and the middle period to exploratory ventures into outer space, the next few decades belong to biology. The prolongation of life to double or triple its current span seems virtually assured, the extension of female fertility into the sixties is more than a distinct possibility, and novel ways of reproducing the human species have moved from science fiction to the laboratory. The question then arises, What will happen when biological reproduction will not only be inadvisable for the sake of collective well-being but superseded by new forms and eventually by nonhuman forms of reproduction?

A number of already existing possibilities may give us a foretaste of what is to come. For example, the separation of conception from gestation means that motherhood can become specialized, permitting some women to conceive and rear many children and others to bear them without having to provide for them. Frozen sperms banks (of known donors) are envisioned from which prospective mothers could choose the fathers of their children on the basis of particularly admired or desired qualities, thereby advancing an age-old dream of selecting a distinguished paternity for their children based on demonstrated rather than potential male achievement. And it would grant men a sort of immortality to sire offspring long after their biological deaths as well as challenge the implicit equation now made between fathers and husbands. Finally, the as yet remote possibility to reproduce the human species without sexual intercourse, by permanently separating sex from procreation, would permit unmarried women (and men) to have children without being married, reduces a prime motive for marriage and may well dethrone—inconceivable as this may seem—the heterosexual couple. All of these pose questions of legal and social policy to plague the most subtle Solon. Who is the father of a child—the progenitor or the provider where these have become legitimately distinct roles? Who is the mother—the woman who conceives the child or the one who carries it to term? Who will decide on sex ratios once sex determination becomes routine? Along with such challenges and redefinitions of human responsibility, some see the fate of heterosexuality itself to lie in the balance. In part of course this rests on one's assumptions about the nature of sexuality and sexual identity.

Anatomy alone has never been sufficient for the classification of human beings into male and female which each society labors to develop and then calls natural. Anatomy is but one—and by no means always a reliable—identifying characteristic. Despite our beliefs, sex identification, even in the strictest physical sense, is by no means clear-cut. Various endeavors to find foolproof methods of classification—for example, for participation in the Olympics—have been unsuccessful, as at least nine separate and often uncorrelated components of sexual phenotype have been identified. But if we cannot count on absolute physical differentiations between the sexes, we do even less well when it comes to their social and psychological attributes. Several decades of research have shown beyond doubt that most of what we mean by the difference between the sexes is a blend of cultural myth and social necessity, which must be learned, painstakingly and imperfectly, from birth on. Once acquired, sexual identity is not fixed but needs to be reinforced and propped up in a myriad of ways of which we are quite unaware.

In the past this complicated learning process was guided by what we may call the categorical reproductive imperative, which proclaimed procreation as an unquestionable social goal and which steered the procreative and sexual capacities and aspirations of men and women toward appropriate channels virtually from birth on. Many other features strengthened these tendencies— symbolism and sentiment, work patterns and friendships, all kinds of subtle and not so subtle rewards and punishments for being a "real" man, a real woman. But once the reproductive imperative is transformed into a reproductive ban, what will be the rationale for the continuance of the exclusive heterosexual polarity in the future? If we keep in mind that only two out of our forty-six chromosomes are sex-carrying, perhaps these two will disappear as their utility subsides. Even without such dramatic changes, already there is speculation that heterosexuality will become but one among several forms of sexuality, these having previously been suppressed by strong social sanctions against sexual deviation as well as their inability to reproduce themselves in standard fashion. More than three decades ago, Olaf Stapleton, one of the most imaginative science fiction writers of the century, postulated the emergence of at least six subsexes out of the familiar ancient polarity. At about the same time, Margaret Mead, in the brilliant epilogue to her book on sex and temperament (*Sex and Temperament in Three Primitive Societies,* William Morrow and Co., New York, 1935), suggested a reorganization and recategorization of human identity not along but across traditional sex lines so as to produce a better alignment between individual capacity and social necessity. In our time we have witnessed the emergence of UniSex (the term is McLuhan's) and predictions which range from the disappearance of sex to its manifold elaboration.

Some are speculating about a future in which only one of the current sexes will survive, the other having become superfluous or obsolescent. Depending on the taste, temperament—and sex—of the particular writer, women and men have alternately been so honored (or cursed). It is not always easy to tell which aspect of sex—the anatomical, psychological, or cultural—the writer has in mind, but as the following comment suggests, much more than anatomy is at stake.

> Does the man and woman thing have a future? The question may not be hypothetical much longer. Within 10 years . . . we may be able to choose the sex of our offspring; and later to reproduce without mating male and female cells. This means it will someday be possible to have a world with only one sex, woman, and thereby avoid the squabbles, confusions, and headaches that have dogged this whole business of sex down the centuries. A manless world suggests several scientific scenarios. The most pessimistic would have society changing not at all, but continuing on its manly ways of eager acquisition, hot competition, and mindless aggression. In which case, half the women would become "men" and go right on getting ulcers, shouting "charge" and pinning medals on each other. (George B. Leonard, "The Man and Woman Thing," *Look,* December 25, 1968)

Long before the demise of heterosexuality as a mainstay of the social order, however, we will have to come to terms with changing sexual attitudes and mores ushered in by what has been called the sexual revolution. This liberalization, this rejection of old taboos, half-truths, and hypocrisies, also means a crisis of identity as men and women, programmed for more traditional roles, search for the boundaries of their sexual selves in an attempt to establish a territoriality of the soul.

Confusion is hardly, of course, a novel aspect of the human condition. Not knowing where we have come from, why we are here, or where we are headed, it could hardly be otherwise. There have always been dissatisfied men and women rejecting the roles their cultures have assigned them or the responsibilities attached to these. But these are the stuff of poetry and drama, grist for the analyst's couch or the priest's confessional, in other words private torments and agonies kept concealed from an unsympathetic world. It is only when such torments become transmuted into public grievance and so become publicly heard and acknowledged that we can be said to be undergoing profound changes akin to what we are experiencing today.

Returning now to our main question—Does the family have a future?—it should be apparent that I expect some basic and irreversible changes in the decades ahead and the emergence of some novel forms of human togetherness. Note that the current scene does not already offer some provocative variations on ancient themes, but most of these gain little public attention, still less approval, and so they are unable to alter professed beliefs and standards. Moreover, every culture has its own forms of self-justification and self-righteousness; and in our eagerness to affirm the intrinsic superiority of our ways, we neglect to note the magnitude of variations and deviations from the ideals we espouse. What are we to make, for example, of such dubious allegiance to the monogamous ideal as serial marriages or secret adulteries? Or, less morally questionable, what of the quasi-organized part-time family arrangements necessitated by extreme occupational and geographic mobility? Consider for a moment the millions of families of salesmen, pilots, seacaptains, soldiers, sailors and junior executives where the man of the house is not often *in* the house. These absentee husbands—fathers who magically reenter the family circle just long enough to be appreciated, leaving their wives in charge of the homes they pay for and of the children they sired, are surely no more than part-time mates. If we know little about the adjustments they have had to make or their children's responses, this is because they clearly do not fit in with our somewhat outmoded stereotyped notions of what family relations ought to be. Or consider another home-grown example, the institution of governesses and boarding schools to rear upper-class children. Where is the upper-class mother and how does she spend her time between vacations and homecoming week-ends? Then there are of course many countries around the world—Israel, Sweden, and socialist countries, some of the African societies—where all or nearly all women, most of them mothers, work outside of the home as a matter of course. And because these societies are free from guilt and ambivalence about the working mother, they have managed to incorporate these realities more gracefully into their scheme of things, developing a number of useful innovations along the way. Thus even in our own day, adaptions and modifications exist and have not destroyed all notions of family loyalty, responsibility, and commitment.

In fact, people may be more ready for change than official pronouncements and expert opinions assume. The spread of contraceptive information and the acceptance of full birth control have been remarkable. The relaxation of many erstwhile taboos has proceeded at breakneck speed, and the use of public forums to discuss such vital but previously forbidden topics as abortion, homosexuality, or illegitimacy is dramatic and startling in a society rooted in Puritanism. A number of studies, moreover, show that the better educated are more open to reexamination and change in all spheres, including the family. Since these groups are on the increase, we may expect greater receptivity to such changes in the future. Even such startling proposed innovations as egg transplants, test-tube babies, and cloning are not rejected out of hand if they would help achieve the family goals most Americans prize. (See "The Second Genesis" by Albert Rosenfeld and the Louis Harris Poll, *Life,* June 1969, pp. 31-46.)

Public response to a changing moral and social climate is of course hard to predict. In particular, as regards family concerns, the reactions of women, so crucially bound up with motherhood and child rearing in their self-definitions, are of especial interest. In this connection one study of more than 15,000 women college students attending four year liberal arts colleges in the United States is relevant for its findings on how such a nationwide sample of young coeds, a group of great future significance, feels about marriage, motherhood, and career. (Charles F. Westoff and Raymond H. Potvin, *College Women and Fertility Values,* Princeton University Press, 1967.) Selecting only those items on which there was wide consensus and omitting details of interest to the specialist, the general pattern of answers was unmistakable. The large majority of these would-be wives and mothers disapproved of large families (three or more children), did not consider children to be the most important reason for marriage, favored birth control and birth planning, and thought it possible for a woman to pursue family and career simultaneously. They split evenly on the matter of whether a woman's main satisfaction should come from family rather can career or community activities, and they were virtually united in thinking that mothers with very young children should not work. The latter strongly identifies them as Americans, I think, where nursery schools and other aids to working mothers—including moral support—are not only lacking but still largely disapproved of.

Thus if we dare to speculate further about the future of the family, we will be on safe ground with the following anticipations: (1) a trend towards greater, legitimate variety in sexual and marital experience; (2) a decrease in the negative emotions—exclusiveness, possessiveness, fear, and jealously—associated with these; (3) greater room for personal choice in the kind, extent, and duration of intimate relationships, which may greatly improve their quality as people will both give and demand more of them; (4) entirely new forms of communal living arrangements in which several couples will share the tasks of child rearing and economic support as well as the pleasures of relaxation; (5) multistage marriages geared to the changing life cycle and the presence or absence of dependent children. Of these proposals, some, such as Margaret Mead's, would have the young and the immature of any age test themselves and their capacities to relate to others in an individual form of marriage which would last only so long as it fulfilled both partners. In contrast to this, older, more experienced, and more mature couples who were ready to take on the burdens of parenthood would make a deeper and longer lasting commitment. Other proposals would reverse this sequence and have couples assume parental commitments when young and, having discharged their debt to society, be then free to explore more personal, individualistic partnerships. Neither of these seems as yet to be particularly appealing to the readers who responded to Mead's proposal as set forth in *Redbook Magazine.* (Margaret Mead, "Marriage in Two Steps," *Redbook Magazine,* July 1966; 'The Life Cycle and Its Variation: The Division of Roles," *Daedalus,* Summer 1967; "A Continuing Dialogue on Marriage: Why Just Living Together Won't Work," *Redbook Magazine* April 1968.)

For the immediate future, it appears that most Americans opt for and anticipate their participation in durable, intimate, heterosexual partnerships as anchors and pivots of their adult lives. They expect these to be freer and more flexible than was true in the past, however, and less bound to duty and involuntary personal restrictions. They cannot imagine and do not wish a life without them.

Speculating for the long-range future, we cannot ignore the potential implications of the emerging cultural taboo on unrestricted reproduction and the shift in public concern away from the family as the central preoccupation of one's life. Hard as it may seem, perhaps some day we will cease to relate to families, just as we no longer relate ourselves to clans, and instead be bound up with some new, as yet unnamed principle of human association. If and when this happens, we may also see a world of Unisex, Multisex, or Nonsex. None of this can happen, however, if we refuse to shed some of our most cherished preconceptions, such as that monogamy is superior to other forms of marriage or that women naturally make the best mothers. Much as we may be convinced of these now, time may reveal them as yet another illusion, another example of made-to-order truths.

Ultimately all social change involves moral doubt and moral reassessment. If we refuse to consider change while there still is time, time will pass us by. Only by examining and taking stock of what is can we hope to affect what will be. This is our chance to invent and thus to humanize the future.

Chapter 2

"Endangered Species" or "Here to Stay": The Current Debate about the Family

The Family as a Haven in a Heartless World

Christopher Lasch

The family in the form familiar to us took shape in the United States and western Europe in the last half of the eighteenth and the first half of the nineteenth centuries, although its antecedents can be traced back to an earlier period. The chief features of the Western family system can be simply, if somewhat schematically, set forth. Compared with practices in most other societies, marriage takes place at a late age, and large numbers of people remain unmarried. As these demographic facts imply, marriages tend to be arranged by the participants instead of by parents and elders; at best the elders have a veto. Young couples are allowed to court with a minimum of interference from adults, on the understanding that their own self-restraint will take the place of adult supervision—an expectation that is not unreasonable considering that courting couples are typically young adults themselves and that young women in particular have been trained from an early age to accept advances from the other sex without compromising their reputation.

At the same time the habits of self-inhibition acquired during courtship are not easily relinquished in marriage, and the Western marriage system therefore gives rise to much sexual tension and maladjustment, which is more keenly felt than it would be elsewhere because marriage is supposed to be based on intimacy and love. The overthrow of arranged marriage was accomplished in the name of romantic love and a new conception of the family as a refuge from the highly competitive and often brutal world of commerce and industry. Husband and wife, according to this ideology, were to find solace and spiritual renewal in each other's company. Especially the woman was expected to serve, in a well-worn nineteenth-century phrase, as an "angel of consolation."

Reprinted by permission of the author and the publisher from *Salmagundi* (Fall 1976), pp. 42–55.

Her mission of mercy extended of course to her children as well, around whom middle-class family life increasingly centered. A new idea of childhood, as Aries has shown, helped to precipitate the new idea of the family. No longer seen simply as a little adult, the child came to be regarded as a person with distinctive attributes of his own, impressionability, vulnerability, and innocence, that required a warm, protected, and prolonged period of nurture. Whereas formerly children had mixed freely in adult society, parents now sought to segregate them from premature contact with servants and other corrupting influences. Educators and moralists began to stress the child's need for play, for love and understanding, and for the gradual, gentle unfolding of his nature. Child-rearing became more demanding as a result, and emotional ties between parents and children were strengthened at the same time that ties to relatives outside the immediate family were greatly weakened. Here was another source of persistent tension in the middle-class family—the emotional overloading of the parent-child connection.

Still another source of tension was the change in the status of women that the new family system required. The bourgeois family simultaneously degraded and exalted women. On the one hand, it deprived women of many of their traditional employments, as the household ceased to be a center of production and devoted itself to childrearing instead. On the other hand, the new demands of childrearing, at a time when so much attention was being given to the special needs of the child, made it necessary to educate women for their domestic duties. Better education was also required if women were to become suitable companions for their husbands. A thoroughgoing reform and extension of women's education was implicit in the new-style domesticity, as Mary Wollstonecraft, the first modern feminist, was one of the first to appreciate when she insisted that if women were to become "affectionate wives and rational mothers," they would have to be trained in something more than "accomplishments" that were designed to make young ladies attractive to prospective suitors. Early republican ideology had as one of its main tenets the proposition that women should become useful rather than ornamental. In the categories immortalized by Jane Austen, women were called on to give up sensibility in favor of sense. Thus bourgeois domesticity gave rise to its antithesis, feminism. The domestication of woman gave rise to a general unrest, encouraging her to entertain aspirations that marriage and the family could not satisfy. These aspirations were one ingredient in the so-called marriage crisis that began to unfold at the end of the nineteenth century.

To summarize, the bourgeois family system, which had its heyday in the nineteenth century and now seems to be slowly crumbling, was founded on what sociologists have called companionate marriage, on the child-centered household, on the emancipation or quasi-emancipation of women, and on the structural isolation of the nuclear family from the kinship system and from society in general. The family found ideological support and justification in the conception of the family as an emotional refuge in a cold and competitive society. Before turning to the late nineteenth-century crisis of the family, we need to examine a little further the last of these social facts—the concept of the family as a haven in a heartless world. This ideal took for granted a radical separation between work and leisure and between public life and private life. The emergence of the nuclear family as the principal form of family life reflected the high value modern society attached to privacy, and the glorification of privacy in turn reflected the devaluation of work. As production became more complex and efficient, work became increasingly specialized, fragmented, and routine. Accordingly work came to be seen as merely a means to an end —for many, the end of sheer physical survival; for others, of a rich and satisfying personal life. No longer regarded as a satisfying occupation in its own right, work had to be redefined as a way of achieving satisfactions or consolations outside work. Production, in this view, is interesting and important only because it enables us to enjoy the delights of consumption. At a deeper level of mystification, social work—the collective self-realization of mankind through its transformation of nature—appears merely as the satisfaction of private wants.

There is an even deeper sense in which work was degraded when it was mechanized and reduced to a routine. The products of human activity, especially the higher products of that activity such as the social order itself, took on the appearance of something external and alien to mankind. No longer recognizably the product of human invention at all, the man-made world appeared as a collection of objects independent of human intervention and control. Having objectified himself in his work, man no longer recognized it as his own. One of the best examples of this externalization of human creativity is the capitalist economy, which was the collective creation of human ingenuity and toil but was described by the classical economists as a machine that ran according to immutable laws of its own, laws analogous to the laws of nature. These principles, even if they had existed in reality instead of merely in the minds of Adam Smith and Ricardo, were inaccessible to everyday observation, and in the lay mind, therefore, the market economy defied not merely human control but human understanding. It appeared as a complex network of abstractions utterly impenetrable and opaque. John Adams once demonstrated his grasp of modern banking and credit by complaining that "every dollar of a bank bill that is issued beyond the quantity of gold and silver in the vaults represents nothing and is therefore a cheat upon somebody." Jefferson and Jackson, as is well known, held the same opinion. If the governing classes labored under such confusion, we can easily imagine the confusion of the ordinary citizen. He lived in a world of abstractions, where the relations between men, as Marx observed, assumed the fantastic shape of relations between things. Thus labor-power became a commodity, measurable in abstract monetary terms, and was bought and sold on the market like any other commodity.

At bottom, the glorification of private life and the family represented the other side of the bourgeois perception of society as something alien, impersonal, remote, and abstract—a world from which pity and tenderness had been effectively banished. Deprivations experienced in the public world had to be compensated in the realm of privacy. Yet the very conditions that gave rise to the need to view privacy and the family as a refuge from the larger world made it more and more difficult for the family to serve in that capacity.

By the end of the nineteenth century American newspapers and magazines were full of speculation about the crisis of marriage and the family. From the 1890s down to the 1930s, discussion of the decline of the family became increasingly intense. Four developments gave rise to a steadily growing alarm: the rising divorce rate, the falling birth rate among "the better sort of people," the changing position of women, and the so-called revolution in morals.

Between 1870 and 1920 the number of divorces increased fifteen times. By 1923, one out of every seven marriages ended in divorce, and there was no reason to think that the trend toward more and more frequent divorce would reverse itself.

Meanwhile "the diminution of the birth rate among the highest races," as Theodore Roosevelt put it in 1897, gave rise to the fear that the highest races would soon be outnumbered by their inferiors, who reproduced, it was thought, with total disregard for their ability to provide for the rising generation. The middle classes, on the other hand, clearly paid too much attention not only to the future but to their own present comfort. In the opinion of conservatives they had grown soft and selfish, especially middle-class women, who preferred the social whirl to the more serious pleasures of motherhood. Brooks Adams, spokesman for crusty upper-class reaction, described the new woman as the "highest product of a civilization that has rotted before it could ripen." Progressives also worried about the declining birth rate, but they blamed it on the high cost of living and rising standards of comfort, which led young men either to avoid marriage or to postpone it as long as possible. Women were not to blame for "race suicide," according to a leading woman's magazine. The "actual cause" was the "cost of living impelling the masses to pauperdom." The American man, with reason, "is afraid of a large family."

The changing status of women was obvious to the most casual observer. More and more women were going to college, joining clubs and organizations of all kinds, and entering the labor force. What explained all this activity and what did it signify for the future of the family? The feminists had a simple answer, at least to the first of these questions: women were merely "following their work out of the home." Industry had "invaded" the family, stripped it of its productive functions. Work formerly carried on in the household could now be carried out more efficiently in the factory. Even recreation and child-rearing were being taken over by outside agencies, the former by the dance-hall and the popular theater, the latter by the school. Women had no choice but to "follow their occupations or starve," emotionally if not in literal fact. Confined to the family, women would become parasites, unproductive "consumers upon the state," as a feminist writer put it in 1910.

Faced with an argument that condemned leisure as a form of parasitism, anti-feminists could have insisted on the positive value of leisure as the precondition of art, learning, and higher forms of thought, arguing that its benefits ought to be extended to the American businessman. But an attack on feminism launched from an essentially aristocratic point of view—an attack that condemned feminism as itself an expression of middle-class moralism and philistinism—hardly recommended itself to those who wished above everything else to preserve the sanctity of the home. American critics of feminism preferred to base their case on the contention that woman's usefulness to society and her own self-fulfilling work lay precisely in her sacred duties as wife and mother. The major premise of feminism—that women should be useful, not ornamental —had to be conceded; even while the conclusions feminists drew from this premise, the conclusions, they would have argued, that followed inevitably, were vigorously repudiated.

For the same reason a total condemnation of the feminist movement had to be avoided. Even the denunciation of "selfishness" was risky. In the mid-nineteenth century, defenders of the home had relied heavily on appeals to woman's duty to sacrifice herself for the good of others; but by 1900 this kind of rhetoric, even when translated into the progressive jargon of "service," had begun to seem decidedly out of date. The view that woman's destiny was to live for others gradually gave way to the view that woman too had a right to self-fulfillment—a right, however, that could best be realized in the home. In a word, the critics of feminism began to argue that motherhood and housewifery were themselves deeply satisfying "careers," which required special training in "homemaking," "domestic science," and "home economics." The invention of such terms expressed an attempt to dignify housework by raising it to the level of a profession. By rationalizing the household and child care, opponents of feminism hoped also to make the family a more effective competitor with the outside agencies that were taking over its functions.

If feminism disturbed the partisans of domesticity with its criticism of the home's inefficiency and its attempt to provide the "restlessness" of modern women with outlets beyond the family, the movement to liberate sexuality from conventional restraints troubled them much more deeply. Feminism at least allied itself with progressivism and with the vision of women's purifying influence over society; indeed the very success with which it identified itself with dominant themes in middle-class culture forced anti-feminists to refrain from attacking it frontally. The "new morality," on the other hand, directly challenged prevailing sexual ethics. It proclaimed the joys of the body, defended divorce and birth control, raised doubts about monogamy, and condemned interference with sexual life on the part of the state or community.

Yet even here the defenders of the family soon learned that unyielding condemnation was by no means the best strategy. In the long run it was no advantage to the family to associate itself with censorship, prudery, and political reaction. Instead of trying to annihilate the new morality, it made more sense to domesticate it—to strip away whatever in the ideology of sexual emancipation was critical of monogamy while celebrating a freer and more enlightened sexuality within marriage. Incidentally this operation provided the housewife with another role to complement her new role of consumer-in-chief —the multifaceted role of sexual partner, companion, playmate, and therapist.

Sex radicals not only called for a revolution in morals, they claimed that such a revolution was already under way. They cited statistical surveys that seemed to show a growing trend toward adultery and premarital sex. Faced with this evidence, the beleaguered champions of marriage executed another strategic retreat. The evidence showed, they argued, that the so-called revolt against marriage was not a revolt against marriage at all, merely an attack on the "sex-monopoly ideal" with which marriage had formerly been rather unnecessarily associated. Since "emphasis on exclusive sex possession" actually had a "destructive effect," it could safely be abandoned. Similarly the "virginity standard"—the requirement that the woman be a virgin at marriage —could be dispensed with. Exclusiveness in sex should be regarded as an ideal to be approximated, not as a standard to be imposed on everyone from without. Each couple should decide for themselves whether they would consider infidelity as evidence of disloyalty.

Another piece of ideological baggage that had to be thrown overboard, according to the emerging body of authoritative opinion on marriage and to spokesmen for arrangements that later came to be known as "open marriage," was the notion that marriage should be free of conflict and tension. Quarrels should be regarded as a normal part of marriage, events that should be taken in stride and even turned to productive purposes. Quarrels might even have a beneficial effect if they were properly "stage-managed" and rounded off with "an artistic consummation."

A fierce attack on romantic love played as important a part in the defense of marriage as in the criticism of marriage. Romantic love, it was thought, set impossibly high standards of devotion and loyalty—standards marriage could no longer meet. By undermining "sober-satisfying everyday life," romance wrought as much havoc as prudery, its twin. In the minds of radicals and conservatives alike, romantic love was associated with illusions, dangerous fantasies, and disease—with consumptive heroines, heroes wasting away with feverish desire, and deathbed farewells; with the overwrought, unhealthy music of Wagner, Strauss, and Puccini. Romantic love threatened both psychic and physical stability. The fashionable talk of marriage as an art conveyed a conception of marriage and the family that drew not so much from esthetics as from science and technology—ultimately from the science of healing. When marriage experts said that marriage was the art of personal "interaction," what they really meant was that marriage, like everything else, rested on proper technique—the technique of stage-managing quarrels, the technique of mutual agreement on how much adultery the marriage could tolerate, the technique of what to do in bed and how to do it. The new sex manuals, which began to proliferate in the twenties and thirties, were merely the most obvious examples of a general attempt to rationalize the life of the emotions in the interest of psychic health. That this attempt entailed a vigorous assault on "illusion" and fantasy is highly significant. It implies a concerted attack on the inner life, which was perceived as a threat to stability, equilibrium, and adjustment to reality. Marriage was to be saved at the expense of private life, which it was simultaneously expected to foster. The therapeutic program eroded the distinction between private life and the marketplace, turning all forms of play, even sex, into work. The experts made it clear that "achievement" of orgasm required not only proper technique but effort, determination, and emotional control.

So far I have spoken of the emergence of the nuclear family and its impact on popular thought, with particular attention to the ways in which the popular mind, led by the guardians of public health and morality, struggled with evidences of the family's growing instability. It remains to be seen how the same questions were dealt with at a more exalted level of thought—sociological theory. The social sciences devoted a great deal of attention to the crisis of marriage and the family. In particular the discipline of sociology, having divorced itself from the evolutionary and historical perspectives that had once dominated it, and having defined its field as the study of contemporary institutions and the social relations to which they gave rise, found it necessary to deal in detail with the contemporary family and what was happening to it. Much of what sociology had to say had already been anticipated in popular debate. Indeed it is clear that the sociology of the family in America arose in part as an answer to popular misgivings about the family. The role of sociology was to soothe those apprehensions with the voice of calm scientific detachment. Taking up certain lines of defense that had been suggested by doctors, social workers, psychotherapists, or scholars writing for a popular audience, sociology restated them in far more elaborate and extensive form, at the same time removing them from the polemical context in which they had originated. Claiming to have no stake in the outcome of investigations into the functions of the family, sociology provided the family with an elaborate ideological defense, which soon found its way back into popular thought and helped to bring about an important revival of domesticity and the domestic virtues in the thirties, forties, and fifties.

In effect, sociology revived the nineteenth-century myth of the family as an oasis and restated it in what looked like scientific form. First it dismissed the evidence of the family's decline by translating it into the language of functional analysis; then it showed that loss of certain functions (notably economic and educational functions) had been compensated by the addition of new ones.

Ernest W. Burgess, founder of a flourishing school of urban sociology at the University of Chicago, was one of the first to propose, in the early twenties, that what the family had lost in economic, protective, educational, religious, and recreational functions, it had made up in "affectional and cultural" functions. According to Burgess, the family had been "reduced" to an affectional group, "united by the interpersonal relations of its members," but the reduction in its size and scope had strengthened, not weakened, the family by enabling it to concentrate on the interplay of "interacting personalities." As the "institutional" functions of the family declined, the "personality" functions, in the words of W. F. Ogburn, took on greater and greater importance.

The rise of functionalism in social science coincided with, and was made possible by, the repudiation of historical approaches. At one time students of the family (and of other institutions as well) had attempted to arrange various institutional forms of the family in an evolutionary sequence or progression. Theoretical arguments about the family usually boiled down to arguments about historical priority. One group of theorists, following Bachofen, Morgan, and Engels, held that marriage had evolved from promiscuity to monogamy and the family from matriarchal to patriarchal forms. Others, like Westermarck, argued that patriarchal monogamy was the original form of the family. By the 1920s, these disputes had begun to seem inconclusive and heavily ideological, with the adherents of the matriarchal theory predicting the imminent demise of the monogamous family and their opponents seeking to demonstrate its permanence and stability. Sociology now rejected more modest historical theories as well—for example, theories that sought to link the decline of the patriarchal, extended family in Europe to changes in social and economic organization. Instead of attempting to explain the family's history, social science now contented itself with analyzing the way it functioned in various cultures. It was not altogether incidental that this functionalist analysis of the family, worked out first by anthropology in company with psychoanalysis and then applied by sociology to the contemporary family, had reassuring implications for the question of the family's future. The great variety of family forms suggested that while the family varied enormously from one culture to the next, in some form it was always found to be indispensable. The family did not evolve or decline, it merely adapted itself to changing conditions. As industry and the state took over the economic, educational, and protective work of the family, society at the same time became more impersonal and bureaucratic, thereby necessitating the creation of an intimate, protected space in which personal relations could continue to thrive. In the words of the urban sociologist Louis Wirth, "the pecuniary nexus which implies the purchasability of services and things has displaced personal relations as the basis of association"—everywhere, that is, except within the family. Joseph Folsom, a specialist in family sociology, noted in 1934 that modern society gave rise to a "generally increased need for intense affection and romance," while at the same time it "increased the difficulty of satisfying this need." As he put it somewhat quaintly, a "cultural lag" had arisen "between the increasing need for love and the practical arrangements to promote it." Ernest R. Mowrer, another family sociologist, argued along similar lines: "One of the most pronounced and striking phases of modern life is the repression of the emotions" —a tendency from which the family alone is exempt. Accordingly the family becomes "all the more important as the setting for emotional expression." In the rest of life, emotions have no place. "A business man is supposed to be cold, unfeeling, and 'hard-boiled.' Exchange . . . is unemotional and objective." The family, on the other hand, satisfies "the desire for response." Pent-up rage as well as pent-up love find expression in domestic life, and although this rage creates tensions in the family it is also a source of its continuing vitality. Familial tension, Mowrer argued, ought to become the primary concern of sociological study, through which it can be understood and therefore kept under control.

By reviving nineteenth-century conceptions of the family in allegedly scientific form, the sociology of the family accomplished something almost brilliant in its way: it stood the evidence of the family's decline on its head. Sociology invoked loss of functions, the drastic shrinkage of the family, and even the rising divorce rate to prove the stability, not the decline, of the family. Academic scholarship demonstrated that it was precisely the loss of its economic and educational importance that permitted the family to discharge its emotional functions more effectively than ever. The "loss of functions," instead of undermining the family, allowed it to come more fully into its own. There was only one trouble with this line of argument—a major one, however, with ramifying theoretical implications. Having abandoned historical analysis, sociology rested its claims to scientific status on a functional analysis of modern society—an analysis, that is, which purported to show how all the pieces fit together to make up a smoothly functioning social order. Yet at the same time it saw the family as in conflict with society—a haven of love in a loveless world. Nor could it argue, except by drastically simplifying the problem, that this conflict was itself functional. The view that family life alone provided people with the emotional resources necessary to live and work in modern society remained convincing only so long as the socializing function of the family was ignored. The family might be a haven for adults, but what about the children whom it had to prepare to live in precisely the cold and ugly world from which the family provided a haven? How could children raised under the regime of love learn to "function" in the marketplace? Far from preparing the young for this ordeal, the family, if it operated as sociology insisted it did operate, could only be said to cripple the young, at the same time that it offered a psychological refuge for the cripples, now grown to maladjusted maturity, that it had itself produced.

For a time, sociology could deal with these problems by ignoring them— that is, by ignoring the family's role in socializing the child. Some writers went so far as to insist that child-rearing had become incidental to marriage. But the rise of the so-called culture-and-personality school in American anthropology soon made this view untenable. The work of Ruth Benedict, Margaret Mead, and others made it clear that in every culture socialization is the main function of the family. A sociology that confined itself to the analysis of marriage could not stand comparison with the theoretical achievements of this new anthropology. The sociology of the family had to provide a theory of socialization or collapse into a rather pretentious form of marital counselling. Specifically it had to explain how an institution organized along very different principles from the rest of society could nevertheless train children to become effective members of society.

This was the problem, in effect, to which Talcott Parsons addressed himself in that part of his general theory which dealt with socialization—in Parsonian terminology, with tension-management and pattern-maintenance. Parsons begins by placing the study of the family in a broader social context—already a considerable advance over the work of his predecessors. According to Parsons, the family's famous loss of functions should be seen as part of the more general process of "structural differentiation"—the basic tendency of modern society. As the social division of labor becomes more and more complex, institutions become more specialized in their functions. To take an obvious example, manufacturing is split up into its various components, each of which is assigned to a special unit in the productive system. Specialization of functions increases efficiency, as is well known. Similarly the family performs its emotional services more efficiently once it is relieved of its other functions, which can be more efficiently carried on in institutions expressly designed for those purposes.

Having established a strong link between the development of the family and other social processes, Parsons now has to consider what other sociologists ignored, the family's role in socializing the child. How does the family, an institution in which social roles are assigned by ascription rather than achievement, train the child to enter a society in which roles are achieved rather than ascribed? The isolation of the family from the rest of the kinship system encourages a high degree of dependency between parents and children, yet at the same time the family has to equip the child to break these ties of dependency and to become an independent, self-reliant participant in the larger world. How does it manage to do both of these things at once, to tie children to their parents and yet to lay the ground work for the severance of those ties?

Briefly, Parsons proposes that the emotional security the family gives to the child in his early years is precisely the psychic foundation of the child's later independence. By providing the child with a great deal of closeness and warmth and then by giving him his head, the isolated nuclear family trains a type of personality ideally equipped to cope with the rigors of the modern world. Permissiveness, which many observers mistake for a collapse or abdication of parental responsibility, is actually a new way of training achievement, according to Parsons. It prepares the child to deal with an unpredictable world in which he will constantly face "unstructured situations." In the face of such contingencies he will have little use for hard-and-fast principles of duty and conduct learned from his parents. What he needs is the ability to take care of himself, to make quick decisions, and to adapt quickly to many types of emergencies. In a slower world, parents could indoctrinate their children with moral precepts adaptable to any foreseeable occasion, but modern parents, according to Parsons, can hope only to provide their young with the inner resources they need to survive on their own. This kind of training requires an intense dependency in early childhood followed by what strikes many foreigners as "incredible leeway" later on. But we should not be deceived by this "leeway." What looks like "abdication" is simply realism.

Youth culture, Parsons argues, is a differentiated part of the socialization system, the function of which is to ease the adolescent's transition from particularism to universality, ascription to achievement. Youth culture provides the adolescent with the emotional security of relationships that are "largely ascriptive" yet take him outside his own family. By providing this kind of "emotional support," the subculture of American adolescents fills an important set of needs, complementing the family on one side and the school on the other. Not only does it take young people out of the family but it helps to select and certify them for their adult roles—for example, by reinforcing appropriate ambitions while discouraging ambitions that are beyond the individual's abilities or his family's means to support.

This summary does not do justice to the elegance of the Parsonian theory of the family. We must press on to a further point: that for its elegance, the Parsonian theory has little capacity to explain empirical events, as any theory must. Far from explaining events, it has been overtaken by them. Writing in 1961, on the eve of an unprecedented upheaval of American youth, Parsons thought young people were becoming less hedonistic and more serious and "progressive," but his theory hardly anticipated the emergence of a youth culture that condemned American society in the most sweeping terms, repudiated the desirability of growing up in the usual way, and sometimes appeared to repudiate the desirability of growing up at all. It would be the height of perversity to interpret the youth culture of the sixties and seventies as a culture that eases the transition from childhood to maturity, when the attainment of adult status and responsibilities is seen by the culture as a betrayal of its ideals, by definition a "sell-out," and therefore becomes in the eyes of young people something to be accepted only with deep feelings of guilt. As for the argument that a heightened dependence in childhood is the basis of increased autonomy in adulthood, it does not explain why, in our society, personal autonomy seems more difficult than ever to achieve or sustain. Nor does it explain why so many signs of a massive cultural and psychological regression should appear just at the historical moment when, according to Parsons, the family has emerged from a period of crisis and has "now begun at least to be stabilized."

It is precisely the instability of the family that most emphatically repudiates the Parsonian theory of it. Youth culture itself has made the family a prime target—not just something to "rebel" against but a corrupt and decadent institution to be overthrown. That the new youth culture represents more than adolescent rebellion is suggested by the way its attack on the family reverberates, appealing to a great variety of other groups—feminists, advocates of the rights of homosexuals, cultural and political reformers of all kinds. Hostility to the family has survived the demise of the political radicalism of the sixties and flourished amid the conservatism of the seventies. Even the pillars of society show no great inclination to defend the family, historically regarded as the basis of their whole way of life. Meanwhile the divorce rate continues to rise, young people avoid or at least postpone marriage, and social life organizes itself around "swinging singles." None of these developments bears out the thesis that "loss of functions" made the family stronger than ever by allowing it to specialize in the work it does best. On the contrary, no other institution seems to work so badly, to judge from the volume of abuse directed against it and the growing wish to experiment with other forms.

Here to Stay: Parents and Children

Mary Jo Bane

Worry about the family is mostly worry about the next generation. Falling birthrates, rising divorce rates, increasing numbers of working mothers, and other indicators of the alleged decline of the family would probably seem much less alarming if adults alone were affected by the making and dissolving of families. People are distressed by these trends not because they signal a decline in the quality and richness of adult lives but because they seem to threaten the next generation. If the trends continue, will there be a next generation? Will it turn out all right? Will it be able to maintain and perhaps even improve the world?

These feelings about the importance of generational continuity lie, I suspect, behind the implicit and explicit comparisons that one generation makes with the generations before it. Modern families and modern methods of child rearing are almost always measured against the families of earlier times. The comparison is usually unfavorable to modern families. In contrast, when mod-

Chapter 1 from *Here to Stay: American Families in the Twentieth Century* by Mary Jo Bane, © 1976 by Mary Jo Bane, Basic Books, Inc., Publishers, New York. Reprinted by permission. Notes omitted. These notes provide detailed documentation of historical and demographic sources and can be found in Bane on pages 159–162.

ern technology and economic institutions are evaluated against earlier times the judgment is far more often made that things are better. In technology, progress is the standard. In social institutions, continuity is the standard, and when change occurs, it is seen as decline rather than advance.

Decline and *advance* are not easily defined terms, of course. What some people see as good child rearing, others may see as stifling repression and yet others as rampant permissiveness. But some agreement probably exists on the basic principles of how a society ought to treat its children: Children should receive secure and continuous care; they should be neither abused nor abandoned. Children should be initiated into adult society with neither undue haste nor unduly long enforced dependency—in other words, allowed to be children and permitted to become adults. Probably most important, Americans believe that children should be wanted both by their parents and by society.

Arguments that modern families are failing their children usually cite rising divorce rates and the rising proportion of mothers working as evidence that children are less well cared for by their parents now than in the past, that their environments are less secure and less affectionate. In addition, statistics on falling birthrates are sometimes used as evidence that modern Americans want and value children less than earlier generations. But data on parental care, family size, and the ties between generations can be used to make a different argument: that discontinuities in parental care are no greater than they were in the past; and that changes in fertility rates may lead to an environment that, according to generally agreed on criteria, is more beneficial for children.

Demographic Facts and the Age Structure of Society

Intergenerational relationships are profoundly influenced by the age structure of society, since that structure determines how many generations are alive at any one time and what proportion of the population has living ancestors or descendants. The age structure can also influence whether a society "feels" mature and stable or young and vibrant. Certain activities or patterns may seem characteristic of a society because they are characteristic of the largest age group in the population.

A combination of birth and death rates creates the age structure of a society. These two rates also determine the rate of growth of the population, which can in turn affect the density and structure of living arrangements. Birth and death rates thus define the demographic context within which the relationships between generations must be worked out. As technology provides the basic facts of economic life, demography defines the basic facts of social life.

Today's great-grandparents were born during a period when the population of America was growing at a rapid rate. The European populations from which the American colonists had come had been relatively stable in size, with death rates balancing birthrates over long-term cycles of prosperity followed by epidemics and famines. In the seventeenth-century, death rates began to fall dramatically and steadily, probably because of general improvements in nutrition and the physical environment. Death rates fell at all ages; not only did mature people live longer, but more infants survived to childhood and more children to maturity. And more women lived to have more children. The result was a rapid population growth that has characterized the United States at least since the U.S. Census began in 1790, and probably much earlier.

Falling death rates, however, have been partially balanced by falling birthrates. In the United States, birthrates have been gradually falling for as long as data have been collected. They probably began to fall about 1800 or possibly earlier, and in the last few years they have fallen below replacement level. If they remain at replacement level, the United States will reach a stable population level about the year 2000. In the United States, therefore, the rate of natural population growth was probably highest in the early and mid-nineteenth century. Around 1800 the population grew at a rate of almost 3 percent per year. By 1880 it was growing at around 2 percent per year and by 1974, at six-tenths of one percent.

A rapidly growing population is different from a stable population in several ways. One is age structure. Demographers find that the average age of populations that are not growing can range from about twenty-seven years when mortality rates are very high (probably characteristic of pre-industrial Europe) to about thirty-eight years when mortality rates are very low (the United States of the future). In contrast, a rapidly growing population is young. The median age of the population of the United States shown in Table 1-1 illustrates the point.

As population growth has slowed down, the American population has become gradually older. This aging is perhaps the most important difference between the world of our great-grandparents and our own world, and contributes to many of the changes that have taken place in family and intergenerational relationships.

It may seem strange that a population becomes younger as death rates fall. As people live longer should the population not become older? The reason it does not is that in all the societies that demographers have studied, death rates

Table 1. Proportion of American Women Who Are Widows, by Age, 1976

Age Group	% Widows
Under 35	1.0
35–39	1.9
40–44	3.2
45–54	7.2
55–64	19.1
65–74	42.0
75+	69.7

are highest both late in life and early in life. Declines in death rates are usually most dramatic among infants. More infants survive, contributing more children to the population. More women survive to reproductive age and contribute even more children to the population. Thus lower mortality rates result in a younger average age of the population even though average life expectancy at birth rises.

Imagine, for example, a population in which half the babies died at birth and half lived to be 50. The average life expectancy would be 25 years, and the average age of the population would also be 25 years. Now imagine that infant mortality rates fell, so that everyone lived to be 50. The average life expectancy would then be 50. The average age of the population would still be 25, if the population remained stable in size. But if birthrates remained the same as they were when death rates were high, the population would be bound to grow, since more women would live to reproductive age and there would be more babies and children than older people. Thus mortality rates would have produced a younger rather than an older population.

Another interesting characteristic of a rapidly growing population, related to its age structure, is that working-age adults comprise a relatively small proportion of the population. Working-age adults (age 15–64) made up 58 percent of the rapidly growing population of the United States in 1880. In contrast, 68 percent of the population of the United States in 1940 was made up of working-age adults. The nonworkers in a rapidly growing population are almost all children, since the proportion of old people is extremely low. On the other hand, when death rates are low and the population is stable in size, almost half of the nonworkers are over 65.

A third feature of a rapidly growing population is that it must every year induct a relatively large number of young people into adulthood and into the work force. More must start work than retire. This can put a strain on adult society in general and on the economy in particular. If the economy is not growing as rapidly as the population, the problem of what to do with young people can become acute.

Changes in the rate of population growth produce changes in the age structure of a society that are in turn reflected in the problems the society must cope with, the mechanisms it uses to do so, and the general feel of the society. In a rapidly growing population, children and adolescents must be more visible. A young, childlike society may be a more congenial place for children to live. But it may not. Children may be more precious when they are relatively rare. A more mature society may have more physical and emotional resources to give to the care of children. It may display a greater ease in inducting children —since there are fewer of them—into the adult society.

Teenagers may cause major social problems when they make up a disporportionately large segment of the population. When they are fewer, especially when the number entering the labor force equals the number retiring, they can be integrated much more easily. This interpretation might partially explain cycles of concern over youth. It might also partially explain societal attitudes toward children. Dr. Spock, after all, advocated permissive child-rearing in the first edition of his book in 1947, when children were relatively rare. He changed his mind in 1968, for a variety of reasons no doubt. But whether Spock realized it or not, he may simply have been reacting to what must have seemed a veritable surfeit of children. In the coming decades, children and adolescents will make up a small proportion of the population. Through this simple demographic change, they may become less of a problem and more of a precious resource.

Childlessness and Family Size

Declining birthrates not only change the position of children in society as a whole, but they can also affect the status of children in individual families. Low birthrates that occur because fewer women are having children should probably be interpreted differently from rates that are low because many women are having a smaller number of children. High rates of voluntary childlessness in the society might reflect a cleavage in the society. If people who did not have children were different from those who did—if, for example, they were better educated or concentrated in the professional occupations—the potential for social conflict would be great. Public support for children would certainly be hard to master if only low-status (or only high-status) parents had children. At the same time, the family environments of children would not necessarily change much. If fewer women had children but still had large numbers, most children would continue to be brought up in large families.

If, on the other hand, low birthrates occurred because most people continued to have children but had fewer of them, political divisions between the childless and others would be less likely. But an important change would take place in the family environments of children. More children would be brought up in small families. The consequences would more likely be beneficial to both the children and the society.

Decreasing family size rather than increasing childlessness accounts for most of the declining fertility in the United States. The U.S. Census first gathered data on the total number of children women had had over their reproductive years in 1910. The census data is probably accurate for women born as early as 1846 and as late as 1935, since most women now complete their childbearing before age 35. The fertility of women born after 1935 can be predicted from two sources: from Census Bureau questions that ask women how many children they expect to have, and from projections of fertility rates based on the number of children they have had so far. These combined sources provide fairly accurate descriptions of the fertility history of women born since the middle of the nineteenth century.

Between 90 and 95 percent of women marry at one time or another. The proportion has fluctuated over the years, with a slight increase in recent decades in the proportion of women marrying. The proportion of married women who have no children has also fluctuated over the years—first up, then down. The childless proportion rose from about 8.2 percent of married women born 1846–55 to a high of over 20 percent of the married women born between 1901 and 1910. Childlessness then fell to 7.3 percent among married women born 1931–35.

It is hard to say why childlessness rose during the nineteenth century, but it may have to do with the unhealthful conditions facing women in the factories or the economic difficulties experienced especially by the immigrants. One explanation for the high rates of childlessness among married women born around the turn of the century is the economic depression of the 1930s. When unemployment rates are high, birthrates almost always fall. In the 1930s unemployment reached a new high and birthrates a new low.

The decline in childlessness since the 1930s is equally hard to explain. It may have to do with improvements in general health and with new medical treatments for sterility and infertility. Involuntary childlessness may have virtually disappeared. Predictions about the future are thus predictions about voluntary childlessness, which is now possible through the relative ease of birth control and abortion.

Predictions might be based on the characteristics of women who remained childless in the past. Among women born before 1920 who were surveyed by the 1970 census, those who were childless were more likely to be black, to have been born in the Northeast, to have married at older ages, to have gone to college, to have lived in urban areas, and to have been married to professional or white-collar workers rather than farmers or laborers. In general, the childless were better educated and better off. High rates of childlessness among blacks are the exception and may be explained by health conditions.

These correlates suggest that childlessness should have increased over time as more women became better educated and better off. But that is the opposite of what actually happened. The cross-sectional data also suggest that childlessness should decrease during hard times since fewer people are well-off. But this too is precisely the opposite of the historical fact. The economic and demographic correlates of childlessness are, therefore, not very useful bases for making predictions about what will happen.

Some predictions can be made, however, on the basis of what women say about the number of children they expect to have. In 1975 less than 5 percent of wives who were interviewed about family plans expected to remain childless. This proportion was relatively constant throughout the age groups. The proportion of women who expect to remain childless went up slightly from 1967–1974, but then went down again in 1975. Better-educated women and white women are more likely to expect to remain childless, but the difference is not great.

The most interesting thing about these figures on expected childlessness is that they are so low. If as few women remain childless as say they expect to, the childless proportion among women born between 1940 and 1955 will be the lowest ever recorded. Even if the rate of childlessness for all women were equal to the expected rate for college women, childlessness would still be at its lowest recorded level. Under either condition, however, the country is due for some upswing in births, as those who have put off having children is due for some upswing in births, as those who have put off having children begin to have them. One problem with the data is that the Census Bureau interviews only married women about their family plans, not unmarried women who may or may not marry and may or may not expect children in the future. Another is that women who now see themselves as putting off children may later be unable to have them, or decide not to. This problem can be partially corrected by making projections from birthrates by age. One demographic study uses these rates to estimate that 10 percent of women born around 1945 will actually remain childless, rather than the 5 percent who expect to. The Census Bureau made a series of projections from similar data, with similar results. These studies project a slightly higher rate of childlessness than that found among women born during the 1930s, but still lower than that among women born 1901–10. It seems safe to say that the vast majority of American women will continue to have at least one child.

Although there has been no systematic increase over the century in the proportion of women who have no children, there has been a systematic and dramatic decrease in the number of children each mother has. The average married woman in colonial Massachusetts may have had as many as eight children. The average mother born 1846–55 had 5.7 children. The average number of children decreased steadily for sixty years, reaching 2.9 children among women born 1911–15. It then rose for a short period during the postwar baby boom; women born 1931–35 have had an average of 3.4 children per woman with children. It is now once again falling. Yet the proportion of women having no children or having only one child has not increased over the century. The big change has thus been in the proportion of women having very large families, a change which has occurred for all races and education levels. Many fewer women have five or more children; many more women have two or three.

Looking at these numbers from the viewpoint of the children illustrates the change that has taken place over four generations. Statistics about average family size do not accurately reflect the size of the family into which the average child is born. The family of the average child is larger than the average family because more children are born into larger families.

If this sounds like a riddle, imagine ten families distributed as follows:

1-child—4 families
2-child—3 families
3-child—2 families
4-child—1 family

The average family size is $4(1) + 3(2) + 2(3) + 1(4) \div 10 = 2$. But the twenty children are distributed as follows:

> 1-child families—4 children
> 2-child families—6 children
> 3-child families—6 children
> 4-child families—4 children

The average child is born into a family of $4(1) + 6(2) + 6(3) + 4(4) = 50$ $\div 20 = 2.5$ children, and has an average of 1.5 brothers and sisters. When large families are included in the calculations the differences between average family size and the average number of brothers and sisters can be very dramatic.

From the point of view of the child, a better indication of family size than average family size is the average number of brothers and sisters that children of different generations have. The great-grandparents of today's children had on the average six brothers and sisters. Their grandparents had five brothers and sisters. Their parents—depression babies—had on the average three brothers and sisters. Today's children may have as few as two. The low birthrates of the depression occurred partly because of high rates of childlessness and only children. There were, however, many large families. In contrast, the low fertility rates of the early 1970s are the product of low rates of childlessness and only children, accompanied by extremely small numbers of large families. Most children in the 1970s are born into two- or three-child families. If these patterns continue, the average child born in the next decade will have only two brothers and sisters.

Small families mean a quite different life for children. Some of the differences are probably detrimental to children, but, on the whole, small families seem to be beneficial. A number of studies suggest that children from small families do better in school and score better on standardized tests than children from large families. Part of the explanation is that smaller families are usually better off financially. But even when these families are equally well-off, children from large families do not get as much education, as good jobs, or as high earnings as children from small families.

One of the most interesting studies on family size and achievement investigated the reasons for the superior performance of children from small families. The study first looked at the amount of time that parents and other adults spent with children. Middle children in large families received considerably less adult care and attention than children in smaller families or than first and last children in larger families. Parental attention must be shared by more people when the family has more children living at home, a condition that affects middle children in large families more than others.

The study then looked at the effect of family size on achievement. It found that a variable representing the child's share of family time and financial resources had a more important effect on achievement, both educational and occupational, than most other background characteristics.

Children from large families seem to be somewhat slower in physical development than children from small families. Emotional and social differences have not been so clearly documented, although there is some evidence that children from small families are more likely to think well of themselves. On the other hand, cross-cultural studies have shown that children who care for younger children are more nurturing and responsible and less dependent and dominant than others. Because children are more likely to have taken care of younger siblings when they come from larger families, smaller families may produce fewer independent and helpful children. In general, though, the trend toward smaller families among all segments of the population has probably done more to increase and equalize cognitive development and schooling than any other demographic trend.

The data on childlessness and family size, in short, do not suggest a societal abandonment of children. A large increase in childlessness now that involuntary childlessness is almost nonexistent would indicate that a substantial portion of the population wanted no children, but this has not occurred. The vast majority of adults have at least one child. Average family size has decreased, but the decline has taken place mostly in larger families. Family size is converging for the entire population on the two- or three-child ideal. These smaller families seem to be advantageous for children rather than a sign of societal indifference.

Living Arrangements of Children

Another indicator of the place of children in the society is whether parents and children live together. Children who live with their parents are certainly better off than children raised in orphanages. They may or may not be better off than children raised by relatives or foster parents. At any rate, whether or not children live with their parents provides some indication of the strength of ties between parents and children.

Many people assume that the rising divorce rates of the last few decades mean that fewer children now live with their parents. This assumption is not completely accurate. The data suggest that the proportion of children who live with at least one of their parents rather than with relatives, with foster parents, or in institutions has been steadily rising.

The U.S. Census has published information about the living arrangements of people only since 1940. Since then the proportion of children living with at least one of their parents in a separate household has gone steadily up, from about 90 percent in 1940 to almost 95 percent in 1970. The increase seems to have occurred for two reasons. The first reason is that the proportion of children who lost a parent through death and divorce combined fell gradually during the first half of the century and probably fell before that as well. Among children born between 1911 and 1920, about 22 percent lost a parent through death and 5 percent had parents divorce sometime before their eighteenth birthday. Gradually declining death rates meant that fewer children lost parents as the century went on. Smaller families had the same effect, since more children were born to younger parents. The result was that about 20 percent of the children born during the 1940s lost parents through death or divorce. Only for children born around 1960 did rising divorce rates begin to counteract the effects of falling death rates. The proportion of children who experienced a parental disruption fell until then; only recently has disruption increased.

The second reason for the rise in the proportion of children living with at least one parent between 1940 and 1970 is a dramatic increase in the proportion of widowed and divorced women who continued living with their children after their marriage ended. In 1940 only about 44 percent of women with children but without husbands headed their own families. The rest must have sent their children to live with their grandparents or other relatives or to orphanages. By 1970 almost 80 percent of divorced, separated, and widowed women with children headed their own families. Some women, especially the young and unmarried, continue to leave their children with their grandparents. Most, however, now keep the family together. The children may not live with both their parents, but they do live with at least one. In 1975, despite rising divorce rates, only 2.7 percent of children under 14 lived with neither of their parents. The aggregate figures do conceal a racial difference: In the same year, 1975, 7.5 percent of non-white children were living with neither parent, compared with 1.7 percent of white children. But for non-whites as well as whites, the percent living with neither parent has been going down, from 9.8 percent for non-whites in 1968 to the present figure.

Although the proportion of children living with at least one parent has risen, rising divorce rates since 1960 have caused a decrease in the proportion of children under 14 living with both parents. In 1960, 88.5 percent of all children under 14 lived with two natural or adoptive parents; by 1974 the number had fallen to 82.1 percent. This trend is likely to continue. Estimates from death and divorce rates indicate that nearly 40 percent of the children born around 1970 will experience a parental death, divorce, or separation and consequently live in a one-parent family at some point during their first eighteen years. The proportion living with neither parent, however, is likely to remain small.

The effects on children of these changes in living arrangements are not well understood. Hardly anyone argues that the divorce or death of parents is good for children, but the extent of the harm done has not been documented. There is some evidence that children from broken homes do not do as well in school as children from unbroken homes. Much of the disadvantage seems to come, however, from the fact that many one-parent homes are also poor. Moreover, children whose parents divorce are no worse off than children whose homes are unbroken but also unhappy. Although the evidence is scanty, it suggests that most children adjust relatively quickly and well to the disruption and that in the case of divorce the disruption may be better than the alternative of living in a tension-filled home.

No studies have looked at the effects on children of various living arrangements after divorce. This is surprising, given the significant change that has taken place over the last thirty years in what normally happens to children. Probably children who stay with their mothers are better off than children with foster parents or relatives, although individual circumstances can vary widely. Staying with the mother may make the event less disruptive and less distressing; only one parent is lost rather than both. The increased tendency of widowed and divorced mothers to keep their children may, therefore, be good for the children.

The effect of the growing tendency of women with children but without husbands to set up separate households rather than live with relatives or friends is less clear. Since single-parent families seem to live on their own whenever they can afford to, they must see advantages to the arrangement. On the other hand, single parents have the almost impossible reponsibility of supporting and caring for a family alone. The absence of other adults to relieve the pressure must increase the tension and irritability of single parents (unless, of course, the presence of other adults would increase tension and irritability even more). Children in separate households gain the undivided attention of their mothers and often establish extremely close supportive relationships. But they lose the company of other adults and the exposure to a variety of adult personalities and role models that larger households might provide. Separate households are clearly what most single parents want, but it would be interesting to know exactly what they give up in having them.

Child Care Arrangements

Like data on living arrangements, data on child care arrangements are often cited as evidence of the state of parent-child relationships. People often talk as if children are best off when they are taken care of exclusively by their mothers. The rise in the proportion of mothers who hold paid jobs is, therefore, cited periodically as an indicator of the decline of the family. Most concern, of course, is focused on young children; Americans have long believed that older children should go to school and play on their own, not be continually supervised by mother. But even care arrangements for young children involve more than simply care by the mother. Care arrangements have changed over the century, but it is not clear that families and mothers have become less important. Nor is it clear whether the changes are good or bad.

The most important activity of contemporary children up to the age of 14 is watching television. The average preschooler seems to watch television about thirty-three hours per week, one-third of his waking hours. The average sixth-grade child watches about thirty-one hours. Since television sets only became common during the 1950s, the importance of television has clearly been a development of the last quarter century. It represents a tremendous change in how children of all ages are cared for. Television is by far the most important new child care arrangement of this century.

The next most important activity of children's waking hours is going to school. Children now spend an average of about nineteen hours a week in school. A larger proportion of children of all ages go to school now than ever before. They start school earlier and stay in school longer. The most dramatic change of the last ten years has been in the proportion of very young children enrolled in nursery school and kindergarten. In 1965 about 27 percent of all 3- to 5-year-olds were enrolled in school; by 1973, 41 percent of this age group were in school.

Other important changes have occurred in the length of the school year and in average daily attendance. In 1880 the average pupil attended school about eighty days per year. By the 1960s the typical school year was 180 days and the average pupil attended about 164 days. Both these changes mean that children enrolled in school spend more time there. School, therefore has steadily gained in importance as a child care arrangement.

Compared with these two dramatic changes in child care arrangements— the growth of television and school—changes caused by mothers working outside the home appear almost trivial. It is true that the proportion of mothers with paid jobs has risen sharply over the last twenty-five years, particularly among mothers of preschool children. In 1950, 12 percent of married women with children under six were in the labor force; by 1974 the proportion had grown to nearly 40 percent. Many of these working mothers arranged their schedules so that they worked only when their children were in school or when fathers were at home to take care of the children. About 70 percent, however, made other child care arrangements. The most common was to have a relative or sitter come to the home and care for the children. Only about 10 percent of the preschool children of working mothers went to day care centers.

How much of a difference these arrangements make in the lives of children depends on what actually happens to them and who actually spends time with them. There is no evidence as to how much time mothers a century ago spent with their children. Undoubtedly, it was less than contemporary nonworking mothers, since mothers of a century ago had more children and probably also had more time-consuming household tasks.

Contemporary nonworking mothers do not spend a great deal of time exclusively with their children. A national study done in 1965 found that the average nonworking mother spent 1.4 hours per day on child care. A study of 1,300 Syracuse families in 1967–68 showed that the average nonworking mother spent sixty-six minutes a day in physical care of *all* family members and forty-eight minutes in other sorts of care on a typical weekday during the school year. The amount of time varied with the age and number of children.

A small 1973 Boston study, by White and Watts, found that of the time they were observed mothers spent about a third interacting with their children (but one expects that mothers being observed by Harvard psychologists might depart somewhat from their normal routines). The children in the study, age 1 to 3, spent most of their time in solitary playing or simply watching what went on around them.

Working mothers spend less time on child care than nonworking mothers, but the differences in the amount of time mothers spend exclusively with their children are surprisingly small. In the Syracuse study, the correlations between the amount of time women spent on physical care of family members and whether or not they are employed were very small, once family size and children's ages were taken into account. When all family members, not just wives, were looked at, the correlations were even smaller. There is some evidence that working mothers especially in the middle class try to make up for their working by setting aside time for exclusive attention to their children. They probably read more to their children and spend more time in planned activities with them than do nonworking mothers.

There is no evidence that having a working mother per se has harmful effects on children. When a mother works because the father is incapacitated, unemployed, or paid poorly, the family may be poor and disorganized and the children may suffer. In these cases, however, the mother's working is a symptom and not a cause of more general family difficulties. In other cases where mothers work, children are inadequately supervised and may get into trouble. Again, though, the problem is general family difficulty. The Gluecks' study of lower-class boys, often cited as evidence that working mothers raise delinquent children, shows no direct link between the mothers' employment and delinquency. It did find that in lower-class homes children of working mothers were less likely to be adequately supervised, and that there was a tie between lack of supervision and delinquency whether the mothers worked or not. In families where the mother's employment is not a symptom of deeper family trouble, children seem not to turn out any differently from other children.

Parents and Teenagers

For the last century or so, Americans have become attuned to the existence and peculiarities of that stage in life between childhood and adulthood that we call adolescence. Adolescence is apparently a creation of relatively recent times; at least its problems have only recently attracted widespread attention. Certainly, as Margaret Mead showed so well, adolescent difficulties do not occur universally. Whatever the distinctive characteristics of the adolescent personality, however, there have been some noticeable changes over the last century in the living and working arrangements of adolescents. The general trend is to tie adolescent boys to parents for an increasing length of time and to begin to liberate adolescent girls.

In mid-nineteenth-century America, it was common practice for young men, and to a lesser extent young women, to leave their parents' house and live for a few years as a lodger or servant in some other older person's house before marrying and setting up independent households. The best information on family structure in the mid-nineteenth century comes from Michael Katz's study of Hamilton, Ontario. Boarders and lodgers were then an important feature of life. In 1851 more than half of the young men aged around 20 were living as boarders in the household of a family other than their own. But industrialization was accompanied by business cycles and increased schooling, which in turn brought striking changes in the lives of young people. By 1861 only a third of Hamilton's young men were living as boarders. More lived at home and went to school. Nearly a third were neither employed nor in school. The nineteenth-century specter of gangs of young men roaming the city streets must have arisen because gangs of young men were indeed roaming the streets.

In the United States also, many young men of the middle and late nineteenth century lived for a time as boarders. Boarding was a different phenomenon, however, in rural and urban areas. In cities young men typically lived with families but worked elsewhere. Rural youth were more often live-in farm help. By 1970, boarding out had virtually disappeared; less than 2 percent of 15- to 19-year-olds were living as boarders or servants. Instead they were living at home and going to school. The rise in school attendance was dramatic. In 1910, about 30 percent of 16- to 19-year-old boys were in school compared to about 73 percent in 1970. The employment situation for teenagers is still, as it was in mid-nineteenth century Hamilton, dreadful. The young men have not been put to work, but they have been induced to stay in school.

Young women, so often forgotten in historical discussions, are working more and going to school more. Typically, young women lived at home performing domestic tasks until they married. In mid-nineteenth-century Hamilton, for example, about 36 percent of the 18- and 19-year-old women were employed and about 5 percent went to school. Another 5 percent were married. The rest must have been living at home, doing domestic chores or doing nothing. During the growth of schooling in the nineteenth century, girls' attendance rates rose even faster than boys'. In 1970 in the United States, young women were still living at home, but they were going to school rather than helping mother. The vast majority (88.6 percent) of the 16- and 17-year-olds and 41.6 percent of the 18- and 19-year-olds were enrolled in school. Most of the rest were working at paid jobs, and some were raising children.

Among both men and women, there seems to have been a slight increase in the last decade in the proportion who live away from their parents during their late teenage years. Even in 1974, however, this group was a minority. Among 18- and 19-year-old men, about 7 percent were married and living with a wife and only about 6 percent were living on their own. Among 18- and 19-year-old women, 21 percent were married and 9 percent were living on their own.

Virtually all 14- to 17-year-olds lived with their parents. The living arrangements of 20- to 24-year-olds will be examined in Chapter Three.

In short, there has been no significant emancipation of teenagers from their families. In comparison with nineteenth-century teenagers in urban areas, in fact, contemporary teenage boys are much more dependent on their parents for shelter and support. What they do at home is another matter, but they do live there.

Children in the Family and Society

In summary, demographic materials suggest that the decline of the family's role in caring for children is more myth than fact. None of the statistical data suggests that parental watchfulness over children has decreased over the span of three generations; much suggests that it has increased. The most important difference between today's children and children of their great-grandparents' and grandparents' time is that there are proportionately fewer of them. They make up a smaller proportion of society, and there are fewer of them per family. Like children born during the 1930s, but unlike children born during the 1950s, children of the 1970s face a predominantly adult world. If the rate of population growth continues to stabilize, the society of the next decades will be older and the families smaller than any previously found in America.

Parent-child bonds also persist despite changes in patterns of disruption and living arrangements after disruption. The proportion of children who lose a parent by death has gone steadily down over the generations. The proportion who live with a parent after a death or divorce has gone steadily up. Even in recent years when family disruptions have begun to rise again to high levels, almost no children have gone to relatives, foster homes or institutions.

The trend toward more mothers in the paid labor force has probably not materially affected parent-child bonds. Even though more mothers work outside the home and more children go to school earlier and longer, the quantity and quality of actual mother-child interaction has probably not changed much. In short, the major demographic changes affecting parents and children in the course of the century have not much altered the basic picture of children living with and being cared for by their parents. The patterns of structural change so often cited as evidence of family decline do not seem to be weakening the bonds between parents and children.

Family Membership, Past and Present

Barbara Laslett

Recent sociological discussions of the family have a curiously contradictory character. The growth of a counterculture in the 1960s and early 1970s both rejected and posed alternatives to traditional forms of the family (Skolnick, 1973). Interpreting student and antiwar activism as a failure in the family's ability to provide coherent socialization experience for its children (Flacks, 1971) led people to question the adequacy of family norms and traditional family life. To use Arlene Skolnick's (1973) phrase, the nuclear family was thought to be "alive, but not well." In contrast to this view, other discussions of the contemporary family emphasize its robustness. Mary Jo Bane (1976:xiv), for instance, concluded that the demographic data she analyzed show "surprising evidence of the persistence of commitments to family life . . ."—that the family is "here to stay."

Marriage and divorce statistics mirror the apparent contradictions exemplified by these views. In the United States, marriage continues to be an exceedingly popular institution. A comparison of marriage rates in twenty-two selected countries (Carter and Glick, 1976:387) shows that in 1965, only Egypt had a higher marriage rate than the United States, while in every year between 1970 and 1974, the United States rate was higher than that of any other country included in their comparison.[1] Of course the high rate of marriage in the United States may well be affected by the fact that Americans also have the highest divorce rate compared to seventeen of these same countries. Although there has been a slight decline in the American remarriage rate since 1974, the divorce rate has been increasing steadily since 1965 (Carter and Glick, 1976:391). Nevertheless, Bane suggests (1976:34) that "it is not marriage itself but the specific marital partner that is rejected."

In addition to marriage and divorce statistics, other aspects of family life have been attracting public and professional interest. Whether the increasing attention to family violence (Steinmetz and Straus, 1975; Gelles, 1974; Steinmetz, 1977) indicates a higher incidence of violence or simply more public discussion of it is difficult to know; in either case, child and wife battering are clear indications of family "troubles." Even the rise in the professions of marriage and family therapy[2] can be interpreted in two ways—as indicating

From *Social Problems*, 25:5 (June 1978), pp. 476–490. Copyright © 1978 by the Society for the Study of Social Problems. Reprinted by permission.

[1]The marriage rate has declined somewhat since 1972 but without changing the status of the United States compared to other countries.

[2]In 1960, the membership of the American Association of Marriage and Family Counselors was 237; by 1976 it had risen to 4230. In every year since 1970 (at which time the membership was 973), the percentage annual increase in membership ranged from twenty-four percent to thirty-seven percent. (American Association of Marriage and Family Counselors, personal communication from administrative offices, Claremont, Calif.)

increasing difficulties within the family or of greater efforts to resolve problems. One may therefore ask, why is the contemporary family "not well—but here to stay"?

Several answers have been given to why the family is not well. Skolnick (1973), for instance, suggests that earlier conceptualization tended to sentimentalize the family and its relationships, to view the family in utopian terms, and to ignore the strains and conflicts which daily life involves. Only recently have conceptualizations derived from conflict theory been applied to family dynamics. Other answers have suggested that large-scale political and economic changes have contributed to the difficulties that the modern family now faces (Flacks, 1971; Zaretsky, 1976).

Functional theory, particularly Parsons, has provided one answer to why the family is "here to stay." The argument is familiar and emphasizes an increasing *division of labor* within and between social institutions—structural differentiation—which has characterized the process of historical change. Under these conditions, the family has assumed a more specialized set of functions for the larger society—that of primary socialization agent for children and the stabilization of adult personalities. Thus, "the family has become *a more specialized agency than before* . . . but (is) not in any general sense less important, because the society is dependent *more* exclusively on it for the performance of *certain* of its vital functions" (Parsons and Bales, 1955:9-10).

Recent statements by social scientists elaborate upon this view of the contemporary family's "socio-emotional specialization." Berger and Kellner (1975), for instance, state that "marriage occupies a privileged status among the significant validating relationships for adults in our society." Providing a very Parsonian explanation for this development, they say

> this character of marriage has its roots in much broader structural configurations of our society. The most important of these, for our purpose, is the crystallization of a so-called private sphere of existence. . . . defined and utilized as the main social area for the individual's self-realization.

Weigert and Hastings (1977) also discuss the significance of the family's specialized role when they say "the basic relationships of the nuclear family . . . are central to the processes of identity formation . . ." And Zaretsky (1976:30) introduces a class dimension into this characterization of the contemporary family when he says

> under capitalism an ethic of personal fulfillment has become the property of the masses of people . . . Much of this search for personal meaning takes place within the family and is no reason for the persistence of the family in spite of the decline of many of its earlier functions.

Noting that in modern society the development of personal identity and the satisfaction of personal needs have become specialized functions of the family leaves two important questions unanswered: 1) how was institutional differentiation at the macro-structural level transformed into individual, emotional, expectations within the family, and 2) can the family, in practice rather than soley in theory, satisfy the demands assigned to it by its functional specialization? The following analysis will address the first of these questions by drawing upon the results of recent research in demographic and family history.[3]

The thesis presented here is that changes in household composition, in the demography of kinship, and in the relationship between the family and other institutions have contributed to the greater emotional significance of the family through their impact on the socialization process. These changes, since the end of the nineteenth century,[4] have caused family membership in the United States to have increased significance for personal identity and emotional gratification. (Aries, 1975, and Shorter, 1975, provide similar arguments about the European family.) In addition, changes in ideology have reinforced the belief that family relationships have become more important for individual development, self-definition, and satisfaction in life.

An analysis which shows *how* family membership has become more significant to individual identity does not, thereby, support a sentimental view, focused only on the positive results of domestic interaction. The intense feelings generated by intimate relationships can be positive or negative, and family relationships may be particularly vulnerable in this respect. In fact, when strong feelings are involved, conflict, abuse, and family dissolution may be more frequent.

Thus, to describe the history of the family's increased importance as a source of personal identity and satisfaction in life is not to say that it successfully satisfies the demands its increasing specialization and importance impose upon it. Several social scientists (Lasch, 1977; Slater, 1970, 1977) have suggested that inherent contradictions within the family make its success unlikely. It is precisely this disparity—between expectations structurally and normatively encouraged and the ability to satisfy them—which is central to understanding the contradictions in contemporary family life.

Family Structure and Socialization

Recent research on the history of the family in Western Europe and North America shows that the membership of most households, both past and present, was—and is—composed primarily of nuclear family members. (See,

---

[3]A more complete formulation, in which macro-economic changes will be more fully discussed, is in preparation as part of the author's study of the family and social change in nineteenth century Los Angeles. For a preliminary statement see B. Laslett, 1978b.

[4]For this discussion, the twentieth century family will be contrasted with the family in earlier historical periods, with full recognition that such a gross dichotomy obscures variation in the rates and timing of the developments important for understanding how historical change has affected the family. See B. Laslett, 1973, for a discussion of why the twentieth century family can legitimately be differentiated from the family in earlier historical periods.

for instance, Anderson, 1971; Demos, 1970; Greven, 1970; Katz, 1975; P. Laslett, 1972, 1977; Parish and Schwartz, 1972; Blumin, 1975; B. Laslett, 1975, 1977). It is important, however, to distinguish the family, defined in terms of the co-resident domestic group, from the kinship group extending beyond the household.

The most frequently used data for investigating the structure of family life in past times are parish records, and census and other types of nominal listings, which usually report information on the co-resident domestic group. Empirical research findings on kinship ties beyond the household are more difficult to obtain and fewer are available. (For some examples, see Anderson, 1971; Plakans, 1977.) While the use of findings about the organization of the co-resident domestic group to discuss family structure in past times has been defended by some scholars (P. Laslett, 1972), its limitations have been criticized by others (Berkner, 1975). Conclusions based on household-level data clearly provide only partial information, since the residential unit is but one way to define the family. (See Goody, 1972, for a further discussion of this issue.)

Dispute over the proper—and possible—unit of analysis in historical family research contributes to contradictory interpretations about how the family has changed. While, as has been suggested, several social scientists argue that the family has become increasingly important, others take an opposite view. Wells (1971:278) in discussing the effects of demographic change on the life cycle of American families, says that there has been a "relative decrease in the importance of children in the life of twentieth-century families . . ." Kobrin (1976) makes a similar argument in relation to the increased proportion of persons living alone in the twentieth century.

There is reason to question these conclusions, however, since some of the same demographic factors on which they are based have increased the availability of kin with whom contact is both possible and likely to occur—particularly parents and grandparents. Although child-rearing as traditionally defined —the care of pre-adult, resident children—may occupy a smaller proportion of the family life cycle in contemporary America than was true in the past, advances in the technology relevant for contact and communication—such as automobiles, highway systems, telephones—mean that residence may no longer be central to the continuation of relationships among family members.

Given the scarcity of empirical research on the nonresidential family in the past, the following discussion will present the results of two research traditions not usually related to each other. It will first examine findings on the household unit and then the demographic changes which have affected the size and structure of the kinship group. The impact of migration and urbanization on the availability of family members will also be discussed. The relation between these research findings—and their importance for understanding the significance of family membership in contemporary society—will be integrated through a discussion of their possible effects on socialization within the family.

Household Composition

As indicated, the nuclear family was in past times the predominant type of co-residential domestic group. This finding does not imply that all people lived in nuclear families for all of their lives; life cycle variation in the kin composition of the residential family has been found in several historical studies (Goody, 1972; Hareven, 1975; Herlihy, 1972; Berkner, 1972; B. Laslett, 1975). Household structure has also been shown to be related to socio-economic characteristics of the head of the household, demographic factors, ethnicity, land-holding patterns, and inheritance practices (Glasco, 1975; Gutman, 1976; Katz, 1975; Coale et al., 1965; B. Laslett, 1975, 1977; Farber, 1972; Berkner and Mendels, in press; Furstenberg et al., 1975). Despite these sources of variation, there continues to be support for the view that the nuclear family household was, and is, the modal category of the co-resident domestic group in most western societies in both the preindustrial past and under comtemporary forms of social and economic organization.

While predominantly nuclear in its kinship structure, the preindustrial and early industrial household was also likely to include others unrelated to the conjugal family unit. Among such persons were servants, boarders, and lodgers, apprentices, employees, and other people's children.[5] (B. Laslett, 1973; Blumin, 1975; Kobrin, 1976). Modell and Hareven (1973) show that "the proportion of urban households *which at any particular point in time* had boarders or lodgers was between fifteen and twenty percent."[6] Today, on the contrary, non-kin are unlikely to be included among the membership of many households. In 1970, only 3.5% of all households included in the federal census had one or more resident members unrelated to the head (U.S. Bureau of the Census, 1973:246).

One characteristic distinguishing the contemporary household from domestic settings in the past, therefore, is that few now contain nonrelatives. But in

[5]The periods of service, apprenticeship, and boarding common for young people in the preindustrial Western experience was not usually spent in the homes of kinsmen, although by the beginning of the twentieth century this may have begun to change.

[6]Overall figures may underestimate the proportion of households which included "strangers within the co-resident domestic group, since taking in boarders was related to the family life cycle. Modell and Hareven (1973), for instance, report that among a sample of native, working-class families in the industrial north in 1890, twenty percent of the families with a resident child under five took in boarders if the household head was under twenty-five years of age compared to thirty-five percent of the households with a child of comparable age but when the head was forty-five years of age or older. Berkner (1972) also finds life cycle variation in the presence of residence agricultural workers among eighteenth century peasant households in Austria.

Taking in boarders has usually been associated with urbanization (Modell and Hareven, 1973) and seems to have been higher in urban than rural areas (B. Laslett, 1977b). There is evidence, however, that it occurred in rural communities as well (Blumin, 1975; Roberts, 1904).

nineteenth century America, interaction with non-kin outside the household was likely to be supplemented by contact with resident non-kin. A large proportion of persons interacted with non-kin as part of the daily life within their homes. Although the qualitative character of such contact cannot be known solely from this kind of evidence—the extent to which non-relatives were integrated into the family's life and affairs—non-kin shared the household where many nineteenth century children and adults lived.

Under contemporary conditions, socialization within the household refers primarily to interactions between parents and their children. The psycho-dynamic structure of this process is, therefore, likely to reflect the personalities and personal histories of individuals linked together by family ties. Thus, identification and role modeling—the processes involved in the psycho-dynamic structure of personality development—are defined primarily by characteristics of individuals within the nuclear family group and become identified with membership in a specific family unit. There is a strong imprint of family membership.

This feature of contemporary household composition has relevance for various stages of growth throughout the life cycle, during which themes develop, are enacted, and become identified with a particular family. According to Hess and Handel (1969:18):

> A family theme is a pattern of feelings, motives, fantasies, and conventional-ized understanding grouped about some locus of concern which has a particu-lar form in the personalities of the individual members. The pattern comprises some fundamental view of reality and some way or ways of dealing with it. In the family themes are to be found the family's implicit direction, its notion of "who we are."

Development and reiteration of such themes is likely to provide the basis for a more heightened sense of differentiation between family and non-family members in the present than in the past, when households included both kin and non-kin.

In adolescence, the influence of non-kin was likely to continue, but was due as much to the adolescents' moving as to the household composition of their families of origin, for adolescence in earlier times was marked by the removal of young adults from their parents' homes. They left to find work, to become servants and apprentices and, some have argued, to get an education and build character (Morgan, 1944; Demos, 1970; Shorter, 1975). This pat-tern seems to have occurred in various parts of Western Europe (see, for in-stance, Anderson, 1971; McBride, 1976; Schofield 1970; Shorter, 1975) and North America (Bloomberg, 1974; Dublin, 1975; Katz, 1975; Little and Laslett, 1977).

Recent historical research shows (Katz, 1975; Bloomberg, 1974; Little and Laslett, 1977) that in the late nineteenth century, at least in the industrializing economies of the new world, adolescents experienced a lengthening period of dependency upon their parents. Prior to that time, many spent their adolescence outside the parental home. Of course visiting home and parents was possible and did take place although how often depended on the terms of the contract governing the life of the servant or apprentice as well as the distance involved. Thus, contact with kin for many adolescents and young adults in the past was more likely to be a special occasion than a daily or weekly occurrence.[7]

These aspects of household composition are likely to have influenced the socialization process of both adults and children in the past, as they do in the present. We can see the significance of these structural changes most clearly in relation to adolescence—a period characterized in contemporary psychological thought (Erikson, 1959) by a search for a separate identity on the part of young adults. The increased identification of the self with a particular family unit, and the greater clarity of boundaries between family and nonfamily members, may have increased the need to differentiate one's self from the family group as part of the transition to adulthood, thereby sharpening parent-child conflict during adolescence.[8] Furthermore, the wish to establish one's own identity is more likely to be experienced by both parents and children as a rejection of and rebellion against the more clearly formulated identity with a particular family. Thus, the search for a separate identity involves questioning parental norms and authority, since it is parents who symbolize in the strongest emotional terms, the norms and authority of the adult world.

Understanding the impact of household composition on socialization within the family should not be limited to the young people involved. Under the conditions of contemporary family living, parents are also more likely than in the past to develop strong identification with their children. Each of the child's developmental stages poses developmental tasks for the parents as well, reawakening themes and conflicts from their own youth and posing the psychological tasks associated with aging. It is not surprising that two contemporary concerns of psycho-dynamic thought center simultaneously on problems of adolescence and "the mid-life crisis." These "crises of growth" reflect the increased intensity of family relationships and the increased importance of family membership for personal identity to which historical changes in household composition have contributed.

Demography and Kinship

Three demographic factors are of particular importance in comparing the size and structure of the kinship group in past and present western societies:

[7]The implications of these changes in residence for the meaning of adolescence is discussed in Little and Laslett, 1977.

[8]Modell et al. (1976) discuss other structural reasons which would explain the greater conflict associated with adolescence in contemporary society.

mortality, age-at-marriage, and fertility. Although several types of kin will be considered, ascendant kin are most relevant for discussing the availability of persons intentionally likely to assume roles in the socialization process, particularly for children.[9]

Mortality

In the past, people simply did not live long enough to form a sizeable pool of older relatives with whom contact was possible. In 1900, the expectation of life at birth (for the white population) in the United States was 48.2 years for males and 51.1 years for females. In 1970, these figures had risen to 68.0 years for males and 75.6 years for females. (U.S. Bureau of the Census, 1975: 56). While some nineteenth century American mortality data is available, questions have been raised about its adequacy (Vinovskis, 1972, 1974); the decline in mortality in the twentieth century, however, when vital registration data have become increasingly available is clearer (see Taeuber and Taeuber, 1958).

Although infant mortality made a major contribution to death rates in earlier times, higher mortality in the past affected adults as well as infants. At age twenty, the expectation of life of white males was 42.4 additional years in 1900 and 50.3 additional years in 1970; the comparable figures for white women are 43.8 and 57.4 additional years, respectively (U.S. Bureau of the Census, 1976:56). One consequence of the changing mortality rates is that "the chances that today's typical bride and groom will both survive the next fifty years (to their golden wedding anniversary) are more than twice as great as were the chances of such survival for their counterparts in 1900–02" (Metropolitan Life, February, 1976). Thus, fewer parents and grandparents were available in earlier historical periods to participate in the socialization of their children and grandchildren.

Differential mortality by sex is also relevant to kin contacts. In twentieth century America, there has been an increasing sex difference in life expectancy. While the length of life (at birth and older ages) of both sexes has increased between 1900 and 1970, the increase for women has been greater than the increase for men, as the expectation of life figures quoted earlier indicate. Findings from contemporary research on the family (Adams, 1968:167) show the importance of parents for continued kin contact among their adult chil-

[9]Demos (1972:656) points out the potential significance of older siblings in the socialization process of children in the large families found in Plymouth Colony. Shorter (1975:26), however, says that in Europe usually only two or three children were in residence simultaneously. Given the tendency for employment to begin at relatively young ages, it is older siblings who were most likely to have left their parents' homes. The residence patterns of adolescents before the end of the nineteenth century (Bloomberg, 1974; Katz, 1975; Little and Laslett, 1977) suggest that the same may have been true in North America.

dren; when parents are alive, contact is greater than after the parents' deaths. The mother's survival may be particularly important in this respect, since women are more active in maintaining family ties (Adams, 1968:27–28). Since women have greater longevity than men, contacts among related adults may be sustained even longer than would be likely without this pattern of differential life expectancy by sex.[10]

Age-at-Marriage

The median age at first marriage in the United States in 1890 was 26.1 years for men and twenty-two years for women; in 1950 it was 22.8 and 20.3 years (U.S. Bureau of the Census, 1976:19); and in 1974 it was 23.1 and 21.1 years, respectively (U.S. Bureau of the Census, 1974:1). The late nineteenth century figures may well represent the high point of an upward trend, since available data indicate that people married younger in the colonial period. (See Wells, 1972 for colonial America, as well as Britain and France at a comparable time period; Farber, 1972; and Sklar, 1974, for late nineteenth and early twentieth century European data.) In the twentieth century, however, compared to the late nineteenth, children are born earlier in their parents' life span and are more likely to survive. Under such circumstances, family members will be available both for more of the individual's life, because of increases in life expectancy of the older generation, and for greater periods of the family life cycle because new families begin at earlier ages.[11]

Fertility

While the pool of potential kin may be affected by declining mortality and age-at-first-marriage, changing fertility rates are also relevant for estimating the size and structure of the kinship group in the present compared to the past. Fertility in the United States has declined (see Coale and Zelnik, 1963; Taeuber and Taeuber, 1957). The question is whether lowered fertility offsets the effects of decreased mortality, so that the number of living relatives per family in the present is no different from in the past.

Historical data to answer this question directly are not available. Goodman, Keyfitz and Pullum (1974), however, provide suggestive material in their estimates of the number of surviving female relatives of different types given the fertility and mortality of the United States in 1967 and Madagascar in 1966, that is, a country with low fertility and low mortality—the modern demographic profile—compared to a society with high fertility and high mor-

---

[10]Linkages along the male line may be stronger when there are economic ties between fathers and their children. The decline in family businesses and self-employment (Blau and Duncan, 1967:41) in the twentieth century would thus lessen the salience of father-adult child contact.

[11]The impact of age-at-marriage on the size of the kinship group is clearly seen where it has been early, not late, and where high fertility has been encouraged. See Gutman (1976) for a discussion of these factors in relation to the black family.

tality—the preindustrial patterns.[12] This analysis shows that three factors are relevant for estimating the number of female kin alive under the two demographic regimes: the age of the woman; the distance of the kinship link between a woman and her relative and whether the relative is an ascendant, descendant, or lateral kin. In general, the results show that in societies with low fertility and low mortality, older relatives are more available and younger relatives are less available. Although some lateral relatives would also be less available under western, industrial demographic conditions, the difference is small. The advantage in terms of the size of the kinship pool does not appear to be marked for one type of society compared to another. Gray's (1977) application of the Goodman, Keyfitz, and Pullum model to 1920, 1930, and 1970 U.S. demographic rates shows, however, that to the extent that there is a difference, more living kin are available to contemporary Americans than was true in earlier periods.

If one differentiates between relatives not in terms of generation but in terms of relational proximity to an individual, another aspect of the kinship structure emerges. The only categories of kin where Goodman, Keyfitz, and Pullum show that the high fertility, high mortality society has a marked advantage over the low fertility, low mortality society is in terms of cousins and granddaughters. Data on social contact between kin in the contemporary United States (Adams, 1968) suggest that interaction is most frequent between closest kin (parents, children and siblings) and falls off sharply as one moves further away from primary bonds. Demos (1970:124) found that the most significant kin connections in Plymouth colony were also those between members of the primary family unit. In the absence of primary family members, however, more distant kin may have been of greater importance (see Greven, 1970). It should be remembered, however, that migration—a significant feature of American life throughout its history—is higher among younger adults. Although proportionately more young adults may have been alive under preindustrial demographic conditions, their availability for purposes of interaction with other family members may not have been as great as numbers alone would suggest.

The demographic factors reviewed have implications for understanding patterns of family interaction and the processes of socialization both within the household and the extended kin group. Glick (1977) says that "the larger the family the larger proportion of time that children are likely to spend interacting with each other, whereas the smaller the family the greater the proportion

---

[12]It could be argued that contemporary Madagascar and preindustrial America are so unalike that the Goodman, Keyfitz, and Pullum (1974) estimates cannot be used even suggestively. There are several reasons to reject this position: 1) The model is purely mathematical and takes account of no other characteristics of Madagascar society except its gross reproduction rate and expectation of life at birth. 2) The demographic rates used to generate the model's estimates for Madagascar are sufficiently close to the pre-industrial American figures to validate their usefulness as suggestive (although certainly not conclusive) indicators.

of time the children are likely to spend interacting with their parents . . ."
Thus, changes in mortality, fertility, and age-at-marriage, as well as changes
in household composition, are likely to affect the processes of role modeling
and identification that occur within the contemporary family. It is likely to
increase the impact of parents in the socialization process. Despite the increased proportion of mothers in the labor force, the overwhelming proportion
of children are cared for by their own parents or other relatives, rather than
by non-relatives (U.S. Bureau of the Census, 1976). Furthermore demographic
changes have also resulted in the availability of more ascendant kin, particularly grandparents, uncles, and aunts, who may elaborate the meaning of
kinship throughout the individual life cycle. Given the increased importance
of family membership established in the early years of the socialization process,
for both children and adults, and the means of contact and communication
which technological advances have made available, common residence is no
longer likely to be as significant a determinant contact as in earlier historical
periods.

Urbanization and Migration

Two factors relevant to the distribution of population also affect the availability of kin with whom contact may occur: (1) urbanization and (2) migration. Although rapid urbanization has been a feature in the American
experience since the early nineteenth century (Potter, 1974), the twentieth
century has witnessed an increasing concentration of population in large urban
centers. Kin may be concentrated in areas where fairly frequent contact is
easier to make and harder to avoid, because of the expansion of the highway
system, the widespread availability of automobiles, air travel, and the telephone.

Migration, a characteristic of American life both in the past and present
(Lee, 1964: 127), has often been used to explain the absence of kin contact
among mobile populations. The act of migration (particularly overseas migration) reduces the pool of potential kin available both to the migrant and the
non-migrant. Furthermore, the process of internal (vs. overseas) migration can
also thin the ranks of kin with whom contact is possible. Here again, literacy
and the technology of communication are important, for once a relative leaves
a community, contact between family members depends on the available
modes of communication. But the impact of migration may also depend on
whether it occurs early or late in the historical development of an area.

In earlier generations, migrating family members established themselves in
places which did not include members of their own kin group. The potential
for kin contact was reduced or eliminated because of migration. First generation migrants would be most lacking in ascendant kin since migration typically
occurs among the younger categories. (See U.S. Bureau of the Census,
1976:122, for data on foreign immigrants by age between 1820 and 1970.) The

likelihood that kin would be found in the place of destination of the next generation of migrants, however, is increased by the simple fact that earlier migration of family members had occurred. Nineteenth as well as twentieth century migrants have been shown to choose their destinations in part because of the presence of kin group members in the new area (Hareven, 1975; McLaughlin, 1971; Hendrix, 1975, 1976). Thus, migration, particularly under modern technological conditions, does not necessarily reduce contact to the degree suggested by earlier authors, although it does, perhaps, render it voluntary (Shorter, 1975).

To summarize, structural factors have created the potential for family membership to become a more salient feature of personal identity in the contemporary period compared to the western, pre-industrial past through its effect on socialization within the household, on the increased number of ascendant kin, and the spatial distribution of the kin group. In addition, developments in the technology of contact and communication and increased literacy make it easier for family members to be in touch with each other whether or not they live close together.

In the earlier period, the co-resident domestic group was less often confined to primary kin group members, while in the present context, more households contain nuclear family members only. Thus, within the home, non-kin are not as likely to diffuse identification with a particular family. Greater numbers of ascendant kin outside the home are available to amplify the identification developed within it.

The Ideology of Family Life

Beliefs about family life in contemporary American society tend to reflect and reinforce the intimacy and intensity which residential and demographic factors make possible. The early Puritan ideology in America emphasized the role of the family as guardian of the public, as well as the private, good. Not only did religion specify the approved relationships between family members —their duties and responsibilities to each other—but it also made it a sacred duty of church members to see that edicts were carried out. It was not sufficient for people to be moral in public—they also had to be moral in private, and religion provided a legitimating ideology for minding other people's family affairs.

In contrast to these beliefs, the idea of the private family and the home as a personal sanctuary grew throughout the nineteenth century. Family life began to be characterized as an oasis, a retreat, a haven from the uncertainties, immoralities, and strains of life in a rapidly changing society (Jeffery, 1972; Sennett, 1970). Elder's (1974) suggestion that "the family as refuge" was one reaction of American families to the Depression of the 1930's indicates that this theme has continued within the twentieth century. Insecurities in public roles and disappointments in the occupational sphere—made all the more painful, perhaps, by a political ideology which emphasizes individual success and advancement—reinforced a belief in the family as the only place where meaningful relationships are possible.

The theme of the family as a retreat can also be found in recent discussions of contemporary non-traditional family forms such as communes and open marriages (Sussman, 1972). These alternative family forms are thought to provide the opportunity for deep and meaningful personal relationships to a greater extent than other types of family living. Thus, the family continues to be seen as a haven from the large society. Sussman (1972:8) says:

> Life is for meaningful relationships on a micro-level where one can control one's own destiny or at least not be subordinated; a level which provides numerous options and optimal freedom for deep relationships.

The ideology of family living, even in its most avant-garde form, continues to emphasize the importance of the family as a refuge from the larger society. This perspective is based on the belief that it is only within the family that a sense of personal control and intimacy can be found (also see, Zaretsky, 1976). Whether or not this belief and the needs it expresses can actually be satisfied within the family is another issue.

The relationship of the family to other social institutions reinforces the search for meaning within the family. One of the features said to characterize modern industrial societies, compared to those which preceded them historically, is an increase in the importance of achieved versus ascribed attributes. In the life of families in Andover, Mass., in the seventeenth century (Greven, 1970), access to arable land was crucial to the adult life of sons. The father's control over land affected many aspects of the son's adult behavior—including when he could marry. The growth of an occupational system emphasizing an individual's educational achievement, and the increasing availability of public education, have loosened the constraints which past authority patterns and practices were likely to impose (Goode, 1963). Family contacts may therefore be less crucial to achieving one's place in the modern occupational world.

But the very fact that family contacts may no longer play such an important part in placing individuals in their public social roles—thus reducing the instrumental usefulness of kin contacts—may serve to increase their socio-emotional importance. In a society whose ideology values individual achievement and scorns nepotism, family membership may be prized simply because it does not have to be earned. The ascribed character of family membership may be experienced as a positive attribute for the very reason that it can be "taken for granted."

The socialization that occurs within the twentieth century American family is likely to contribute to the "taken for granted" character of family relationships. As the differentiation between the norms, values, and location of the family compared to other institutions has increased, the differences between the family and other areas of social life have sharpened. The contemporary family's private character (B. Laslett, 1973), by providing a "backstage area" (Goffman, 1959) where persons can relax from performing their public roles, contributes to an ideology that defines the family primarily in socio-emotional terms. What is frequently forgotten in these formulations, is that performers not only relax backstage, but they also prepare for—and sometimes rehearse —their public roles. Thus, the potentially contradictory and confusing messages communicated within the domestic setting can create discrepancies between the ideology and actuality of contemporary family life.

Changes in economic organization within the general society may have affected the emotional meaning of family relationships in other ways. In the past, when the family was the unit of production as well as the unit of consumption, work and family roles were intertwined to a greater extent than in the present. The systematic separation of home and work activities which began in nineteenth century America, the decline in proprietorship in the contemporary period, and the increase in the salaried and bureaucratic sector of the economy (Blau and Duncan, 1967) means that fewer family members may be working together than was true in an earlier period. In the past, relations between employers and employees, masters and servants or apprentices, and parents and children shared greater emotional similarity than is true today (see P. Laslett, 1971; Farber, 1972; Douglas, 1921:55). But it is precisely a decline in the intertwining of what we now see as diverse social roles which permits the intensification of the emotional aspects of family relationships.

A similar argument can be made in relation to the family as educator. Before public schooling was widely available, much education occurred in the home (Cremin, 1974). Removing the requirement that parents teach, monitor, and correct their children's intellectual development reduces potential conflict between aspects of their behavior as parents. Today, parents do not have to satisfy the sometimes contrary demands of expecting achievement in the sphere of cognitive development while simultaneously providing socio-emotional resources for their children's psychological development.

This argument is not meant to imply that parents are less concerned about the educational achievement of their children. The opposite may be true. (See LeVine, 1974, for a discussion of how parents' goals for their children affect child-rearing behavior.) Alice Rossi (1968) has suggested that in the absence of clear-cut standards, mothers and fathers often use children's report cards and pediatricians' reports to judge their performance as parents. But the availability of institutions to foster their children's attainment of instrumental skills outside the home permits and encourages a greater concentration on the affective character of the relationships within it.

Structural conditions within the household which contribute to the increased emotional intensity of comtemporary parent-child relations, are reinforced by the relations between the family and other social institutions. Children's educational and occupational attainments are more likely to take on greater psychological meaning—to become reflections or extensions of parents' personal fantasies and ambitions. The possibility of testing these fantasies against reality—or understanding what makes fantasies more or less possible ambitions—is not as available to modern parents who share less of an experiential world with their children than did parents in the pre-industrial period.

Social contact outside the residential unit may help to confirm or diminish the importance of family membership for personal identity. Frequent interaction between extended family members provides a basis for the continuing reaffirmation of the sense of membership generated within the residential family. Many studies since World War II show the importance of contact between kin compared to non-kin in the United States (Axelrod, 1956; Greer, 1956; Bell and Boat, 1957; Sussman and Burchinal, 1962; Lawson, 1974). Thus, the importance of kinship is not only theoretical. It is real, since it appears to provide the most significant basis for interaction when options are available. That this is true even when technology which makes contact easier also makes it a matter of choice (Shorter, 1975), is testimony to the salience of family membership in contemporary America.

Conclusions

The preceding analysis suggests that the significance of family membership has changed in the United States. Changes in household composition and the demography of kinship, in the technology of communication and the spread of literacy, in the ideology of family life and the relationship of the family to other social institutions have affected the process of socialization in ways increasing the family's salience in the formation of personal identity. Earlier fears that urbanization and industrialization would weaken "the bonds of kinship" (Wirth, 1938) have not been bourne out. To the contrary, the historical changes that have been described have resulted in an "intensified . . . weight of meaning attached to the personal relations of the family" (Zaretsky, 1976:66).

But if this has occurred, why are there the family problems and strains noted at the beginning of this paper? Weibert and Hastings (1977) suggest that the contemporary family's "specialized function of affectivity and expressivity for the sustenance of emotionally charged personal identities" also makes it a particularly powerful source of pain and conflict. In addition, the specialized and bureaucratic organization of modern life has made the family one of the few *locations* where the expression of strong feeling is legitimate, thus increasing the likelihood that emotionally charged interactions—both positive and negative—will occur.

Perhaps the most important question to be asked about the modern family is not whether it is "here to stay" but whether it can sustain and satisfy the search for meaning and the weight of expectation that it has come to have. The contradiction implied by saying the contemporary family is "here to stay, but not well" can be understood only when the second question posed at the beginning of this paper has been answered: Does, and can, the family have the resources—both material and emotional—to satisfy the demands which are placed upon it in contemporary American society?

References

Adams, Bert N.
   1968   *Kinship in an Urban Setting.* Chicago: Markham
Anderson, Michael
   1971   *Family Structure in Nineteenth Century Lancashire.* Cambridge: Cambridge University Press.
Aries, Philippe
   1975   "La famille." *Encounter* 45(August):7–12.
Axelrod, Morris
   1956   "Urban structure and social participation." *American Sociological Review* 21(February):13–18.
Bane, Mary Jo
   1976   *Here to Stay: American Families in the Twentieth Century.* New York: Basic Books.
Bell, Wendell and Marion D. Boat
   1957   "Urban neighborhood and informal social relations." *American Journal of Sociology* 62(January):391–398.
Berger, Peter, and Hansfried Kellner
   1975   "Marriage and the construction of reality." Pp. 219–233 in Dennis Brisset and Charles Edgley (eds.) *Life As Theatre: A Dramaturgical Sourcebook.* Chicago: Aldine.
Berkner, Lutz K.
   1972   "The stem family and the development cycle of the peasant household: An Eighteenth-century Austrian example." *American Historical Review* 77(April):398-418.
   1975   "The use and misuse of census data for the historical analysis of family structure." *Journal of Interdisciplinary History* 6(Spring):721–738.
Berkner, Lutz K., and Franklin F. Mendels
   forth-   "Inheritance systems, family structure and demographic patterns in western Europe
   coming   (1700–1900)."Mimeographed.
Blau, Peter M., and O. D. Duncan
   1967   *The American Occupational Structure.* New York: John Wiley.
Bloomberg, Susan
   1974   "The household and the family: The effects of industrialization on skilled workers in Newark, 1840–1860." A paper presented at the meetings of the Organization of American Historians, Denver.
Blumin, Stuart M.
   1975   "Rip Van Winkle's grandchildren: Family and household in the Hudson Valley, 1800–1860." *Journal of Urban History* 1(May):293–315.
Carter, Hugh, and Paul C. Glick
   1976   *Marriage and Divorce: A Social and Economic Study,* revised edition. Cambridge, Mass.: Harvard University Press.
Coale, Ansley J., and Melvin Zelnik
   1963   *New Estimates of Fertility and Population in the United States.* Princeton, N.J.: Princeton University Press.
Coale, Ansley J. et al.
   1965   *Aspects of the Analysis of Family Structure.* Princeton, N.J.: Princeton University Press.
Cremin, Lawrence A.
   1974   "The family as educator: Some comments on the recent historiography." *Teachers College Record* 76(December):250–265.
Demos, John
   1970   *A Little Commonwealth.* New York: Oxford University Press.

1972   "Demography and psychology in the historical study of family life: A personal report."
        Pp. 561–570 in Peter Laslett (ed.), *Household and Family in Past Time.* Cambridge:
        Cambridge University Press.
Douglas, Paul H.
1921   *American Apprenticeship and Industrial Education. Studies in History, Economics and
        Public Law XCI,* New York: Columbia University Press.
Dublin, Thomas
1975   "Women, work and the family: Women operatives in the Lowell Mills, 1830–1860."
        Feminist Studies 3(Summer):30–39.
Elder, Glen H., Jr.
1974   *Children of the Great Depression: Social Change in Life Experience.* Chicago: Univer-
        sity of Chicago Press.
Erikson, Erik H.
1959   "Identity and the life cycle." *Psychological Issues,* 1.
Farber, Bernard
1972   *Guardians of Virtue: Salem Families in 1800.* New York: Basic Books
Flacks, Richard
1971   *Youth and Social Change.* Chicago: Markham
Furstenberg, Frank F., Jr., Theodore Hershberg, and John Modell
1975   "The origins of the female-headed black family: The impact of the urban experience."
        Journal of Interdisciplinary History 6(Autumn):211–233.
Gelles, Richard J.
1974   The violent home: A study of physical aggression between husbands and wives. Beverly
        Hills, Calif.: Sage Publications.
Glasco, Laurence A.
1975   "The life cycle and household structure of American ethnic groups: Irish, Germans,
        and native-born whites in Buffalo, New York, 1855." *Journal of Urban History*
        1(May):399–364.
Glick, Paul C.
1977   "Updating the life cycle of the family." *Journal of Marriage and the Family* 39(Feb-
        ruary):5–13.
Goode, William J.
1963   *World Revolution and Family Patterns.* New York: Free Press.
Goodman, Leo A., Nathan Keyfitz, and Thomas W. Pullum
1974   "Family formation and the frequency of various kinship relationships." *Theoretical
        Population Biology* 5(February):1–27.
Goody, Jack
1972   "The evolution of the family." Pp. 103–124 in P. Laslett (ed.), *Household and Family
        in Past Time.* Cambridge: Cambridge University Press.
Gray, Anke Van Hilst
1977   "Who was really there? An historical look at available kin." An empirical paper
        presented to the Department of Sociology, University of Southern California.
Greer, Scott
1956   "Urbanism reconsidered." *American Sociological Review* 21(February):22–25.
Greven, Philip
1970   *Four Generations: Population, Land and Family in Colonial Andover, Massachusetts.*
        New York: Cornell University Press.
Gutman, Herbert G.
1976   *The Black Family in Slavery and Freedom, 1750–1925.* New York: Pantheon.
Hareven, Tamara K.
1975a   "Family time and industrial time: Family and work in a planned corporation town,
        1900–1924." *Journal of Urban History* 1(May):365–389.
1975b   "The laborers of Manchester, New Hampshire, 1912–1922: The role of family and
        ethnicity in adjustment to industrial life." *Labor History* 16(Spring):249–265.
Hendrix, Lewellyn
1975   "Kinship and economic-rational migration: A comparison of micro- and macro-level
        analyses." *Sociological Quarterly* 16(Autumn):534–543.
1976   "Kinship, social networks, and integration among Ozark residents and out-migrants."
        Journal of Marriage and the Family 38(February):97–104.

Herlihy, David
1972   "Mapping households in medieval Italy." *Catholic Historical Review* 58(April):1–24.
Hess, Robert D., and Gerald Handel
1967   "The family as a psychosocial organization." Pp. 10–29 in Gerald Handel (ed.), *The Psychosocial Interior of the Family: A Source Book for the Study of Whole Families.* Chicago: Aldine.
Jeffrey, Kirk
1972   "The family in utopian retreat from the city: the nineteenth century contribution." *Soundings* 40(Spring):21–41.
Katz, Michael B.
1975   *The People of Hamilton, Canada West.* Cambridge, Mass.: Harvard University Press.
Kobrin, Frances E.
1976   "The fall in household size and the rise of the primary individual in the United States." *Demography* 31(February):127–138.
Lasch, Christopher
1977   *Haven in a Heartless World: The Family Besieged.* New York: Basic Books.
Laslett, Barbara
1973   "The family as a public and private institution: An historical perspective." *Journal of Marriage and the Family* 35(August):480–492.
1975   "Household structure on an American frontier: Los Angeles, California, in 1850." *American Journal of Sociology* 81(July):109–128.
1977   "Social change and the family: Los Angeles, California, 1850–1870." *American Sociological Review* 42(April):269–291.
1978a   "Household structure and the social organization of production: Los Angeles, California, in 1850." A paper to be presented at the IXth World Congress of Sociology, Uppsala, Sweden.
1978b   "Strategies for survival: An historical perspective on the family and development." A paper to be presented at the IXth World Congress of Sociology, Uppsala, Sweden.
Laslett, Peter
1971   *The World We Have Lost.* Second Edition. London: University Paperbacks.
1972   *Household and Family in Past Time.* (Ed.) Cambridge: Cambridge University Press.
1977   *Family Life and Illicit Love in Earlier Generations.* Cambridge: Cambridge University Press.
Lawson, John E., Jr.
1974   *The Impact of the Local Metropolitan Environment on the Patterning of Social Contacts.* Ph.D. dissertation, Dept. of Sociology, University of Southern California.
Lee, Everett S.
1964   "Internal migration and population redistribution in the United States." Pp. 123–136 in Ronald Freedman (ed.), *Population: The Vital Revolution.* Garden City, N.Y.: Anchor Books.
LeVine, Robert A.
1974   "Parental goals: A cross-cultural view." *Teachers College Record* 76(December):226–239.
Little, Margaret, and Barbara Laslett
1977   "Adolescence in historical perspective: The decline of boarding in 19th century Los Angeles." A paper presented at the annual meetings of the American Sociological Association, Chicago.
McBride, Theresa M.
1976   *The Domestic Revolution: The Modernization of Household Service in England and France, 1820–1920.* New York: Holmes and Meier.
McLaughlin, Virginia Yans
1971   "Working class immigrant families: first generation Italians in Buffalo, New York." A paper delivered before the Organization of American Historians, New Orleans.
Metropolitan Life
1976   "Likelihood of a golden wedding anniversary." *Statistical Bulletin,* 57(February):4–7.
Modell, John, and Tamara K. Hareven
1973   "Urbanization and the malleable household: an examination of boarding and lodging in American families." *Journal of Marriage and the Family* 35(August):467–479.

Modell, John, Frank Furstenberg, and Theodore Hershberg
1976   "Social change and transitions to adulthood in historical perspective." *Journal of Family History* 1(Autumn):7–32.
Morgan, Edmund S.
1944   *The Puritan Family.* New York: Harper.
Parish, William L., and Moshe Schwartz
1972   "Household complexity in nineteenth-century France." *American Sociological Review* 37(April):154–173.
Parsons, Talcott, and Robert F. Bales
1955   *Family, Socialization and Interaction Process.* Glencoe, Ill.: Free Press.
Plakans, Andrejs
1977   "Identifying kinfold beyond the household." *Journal of Family History* 2(Spring):3–27.
Potter, J.
1974   "Demography: the missing link in American history." A paper presented at the meetings of the Organization of American Historians, Denver.
Roberts, Peter
1904   *Anthracite Coal Communities.* New York: Macmillan.
Rossi, Alice S.
1968   "Transition to parenthood." *Journal of Marriage and the Family* 30(February):26–39.
Schofield, R. S.
1970   "Age-specific mobility in an eighteenth century rural English parish." *Annales de demographie historique:*261–274.
Shorter, Edward
1975   *The Making of the Modern Family.* New York: Basic Books.
Sennett, Richard
1970   *Families Against the City: Middle Class Homes of Industrial Chicago, 1872–1890.* Cambridge, Mass.: Harvard University Press.
Sklar, June L.
1974   "The role of marriage behaviour in the demographic transition: The case of eastern Europe around 1900." *Population Studies* 28(July):231–248.
Skolnick, Arlene
1973   *The Intimate Environment: Exploring Marriage and the Family.* Boston: Little, Brown.
Slater, Philip
1970   *The Pursuit of Loneliness: American Culture at the Breaking Point.* Boston: Beacon Press.
1977   Footholds: Understanding the Shifting Sexual and Family Tensions in Our Culture. New York: E. P. Dutton.
Steinmetz, Suzanne K.
1977   *The Cycle of Violence: Assertive, Aggressive and Abusive Family Interaction.* New York: Praeger.
Steinmetz, Suzanne K., and M. A. Straus (eds.)
1974   *Violence in the Family.* New York: Dodd, Mead & Co.
Sussman, Marvin B. (ed.)
1972   *Non-Traditional Family Forms in the 1970s.* Minneapolis, Minn.: National Council on Family Relations.
Sussman, Marvin B., and L. G. Burchinal
1962   "Kin family network: unheralded structure in current conceptualization of family functioning." *Marriage and Family Living* 24.
Taeuber, Conrad, and Irene B. Taeuber
1958   *The Changing Population of the United States.* New York: Wiley
U.S. Bureau of the Census
1973   *Census of Population: 1970.* Subject Reports. Final Report PC(2)-4A. Family Composition. Washington, D.C.: U.S. Government Printing Office.
1974   *Current Population Reports,* Series P–20, No. 271. "Marital Status and Living Arrangements: March 1974." Washington, D.C.: U.S. Government Printing Office.
1976   *Current Population Reports,* Series P–20, No. 298. "Daytime Care of Children: October 1974 and February 1975." Washington, D.C.: U.S. Government Printing Office.
1976   *The Statistical History of the United States: From Colonial Times to the Present.* Washington, D.C.: U.S. Government Printing Office.

U.S. Dept. of Health, Education and Welfare
    1975   *Vital Statistics of the United States, 1970.* Vol. 1—Natality. Public Health Service. Rockville, Md.: National Center for Health Statistics.
Vinovskis, Maris A.
    1972   "Mortality rates and trends in Massachusetts before 1860." *Journal of Economic History* 32(March):184–213.
    1974   "The demography of the slave population in antebellum America." *Journal of Interdisciplinary History* 5(Winter):459–467.
Weigert, Andrew J., and Ross Hastings
    1977   "Identity loss, family and social change." *American Journal of Sociology* 82(May):1171–1185.
Wells, Robert
    1971   "Demographic change and the life cycle of American families." *Journal of Interdisciplinary History* 2(Autumn):273–282.
    1972   "Quaker marriage patterns in a Colonial perspective." *William and Mary Quarterly, Third Series* 24(July):415–442.
Wirth, Louis
    1938   "Urbanism as a way of life." *American Journal of Sociology* 44(July):3–24.
Zaretsky, Eli
    1976   *Capitalism, the Family and Personal Life.* New York: Harper & Row.

2

Sexuality and Sex Roles

Introduction

Chapter 3   The Social Meaning of Sexuality

Blumstein and Schwartz
Bisexuality: Some Social Psychological Issues

Morton Hunt
Marital Sex

Lillian Breslow Rubin
Blue-Collar Marriage and the Sexual Revolution

Chapter 4   Men's Roles

Deborah S. David and Robert Brannon
The Male Sex Role

Kay M. Tooley
"Johnny, I Hardly Knew Ye": Toward Revision of the Theory of
Male Psychosexual Development

Mirra Komarovsky
Cultural Contradictions and Sex Roles

Chapter 5   Women's Roles

Barbara Ehrenreich and Deirdre English
Reflections on the "Woman Question"

Ann Oakley
The Sociology of Housework

Starr Roxanne Hiltz
Widowhood: A Roleless Role
Janet Zollinger Giele
Changing Sex Roles and Family Structure

Introduction

American society has recently experienced both a sexual revolution and a sex-role revolution. The first has liberalized attitudes towards erotic behavior and expression; the second has changed the roles and statuses of women and men in the direction of greater equality. Both revolutions have been brought about by the rapid social changes of recent years, but both revolutions also represent a belated recognition that traditional beliefs and norms did not reflect how people actually behaved and felt.

In terms of scholarship, the main effect thus far of the two revolutions is on awareness and consciousness. For example, much social science writing was suddenly revealed to have been based on sexist assumptions. Many sociologists and psychologists took it for granted that women's roles and functions in society reflected universal physiological and temperamental traits. Since in practically every society women were subordinate to men, inequality was interpreted to be an inescapable necessity of organized social life. Such analysis suffers from the same intellectual flaw as the idea that discrimination against nonwhites implies their innate inferiority. All such explanations fail to analyze the social institutions and forces producing and supporting the observed differences. In approaching the study of either the physical or the social relations between the sexes, it is therefore important to understand how traditional stereotypes have influenced both popular and professional conceptions of sexuality and sex differences.

The articles reprinted in this section on the male and female sex role develop this theme in different ways but generally examine how stereotyping influences and sets limits on male and female socialization. These limits rob both men and women of a broader potential, for example, gentleness for men, achievement for women. Stereotyping thus diminishes the capacity of both men and women to fulfill a broader potential than conventional sex roles dictate.

The conventional idea of sexuality defines sex as a powerful biological drive continually struggling for gratification against restraints imposed by civilization. The notion of sexual instincts also implies a kind of innate knowledge: A person intuitively knows his or her own identify as male or female, he or she knows how to act accordingly, and he or she is attracted to the "proper" sex object—a person of the opposite gender. In other words, the view of sex as biological drive pure and simple implies "that sexuality has a magical ability, possessed by no other capacity, that allows biological drives to be expressed directly in psychological and social behaviors" (Gagnon and Simon 1970, p. 24).

The whole issue of the relative importance of biological versus psychological and social factors in sexuality and sex differences has been obscured by polemics. On the one hand, there are the strict biological determinists who declare anatomy is destiny. On the other hand, there are those who argue that all aspects of sexuality and sex-role difference are matters of learning and social conditioning.

There are two essential points to be made about the nature versus nurture argument. The first is that extreme positions overlook the connection between biology and experience. Research into the development of sex differences suggests not an opposition between genetics and environment but an interaction:

> In the theory of psychosexual differentiation, it is now outmoded to oppose or juxtapose nature vs. nurture, the genetic vs. the psychological, or the instinctive vs. the environmental, the innate vs. the acquired, the biological vs. the psychological, or the instinctive vs. the learned. Modern genetic theory avoids these antiquated dichotomies. ... (Money and Ehrhardt 1972, p. 1)

The second and related point concerns a misconception about how biological forces work. Both biological determinists and their opponents assume that if a biological force exists, it must be overwhelmingly strong. But the most sophisticated evidence concerning both psychosexual development *and* erotic arousal suggests that physiological forces are gentle rather than powerful. Acknowledging the possible effects of prenatal sex hormones on the brains of human infants, Robert Stoller thus warns against "biologizing":

> While the newborn presents a most malleable central nervous system upon which the environment writes, we cannot say that the central nervous system is neutral or neuter. Rather, we can say that the effects of these biological systems, organized prenatally in a masculine or feminine direction, are almost always ... too gentle in humans to withstand the more powerful forces in human development, the first and most powerful of which is mothering ... (Stoller 1972, p. 211).

Striking evidence of the independence of sexual identity and activity from biological determinants comes from studies of hermaphrodites and other "sex errors of the body." A program of research into the psychological effects of such errors has been carried out by John Money and his associates (1961, 1965). Their most significant conclusion is that the sense of gender identity— I am a boy, or I am a girl—is a product of social learning rather than of anatomy and physiology. The experience of the English writer James Morris, who became Jan Morris, illustrates that our gender identity can be of one sex while our sexual organs may be of the other. Morris's experience, while real, is statistically extreme. By contrast, the study by Blumstein and Schwartz reprinted in Chapter 3 shows that sexual choice—is one attracted to men or women or both?—is more uncertain and more complex than the concept of male or female ordinarily implies.

When we think about the current liberalization of sexual behavior and attitudes in recent times, we tend to think of such striking phenomena as the transformation of men into women and vice versa, group sex, the new openness about homosexuality, and aspects of unconventional or taboo sexuality. Yet equally significant, if not so spectacular, are changes in sexual behavior within marriage. Morton Hunt argues in his selection in Chapter 3 "a dramatic and historical change has taken place in the practice of marital coitus in America." If Hunt's data are correct, there has been a great increase in marital eroticism in recent years; married people of all ages are having sex relations more often; they are spending more time in foreplay and intercourse; and they are engaging in formerly taboo activities such as oral sex. Hunt argues that women appear to be equal, rather than reluctant, participants in the increased eroticism. He thus notes that many more women report having regular orgasms than they did in the past, and only a tiny fraction complain that their husbands are too demanding sexually in contrast to the two-thirds majority who made that complaint in the past.

It would be a mistake however, to think that the sexual revolution has brought nothing but uninhibited joy. It has also produced new problems and anxieties. Lillian Rubin's selection deals with the difficulties experienced by blue-collar couples trying to cope with the new sexuality. For wives caught between the new standards for sexual performance and their own and their husbands' earlier training, having an orgasm can often seem to be just another chore in a life already full of chores. Middle-class women, more comfortable with the idea of sexual experimentation, feel guilty about the hang-ups that may prevent them from acting on their liberated beliefs. For their part, men who encourage their wives to be more erotically active may be turned off if the women become so. As in other areas of social life, those who intend a certain outcome may unintentionally achieve its opposite. Thus, the movement toward sexual liberation may inadvertently result in sexual repression.

Chapter 3

The Social Meaning of Sexuality

Bisexuality: Some Social Psychological Issues

Philip W. Blumstein and Pepper Schwartz

The scientific study of human sexuality has not reached a stage of conceptual maturity. Any scientific endeavor must, as an important early step, develop a workable number of abstractions to simplify a complex universe of phenomena. The study of sexuality has had little success at such a task because it has failed to address an even more fundamental problem, i.e., to recognize and map the complexity and diversity of the very sexual phenomena under scrutiny. It is not difficult to understand why sex research is replete with oversimplifications masquerading as scientific abstractions. By and large, investigators working with sexual data have accepted uncritically the pervasive cultural understandings of sexuality and have assumed there to be a simple and "correct" conceptual scheme readily modifiable to the requirements of scientific rigor. As a result of our continuing study of sexual identity we have been led to quite the opposite view and have become disaffected with scientific conceptions that simply reflect the prejudices of folk wisdom. Indeed, the most fundamental conclusion from our research has been that the closer we probe such questions as how people come to define themselves sexually or how their erotic and affectional biographies are structured, the more—not less—the data defy organization in terms of the classical simplicities.

Escaping scientists' borrowed conceptions of sexuality is difficult indeed, because these lay notions, we feel, play a very important part in shaping the actual sexual data themselves. We take the simple position that personal views about sexuality in the abstract reflect wider cultural understandings, and affect, in turn, the concrete constructions people place on their own feelings and experiences, and thereby affect their behavior. So it is essential to accept

From the *Journal of Social Issues,* Vol. 33, No. 2 (1977), pp. 30–45. Copyright © 1977 by the Society for the Psychological Study of Social Issues. Reprinted by permission.

cultural understandings of sexuality as crucial data, while at the same time rejecting the scientific validity of their underlying premises.

Guiding our primary cultural understandings concerning sexuality are three related dichotomies: gender (female versus male), sex role (feminine versus masculine), and affectional preference (homosexual versus heterosexual). Although departures from these dichotomies can be accommodated (e.g., transsexualism has been allowed to emerge as both a concept and as an empirical reality), the very extraordinariness that accompanies such departures reflects and reinforces the cultural simplifications.

Bisexuality is another conceptual loose-end which has been forced by recent media events into a precarious niche in an otherwise neat conceptual apparatus. There is certainly nothing new in the fact that some people do not limit their lifetime of sexual experiences to one sex or the other. In fact, sex researchers over the years have presented compelling evidence of bisexuality in both our own culture and elsewhere around the world (Ford & Beach, 1951). Nevertheless it seems clear that such behavior has been seen as a curiosity, and no attempt has been made to integrate the occasional data on bisexuality into any coherent scientific view of sexuality, nor to modify the hegemony of dichotomous concepts.

As far back as 1948, Kinsey admonished sex researchers to think of sexuality in general, and sex-object choice in particular, in terms of a continuum rather than as a rigid set of dichotomous categories (Kinsey, Pomeroy, & Martin, 1948). His studies found the "37% of the total male population had had at least some overt homosexual experience to the point of orgasm between adolescence and old age," and that between 8% and 20% of females (depending on marital status and education) had made at least incidental homosexual responses or contacts in each of the years between 20 and 35 years of age (Kinsey, Pomeroy, Martin, & Gebhard, 1953). These data, as revolutionary as they were, need to be contrasted with the findings that only 4% of Kinsey's white males and between 0.3% and 3% of his females were exclusively homosexual after the onset of adolescence. The inescapable—but often escaped—conclusions from Kinsey et al.'s findings are that a mix of homosexual and heterosexual behaviors in a person's erotic biography is a common occurrence, and that it is entirely possible to engage in anywhere from a little to a great deal of homosexual behavior without adopting a homosexual lifestyle.

The implications of viewing human sexuality as being plastic and malleable have never really been exploited. Even the word *bisexuality* gives a misleading sense of fixedness to sex-object choice, suggesting as it does a person in the middle, equidistant from heterosexuality and from homosexuality, equally erotically disposed to one gender or the other. Our data show that exceedingly few people come so neatly packaged; thus if we were to be really true to Kinsey's idea of a sexual continuum, we would instead use the preferable term, *ambisexuality,* connoting some ability for a person to eroticize both genders under some circumstances. However, *bisexuality* seems to have already become entrenched in our language, and we will have to settle for it, rather than the term Kinsey would have preferred. Indeed, even though we are indebted to Kinsey for his insistence on a homosexual/heterosexual continuum, we must emphasize that this view also misleads by focusing on the individual, with his or her sexual "place" as a unit of conceptualization, rather than on the sexual behavior (with all of its antecedents and subjective meanings) as a unit for theorizing.

Kinsey et al.'s data were not the only ones indicating that homosexual and heterosexual behavior could be incorporated in a single sexual career. Other studies have pointed to a bisexual phenomenon, although they have never dealt with the question of bisexuality per se. McCaghy and Skipper (1969), for example, argued that because of the social organization of the occupation of striptease, many of the women become involved in homosexual relationships, although they often continue to have heterosexual involvements. Furthermore, it has been well documented that women in correctional institutions commonly develop homosexual relationships within a well-articulated, quasi-kinship system (Giallombardo, 1966, 1974; Ward & Kassebaum, 1965). While the homosexual liaisons seem to be very important for the psychological well-being of the inmates and serve as a major foundation for the social organization of the institutions, the homosexuality is for most inmates situational. Most of those women and girls who were committed to a heterosexual lifestyle before incarceration return to the same pattern upon release.

The existence in our society of bisexuality in males has received somewhat greater documentation. Studies of prisoners (Kirkham, 1971; Lindner, 1948; Sykes, 1958) have repeatedly shown a fair incidence of homosexual behavior and the development of homosexual liaisons among men who had no prior homosexual experience and who would return to exclusive heterosexuality upon release. A study of brief homosexual encounters in public restrooms (Humphrey, 1970) demonstrated that a sizeable number of men who take part in "tearoom" activities are heterosexually married and do not consider themselves to be homosexual. Ross (1971) has reported that some of the men in his sample of self-identified homosexual men who were married to women had ongoing sexual relationships with their wives. Reiss (1961) interviewed teenage male prostitutes who engaged in homosexual relations with adult men, while maintaining a heterosexual self-perception and an otherwise heterosexual career. Reiss viewed this duality as a reflection of the legitimizing effects of peer group norms, the depersonalized nature of the sexual relations, and the financial gain that could be used as a neutralization technique.

What has been obscured in all of this haphazard treatment of bisexuality is that these sexual data can be used to address more general questions of theoretical importance. Bisexuality illustrates and illuminates important facets of processes of self-labeling, of the plasticity of human sexuality, and of the differences between the erotic and emotional socialization of men and women in our society.

The Present Study

In our study of bisexuality, we were interested in four major questions. First, in deference to Kinsey et al.'s observation of sexual fluidity, we were particularly interested in how sexual object choice develops, and how this development fits into the life experiences of the individual. Is bisexuality, for example, a continuous theme throughout a person's life, foreordained by events occurring in childhood and adolescence—as much of psychosexual theory (e.g., Fenichel, 1945) would argue—or does it emerge and change with the buffeting of events and circumstances throughout the life cycle? Second was the question of self-definition. When does a pattern of sexual or other social behaviors give rise to a person's sense of his or her sexual identity, and when are they simply behaviors with no further implications? Our third concern was with the circumstances and conditions that either encourage or allow, discourage or prevent, the development of bisexual behavior. And finally, our fourth interest was in how these three things—continuity, self-definition, and causal factors —would differ between males and females in our society. What might a comparison of the processes of becoming a bisexual woman and the processes of becoming a bisexual male tell us about male and female sexuality in general?

Our observations in response to these four questions are based on lengthy semistructured interviews with 156 people (equally divided between men and women), who had had more than incidental sexual experience with both men and women. We also interviewed a number of persons who had strong feelings about bisexuality as it pertained either to their own lives or to groups to which they belonged. The interviews were conducted in Seattle, New York, Berkeley, San Francisco, and a few other locations between 1973 and 1975. The respondents ranged in age from 19 to 62, and reflected a broad spectrum of occupations, educational levels, and sexual histories. Most of those interviewed were recruited through advertisements in taverns, restaurants, churches, universities, voluntary associations, and even a few embryonic bisexual rap groups. A large number of respondents were from a "snowball" sample or were personal contacts of the authors. The interviews generally lasted between 1½ and 3 hours and were tape-recorded. They covered the following areas of the respondents' lives: sexual and romantic history, family relationships and background, preferred sexual behaviors and fantasies, and most important, critical events in the formation of a sexual identity and the development of a sexual career. These interviews were conducted against a backdrop of several years of formal and informal observation and interviews with self-identified male and female homosexuals.

While our respondents constitute a very diverse and heterogeneous group, they are certainly not representative of anything but themselves. It is quite inappropriate to think in terms of random sampling of a specifiable universe of persons when dealing with underground populations or sexual minorities (Bell, 1974; Weinberg, 1970), and it was our intention to find any bisexuals we could and explore with them any themes that they might have shared in their socio-sexual development. Because the sample was heterogeneous we are quite confident that we are not simply describing the idiosyncrasies of a unique set of persons, and that we are able to suggest some regularities that exist among a broad group of people in the present cultural and historical context. But we also feel that to place great stock in the frequencies of response patterns would give a misleading sense of concreteness to what we have observed. Therefore we have chosen to present data only when patterns occurred with sufficient regularity to deserve interpretation, and to present data in the form of verbatim responses that represent (perhaps with a prejudice to more articulate statements) a class of responses that were found among a sizeable number of respondents. In this paper we present a general discussion of how our interview data were used to address the four guiding questions outlined above. (For other treatments of this material see Blumstein & Schwartz, Note 1, 1976, in press.)

The Erotic Biography of Respondents

We found no such thing as a prototypic bisexual career. This is not to say there are no patterns to the lives of our respondents, but rather no single or small number of patterns seems to predominate among those who call themselves bisexual, or among those whose behavior might be given that label. For example, a sizeable number of male respondents and the majority of the females had no homosexual experiences prior to adulthood. Furthermore, the occurrence of family patterns often claimed to predict a nonheterosexual adaptation (e.g., boys with weak distant fathers and overwhelming mothers) was quite rare. A few respondents had early sexual experiences that might be termed traumatic, but their adult lives had very little else in common. Major themes in psychosexual theory were of little utility in understanding our respondents.

Perhaps the most interesting finding was that many respondents, who had once seemed well along the road to a life of exclusive heterosexuality or of exclusive homosexuality, made major changes in sex-object choice. For example, early in the study we interviewed a young professional woman who referred to herself as "purely and simply gay," even though she had had sexual experience with men. In recounting her life history she mentioned that at the age of 7 or 8 she habitually initiated sexual contacts with her friends at pajama parties. Eventually one girl's mother learned about it, and our respondent was castigated by her friends' families, her friends, and her own family. If that stigmatizing experience were not enough to plant the seeds of a deviant self-definition, in adolescence she was the victim of a brutal sexual assault by a group of boys. She pointed to both of these experiences as reasons she had become a lesbian 10 years prior to the interview. We found her analysis convincing since it was so consistent with prevailing views on the psycho-development of lesbianism (e.g., Wilbur, 1965). Then, a year later she wrote to tell us she was in love with a man and they planned to marry.

Clearly, this woman's early experiences, as well as her 10 years of lesbian relationships and her active adherence to a lesbian self-label, did not guarantee that she would not experience a significant change in her life. Other interviews like this one, some starting with homosexual identification, some with heterosexual, suggested to us that while childhood and adolescent experiences do have a place in developing sexuality, their effects are far from immutable. For the majority of respondents, pivotal sexual experiences occurred in adulthood, and those whose experiences or fantasies stemmed from adolescence or childhood were no more or less likely to make a subsequent change than the larger group.

We were continually surprised at how discontinuous our respondents' erotic biographies could be. For example, a number of men who had decided they were homosexual at an early age and lived in almost exclusively homosexual networks later met women with whom they had sexual relationships for the first time in their lives. A very large number of both male and female respondents had made at least one full circle—an affair with a man, then one with a woman, and finally back to a man, or vice versa. For example, one woman of about 45 had been married and had three children. After divorcing and having several heterosexual relationships, she fell in love with another woman of her own age, and they began the first homosexual relationship that either of them had experienced. Neither had ever had any homosexual fantasies prior to their meeting. After a three-year relationship, they broke up and our respondent had a number of brief affairs with both women and men. Our interview captured her at this point in her life, but she reflected that in each of her relationships she considered herself to *be* what was implied by the gender of the person with whom she was amorously involved: homosexual when with a woman, heterosexual when with a man. She wondered aloud whether perhaps *bisexual* might be a more appropriate term.

It is clear from these cases that it was crucial for us to have the respondent's retrospective report as well as some longitudinal data. Fortunately, we were able to retain contact after the interview with about a quarter of our sample. It is misleading to try to understand anything about the achievement of sexual identity or about the importance of sexual events in a person's life without longitudinal observation. Speaking to respondents more than once was important, too, because they often tended to see more continuity in their lives than we found. It was very common for them to say that prior changes in sex-object choice were part of a past history of self-misperception, and that they had finally found their sexual "place." A follow-up interview often contradicted their assertions.

Our conclusion was that classical notions of the immutability of adult sexual preference are an overstatement and often misleading. Because of the unrepresentativeness of our sample, we cannot speculate about how widespread such erotic malleability is in our society. Perhaps there are many people who have undergone major life changes. The ease with which we found respondents with such a background suggests that it is more than a rare occurrence. Perhaps there are many people who could experience such monumental changes if they were not insulated from precipitating circumstances; or perhaps the vast majority would not be subject to such changes under any circumstances. If future research proves bisexual potential to be relatively rare, then classic developmentalist approaches that view childhood socialization to be all-important will be vindicated. If, on the other hand, the potential is not uncommon, then approaches that emphasize the situational emergence of human behavior will be supported. From our data, we conclude that (a) sex-object choice and sexual identification can change in many ways and many times over the life cycle, (b) the individual is often unaware of his or her ability to change, and (c) childhood and adolescent experiences are not the final determinants of adult sexuality.

Sexual Behavior and Sexual Identity

In our early interviews it became clear that people often adopted homosexual or bisexual self-identifications without having any homosexual experience. It was equally clear that, for many people, extensive homosexual experience had no effect on their heterosexual identity. For example, one male respondent recalled:

> I had this affair with a gay guy for almost a year. We were good friends and we became identified as a couple after a while. I think he basically saw me as a straight person who was kind of stepping over the imaginary line for a while. I was also sleeping with a woman, and, while I liked them both, I thought I was heterosexual as a person.

Another female respondent recalled her first homosexual encounter:

> It was a great experience. I think everyone should have it. Before this happened, I was really hung up. When I got involved with another woman, I realized how nice it was. It was really enlightening. I think heterosexually though, so I don't feel any big drives to repeat it. But I probably will if the opportunity comes along.

Still other respondents could have a single erotic encounter with a person of either the same or opposite gender and decide unequivocally what they "really were." As one woman reported:

> The first time Linda touched me, I went weak. The men I had made love with were so clumsy and awkward by comparison. I just realized who I was, that I was gay, and men were OK, but not the main thing.

On the other hand, experience with both genders could be seen as confirmation of a bisexual identity. One respondent told us how it had seemed reasonable to him:

> "Well," I thought as this guy climbed in my bed, "What the hell? Why shouldn't I? There's no reason why I should cut off my nose to spite my face. It's going to be fun; it's been fun before, and why can't I have the best of both possible worlds?" Bisexuality seemed like me.

We feel that certain conditions were significant in making a sexual event either crucial or irrelevant in the process of assuming a sexual identity.

Labelling. Consistent with what sociologists have noted in regards to other self-definitions (Becker, 1973), events or behaviors that produced a public reaction or otherwise affected the reactions other people made to our respondents were important in providing a bisexual self-definition (or homosexual or heterosexual). Such events were particularly significant during adolescence, when peer-group definitions have tremendous power over people. Several male respondents, who had been labelled the "class sissy," had felt that surely they must be sexually odd, and that their oddness was recognized by their peers. They had believed that their peers knew more about them than they had known themselves, and this was often self-fulfilling when it came to sex-object choice. Interestingly, such labelling processes seemed to be more important for males than females in the assumption of a homosexual or bisexual identity in adulthood. In contrast, boys and girls who escaped such labelling, even though some of their behavior might be homosexual, seemed somewhat less apt to apply deviant labels to themselves. For example, we interviewed two men who had been successful high school athletes. They shared a sexual relationship throughout high school and also had sexual relations with girls. They were never ridiculed or stigmatized in high school, even though their inseparability was well-known. Because so much of these men's behavior was considered sex-role appropriate, they escaped a homosexual label from others who might suspect their relationship. The two continued their homosexual activities into adulthood, one finally deciding he was homosexual, the other preferring to be bisexual.

Conflicting Events. The ability to perform sexually with a person of the opposite gender was not sufficient to inhibit the adoption of a homosexual identity, nor was it necessary for a bisexual identification. But it did seem to increase the likelihood of the latter. Many respondents seemed to be caught up in dichotomous thinking about sexuality, and struggled to resolve conflicting events (sexual experiences, attraction, or fantasies directed at both genders) by emphasizing one set of events as more plausible than the other. Commonly, one set of explanatory events was adduced for one's heterosexual behavior and a completely different set for one's homosexual behavior. For example, a male respondent reported:

> I'm straight, but I need outlets when I'm away from home and times like that. And it's easier to get with men than women. So I go into the park, or at a rest station on the highway and get a man to blow me. I would never stay

the night with one of them, or get to know them. It's just a release. It's not like sex with my wife. It's just a way to get what you need without making it a big deal. And it feels less like cheating.

While attempts to balance the two sets of conflicting information might have offered the chance of deciding one was bisexual, for most of our respondents (especially men) fairly strong heterosexual feelings and a good deal of heterosexual experience from an early age were necessary for a bisexual identification to compete with a homosexual identity. Our cultural logic holds that it is almost impossible to have only some homosexual feelings. The idea is seldom questioned that a single homosexual act or strong homosexual feelings reveal the "true person." Hence, since we have no imagery for partial states of being, the individual often reinterprets past events as further confirmation of his or her undeniable homosexuality. As one respondent said:

I was married for four years when I started to have these fantasies about a guy I worked with. I would get these fantasies and I would have to masturbate. I think that this was just the most mature crush I had, because when I think back on it, there had been lots of others, although I didn't know what they were then. I began to think I was homosexual about this time, even though I was still sleeping with my wife and enjoying it. But I felt guilty, and I was worried she would find out what I really was.

Of course, interpretations of respondents' erotic recollections are indeed risky, and commonly the present shapes the past more than the reverse. Nevertheless, it seemed clear that most respondents actively searched their memories for significant events that would help confirm their lay hypotheses concerning present events and feelings.

Among our interviewees, it seems that sexual attraction, as well as enjoyable sexual experience with both genders, helped people adopt a bisexual identity. Another factor was the emotional response to persons of either gender. Whom a person loved seemed to have an impact somewhat independent of whom that person eroticized. This was particularly true of women, since love and sexuality are customarily such interwoven themes in female erotic socialization. But it was also true of a sizeable number of males. It was not uncommon for a nonsexual but deeply emotional attachment between two people of the same gender who had no prior homosexual feelings to develop into a sexual relationship, and sometimes a shift to a bisexual identification for both partners. On the other hand, if a person (mostly men) could relate sexually to men and women but could only love one or the other, then that person would not likely assume a bisexual label.

Reference Group Contact. Sexual behavior and sexual identification both seem to vary by whether the respondent was a social isolate, was involved in an ongoing relationship, or was part of a sexual community. By the latter we mean subcultural groups that have formed and organized around members' sexual similarities, e.g., the various gay subcultures. So, for example, some respondents were strongly committed to particular homosexual relationships for a number of years without assuming a homosexual identity if they were not involved in the gay community. When most of their friends were homosexual, respondents were likely to be treated as homosexual and come to define themselves as such.

Our conclusion, after noticing the regularity in the differences of sexual identity depending on subculture membership and involvement, was that the social ratification of identities provided by such groups can be very powerful (Berger & Luckmann, 1966). Repondents who were ambivalent or questioning about their bisexual attractions or behaviors often encountered people in the gay world who could provide easy vocabularies for interpreting these feelings and acts (Blumstein & Schwartz, 1976, in press). Sometimes they were told that heterosexual attractions were only a cop-out or an aspect of false consciousness, that the respondent was really denying his or her true sexuality, being unwilling to come to grips with being a homosexual. After varying amounts of personal struggle, some respondents found this explanation plausible and moved toward adoption of a homosexual identity, developed a gay lifestyle, and concentrated on homosexual relationships. Others, finding the gay world unsympathetic or incredulous when it came to their bisexuality, either left the community for periods of time or kept their bisexual feelings private. For example, one woman who had a lesbian identification fell in love with a man and felt compelled to leave her women's collective because the other members would not grant support or legitimacy for her new relationship and asserted that it was simply "neurotic acting out."

We do not mean to paint the homosexual communities as villains in thwarting people's bisexuality. Indeed, respondents were much more likely to report hostility to their lifestyles among heterosexuals (who could not appreciate the distinction between bisexual and homosexual) than among homosexuals, and many reported a great deal of support for a bisexual identification among homosexual friends. But in both the straight and gay communities, the fact that respondents had had homosexual relationships tended to define an identity for them, while their heterosexual relationships were considered somehow irrelevant or a passing fancy.

The final step, we began to see, especially in the San Francisco area, was a deliberate attempt to create a bisexual community, where members could come together to give mutual support and to share with one another a collective wisdom for developing a bisexual lifestyle. Although it is premature to know, it seems very likely that such institutions as bisexual rap groups will increasingly support people's assumption of a bisexual identification.

Circumstances Conducive to Bisexuality

While there is a wide array of situations or conditions that serve to introduce people to novel sexual experiences, we found three themes to be particularly prevalent among our respondents. The first of these was experimentation in a friendship context. Many respondents (especially women) progressed to a sexual involvement from an intense emotional attachment with a person of the gender they had never before eroticized. A male with a homosexual identification might develop a casual experimental heterosexual relationship with a close woman friend at a point in his life where he seemed perfectly comfortable with his homosexuality. Several previously heterosexual men who came to a bisexual identity in their 30s reported they had had early homosexual experiences with close teen-age friends when heterosexual relations were somewhat limited. They had treated these experiences as irrelevant teen-age play, until adult experiences precipitated reconsideration. A few respondents with no previous homosexual experience reported that they were able to eroticize adult male friendships. A few lesbians reported being able to develop sexual involvements with male friends, especially homosexual men whose sexual politics they found less objectionable. The most common finding, however, was that previously heterosexual women who developed deep attachments to other women, e.g., as college roommates or later in life when involved in the women's movement, ultimately shifted these feelings into the erotic arena and began long-term homosexual relationships.

Bisexual encounters also emerged frequently in such liberal hedonistic environments as group sex, "three ways," and other combinations. These often proved a less threatening arena for sexual experimentation for heterosexuals than would a dyadic homosexual encounter. Females found these experiences less difficult than males, who were customarily the instigators of the event. These occurrences were understood to be pleasure seeking in a diffuse sense, rather than a specific act with stigmatizing implications for one's sexual identity. Focus was on the good feelings rather than on the gender of the person providing them.

The third pattern was supported by a number of erotically based ideological positions. For example, some people came to a bisexual identification (occasionally without any corresponding behavior) because of adherence to a belief in humanistic libertarianism. They felt that everyone should be free and able to love everyone in a perfect erotic utopia. For them, love meant sex, which was seen as a means of communication and "becoming human." Encounter groups or group massages often progressed to a sexual stage. As one respondent explained, "It only made sense. We had all been psych majors, and every psych major learns that we are all inherently bisexual." How much of this ideology preceded the behavior and how much provided post hoc legitimacy is, of course, difficult to assess.

Many of the women in our study decided to experiment with homosexual relationships because they felt encouraged by the tenets of the women's movement to examine their feelings towards other women and to learn to be close to them. The movement had encouraged them to respect and like other women, and for many this novel feeling was closely akin to the feelings they had felt with those men whom they had eroticized. Sometimes these women instigated sexual encounters for ideological rather than erotic reasons, but soon developed erotic responses and became more generally physically attracted to other women. In some cases the homosexual attraction became a dominating force in the women's lives; in other cases it coexisted with heterosexual responses; and in still other cases it never established any prominence and homosexual behavior was discontinued (although a political bisexual self-identification was sometimes retained).

Differences between Women and Men

There were a great many differences in the bisexual behavior of male and female respondents, which seemed quite consistent with what we know about general patterns of male and female sexuality (Gagnon & Simon, 1973). Most prominently, men and women differed in the ease with which they incorporated homosexual activity into their lives. Women found initial experiences much less traumatic than men, and they were less likely to allow a single experience or a few experiences to lead them to an exclusive homosexual identification. Women often felt that such activities were a natural extension of female affectionate behavior and did not have implications for their sexuality. Men, on the other hand, were much more preoccupied with what the experience meant for their masculinity, sometimes fearing that they might never again be able to respond erotically to a woman. Some men insulated themselves from the homosexual implications of homosexual behavior by exclusively engaging in either impersonal sex as in public restrooms (Humphreys, 1970), or in homosexual acts where they took what they considered to be the masculine role, i.e., the insertor role in fellatio or sodomy. As one man recounted, "There are four kinds of men: men who screw women, men who screw men and women, men who screw men, and then there are the queers (i.e., the ones who *get* screwed)."

For men, both their first heterosexual and first homosexual experience were very likely to be with strangers (prostitutes, "bad girls," homosexual tricks), whom they would probably never see again. The predominant pattern among women was for sex to occur with a close friend, and this to them was a natural and logical outgrowth of a strong emotional attachment. The realization that they were in love with a person (of the same or opposite gender) was often a prerequisite for sexual attraction, sexual behavior, or a change in sexual identity.

Males reported much more difficulty coping with homosexual behavior and developing a homosexual identification than women. We attribute this to the stigma attached to homosexuality among American men (more than among women). Masculinity is a major element in men's sense of self-worth, and homosexuality, in the popular imagination, implies impaired masculinity.

Conclusion

This study has been part of our ongoing research on sexual identity and how it reflects the interaction of social forces, cultural perspectives, and psychological processes. We chose bisexuality as a vehicle of inquiry because we feel it has a strategic capacity for illuminating more general issues in the study of human sexuality. We view our research as exploratory, but we feel that when more investigators have addressed themselves to the phenomenon of bisexuality the accumulated evidence will help transform the way science views human sexuality. We anticipate that the perspective which emerges will reflect a number of thematic questions. What is the nature of the relationship between people's sexual experiences and the ways they make sense of their sexuality? How do cultural and subcultural understandings regarding sexuality affect sexual experience and sexual identification? How much of sexuality can be understood by focusing on the continuities among males and the continuities among females, irrespective of affectional preference or sexual lifestyle? How much of adult sexuality is determined by socialization experiences and how much reflects adult experiences and events? And finally, what do the answers to these questions tell us about the variability and plasticity of sexual behavior and sexual definitions?

Reference Note

1. Blumstein, P.W., & Schwartz, P. *Bisexuality.* Paper presented at the meeting of the American Sociological Association, New York, August 1976.

References

Becker, H. S. *Outsiders: Studies in the sociology of deviance* (Rev. ed.). New York: Free Press, 1973.

Bell, A. P. Homosexualities: Their range and character. In *Nebraska Symposium on Motivation.* Lincoln: University of Nebraska Press, 1974.

Berger, P. L., & Luckmann, T. *The social construction of reality: A treatise in the sociology of knowledge.* Garden City, N.Y.: Doubleday, 1966.

Blumstein, P. W., Shcwartz, P. Bisexuality in women. *Archives of Sexual Behavior,* 1976, 5, 171–181.

Blumstein, P. W., & Schwartz, P. Bisexuality in men. *Urban Life,* in press.

Fenichel, O. *The psychoanalytic theory of neurosis.* New York: Norton, 1945.

Ford, C. S., & Beach, F. A. *Patterns of sexual behavior.* New York: Harper & Row, 1951.

Gagnon, J. H., & Simon, W. *Sexual conduct: The social sources of human sexuality.* Chicago: Aldine, 1973.

Giallombardo, R. *Society of women.* New York: Wiley, 1966.

Giallombardo, R. *The social world of imprisoned girls.* New York: Wiley, 1974.

Humphreys, L. *Tearoom trade: Impersonal sex in public restrooms.* Chicago: Aldine, 1970.

Kinsey, A. C., Pomeroy, W. B., & Martin, C. E. *Sexual behavior in the human male.* Philadelphia: W. B. Saunders, 1948.

Kinsey, A. C., Pomeroy, W. B., Martin C. E., & Gebhard, P. H. *Sexual behavior in the human female.* Philadelphia: W. B. Saunders, 1953.

Kirkham, G. L. Homosexuality in prison. In J. M. Henslin (Ed.), *Studies in the sociology of sex.* New York: Appleton-Century-Crofts, 1971.

Lindner, R. Sexual behavior in penal institutions. In A. Deutsch (Ed.), *Sex habits of American men.* New York: Prentice-Hall, 1948.

McCaghy, C. H., & Skipper, J. K., Jr. Lesbian behavior as an adaptation to the occupation of stripping. *Social Problems.* 1969, 17, 262–270.

Reiss, A. J. Jr. The social integration of queers and peers. *Social Problems,* 1961, 9, 102–120.

Ross, H. L. Modes of adjustment of married homosexuals. *Social Problems,* 1971, 18, 385–393.

Sykes, G. *The society of captives.* Princeton, N. J.: Princeton University Press, 1958.

Ward, D. A., & Kassebaum, G. G. *Women's prison: Sex and social structure.* Chicago: Aldine, 1965.

Weinberg, M. S. Homosexual samples: Differences and similarities. *Journal of Sex Research,* 1970, 6, 312–325.

Wilbur, C. B. Clinical aspects of female homosexuality. In J. Marmor (Ed.), *Sexual inversion: The multiple roots of homosexuality.* New York: Basic Books, 1965.

Marital Sex

Morton Hunt

The Western Tradition Concerning Marital Sexual Pleasure

Every human society has forbidden sex between at least some kinds of partners, and sexual relations in all but one kind of partnership have been forbidden by at least some societies. The one universal exception, the one partnership within which sexual activity is everywhere deemed acceptable, is the husband-wife relationship. But the universal acceptability of marital sex is not at all the same thing as universal freedom for husbands and wives to seek maximum enjoyment from their sexual activities; the social legitimacy of marital coitus does not necessarily signify the emotional legitimacy of pleasure. Accordingly, even though marital coitus has been approved everywhere, there are great variations, from society to society, in the precise sexual activities permitted to husbands and wives, in the inner feelings accompanying those activities and in the kinds of satisfaction they have obtained from their physical relationship.

Western civilization has long had the rare distinction of contaminating and restricting the sexual pleasure of married couples more severely than almost any other. From the beginnings of Christianity, marital sex was viewed not as a positive good, nor as a joy to be made the most of, but as an unavoidable lesser evil, preferable only to the far worse one of sex outside of marriage. Saint Paul formulated the doctrine in his *First Epistle to the Corinthians.* "I would that all men were even as I myself (i.e., celibate)," he wrote. ". . . I say therefore to the unmarried and widows, it is good for them if they abide even as I. But if they cannot contain, let them marry: for it is better to marry than to burn."

Later, various fathers of the church carried this antihedonistic and antisexual philosophy much further: Even marital sex, they said, was sinful if it was thoroughly enjoyable. In the 3rd Century A.D., for instance, Clement of Alexandria warned that married coitus remained sinless only if delight was restrained and confined, and in the 5th Century Saint Jerome asserted that "he who too ardently loves his own wife is an adulterer." By the 7th Century it was established church dogma that married intercourse was so incompatible with spiritual exercises that husbands and wives must abstain from sex for three days before taking communion. The same church that had made marriage a holy act thus characterized the essential sexual part of it as an unholy, even though permissible, lapse from purity.

Such was the view that pervaded Western society and severely restricted the ability of men and women to take pleasure in married sexual relations. Although somewhat mitigated during periods of liberalism or learning, it remained generally dominant until modern times; indeed, in America in the late 18th and the 19th Century, its blighting effect was particularly strong, being intensified by the prudish middle-class view of the "good" woman as ethereal, passive and far above having any lustful or passionate feelings. Women's liberationists often assert that this view was part of the apparatus of male dominance, and that it was deliberately promulgated by men to keep women subordinate and enslaved; but although it may indeed have helped to do so, men did not consciously create it for that purpose. Its roots lay not in male dominance but in middle-class puritanism and the fundamentalist explanation of sin, which dichotomized womanhood into sinner and saint, Eve and Mary, whore and mother, minion of Satan and handmaiden of Christ. Besides, in many a non-Christian society, wives, although thoroughly subjugated, were quite capable of being highly sexual and passionate in marriage, these qualities being highly praised in them by men, as is apparent from even the most casual inspection of such classic Near Eastern marriage and sex manuals as the *Kama Sutra* and *The Perfumed Garden of the Shaykh Nefzawi.* In any case, even if the Christian-bourgeois view of woman helped keep her enslaved, it cost her oppressor dearly; he may have the right to enjoy her favors whenever he wished, but it was the right to relieve himself in a silent, inert, unresponding and unseen receptacle (inky darkness being the rule), who did her "conjugal duty" by allowing him to "take his pleasure."

Some wives, nonetheless, did enjoy sex, particularly (if we may trust playwrights and satirists) those wives of the very highest and the very lowest social levels. But in the 19th Century the majority of middle-class and working-class women found intercourse only tolerable at best; and a substantial minority regarded it as revolting, messy, vulgar, animalistic, shameful and degrading. Dr. William Hammond, an expert on sexual matters and onetime surgeon-general of the United States, asserted in a widely used medical textbook that, aside from prostitution, it was doubtful that women felt the slightest pleasurable sensation in one-tenth of their intercourse. No reliable survey data on the matter exist, but at the end of the century many of the best-informed American and European doctors believed that female frigidity was widespread and perhaps even prevalent, their estimates of its incidence in American and European women running anywhere from 10 to 75 percent.

But during the early part of the 20th century the liberation and legitimation of human sexual enjoyment—even by the female—got under way. Freud opened up to view the hidden interior of human desire; women started struggling out of their bonds of helplessness, subservience and purity; and marital intercourse began to be viewed as a positive and healthful activity rather than a shameful and somewhat debilitating indulgence. Liberal doctors, scholars and feminists—Havelock Ellis, Ellen Key, Marie Stopes and Theodor Van de Velde, among others—argued for long and careful wooing of the wife by the husband, praised the aesthetic aspects of varied techniques of lovemaking and preached the emotional and physical importance of mutual orgasm.

In the 1930s and 1940s, when Kinsey was doing his fieldwork, writers and social critics ranging from Sinclair Lewis to Philip Wylie were still scornfully portraying the typical American marital sex act as a crude, hasty, wordless Saturday-night grappling. But Kinsey's data partially gave them the lie; his figures proved that the early phase of sexual liberation had already had a considerable ameliorating effect. The younger married women in Kinsey's sample, for instance, were having somewhat less marital intercourse, at any given age, than older women had had at that same age, undoubtedly because wives' own wishes were beginning to count; but at the same time the percentage of such intercourse resulting in female orgasm was climbing, with something like a fifth more of the younger women than the older ones having orgasm most or all of the time, in any given year of married life. At almost every age, in almost every stage of marriage and in nearly every detail—the degree of nudity during intercourse, the kinds of foreplay used, the use of positional variations—the difference between the older and the younger generation, though not large, were consistently in the direction of greater freedom, pleasure and mutuality. The beginnings of sexual egalitarianism and the legitimation of pleasure were changing marital sex as nothing else had in nearly two millenia.

Everything we have seen thus far in this survey points to the fact that since Kinsey's time those liberating forces have vastly increased in power. Accordingly, sex within marriage should now be far more sensuous, uninhibited and mutually satisfying; yet today there seems to be more and harsher criticism of married sex than ever. Many of the shriller voices in the women's-liberation movement portray married intercourse as male-chauvinist exploitation of the female body, with husbands being clumsy, hasty, brutal and selfish, and making no effort to delight or satisfy their wives, let alone consider, in the first place, whether their wives wish to be made love to. Many sexologists, moreover, have made sweeping statements about the prevalence of sexual incompetence or inadequacy in contemporary marriage. Masters and Johnson, for instance, have repeatedly said—while admitting it to be only a guess—that perhaps 50 percent of all American marriages suffer from sexual dysfunction of one sort or another. Critics of monogamous marriage, and advocates of extramarital relations, have in increasing numbers scornfully portrayed married intercourse as stereotyped, dull and constricted, and nonmarital intercourse as varied, exciting and free.

But our survey data appear to contradict this picture of contemporary married sex. They do not lead us to deny that there is still male chauvinism in many a marriage bed, or that many married people have sexual problems, or that for many people married sex eventually becomes overfamiliar and unexciting. They do, however, lead us to dispute the charge that these negative aspects of married sex are more prevalent or severe today than formerly (we believe, in fact, that the opposite is true), and to disagree with the assertion that they are the predominant and essential characteristics of contemporary marriage. How, then, is one to explain the widespread criticism of married sex? The answer, we think, is that the progress our society has made toward fuller and freer sexuality has revolutionized our expectations and made many of us so intolerant of our dissatisfactions that we forget the improvement that has taken place in our lives; like all partially liberated people, we are more discontented now than we were before our lot began to improve.

Yet improvement is widespread and real. The present survey, as we are about to see, indicates that since Kinsey's time marital sex in America has become a good deal more egalitarian (with husbands being more considerate of their wives' needs, and wives assuming more responsibility for the success of intercourse); that husbands and wives are much freer in terms of the kinds of foreplay and coital positions they use; that the conscious pursuit of sensuous pleasure in marriage has become much more acceptable to both sexes; and that there is a considerable increase in the percentage of marital sexual experiences that yield genuine satisfaction to both persons.

Contemporary Forces Tending to Liberate Married Sexual Behavior

Indeed, one could argue that the principal effect of sexual liberation upon American life has been to increase the freedom of husbands and, even more so, of wives to explore and enjoy a wide range of gratifying sexual practices within the marital relationship. Most discussions of sexual liberation concentrate upon its meaning for the unmarried, the unfaithful and the unconventional; but by far the largest number of people whose sexual behavior has been influenced by it are faithful (or relatively faithful) husbands and wives. All those social developments which have made male and female expectations of sex more nearly compatible, which have emancipated men and women from the guilt and inhibitions generated by fundamentalist religion, and which have broadened the average person's repertoire of sexual acts have affected sexual behavior within marriage as much as outside it; for marriage is not an enclave, impervious to outside influences, but a porous thing, penetrated through and through by the currents of the social milieu.

The most obvious of the openings through which external influences enter marriage is, of course, the sum total of attitudes and experiences that the partners bring with them at the outset. We have seen that the sexual attitudes of most young unmarried persons have become much more permissive in recent years, that this has brought about an increase in the amount—and an improvement in the caliber—of premarital sexual experience, and that while the overall change has been greater for females, it has been substantial even for males, especially those of the educated middle class. It would seem obvious that for a large proportion of younger married adults the difficulties of achieving sexual adjustment in marriage must have been reduced and that the range of sexual practices acceptable within most marriages must have been broadened.

Some experts have disputed the beneficent influence of premarital experience; in fact, a number of minor studies have shown small positive correlations between premarital sexual conservatism—specifically, virginity in females—and successful marriage, and a few sociologists and marriage researchers, among them Harvey Locke, Paul Popenoe, Ernest Burgess and Paul Wallin, have therefore held that premarital sexual experience does little or nothing to promote marital sexual adjustment or marital happiness. But men and women with generally conservative attitudes are very likely to have different expectations of marriage from men and women with generally liberal attitudes, and marriages that the former rate "successful" or "happy" might not seem so to the latter. Similarly, most of the survey data on sexual adjustment come from self-appraisals, but the severely inhibited man or semifrigid woman is apt to term his or her married sex life satisfactory if it involves minimal demands and yields modest rewards, while the more liberated man or woman would probably view such a sex life as disappointing and perhaps even as a severe deprivation.

If we turn to objective and quantifiable activities rather than subjective self-appraisal, we find impressive evidence that successful premarital sexual experience does, indeed, bear a positive relationship to married sexual satisfaction for the wife and hence, inferentially, for the husband. Terman, Burgess and Wallin, and Kinsey all reported positive correlations between premarital orgastic experience for the woman and her orgastic regularity within marriage. Kinsey, for instance, found that 57 percent of the females who had had 25 or more coital orgasms before marriage were having orgasms nearly all the time even in the first year of marriage, as compared with 29 to 44 percent of the females who had had no premarital coital experience. Such data, alone, do not prove that the prior experience is the cause of the later success, for it could be that innately responsive females are more receptive to premarital experience and, by the same token, more responsive within marriage. But Kinsey, anticipating this argument, pointed out that for most females orgastic capacity develops only with years of experience, so that premarital experience tends to shorten the time necessary to achieve sexual success within marriage—a crucially important point, in view of the fact that more marital breakups occur in the first and second years of marriage than any subsequent ones.

Whether or not women had had premarital coitus, however, Kinsey found their orgastic regularity increasing with the duration of the marriage, and continuing to improve even up to the twentieth year of marriage, a phenomenon most experts attributed to such internal processes in the marriage as the growth of intimacy and trust, growing familiarity of the partners with each other's physical needs, the slow wearing away of inhibitions, and the growing willingness of the wife to learn from the husband and to make little experiments at his suggestion. Today, however, the continuing improvement of the marital sexual relationship, though it still owes much to these internal factors, also owes a good deal to various external ones. For one thing, nowadays it grates on many a female to have her husband appropriate the role of teacher and innovator; she is willing to have him do so sometimes, provided he plays the role of pupil and follower at other times. In an egalitarian relationshp, each partner is a source of suggestions and innovations, and with the society around them having become so permissive about the publishing, portraying and discussing of details of sexual technique, each partner has easy access to information and stimuli. A generation or more ago it was almost always the husband who suggested some novel activity—rear-entry coitus, say, or fellatio, or watching the action in a mirror—often to the alarm of the naïve wife, who feared her mate might be giving voice to some perversion or abnormality. Today the young wife is as likely as her husband to have heard and read about these and even far more fanciful novelties, thanks to the bumper crop of best-selling sex manuals, candid magazine articles and erotic novels, and to the new openness of talk about such things among her peers. Moreover, she is nearly as likely as her husband to regard such things as nornal, intriguing and worth trying. What young males, and to a greater extent young females, may not have known at the outset of marriage they no longer must discover for themselves or do without; indeed, they can scarcely avoid learning from the outside much of what was known to the ancient writers on the amorous arts, and a good deal that would have astonished even those venerables.*

All of this tends to liberalize the attitudes of both partners in marriage, to increase their repertoire of physical acts and to bring them closer to each other in their expectations and requirements. The sex manuals of the Van de Velde generation held that marital intercourse should always be "person-centered" (the term is Professor Reiss's)—that is, a primarily communicative and emotional act on the part of both partners—although in fact this was more typi-

---

*We are unable, for instance, to find in the Hindu, Arabian or Chinese erotic guidebooks or in Japanese erotic art any reference to the use of edible substances applied to and licked off the genitals, the application of crushed ice to the genitals at the moment of orgasm, or analingus, although these are among the variations advocated in some contemporary sex manuals.

cally the female attitude than the male one. Many of today's sex manuals pay only lip service to the communicative and emotional aspects of intercourse, stressing instead its earthy, sensuous, appetitive side—the "body-centered" attitudes that used to be regarded as typically male. Male and female attitudes, as we measured them, still show some differences along this dimension, but our evidence suggests that American husbands and wives are moving toward a middle ground in which each can be both person-centered and body-centered, enjoying intercourse for both reasons at the same time, or, on occasion, for either one alone. This shift, we think, is due in considerable part to the continuing impact upon young married people of external influences and sources of information.

A number of items in our questionnaire survey indirectly indicate the impact of outside influences, but the most direct evidence comes from our interviews. Most of our middle-aged interviewees said that while they had recently become more permissive in their attitudes, their marital sex habits were too well established to be changed—and some of them candidly regretted that this was the case. But other middle-aged persons, and nearly all married persons under 35, said that books, magazines, films, erotic materials and discussions with friends had been important factors in expanding and liberating their married sex life. Here are a few typical comments:

FEMALE, 45, BLUE-COLLAR HOMEMAKER: After we'd been married a while, we felt there was a lot happening that we didn't understand, so I asked my husband if him and I should try to read up on it. So he went out and bought three books, and through them we found all different ways of caressing, and different positions, and it was very nice,because we realized that these things weren't dirty. Like I could say to my husband, "Around the world in eighty days!" and he'd laugh and we'd go at it, relaxed and having fun. Also, men talk about sex with each other, you know, and sometimes he'll come home and say, "Here's a thing I just heard about, and let's try it," and I'll say "Fine," and we do.

FEMALE, 28, BUSINESSWOMAN: By now, we have what I'd call a pretty wide range of specialties. We experimented even at the beginning, but we were pretty timid; it was reading and talking to friends that made the difference. We went through the *Kama Sutra,* and Henry Miller, and Frank Harris, and some of De Sade, and some of it was ridiculous, but a lot was eye-opening and stimulating. Even blue movies have sometimes given us an idea or two, although mostly they're just for laughs.

FEMALE, 37, WAITRESS: What changed our sex life was that a bunch of us girls on the same block started reading books and passing them around—everything from how-to-do-it sex books to real porno paperbacks. Some of the men said that that stuff was garbage, but I can tell you that my husband was always ready to try out anything I told him I'd read about. Some of it was great, some was awful—we just about wrecked my back, once, with this hassock bit—and some was just funny, like the honey business.

FEMALE, 34, TEACHER: All of a sudden, I kept hearing and reading about this multiple-orgasm thing, and I'd never realized before that it was normal.

It sounded like the greatest, so my husband and I talked it over and decided
to make a special try to see if I could. And I did, and wow!—I was really
bowled over. He felt pretty proud of himself, too. We don't try for it as a
regular thing, but whenever we do, it's really special.

MALE, 26, GRADUATE STUDENT: My wife was never willing to fool
around as much as she now is. Not that we didn't have good, open sex, but
in the last year she seems to have learned to *abandon* herself to it. I think
this has come about from her exposure to other people's opinions—some of
our friends talk quite openly about these things—and from reading things,
like the Masters and Johnson studies, and even popular stuff like *The Sensuous Woman,* which is sometimes silly and overstated but makes a good case
for itself.

MALE, 26, MECHANIC: My wife works, and at lunchtime she and all the
girls talk about things, and she comes home one time and tells me she hears
there's nothing like pornography for a turn-on. So I go along with it; I go out
and buy an armful of stuff—mostly picture magazines—and bring it home.
First, it embarrasses her, but then she gets to see it differently, and to like
some of the things she sees. Same way with a stag film I borrowed and brought
home to show her. Personally, I think it's good and wholesome; it stimulates
and opens the mind.

MALE, 33, COLLEGE INSTRUCTOR: Both my wife and I are terribly
old-fashioned, but since being married our ideas about sex have changed a lot,
partly from maturity, but largely from the influence of the common culture
—all the things one reads and hears about, the common coin, so to speak.
Even a film can affect our life. Recently we saw a rerun of *I Am Curious,
Yellow,* and came home and promptly tried out a position we had never
thought of before—the one on the railing—and frankly, it seemed more
trouble than it was worth, but we rather enjoyed making the experiment.

In addition to all the preceding milieu influences, which can be loosely
termed didactic, there are three others worth mentioning that fall in somewhat
different categories. The first is therapy; to be sure, most forms of therapy are
partly informational, but primarily they involve conditioning and training.
Clinics specializing in sex therapy, many of them patterned upon that of
Masters and Johnson and using similar methods, have proliferated around the
country; a survey by the *New York Times* in October 1972 located several
dozen sex clinics in 20 cities, and many more must exist in other cities. The
Masters-Johnson techniques have, however, had an even wider impact through
the avenue of general-practice medicine and through the direct adoption, by
readers, of the techniques of sex therapy described in their second book,
Human Sexual Inadequacy.

The second special influence is that of contraception, which has achieved a
new level of effectiveness and simplicity in recent years in three forms: pill,
I.U.D. and vasectomy. Many millions of married couples have adopted one or
another of these methods, and the simplicity and freedom from worry they

provide has often brought new spontaneity and joyousness into married inter-course. Among the couples in our interview sample who were most enthusias-tic about their sexual life were some who, desiring no more children, had sought the total security of vasectomy—and were dumbfounded at how much more excitement and delight they got from their sexual relationship as a result.

Finally, women's liberation has altered the sexual relationships of countless married couples—often for the better, sometimes for the worse. The topic is far too complex to be treated adequately here. but we must at least mention it because so many questionnaire responses reveal its influence. The beneficial effects have, in general, been an extention of those changes associated with the gradual emancipation of woman from her subservient, asexual, passive 19th-Century image. The harmful effects have come about in transferring to the sexual arena antagonisms and power struggles between husband and wife that have been exacerbated by the liberation movement. Even though a revision of the power balance between man and wife is often called for, the sexual relation-ship of the couple may suffer as a consequence. Many an angry woman gets even by deciding that her husband is a lousy lover and that she'll have no more of him except on her own terms; and many a man with traditional attitudes, alarmed or repelled by the new kind of woman, loses his drive or sexual self-assurance. Four out of five sexologists in a round-table discussion in the journal *Medical Aspects of Human Sexuality* held that impotence was defi-nitely on the rise; and a team of three psychiatrists writing in *Archives of General Psychiatry* recently identified a syndrome they called "the new impo-tence"—the failure of the male to function as a result of the new assertiveness of women, which some men find so threatening that they cease being able to act as men.

Even a liberated and reasonably secure male, furthermore, might well find at least one by-product of the women's-liberation movement too demanding for his taste. Psychiatrist Mary Jane Sherfey, borrowing loosely from Masters and Johnson and spinning her own version of prehistory, concocted a theory not long ago that all normal women are not only capable of multiple orgasms but that without some intervening force to stop them, they would all, by nature, be sexually insatiable. It was the male, says Dr. Sherfey, who forcibly suppressed female sexuality at the dawn of history to make civilized life possible (ungoverned, woman's sexual drive was too strong, impelling and aggressive to permit a settled family life) and who has kept telling woman ever since that she needs only one orgasm, if any, per coition. As we have already noted, some militant feminists, finding this theory a powerful weapon against men, have written pridefully about the female orgasm potential and urged women to use fingers or vibrators to enjoy themselves without stint, rather than seek their primary gratification in marital coitus. But this can only seem an unhealthy and pathogenic view, except to those women who regard all marital intercourse, and marriage itself, as forms of enslavement by the male enemy.

Frequency of Marital Coitus a Generation Ago and Today

As we saw earlier. the Kinsey data show that the earlier stage of the liberation of women brought about a small but distinct decrease in the average frequency of marital intercourse. One might wonder, therefore, whether the later, and virtually explosive, stage of liberation of women that has taken place in the past decade has not greatly accentuated that trend and brought about something close to a sexual standoff within contemporary marriage. This is, indeed, the impression one gets from the writings of many critics and satirists of modern marriage. But critics and satirists, even if they are portraying something real, may be misled as to how widespread that reality is. To know whether what they see and portray is the general rule, we must turn to statistically representative survey data. Our own data tell a different story, contradicting both what the critics of marriage say and what the extrapolation of Kinsey's data seemed to forecast: We find that, by and large, contemporary marriages involve higher frequencies of marital intercourse than did those of a generation ago. With the smug assurance of hindsight, one can say that this was implicit in the Kinsey data. For although in his time the frequency of marital coitus was declining due to the wife's rising status and her growing right to have a voice in sexual matters, the regularity of her orgasm in marital coitus was rising due to a multitude of sexually liberating factors. This increase in orgastic reliability and overall sexual satisfaction eventually offset the forces that caused the initial drop in coital activity. Such, at least, is our interpretation of the data we are about to present in this and the next two sections of this chapter.

First, then, let us see exactly what has happened to the frequency of marital intercourse. In the past several generations a number of researchers have published estimates or survey data on this matter, but nearly all of the pre-Kinsey studies were based on small or special samples—patients in treatment, volunteer respondents and the like—or on groups covering too wide an age span to yield meaningful frequency data. The more recent studies are, in general, statistically more sophisticated; but because of the difficulty of gathering data in this area, they have often been based on what is most easily available, even when it is manifestly biased. A recent study published in the *Journal of Urology,* for instance, gives data on coital frequency based on information collected from 2801 male patients receiving urological treatment, over half of whom had prostatic hypertrophy or prostatitis. But since it is highly likely that these disorders either made for unusual frequencies in them, or, conversely, were the result of unusual frequencies, these frequency data are a poor guide to normal behavior. Even the respected sociologist Robert Bell, seeking to gather data on the coital frequency of contemporary wives, sent out batches of questionnaires to colleagues in the field of family sociology, who handed them out at their own discretion. The returned sample—60 percent of the distributed questionnaires—is strongly biased in the direction of higher-educated employed women, and further distorted by the silence of the 40 percent who accepted questionnaires but decided not to tell about themselves. Professor Bell's study is useful, within limits, but is hardly a reliable measurement of the changes in behavior of the general population since Kinsey.

For such reasons, the best comparisons we can make are those between our own data and those reported by Kinsey in his 1948 volume on the American male and his 1953 volume on the American female. Like Kinsey, however, we can repeat only what our respondents told us, which means that our data may involve subjective distortion—not outright lies, but underestimates or overestimates caused by the individual's feeling that he or she is having too little, or too much, coitus. Terman, Kinsey, Clark and Wallin, and Levinger have interviewed husband-wife pairs separately and compared their answers as to coital frequency: In some pairs, the spouses give different estimates; and when these estimates are correlated with desired frequency, it turns out that a partner who desires more coitus than he or she is having tends to understate the actual frequency, while one who desires less tends to overstate the actual frequency. All who have researched this matter, prior to the present survey, agree that the bulk of such distortions lies in the direction of husbands wanting more intercourse than they were having, and hence giving lower estimates of actual intercourse than wives, and of wives wanting less than they were having, and hence giving higher estimates than husbands.

How much credence, then, can we put in data gathered in such fashion? Kinsey offered a careful analysis of male-female differences in estimates of frequency, based on interviews with over 700 husband-wife pairs. He found that most of them gave substantially the same estimates, and the differences in the remainder averaged out to be rather small. It was, therefore, Kinsey's opinion that the averages derived from each sex were valid and reliable, even though slightly different. Clark and Wallin disagreed, but most other sex researchers have accepted Kinsey's view and used his data. Recently sociologist J. Richard Udry and pediatrician Naomi M. Morris concocted an ingenious experiment that indicated that most females, at least, tell the truth about coital frequency. Udry and Morris, using a cover story to the effect that they were trying to correlate sexual behavior with hormone levels, obtained daily first-morning urine specimens from 58 female subjects plus reports as to whether or not the women had had coitus in the last 24 hours. They found, by microscopic examination of the urine specimens for spermatozoa, that the reports of coitus or no coitus were generally correct.

All of which gives us good grounds for regarding the coital-frequency estimates of husbands and wives as reasonably trustworthy, even if slightly discrepant. Although the undersatisfied and the oversatisfied may distort their estimates somewhat, these people are in the minority; moreover, part of their distortions cancel each other out. The net result is that such distortions, though individually significant, have only a minor effect on the overall averages for all males and all females. If, therefore, we find that our data show consistent differences from Kinsey's, and of a magnitude considerably larger than the discrepancy between male and female averages, we can take this as evidence that significant change has taken place in the past generation.

And we do find such evidence. The data show that there has been an important, even historic, increase in the typical (median) frequency of marital coitus throughout the population. Convincingly, both husbands and wives report such increases. Moreover, the frequency is higher in every age group of each sex than for comparable groups in Kinsey's time.

Table 1. Marital Coitus: Frequency Per Week as Estimated by Husbands, 1938–1946 and 1972*

1938–1946 (Kinsey)			1972 (Present survey)		
Age	Mean	Median	Age	Mean	Median
16–25	3.3	2.3	18–24	3.7	3.5
26–35	2.5	1.9	25–34	2.8	3.0
36–45	1.8	1.4	35–44	2.2	2.0
46–55	1.3	.8	45–54	1.5	1.0
56–60	.8	.6	55 & over	1.0	1.0

It is hardly possible to overstate the importance of this finding and what it tells us about the net effect of the twin (and sometimes opposing) forces of sexual liberation and women's liberation. We present the data in detail in Tables 1 and 2 followed by our comments. The figures given in these tables are, of course, group averages and do not indicate the vast range of individual variation; among our 35-to-44-year-old males, for instance, the median rate of marital coitus is just under 100 per year, but some men in that group had intercourse with their wives only two or three times per year, and others several hundred times. Both of these are obvious extremes, but no one should take our group averages to represent norms to which all should seek to con-

Table 2. Marital Coitus: Frequency Per Week as Estimated by Wives, 1938–1949 and 1972*

1938–1949 (Kinsey)			1972 (Present survey)		
Age	Mean	Median	Age	Mean	Median
16–25	3.2	2.6	18–24	3.3	3.0
26–35	2.5	2.0	25–34	2.6	2.1
36–45	1.9	1.4	35–44	2.0	2.0
46–55	1.3	.9	45–54	1.5	1.0
56–60	.8	.4	55 & over	1.0	1.0

*In both tables, Kinsey's data have been adapted by recalculating his five-year cohorts into ten-year cohorts to facilitate comparison with our own. The dates 1938–1946 and 1938–1949 refer to the years during which the interviews were conducted on which Kinsey's data are based; our own fieldwork was done, as indicated, in 1972. Our data are based on our white sample; as usual in making direct comparisons with Kinsey's data, we have omitted our blacks to make the samplers more closely comparable.

form. We present both kinds of averages—means and medians—in Tables 1 and 2, since it is meaningful that both measures show increases since Kinsey's time. The means are the better measure of the total coital activity of each group, but tend to exaggerate the coital rate of the typical member of the group. The medians are better indicators of the typical frequency, since they represent the level of activity of the midpoint of a group, above which lie half the cases and below which lie the other half when ranked in the order of the frequency of marital coitus.

In the male table (Table 1) every 1972 mean and median is higher than the corresponding 1938–1946 mean and median, in many cases by anywhere from a quarter to a half—a very substantial and remarkable change in a single generation. In the female table (Table 2) the increases are generally somewhat smaller but consistently in the same direction. The difference between the size of the increases shown in the male table and those shown in the female table is very likely due to an increase in perceptual accuracy by women. If, as we have suggested, the social emancipation of women in the past generation has made wives less apt to have marital coitus unwillingly than used to be the case, it would follow that they would be less likely to overestimate its frequency. If this is correct, then the increases shown in the female estimates must understate the change since Kinsey's time, since the 1938–1949 estimates were somewhat higher than reality, and the 1972 estimates closer to it. There is no corresponding reason to suppose that the 1972 estimates by males underestimate coital frequency any more or less than the 1938–1946 estimates. In any event, if we were to make the reasonable and conservative assumption that the actual truth lies about halfway between the averages derived from male estimates and those from female estimates, we would find increases in marital coital frequency of the order of magnitude shown in Table 3.

It thus appears that there has been a dramatic reversal of the decline in marital coital frequency that had taken place in the generation prior to the time of Kinsey's fieldwork. Since, as we have suggested, marital coitus today is very likely to represent the desires of both partners rather than of the husband alone, the rise in coital frequency must mean that, in general, today's wives find marital intercourse more rewarding than did their counterparts of a

Table 3. Marital Coitus: Frequency Per Week, Male and Female Estimates Combined, 1938–1946/9 and 1972

1938–1946/9 (Kinsey)		1972 (Present survey)	
Age	Median	Age	Median
16–25	2.45	18–24	3.25
26–35	1.95	25–34	2.55
36–45	1.40	35–44	2.00
46–55	.85	45–54	1.00
56–60	.50	55 & over	1.00

generation ago. As confirmation, we cite the fact that only about a tenth of our entire married female sample reported finding marital sex either neutral or unpleasant in the past year, and that even within this small minority, only a quarter said they would prefer less frequent intercourse with the spouse. In contrast, of the great majority of women who found their marital coitus mostly pleasurable or very pleasurable nearly three-quarters said the frequency was just about right, and a quarter would like it to be higher.

The general explanation of wives' increased appetite for marital coitus, it seems obvious, is that recent developments in sexual liberation have done much to rid women of those culturally created inhibitions, including the inability to convey their wishes to their husbands, that formerly stifled both desire and responsiveness. In addition, one other aspect of sexual liberation deserves special mention: This is the stimulative effect of printed and visual materials dealing with sex, which are now virtually omnipresent in daily life. Many of these materials not only convey new ideas but are meant to be erotically arousing. They succeed in the latter intent because sexual liberation has made most people more receptive to such stimuli than their counterparts of 20 or 25 years ago. Up to twice as many of the males and up to four times as many of the females in our sample as in Kinsey's say they can be sexually aroused by depictions of the nude body and by literature, pictures or film portraying sexual activities. Interestingly enough, our data show that married females are much more arousable by erotic stimuli of various sorts, including out-and-out pornography, than are single females. This is probably because, despite the liberating developments of the past generation, erotic feelings still arise most freely, for most women, within the security of total interpersonal commitment. In any case, erotic stimuli of one sort or another are encountered anywhere from once a month to several times a week by more than four out of ten husbands and nearly three out of ten wives in the younger half of our sample—and according to studies made for the Commission on Obscenity and Pornography, each such exposure tends to increase the sexual activity between married partners for the ensuing couple of days.*

It is particularly noteworthy that the increases in coital frequency shown in Tables 1, 2, and 3 extend to older groups; sexual liberation, which in many ways seems associated with the young, is evidently having important effects throughout the population, making it possible for husbands and wives to remain somewhat more interested and active in marital coitus even after many years of marriage than used to be the case. The following are some of the factors probably associated with this shift:

---

*Even those females who deny being aroused by erotic stimuli may well respond with higher coital rates in the day or two after exposure. One study made for the Commission on Obscenity and Pornography found that many of the females who expressed disgust or annoyance when viewing pornographic films nevertheless had distinct clinical symptoms of arousal. In Freudian terms, the ego disapproved but the id responded.

- Increases in the variety of techniques used in foreplay and of positions used in intercourse . . . are keeping marital coitus more interesting.
- Sexual liberation has begun to counteract the puritan-bourgeois notion that sex is unsuitable and disgraceful for the middle-aged or elderly. Kinsey, Masters and Johnson, Isadore Rubin and others have shown that desire and physical capacity, though they wane with age (more in the male than in the female), do not disappear in physically healthy persons, except for psychological reasons, until late in the eighth decade of life.
- Many older females used to lose interest in coitus because of the discomfort and irritation it caused after postmenopausal hormone deprivation had resulted in tissue inelasticity and in a lack of lubricating secretion. These postmenopausal changes are now easily controlled by estrogen-replacement therapy, and many women who once discouraged coitus are now continuing enjoyable coital activity with their husbands.

Another interesting change revealed by the data is a shift in the nature of the discrepancies between the male and female estimates of frequency. In Kinsey's data, young females gave higher frequency estimates than did young males, while among older persons the opposite was true. The explanation, valid at that time, was that young women wanted less than they were having, while older men were unable to provide as much as their wives wanted. Our own data show a very different picture: In the younger half of the sample it is the males, not the females, who give the higher estimates, though the reason can hardly be waning abilities (more likely, it is that liberated young females perceive their coital frequencies as lower than they would like). In the older half of the sample, desire and ability, on the part of both sexes, seem to be in accord, since there are no discrepancies whatever.

In Kinsey's time, education and occupational status, though they bore important relationships to the frequency of masturbation and premarital coitus, had little or no relationship to the frequency of marital coitus. Nor do they today, according to our own data. Religion, on the other hand, did have an important relationship to marital coital frequency in Kinsey's time, and still does. Kinsey reported that less-devout husbands had 20 to 30 percent more marital intercourse than devout ones because the latter carried over into marriage their premarital moral view of sex. For females, however, devoutness did not affect frequency because, according to Kinsey, the male had more control over the frequency of intercourse than the female. Today, religion is still an inhibiting influence on marital coital frequency, but few husbands— especially among the young—are now wholly or principally in control of coital frequency; devoutness in the wife is now likely to cut down on coital frequency, but paradoxically, devoutness in the husband, is not. Perhaps sexual liberation has affected churchgoing males more than churchgoing females; or perhaps the balance of power has been reversed. In any event, the curious figures are given in Table 4.

In sum, we find a considerable increase in the frequency of marital intercourse at every age level, as compared to the same age levels a generation ago.

Table 4.   Marital Coitus: Median Frequency Per Week, by Regularity of Church
Attendance, Under 35 Males and Females

	Regular churchgoers	*Non-churchgoers*
Females' estimates	2.0	3.0
Males' estimates	3.0	3.0

Apparently, it is not just the young and single who are currently having more
active sex lives than their counterparts in Kinsey's time, but married Americans of every age. Sexual liberation has had its greatest effect, at least in
numerical terms, within the safe confines of the ancient and established institution of monogamous marriage.

Blue-Collar Marriage and the Sexual Revolution

Lillian Breslow Rubin

> Experimental? Oh, he's much more experimental than I am. Once in awhile,
> I'll say, "Okay, you get a treat; we'll do it with the lights on." And I put the
> pillow over my head. [Thirty-year-old woman, married twelve years]

> Experimental? Not Ann. I keep trying to get her to loosen up; you know, to
> be more—What would you call it?—adventurous. I mean, there's lots of
> different things we could be doing. She just can't see it. Sometimes I mind;
> but then sometimes I think, "After all, she was brought up in a good family,
> and she always was a nice, sweet girl." And that's the kind of girl I wanted,
> so I guess I ain't got no real right to complain. [Twenty-seven-year-old man,
> married seven years]

These comments, typical of a significant number of the fifty white working-
class couples* with whom I spoke, made me wonder: Is *this* the revolution in
sexual behavior I had been reading about? And if so, were these the issues of
the working class alone? To answer the second question, I also talked with

Adapted from Chapter 8 of *Worlds of Pain: Life in the Working-Class Family* by Lillian
Breslow Rubin, © 1976 by Lillian Breslow Rubin, Basic Books, Inc., Publishers, New York.
Reprinted by permission.
     *For the purpose of this study, class was defined by both education and occupation. All the
families were intact, neither husband nor wife had more than a high-school education, and the
husband was employed in what is traditionally defined as a blue-collar occupation. In addition,
because I was interested in studying relatively young families, the wife was under 40 and at least
one child under 12 was still in the home. Median age of the women was 28; of the men, 31.

twenty-five professional middle-class couples whose characteristics matched the working-class group in all but education and occupation.

Not one couple is without stories about adjustment problems in this difficult and delicate area of marital life—problems not just in the past, but in the present as well. Some of the problem areas—such as differences in frequency of sexual desire between men and women—are old ones. Some—such as the men's complaints about their wives' reluctance to engage in variant and esoteric sexual behaviors—are newer. All suggest that there is, in fact, a revolution in sexual behavior in the American society that runs wide and deep—a revolution in which sexual behaviors that formerly were the province of the college-educated upper classes now are practiced widely at all class and education levels.

The evidence is strong that more people are engaging in more varieties of sexual behavior than ever before—more premarital, post-marital, extra-marital sex of all kinds. In 1948, for example, Kinsey found that only 15 percent of high-school- educated married men ever engaged in cunnilingus, compared to 45 percent of college-educated men. But the world changes quickly. Just twenty-five years later, a national survey shows that the proportion of high-school-educated men engaging in cunnilingus jumped to 56 percent.[1] And among the people I met, the figure stands at 70 percent.

But to dwell on these impressive statistics which tell us what people *do* without attention to how they *feel* about what they do is to miss a profoundly important dimension of human experience—that is, the *meaning* that people attribute to their behavior. Nowhere is the disjunction between behavior and attitude seen more sharply than in the area of sexual behavior. For when, in the course of a single lifetime, the forbidden becomes commonplace, when the border between the conceivable and the inconceivable suddenly disappears, people may *do* new things, but they don't necessarily *like* them.

For decades, novelists, filmmakers, and social scientists all have portrayed working-class men as little more than boorish, insensitive studs—men whose sexual performance was, at best, hasty and perfunctory; at worst, brutal—concerned only with meeting their own urgent needs. Consideration for a woman's needs, variety in sexual behaviors, experimentation—these, it is generally said, are to be found largely among men of the upper classes; working-class men allegedly know nothing of such amenities.[2]

If such men ever lived in large numbers, they surely do no longer. Morton Hunt's study, *Sexual Behavior in the 1970's,* which does not control for class but does give data that are controlled for education, provides evidence that men at all educational levels have become more concerned with and more sensitive to women's sexual needs—with the greatest increase reported among high-school-educated men. Comparing his sample with the 1948 Kinsey data on the subject of foreplay, for example, he notes that Kinsey reported that foreplay was "very brief or even perfunctory" among high-school-educated husbands, while college-educated husbands reported about ten minutes.

Twenty-five years later, Hunt found that the median for non-college and college-educated husbands was the same—fifteen minutes. Similar changes were found in the variety of sexual behaviors, the variety of positions used, and the duration of coitus—with especially sharp increases reported among high-school-educated men.

Not surprisingly, it is the men more often than the women who find these changing sexual norms easier to integrate—generally responding more positively to a cultural context that offers the potential for loosening sexual constraints. For historically, it is men, not women, whose sexuality has been thought to be unruly and ungovernable—destined to be restrained by a good (read: asexual) woman. Thus, it is the men who now more often speak of their wish for sex to be freer and with more mutual enjoyment:

> I think sex should be that you enjoy each other's bodies. Judy doesn't care for touching and feeling each other though.

. . . who push their wives to be sexually experimental, to try new things and different ways:

> She thinks there's just one right position and one right way—in the dark with her eyes closed tight. Anything that varies from that makes her upset.

. . . who sometimes are more concerned than their wives for her orgasm:

> It's just not enjoyable if she doesn't have a climax, too. She says she doesn't mind, but I do.

For the women, these attitudes of their men—their newly expressed wish for sexual innovation, their concern for their wives' gratification—are not an unmixed blessing. For in any situation, there is a gap between the ideal statements of a culture and the reality in which people live out their lives—a time lag between the emergence of new cultural forms and their internalization by the individuals who must act upon them. In sexual matters, that gap is felt most keenly by women. Socialized from infancy to experience their sexuality as a negative force to be inhibited and repressed, women can't just switch "on" as the changing culture or their husbands dictate. Nice girls don't! Men *use* bad girls but *marry* good girls! Submit, but don't enjoy—at least not obviously so! These are the injunctions that have dominated their lives—injunctions that are laid aside with difficulty, if at all.

The media tell us that the double standard of sexual morality is dead. But with good reason, women don't believe it. They know from experience that it is alive and well, that it exists side-by-side with the new ideology that heralds their sexual liberation. They know all about who are the "bad girls" in school, in the neighborhood; who are the "good girls." Everybody knows! Nor is this knowledge given only among the working class. The definition of "good girl" and "bad girl" may vary somewhat according to class, but the fundamental ideas those words encompass are not yet gone either from our culture or our consciousness at any class level.

We need only to look at our own responses to two questions to understand how vital the double standard remains. When we are asked, "What kind of woman is she?" we are likely to think about her sexual behavior; is she "easy" or not. But the question, "What kind of man is he?" evokes thoughts about what kind of work he does; is he strong, weak, kind, cruel? His sexual behavior is his private business, no concern of ours.

Whether these issues are especially real for working-class women, or whether women of that class are simply more open in talking about them than their middle-class counterparts, is difficult to say. Most of the middle-class women I spoke with came to their first sexual experiences at college where, during the early-to-middle 1960's, they suddenly entered a world where sexual freedom was the by-word. These were the years when it was said, "Sex is no different than a handshake"; when it was insisted that if women would only "do what comes naturally," they'd have no problems with sexual enjoyment; when the young women who did have such problems experienced themselves as personally inadequate; when it was "uncool" for a girl to ask questions about these issues—even, God forbid, to say no. Thus for well over a decade, these college-educated women have lived in an atmosphere that was at once sexually permissive and coercive—permissive in that it encouraged them to unfetter and experience their sexuality; coercive, in that it gave them little room to experience also the constraints upon that sexuality that their culture and personal history until then had imposed upon them. That combination, then, would make them at once less guilty about their sexuality *and* less ready to speak of the inhibitions that remain.

All that notwithstanding, one thing is clear. Among the people I met, working-class and middle-class couples engage in essentially the same kinds of sexual behaviors in roughly the same proportions. But working-class wives express considerably more discomfort about what they do in the marriage bed than their middle-class sisters.

Take, for example, the conflict that engages many couples around the issue of oral-genital stimulation. Seventy percent of the working-class and 76 percent of the middle-class couples engage in such sexual activity. A word of caution is necessary here, however, because these gross figures can be misleading. For about one-third of each group, engaging in oral-genital stimulation means that they tried it once, or that it happens a few times a year at most. Another 30 percent of the middle-class couples and 40 percent of the working-class couples said they have oral sex only occasionally, meaning something over three times but less than ten times a year. Thus, only about one-fourth of the working-class couples and one-third of the middle-class couples who engage in oral sex use this sexual mode routinely as a standard part of their repertoire of sexual techniques. Still, fewer of the working-class women say they enjoy it unreservedly or without guilt. Listen to this couple, married twelve years. The husband:

> I've always been of the opinion that what two people do in the bedroom is fine; whatever they want to do is okay. But Jane, she doesn't agree. I personally like a lot of foreplay, caressing each other and whatever. For her, no. I

think oral sex is the ultimate in making love; but she says it's revolting. [With a deep sigh of yearning] I wish I could make her understand.

The wife . . .

I sure wish I could make him stop pushing me into that (Ugh, I even hate to talk about it), into that oral stuff. I let him do it, but I hate it. He says I'm old-fashioned about sex and maybe I am. But I was brought up that there's just one way you're supposed to do it. I still believe that way, even though he keeps trying to convince me of his way. How can I change when I wasn't brought up that way? [With a pained sigh] I wish I could make him understand.

Notice her plaintive plea for understanding—"I wasn't brought up that way." In reality, when it comes to sex, she, like most of us, wasn't brought up *any* way. Girls generally learn only that it's "wrong" before marriage. But what that "it" is often is hazy and unclear until after the first sexual experience. As for the varieties of sexual behavior, these are rarely, if ever, mentioned to growing children, let alone discussed in terms of which are right or wrong, good or bad, permissible or impermissible.

Still, the cry for understanding from both men and women is real. Each wishes to make the other "understand," to transform the other into oneself for a brief moment so that the inner experience can be apprehended by the other. Yet, given the widely divergent socialization practices around male and female sexuality, the wish is but another impossible fantasy. The result: he asks; she gives. And neither is satisfied with the resolution. Despairing of finding a solution with which both are comfortable, one husband comments . . .

Either I'm forcing my way on her or she's forcing her way on me. Either way, you can't win. If she gives in, it isn't because she's enjoying it, but because I pushed her. I suppose you could say I get what I want, but it doesn't feel that way.

It's true, on the question of oral sex, most of the time, she "gives in— hesitantly, shyly, uncomfortably, even with revulsion. Sometimes women act from a sense of caring and consideration . . .

We don't do it much because it really makes me uncomfortable, you know [making a face], a little sick. But sometimes, I say okay because I know it means a lot to him and I really want to do it for him.

Sometimes from a sense of duty . . .

Even though I hate it, if he needs it, then I feel I ought to do it. After all, I'm his wife.

Sometimes out of fear of losing their men . . .

He can find someone to give it to him, so I figure I better do it.

Sometimes out of resignation and a sense of powerlessness . . .

I tell him I don't want to do it, but it doesn't do any good. If it's what he wants, that's what we do.

And sometimes it is offered as a bribe or payment for good behavior—not surprising in a culture that teaches a woman that her body is a negotiable instrument:

> He gets different treats at different times, depending on what he deserves. Sometimes I let him do that oral stuff you're talking about to me. Sometimes when he's *very* good, I do it to him.

While most of the working-class women greet both cunnilingus and fellatio with little enthusiasm or pleasure, cunnilingus is practiced with slightly greater frequency and with slightly less resistance than fellatio. Partly, that's because many women are talked into cunnilingus by their husbands' "If-I'm-willing-why-do-you-care?" argument . . .

> I don't like him to do it, but I can't figure out what to say when he says that I shouldn't care if *he* doesn't.

. . . and partly, and perhaps more important, because cunnilingus is something that is done *to* a woman—an act not requiring her active engagement as fellatio does; and one, therefore, not quite so incongruent with her socialization to passivity. In all areas of life, she has been raised to wait upon the initiative of another, to monitor both behavior and response carefully so as not to appear too forward or aggressive. Nowhere are these lessons more thoroughly ingrained than in her sexual behavior; nowhere has she learned better to be a reflector rather than a generator of action. Thus, fellatio, perhaps more than any other sex act, is a difficult one for a woman.

Even those women who do not express distinctly negative feelings about oral sex are often in conflict about it—unsure whether it is really all right for them to engage in, let alone enjoy, such esoteric sexual behavior, worrying about whether these are things "nice girls" do. One twenty-eight-year-old mother of three, married ten years, explained . . .

> I always feel like it's not quite right, no matter what Pete says. I guess it's not the way I was brought up, and it's hard to get over that. He keeps telling me it's okay if it's between us, that anything we do is okay. But I'm not sure about that. How do I know in the end he won't think I'm cheap.

> Sometimes I enjoy it, I guess. But most of the time I'm too worried thinking about whether I ought to be doing it, and worrying what he's *really* thinking to get much pleasure.

"How do I know he won't think I'm cheap?"—a question asked over and over again, an issue that dominates these women and their attitudes toward their own sexuality. Some husbands reassure them . . .

> She says she worries I'll think she's a cheap tramp, and she doesn't really believe me when I keep telling her it's not true.

Such reassurances remain suspect, however, partly because it's so hard for women to move past the fears of their own sexuality with which they have been stamped; and partly because at least some men are not without their own ambivalence about it, as is evident in this comment from one young husband . . .

> No, Alice isn't that kind of girl. Jesus, you shouldn't ask questions like that. [A long, difficult silence] She wasn't brought up to go for all that [pause] fancy stuff. You know, all those different ways and [shifting uncomfortably in his chair, lighting a cigarette, and looking down at the floor] that oral stuff. But that's okay with me. There's plenty of women out there to do that kind of stuff with. You can meet them in any bar any time you want to. You don't have to marry those kind.

As long as that distinction remains, as long as men distinguish between the girl they marry and the girl they use, many women will remain unconvinced by their reassurances and wary about engaging in sexual behaviors that seem to threaten their "good girl" status.

Those assurances are doubly hard to hear and to believe when women also know that their husbands are proud of their naivete in sexual matters—a pride which many men take little trouble to hide.

> It took a long time for me to convince her that it didn't have to be by the books. She was like an innocent babe. I taught her everything she knows.

Even men whose wives were married before will say with pleasure . . .

> It's funny how naive she was when we got married. She was married before, you know, but still she was kind of innocent. I taught her just about everything she knows.

For the women, the message seems clear: he wants to believe in her innocence, to believe in the special quality of their sexual relationship, to believe that these things she does only for him. She is to be pupil to his teacher. So she echoes his words—"He taught me everything I know." Repeatedly that phrase or a close equivalent is used as women discuss their sexual behavior and their feelings about it. And always it is said with a sure sense that it's what her husband wants and needs to believe, as these incongruent comments from a woman now in her second marriage show.

> One thing I know he likes is that he taught me mostly all I know about sex, so that makes him feel good. It also means that I haven't any habits that have to be readjusted to his way or anything like that.
> *That seems a strange thing to say when you were married for some years before.*

Startled, she looked at me, then down at her hands uncomfortably.

> Yeah, I guess you'd think so. Well, you know, he likes to feel that way so why shouldn't he, and why shouldn't I let him?

Given that knowledge, even if it were possible to do so on command, most women would not dare risk unleashing their sexual inhibitions. From where a woman stands, the implicit injunction in her husband's pride in her innocence is that her sexuality be restrained. And restrain it she does—a feat for which she is all too well trained. The price for that training in restraint is high for both of them, however. He often complains because she doesn't take the initiative . . .

> She never initiates anything. She'll make no advances at all, not even subtleties.

She often replies . . .

> I just can't. I guess I'm inhibited, I don't know. All I know is it's very hard for me to start things up or to tell him something I want.

On the other hand, not infrequently when women put aside that restraint and take the initiative, they may find themselves accused of not being feminine enough.

> It isn't that I mind her letting me know when she wants it, but she isn't very subtle about it. I mean, she could let me know in a nice, feminine way. Being feminine and, you know, kind of subtle, that's not her strong point.

Sensitive to the possibility of being thought of as "unfeminine" or "aggressive," most women shy away from any behavior that might bring those words down upon their heads. For it is painful for any woman of any class to hear herself described in these ways.

> I don't like to think he might think I was being aggressive, so I don't usually make any suggestions. Most of the time it's okay because he can usually tell when I'm in the mood. But if he can't, I just wait.

These, then, are some of the dilemmas and conflicts people face around the newly required and desired sexual behaviors. Among working-class women, isolation and insulation compound their problems. It is one thing to read about all these strange and exotic sexual behaviors in books and magazines, another to know others like yourself who actually do these things.

> He keeps trying to get me to read those books, but what difference would it make? I don't know who those people are. There's a lot of people do lots of things; it doesn't mean I have to do them.

If the books aren't convincing, and it's not culturally acceptable to discuss the intimate details of one's sex life with neighbors, friends, co-workers, or even family, most women are stuck with their childhood and adolescent fears, fantasies, and prohibitions. Small wonder that over and over again during my visit the atmosphere in the room changed from anxiety to relief when subjects such as oral sex were treated casually, with either the implicit or explicit understanding that it is both common and acceptable sexual practice.

> Jim keeps telling me and telling me it's okay, that it's not dirty. But I always worry about it, not really knowing if that's true or not. I read a couple of books once, but it's different. I never talked to anyone but Jim about it before. [Smiling, as if a weight had been lifted from her shoulders] You're so cool about it; talking to you makes it seem not so bad.

In contrast, discussion of these issues with the middle-class women was considerably more relaxed. Regardless of their own feelings about engaging in oral sex, it was clear that most middle-class women recognize that it is a widely practiced and acceptable behavior. In fact, more often than not, they tended to feel guilty and uncomfortable about their own inhibitions, not because they weren't able to please their husbands but because they believed their constraint relfected some inadequacy in their personal sexual adjustment. It was also from middle-class women that I more often heard complaints when their husbands were unwilling to experiment with oral-genital sex. Of the working-class couples who never engage in oral sex, only one woman complained about her husband's unwillingness to do so. Of the middle-class couples in a similar situation, four women offered that complaint.

But it is also true that, generally, the husbands of these middle-class women send fewer ambiguous and ambivalent messages about their wives' sexuality, tend less to think in good girl-bad girl terms, more often expect and accept that their wives had other sexual experiences before they met. Further, these middle-class women are more often in contact with others like themselves in an environment where discussion of sexual issues is encouraged—a course in human sexuality, a women's group, for example.

Still, the recitation of these differences in experience ought not to be read to suggest that middle-class women are now sexually free and uninhibited. The most that can be said on that score is that more of them live in an atmosphere that more seriously encourages that goal, hence more—especially those under thirty—may be closer to its attainment. Meanwhile, at all class levels, most women probably feel comfortable enough with their own sexual responses to be willing participants in sexual intercourse. But when it comes to oral sex—especially among the working class—generally they submit just as their mothers before them submitted to more traditional sexual behaviors.

Sexual conflicts in marriage are not always constellated around such exotic issues, however; nor, as I have said, are any of them the exclusive problem of a particular class. Thus, although what follows rests on material taken from my discussions with working-class couples, much of it applies to the professional middle class as well. True, the middle-class couples more often are able to discuss some of their issues more openly with each other. But despite the current, almost mystical, belief in communication-as-problem-solving, talk doesn't always help. True, middle-class couples much more often seek professional help with these problems. But sexual conflicts in a marriage are among the most intractable—the recent development and proliferation of sex therapies notwithstanding. Those therapies can be useful in dealing with some specific sexual dysfunction—prematurely ejaculating men or nonorgasmic women. But the kinds of sexual conflicts to be discussed here are so deeply rooted in the socio-cultural mandates of our world that they remain extraordinarily resistant regardless of how able the psychotherapeutic help we can buy. Thus, while there are subtle differences between the two classes in the language and tone with which the problems are dealt, in the amount of discussion about them, and in their ability and willingness to seek professional help, in this instance, those differences are not as important as the similarities that remain.

In fact, the earliest sexual problems rear their heads with the couple's first fight. Regardless of what has gone before, at bedtime, he's ready for sex; she remains cold and aloof. Listen to this couple in their mid-to-late-twenties, married nine years. The wife . . .

> I don't understand him. He's ready to go any time. It's always been a big problem with us right from the beginning. If we've hardly seen each other for two or three days and hardly talked to each other, I can't just jump into bed. If we have a fight, I can't just turn it off. He has a hard time understanding that. I feel like that's all he wants sometimes. I have to know I'm needed and wanted for more than just jumping into bed.

The husband . . .

> She complains that all I want from her is sex, and I try to make her understand that it's an expression of love. I'll want to make up with her by making love, but she's cold as the inside of the refrig. Sure I get mad when that happens. Why shouldn't I? Here I'm trying to make up and make love, and she's holding out for something—I don't know what.

The wife . . .

> He keeps saying he wants to make love, but it just doesn't feel like love to me. Sometimes I feel bad that I feel that way, but I just can't help it.

The husband . . .

> I don't understand. She says it doesn't feel like love. What does that mean, anyway? What does she think love is?

The wife . . .

> I want him to talk to me, to tell me what he's thinking about. If we have a fight, I want to talk about it so we could maybe understand it. I don't want to jump in bed and just pretend it didn't happen.

The husband . . .

> Talk! Talk! What's there to talk about. I want to make love to her and she says she wants to talk. How's talking going to convince her I'm loving her.

In sex, as in other matters, the barriers to communication are high; and the language people use serves to further confuse and mystify. He says, "I want to make love." She says, "It doesn't feel like love." Neither quite knows what the other is talking about; both feel vaguely guilty and uncomfortable—aware only that somehow they're passing each other, not connecting. He believes he already has given her the most profound declaration of love of which a man is capable. He married her; he gives her a home; he works hard each day to support her and the children.

> What does she want? Proof? She's got it, hasn't she? Would I be knocking myself out to get things for her—like to keep up this house—if I didn't love her. Why does a man do things like that if not because he loves his wife and kids? I swear, I can't figure what she wants.

This is one time when *she* knows what she wants.

> I want him to let me know in other ways, too, not just sex. It's not enough that he supports us and takes care of us. I appreciate that, but I want him to share things with me. I need for him to tell me his feelings. He keeps saying no, but to me, there's a difference between making love and sex. Just once, I'd like him to love me without ending up in sex. But when I tell him that, he thinks I'm crazy.

For him, perhaps, it *does* seem crazy. Split off, as he is, from the rest of the expressive-emotional side of himself, sex may be the one place where he can allow himself the expression of deep feelings, the one place where he can experience the depth of that affective side. His wife, on the other hand, closely connected with her feeling side in all areas *but* the sexual, finds it difficult to be comfortable with her feelings in the very area in which he has the greatest—sometimes the only—ease. She keeps asking for something she can understand and is comfortable with—a demonstration of his feelings in non-sexual ways. He keeps giving her the one thing he can understand and is comfortable with—his feelings wrapped up in a blanket of sex. Thus do husbands and wives find themselves in an impossibly difficult bind—another bind not of their own making, but one that stems from the cultural context in which girls and boys grow to adulthood.

I am suggesting, then, that a man's ever-present sexual readiness is not simply an expression of urgent sexual need but also a complex compensatory response to a socialization process that *constricts the development of the emotional side of his personality in all but sexual expression.* Conversely, a woman's insistent plea for an emotional statement of a nonsexual nature is a response to a process that *encourages the development of the affective side of her personality in all but sexual expression.* [3]

Such differences between women and men about the *meaning* of sex make for differences between wives and husbands in frequency of desire as well—differences which lead to a wide discrepancy in their perceptions about the frequency of the sexual encounter. [4] Except for a few cases where the women are inclined to be more sexually active than the men, he wants sex more often than she. To him, therefore, it seems as if they have sex less often than they actually do; to her, it seems more often. But the classical caricature of a wife fending off her husband's advances with a sick headache seems not to apply among working-class women. Once in awhile, a woman says . . .

> I tell him straight. I'm not in the mood, and he understands.

Mostly, however, women say . . .

> I don't use excuses like headaches and things like that. If my husband wants me, I'm his wife, and I do what he wants. It's my responsibility to give it to him when he needs it.

Whether she refuses outright or acquiesces out of a sense of duty or responsibility, the solution is less than satisfactory for both partners. In either case, he feels frustrated and deprived. He wants more than release from his own sexual tension; he wants her active involvement as well. Confronted with his ever-present readiness, she feels guilty . . .

> I feel guilty and uncomfortable when he's always ready and I'm not, like I'm not taking care of him.

. . . coerced . . .

> I feel like it hangs over my head all the time. He always wants it; twice a day wouldn't be too much for him. He says he doesn't want me just to give in to him, but if I didn't he'd be walking around horny all the time. If we waited for me to want it, it would never be enough for him.

. . . and also deprived . . .

> Before I ever get a chance to feel really sexy, he's there and waiting. I'd like to know what it feels like sometimes to really want it that bad. Oh, sometimes I do. But mostly I don't get the chance.

Thus, she rarely has the opportunity to experience the full force of her own sexual rhythm, and with it, the full impact of her sexuality. It is preempted by the urgency and frequency of his desires.

Finally, there is plenty of evidence that the battle between the sexes is still being waged in the marriage bed, and in very traditional ways. Several couples spoke of their early sexual adjustment problems in ways that suggest that the struggle was not over sex but over power and control. Often in the early years, when she wants sex, he's tired; when he wants sex, she's uninterested. For many couples, the pattern still repeats itself once in awhile. For about one-fifth of them, the scenario continues to be played out with great regularity and sometimes with great drama, as this story of one early-thirties couple illustrates.

In six months of premarital and ten years of marital coitus, the woman had never had an orgasm.

> We had sex four or five times a week like clockwork all those years, and I just laid there like a lump. I couldn't figure out what all the noise was about.

Asked how he felt about her passivity during that period, her husband—a taciturn, brooding man, whose silence seemed to cover a wellspring of hostility —replied . . .

> If she couldn't, she couldn't. I didn't like it, but I took what I needed. [After a moment's hesitation] She's always been hard to handle.

A year ago, attracted by ideas about women's sexuality that seemed to her to be "in the air," she began to read some of the women's literature on the subject. From there, she moved on to pornography and one night, as she tells it . . .

> The earth shook. I couldn't believe anything could be so great. I kept wondering how I lived so long without knowing about it. I kept asking Fred why he'd never made me understand before. [Then, angrily] But you'll never believe what happened after that. My husband just lost interest in sex. Now, I can hardly ever get him to do it any more, no matter how much I try or beg him. He says he's too tired, or he doesn't feel well, or else he just falls asleep and I can't wake him up. I can hardly believe it's happening sometimes. Can you imagine such a thing? I even wonder whether maybe I shouldn't have made such a big fuss about it. Maybe it scared him off or something.

Her husband refused my attempts to explore the issue with him, insisting that all is well in their sex life, but adding . . .

> She's always asking for something, or hollering about something. I don't have any control around this house any more. Nobody listens to me.

It would seem, then, that as long as he could "take what I needed," he could feel he was asserting some control over his wife and could remain sexually active and potent. When she unexpectedly became an assertive and active participant in the sex act, the only possibility for retaining control was to move from the active to the passive mode. Thus, he felt impotent. His wife, now acutely aware of her sexual deprivation, is left torn between anger, frustration, and the terrible fear that somehow she is responsible for it.

A dramatic story? Certainly, but one whose outlines are clear in 20 percent of these marriages where three women complained about their husbands' impotence and seven about sexual withholding—not surprisingly, a problem most of the men were unwilling to talk about. In the three cases where the husband did address the issue at all, either he denied its existence, "It's no problem; I'm just tired;" or blamed his wife, "She doesn't appeal to me," or "She's too pushy." The last has been a subject of recent concern expressed publicly by psychologists and widely publicized in the mass media. The performance demands being laid on men are extraordinary, we are told, and women are cautioned that their emergent assertiveness—sexual and otherwise— threatens the sexual performance of their men. The time has come, these experts warn, to take the pressure off.

Nowhere, however, do we hear concern about the effects of the performance demand on women. Yet, never in history have heavier demands for sexual performance been laid on them. Until recently, women were expected to submit passively to sex; now they are told their passivity diminishes their husbands' enjoyment. Until recently, especially among the less educated working class, orgasm was an unexpected gift; now it is a requirement of adequate sexual performance.[5] These new definitions of adequacy leave many women feeling "under the gun"—fearful and anxious if they do not achieve orgasm;

if it does not happen at the "right" moment—that is, at the instant of their husbands' ejaculation; or if they are uncomfortable about engaging in behaviors that feel alien or aberrant to them.[6] If anxiety about one's ability to perform adequately has an untoward effect on the male orgasm, is there any reason to believe it would not inhibit the female's as well?

In fact, the newfound concern with their orgasm is a mixed and costly blessing for many women. For some, it has indeed opened the possibility for pleasures long denied. For others, however, it is experienced as another demand in a life already too full of demands. Listen to this thirty-five-year-old woman who works part time, takes care of a house, a husband, six children, and an aging, sick father . . .

> It feels like somebody's always wanting something from me. Either one of the kids is hanging on to me or pulling at me, or my father needs something. And if it's not them, then Tom's always coming after me with that gleam in his eye. Then, it's not enough if I just let him have it, because if I don't have a climax, he's not happy. I get so tired of everybody wanting something from me all the time. I sometimes think I hate sex.

While it is undoubtedly true that more women have more orgasms more often than ever before—and that most of them enjoy sex more than women in earlier generations—it is also true that there are times when a husband's wish for his wife's orgasm is experienced as oppressive and alienating—when it seems to a woman that her orgasm is more a requirement of his pleasure than her own. We may ask: How rational are these thoughts? And we may wonder: Why should it be a matter of question or criticism if, in the course of pleasuring their wives, men also pleasure themselves? When phrased that way, it should not be questioned! But if we look at the discussion around female orgasm or lack of it a little more closely, we notice that it is almost invariably tied to male pleasure. If a woman doesn't have an orgasm, it is a problem, if not for her, then because both her man's pleasure and his sense of manhood are diminished. Can anyone imagine a discussion of male impotence centering around concern for women? In fact, when we talk about the failure of men to achieve erection or orgasm, the discourse takes place in hushed, serious, regretful tones—always in the context of concern about how those men experience that failure. How many of us have ever thought, "What a shame for his woman that he can't have an erection." Any woman who has shared that experience with a man knows that her concern was largely for him, her own frustration becoming irrelevant in that moment. Any man who has experienced impotence knows that his dominant concern was for the failure of his manhood.

It is not surprising, therefore, that several of the women I talked to were preoccupied with their orgasm, not because it was so important to them, but because their husbands' sense of manhood rested on it. Holding her head, one woman said painfully . . .

> I rarely have climaxes. But if it didn't bother my husband, it wouldn't bother me. I keep trying to tell him that I know it's not his fault, that he's really a

> good lover. I keep telling him it's something the matter with me, not with him.
> But it scares me because he doesn't believe it, and I worry he might leave me
> for a woman who will have climaxes for him.

With these final words, she epitomizes the feelings of many women, whether
orgasmic or not, at least some of the time: *her orgasm is for him, not for her.*
It is his need to validate his manhood that is the primary concern—his need,
not hers. For women of the working class, who already have so little autonomy
and control over their lives, this may well be experienced as the ultimate
violation.

To compound the anxiety, now one orgasm is not enough. One woman,
having read that some women have multiple orgasms, worried that her husband would soon find out.

> It's really important for him that I reach a climax, and I try to every time.
> He says it just doesn't make him feel good if I don't. But it's hard enough
> to do it once! What'll happen if he finds out about those women who have
> lots of climaxes?

These, then, are some dimensions of sexual experience in the 1970's that are
buried under the sensational reports of changing sexual mores. Undoubtedly,
there is a loosening of sexual constraints for both women and men; undoubtedly, more people are enjoying fuller sexual experiences than ever before.
Certainly, it is important that these changes are discussed publicly, that the
subject of sex has come out of the closet. But that is not enough. For we must
also understand that such changes are not without cost to the individuals who
try to live them out, who must somehow struggle past powerful early training
to a new consciousness. For women especially—women of any class—that
training in repressing and inhibiting their sexuality makes this a particularly
difficult struggle.

It is both sad and ironic now to hear men complain that their wives are too
cautious, too inhibited, or not responsive enough in bed. Sad, because the
deprivation men experience is real; ironic, because these are the costs of the
sexual limitations that generations of their forebears have imposed on women.
Changing such historic patterns of thought and behavior will not be easy for
either men or women. For certainly, many men are still not without ambivalence about these sexual issues with reference to their women—a subtlety that
is not lost on their wives. But even where men unambivalently mean what they
say about wanting their wives to be freer in the marriage bed, it will take time
for women to work through centuries of socially mandated denial and repression . . .

> All I know is, I can't just turn on so easy. Maybe we're all paying the price
> now because men didn't used to want women to enjoy sex.

. . . and probably will require their first being freer in other beds as well.

> I was eighteen when we got married, and I was a very young eighteen. I'd
> never had any relations with anybody, not even my husband, before we were

married. So we had a lot of problems. I guess I was kind of frigid at first. But you know, after all those years when you're holding back, it's hard to all of a sudden get turned on just because you got married.

Yes, it is "hard to all of a sudden get turned on just because you got married." And as long as women's sexuality continues to be subjected to capricious demands and treated as if regulated by an on-off switch—expected to surge forth fully and vigorously at the flick of the "on" switch and to subside quietly at the flick of the "off"—most women will continue to seek the safest path, in this case, to remain quietly someplace between "on" and "off."

1. Morton Hunt, *Sexual Behavior in the 1970's* (Chicago: Playboy Press, 1974). This study, conducted for *Playboy* magazine, included a representative sample of urban and suburban adults, of whom 982 were men and 1,044 were women. Seventy-one percent of the sample were married (not to each other), 25 percent were never married, and 4 percent had been married.
2. For a good description of this stereotype, see Arthur B. Shostak, "Ethnic Revivalism, Blue-Collarites, and Bunker's Last Stand." In *The Rediscovery of Ethnicity*, edited by Sallie TeSelle (New York: Harper Colophon, 1973). See also Mirra Komarovsky, *Blue Collar Marriage* (New York: Vintage Books, 1962) who, while noting that the stereotype applies to "only a small minority" of the families she studied, found that only 30 percent of the women said they were very satisfied with their sexual relations. And some of the data she presents do indeed validate the stereotype more forcefully and very much more often than among my sample where it is practically nonexistent.
3. Cf. William Simon and John Gagnon, "On Psychosexual Development." In *Handbook of Socialization Theory and Research*, edited by David A. Goslin (Chicago: Rand McNally, 1969) and John Gagnon and William Simon, *Sexual Conduct: The Social Sources of Human Sexuality* (Chicago: Aldine Publishing, 1973) whose work is a major contribution toward understanding the differences in male-female sexuality as an expression of the differential socialization patterns for women and men. These authors also point to the masculine tendency to separate love and sex and the feminine tendency to fuse them. They suggest, in fact, that the male "capacity for detached sexual activity, activity where the only sustaining motive is sexual . . . may actually be the hallmark of male sexuality in our culture." For an exploration of the ways in which social structure and personality intersect from the psychoanalytic perspective, see Nancy Chodorow, *The Reproduction of Mothering: Family Structure and Feminine Personality* (Berkeley: University of California Press, 1977, forthcoming), who argues that the root of the differences in male-female personality and the concomitant differences in the development of psychosexual needs and responses lie in the social structure of the family.

See also Ben Barker-Benfield, "The Spermatic Economy: A Nineteenth Century View of Sexuality." In *The American Family in Social-Historical Perspective*, edited by Michael Gordon (New York: St. Martin's Press, 1973) for a portrait of nineteenth century definitions of male and female sexuality and the fear and abhorrence with which men viewed female sexuality in that era.
4. It is for this reason that studies relying on the recollection of only one spouse for their data —as most do—risk considerable distortion. Thus, for example, when Morton Hunt reports that almost 26 percent of the married women ages twenty-five to thirty-four report having sexual intercourse between 105 and 156 times a year, we know only that this is the wife's perception, and we can assume that the recollection is filtered through her *feelings* about the frequency of the sexual encounter.
5. Again, Hunt's data, while not controlled for class, are suggestive. Using the 1948 Kinsey data as a comparative base, he reports that marital coitus has increased in frequency at every age and educational level. Comparing the Kinsey sample with his own at the fifteenth year of marriage, Hunt reports "a distinct increase in the number of wives who always or nearly always have orgasm (Kinsey: 45 percent; *Playboy:* 53 percent) and a sharp decrease in the number of wives who seldom or never do (Kinsey: 28 percent; *Playboy:* 15 percent)."

6. For a rebuke of the self-styled male "experts" on women's sexuality that is both wonderfully angry and funny as it highlights the absurdity of their advice to women, see Ellen Frankort, *Vaginal Politics* (New York: Bantam Books, 1973): 172–180. She opens this section of her book, entitled "Carnal Ignorance," by saying:

> For the longest time a woman wasn't supposed to enjoy sex. Then suddenly a woman was neurotic if she didn't achieve orgasm simultaneously with her husband. Proof of a woman's health was her ability to come at the very moment the man ejaculated, in the very place he ejaculated, and at the very rate ordained for him by his physiology. If she couldn't, she went to a male psychiatrist to find out why.

Chapter 4

Men's Roles

The Male Sex Role

*Deborah S. David and
Robert Brannon*

Sex as a Learned Social Role

By far the most complex, demanding and all-involving role that members of our culture must ever learn to play is that of male or female. "Casting" takes place immediately at birth, after a quick biological inspection, and the role of "female" or "male" is assigned. It is an assignment that will last one's entire lifetime and affect virtually everything one ever does. A large part of the next 20 years or so will be spent in gradually learning and perfecting one's assigned sex-role: slowly memorizing what a "young lady" should do and should not do, how a "little man" should react in each of a million frightening situations—practicing, practicing, playing house, playing cowboys, practicing—and often crying in confusion and frustration at the baffling and seemingly endless task.

Children often confuse sex roles and make "inappropriate" choices. When a little girl announces that she plans to be a fireman, adults merely smile. They know she doesn't yet have it right, but they're not worried. By the time it matters, she will have learned her sex role so thoroughly that it simply will never occur to her to be a fireman. In the meantime she has other things to learn: there are new dolls to play with and take care of, pretty clothes to try on, shiny black patent-leather shoes—and as a special reward she may help mommy with housework and stir the batter in the big white bowl. No one ever really tells her to be "domestic" or "esthetic" or "maternal"—*but she's learning.*

A little boy meanwhile is learning other things. Balls and bats have miraculously appeared to play with; realistic toy pistols; and trains, blocks, and marbles. The shoes he finds in his closet are sturdy enough to take a lot of wear, and just right for running. One day there is an old tire hanging by a rope from a tree in the back yard, just right for swinging. No one every really tells him to be "active" or "aggressive" or "competitive" *but somehow, he's learning.*

From Deborah David and Robert Brannon, *The 49% Majority: The Male Sex Role,* pp. 8–28, © 1976, Addison-Wesley, Reading, Massachusetts. Reprinted by permission.

The groundwork for proper sex-role behavior is laid during these childhood years, but there is still a certain tolerance for mistakes, and different levels of maturity. With the arrival of adolescence the game rather suddenly becomes real. Teenagers must begin to perform sex roles (sometimes exaggerated caricatures of the adult roles) correctly, or face a kind of cruelty and ridicule from each other which has few human counterparts—and which most adults have mercifully forgotten. How one *dresses, speaks, looks, walks, eats, relaxes— everything suddenly matters.* "Look at how Sam throws a ball! Hey, throw it here, Samantha!" "Watch how Betty walks; she looks like a horse!" Cruel, cutting remarks, hurts that may last for a lifetime . . . and nowhere to hide. The teenager can retreat to home and parents but not for long; tomorrow, the same snickering, judging schoolmates must be faced.

Little wonder that detailed sex-role learning takes place fast in adolescence, and remarkably uncritically. Exactly why is it that girls eat in small bites? Why do boys not like poetry? *Who cares,* just get it right! Why is it that boys "like sex" and girls don't? Never mind. Just get it right, or else! Why do girls wear make-up? Boys hold doors? Girls wait to be called? Boys drive the car? We are too busy learning these never-ending rules to question them. The crucial practicing of sex-role behaviors takes place during these anxiety-filled years, and personalities emerge and begin to harden around habits and styles adopted by teenagers wanted desperately to fit in, to be liked and accepted by their equally anxious classmates. The *deeper* cultural images of maleness and femaleness are seldom articulated. Their assumptions are implicit, however, for they hold together and make whatever sense there is to the welter of specific rules and customs. Males are strong, females are weak; males are aggressive, females are passive; males are coarse, and direct, females sweet, and emotional. In time the exaggerated rigidity of teenage sex roles will soften and mellow, but these basic role-concepts remain embedded in the knowledge and assumptions of virtually every member of our culture. Men are just "naturally" one way, and women another; how could it be otherwise?

It comes as a surprise to most Americans to learn that in other societies what we so automatically assume is "male" may not be viewed as male at all. In a study of three societies in New Guinea, anthropologist Margaret Mead (1935) described three patterns of sex-appropriate behavior and personality which are in striking contrast to those assumed by Americans. Among the mountain-dwelling people known as the Arapesh, both sexes aspire to a pattern which strongly resembles the personality associated with the female role in our culture. Both male and female Arapesh tend to be passive, cooperative, peaceful, and greatly concerned with nourishing and growing living things. The father as well as the mother is said to "bear a child"; it is believed that only the continual caring and participation of the father can make a child grow in the mother's womb or continue to healthy adulthood. Sexual interest is relatively low, and the preferred sexual style is passive for both sexes. The role of authority figure is repugnant to both women and men. Leaders are selected during childhood and specifically trained to be more assertive; otherwise there might be no takers for leadership positions in the tribe.

Less than 80 miles from the Arapesh dwell the Mundugumor, who present a remarkable contrast in temperament and behavior. For both males and females the ideal is an aggressive and belligerent style which almost parodies our own male sex role. "Both men and women," the anthropologist discovered, "are expected to be violent, competitive, aggressively sexed, jealous, and ready to see and avenge insult, delighting in display, in action, in fighting" (Mead, 1968, p. 213). Hostility and aggressiveness are omnipresent and pervade the whole social order, giving it a constantly competitive and violent atmosphere. The mother spends little time with her offspring, nursing them as seldom as possible, weaning them early and abruptly.

A third tribe in this area of New Guinea is the Tchambuli, who have preferred traits which differ sharply for the sexes, but along lines essentially *opposite* to our own. Males are expected to be sensitive, artistic, nervous, gossipy, fond of adornment, and emotionally dependent. The Tchambuli male, with "his delicately arranged curls," his "flying fox skin highly ornamented with shells, his mincing step and self-conscious mein" lives mainly for art and sees the world as an audience for his flute-playing, dancing, carving, and skill at creating costumes.

Tchambuli females must be competent, dominating, practical, and efficient; they actually run almost all of the important domestic and economic institutions. Females are also the sexual aggressors: the male is less interested in sex, and more passive: " . . .he holds his breath and hopes" (*Ibid.*, p. 241).

When we add to these three societies the case of our own, in which males are expected to be aggressive and dominant and females sensitive and passive, it becomes clear that every major combination of roles is represented in human cultures. Mead's provocative conclusion was that:

> Many, if not all, of the personality traits which we have called masculine or feminine are as lightly linked to sex as are the clothing, the manners, and the form of head-dress that a society at a given period assigns to either sex . . . the evidence is overwhelmingly in favor of social conditioning.(*Ibid.*, p. 260)

The discovery that most of what we associate with being male or female is actually a learned social role does not mean that biology is totally irrelevant. Prior to acquiring the appropriate role there may be innate differences among individuals which make learning a certain role more difficult for some than others. The culture acts, however, to encourage some human potentials and suppress others, and most human beings seem to be flexible enough to learn whatever the culture dictates, at least reasonably well. The Tchambuli male who finds himself inclined to be calm, practical, and unartistic will have doubts about his "manliness," and try to cultivate the more masculine traits of nervousness and esthetic appreciation. The American male who is naturally shy or passive will often realize that these qualities are not considered manly and try to either change or compensate for them. Both are likely to succeed, for whatever the sex-role profile of a given culture, most people are able to approximate it by the time they reach adulthood.

A strong indication of the predominant power of social role learning over natural and biological factors may be found in the cases of occasional individuals who were mistakenly identified at birth due to physical abnormalities and raised in the sex-role category opposite to that of their primary biological make-up. Money and Ehrhardt (1972) studied a number of these individuals and concluded that sex-role identification and satisfaction were not correlated with chromosomal, gonadal, hormonal, or external genital characteristics, but were very strongly related to being *raised* as a member of one or the other sexual classifications. In such cases they report that surgery to alter the biological sex features is more successful than trying to change the effects of socialization.

Dimensions Of The Male Sex Role

Now let's return to the specifics of the male sex role in our own culture. We already know some of the broad outlines, but there are seeming inconsistencies in the common-sense view of masculinity. One senses that there is not one ideal image of the "real man" in our society but several. Consider, for example, the following male stereotypes, each of which in one way or another strikes us as distinctively masculine:

- The football player: big, tough, and rugged, though not precisely a towering intellect;
- The jet-set playboy: usually sighted in expensive restaurants or fast convertibles, accompanied by a beautiful woman (whom he's ignoring);
- The blue-collar brawler: a quick temper with fists to match; nobody better try to push *him* around;
- The big-shot businessman: the Babbitt traveling salesman Rotary Club booster type of expansive back-slapper;
- The Don Juan: he's smooth, smoldering, and totally irresistible to women; a super-stud on the prowl;
- The strong, simple working man: he's honest, solid, direct, and hardworking;
- The Truly Great Man: a statesman, prophet, scientist, deep thinker, awesome genius.

They don't look, act, or sound very much alike, but somehow these images all seem distinctively masculine to at least some of us. Does this mean that the male role is so infinitely flexible that anything a man does can seem "manly"? No; most male images and examples are by no means as masculine as these selected examples. The image of the "average guy," the man-in-the-street, is not especially masculine; many successful, familiar, and popular male personalities seem anything but manly.

The answer is that the male role is demanding but, except on a few points, not very specific. There seem to be several basic routes, and many specific variations, to fulfilling the minimum demands of the role. A man can in some sense choose what to "specialize" in—how to project a viable masculine image, choosing from among the options the role provides. In choosing, he is likely to be influenced by his age, class, ethnic subgroup, and physique, as well as individual talents and capacities. There are many acceptable combinations and certain styles become "fads" after they're popularized by movie stars or public personalities. As with other cultural fashions, there are changes over time. Beneath all the permutations, however, are a small number of basic themes which pervade and ultimately define the male sex role. I believe that there are four such general themes, or dimensions, which underlie the male sex role we see in our culture. Each has subparts and complexities and at some points they overlap, but the following four themes seem to comprise the core requirements of the role:

1. No Sissy Stuff: the stigma of all stereotyped feminine characteristics and qualities, including openness and vulnerability.
2. The Big Wheel: success, status, and the need to be looked up to.
3. The Sturdy Oak: a manly air of toughness, confidence, and self-reliance.
4. Give 'Em Hell!: the aura of aggression, violence, and daring.

There may seem to be a mechanistic quality to such an inflexible listing and a model which proposes to examine sex roles in terms of four (or any other number of) components. Obviously such a model overstates what is definitely known about sex roles. Remember also that there are many human traits and characteristics (e.g. generosity, loyalty), which are not strongly associated with either male or female sex roles. Some widely admired male images—*Zorba The Greek* or Sam-the-Lion in *The Last Picture Show* are good examples—combine masculine qualities with unmasculine ones in a very appealing way. But our focus here is on the pure case, the purely masculine part of a man's image. This discussion is focused primarily on the male role in the present-day United States. Much of it is relevant to other areas of Western culture, but there are also national variations which we won't be able to consider here.

Finally, a note about the kinds of evidence we shall consider. As a behavioral scientist I look for and prefer experimental data where it's available. Only a controlled experiment can definitively prove causal relationships between variables (Cronbach, 1957; Campbell & Stanley, 1963). However, such evidence is necessarily limited to factors which can be manipulated by the experimenter. Observational and correlational studies are less conclusive but have greater scope, for nature has been experimenting since the dawn of time on a far grander scale than man can contemplate. By carefully studying covariations among events, social scientists can extend the scope of science far beyond the controlled certainty of the laboratory.

Writers and novelists have no "controls" at all, but sometimes they show enormous powers of analysis. It has often been observed that novelists are among the greatest psychologists. Freud acknowledged the genius of those writers who can draw "from the whirlpool of their emotions the deepest truths, to which we others have to force our way"; "they draw on sources not yet accessible to science" (quoted in Stone and Stone, 1966). Men and masculinity have provided the subject matter for countless great writers in all ages. So to explore this familiar but strangely uncharted domain of masculinity, we'll consider material and insights from all these sources.

1. No Sissy Stuff: the Stigma of Anything Vaguely Feminine.

The earliest lesson: don't be like girls, kid, be like . . . like . . . well, not like girls. Children of both sexes initially identify most strongly with their mothers, the usual caretakers of infants and children (Hartley, 1959; Lynn, 1969; Schaffer and Emerson, 1964). As a child gradually becomes aware that there are two adult sexes, one of which he or she will grow up to be, the first major difference in the psychological development of males and females takes place. While the young female may continue to identify with her mother, the boy must gradually switch to a new source of identification, a process often made difficult by the absence of the father during daytime hours:

> The girl has her same-sex parental model for identification with her more hours per day than the boy has his same-sex model with him. Even when home, the father does not usually participate in as many intimate activities with the child as does the mother, e.g., preparation for bed and toileting . . . Despite the shortage of male models for direct imitation, a somewhat stereo-typed and conventional masculine role is spelled out for the boy, often by his mother, women teachers, and peers in the absence of his father and male models . . . Consequently, males tend to identify with a culturally defined masculine role, whereas females tend to identify with their mothers. (Lynn, 1969, pp. 24-26)

Since boys must learn to perform a masculine role for which there are few models in their immediate environment, one might expect that adults would be relatively tolerant of early mistakes. The reality is that parents are substantially more concerned that boys conform to the male role than girls to the female; both parents, but especially fathers, express substantial displeasure when boys display "feminine" qualities (Lansky, 1967; Goodenough, 1957). Summarizing a number of studies of preschool children, Hartley concludes:

> Demands that boys conform to social notions of what is manly come much earlier and are enforced with much more vigor than similar attitudes with respect to girls . . . and at an early age, when they are least able to understand either the reasons for or the nature of the demands. Moreover, these demands are frequently enforced harshly, impressing the small boy with the danger of deviating from them, while he does not quite understand what they are. (Hartley, 1959, p. 458)

Surrounded by adult females, offered few positive images of what he is expected to be, but chastised and sometimes shamed for being a "sissy" if he emulates girls and women, the young male child is likely to feel:

> . . .an anxiety which frequently expresses itself in over-straining to be mascu-
> line, in virtual panic at being caught doing anything traditionally defined as
> feminine, and in hostility toward anything even hinting at "femininity,"
> including females themselves. (*Ibid.*, p. 458)

This terror of being a sissy, at an age when the child can hardly understand
the meaning of that accusation, let alone ignore it, apparently leaves a deep
wound in the psyche of many males. It has a clear embodiment in the adult
male sex role:

A "real man" must never, never resemble women, or display strongly stereotyped feminine characteristics. This simple rule is applied to almost every
aspect of life and explains a great deal about what is and isn't considered
masculine. Women are smaller, have less hair and higher-pitched voices, so
boys lucky enough to be big, hairy, and deep-voiced start off with an advantage. People automaticaly describe such males as more masculine (Gilkinson,
1937). "Develop a deep, manly voice," advises the Charles Atlas home improvement course, "and watch your confidence improve."

Women are thought to be neat and tidy, so a man who seems too fastidious
will draw wise-cracks. Will Rogers' mother tried scolding and begging her
defiant youngster to keep his shirt tail in, all to no avail. Finally she found a
sure-fire method: she simply sewed a patch of frilly white lace to the tail of
every shirt he owned.

Women wear cosmetics and sweet-smelling toilet waters too, so no two-
fisted man would be caught dead in that junk. "Men are actually hungry to
buy scents and cosmetics," one product researcher confided, "But the product
has to have a name like Command, Tackle, Brut, Bullwhip, or Hai Karate and
have FOR MEN stamped all over the goddam bottle." (One favorite men's
scent was originally a women's cologne—until it was renamed *English Leather.*)
When teen-agers first began to wear their hair longer in the late 1960's, most
older men were incredulous, sometimes outraged. This was no harmless fad
. . . those kids look like . . . like . . . well, like women!

The stigma of femaleness applies to almost everything: vocabulary, food,
hobbies, and even choice of a profession. Pastimes such as knitting, flower
arranging, and needlepoint are so strongly regarded as feminine that it made
the news when a professional football player (a linesman, at that) revealed his
hobby of *needlepoint.* "Aren't you afraid people will think you're a sissy?" an
incredulous reporter asked the 230-pound giant. Art, poetry, music, and virtually all "fine arts" are seen as somewhat feminine pursuits; men who enjoy,
create, or even write about these things are widely assumed to be less manly
than men who ignore them. Male ballet dancers train harder and are actually
in better physical shape than the average professional football player (Chass,
1974), yet their masculinity is highly suspect to most American males. Sports
writers, coaches, truck drivers, engineers, and military men, in contrast, are
automatically seen as masculine regardless of their physical condition. Their

professions place them safely in a man's world—far away from anything that might interest a woman. The threat to this masculine isolation probably explains more of the opposition to women's attempts to enter professional sports than the economic competition reasons usually cited.

If everything associated with females is so potentially stigmatizing, it's not hard to guess how much real intimacy with women themselves a manly man is expected to want. Writing about the social life of men in the typical Western adventure movie, Manville concludes:

> Girls are nice to take your hat off to on Sunday morning when you meet one of them on her way to church, and there's another kind of lady with whom you enjoy a drink in the saloon on a Saturday night when you're ready for fun . . . But a woman as a friend, or deeply moving lover, or equal-partner wife? Never! (Manville, 1969)

Men who are most intensely concerned with their own masculinity seldom desire close contact with women. "A highly intelligent man should take a primitive woman," wrote another hard-driving bully-boy, Adolph Hitler. "Imagine if on top of everything else I had a woman who interfered with my work." (cf. Spiegelman and Schneider, 1974)

Openness and Vulnerability. Women are permitted and even expected to be "emotional"; they're allowed to show when they're feeling anxious, depressed, frightened, happy, loving, and so forth. This kind of openness about feelings, especially ones which cast the feeler in a weak or "unfavorable" light, is strongly prohibited for men. It's not that men can never show *any* emotions. Open displays of anger, contempt, impatience, hostility or cynicism are not difficult for most men. But emotions suggesting vulnerability and even extremely positive feeling such as love, tenderness, and trust are almost never acceptable.

Try to imagine two rugged he-men standing eye to eye and saying: "I've been so upset since we had that argument I could hardly sleep last night. Are you sure you're really not mad at me?" "Heck, Jim, you mean so much to me, I get so much from our friendship . . . I was just afraid that you'd hold a grudge against me." Men do have these emotions and feelings, but we try like hell never to show them. When a male friend does start to say something like that, there are husky cries of "Get a grip on yourself," "Pull yourself together, man," or "Stiff upper lip, old boy."

Some men become so skilled at hiding feelings that their wives and closest friends don't know when they're scared, anxious, depressed, or in pain. They didn't get to be that way accidentally, though. Marc Fasteau remembers consciously practicing the style while in college:

> I tried to maintain a flat, even tone in conversation. I discussed only issues, the larger the better. I worried about every instance of doubt, of self-consciousness, of emotion, of not being in control of groups I was in. The men I admired seemed to feel none of these things. Since I did, how could I play the game? (Fasteau, 1974, p. 125)

Probably no action is more stereotypically feminine or humiliating for a man than crying. One businessman who had an outstanding performance record with his company learned at an executive meeting that a project he had spent a year developing was being taken over by someone else, for fairly arbitrary reasons; he broke down and cried. He was told later that he was totally discredited with his colleagues, had no future with the company, and should look for another job (Fasteau, 1974, p. 123).

Jourard (1971) has developed an index of how much personal information people reveal to others with whom they interact. He finds that men reveal far less than women, no matter who the audience, and that both sexes reveal less to men than to women. Revealing yourself to a man can be dangerous.

Once as a freshman in college I found myself sitting with a stranger in the college cafeteria. I had been undergoing a lot of changes in my thinking about religion that year, and I guess I was in a talkative mood, because I told him all about it: what I'd believed until recently, and the changes I was going through. "Very interesting," he said, puffing on his cigarette with a bored, distant look; not one word about his own religious doubts or convictions. I felt like such a damn fool, it was all I could do to get through the meal and leave the table.

Years later, in a men's consciousness-raising group, I met a man who was incredibly open about his feelings. He could and did say that he loved our group, and what it had meant in his life, and even—get this!—how much he *cared* about another man, right to his face! We had a lot of other things in common and I was enormously drawn to him—but hell! Didn't he know how "uncool" that was? When he would reveal himself in that way, I would involuntarily look at the floor and squirm in embarrassment. I'd like to say I don't react that way to men any more—but I can't.

Male Friendship and the (Gulp!) Unspoken Fear. When men want to express affection to one another, their means are rather limited. In the place of directness, we've developed ritualized gestures which are safer, and a lot more ambiguous; often, in fact, they parody hostility and aggression. Two old friends will celebrate their reunion by slugging each other on the arm. Instead of "I hope you make a good impression today," we say "Give 'em hell."

The unspoken fear which bedevils friendships between men is, of course, the fear of being seen as a homosexual. Surveys have shown that a majority of all men have been worried about being latent homosexuals at some point in their lives. Almost 40% told Kinsey they had actually had what they thought was a homosexual experience since adolescence, yet their descriptions of these events sounded more friendly than erotic (Kinsey, Pomeroy, and Martin, 1948). Fears of being a latent homosexual are many times more common among men than among women (Hoffman, 1969). Why?

The answer is that the male role so totally prohibits tenderness and affection toward members of the same sex that few men can live a normal lifetime without experiencing supposedly forbidden feelings. Many men inevitably find that they care deeply for—and even love—another man, but believe these warm feelings abnormal and unnatural. Thus the secret, gnawing fear that "I must be one of *those* . . ."

Like the majority of men (as I was greatly relieved to find out later!), I secretly feared at one time in my life that I was a "latent homosexual." In college the affection and caring I felt for my three roommates worried me, because I could sense that it wasn't really *all that* different from the affection I felt for the girlfriends I knew best and liked most. If the truth be known, I cared more genuinely for my male friends at this time than for any female I knew. What's worse, when we were sprawled out somewhere watching TV or reading, and our legs or arms would touch comfortably, it was . . . well, pleasant! Once one of my roommates and I were lying on our old sofa, talking and drinking beer. For some reason—as I recall there wasn't much room— he put his head in my lap with some wisecrack about getting comfortable. We continued talking. But I felt a closeness, a sort of emotional bond that hadn't been there before. And . . .after a while, I felt a very real desire to lightly stroke his hair, the way I would have done had he been a woman. Finally, I said something brilliant, like "Get off me you lazy sonofabitch, you're gettin' heavy."

That seems pretty stupid now, but I don't think my fears were unusual, or my caution unjustified. Men do not take "mistakes" of this sort lightly.

2. The Big Wheel: Success, Status, and the Need to be Looked up To.

> A man can't go out the way he came in, Ben; a man has got to add up to something! (Willie Loman in *Death of a Salesman,* Miller, 1971)

One of the most basic routes to manhood in our society is to be a success: to command respect and be looked up to for what one can do or has achieved. There are several basic ways to accomplish this, but by definition this kind of status is a limited commodity which not every man can achieve.

Wealth and Fame. The most visible and sought-after source of status in our society is what we loosely refer to as "being a success." Success is usually defined in terms of occupational prestige and achievement, wealth, fame, power, and visible positions of leadership. These things usually tend to be correlated; however, *extremely* high standing on any one of them seems to have a very special status quality. The tycoon, the congressman, the movie star, and the sports hero enjoy an automatic kind of status, and will often be viewed as masculine role-models on this basis alone. There's something ineffably masculine about the word "millionaire" or even "the richest man in town." It's also quite helpful to be President of the United States, author of a best-selling novel, or even conductor of a symphony orchestra. Really massive doses of success at almost *anything,* in fact, seem so inherently manly that the "world's Greatest" artist, pianist, chef, hair-dresser, or tiddlywink player is to some extent protected from the taint of unmasculine activity which surrounds less successful members of his profession. Intellectual prominence is also valuable in the right circles, but for most people nothing succeeds quite so well as money. "If Karl, instead of writing a lot about capital, had made a lot of it," said Anna Marx about her famous son, "it would have been much better" (Spiegelman and Schneider, 1974, p. 49).

The Symbols of Success. Simply being a doctor, lawyer, or moderately successful businessman is enough to qualify as success in most social circles. A man who has launched a successful career and is earning an impressive salary can usually enjoy the respect of his family, friends, relatives, co-workers, employees—everyone who is *aware* of his accomplishments. Unfortunately, though, neighbors, casual visitors, passing motorists, and the waiter at The Ritz may not happen to know who's Vice President for Local Sales at Crump Amalgamated—to them he's just a middle-aged schlepper with thinning hair and a pot belly. The answer is simple: a $300 hand-made suit, glove-leather Gucci shoes, and a hand-made attache case of unborn calf.

These symbols are wasteful, of course, but in another more psychological way, they make sense. Quadraphonic stereos playing dusty old Lawrence Welk albums; hosts serving Chivas Regal to business friends who couldn't tell it from Old Overshoe; we may chuckle at what seem to be foolish excesses, but the rewards are not what they seem. What's a little wasted money compared with the precious feeling of Being A Man?

What about men to whom real financial success is out of reach, temporarily or permanently, for reasons of age, social class, or race? Many hunger for it anyway, and seize on its smallest symbols in a parody of material success, for even the fleeting feeling of "being a man" can be precious. Kenneth Clark (1965) has described young black men with menial jobs, who carry empty briefcases to and from work. One such youngster wore a white shirt and tie downtown each day to what he said was his "management trainee" job in a large department store; in reality he was a stock-boy.

Other Routes to Status. Men who haven't "made it" by the standards of the mainstream often find other battlegrounds to fight on, other routes to status before smaller but highly appreciative audiences. A neighborhood bar may have a champion dart thrower, with a standing bet to lick any man in the house. A mailroom may have its fastest sorter, a men's club its stalwart whose record for beer drinking has never been equaled. In truth almost anything pursued seriously can become a source of status. Specialized subgroups often develop their own status ranking systems, sometimes very different from or even opposite to the mainstream male role. Aggressive violence plays a minor part in the general cultural male role, as we'll see later, but in certain juvenile street gangs it serves as the major "currency" on which reputations are based.

Miller (1967) reports that lower-status gang members committed four to six times as many violent, illegal crimes as the high-status members, who had already "made it." Once the low-status men have acquired reputations for bloodthirsty recklessness, they too can "retire" to the relative ease (and safety) of senior status.

One of the most interesting examples of subgroup status is found in the encounter-group, clinically oriented "human potential" movement. In the mainstream male role, showing tender or fearful emotions is distasteful and embarrassing, while being "sensitive" to other people's emotions is fairly irrelevant. In the clinical counter-culture, sensitivity and being "in touch with one's emotions" have been redefined as extremely good. Naturally, the subgroup leaders who are most awesomely in touch with every emotion and can "sense" things in other people that no one else can are . . .men! At such gatherings as Humanistic Psychology and Orthopsychiatry conventions, these super-sensitive Gurus glide around like whacked-out birds of paradise in beads and Indian gowns, followed by their retinues of admirers.

Being "Competent". Ask any man a factual question and you'll get an answer," says a single woman I know. "He may not know a damn thing about it, but he'll make up something rather than say he doesn't know." Men feel a strong need to seem knowledgeable, on top of things, and generally equal to any situation that arises. When a husband and wife are driving in a car and get lost, it's almost always the woman who suggests stopping to ask directions of someone. When a car won't start, men gather around like flies to peer intently at the mysterious innards. "She's probably flooded," sombody grunts knowledgeably.

The act of lovemaking was once considered a natural function, and the male's prerogative at that. With the widespread discussion of female orgasm, not to mention multiple orgasm, and the appearance of hundreds of sex manuals telling men how to bring any woman to the brink of ecstasy in 35 easy steps, a whole new proving ground for male competence (and status) has appeared. "And I didn't have to consult my sex manual even once!" crowed Woody Allen after his night of debauchery in *Play It Again Sam.* "My husband has studied those things so much," said one med student's wife, "I can tell when he's flipping from page forty-one to forty-two."

The Breadwinner Role. Most men seek and long for at least part of their lives in which they feel like a "big wheel." Status of course is a relative thing: A man whose wife looks up to him can feel like a "real man" in relation to her, but not necessarily to anyone else. A shopkeeper who is feared and respected by his employees may feel sublimely masculine at work—but he doesn't look or feel manly when he's asking for a loan at the bank or being ignored by the maitre d' in a fancy restaurant. The famous "fragile male ego" that marriage manuals warn women to be so careful of is one symptom of the status vulnerability most average men must endure. ("Better to let him win a few games of checkers than to put up with a sullen, humiliated man for the rest of the evening," one such guide cautions young women.) For many men the need to feel important is most usually met in role-dictated dominance/submission interactions with women or with traditional labor divisions in the family.

In the traditional nuclear family the male is the only paid worker, the Breadwinner, the Sole Provider. Even if his job is dull and routine, he leaves the home, labors, and returns with "food for the table"—a computerized paycheck with federal, state, and local withholdings, perhaps—but a direct descendant of Neanderthal's haunch of bison. This bastion of status within the family is traditionally available to virtually every male, a haven in which one basic demand of the male role can be satisfied. When unemployment occurs on a wide scale, such as when the chief industry in a small community fails, the psychological consequences to men are often as severe as the economic.

Despite the importance of having a job, an astounding proportion of men do not especially like what they do for a living, the way they spend approximately two-thirds of their waking hours for the better part of their lives. In a series of interviews I conducted to pretest a questionnaire on masculinity, men's answers about their jobs were notably unenthusiastic. "Well, it's a living," said a restaurant manager. "I guess I like it—I been doing it 15 years," said a window dresser. "Hell, I gotta eat," said a car salesman.

These are all men who are far from the pinnacle of success (as are most of us), so perhaps it's not surprising they don't see their jobs as heaven on earth. But a member of my men's consciousness-raising group had a different problem with his job. He's an executive with one of the largest corporations in America, in his early forties, and was making over $50,000 a year in an assignment he actually enjoyed and was good at. *His* problem was an impending promotion. Having proven his competence at this level of the company hierarchy, he was expected to move on to the next level. It meant more money but a substantially different kind of work, which he was fairly sure he wouldn't like as well, and he'd have to commute a lot further. It made sense to stay where he was . . .but he couldn't. For one thing that would label him as a "quitter" in the company, and his chances of ever being promoted later would evaporate. For another he really couldn't resist the urge to move upward, or live with a reputation as a guy who was headed nowhere. He accepted the promotion, and, as predicted, hated his new assignment.

To the blue-collar worker struggling to make ends meet, such executives are a privileged class of rich mandarins, and obviously, in a way, they are. But based on some close observations I'd say there's another fact that's relevant. They're not very happy.

3. The Sturdy Oak: A Manly Air of Toughness, Confidence, and Self-Reliance.

> If you can keep your head when all about you
> Are losing theirs and blaming it on you,
> If you can trust yourself when all men doubt you,
> But make allowance for their doubting too; . . .
>
> If you can force your heart and nerve and sinew
> To serve your turn long after they are gone,
> And so hold on when there is nothing in you
> Except the Will which says to them: "Hold on!" . . .
>
> If you can fill the unforgiving minute
> With sixty seconds' worth of distance run,
> Yours is the Earth and everything that's in it,
> And—which is more—you'll be a Man, my son!
>   (From "If," by Rudyard Kipling)

> You had to have some quality that was hard to pin down, a certain kind
> of confidence, a little swagger but not in a boastful way, an easiness, a style,
> an air of casual good nature, of leadership that wasn't sought but seemed to
> come natural. You couldn't pin it down, but you could see it in a person.
> (Wakefield, 1970, p. 195)

There's another basic theme in our culture's positive prescription for masculinity which has little to do with success or traditional measures of social
status and has seldom been noticed or mentioned by social science. Some of
the widely admired figures in American motion pictures are men who conspic-
uously *lack* social status: William Holden in *Stalag 17,* Bogart in *The African
Queen,* Paul Newman in *Cool Hand Luke,* Marlon Brando in *Streetcar Named
Desire,* John Wayne in *True Grit,* and many more. What they have is harder
to identify, for it seems more a matter of style than tangible achievement, and
its ingredients are variable. There's a distinct sense of strong manliness, however, not usually belligerent or looking for trouble, but tough and self-pos-
sessed, which somehow emerges from the variable combination of quiet
confidence, self-reliance, determination, indifference to opposition, courage,
and seriousness. Most of all, there's a sense of mental and physical toughness
—the big and little signs which signal that "here is a man," a force to be
reckoned with, not a straw that blows with the changing wind. It doesn't
matter so much *what* he's doing, whether holding "the system" together, like
Marshall Dillion of *Gunsmoke,* or striking at its very foundation, like John
Galt of *Atlas Shrugged;* what matters is *how* he's doing it. There's a self-
confidence and seriousness in all these figures which demands respect even in
defeat.

There is something rather unreal about this formidable creature that every
one of us is supposed to be—something illogical, impossible, and, for most of
us, deeply thrilling. Growing up in America as life became increasingly civilized, urban, and complex, we sat in darkened movie theatres and watched

these unreal men, fashioned as much by a collective cultural demand as by some Hollywood script writer, larger and far more compelling than our real lives. We watched Gary Cooper standing all alone on that long, dusty street, in *High Noon,* watched by the town that would not stand beside him: ready to die, but not to run. Usually the man we longed to be was big and fast on the draw like that, but sometimes it was a seemingly ordinary guy who showed real strength when the chips were down. Montgomery Clift's unforgettable Corporal Prewitt, in *From Here to Eternity,* couldn't be broken by anything a whole army could dish out, and he showed us that "real men" come in all sizes. The moving *Nothing But a Man* showed us that they come in all colors too; the film's battered hero finally turns on his Uncle-Tom father-in-law, who is berating him to accept white supremacy, and delivers the punch line of a powerful film: "You been bendin' down so long, you don't know how to stand up straight; you ain't a man at all."

A man cannot always win in this world, but he can always stand his ground win or lose ... *stand up straight;** something in that metaphor of standing captures the image of nonbelligerent strength we so admire. A joke about an old German Jew and a young Nazi illustrates it well: A Nazi soldier is watching an old Jew hobble by. As the man passes, he shouts: "Swine!" The old Jew slowly turns and replies: "Cohen, pleased to meet you." Even in desperate circumstances, a man can stand up and be a *mensch.*

Another of these Sturdy Oak qualities is self-reliance—the idea that a man should always be "his own man," should think for himself. One of the most popular motion pictures in recent years was *A Man for All Seasons* (Best Picture of 1966), the story of Sir Thomas More's fight to the death against Henry VIII. Few of the modern viewers so enthralled by this 16th century story could have had much enthusiasm for More's position—that divorce was immoral. What was so majestic was the spectacle of one man's personal conviction arrayed against the might of imperial England, refusing to accept any compromise which would save his life.

Strong and independent in action, the *style* of such a man is calm and composed, unimpressed by pain or danger. "Of course it hurts," smiled Peter O'Toole as *Lawrence of Arabia,* as a match burned into his fingertips; "the trick, you see, is not to *care* that it hurts." It goes far beyond the mere avoidance of "feminine" emotionality; it's the cultivation of a stoic, imperturbable persona, just this side of catatonia. A "real man" never worries about death or loses his manly "cool."

> "To hell with the handerchief," said Walter Mitty scornfully. He took one last drag on his cigarette and snapped it away. Then, with that faint, fleeting smile playing about his lips, he faced the firing squad; erect and motionless, proud and disdainful, Walter Mitty the Undefeated, inscrutable to the last. ("The Secret Life of Walter Mitty," James Thurber, 1964)

*As the Everly Brothers would wail in a popular song called *Cathy's Clown:* "A man can't crawl, he's got to stand tall, or he's not a man at all."

Physical Strength, Athletic Prowess. For adults, athletic skill by itself is not strongly related to the appearance of masculine toughness. Famous sports figures such as Tom Seaver, Bob Cousey, Sandy Koufax, and Rod Laver are obviously skillful, but they don't have an exceptionally tough, or masculine, public image. Their reputations as celebrities are based as much on status and public exposure as on being sports figures *per se.* Professional athletes who do have a strong image of manliness aren't always the most successful, but they usually embody one of the traits we'll examine in the next section. They have a reputation for being unnecessarily violent (e.g., Ty Cobb, Derek Sanderson, Marlin McKeever) or they're famous for their off-the-field hell-raising (Paul Hornung, Babe Ruth, Billy Kilmer, Joe Kapp).

Physical size and strength are more directly relevant to the Sturdy Oak image. A physically big man is usually able to stand up to physical intimidation more easily than a small one, so he may be called on less often to prove himself. But when a big man loses to a smaller man or appears to have no "guts" in the crunch, he becomes an object of scorn, the butt of innumerable jokes and stories. *The Harder They Fall* was a popular Bogart film about a titanic boxer from South America who bowls over his seemingly terrified opponents—in fixed fights. He really can't take a punch, you see, but nobody knows that. When he finally faces an honest fighter he crumbles, and his total disgrace is symbolized by a bout of crying. The hard-bitten sports writer (Bogart), at a fraction of the giant's body weight, is obviously much more of a Man.

The Sturdy Oak and the Average Guy. The need to be seen as a tough customer operates on Park Avenue as well as the gridiron. In executive jobs in which effectiveness can't be gauged directly, promotions often go to a man who has built the best reputation for toughness. In one company it's fairly common practice for a new regional manager to fire 15 of his 60 branch managers, without regard to competence, just to show his superiors he's tough enough to handle the new job. At another large corporation it was once arranged for someone to rise from the audience during a presentation by a new manager, walk up to the charts he was using and throw them to the floor, stomp on them, and return to his seat. If the speaker kept his cool while this happened, and then continued his presentation without appearing upset, he had passed the test (Fasteau, 1974, p. 123).

The kind of confidence and toughness required by a test like this, and portrayed so often in popular fiction, is an idealized image, not an accurate picture of the way flesh-and-blood males usually behave. Yet this deeply socialized ideal can exert a powerful strain on men's attitudes, values, and judgments; it can kindle a sudden longing in the mildest of men to appear tough and decisive, whether or not the situation calls for it. A businessman may cling to a losing investment rather than concede that he miscalculated. A father may decide on a stern punishment for his son and stick to it, when understanding and support are what's needed. A husband may insist on lifting heavy objects or fighting a fire in the attic by himself. Women sometimes reinforce this need, for reasons related to their own sex role and the desire to feel sheltered and protected. As one young woman candidly put it "I want a real man, someone I can lean on, depend on." But the man's inner response is often: "Oh God! How can I be that? I don't know the answers; I'm as scared as she is." Like Willie Loman in Arthur Miller's *Death of a Salesman,* we often respond with bluster and braggadocio that fools almost no one; how many women must privately say, like Willie's wife "He's only a little boat looking for a harbor."

4. Give 'Em Hell: The Aura of Aggression, Violence, and Daring

There is nothing inherently or necessarily bad about being a success, earning respect, or having confidence and determination. It can be oppressive to *have to be* these things, but the qualities themselves are not inherently undesirable by usual standards.

There is another deep and rich vein in the male sex role that also smacks of strength and toughness but is *not* fundamentally wholesome, constructive, or benign. It is the need to hurt, to conquer, to embarrass, to humble, to outwit, to punish, to defeat, or most basically, in Horney's useful phrase, "to move against people." Like the other deep themes in the male role, this behavior takes many forms, some more disguised than others. But whereas what we have called the Sturdy Oak qualities encompass essentially defensive resources, the underlying theme here is one of attack.

This male penchant for moving against people is not always directed at the strong and powerful, however. There is a disturbing experiment by Titley and Viney (1969) in which aggression (in the form of electric shocks) toward a helpless victim was studied. Women tended to deliver less intense shocks to a victim who appeared to be physically disabled than they did to a normal victim. Men did exactly the opposite. . . .

"Johnny, I Hardly Knew Ye": Toward Revision of the Theory of Male Psychosexual Development

Kay M. Tooley

Theoretical discussions about psychosexual development and sexual identity have focused on male development as baseline and female development as a variation from that norm. This is a proper and inevitable history for the science/art of psychoanalysis, originating as it did in self-observation and self-report. Most of the selves observed and reported were male. The language, metaphor, and psychic history were male. Since Freud, and including him, there has been considerable dissatisfaction with the revised female editions of psychosexual development, which has led to complicated and almost impenetrable revisions of revisions of that original theory. Female consultants were admitted to the mysteries, coached in the language and metaphor, and invited to, now, please tell us, "What does a woman want?" Practicing therapists seem to be surprisingly unaware that female patients also coached in the historical male metaphor by interpretation (and under a heavy economic and emotional pressure not to "resist" such interpretations), are highly likely to speak the language that makes sense to the therapist—and thus to confirm his theoretical bias.

Fortunately, men and women have more common history as human beings than divergent history as sexual beings. Fortunately, metaphor is a strong cognitive tool, often translatable by the listener into something usefully applicable to her own situation. As a result, women patients are often helped considerably by the analytic method which, again fortunately, often leaves the theory far behind in its individual practical application. However, women patients are complaining more frequently that "often" and "oblique" are not enough, that they are tired of hand-me-down, theory-based interpretations; they are "resisting" by leaving treatment with male therapists in search of women practitioners—who may or may not represent an improvement. "The psychology of women," as it now exists, is a shadowy negative of the psychology of men, and can be successfully formulated only if male psychology is reassessed and considerably revised.

A problem in revision of theory is escaping the reification of ideas and language inevitable in any theory and technique with a history. One must find a different language, a different perspective, for both viewing and evaluating the familiar data of human experience upon which theory is based. This essay

From the *American Journal of Orthopsychiatry,* Vol. 47, No. 2 (April 1977), pp. 184–195. Copyright © 1977 the American Orthopsychiatric Association, Inc. Reproduced by permission.

"Johnny, I Hardly Knew Ye," [11] is an early Irish war-protest song sung by a woman to a mutilated returning soldier-husband.

will employ a female perspective on male sexual development, and a conceptual framework more akin to developmental psychology than to psychoanalysis. An effort will be made to relate this perspective and language to common clinical truisms observed so widely for such a long period of time as to be generally accepted as knowledge gained from everyone's professional experience. The thesis to be defended is that male theorists and practitioners have made virtues of the harsh facts of male socialization; that these practices have unhappy repercussions in the male ego and in the culture as a whole; and that these harsh realities are modifiable only if they are identified and understood.

To begin with a metaphor, suppose we had studied two groups of males who had been divided into group A and group B at age eight on the basis of teacher observation and evaluation, test assessments, and developmental history. Group A boys walked earlier, talked earlier, made an easier adjustment to school, learned to read better and faster, and were relaxed and comfortable in the school environment. Group A boys also were rarely enuretic or assaultive or hyperkinetic. They contributed only about 20% of the group referred for psychotherapy. Group A boys had better interpersonal skills and a more highly developed capacity for empathy. Group B boys, conversely, showed significantly more immaturity, symptomatic behavior, and lack of capacity for adjusting to different environments. They contributed 80% of the child guidance population and the population of children referred for remedial education. Furthermore, group A and group B boys are known to be equal in number, to have the same cultural and socioeconomic background and the same access to inherited capabilities.

On the basis of such differences, we would infer that group A had had a much more benign growth-inducing parenting in the important preschool years than did group B. Furthermore, we would be most interested in investigating further just how child-rearing practices differed from group A to group B. Observation and interviews with the parents would establish that corporal punishment and shaming were less often used with the group A boys, and that they were permitted much more physical closeness and cuddling that were those in group B—and until a later age. Group B boys were discouraged in their efforts to be close even when their siblings were not; they were encouraged to play at a considerable distance from mother, while group A mothers encouraged their children to play close by, particularly in strange and potentially frightening circumstances. Mothers talked more often and at greater length with their Group A children from infancy than with the group B children. They also confessed they had felt closer, warmer, and more at ease with their group A children, usually on the basis of perceived similarity: "He looks like my side of the family." However, fathers also treated their group A children more gently and affectionately than their group B children. Both parents were less likely to stress performance with their group A children. In spite of this, group A children learned skills such as talking, feeding, and dressing themselves earlier, and generally had an earlier and easier toilet training. Their better school performance has been mentioned previously.

Of course, the group A children are girls and the group B children are boys. [1, 2, 7, 12, 13, 14, 15, 17, 18, 19, 20, 21, 26] However, in converting these observations into theories of child development, we have stoutly resisted what seems an obvious conclusion: that girls are more intelligently, kindly, and gently reared than boys, and that this has positive effects that are readily observable in the latency period.* When other factors are held constant—socioeconomic background, genetic endowment, access to education—the child who performs better socially and intellectually (we would usually infer) has had a superior preschool home experience than his less well adjusted counterpart.

To examine the impact on little boys of this subtly disadvantageous handling, we must remember that most little boys have sisters. Those who do not have sisters receive just as much physical punishment and physical rejection (independence training) because that is what this society tends to prescribe for boys. Psychoanalytic theory acknowledges the presence of sisters in families to establish the basis for castration complex ("upon observing his little sister's penisless state . . . ," etc.). From developmental psychology, we can infer that young boys have an opportunity to observe quite a lot more: their sisters are spanked much less, cuddled much more, spoken to more often and more gently, and praised more often whether older or younger. Boys' desires to cuddle and experience physical closeness are discouraged with varying degrees of harshness.

Physical rejection is evidenced quite early in mother-son interactions.[10] One suspects that boys' early and obvious genital reaction to physical pleasure worries their mothers. It seems "sexual," and this tends to make mothers uneasy. Feeling guilty about stimulating "sexual" reactions in their sons, they may impose physical separation and isolation from their person both earlier and more drastically than they do with their daughters (which predisposes males to the depressive-aggressive world view that will be discussed later). Maternal implementation of the separation-individuation task is also significantly different for boys and girls. A central aspect of the mothers' functioning in this task is supervision of the mindless motility of their toddlers: mothers make sure that toddlers do not learn about the physical environment too harshly and too early.[25] Little boys are more restless and more motile from birth;[18] they, more likely than their sisters, will climb fifteen times to the top of the table. Fatigue and resentment may lead mothers to allow boys, more often than girls, to learn about falls and bumps from experience. Boys learn about the hard and painful unyieldingness of the physical world at a time when their physical and mental development does not permit the lesson to be readily mastered. Little girls get hurt less and later, and so more easily learn to "be

---

*That girls lose this developmental impetus in adolescence is another important social phenomenon but beyond the scope of this paper.

careful." Boys feel more pain, and consequently more anger at their physical environment—and this at a stage of development when "world" is insufficiently differentiated from mother. Thus, mother-son alienation received another reinforcement. Little boys' anger is complementary to their mothers' sense of guilt, a complementarity resurrected in adult male-female relationships. (He blames her for what is unsatisfactory in his life, and she accepts the blame). If, on top of all this, sex-typing is enforced in their families, little boys (who, as yet, have no concept of their fathers' work) are made to feel ashamed of their wish to join mothers and sisters in the cooking, cleaning, and other household activities that make up the day.

As they move into latency, boys find that their sisters are permitted tomboyish activities to a much greater degree than boys are permitted girlish activities. Furthermore, any budding expertise their sisters show in male domains is likely to elicit parental satisfaction and compliments, often a simultaneous source of pain and shame for young boys: "She swims (or "plays baseball" or "fixes bicycles") better than he does!" It is no wonder that males often carry to adulthood a terror and hatred of competitive and competent females, and indeed feel "castrated" in observing their performance.

Now is the time, perhaps, for a slight digression. It is a clinical corollary that a fear which is excessively preoccupying and only remotely probable often indicates an unconscious wish. Thus, the wealthy man who spends his conscious hours in an anxious horror of poverty might well unconsciously wish to be rid of his money. A woman whose frequent fear of rape dominates her thinking and activity might be supposed to wish unconsciously to be raped. A man who worries all his life about losing his penis might be supposed unconsciously to wish for that state. Other writers have pointed out that castration fear has all of the hallmarks of a reaction formation—a wish to be penisless, which is unacceptable to the conscious and rational mind.[10] Some have related to it womb envy; others have hypothesized a prehistoric past leaving a racial memory of matriarchy—a time in history of the human race when it was decidedly more advantageous and pleasant to be a woman.[27] But a thesis pursued in this paper is that men have a personal past, repressed and distorted by adulthood, in which it must have seemed to them that it was much more pleasant and advantageous to be a girl. Like most childhood traumas, when the circumstances are known and interpreted the wish is much less shaming and irrational. Historically, the wish in the little boy to be penisless is sensible, a realistic judgment based on daily observation and experience. A castration wish is ego-alien to the adult male only because repression has obscured the excellent reasons for it. Instead, his ego translates the wish in currently reasonable terms: to wish to be castrated is to wish to be disfigured, maimed, unsexed.

The child's practical, although inaccurate, observation is that "no penis" equals "girl." The adult male has learned that castration does not equal woman but only non-man. (This point has occasioned much mysterious confusion in psychoanalytic theory.) Hence, the childish and conscious castration wish must be transmuted into postchildhood castration fear. The boy's wish to be female, based on a realistic perception of girls' favored treatment, is not supported by adult perceptions (women do not have a favored status in adult society) and is thus even more unacceptable to the man's conscious ego. "Penis envy" in adult women is much less at odds with current reality perceptions —seems much less "crazy" to the observing ego—because money, power, and freedom of choice are more available to adult men that to adult women. This represents a complete shift in the status quo of the sexes from their preschool days.

The girl, with the experience of warm and successful relationships within the home, steps into the school society with confidence. The little boy hesitates; the new situation seems to him to promise even less than the one he is leaving. He retreats and focuses his need for pleasure and self-approval on his body, specifically his penis. He has learned to cathect his whole body much less than girls do, because important others have seemed to cathect it less. It is the same body that was underprotected in the separation-individuation phase, the body that was the source of frequent pain at that time. Socialization practices in respect to the boy have emphasized that the expression of grief over pain is babyish and unmanly. Further, experiencing pain and inflicting it on others is presented as "fun" for the boy but not for the girl. This implements the retreat from the cathexis of the whole body to the cathexis of the penis, and a retreat from object relationships to a preference for part-object relationships.

The boy turns his interest away from the world of people to the world of objects and things (in which he shows an early competence, in contrast to the girl's early interpersonal and language competence). His already present anger and sense of rejection[24] is enlarged by his recognition that the new caretakers, teachers, are also put off by his fidgety action-oriented mode, his aggression, and his relative lack of interpersonal skills.[16] Masturbation becomes for him a dependable and always accessible source of reassurance and tension release. The latency expansion in his cognitive development consolidates his early predisposition for genital preoccupation and for the genitalization of his life experience. His competence in the world of things gains instinctual impetus from a focus on the "penis-like" aspect of things. Here we are indebted to the huge accumulation of psychoanalytic case descriptions that have unearthed the "penis perception" as the basis of the male cognitive experience: "treeness" is *trunk*, not leaf or fruit; "eyeness" is orbs with a projection between, not a hollow receptable of sensation; cars are powerful thrusting objects, not warm and relatively effortless means of being carried about; birds are erectile tissue, not free-moving nesting creatures; and the same with fish and dragons and tadpoles and dinosaurs and mosquitos, telephone poles and toothpicks, knives and feathers, toes and teeth, and everything that moves and is and does (and is threatened) on the face of the earth.

In this symbolic language, leaves are never separated offspring that wither and die. They are separated penises, so that even fear of death can be diluted to fear of castration. Concern with the penis substitutes for concern about all other threatening life relationships. This aids in averting anxiety and promoting autonomy; but while the advantages have been well publicized in the literature on male sexuality, the dangers and drawbacks to individual men and the civilization they control have gone unrecognized, unstated, and unconsidered.

In his lonely, angry state, the little boy feels that his penis is all he has; he will treasure it, worry about it, protect it all of his life, often distorting his entire life experience, his judgment of the world, into a genital-endangering conspiracy of other men, women, even children who would emasculate him if he were off-guard for a moment. It is at this point that we are indeed trapped by our male-evolved conceptual language, in which male attributes are implicitly good and healthy, female attributes the obverse.[4] ("Aggressive," in this conceptual language, conveys "assaultive" as well as "assertive"; "autonomous" connotes "unrelated" as well as "inner directed." As applied to women, "passive" means "inert" as well as "receptive"; "submissive" suggests "obedience" as well as the capacity for compromise and reconciliation.)

When research subjects are of late adolescent rather than of latency age, reports of findings are so dominated and so hopelessly confounded by stereotypical language that one must turn to the operational definition to understand what is in fact being measured. For example, if an adolescent is found to be easily mobilized by peer opinion to turn on a scapegoat, does this measure capacity for aggression or for group compliance? It is a truism among motivational researchers that their measures "work" for men but not for women. In other words, men know what motivates men, but not what motivates women. Back we go to, "What does a woman want?" Not such a puzzle: enough freedom of opportunity to test her head and heart, and enough money and power to insulate her from poverty and physical insult. Not so different from what a man wants. The deeper question, instead, concerns how a woman's strategy for achieving what she wants compares to a man's; the differences are great.

One study, which has taken the language of experimentation carefully into account, will be considered here in some detail. Goldstine[8] used projective measures (TAT) to examine the interpersonal modes and world views of male and female college students. Although her findings are familiar, the language of her summary—the processing of surplus meanings and surplus values of descriptive words—is unusual. It should be kept in mind that neither the young men nor the young women in this study had yet tested the outside world of work and hard reality, so that the views expressed had to be shaped largely by early socialization.

Goldstine found that the college men studied differed markedly from the women in their commitment to an "impersonal" rather than an "interpersonal" orientation. Males did not see the world they were about to enter as a place of potential satisfaction, and did not expect people to like them, protect them, and support them. These college men, again in contrast to the women, tended to define relationships in terms of their potential for hurt and frustration; they preferred to terminate relationships and withdraw, rather than work to improve them. Males conceptualized a dog-eat-dog world in which their own well-being must come at someone else's expense; conversely, the well-being of others was viewed as a source of personal chagrin and deprivation.

Here, it might be argued that these young men were merely expressing accurate reality testing. But the point is precisely that the dominant definition of "reality" is shaped largely by this masculine bias,[22] which holds that gratification of another invariably diminishes one's own possibility of being gratified —a depressive world view familiar to all clinicians and characterized by the absence of a clear concept of "enough" (enough guns, enough butter, enough money, enough possessions, enough power, enough motility).

Goldstine's male subjects expressed a need to preserve a sense of power by choosing to take rather than to be given to ("dominant" rather than "submissive," in the established terminology), to coerce rather than to convince; they preferred to leave rather than face their long-endured fear of being left. No wonder the civilized virtues of compromise, and openness to the ideas, needs, and desires of others are, in practice, so often and so easily discarded; male psychology perceives these qualities as feminine "submissiveness" and "passivity"—as emasculation. Fear of emasculation, whether expressed as the boyhood fear of castration or the grownup male fear of impotence, remains the core organizer of adult male life experience, a natural outgrowth of the little boy's defensive phallocentrism. (One writer,[9] attempting to make a virtue of the harsh necessities of male socialization, pointed out the male's superior "self-boundary," in contrast to female "boundarylessness." To the present writer, a more apt comparison would be between two different kinds of boundaries: the Berlin Wall, for example, patrolled night and day, and the US-Canada border. The difference lies in the perception of the outsider as enemy.)

By adulthood, the penis carries such a heavy responsibility for the whole range of self-esteem and pleasure possibilities that its functioning is a source of great anxiety for the man. Any negative feedback from the environment may trigger impotence and a typically male effort to externalize blame for this impotence. This disproportionate anger, evoked by small and inevitable life insults, constitutes a constant problem, even a danger for the man. Should a co-worker get his promotion (and even though other gratifying work possibilities remain), the man is not just momentarily discouraged, but is "emasculated" by a malevolent powerful male; the result is much greater fear, anger, and demoralization than the event warrants. If a neighbor runs the lawnmower over his daffodils, the man hasn't lost a few flowers that were going to fade in a week anyway; he has been "castrated." If another car cuts in front of him on the expressway, it is not a fleeting annoyance, not even a dangerous fleeting annoyance; it's a major operation—a castration. This exaggerated response to minor incidents is often justified to the conscious male ego by "the *principle of the thing!*"

Women have always been mystified by male willingness to bloody each other over incidents that seem trivial, while men have been incensed because women do not seem to give a comparable damn about the "principle of the thing" ("deficient superego"). Men's hearts—bruised, battered, strained through a lifetime of such daily anger and fear—break down in middle age at four times the rate of women's (even when the circumstances, such as life stress, are taken into account). Medical efforts have been made to salve those hearts with estrogen, as though one could confer belatedly some balm of female durability. I am suggesting that it is not the stressfulness of their lives but the surplus meaning of the daily small "castrations" and "emasculations," and the consequent rage and fear, that wears out too many men too early.

Cultural pressures and socialization practices have, by adulthood, placed a heavy responsibility on the male genital, far heavier than nature ever intended. Successful sex therapy for impotence involves divesting the penis of a symbolic responsibility for all forms of pleasure, competence, and achievement. Such therapy frequently involves a phase in which men are specifically forbidden intercourse and encouraged belatedly to explore the possibilities of the whole body's sensuality without the internal demand to prove himself in a sexual athletic competition. Unfortunately, as women become freer to express enthusiasm for intercourse, men are becoming more frequently impotent. Goldstine's work would indicate that it fits better with the masculine stereotype to "take" pleasure from a somewhat unwilling donor, rather than to cooperate in a pleasure-seeking enterprise. "Co-operation" is a rather alien concept. To the man, it seems instead a "competition" in which the evidence that he is "finished" is unconcealable, while her state remains a mystery. Stoller[23] has added another insight: much of male sexual arousal is at base vengeful, a retaliation against a depriving mother. Woman's past unwillingness to gratify is undone by each sexual encounter, and present unwillingness is itself a component of his satisfaction.

Inevitably, men turn the fear of emasculation and impotence on women, because historically and unconsciously it was woman who devalued their penises to begin with. As mentioned above, women accept the projection of blame because of their own conflict over managing both the little boy's sexuality and his need for dependency gratification. It is also true that women are much safer targets for aggression that are other men. A case in point is the long submerged but widespread tradition of wife-beating, conceived as properly masculine and quite legal. Neither male nor female mental health experts would approve of wife-beating. However, male practitioners, along with the rest of the male world, do fear and distrust the active and independently achieving female, widely felt to be "castrating" and "unfeminine." I would suggest that a competent, competitive, female peer evokes a memory not of mother, daughter, or wife, but of *sister,* that formidable rival of old. Their barometer of self-esteem may indeed register alarm if men must deal with her again, and they will refuse to deal with her if they can—and they can and do.

The profession is guilty of promoting another pernicious myth that involves the same propaganda of inertness as the above; that is, the myth of motherhood as a passive experience—mother eternally rocking and breastfeeding her infants—a fantasy that provides sure and certain indication of a traumatic dependency weaning in the male professionals who, along with other men, prefer it. It is an attempt to rewrite developmental history to dethrone retrospectively the "giantess of the nursery"—that busy, absolute monarch of the preschool world who coerces and trains and forbids, as well as dispenses at will, naps and cookies and spankings and kisses.

Discussion

This paper has proposed a need for a reordering of traditional hypotheses about male psychosexual socialization. It has been suggested that current theory represents a defensive effort to make virtues of the harsh realities of male socialization. In counterpoint, this essay reaffirms what other writers have suggested: "the psychology of women . . . represent[s] a deposit of the desires and disappointments of men"[10] (p. 326).

There are implications for clinical practice in a reformulation of the theory of male development—the same imperatives the mental health professions have always acknowledged: If there are practices and beliefs that poison human relationships, restrict human potential, and limit capacity for available enjoyment and pleasure, then we have an obligation to work to identify them, to counteract them, and to modify the practices and beliefs that gave rise to them.

Are the facts of male socialization modifiable? He *is* born with higher motility, and his genital difference *will* be grounds for lack of maternal empathic identification. Mothers have sensed that there is a lack in their capacity to understand and care for all of their children; as a result, they have invited a host of surrogates—Freuds and Spocks and Gesells—into the nursery to replace the missing expertise of a crucial, long-absent figure who does understand little boys, who does value motility, and who has a high investment in the welfare of his family. I am referring, of course, to fathers. It is time for fathers to come out of the closet where they have been half-ashamedly treasuring their pleasure, pride, and interest in their babies, and where their contributions have been classified as a kind of second-rate imitation of mothering. Fathers have, on occasion, been assigned the valuable function of "mothering" mothers in the demanding postnatal years.[5] This is an important and too often underestimated function. However, we need to confront a different question. What attitudes and services can fathers supply babies and small children that mothers cannot? I submit that the sad lacks in a small boy's life result from his father's exile, not from his mother's malevolence, although I can certainly understand why male analysts and analysands might have perceived this differently.[6]

Let us consider the question of male motility—a problem from the earliest days of life. A wakeful baby is often a crying baby, one more likely to arouse a sense of maternal ineffectiveness. A highly mobile toddler is more likely to need constant surveillance and pursuit, resulting in more maternal anxiety, fatigue, and resentment—as will a four-year-old who *must* crawl through the sewer under construction in the next block. Who, mother or father, is more likely to see this active exploration as muscular achievement, as brave mischief, as a valuable and not merely dangerous quality? If a two-and-a-half-year-old is still in diapers, although his sisters were "clean" by eighteen months, and if he grows into an eight-year-old who can't pass a mud puddle without giving in to a desire for total immersion, which of his parents will be better able to dredge up empathic memories of being thought "messy?" Fathers can and will, if we permit and even teach them to be affectionate and sympathetic toward their own little-boy selves.

Most mothers, most of the time, are fond of fathers (having had in their own past considerable loving experience with the genre). If fathers are present when their sons are acting up, if they cope with these behaviors and process them as positive, mothers will come to see them as positive also. The inborn qualities of the little male may come to be a source of *parental* pride, rather than *maternal* concern.

Similarly, if an infant male's penile erection after a warm bath or after baby play is greeted by the amused appreciation of his father, it is not going to be viewed as a perversion by his mother—no matter what the experts say. (As a matter of fact, we must confront the possibility that mothers are simply going to be much less interested in experts if fathers are available to do fathering.) If it is true that women generally enjoy a wider sensual experience and a greater interpersonal tolerance, It is also true that men generally enjoy a greater freedom and ease about sexuality. If a woman alone feels guilty about a male infant's obvious sexual/sensual response, a woman with her husband at her elbow will feel secure with the world's finest chaperone. At the very least, that baby boy might be quickly shifted to the different lap of a different playmate rather than relegated with affective coolness to the floor or the playpen. (I can feel my male colleagues beginning to fret about homosexuality and would remind them that there is no evidence that homosexuality results from warmly collaborative parenting. It is more likely to result from the separation and alienation of the sexes, which our own theories have done considerable to foster.)

If little boys had a less traumatic dependency weaning relative to little girls, they might be less aggressive, less distrustful, and certainly less hostile to women; they might have more highly developed interpersonal skills and verbal skills. As a consequence, elementary school would not compound the trauma of the preschool environment. The boys would not need to retreat into narcissistic reliance on the penis. They would have the skills and the affective "bank account" to develop confidence in their ability to obtain affection and earn approval.

And then would come the millenium. (One is due in only 23 years.) The long reign of terror of King Oedipus would be over at last. We could exorcise the fearful demon who insists that if good things are shared they are lost, and that "too much" is the only possible antidote to "too little." Man's ancient grievance against woman, whose insistence on her freedom to know and to choose caused his expulsion from the Garden of Eden, could be softened by an understanding that there are other gardens, other possibilities for peace and comfort; he would no longer need to restrict, punish, and coerce her in retaliation for his expulsion.

The physical environment might become something to be mutually tended and nurtured as the sum of all possible gardens, rather than an object that must be walled, defended, assaulted, and despoiled if needs are to be met. When we look back at a long life and say, "I've had enough!", it may be an expression of hopes fulfilled rather than an exclamation of angry despair.

"And they never will get our sons again, Johnny, I'm swearin' to ye!"[11]

References

1. Anastasi, A., and Foley, J. 1949. *Differential Psychology: Individual and Group Differences in Behavior* (2nd Ed.). Crowell-Collier-Macmillan, New York.
2. Bardwick, J. 1971. Dependency, passivity, and aggression. In *Psychology of Women,* J. Bardwick, ed. Harper and Row, New York.
3. Bermann, E. 1973. *Scapegoat: The Impact of Death-Fear on an American Family.* University of Michigan Press, Ann Arbor.
4. Broverman, I. et al. 1970. Sex role stereotypes and clinical judgments of mental health. *J. Consult. Clin. Psychol.* 34:1–7.
5. Cohen, M. 1966. Personal identity and sexual identity. *Psychiatry* 29:1–14.
6. Earls, F. 1976. The fathers (not the mothers): their importance and influence with infants and young children. *Psychiatry* 39:209–226.
7. Goldberg, S., and Lewis, M. 1972. Play behavior in the year old infant: early sex differences. *In Readings on the Psychology of Women,* J. Bardwick, ed. Harper and Row, New York.
8. Goldstine, T. 1974. Impersonal and interpersonal orientations in the concept of autonomy: a study of sex differences. Doctoral dissertation, University of Michigan, Ann Arbor.
9. Gutmann, D. 1975. Women and the conception of ego strength. *Merrill Palmer Quart.* 11:229–240.
10. Horney, K. 1926. The flight from womanhood. *Inter. J. Psychoanal.* 7:324–339.
11. "Johnny, I hardly knew ye." Irish folk song (author unknown). In *Songs of Mother Ireland.* Associated Recordings Company, London, W. 10.
12. Kagan, J. 1964. Acquisition and significance of sex-typing and sex-role identity. In *Review of Child Development Research,* M. Hoffman and L. Hoffman, eds. Russell Sage Foundation, New York.
13. Kagan, J., and Lewis, M. 1965. Studies of attention in the human infant. *Merrill Palmer Quart.* 11:95–127.
14. Kelly, F., and Berry, C. 1931. *Special Education: The Handicapped and the Gifted.* White House Conference on Child Health and Protection, Appleton, New York.
15. Kopel, D., and Geerded, H. 1933. A survey of clinical services for poor readers. *J. Ed. Psychol. Monogr.* 13:209–224.
16. Lippitt, R., and Gold, M. 1959. Classroom social structures as a mental health problem. *J. Soc. Issues* 15:40–50.

17. Maccoby, E. 1966. Sex differences in intellectual functioning. In *The Development of Sex Differences,* E. Maccoby, ed. Stanford University Press, Stanford, Calif.
18. Moss, H. 1967. Sex, age, and state as determinants of mother infant interaction. *Merrill Palmer Quart.* 13:19–36.
19. Schaefer, E., and Bayley, N. 1963. Maternal behavior, child behavior, and their intercorrelations from infancy through adolescence. *Monogr. Soc. Res. Child Develpm.* (28):3.
20. Schuell, H. 1947. *Differences Which Matter: A Study of Boys and Girls.* Bon Boeckman-Jones, Austin, Texas.
21. Sears, R., Ran, L., and Alpert, R. 1965. *Identification and Child Rearing.* Stanford University Press, Stanford, Calif.
22. Simmel, G. "Philosophische Kultur" (unavailable in English). See citation in, HORNEY. K., above.
23. Stoller, R. 1976. Sexual excitement. *Arch. Gen. Psychiat.* 33:899–909.
24. Terman, L., and Tyler, L. 1954. Psychological sex differences. In *A manual of Child Psychology,* L. Carmichael, ed. John Wiley, New York.
25. Tooley, K. 1974. Words, actions and 'acting out': their role in the pathology of violent children. *Inter. Rev. Psycho-Anal.* 1:341–351.
26. Witkin, H. et al. 1962. *Psychological Differentiation.* John Wiley, New York.

Cultural Contradictions and Sex Roles: The Masculine Case

Mirra Komarovsky

In a rapidly changing society, normative malintegration is commonly assumed to lead to an experience of strain. Earlier research (Komarovsky, 1946) on cultural contradictions and the feminine sex role showed that women at an eastern college suffered uncertainty and insecurity because the norms for occupational and academic success conflicted with norms for the traditional feminine role. A replication (Wallin, 1950) at a western university reported agreement in the questionnaire data, but the interview material led the investigator to conclude that the problem was less important to the women than the earlier study had suggested. However, Wallin pointed out that, in his replication, the respondents were oriented to marriage, while the Komarovsky study had included an appreciable number of women oriented to careers. This finding tended to support the view that women who were satisfied with the traditional female role would show less strain when confronted with contrary expectations than women who hoped to have both a rewarding career and a rewarding marriage.

Men are also confronted with contradictory expectations. For example, the traditional norm of male intellectual superiority conflicts with a newer norm of intellectual companionship between the sexes. This research investigated the

Reprinted from the *American Journal of Sociology* (January 1973), pp. 873–884, by permission of The University of Chicago Press. © 1973 by The University of Chicago. All rights reserved. A full report of the findings has been published in Mirra Komarovsky, *Dilemmas of Masculinity: A Study of College Youth,* New York: W. W. Norton & Co., 1976.

extent of masculine strain experienced by 62 college males randomly from the senior class of an Ivy League male college. The study included a variety of status relationships, but the results reported here deal with intellectual relationships with female friends and attitudes toward working wives.

Methods

Each of the 62 respondents contributed a minimum of three two-hour interviews and also completed a set of five schedules and two psychological tests, the California Personality Inventory and the Gough Adjective Check List. The psychological tests were interpreted by a clinical psychologist. The 13-page interview guide probed for data on actual role performance, ideal role expectations and limits of tolerance, personal preferences, perception of role partner's ideal expectations, and relevant attitudes of significant others. Direct questions on strains came only at the end of this sequence. Extensive use was made of quasi-projective tests in the form of brief episodes. The total response rate of the original sample ($N = 79$) was 78%.

Intellectual Relationships with Female Friends

When fewer women attended college, the norm of male intellectual superiority might have had some validation in experience. But today college women are more rigorously selected than men in terms of high school academic performance (*Princeton Alumni Weekly,* 1971). Nevertheless, social norms internalized in early childhood are resistant to change. The first question for this research was, How many men would show insecurity or strain in their intellectual relationships with women when confronted with both bright women and the traditional norm of male superiority?

The Troubled Third

Of the 53 men for whom the data were available (six did not date, three could not be classified reliably), 30% reported that intellectual insecurity or strain with dates was a past or current problem. This number included men who, having experienced stress, sought to avoid it by finding dates who posed no intellectual threat. The following excerpts from interviews illustrate the views of this troubled third:

> I enjoy talking to more intelligent girls, but I have no desire for a deep relationship with them. I guess I still believe that the man should be more intelligent.
>
> *   *   *
>
> I may be a little frightened of a man who is superior to me in some field of knowledge, but if a girl knows more than I do, I resent her.
>
> *   *   *

> Once I was seeing a philosophy major, and we got along quite well. We shared a similar outlook on life, and while we had some divergent opinions, I seemed better able to document my position. One day, by chance, I heard her discussing with another girl an aspect of Kant that just the night before she described to me as obscure and confusing. But now she was explaining it to a girl so clearly and matter-of-factly that I felt sort of hurt and foolish. Perhaps it was immature of me to react this way.

The mode of strain exemplified by these men might be termed "a socially structured scarcity of resources for role fulfillment." Apart from the ever-present problem of lack of time and energy, some social roles are intrinsically more difficult to fulfill, given the state of technical skills, the inherent risks, or other scarcities of facilities. The strain of a doctor called upon to treat a disease for which modern medicine has no cure is another case in point.

Selective dating and avoidance of superior women solved the problem for some troubled youths, but this offered no solution for six respondents who yearned for intellectual companionship with women but dreaded the risk of invidious comparisons. The newly emerging norm of intellectual companionship with women creates a mode of strain akin to one Merton and Barber (1963) termed "sociological ambivalence." Universalistic values tend to replace sex-linked desiderata among some male undergraduates who now value originality and intelligence in female as well as in male associates. The conflict arises when, at the same time, the norm of masculine intellectual superiority has not been relinquished, as exemplified in the following case: "I am beginning to feel," remarked one senior about his current girl friend, "that she is not bright enough. She never says anything that would make me sit up and say, 'Ah, that's interesting!' I want a girl who has some defined crystal of her own personality and does not merely echo my thoughts." He recently met a girl who fascinated him with her quick and perceptive intelligence, but this new girl made him feel "nervous and humble."

The problem of this youth is to seek the rewards of valued attributes in a woman without arousing in himself feelings of inferiority. It may be argued that in a competitive society this conflict tends to characterize encounters with males as well. Nonetheless, if similar problems exist between two males, the utility curve is shaped distinctively by the norm of male intellectual superiority because mere equality with a woman may be defined as a defeat or a violation of a role prescription.

The Adjusted Majority

The 37 students who said that intellectual relationships with dates were not a problem represented a variety of types. Eleven men felt superior to their female friends. In two or three cases, the relationships were judged equalitarian with strong emphasis on the rewards of intellectual companionship. In contrast, several men—and their dates—had little interest in intellectual concerns. In a few instances the severity of other problems overwhelmed this one.

Finally, some eight men were happily adjusted despite the acknowledged intellectual superiority of their women friends. What makes for accommodation to this still deviant pattern?

In seven of the eight cases, the female friend had some weakness which offset her intellectual competence, such as emotional dependence, instability, or a plain appearance, giving the man a compensating advantage. A bright, studious, but relatively unattractive girl may be acceptable to a man who is not as certain of his ability to win a sexually desirable female as he is of his mental ability. In only one of the eight cases the respondent admitted that his steady girl was "more independent and less emotional, actually a little smarter than I. But she doesn't make me feel like a dunce." Her superiority was tolerable because she provided a supportive relationship which he needed and could accept with only mild, if any, emotional discomfort.

Another factor which may account for the finding that 70% of the sample reported no strain is the fact that intellectual qualities are no longer considered unfeminine and that the imperative of male superiority is giving way to the ideal of companionship between equals. This interpretation is supported by responses to two standard questions and by the qualitative materials of the interviews. A schedule testing beliefs on 16 psychological sex differences asked whether the reasoning ability of men is greater than that of women. Only 34% of the respondents "agreed" or "agreed somewhat," while 20% were "uncertain"; almost half "disagreed" or "disagreed somewhat."

Another question was put to all 62 respondents: what are for you personally the three or four most desirable characteristics in a woman (man) who is to be close to you? Of all the traits men desired in a woman, 33% were in the "intellectual" cluster, in contrast with 44% of such traits if the friend were male. The fact that the sex difference was not larger seems significant. The major difference in traits desired in male and female intimates (apart from sexual attractiveness and love) was the relative importance of "social amenities and appearance" for women.

The qualitative data amply document the fact that the majority of the respondents ideally hoped to share their intellectual interests with their female as well as their male friends. To be sure, what men occasionally meant by intellectual rapport with women was having an appreciative listener: "I wouldn't go out," declared one senior, "with any girl who wasn't sharp and perceptive enough to catch an intellectual subtlety." But for the majority a "meaningful relationship" with a woman included also a true intellectual interchange and sharing. As one senior put it, "A guy leaving a movie with his date expects her to make a stimulating comment of her own and not merely echo his ideas." Another man wanted a date with whom he could "discuss things that guys talk about," and still a third man exclaimed: "What I love about this girl is that she is on my level, that I can never speak over her head."

It is this ideal of intellectual companionship with women, we suggest, that may explain the relative adjustment of the men in this sphere. As long as the expectation of male superiority persisted, anything near equality on the part of the woman carried the threatening message to the men: "I am not the intellectually *superior* male I am expected to be." But when the ideal of intellectual companionship between equals replaces the expectation of male superiority, the pressure upon the man eases and changes. Now he need only reassure himself that he is not inferior to his date, rather than that he is markedly superior to her. Once the expectation of clear superiority is relinquished, varieties of relationships may be accommodated. Given a generally similar intellectual level, comparative evaluations are blurred by different interests, by complementary strengths and weaknesses, and occasionally by rationalizations ("she studies harder") and other devices.

One final explanation remains to be considered. May the intellectual self-confidence of the majority be attributed in part to women's readiness to play down their intellectual abilities? That such behavior occurs is attested by a number of studies (Komarovsky, 1946; Wallin, 1950).

When respondents were asked to comment upon a projective story about a girl "playing dumb" on dates, the great majority expressed indignation at such "dishonest, condescending" behavior. But some three or four found the behavior praiseworthy. As one senior put it, "Her intentions were good; she wanted to make the guy feel important."

Although we did not interview the female friends of our respondents, a few studies indicate that such playing down of intellectual ability by women is less common today than in the 1940s. Questionnaires filled out at an eastern women's college duplicated earlier studies by Wallin (1950) and Komarovsky (1946). The 1970 class was a course on the family, and the 1971 class probably recruited a relatively high proportion of feminists. Table 1 indicates that the occasional muting of intellectual competence by women may have played some role in the adjustment of the men, but it would appear to be a minor and decreasing role.

The hypothesis that the emerging ideal of intellectual companionship serves as a buffer against male strain needs a test which includes (as our study did not) some index of intellectual ability as well as indices of norms and of strain. Of the 27 men who disagreed with the proposition that the reasoning ability of men is greater than that of women, only five reported intellectual insecurity with women, whereas of the 34 men who believed in masculine superiority or were uncertain, nine experienced strain. Most troubled were the 12 men who were "uncertain"; four of them were insecure with women. Case analyses suggest that the interplay between a man's experience, personality, and beliefs is complex. For example, one traditional man, having confessed feelings of intellectual insecurity on dates, clung all the more tenaciously to the belief in superior male reasoning ability.

Some men took the "liberal" position on sex differences as a matter of principle. Of the nine black students, eight rejected the belief in male superiority, perhaps because they opposed group comparisons in intelligence. Again,

Table 1.   Readiness of Women to Play Down Intellectual Abilities (%)

	Wallin 1950 (N = 1963)	Sociology Class 1970* (N = 33)	Advanced Sociology Class 1971* (N = 55)
When on dates how often have you pretended to be intellectually inferior to the man?			
Very often, often, or several times	32	21	15
Once or twice	26	36	30
Never	42	43	55
In general, do you have any hesitation about revealing your equality or superiority to men in intellectual competence?			
Have considerable or some hesitation	35	21	13
Very little hesitation	39	33	32
None at all	26	46	55

*Mirra Komarovsky, unpublished study.

in some cases, the direction of the causal relation was the reverse of the one we posited: men who felt in fact intellectually superior were hospitable to the "liberal" ideology. In view of these complexities, our suggestive results as to the positive association between egalitarian norms and the absence of strain remain to be tested in larger samples.

Attitudes Toward Future Wives' Occupational Roles

The ethos on the campus of this study clearly demanded that men pay at least lip service to liberal attitudes toward working wives. If the initial responses to structured questions were accepted as final, the majority would have been described as quite feminist in ideology. But further probing revealed qualifications which occasionally almost negated the original response. For example, an affirmative answer to a proposition, "It is appropriate for a mother of a preschool child to take a fulltime job," was, upon further questioning, conditioned by such restrictions as "provided, of course, that the home was run smoothly, the children did not suffer, and the wife's job did not interfere with her husband's career." The interview provided an opportunity to get an assessment of normative expectations, ideal and operative, as well as of actual preferences. The classification of attitudes to be presented in this report is based on the total interview. Preferences reported here assume that a wife's paycheck will not be an economic necessity. The overwhelming majority were confident that their own earnings would be adequate to support the family.

Throughout the discussion of working, only two or three men mentioned the temptation of a second paycheck.

Four types of response to the question of wives' working may be identified. The "traditionalists," 24% of the men, said outright that they intended to marry women who would find sufficient fulfillment in domestic, civic, and cultural pursuits without ever seeking outside jobs. "Pseudo-feminists," 16% of the men, favored having their wives work, at least when the question was at a high level of abstraction, but their approval was hedged with qualifications that no woman could meet.

The third and dominant response included almost half (48%) of the respondents. These men took a "modified traditionalist" position which favored a sequential pattern: work, withdrawal from work for child rearing, and eventual return to work. They varied as to the timing of these stages and as to the aid they were prepared to give their wives with domestic and child-rearing functions. The majority saw no substitute for the mother during her child's preschool years. Even the mother of school-age children, were she to work, should preferably be at home when the children return from school. Though they were willing to aid their wives in varying degrees, they frequently excluded specific tasks, for instance, "not the laundry," "not the cleaning," "not the diapers," and so on. Many hoped that they would be "able to assist" their wives by hiring maids. The greater the importance of the wife's work, the more willing they were to help her. (One senior, however, would help only if his wife's work were "peripheral," that is, not as important to her as her home.)

The last the "feminist" type, was the smallest, only 7% of the total. These men were willing to modify their own roles significantly to facilitate their future wives' careers. Some recommended a symmetrical allocation of tasks—"as long as it is not a complete reversal of roles." In the remaining 5% of the cases, marriage was so remote that the respondents were reluctant to venture any views on this matter.

The foregoing summary of types of male attitudes toward working wives fails to reveal the tangled web of contradictory values and sentiments associated with these attitudes. We shall presently illustrate a variety of inconsistencies. But underlying them is one basic problem. The ideological support for the belief in sharp sex role differentiation in marriage has weakened, but the belief itself has not been relinquished. Increasing skepticism about the innate character of psychological sex differences and some convergence in the ideas of masculinity and femininity (see McKee and Sherriffs, 1957, 1959) have created a strain toward consistency. The more similar the perceptions of male and female personalities (see Kammeyer, 1964), the more universalistic must be the principles of evaluation applied to both sexes. "If you could make three changes in the personality of the girl friend who is currently closest to you, what would they be?" we asked the seniors. Universalistic values were reflected in the following, as in many other responses: "I would like her to be able to set a goal for herself and strive to achieve it. I don't like to see people slacking off." Earlier cross-sex association in childhood and early adolescence (see Udry, 1966) has raised male expectation of enjoying an emotional and intellectual companionship with women. These expectations, however, coexist with the deeply rooted norm that the husband should be the superior achiever in the occupational world and the wife, the primary child rearer. One manifestation of this basic dilemma is the familiar conflict between a value and a preference. "It is only fair," declared one senior, "to let a woman do her own thing, if she wants a career. Personally, though, I would want my wife at home."

More interesting are the ambivalent attitudes manifested toward both the full-time homemaker and the career wife. The image of each contained both attractive and repellent traits. Deprecating remarks about housewifery were not uncommon, even among men with traditional views of women's roles. A conservative senior declared, "A woman who works is more interesting than a housewife." "If I were a woman," remarked another senior, "I would want a career. It must be boring sitting around the house doing the same thing day in, day out. I don't have much respect for the type of woman whom I see doing the detergent commercials on TV."

But the low esteem attached by some of the men to full-time homemaking coexisted with other sentiments and convictions which required just such a pattern for one's wife. For example, asked about the disadvantages of being a woman, one senior replied, "Life ends at 40. The woman raised her children and all that remains is garden clubs and that sort of thing—unless, of course, she has a profession." In another part of the interview, this young man explained that he enjoyed shyness in a girl and detested aggressive and ambitious women. He could never be attracted to a career woman. It is no exaggeration to conclude that this man could not countenance in a woman who was to be his wife the qualities that he himself felt necessary for a fulfilled middle age.

A similar mode of contradiction, incidentally, was also disclosed by some seniors with regard to women's majors in college. "There are no 'unfeminine' majors," declared one senior. I admire a girl who is premed or prelaw." But the universalistic yardstick which led this senior to sanction and admire professional goals for women did not extend to the means for their attainment, as he unwittingly revealed in another part of the interview. Questioned about examples of "unfeminine" behavior, this senior answered: "Excessive grade consciousness." If a premed man, anxious about admission to a good medical school, should go to see a professor about a C in chemistry, this senior would understand although he would disapprove of such preoccupation with grades. But in a woman premed he would find such behavior "positively obnoxious."

If the image of the full-time homemaker contained some alienating features, the main threat of a career wife was that of occupational rivalry, as illustrated in the following excerpt from the interviews. A senior speaks:

I believe that it is good for mothers to return to fulltime work when the children are grown, provided the work is important and worthwhile. Otherwise, housewives get hung up with tranquilizers, because they have no outlet for their abilities. . . . Of course, it may be difficult if a wife becomes successful in her own right. A woman should want her husband's success more than he should want hers. Her work shouldn't interfere with or hurt his career in any way. He should not sacrifice his career to hers. For example, if he is transferred, his wife should follow—and not vice versa.

In sum, work for married women with grown children is approved by this young man, provided that the occupation is of some importance. But such an occupation is precisely one which carries a threat to the husband's pride.

The expectation that the husband should be the superior achiever appears still to be deeply rooted. Even equality in achievement of husband and wife is interpreted as a defeat for the man. The prospect of occupational rivalry with one's wife seems intolerable to contemplate. "My girl friend often beats me in tennis," explained one senior. "Now, losing the game doesn't worry me. It in no way reduces my manhood. But being in a lower position than a woman in a job would hurt my self-esteem."

Another student, having declared his full support for equal opportunities for women in the occupational world, added a qualification: "A woman should not be in a position of firing an employee. It is an unpleasant thing to do. Besides, it is unfair to the man who is to be fired. He may be a very poor employee, but he is still a human being and it may be just compounding his unhappiness to be fired by a woman."

In sum, the right of an able woman to a career of her choice, the admiration for women who measure up in terms of the dominant values of our society, the lure but also the threat that such women present, the low status attached to housewifery but the conviction that there is no substitute for the mother's care of young children, the deeply internalized norm of male occupational superiority pitted against the principle of equal opportunity irrespective of sex —these are some of the revealed inconsistencies.

Such ambivalences on the part of college men are bound to exacerbate role conflicts in women. The latter must sense that even the men who pay lip service to the creativity of child rearing and domesticity reserve their admiration (if occasionally tinged with ambivalence) for women achievers who measure up in terms of the dominant values of our society. It is becoming increasingly difficult to maintain a system of values for women only (Komarovsky, 1953).

Nevertheless, to infer from this account of male inconsistencies that this is an area of great stress for them would be a mistake. It is not. By and large, the respondents assumed that the women's "career and marriage" issue was solved by the sequential pattern of withdrawal and return to work. If this doomed women to second-class citizenship in the occupational world, the outcome was consistent with the conviction that the husband should be the superior achiever.

Men who momentarily worried about the fate of able women found moral anchorage in their conviction that today no satisfactory alternative to the mother's care of young children can be found. Many respondents expressed their willingness to help with child care and household duties. Similarly, many hoped to spend more time with their own children than their fathers had spent with them. But such domestic participation was defined as assistance to the wife who was to carry the major responsibility. Only two or three of the men approved a symmetrical, rather than a complementary, allocation of domestic and occupational roles. An articulate senior sums up the dominant view:

> I would not want to marry a woman whose only goal is to become a housewife. This type of woman would not have enough bounce and zest in her. I don't think a girl has much imagination if she just wants to settle down and raise a family from the very beginning. Moreover, I want an independent girl, one who has her own interests and does not always have to depend on me for stimulation and diversion. However, when we both agree to have children, my wife must be the one to raise them. She'll have to forfeit her freedom for the children. I believe that, when a woman wants a child, she must also accept the full responsibility of child care.

When he was asked why it was necessarily the woman who had to be fully responsible for the children, he replied:

> Biology makes equality impossible. Besides, the person I'll marry will want the child and will want to care for the child. Ideally, I would hope I'm not forcing her to assume responsibility for raising the children. I would hope that this is her desire and that it is the happiest thing she can do. After we have children, it will be her career that will end, while mine will support us. I believe that women should have equal opportunities in business and the professions, but I still insist that a woman who is a mother should devote herself entirely to her children.

The low emotional salience of the issue of working wives may also be attributed to another factor. The female partners of our respondents, at this particular stage of life, did not, with a few exceptions, force the men to confront their inconsistencies. Apparently enough women will freely make the traditional-for-women adjustments—whether scaling down their own ambitions or in other ways acknowledging the prior claims of the man's career. This judgment is supported by the results of two studies of female undergraduates done on the same campus in 1943 and 1971 (Table 2). The big shift in postcollege preferences since 1943 was in the decline of women undergradutes who opted for full-time homemaking and volunteer activities. In 1971, the majority chose the sequential pattern, involving withdrawal from employment for child rearing. The proportion of committed career women who hope to return to work soon after childbirth has remained constant among freshmen and sophomores.

If women's attitudes have not changed more radically in the past 30 years it is no doubt because society has failed to provide effective supports for the woman who wishes to integrate family life, parenthood, and work on much the same terms as men. Such an option will not become available so long as

Table 2. College Women's Attitudes toward Work and Family Patterns (%)

	Random Sample of Sophomore Class at Women's Liberal College, 1943 (N = 78)	Class in Introductory Sociology, Same College 1971 (N = 44)
Assume that you will marry and that your husband will make enough money so that you will not have to work unless you want to. Under these circumstances, would you prefer:		
1. Not to work at all, or stop after childbirth and decide later whether to go back	50	18
2. To quit working after the birth of a child but definitely to go back to work. . . .	30	62
3. To continue working with a minimum of interruption for childbearing.	20	20

Source: Mirra Komarovsky, unpublished studies.

the care of young children is regarded as the responsibility solely of the mother. In the absence of adequate child care centers, an acceptance of a symmetrical division of domestic and work responsibilities, or other facilitating social arrangements, the attitudes of the majority of undergraduates reflect their decision to make some kind of workable adjustments to the status quo, if not a heroic struggle to change it.

Summary

Role conflicts in women have been amply documented in numerous studies. The problem underlying this study was to ascertain whether recent social changes and consequent malintegration with regard to sex roles have created stressful repercussions for men as well as for women. In a randomly selected sample of 62 male seniors in an Ivy League college, nearly one-third experienced some anxiety over their perceived failure to live up to the norm of masculine intellectual superiority. This stressful minority suffered from two modes of role strain: scarcity of resources for role performance and ambivalence. The absence of strain in the majority may be explained by a changed role definition. Specifically, the normative expectation of male intellectual superiority appears to be giving way on the campus of our study to the ideal of intellectual companionship between equals. Attitudes toward working wives abounded in ambivalences and inconsistencies. The ideological supports for the traditional sex role differentiation in marriage are weakened, but the emotional allegiance to the modified traditional pattern is still strong. These inconsistencies did not generate a high degree of stress, partly, no doubt, because future roles do not require an immediate realistic confrontation. In addition, there is no gainsaying the conclusion that human beings can tolerate a high degree of inconsistency so long as it does not conflict with their self-interest.

References

Kammeyer, Kenneth. "The Feminine Role: An Analysis of Attitude Consistency." *Journal of Marriage and the Family,* 26 (August 1964): 295–305.

Komarovsky, Mirra, "Cultural Contradictions and Sex Roles." *American Journal of Sociology,* 52 (November 1946): 182–189.

Komarovsky, Mirra, *Women in the Modern World, Their Education and Their Dilemmas.* Boston: Little, Brown, 1953.

McKee, John P., and Alex C. Sherriffs, "The Differential Evaluation of Males and Females." *Journal of Personality,* 25 (March 1957): 356–363.

McKee, John P., and Alex C. Sherriffs, "Men's and Women's Beliefs, Ideals, and Self-Concepts." *American Journal of Sociology,* 64 (1959), no. 4: 456–363.

Merton, Robert K., and Elinor Barber. "Sociological Ambivalence." In *Sociological Theory, Values and Socio-cultural Change,* edited by E. A. Tiryakian. Glencoe, Ill.: Free Press, 1963.

Princeton Alumni Weekly, February 23, 1971, p. 7.

Udry, J. Richard. *The Social Context of Marriage.* Philadelphia: Lippincott, 1966.

Wallin, Paul. "Cultural Contradictions and Sex Roles: A Repeat Study." *American Sociological Review,* 15 (April 1950): 288–293.

Chapter 5

Women's Roles

Reflections On The "Woman Question"

Barbara Ehrenreich and Deirdre English

"If you would get up and do something you would feel better," said my mother. I rose drearily, and essayed to brush up the floor a little, with a dustpan and small whiskbroom, but soon dropped those implements exhausted, and wept again in helpless shame.

I, the ceaselessly industrious, could do no work of any kind. I was so weak that the knife and fork sank from my hands—too tired to eat. I could not read nor write nor paint nor sew nor talk nor listen to talking, nor anything. I lay on the lounge and wept all day. The tears ran down into my ears on either side. I went to bed crying, woke in the night crying, sat on the edge of the bed in the morning and cried—from sheer continuous pain. Not physical, the doctors examined me and found nothing the matter.

It was 1885 and Charlotte Perkins Stetson had just given birth to a daughter, Katherine. "Of all angelic babies that darling was the best, a heavenly baby." And yet young Mrs. Stetson wept and wept, and when she nursed her baby, "the tears ran down on my breasts. . . . "

The doctors told her she had "nervous prostration." To her, "a sort of gray fog [had] drifted across my mind, a cloud that grew and darkened." The fog never entirely lifted from Charlotte Perkins Stetson (later Gilman). Years later, in the midst of an active life as a feminist writer and lecturer, she would find herself overcome by the same lassitude, incapable of making the smallest decision, mentally numb.

Depression struck Charlotte Perkins Gilman when she was only 25 years old, energetic and intelligent, a woman who seemed to have her life open before her. It hit young Jane Addams—the famous social reformer—at the same time of life. Addams was affluent, well educated for a girl, ambitious to study medicine. Then, in 1881, at the age of 21, she fell into a "nervous depression" that paralyzed her for seven years and haunted her long after she began her work at Hull House in the Chicago slums. She was gripped by "a sense of futility, of misdirected energy" and was conscious of her estrangement from "the active, emotional life" within the family, which had automatically embraced earlier generations of women. "It was doubtless true," she later wrote of her depression, "that I was 'Weary of myself and sick of asking what I am and what I ought to be.' "

Margaret Sanger—the birth control crusader—was another case. She was 20 years old, happily married, and, physically at least, seemed to be making a good recovery from tuberculosis. Then she stopped getting out of bed, refused to talk. In the outside world, Theodore Roosevelt was running for president on the theme of the "strenuous life." But when relatives asked Margaret Sanger what she would like to do, she could only say, "Nothing." "Where would you like to go?" they persisted. "Nowhere."

Ellen Swallow (later Ellen Richards—founder of the early twentieth century domestic science movement) succumbed when she was 24. She was an energetic, even compulsive, young woman; and, like Addams, felt estranged from the intensely domestic life her mother had led. Returning home from a brief period of independence, she fell into a depression that left her almost too weak to do household chores. "Lay down sick. . . . " she entered in her diary. "Oh so tired. . . ." And on another day, "Wretched," and again, "Tired."

It was as if these women had come to the brink of adult life and then refused to go on. They stopped in their tracks, paralyzed. The problem wasn't a lack of things to do. Charlotte Perkins Gilman, like Jane Addams, felt "intense shame" that she was not up and about. All of them had family responsibilities to meet; all but Jane Addams had houses to run. They were women with other interests too—science or art or philosophy—and all of them were passionately idealistic. And yet, for a while, they could not go on.

For, in the new world of the nineteenth century, what was a woman to do? Did she build a life, like her aunts and her mother, in the warmth of the family —or did she throw herself into the nervous activism of a world that was already presuming to call itself "modern"? Either way, wouldn't she be ridiculous, a kind of misfit? Certainly she would be out of place if she tried to fit into the "men's world" of business, politics, science; but in an historical sense, perhaps even more out of place if she remained in the home, isolated from the grand march of industry and progress. "She was intelligent and generous," Henry James wrote of the heroine in *Portrait of a Lady;* "it was a fine free nature; but what was she going to do with herself?" Certainly the question had been asked before Charlotte Perkins Gilman's and Jane Addams's generation, and certainly other women had collapsed because they did not have the answers. But only in the last 100 years or so in the Western world has the private dilemma surfaced as a gripping public issue—the "Woman Question" or the "Woman Problem." The misery of a Charlotte Gilman or a Jane Addams, the crippling indecisiveness, was amplified in the nineteenth and twentieth centuries among tens of thousands of women. A minority transformed their numbness into anger and became activists in reform movements; many—the ones whose names we don't know—remained permanently depressed, bewildered, sick.

Men—men of the "establishment" who were physicians, philosophers, scientists—addressed themselves to the Woman Question too in a constant stream of books and articles. For while women were discovering new questions and doubts, men were discovering that women were themselves a question, an anomaly when viewed from the busy world of industry. They couldn't be included in the men's world, but they no longer seemed content with their traditional place. "Have you any notion how many books are written about women in the course of one year?" Virginia Woolf later asked an audience of women. "Have you any notion how many are written by men? Are you aware that you are, perhaps, the most discussed animal in the universe?" Woman had become an issue, a social problem—something to be investigated, analyzed, and solved.

The Woman Question arose in the course of an historic transformation—the industrial revolution—whose scale later generations have still barely grasped. Marx and Engels—usually thought of as the instigators of disorder rather than the chroniclers of it—were the first to comprehend the cataclysmic nature of these changes. An old world was dying and a new one was being born:

> All fixed, fast-frozen relations, with their train of ancient and venerable prejudices and opinions, are swept away, all new-formed ones become antiquated before they can ossify. All that is solid melts into air, all that is holy is profaned, and man is at last compelled to face with sober senses his real conditions of life and his relations with his kind.

Incredible, once unthinkable, possibilities opened up as all the "fixed, fast-frozen relations"—between man and woman, between parents and children, between rich and poor—were thrown into question. Over 150 years later, the dust has still not settled.

On the far side of the industrial revolution was what we will call, for our purposes, the "old order." Historians mark off many "eras" within these centuries of agrarian life, royal lines, national boundaries, military technology, fashions, art, and architecture—all evolved and changed throughout the old order. Nevertheless, for all the visible drama of history, the lives of ordinary people, doing ordinary things, changed very little:

> Routine predominates at the level of everyday life: corn is sown as it was always sown, maize planted, rice fields levelled, ships sail the Red Sea as they have always sailed it.[1]

Three patterns of social life in the old order gave it consistency. First, the old order was unitary. Life for the great majority of people was not marked off into different spheres of experience: work and home, public and private, sacred and secular. Production (of food, clothing, tools) took place in the same rooms or outdoor spaces where children grew up, babies were born, couples came together. The family relationship was not secluded in the realm of emotion; it was a working relationship. Biological life—sexual desire, nursing babies, sickness, the progressive infirmity of age—impinged directly on the group activities of production and play. Ritual and superstition affirmed the unity of body and earth, biology and labor: menstruating women must not bake bread; conception is most favored at the time of the spring planting; sexual transgressions will bring blight and ruin to the crops. The human relations of family and village, knit by common labor as well as sex and affection, were paramount. There were marketplaces, but there was not yet *a* market to dictate the opportunities and activities of ordinary people. If people went hungry, it was not because the price of their crops fell, but because the rain did not.

The old order was patriarchal: authority over the family was vested in the elder males, or male. He, the father, made the decisions that controlled the family's work, purchases, marriages. Under the rule of the father, women had no complex choices to make, no questions as to their nature or destiny: the rule was simply obedience. At home was the father, in church was the priest or minister, at the top were the "town fathers," the local nobility, or, as they put it in Puritan society, "the nursing fathers of the Commonwealth"—above all was "God the Father."

And yet, to a degree that is almost unimaginable from our vantage point within industrial society, the old order was gynocentric: the skills and work of women were indispensable to survival. Woman was always subordinate, but she was far from being a helpless dependent. Consider a woman in colonial America:

> It was the wife's duty, with the assistance of daughters and women servants, to plant the vegetable garden, breed the poultry, and care for the dairy cattle. She transformed milk into cream, butter and cheese, and butchered livestock as well as cooked the meals. Along with her daily chores the husbandwoman slated, pickled, preserved, and manufactured enough beer and cider to see the family through the winter.
>
> Still, the woman's work was hardly done. To clothe the colonial population, women not only plied the needle, but operated wool carders and spinning wheels—participated in the manufacture of thread, yarn and cloth as well as apparel. Her handwrought candles lit the house; medicines of her manufacture restored the family to health; her homemade soap cleansed her home and family. . . . [2]

It was not only woman's productive skills that gave her importance in the old order. She knew the herbs that healed, the songs to soothe a feverish child, the precautions to be taken during pregnancy. All women were expected to have learned, from their mothers and grandmothers, the skills of raising children, healing common illnesses, nursing the sick.

So there could be no Woman Question in the old order. Woman's work was cut out for her; the lines of authority that she was to follow were clear. She could hardly think of herself as a "misfit" in a world that depended so heavily on her skills and her work. Nor could she imagine making painful decisions about the direction of her life, for, within the patriarchal order, all decisions of consequence would be made for her by father or husband, if they were not already determined by tradition. The Woman Question awaits the arrival of the industrial epoch.

The market had been gaining ground inch by inch throughout the late Middle Ages. But only in the nineteenth century, with industrialization and the development of modern capitalism, did it come to replace nature as the controlling force in the lives of ordinary people. Food prices came to regulate existence as surely as rainfall and temperature once had—and seemed just as arbitrary. Depressions became calamities on the scale of famines or epidemics.

With the triumph of the market, the settled patterns of life that defined the old order were shattered irrevocably. The old unity of work and home, production and family life, was necessarily and decisively ruptured. Henceforth the household would no longer be a more or less self—contained unit, binding its members together in common work. When production entered the factory, the household was left with only the most personal biological activities—eating, sex, sleeping, caring for the young and the sick and the aged, and (until the rise of institutional medicine) giving birth, and dying. Life was experienced as being divided into two distinct and opposing spheres: a "public" sphere of endeavor, governed ultimately by the market; and a "private" sphere of intimate relationships and individual biological existence.

To go from a society organized around household production to one organized around largescale factory production, from a society ruled by seasons and climate to one ruled by the market, was to reach into the heart of human social life and uproot the deepest assumptions. Everything that had been "natural" was overturned. What had unquestionably been "human nature" appeared archaic; what had been accepted for centuries as human destiny was no longer acceptable and, in most cases, was not even possible.

For men, private life took on a sentimental appeal in proportion to the coldness and impersonality of the "outside" world. Men looked to the home to fulfill both the bodily needs denied at the workplace and the human solidarity forbidden in the market.

The lives of women—always much more confined by nature and social expectation than those of men—were thrown into confusion. In the old order, women had won their survival through participation in the shared labor of the household. Outside of the household there was simply no way to earn a livelihood and no life for a woman. Women could be, at different ages or in different classes, wives, mothers, daughters, servants, or "spinster" aunts, but these are only gradations of the domestic hierarchy. Women were born, grew up, and aged within the dense human enclosure of the family.

But with the collapse of the old order, there appeared a glimmer, however remote to most women, of something like a choice. It was now possible for a woman to enter the market herself. That might mean low wages and miserable working conditions, loneliness and insecurity; but it also meant the possibility —unimaginable in the old order—of dignity and independence from the grip of the family.

These were the frustratingly ambiguous options that began to open up to women in the late eighteenth and early nineteenth centuries. In most cases, of course, the "choice" was immediately foreclosed by circumstances: some women were forced to seek paid work no matter how much their working disrupted the family; others were inescapably tied to family responsibilities no matter how much they needed or wanted to work outside. But the collapse of the old order had broken the pattern that tied every woman to a single and unquestionable fate.

The impact of the change was double edged. It cannot simply be judged as a step forward or a step backward for women (even assuming that that judgment could be made in such a way as to cover all women—the black domestic, the manufacturer's wife, the factory girl, and so on). Industrial capitalism freed women from the endless round of household productive labor, and in one and the same gesture tore away the skills that had been the source of women's unique dignity. It loosened the bonds of patriarchy, and at once slapped on the chains of wage labor. It "freed" some women for a self-supporting spinster-hood, and conscripted others into sexual peonage. And so on.

From these changes—the backward steps as well as the forward ones—the Woman Question emerged. For women generally—from the hardworking women of the poorer classes to the cushioned daughters of the upper classes —the Woman Question was a matter of immediate personal experience: the consciousness of possibilities counterposed against prohibitions, opportunities against ancient obligations, instincts against external necessities. The Woman Question was nothing less than the question of how women would survive, and what would become of them, in the modern world. The women who lost years of their youth to nervous depression, the women who first tasted the "liberation" of grinding jobs and exploitative sex, the women who poured their hearts into diaries while their strength drained into childbearing and child rearing, worked out the Woman Question with their lives.

The Woman Question also entered the realm of public life as an "issue" subject to the deliberations of scholars, statesmen, and scientists. Here is Freud:

> Throughout history people have knocked their heads against the riddle of the nature of femininity. . . . Nor will *you* have escaped worrying over this problem—those of you who are men; to those of you who are women this will not apply—you are yourselves the problem.

Freud projected his own age's obsession with the Woman Question to a universal and timeless status. Yet the old patriarchs would never have raised such a question. To them, the nature and purpose of women posed no riddle. But the old ways of thinking about things—which posited a static, hierarchical social order presided over by the Heavenly Father—were already losing their credibility when Freud wrote. The new age needed a new way of explaining human society and human nature. That way, as it developed in the last three centuries, was not accepting, but questioning; not religious, but scientific.

Ever since the beginning of the seventeenth century, when Galileo faced the Inquisition over the issue of whether the earth was the center of the universe, science had set itself up as antagonistic, or at best, disdainful of religious doctrine and traditional authority in all fields. Galileo, and the scientists who followed him, claimed the entire observable world—stars, tides, rocks, animals, and "man" himself—as an area for unfettered investigation, much as businessmen were laying claim to the marketplace as a secular zone, free of religious or feudal interference. Science grew with the market. It took the most revolutionary aspects of the business mentality—its loyalty to empirical fact, its hard-headed pragmatism, its penchant for numerical abstraction—and hammered them into a precision tool for understanding and mastering the material world.

Science mocked the old patriarchal ideology, ripped through its pretensions, and left it as we know it today—a legacy of rituals, legends, and bedtime stories told to children. Science in the eighteenth and nineteenth centuries was the sworn enemy of ghosts and mystery and mumbo jumbo—the traditional trappings of patriarchy—and an old friend to revolutionaries. Socialists like Karl Marx and feminists like Charlotte Perkins Gilman were devotees of science as a liberating force against injustice and domination.

We are indebted, then, to the critical and scientific spirit that arose with the market for the defeat of the patriarchal ideology that had for centuries upheld the patriarchal tyranny. But to be opposed to patriarchal structures of authority is not necessarily to be *feminist* in intent or sensibility. The emerging world view of the new age was, in fact, distinctly *masculinist*. It was a world view that proceeded from the market, from the realm of economic or "public" life. It was by its nature external to women, capable of seeing them only as "others" or aliens. We call this new outlook "masculinist" to distinguish it from traditional patriarchal ideology.

Patriarchal ideology subordinated women too, of course, but it was not formed in some realm other than that inhabited by women. Masculinist opinion, however, proceeded from the male half of what had become a sexually segregated world. It reflected not some innate male bias but the logic and assumptions of the market.

The masculinist view of human nature almost automatically excludes woman and her nature. Whether expressed in popular opinion or in learned science, it is biased not only toward biological man and his nature, but specifically toward capitalist man, the "economic man" of Adam Smith's economic theories. To economic man, the inanimate things of the marketplace—money and the commodities that represent money—are alive, and possessed of almost sacred significance. Conversely, things truly alive are, from a strictly "rational" point of view, worthless except as they impinge on the market and affect one's economic self-interest: employees are "production factors," a good wife is an "asset," and so on. Masculinist ideology comes to identify transactions of economic man with the laws of human nature.

From this vantage point, woman inevitably appears alien, mysterious. She inhabits (or is supposed to inhabit) the "other" realm, the realm of private life, which looks from the market like a preindustrial backwater, or a looking-glass land that inverts all that is normal in the "real" world of men. Economic man is an individual, a monad, connected to others only through a network of impersonal economic relationships; woman is embedded in the family, permitted no individual identity apart from her biological relationships to others. Economic man acts in perfect self-interest; a woman cannot base her relationships within the family on the principle of quid pro quo: she *gives*.

It appears, from a masculinist perspective, that woman might be a more primitive version of man—not because there is prima facie evidence of her lower intelligence, but because of her loving and giving nature, which is itself taken as evidence of lower intelligence, or basic irrationality. Rousseau's "noble savage," like his ideal woman, was compassionate and nurturing: the bond between people "must have been much closer in the state of nature than in a rational state of mind." And Darwin found that:

> Woman seems to differ from man in mental disposition, chiefly in her greater tenderness and less selfishness. . . .
> It is generally admitted that with woman the powers of intuition, or rapid perception, and perhaps of imitation, are more strongly marked than in man; but some, at least, of these faculties are characteristic of the lower races, and therefore of a past and lower state of civilization.

Everything that seems uniquely female becomes a challenge to the rational scientific intellect. Woman's body, with its autonomous rhythms and generative possibilities, appears to the masculinist vision as a "frontier," another part of the natural world to be explored. A new science—gynecology—arose in the nineteenth century to explore and subdue this strange territory and concluded that the female body is not only primitive, but deeply pathological. Woman's psyche, of course, became an acknowledged scientific enigma, like the inner substance of matter, or the shape of the universe. The early twentieth century American psychologist G. Stanley Hall called it "terra incognita," and when Freud wrote of the "riddle of the nature of femininity" he spoke for generations of scientists who puzzled over the strange asymmetry of nature that had made only one sex fully normal.

The discovery of woman as an anomaly—a question—quite apart from woman's discovery of her own questions and options in the new order: this was the essential masculinist perception. Patriarchal ideology had seen women as inferior, but always as organically linked to the entire hierarchy that extended from the household to the heavens. Now those links were broken; patriarchal ideology, which had been the organizing principle of human society for centuries, lay tattered and demoralized. Yet woman was not freed by its downfall, but became a curiosity, a question in the minds of men, a social issue that somehow would have to be resolved.

Within the framework of the masculinist outlook, only two answers to the Woman Question were possible. We call them "rationalist" and "romantic," though many people would call them, after a quick glance, "feminist" and "male chauvinist." But it is not that simple. Although they are opposed to each other, they emerged from the same ground and they grew together, back to back, as the masculinist culture developed. At any given moment, each answer had its proponents, and neither could be completely put to rest. But ultimately one came to dominate Anglo-American and Western culture in general from the early nineteenth century until the rise of the women's liberation movement in our own day. That choice was overwhelmingly for the romantic solution, enforced in real life with all the weight of the economy and the persuasion of scientific authority.

The rationalist answer is, very simply, to admit women into modern society on an equal footing with men. If the problem is that women are in some sense "out," then it can be solved by letting them "in." Sexual rationalism shares the critical spirit of science: it mocks the patriarchal myths of female inferiority, denounces modern "sex roles" as arbitrary social inventions, and dreams of a social order in which women and men will be not only equal, but, insofar as possible, functionally interchangeable. Born in the exuberantly clear-headed days of the French Revolution and nurtured by every succeeding wave of social movement, sexual rationalism is a radical ideology.

But the sexual rationalist position, though radical, is no less masculinist. It looks out from the market at the world of women, critical of that world, but largely uncritical of the market, except insofar as it has excluded women. Charlotte Perkins Gilman, perhaps the most brilliant American proponent of the sexual rationalist position, held that the home was "primitive" and that women, as a result of their confinement to it, suffered from "arrested development" to the point where they had become almost a separate species. Betty Friedan, the best known sexual rationalist of our period, found the home a "trap" and housewives stunted in mind and spirit. But in recoiling, justifiably, from "woman's sphere" (and not so justifiably from the women in it), sexual rationalism rushes too eagerly into the public sphere as men have defined it. "We demand," wrote South African feminist Olive Schreiner—a sexual rationalist in the spirit of Charlotte Perkins Gilman—that "we also shall have our share of honored and socially useful human toil, our full half of the labor of the Children of Woman. We demand nothing more than this, and we will take nothing less. This is our 'WOMAN'S RIGHT!'"[3]

The rationalist feminist seldom questions the nature of that toil and whom it serves. Gilman, and to an even greater degree Friedan, saw women entering "fulfilling" careers—presumably in business and the professions—with no evident concern about the availability of such jobs to all women, much less about the larger social purpose of the available occupations. The sexual rationalist program is one of assimilation, with ancillary changes (day care, for example) as necessary to promote women's rapid integration into what has been the world of men.

The industrial revolution made the rationalist program seem not only achievable but inevitable. The bulk of women's old labor had been removed to the factories: why shouldn't the remaining domestic activities follow suit? The sphere of "private life" would be, in effect, dismantled. Gilman urged that restaurants, kindergartens, housecleaners be set up "on a business basis" to take over women's chores. Freed of this "clumsy tangle of rudimentary industries," the family would become a voluntary association of individuals. Women would no longer be identified by a mere sexual or biological connection to other people, but by their independent endeavors in the public world. From a nineteenth century vantage point, these developments seemed likely to happen by themselves. The machine was eliminating the importance of muscular differences between the sexes, and the factory was proving itself far more efficient than the home. The market had taken over so many of women's activities, from clothes making to food processing—what was to stop it from swallowing up the home and family and spitting out autonomous, genderless individuals?

It was, in large part, the horror of such a prospect that inspired the other answer to the Woman Question: sexual romanticism. In keeping with the masculinist spirit, sexual romanticism sees women as anomalous, half outside the world of men. The rationalist rebels against this situation; the romantic finds comfort in it. Sexual romanticism cherishes the mystery that is woman and proposes to keep her mysterious by keeping her outside.

Just as sexual rationalism is linked historically to a larger stream of rationalist thinking, sexual romanticism emerged with the "romantic movement" of the eighteenth and nineteenth centuries. Rationalism welcomed the new age of industrial capitalism; romanticism shrank back from it in revulsion. It was a brutal world, not even tempered by the charitable paternalism and noblesse oblige of feudal times. Where middle-class revolutions had made men free, that freedom consisted of the solitary right to sink or swim, to "make it" or be crushed by those who were making it. The romantic spirit reached with nostalgia for the old order, or for imaginary versions of it: a society not yet atomized, but linked organically in trust and mutual need, enlivened by the warmth of "irrational" passions, and enriched by the beauty of untouched nature.

Nothing could be more abhorrent from a romantic standpoint than the sexual rationalist program. To dissolve the home (by removing the last domestic chores and letting women out to work) would be to remove the last haven from the horrors of industrial society. Communal dining halls, child-care services, and housekeeping services would turn out to be outposts of the hated factory—or factories themselves—imposing their cold and regimented operations on the most intimate and personal details of life. Economic man must have consolation for his lonely quest, a refuge from the market. Sexual romanticism asserts that the home will be that refuge, woman will be that consolation. The English critic and author John Ruskin lays out exactly what the sexual romanticist seeks in "women's sphere":

> This is the true nature of home—it is the place of peace; the shelter, not only from all injury, but from all terror, doubt and division. In so far as it is not this, it is not home; so far as the anxieties of the outer life penetrate into it, and the inconsistently minded, unknown, unloved or hostile society of the outer world is allowed by either husband or wife to cross the threshold it ceases to be a home; it is then only a part of the outer world which you have roofed over and lighted fire in. But so far as it is a sacred place, a vestal temple, a temple of the hearth watched over by household gods . . . so far it vindicates the name and fulfills the praise of home.

Here will be preserved a quaint and domesticated version of patriarchy, as if nothing had ever happened in the world outside.* There is in the romantic spirit a passionate and humanistic rejection of the market but it settles for only this furtive and half-hearted rebellion: not to overthrow the market, but to escape from it—into the arms of woman. The deity who makes Ruskin's ideal home sacred is no vengeful patriarch, capable of driving out money lenders and idolators, but a mere "household god."

The romantic imagination feverishly set out to construct a woman worthy of occupying Ruskin's "vestal temple." The guidelines were simple: woman should be, in every feature, a counterpoint to the market; she should be the antithesis of economic man. Now, from our perspective, there is a real basis to this romantic construction: there is a strength in women's nurturance that does contradict the rules and assumptions of the market, and that is potentially opposed to the market. But the romantics had no interest in discovering the authentic strengths and impulses of women—any more than they had, in most cases, in authentically attacking the inhumanity of the market. The romantic construction of woman is as artificial as the 16-inch waist and three-foot-wide hooped skirts popular in the mid-nineteenth century. Economic man is rational; therefore romantic woman is intuitive, emotional, and incapable of quanti-

---

*The romantic nostalgia of the nineteenth century was not reserved for women. The primitive peoples uncovered by expanding Euro-American capitalism lived, like women of the industrial countries, in the shadowy realm outside the market. To the romantic imagination, they shared with women generally the human qualities denied by the market, and gladdened the world with their pastoral simplicity. In the words of psychologist G. Stanley Hall: "Nearly all savages are in many respects children or youth of adult size. . . . They are naturally amiable, peaceful among themselves, affectionately lighthearted, thoroughly goodnatured, and the faults we see are those we have made. They live a life of feeling, emotion, and impulse, and scores of testimonials from those who know them intimately and who have no predilection for Rousseau-like views are to the effect that to know a typical savage is to love him." Hall castigated imperialist attempts to "commercialize them and overwork them." They must be allowed to remain outside the market, "to linger in the paradise of childhood," for without their refreshing charm "our earthly home would be left desolate indeed."

tative reasoning. Economic man is competitive; she is tender and submissive. Economic man is self-interested; she is self-effacing, even masochistic. A popular Victorian poem depicts the result of all these negations: a creature who was supposed to be all that is "human" (as opposed to "economic") and ends up being subhuman, more like a puppy than a priestess:

> Her soul, that once with pleasure shook
> Did any eyes her beauty own,
> Now wonders how they dare to look
> On what belongs to him alone;
> The indignity of taking gifts
> Exhilarates her loving breast;
> A rapture of submission lifts
> Her life into celestial rest;
> There's nothing left of what she was;
> Back to the babe the woman dies,
> And all the wisdom that she has
> Is to love him for being wise.*

The sexual rationalist who does not gag on the foregoing lines can respond with a certain cynical impatience: the lovely wife of romantic yearnings is in fact her husband's financial dependent and ward. Charlotte Perkins Gilman argued that she was a kind of combined housemaid-prostitute, earning her keep.

Yet from the Victorian ideal of the nineteenth century to the feminist mystique of the mid-twentieth century, sexual romanticism triumphed over sexual rationalism. When the cataclysmic transition from the old order ended in the United States and Europe, when society began to re-form itself into something that could be once again called an "order," a settled and reproducible way of life, that new order rested heavily on the romantic conception of woman and the home. Sexual rationalism, which had seemed to be as inevitable as technological progress, remained a dissident stream, associated with bohemianism, radicalism, and feminism.** The dominant ideology defined

---

*It has become common today to confuse this kind of romanticist goo with patriarchal ideology. But the two views of women are fundamentally incompatible. Patriarchy's women were not gushing, limp-wristed creatures; they were hard workers and stout partners. At the same time, patriarchal ideology never for a moment dreamed of ascribing women moral superiority, as the romantics did in making women the custodians of the Sacred. Patriarchal ideology rested on the assumption of women's moral inferiority and their utter dependency on males to mediate and interpret scripture. Sexual romanticism draws heavily on archaic imagery, but that is only nostalgia—a product of the new epoch, not a continuation of the old order.

**Feminism has oscillated between romantic and rationalist ideas. The first generation of American feminists (Susan B. Anthony, Elizabeth Cady Stanton, etc.) were unswerving sexual rationalists, but the second generation—which came to maturity in the 1880s and 1890s—unhesitantly embraced sexual romanticism, arguing that women should have the vote not because it was their *right,* but because they were mothers, "the guardians of the race." Contemporary feminism is overwhelmingly rationalist, but it is not without undercurrents of romanticism: for example, feminists who reject "integration" and aspire to resurrect a pretechnological matriarchate, or rule by women. Women have pinned their hopes on technological "progress," or they have sought vindication in a remote and imagined past—both in the name of feminism.

woman as a perpetual alien, and the home as an idyllic refuge from the unpleasant but "real" world of men. Sexual romanticism triumphed not only because it was psychologically comforting to a majority of men (and many, many women), but also for a pragmatic reason that the sexual rationalists of the early industrial period could never have foreseen. Sexual romanticism, it turned out, meshed ideally with the needs of the maturing economy, which would increasingly depend on the economic pattern of individual domestic consumption to fuel its growth. This pattern produced a new kind of woman's work, based on the management of private family spending, and requiring a woman's full-time attention to the home. Just as important, the "romanticized" woman makes a more convenient worker when she is needed by industry: she is supposed to work for low wages, typically in work that requires submissiveness and/or nurturance, and quickly goes back where she "belongs" when the jobs run out.

But the legitimacy of this new sexual-economic order has been secured only through great effort. The romantic solution, by its very nature, cannot be justified by direct application of the laws and assumptions of the market. There is nothing in the logic of the market that can distinguish between male and female (or black and white) workers, consumers, owners, or investors. And the revolutionary new ideas of "equality" and "liberty" that the rising middle class had once hurled in the face of monarchs were implicitly oblivious to gender, as feminists have always been quick to point out. In fact, the tenets of the business world, and the political ideals of the class who dominated that world, had opened the ground for sexual rationalism. Sexual romanticism was forced to seek legitimacy from some authority higher than either economic realism or political idealism.

That authority was science. For over a hundred years, the romantic answer to the Woman Question would be articulated not in political, or aesthetic, or moral terms, but in the language of science. But the "science" that rose to the defense of sexual romanticism was a pale, and not wholly legitimate, descendant of the science that had once challenged the authority of kings and popes. By the end of the nineteenth century, the men and women who spoke most loudly in the name of science, who interpreted it to a larger public, and who sought to translate it into social policy, were seldom, even by the most generous definition, scientists.

The new representative of science was the expert. His business was not to find out what was true, ferreting out folly, prejudice, and obfuscation wherever they appeared. His job was to tie the ideology of sexual romanticism to the everyday organization of life with all the strength of scientific authority. His allegiance to science was, in the end, a matter of public relations more than principle: if the truth threatened to undermine his commitment to sexual romanticism, he betrayed science and found a new "truth."

The experts who arose near the turn of the century as authorities on the lives of women—professional physicians, psychologists, domestic scientists, parent educators, and so on—each claimed a specialized body of scientific knowledge.

Their careers rested on this claim. Without a connection to science they had no legitimacy, no audience for their ideas, no market for their skills. Their principal client was the woman sequestered in her "sphere," where her everyday activity was the object of their surveillance, judgment, and constantly updated advice. It was to their own economic advantage to advance "scientific" theories of woman's (romanticized) nature, and to strengthen the ties—of anxiety and self-doubt—that bound woman to her corner of a sexually segregated world.

Physicians were the first of the new experts. With claims to knowledge encompassing all of human biological existence, they were the first to pass judgment on the social consequences of female anatomy and to prescribe a "natural" life plan for women. In the twentieth century, psychomedical experts extended their authority to define woman's domestic activities down to the smallest detail of household management, marital relations, and child raising.

The experts' rise to power over the lives of women depended in part on their own vigorous efforts at self-promotion, in part on the sponsorship of the very wealthy; but it depended also on the real needs of women. The Woman Question, as a subjective dilemma in the lives of women, is born again with each new generation, as it has been since the collapse of the old order. Women no longer could—or would—look for answers from fathers, grandmothers, or priests. To women confronted with new sets of choices, or trying to contain themselves in the shrunken realm of the household, the new experts appeared not only as authorities, but as potential allies.

It was not only gullible women, or conservative women, who embraced the dominion of the experts, but independent-minded and progressive women, even feminists. They welcomed the expert because he seemed to stand for all that was forward looking and scientific, and to oppose all the oppressive reminders of the old order. Margaret Sanger, still a heroine to many feminists, was responsible for guiding the birth control movement out of the grass roots and into the hands of the medical profession—an achievement that she certainly did not see as regressive. Ellen Richards, a reformer in her own right, worked to carve out a new area of expertise (domestic science) that would preside over the most mundane routines of domestic life. Charlotte Perkins Gilman, Ellen Richards, Margaret Sanger, and—it could be argued—Jane Addams, were all, in their different ways, firm believers in the progressive character of science and its representative experts.

In many ways the relationship between women and the experts was not unlike the conventional relationship between women and men. The experts wooed their female constituency, promising the "right" and scientific way to live, and women responded—most eagerly in the upper and middle classes, more slowly among the poor—with dependency and trust. It was never an equal relationship, for the experts' authority rested on the denial or destruction

of women's autonomous sources of knowledge: the old networks of skill sharing, the accumulated lore of generations of mothers. But it was a relationship
that has lasted right up to our own time, when women have begun to discover
that the experts' answer to the Woman Question is not science at all, but only
the ideology of the masculinist society dressed up as objective truth.

1. Fernand Braudel, *Capitalism and Material Life, 1400–1800,* Harper & Row, 1973.
2. Mary P. Ryan, *Womanhood in America,* Franklin Watts, 1975
3. *Women and Labor,* Frederick A. Stokes and Company, 1911.

The Sociology of Housework   *Ann Oakley*

(a) Feelings About Housework

The principal aim of the study was to conceptualize housework as work,
rather than simply as an aspect of the feminine role in marriage. In this way
it differs from previous sociological surveys of family life or women's domestic
situation. The concept of 'satisfaction with housework', analogous with the
notion of job satisfaction in the employment sphere, follows from the
housework-as-work perspective.

1. The major finding here is that dissatisfaction with housework predomi-
nates. Seventy per cent of the women interviewed came out as 'dissatisfied' in
an overall assessment of feelings expressed about housework during the course
of a long depth interview. This figure lays to rest the idea that only a tiny
minority of women are discontented housewives.

2. Monotony is a common experience. Three-quarters of the sample report
it, and eighty per cent of these are dissatisfied with housework. Fragmentation
—a characteristic of work related to monotony—is also experienced by the
majority of housewives, but is not associated with work dissatisfaction. The
reason for this lack of connection appears to be the expectation that housework
must necessarily be fragmented work; women are not made dissatisfied by an
outcome they predict. Excessive pace in work, a second characteristic of work
often associated with monotony in studies of industrial workers' attitudes, is
reported by half the sample. Like fragmentation, it is unrelated to work satisfaction patterns. All three of these experiences—monotony, fragmentation and
excessive pace—show a higher incidence among housewives than among factory workers. In this respect housewives have more in common with assembly

Reprinted by permission of Martin Robertson & Company Ltd., London, 1974. Subsequently
published by Pantheon Books, New York, 1975, from Ann Oakley, *The Sociology of Housework,*
pp. 182–189. References cited in the original have been deleted.

line workers than with factory workers engaged in more skilled and less repetitive work.

3. Loneliness is a frequent complaint. Most of the women who are dissatisfied with housework report a low level of social interaction with others. This parallels the finding from industrial sociology that the opportunity to engage in social relationships with other workers is one of the most prized aspects of any job.

4. Autonomy is the most highly valued dimension of the housewife role. 'Being one's own boss'—a phrase used by nearly half the sample—and exercising control over the pace of work is a facet of housewifery which contrasts favourably with employment work.

5. Housework is the most disliked aspect of 'being a housewife'.

6. Another disadvantage is the low status of the housewife role: the low social prestige and trivialization of housework implied by the phrase 'just a housewife'. A perception of low status is related to housework dissatisfaction —more of those who complain about their status are dissatisfied than satisfied.

7. Attitudes towards the separate tasks that make up housework show considerable variation between tasks, although not between women. The most liked tasks are (in order) cooking, shopping, washing, cleaning, washing up and ironing. The consistency between different women's answers follows from the fact that particular work conditions or contexts are experienced as more satisfying than others. For example, the opportunity to talk to other people while working, having enough time in which to complete tasks, and possessing the right environment or tools of work, are conditions which promote a positive attitude to housework activities. While the *heterogeneity* of housework duties is emphasized in these findings, so also is the *similarity* of the experiences women cite as leading to enjoyment of these duties.

8. Housewives have a long working week. The average in this sample is seventy-seven hours, with a range from forty-eight (the only housewife employed full time at the time of interview) to 105.

9. An important dimension of work behaviour is the felt need to specify standards and routines to which the housewife must adhere in the course of work performance. This process has a number of origins and functions. First, it appears to be a means of creating unity out of a collection of heterogeneous work tasks. Secondly, it is a way of expressing the feeling of personal responsibility for housework. Thirdly, it establishes a means of obtaining reward in housework—satisfaction can be gained daily from successful adherence to these standards and routines. An incidental function is that of job enlargement. There is a relationship between the extent of standards- and routine-specification and the number of hours worked; the majority of those housewives with a 'high' specification work seventy or more hours a week.

With the provision of these job definitions women relinquish, to a considerable extent, the experience of autonomy. For a day-to-day control over work rhythms is substituted a psychological need to follow certain rules. These become 'objectified' i.e. are felt as, in some sense, *external* to the housewife as worker.

10. The relationship between the specification of standards and routines and work satisfaction patterns is in the direction of more satisfaction in the high specification group. This draws attention to the importance of self-reward; by attaining the standards and repeating the routines they set themselves, women may be able to gain a measure of psychological satisfaction. The corollary to this is that a failure to achieve one's pre-set goals may bring about substantial dissatisfaction.

11. Experiences connected with women's performance of jobs outside the home have some bearing on their satisfaction with work in the home. All the women who held high status jobs in the past (such as computer programmer, manicurist, fashion model) are dissatisfied with housework. This phenomenon can be described as a case of incongruency between the housewife's separate statuses: the high status of one's previous job contrasts with the low status of being a housewife, and the resulting stress pushes the balance in favour of present dissatisfaction.

The factor of satisfaction with employment work is also important. Dissatisfaction with housework is higher among those who report work satisfaction in a previous job; in the women's comments housework is unfavourably compared with employment work which, whatever the particular nature of the work, offers company, social recognition and financial reward.

(b) Orientation to the Housewife Role

A second group of findings is very closely connected to the first group, but is separated by a conceptual distinction which at first sight appears trivial. In fact this distinction is of fundamental importance, both to an analysis of the housewife's situation, and to the wider question of how the research interconnects with the women's liberation issue.

The concept of *feelings about housework* relates to women's approaches and responses to the daily experience of doing housework. By contrast, the concept of women's *orientation to the housewife role* describes the relationship between the notion of 'being a housewife' and the psychological identity of women. While the former is a question of job satisfaction in the home, the latter refers to the whole construction of psychological femininity and its 'fit' in a social world predicated on gender differences. The sense of self as a housewife (or not) is a deeply rooted facet of self-identity as feminine; the equation of femininity with housewifery is basic to the institution of family life and to the gender divisions which obtain in the paid work world (the existence of low paid women's jobs being a structural feature of this world).

The discontinuity between the two concepts—feelings about housework and orientation to the housewife role—is, of course, only partial; the two have a degree of overlap. Nevertheless, a differentiation between factors that could be subsumed under the heading of one concept rather than the other was an important feature of the way the research developed. Four conclusions in particular can be identified as relating to orientation to the housewife role.

1. The extent to which housewives are personally identified with the housewife role shapes their whole orientation to it. The majority of the women in the sample have a high or medium identification; a low identification is uncommon. A high personal identification with the role of housewife means that the performance of housework is felt to be one's personal responsibility.
2. The level of identification with the housewife role is related to the way housework is done. Those women with a high identification were likely to have a high specification of standards and routines.
3. In the shaping of domestic role identification in women, the function of the mother as role model is all-important. Mothers are frequently mentioned as influences over women's own housework behaviour; there may not be direct imitation of the mother's way of doing housework, but both imitation and rebellion are essentially aspects of the same identification process.
4. Paralleling the importance of an underlying identification with the housewife role are declared beliefs in favour of 'natural' feminine domesticity, and opposed to a similar degree of domesticity in men. Women locate their orientation to the housewife role within the context of a general view of feminine and masculine roles, according to which the place of each sex is clearly and differently defined. This definition of appropriate gender role behaviour thus covers not only the equation of femaleness with housewifery, but also the patterning of the division of labour between the housewife and her husband.

The distinction between feelings about housework and orientation to the housewife role has manifold implications. In the first place, it enables us to explain certain apparent disagreements on the subject of women's satisfaction or dissatisfaction with domesticity which abound in popular discussion, and which may also be found in academic research. Secondly, this distinction offers a unified understanding of both social class *differences* and *similarities* in housework attitudes/satisfactions. These two particular advantages of distinguishing between the two concepts can be illustrated by taking the prototype of a common conversation today—one which contains the two alternative propositions that women are 'happy' and 'unhappy' as housewives:

> A I don't understand why everyone talks as though all housewives have a miserable time. Lots of women like being housewives.
> B It's ridiculous to pretend that anyone actually *likes* cleaning floors and washing dishes—how can they? Housework is awful work. It's lonely and boring. There's nothing to show for it—it's all got to be done the next day. You don't get paid for it, either.
> A That may be your view, but the plain fact is that most women want to get married and become housewives. They don't complain about it—it's very important to them to look after their homes and their children, and they don't

really have any other ambition. It's only a small minority of militant women who put your point of view. You're *degrading* the housewife. There's nothing wrong with being a housewife and liking it. Running a home is more satisfying than doing a dreary office or factory job.

B But being a housewife is the only option open to many women. It's because there's no alternative that they say they like being housewives—that they like housework. If things were different they might declare their real feelings . . .

Participant A in this conversation is talking about women's relationship to the housewife role, whereas participant B is focusing on feelings about housework. A is not saying that women like housework—only that they like being housewives. Similarly, B is saying women dislike housework but is not arguing that women dislike being housewives. The disagreement is spurious. It is caused by a failure to see that the values of the two factors—feelings about the work, and approach to the role—may not coincide. A woman may be positively oriented to the housewife role but dislike housework; or she may be negatively disposed towards housewifery—not feeling herself to be a housewife —but at the same time enjoy doing housework.

A similar concentration on one or other of the two factors helps to explain why some studies of women's domestic situation emphasize satisfaction, while others highlight dissatisfaction. For example, Mirra Komarovsky's *Blue Collar Marriage* and Lee Rainwater, Richard Coleman and Gerald Handel's *Workingman's Wife* both offer portraits of the working-class woman's life in America, but their conclusions on the whole disagree; Komarovsky stresses the women's satisfaction with housewifery and Rainwater and his colleagues draw attention to the frustrations and dissatisfactions of housework. While Komarovsky focuses on feelings about the role as such, the other study asks questions specifically about daily routine and about feelings towards household tasks. The working-class woman in this study 'characterizes her daily life as "busy," "crowded," "a mess," "humdrum," "dull, just dull" . . . They see themselves as "hard working" women' whereas Komarovsky's subjects 'accept housewifery'. This sharp contrast in the tone of the two conclusions stems from the different approaches adopted. The authors of *Workingman's Wife* turn the spotlight on feelings about housework; in *Blue Collar Marriage* Komarovsky is concerned with the acceptance/non-acceptance of the housewife role.

(c) Social Class

How is an explanation of social class differences aided by the distinction between orientation to the housewife role and feelings about housework?

Some clear differences between working-class and middle-class women did emerge in the interviews; there were also ways in which the two groups were similar. The incidence of dissatisfaction with housework, attitudes to work tasks, the specification of standards and routines, and identification with the housewife role are some of the most important dimensions on which no class difference is manifested. On the other hand considerable class differences were shown in answers to the question 'Do you like housework?' and in responses to a 'test' of self-attitudes given half way through the interview. Broadly speaking, these two components of the interview show working-class women as much more closely involved with the housewife role and with domestic interests and activities generally. 'Like' or 'don't mind' answers to the 'Do you like housework?' question, which were provided chiefly by the working-class housewives in the sample, were interpreted (pages 66–8) as statements symbolizing an attachment to the norm of feminine satisfaction with housework—this norm being more characteristic of working-class than middle-class communities, the adherence to it being facilitated by the more typically 'working-class' mode of language use.

The conjunction of these differences and similarities between the classes can be summed up by saying that, while similar feelings about housework are shared by working-class and middle-class housewives, their orientation to the housewife role tends to differ. The working-class orientation is, on the whole, more positive: there is a strong motivation to declare a personal identification with domesticity, and this, in turn, leads to a search for satisfaction in housework. Correspondingly, the middle-class tendency is towards a disengagement from the housewife role on a verbal and cognitive level (despite an underlying childhood identification with the mother-housewife): instead of a striving after satisfaction with housework there tends to be a recognition of housework dissatisfaction. It is important to note, however, that neither outcome is guaranteed. A woman who wants to be satisfied as a housewife may find that this orientation cannot over-ride the routine daily dissatisfactions of doing housework. Similarly, the recognition of housework dissatisfaction as a possibility (or even probability) may enable some satisfaction to be felt.

It is on the dimension of work attitudes and feelings that the identity of experience between working-class and middle-class women is most in evidence. This, on its own, constitutes a main finding of the study. The incidence of dissatisfaction with housework among the two class groups is the same. If one substitutes the women's education for the social class categorization based (chiefly) on husband's occupation, there is still no differentiation: housewives with an early-completed education are no more likely than those whose education was more prolonged to be satisfied with housework. A finding from industrial sociology was cited in Chapter 4 to support this conclusion. In his study of Detroit automobile workers Arthur Kornhauser shows that occupational differences in 'mental health' (broadly equivalent to 'satisfaction') persist apart from the influence of education. The proportion of workers having good mental health consistently decreases with level of skill required by the job for each of three educational categories separately. In other words the level of skill obtaining in a job, rather than the worker's educational background, is the factor associated with differences in mental health. Applied to the case of the housewife, one could suggest that it is the nature of housework as a job that makes dissatisfaction with it likely. This influence may be stronger than the effect of education or any experience related to social class membership. Such a conclusion requires some revision of the conventional sociological assumption that the unhappy housewife is a purely middle-class phenomenon. Together with other findings it may also be taken as evidence against the appropriateness of the usual approach which assigns women to one social class or another on the basis of their husband's occupation. In some cases the lines drawn may be spurious ones, i.e. there may be no significant differences between women which parallel the class division; the class boundaries thus constructed may actually divert attention from meaningful contrasts which do exist.

Widowhood: A Roleless Role   *Starr Roxanne Hiltz*

The death of a spouse is one of the most serious life crises a person faces. The immediate emotional crisis of bereavement, if not fully worked through, may result in symptoms of mental disorder. During the first few days of bereavement, sacred and secular guidelines define the proper mourning role for the widow. Over the longer term, however, there is generally a need for a total restructuring of the widow's life, as she finds herself much poorer, socially isolated, and left without a meaningful life pattern.

Widowhood can thus be defined more by a collapse of old roles and structural supports than by norms and institutions which specify or provide new role relationships and behavior patterns. Lopata (1975a) concludes from her data that American society has been phasing out the traditional status role of "widow" as an all-pervasive lifelong identity: "Usually, widowhood is a temporary stage of identity reconstruction, and this is the major problem. The direction of movement out of it is not clearly specified" (1975a, p. 47). Widowhood is best conceptualized as a negatively evaluated social category where the individual loses the central source of identity, financial support, and social relationships. It is a "roleless role."

This article reviews selected works by sociologists, psychologists, and social workers on widowhood in American society. Emphasis is upon studies which examine the factors related to the change or dissolution of old role relationships and their replacement by new ones; aspects of widowhood which are related to the structure and functioning of the American family as a whole;

From *Marriage and Family Review,* 1:6 (November/December 1978), pp. 1–10. Reprinted by permission of The Haworth Press, Inc.

and the recent emergence of social service programs aimed at aiding widows in reshaping their lives and identities.

Demographic Characteristics

Widowhood is shared by a very large number of women. In 1976, there were about 10,020,000 widows in the United States, and their numbers have been increasing by about 100,000 a year (Bureau of the Census, Note 1). This is about 13% of all women over the age of 18. Growth in the number and proportion of women who are widows is certain to continue for the rest of this century, since Census projections (Note 2) indicate an increase of 43% in the size of the total population over 65 by the year 2000.

The genesis of widowhood as a social problem in America can be traced to the combined operation of demographic changes and the persistence of a set of values which defines a married woman mainly in terms of her role as a wife.

Currently, American women have a life expectancy of 79, about seven years longer than American men. If demographic patterns were used to suggest marital arrangements, it would make sense for older women to marry younger males. However, our cultural norms and opportunities are such that the initial mortality differences are compounded by the tendency for women to marry older men. Since only about 5% of previous cohorts of American women never married at all, the inevitable result is that ever-larger proportions become widows and remain so for an increasing number of years. (See Table 1; figures are from U.S. Bureau of the Census, Note 3.)

Though the modal age for widowhood is above fifty, a recent detailed study by the Bureau of the Census shows that the majority of women whose first husbands die are widowed before the age of fifty. The younger the age at widowhood, the more likely a woman is to marry, but overall, less than a third of these widows ever remarry. Some of the very detailed demographic data available from this study are summarized in Table 2 below. (Bureau of the Census, 1977, p. 15; Note 4)

Table 1. Proportion of American Women Who Are Widows, by Age, 1976

Age Group	% Widows
Under 35	1.0
35–39	1.9
40–44	3.2
45–54	7.2
55–64	19.1
65–74	42.0
75+	69.7

Table 2.   Women Whose First Marriage Ended in Widowhood, by Age at Widowhood, Percent Remarried, and Median Years Widowed at Survey Date: June 1975

Age at Widowhood	Number (In Thousands)	Percent Remarried	Median Years Widowed
14 to 29	1,143	77.4	5.7
30 to 39	1,090	48.7	4.4
40 to 49	1,436	26.7	10.6
50 to 75	3,107	6.4	9.3
Total	6,778	29.5	—

Widowhood Roles

Most preindustrial societies have very clear roles for widows. For example, in traditional Indian society, a Brahmin widow was supposed to commit *suttee* by throwing herself on her husband's funeral pyre. If she did not do this, she was condemned to live out her life dressed in a single coarse garment, with shaven head, eating only one meal a day, and shunned by others as "unlucky." Another extreme solution, practiced in many African societies, was an immediate (automatic) remarriage, in which the wife and children were "inherited" by a younger brother of the deceased or by some other heir, and the widow became one of his wives in a polygamous family. (See Lopata, 1972, for further descriptions of these customs and those of many other societies in regard to widows.) Even if such prescribed actions and roles were not particularly desirable from the widow's point of view, at least it was clear what she was to do with the rest of her life.

The new widow in American and other (Western) industrialized societies has lost not only a husband, but her own main functions, reason for being, and self-identity. In spite of the emergence of "women's liberation," most women who are becoming widows today have defined themselves primarily as wives and mothers. Lopata sums up the situation in *Widowhood in an American City,* a study of Chicago widows:

> In spite of the rapid industrialization, urbanization, and increasing complexity of the social structure of American society, the basic cluster of social roles available to, and chosen by, its women has been that of wife-mother-housewife. This fact imposes some serious problems upon the last stage of their lives, similar to the problems of retirement in the lives of men who had concentrated upon their occupational roles. The wife-mother-housewife often finds herself with children who are grown, absent from her home, and independent of her as a basic part of their lives; her husband has died, and her household no longer contains a client segment. (Lopata, 1973c, pp. 87–88)

Caine, in her poignant account of her own bereavement and eventual readjustment with professional help, has written a most moving description of the effects of the wrenching away of one's social and self-identity that occurs with the death of a husband:

> "Widow" is a harsh and hurtful word. It comes from the Sanskrit and means "empty." . . .
>
> After my husband died, I felt like one of those spiraled shells washed up on the beach. Poke a straw through the twisting tunnel, around and around, and there is nothing there. No flesh. No life. Whatever lived there is dried up and gone.
>
> Our society is set up so that most women lose their identities when their husbands die. Marriage is a symbiotic relationship for most of us. We draw our identities from our husbands. We add ourselves to our men, pour ourselves into them and their lives. We exist in their reflection. And then . . . ? If they die . . . ? What is left? It's wrenching enough to lose the man who is your lover, your companion, your best friend, the father of your children, without losing yourself as well. (Caine, 1974, pp. 181, 1)

It should be noted that Caine had a fine job for many years before her husband died, but yet this did not alleviate the necessity and pain of totally restructuring her social role.

Remarriage is not a likely solution. There are fewer than two million widowers in the United States, one for every five widows, and they are likely to marry younger women. Cleveland and Gianturco (1976), in a retrospective study of North Carolina data, for instance, concluded that less than 5% of women widowed after age 55 ever remarry.

As Lopata points out:

> Life styles for American widows are generally built upon the assumption that they are young and can soon remarry or that they are very old and removed from the realm of actual involvement. The trouble is that most widows are neither, but the society has not taken sufficient cognizance of this fact to modify the facilities and roles available to them. (Lopata, 1973c, p. 17)

A woman is likely to spend as much time as a widow as she does raising children. Although she was socialized all through her early life for the wife-and-motherhood role, she typically has had no preparation at all for the widowhood role. The whole subject has been taboo, and few women prepare ahead of time for widowhood.

Despite the statistical data and personal tragedies that make widowhood a major social problem "encompassing increasing numbers of women and their families and indirectly affecting many others" (Berardo, 1968, p. 200), until recently there has been little sociological research or social service resources to deal with it.

There was only some early work by Elliot (1930, 1933, 1946, 1948) and a study of British widows (Morris, 1958). However, several large-scale and/or long-term research projects on widowhood have appeared in the late 1960s and early 1970s, and will form the main basis for the findings surveyed here:

1. Two major studies by Lopata. *Widowhood in an American City* (1973c) was based on interviews with 301 Chicago widows and examined the role behavior of widows as mothers, in-laws, friends, and in the wider community. Her most recent study of support systems for widows draws on a survey of 1,169 (Chicago area widowed Social Security beneficiaries (Lopata, Note 4). It describes the present and needed personal, economic, and social service supports available to the widowed. Lopata's work on the widowed is by far the most extensive. (See also Lopata, 1969, 1970, 1971, 1973a, 1973b, 1975a, 1975b, Note 3, Note 5, Note 6.)

2. The work of members of the Laboratory of Community Psychiatry at Harvard Medical School includes: (a) studies of bereavement as a set of psychological and medical symptoms (Glick, Weiss, & Parkes, 1974; Maddison, 1968; Parkes, 1964a, 1964b, 1965, 1975); (b) a widow-to-widow program (Silverman, 1966, 1969, 1970, 1972; Silverman & Cooperband, 1975; Silverman & Englander, 1975); and (c) Weiss's work on widowhood as a "transitional state." Similar to separation and divorce, widowhood requires not only resolution of "unfinished business" in old role relationships, but also the construction of a new self-identity. Weiss has developed seminars for the bereaved (1969, 1974, 1976).

3. Another major project is on crisis intervention with families of the bereaved aged in the Bronx, New York, at Monterfiore Hospital, which focuses on the impact of professional intervention upon physical and psychiatric health (Gerber, Rusalem, Hannon, Battin, & Arkin 1975: (Gerber, Wiener, Battin, & Arkin, 1975; Schoenberg et al., 1975).

4. A program of research on the Widows Consultation Center in New York City (Hiltz, 1974, 1975, 1977) focuses on social service programs designed to help widows rebuild their lives, and how these services were helpful to the clients.

There are also some smaller scale studies based on analysis of a single set of survey or other data. Adams (1968) studied strains between middle-class widows and their grown sons. Chevan and Korson (1972, 1975) document the unwillingness of American widows to live with children or others rather than head their own household. Results of a sample survey of widowed and married Los Angeles women aged 45–74 suggest that the lower income and employment status of widows accounts for their lower morale, since differences in morale scores disappeared when these status factors were removed (Morgan, 1976). Secondary analysis by Harvey and Bahr (1974) examined the relationship between the morale of widows and their various "affiliations,' or roles, and included an examination of the effects of moving from a full-time housewife role to full-time work for widows who also have to cope with children at home. A report by Lucy Mallan for the Social Security Administration (1975) focuses on the contribution of Social Security benefits to the economic status of widows and their families.

Grief as a Kind of Illness: Effects on Role Performance

The emotional and psychological traumas of grief and mourning involve "letting go" of the emotional ties and roles centered on the husband. If this working through of grief is successfully accomplished, the widow can face a second set of problems having to do with building a new life, a new set of role relationships, and a new identity.

Much of the psychological literature on grief represents an elaboration of Freud's theories. For Freud, grief or "grief work" is the process by which bereaved persons struggle to disengage the loved object. The emotional bond is fused with energy, bound to memories and ideas related to former interations with the loved person. The mourner has to spend time and effort to bring to consciousness all of these memories in order to set free the energy, to break the tie (Freud, 1917/1957).

Building on the Freudian theory is the classic study by Lindermann in 1944. Based on a study of survivors of the Coconut Grove fire, it established the theory that "normal" bereavement consists of the following stages:

1. Numbness and disbelief, a tendency to deny the death, not to accept the fact that "he is *really* dead, gone forever." This numbness often extends for several weeks beyond the funeral.
2. This is followed by emotional reactions such as crying, often accompanied by such psychosomatic symptoms as headache and insomnia; feelings of guilt, "If I had done so-and-so, maybe he wouldn't have died"; expressions of anger, "Why me! It is so unfair!"; hostility or blame, "The doctors killed him"; and often preoccupation with memories of the deceased and an idealization of him.
3. Feelings of sadness and loneliness, which are often incapacitating, depression, loss of customary patterns of conduct and of motivation to try to go on living, is another stage. This may be followed by a recovery phase.

At one time "grief," as in the extended "pining away" of the third stage, was recognized as a cause of death and listed on death certificates. As Glick et al. (1974) have concluded from their extensive studies of bereavement, "the death of a spouse typically gives rise to a reaction whose duration must be measured in years rather than in weeks" (1974, p. 10).

A variety of grief reactions may occur when the mourner does not express emotion or refuses to deal with the loss. These include delay of the grief reactions for months or even years; overactivity without a sense of loss; indefinite irritability and hostility toward others; sense of the presence of the deceased; acquisition of the physical symptoms of the deceased's last illness; insomnia; apathy; psychosomatically based illnesses such as ulcerative colitis; and such intense depression and feelings of worthlessness that suicide is attempted (Parkes, 1972, p. 211; Van Coevering, Note 7, p. 6).

One tendency is to reconstruct an idealized version of one's deceased husband and of the role relationship with him before the death. Referred to as "husband sanctification," Lopata (Note 6) reports that three-quarters of the Chicago area current and former beneficiaries of Social Security define their late husband as having been "extremely good, honest, kind, friendly, and warm" (Note 6, pp. 4–5). Sanctification is especially likely among women who rank the role of wife above all others. It is an attempt to continue defining oneself primarily in terms of the now-broken role relationship. Lopata views this as an effort to "remove the late husband into an other-worldly position as an understanding but purified and distant observer" (Note 6, p. 30), so that the widow is able to go about reconstructing old role relationships and forming new ones.

There are several factors related to severe or prolonged grief. Sixty-eight widows and widowers under the age of 45 were interviewed shortly after the spouse died and again a year later in the Harvard Bereavement Study. An "outcome score" was obtained from depth interview material and answers to questions on health; increased consumption of alcohol, tranquillizers, and tobacco; self-assessment as "depressed or very unhappy"; and "wondering whether anything is worthwhile anymore." Three classes of strongly correlated and intercorrelated variables predict continued severe bereavement reactions 13 months after the death (Parkes, 1975, pp. 308–309):

1. Low socioeconomic status, i.e., low weekly income of the husband, Spearman's rho correlation of .44; low occupational status, .28.
2. Lack of preparation for loss due to noncancer deaths, short terminal illness, accident or heart attack, or failure to talk to the spouse about the coming death, correlations of .26 to .29.
3. Other life crises preceding spouse's death, such as infidelity and job loss, correlations of .25 to .44.

It is interesting that a poor outcome is likely if the marriage relationship was troubled before the death; folk wisdom would have it that the widow would be "glad to be rid of him." Psychologically debilitating guilt over having wished the death of the husband seems to be very strong in such cases, however. Another problem is the amount of "unfinished business" (Blauner, 1966) left by the removal of the husband through death. Parkes concludes that for his young respondents, including widowers as well as widows, "When advance warning was short and the death was sudden, it seemed to have a much greater impact and to lead to greater and more lasting disorganization" (Parkes, 1975, p. 313).

However, a British study of mostly older widows and widowers (Bornstein, Clayton, Halikas, Maurice, & Robin, 1973) did not show a similar relationship. Perhaps, in old age, death, even "without warning," is not shocking, since it has commonly been encountered previously among one's reference group of friends, relatives, and their spouses. In a study of "anticipatory grief" among the elderly, an extended period of chronic illness of the spouse was associated with poorer medical adjustment six months after death for widowers (Gerber, Rusalem, Hannon, Battin, & Arkin 1975). This suggests that any intervention should be introduced during such a period.

Emotional problems related to grief or bereavement were by far the most prevalent problems reported by the clients of the Widows Consultation Center, both initially and at the time of the follow-up about one year later (see Table 3). These are not independent of the problems relating to income, friends, and family. Disturbance and dissolution of the widow's main social relationships and removal of the main source of income require finding new friends and activities, a job, often less expensive housing; and similar adjustments. Any major change in role relationships and living patterns is stressful, and causes emotional disturbance. But many changes in one's life circumstances and behavior patterns simultaneously are especially likely to be associated with extreme emotional stress and such symptoms as mental illness, heart attacks, and suicide.

Given the severe and persistent emotional, psychological, and psychosomatic aspects of even "normal" grief, it becomes impossible for a widow to carry out her usual role relationships and to cope with the problems of change in financial and social status that are thrust upon her.

Financial Problems

The subsequent life changes and problems faced by the widow indicate that widowhood is a role for which there is no comparable role among males. Glick and associates (1974) summarize the difference between their samples of widows and of widowers: "Insofar as the men reacted simply to the *loss of a loved other,* their responses were *similar* to those of widows, but insofar as men reacted to the *traumatic disruption of their lives,* their responses were *different"*

Table 3. Self-Reporting of Problems by Widows in Response to Structured Questions at Time of Follow-up Interview

Problem Area	Problem When Came to Center	Problem Now	N^a
Emotional upset	80%	68%	174
Relations with family	39%	32%	221
Finding a job	49%	39%	230
Living quarters	32%	31%	227
Friends	53%	49%	220
Government agencies	19%	15%	222
Managing finances	68%	51%	218
Relations with men	30%	44%	146

N^a includes only those who responded to the structured question.
Source: Follow-up interviews, N = 259.

(Glick et al., 1974, p. 262). This differential impact is found in the financial impact of the death. For the widow, it almost always means the loss of the main source of financial support for the family and a consequent lowering of the standard of living. Overall, widows in 1970 constituted 19% of the female population over 14, but 24% of those with an income under $1,000 and 36% of those living on between $1,000 and $2,999 (U.S. Bureau of the Census, Note 2). In Lopata's sample of Chicago widows, 60% had annual family incomes under $3,000 (1973c, p. 37).

Mallan's 1975 study found that Social Security benefit increases between 1967 and 1971 has "lessened the likelihood that young widows, with one to three children, would be poor" (1975, p. 18). However, three-quarters of old widows around the age of 60, not yet eligible for retirement benefits but not working, were found to be in poverty.

The dynamics of their situation is partially explained by a survey of 1,744 widows whose husbands had died in 1966, conducted by the Life Insurance Agency Management Association in 1968–69 and published in 1970 (Note 8). They found that for 28% there was at least a year between the onset of the final illness or disability and the death. This is a financially and emotionally draining experience. Only two-thirds of all widows with medical bills received any health insurance payments, and for them the health insurance paid an average of 77% of the bill. Final expenses were $3,600, on the average, with life and health insurance combined covering only 64% of the final expenses. For the remainder, the widows had to deplete savings or use income from their Social Security, earnings, or other sources.

By two to three years after the onset of widowhood, the incomes of the widows' families were down an average of 44% from previous levels, and 58% had incomes that fell below the amount that would have been necessary to maintain their family's former standard of living. This occurred even among those who received life insurance benefits. After final expenses, 44% had used up part of this for living expenses, and 14% had consumed all of it.

In addition to financially devastating final expenses which wipe out savings, widows are entitled to no Social Security benefits at all unless they have dependents or are over 60. After 60 years of age, they are entitled only to a portion of what would have been their husband's benefits. The final explanation for the high probability of poverty among widows is that because of age, low level of skill and education, and lack of experience, they are often unable to obtain employment. In other words, neither the private economy nor the public welfare system is currently structured to provide economic support to widows in late middle age.

Finding New Social Roles

Before widowhood, a married woman defines herself and relates to others mainly in terms of her status as somebody's wife. At widowhood, most of her role relationships will have to adjust and some will terminate. She will have to establish new role relationships if her life is to be a satisfying one. For example, she is unlikely to maintain close ties with friends and relatives who belonged to social circles maintained with her husband. Changes in finances can require changes in other spheres of life, such as movement into the work force. A change in residence may result in loss of contact with neighbors. Often, in settling her husband's estate, she has to deal with lawyers and insurance agents and has to take on the role of businesswoman (Lopata, 1975a, p. 48).

The difficulties an older woman in our society is likely to encounter in establishing such a new set of role relationships is affirmed by Professor Lopata. She found that half of the widows in her sample considered loneliness their greatest problem, and another third listed it second. Social isolation was listed by 58%, who agreed with the statement "One problem of being a widow is feeling like a 'fifth wheel' " (Lopata, 1972, pp. 91, 346).

Lopata's work focuses on the widow's role relationships in regard to motherhood, kin relationships, friendship, and community involvement, including employment. Among her findings are that "women who develop satisfactory friendships, who weather the transition period and solve its problems creatively, tend to have a higher education, a comfortable income, and the physical and psychic energy needed to initiate change" (Lopata, 1972, p. 216). These women are not the "average" widow, who is likely to have a high school education or less, low income, depleted physical energy due to advancing age, and depleted psychic energy due to the trauma of bereavement and its associated problems.

The importance of maintaining or establishing supportive role relationships with an understanding "other" such as an old friend, neighbor, or supportive professional or paraprofessional, has been emphasized in many studies. For instance, Maddison and Raphael (1975) emphasize their "conviction that the widow's perception of her social network is an extremely important determinant of the outcome of her bereavement crisis" (1975, p. 29). "Bad outcome" women had no one to whom they could freely express their grief and anger.

Disruption of Family Relationships

The death of the husband tends to cause strain in relationships with children, in-laws, and even one's own siblings and other relatives. Thirty-nine percent of the clients of the Widows Consultation Center reported that relationships with family members were a problem at the time they came to the Center. Problems with children were reported by more clients (31%), compared to in-laws (8%) and siblings (6%).

The problems with children were twofold: a perceived coldness or neglect to give the widow as much "love" and support and time as she thought she was entitled to (17%), and what the widow considered serious behavioral problems with the children, such as taking drugs or withdrawing from employment and from communication with the mother (15%) (Hiltz, 1977, pp. 64–65).

What is seen as "neglect" or "coldness" by the widow may be viewed as an unfair and unpleasant burden by the child, especially sons. For example, Adams (1968) found that grown middle-class sons perceived their obligations to their mother as a "one-way" or unreciprocated pattern of aid and support-giving. This typically results in a son's loss of affection for the mother and his resentment of her dependence upon him.

For younger widows with dependent children, there are difficulties in maintaining the maternal role of effectively responding to the child's needs. Taking a sample of 19 cases of widows with children under 16 from follow-up 3 years after bereavement, Silverman and Englander found that most parents and children avoided talking about the death to one another. Common reactions of the child were fear that they would lose the surviving parent, too; the assumption by the child of new family responsibilities; and poor school work related to rebellion and social withdrawal (Silverman & Englander, 1975, p. 11).

Role relationships to in-laws may be cut off entirely if the widow does not find them pleasant and supportive. As Lopata (Note 4) points out, this is a unique kind of institutional arrangement, since the patriarchal family traditionally had vested rights over the wife and the offspring of a marriage. However, "American widows are free to move away from their in-laws, if they were living nearby, and even to lose all contact with them. They are free to cut the ties between their children and that side of the family and even to remarry and change the name of the unit" (Note 4, p. 3). However, none of the studies seem to include the impact of such decisions on the role relationship between paternal grandparents and grandchildren, and on the emotional pain that may be caused if the relationship is severed.

Intervention Strategies and Their Effectiveness

Findings from recent research projects have sustained the premise that social service or intervention programs to help the widow cope and build a satisfactory network of role relationships do work. One such project involving intervention in the life of the widow is the "Widow-to-Widow" program. Five widows were originally recruited as aides, chosen as having personal skills in dealing with people and as representatives of the dominant racial and religious groups in the community. The aide wrote the new widow a letter saying that she would call on her at a particular time. This usually occurred three weeks after the death, unless the widow telephoned and requested no visit. Of the 91 widows located in the first seven months of the program, 64 accepted contact, half by visit and half by telephone, an overall acceptance rate of 60%. The aides offered friendship as well as advice and assistance with specific problems. In addition, group discussion meetings and social events such as a cookout were organized to which all of the widows were invited (Silverman, 1969, pp. 333–337). As Silverman describes the role of the aide, she "encourages, prods, insists, and sometimes even takes the widow by the hand and goes through the motions with her" (1972, p. 101).

On the basis of this project and one other, Silverman and Cooperband conclude that "the evidence points to another widow as the best caregiver. . . . This other widow . . . can provide a perspective on feelings; she provides a role model; she can reach out as a friend and neighbor" (Silverman & Cooperband, 1975, p. 11).

Some psychiatrists and social workers question the advisability of using untrained recent widows to give aid to other widows, without available referral to professionals. For instance, they point to abnormal grief reactions experienced by widows visited by aides, including two who died, who may have responded to professional intervention. Also, unresolved elements of her own grief might lead the widow-aide to excessive reliance upon her own methods of coping, overlooking or negatively responding to other possibilities (Kahana, 1975). "The danger is that unresolved or unrecognized grief may adversely influence the aide in trying to assist the newly bereaved widow. . . . Some of the people who say 'I know how you feel' may really mean 'I know how I feel' " (Blau, 1975, pp. 36–37).

The Widows Consultation Center's casework service was to provide a single central source of help to eliminate the frustration and despair experienced by clients in going from one agency to another in a search for information, directions, and assistance. Individual counseling with a caseworker included referrals or assistance in dealing with agencies such as the Social Security Administration or the New York Housing Authority, or on emotional, social, or family problems. For problems best dealt with by referral, counseling rarely went beyond one session. For emotional problems, however, counseling generally involved many meetings.

Group discussion or therapy sessions, with groups of three to ten widows, met weekly with a professional leader. They varied, depending upon the participants, from fairly casual sharing of experiences as widows to explicitly therapeutic groups. (See Hiltz, 1975, for a description of these groups.)

Social activities and recreational events were organized for the Center's clients. These social get-togethers were initiated slowly, with the first year's activities most typically a monthly tea at the Center preceded by a brief lecture on some topic of apparent interest to widows, such as a book on widowhood. By the third year, a part-time social worker was hired to organize and conduct social activities, such as Sunday afternoon sessions at the local "Y," weekend bus trips, and free theater parties.

Special professional consultation about legal or financial problems was arranged through caseworkers, who made appointments for clients who seemed to need expert advice. The financial consultant was a well-known writer on personal finance, who did not recommend specific investments but gave generalized advice on types of investments, budgeting, and allocation of funds.

The main criterion of effectiveness used in this study was the widows' own feelings about whether or not the WCC had helped them with each problem area identified by each widow at the time she came to the Center. Widows felt the Center had been most helpful with emotional problems. Overall, 53% of widows questioned about this area said that the Center had been helpful to them, and this increases to 80% for those with five or more visits to the Center.

When asked "Overall, would you say that the Widows Consultation Center was a great deal of help to you, of some help, or no help at all?"; 33% said "of some help"; and 30% said "no help." These results become more favorable as the number of private interviews, group therapy sessions, or social activities attended increases. For example, less than a third of those who had only one or two private interviews felt that the Center had given them a "great deal of help," compared to 79% of those who had five or more private consultation sessions. These findings support the feelings of the caseworkers that they achieved much more success in helping their clients with a supportive case-work process that extended over some period of time, rather than a one- or two-visit process.

Building on his work with the separated, sociologist Weiss and his colleagues developed a program of eight "seminars" for the bereaved. Each of eight weekly meetings begins with a lecture of about 45 minutes on some aspect of bereavement. After each lecture, small discussion groups are formed to discuss various subjects according to members' interests. There is a wine and cheese party at the last meeting, and then a "reunion" of the group about six weeks after the last meeting (Weiss, 1976, Note 9). This program is monitored and evaluated with follow-up interviews of participants.

The Widows Consultation Centre in Winnipeg, built upon the experiences of the New York WCC, modified the service model in several respects, resulting in greater economy. It provides a more financially feasible model for the majority of communities than the original WCC, and incorporates techniques developed by Silverman and Weiss. Rather than creating a completely new and independent agency, it was decided by the Winnipeg WCC that "it would be preferable that such a service should be developed as an expansion of an existing agency. The Y.W.C.A. was thought to be most appropriate for this purpose because of its community acceptability and because it had already done some work in the area of programming for widows" (DeGraves, Note 10, Note 11). The Winnipeg WCC operates with only one professional social worker who does all the counseling, supervises twice-a-month social programs, supervises three visiting widows in a widow-to-widow program, and serves as the group leader for a therapeutic discussion group which is now modeled on Weiss's seminars at the Harvard Medical School (DeGraves, Note 12). Since this is a service-oriented agency, there are no reliable data on the effectiveness of the various components of the program.

The Montefiore Hospital Project with the bereaved aged is the only controlled experiment on the effectiveness of therapeutic intervention. A large number of the elderly are assigned for primary medical care to an internist at the hospital. Therefore, there was an opportunity to work with medical records of a large population in designing an intervention program. The families of all persons who died in the hospital were assigned, on a two-to-one basis, to brief therapeutic intervention of six months or less by a psychiatric social worker and a psychiatric nurse; or to no treatment. In addition, every third bereaved spouse was matched by age, sex, and number and sex of children with a nonbereaved patient of the hospital. The intervention consisted of client-centered treatment over the telephone or in person with helping the bereaved to express their feelings and understanding their emotional reactions, and assisting with current problems and future plans. Dependent variables were almost entirely medical indicators, such as visits to doctors, major and minor illnesses, and prescription of medicines. In reporting the results of the experiment, Gerber, Wiener, Battin, and Arkin (1975) conclude:

> The results for 75 per cent (five of the seven) of the measures of therapeutic outcome tend to suggest that the type of brief therapy we offered was to some extent medically beneficial. . . . From our experience it appears that a therapeutic service to the bereaved will begin to have a positive impact approximately three months after the intervention begins (Gerber et al., 1975, p. 330)

However, the authors caution, "We actually have limited knowledge about which type of service (individual versus group therapy), which intervention orientation (long-term versus lay support) produces the most effective result" (1975, p. 312). I would add to this list a distinction between socially oriented peer groups and professionally led therapeutic groups, and the distinction between projects which systematically seek out all widows in a community and those which depend on client initiative. What is needed at this point is a large-scale project which systematically experiments with the effectiveness of various individual and combined techniques for widows of various ages, life situations, and severity of grief.

Summary

Studies of widowhood during the last decade have given us an understanding of the fact that widows in American society must forge a total emotional, financial, and social reorganization of their lives, at a time when their resources for such a task are generally inadequate. There are many areas in which the "broad picture" of the problems faced by widows must be filled in by much more detail. Strategies to prevent deterioration in communication and quality of relationship between the newly widowed mother and her dependent or grown children is one example of an area in which such research would be particularly valuable. At the societal level, we need to explore what mix of private and public efforts can replace the likelihood of poverty created by the current Social Security "blackout period" and lack of job opportunities for older widows with some assurance of financial security. Finally, we need to forge a stronger relationship between social service programs and social research, so that knowledge of successful and unsuccessful strategies in helping widows to build a socially and financially supportive set of role relationships becomes cumulative and shared.

Reference Notes

1. U.S. Bureau of the Census. Marital status and living arrangements, March 1976. In *Current population reports: Population characteristics,* Series p-20, No. 36. Washington, D.C.: Author, 1977.
2. U.S. Bureau of the Census. Population characteristics, marital status and living arrangements, March 1972. In *Current population reports,* Series P-20, No. 42. Washington, D.C.: U.S. Government Printing Office, 1972.
3. U.S. Bureau of the Census. Number, timing and duration of marriages and divorces in the U.S., June 1975. In *Current Population Reports,* Series P-20, No. 297. Washington, D.C.: U.S. Government Printing Office, 1976.
4. Lopata, H. Z. *Support systems involving widows in a metropolitan area of the United States.* Unpublished manuscript, Loyola University Center for the Comparative Study of Social Roles, 1977.
5. Lopata, H. Z. *Widowhood: Societal factors in lifespan disruptions and alternatives.* Paper presented at the Fourth Lifespan Developmental Psychology Conference, Morgantown, W.Va., May 1974.
6. Lopata, H. Z. *Widowhood and husband sanctification.* Paper presented at the 71st annual meeting of the American Sociological Association, New York City, August 1976.
7. Van Coevering, V. *Developmental tasks of widowhood for the aging woman.* Paper presented at the annual meeting of the American Psychological Association, September 1971.
8. Life Insurance Agency Management Association. *The widows study* (Vol. 1, *The onset of widowhood;* Vol. 2, *Adjustment to widowhood: The first two years*). Author, 1970.
9. Weiss, R. Personal communication, August 1976.
10. DeGraves, D. *The widow-to-widow program.* Unpublished manuscript, 1975. (Available from the Widows Consultation Centre, 447 Webb Place, Winnipeg, Manitoba, Canada.)
11. DeGraves, D. *The widows consultation centre.* Unpublished manuscript, 1975. (Available from the Widows Consultation Centre, 447 Webb Place, Winnipeg, Manitoba, Canada.)
12. DeGraves, D. Personal communication. 1977.

References

Adams, B. The middle-class adult and his widowed or still-married mother. *Social Problems.* 1968, *16,* 50–59.
Berardo, F. M. Widowhood status in the United States: Perspective on a neglected aspect of the family life cycle. *The Family Coordinator,* 1968, *17,* 191–203.
Blau, D. On widowhood: Discussion, *Journal of Geriatric Psychiatry,* 1975, *8,* 29–40.
Blauner, R. Death and social structure, *Psychiatry,* 1966, *29,* 387–394.
Bornstein, P. E., Clayton, P. J., Halikas, J. A., Maurice, W. L., & Robin, E. The depression of widowhood at 13 months. *British Journal of Psychiatry,* 1973, *122,* 561–566.
Caine, L. *Widow,* New York: Wm. Morrow & Co., 1974.
Chevan, A., & Korson, H. The widowed who live alone: An examination of social and demographic factors. *Social Forces,* 1972. *51,* 43–53.
Chevan, A., & Korson, H. Living arrangements of widows in the United States and Israel, 1960 and 1961. *Demography,* 1975, *12,* 505–518.
Cleveland, W. P., & Granturco, D. T. Remarriage probability after widowhood: A retrospective method. *Journal of Gerontology,* 1976, *31,* 99–103.
Elliot, T. D. The adjustive behavior of bereaved families: A new field for research. *Social Forces,* 1930, *8,* 543–549.

Elliot, T. D. A step toward the social psychology of bereavement. *Journal of Abnormal and Social Psychology,* 1933, *27,* 380–390.

Elliot, T. D. War bereavements and their recovery. *Marriage and Family Living,* 1946, *8,* 1–6.

Elliot, T. D. Bereavement: Inevitable but not insurmountable. In H. Berker & A. Hill, *Family, marriage and parenthood.* Boston: D. C. Heath, 1948.

Freud, S. Mourning and melancholia. In J. Strachey (Ed. and trans.), *The Standard Edition of the Complete Psychological Works of Sigmund Freud* (Vol. XIV). London: The Hogarth Press and the Institute for Psycho Analysis, 1957. (Originally published 1917.)

Gerber, I., Rusalem, R., Hannon, N., Battin, D., & Arkin, A. Anticipatory grief and aged widows and widowers. *Journal of Gerontology,* 1975, *30,* 225–229.

Gerber, I., Wiener, A., Battin, D., & Arkin, A. M. Brief therapy to the aged bereaved. In B. Schoenberg, I. Gerber, A. Wiener, A. Kutscher, D. Peretz & C. Carr. (Eds.), *Bereavement: Its psychosocial aspects.* New York: Columbia University Press, 1975.

Glick, I. O., WEiss, R., & Parkes, C. M. *The first year of bereavement.* New York: John Wiley & Sons, 1974.

Harvey, C. D., & Bahr, H. M. Widowhood, morale, and affiliation. *Journal of Marriage and the Family,* 1974, *36,* 97–106.

Hiltz, S. R. Evaluating a pilot social service project for widows: A chronicle of research problems. *Journal of Sociology and Social Welfare,* 1974, *1,* 217–224.

Hiltz, S. R. Helping widows: Group discussions as a therapeutic technique. *The Family Coordinator,* 1975, *24,* 331–336.

Hiltz, S. R. *Creating community services for widows: A pilot project.* Port Washington, N.Y.: Kennikat Press, 1977.

Kahana, R. J. On widowhood: Introduction. *Journal of Geriatric Psychiatry,* 1975, *8,* 5–8.

Levin, S. On widowhood: Discussion. *Journal of Geriatric Psychiatry,* 1975, *8,* 57–59.

Lindemann, E. The symptomatology and management of acute grief. *American Journal of Psychiatry,* 1944, *101,* 141–148.

Lopata, H. Z. Loneliness: Forms and components. *Social Problems,* 1969, *17,* 248–262.

Lopata, H. Z. The social involvement of American widows. *American Behavioral Scientist,* 1970, *14,* 41–57.

Lopata, H. Z. Widows as minority groups. *Gerontologist,* 1971, *11,* 67–77.

Lopata, H. Z. Role changes in widowhood: A world perspective. In D. Cowgill & L. Holmes (Eds.), *Aging and modernization.* New York: Appleton-Century-Crofts, 1972.

Lopata, H. Z. Living through widowhood. *Psychology Today,* July 1973, pp. 87–92. (a)

Lopata, H. Z. Self identity in marriage and widowhood. *Sociological Quarterly,* 1973, *14,* 407–418. (b)

Lopata, H. Z. On widowhood: Grief, work, and identity reconstruction. *Journal of Geriatric Psychiatry,* 1975, *8,* 41–55. (a)

Lopata, H. Z. Widowhood: Societal factors in life-span disruption and alternatiives. In N. Datan & L. H. Ginsberg (Eds.), *Life span development psychology: Normative life crisis.* New York: Academic Press, 1975, (b)

Maddison, D. Relevance of conjugal bereavement for preventive psychiatry. *British Journal of Medical Psychology,* 1968, *41,* 223–233.

Maddison, D., & Raphael, B. Conjugal bereavement and the social network. In B. Schoenberg, I. Gerber, A. Wiener, A. Kutscher, D. Peretz, & C. Carr. (Eds.), *Bereavement: Its psychosocial aspects.* New York: Columbia University Press, 1975.

Mallan, L. B. Young widows and their children: A comparative report. *Social Security Bulletin* (U. S. Department of Health, Education and Welfare Publication No. SSA-75-700), May 1975, pp. 3–21.

McCourt, W. F., Bornett, R., Brennan, J., & Becker, A. We help each other: Primary evaluation for the widowed. *American Journal of Psychiatry,* 1976, *133,* 98–100.

Morgan, L. A. A Re-examination of widowhood and morale. *Journal of Gerontology,* 1976, *31,* 687–695.

Morris, P. *Widows and their families.* London: Routledge & Kegan Paul, 1958.

Parkes, C. M. Effects of bereavement on physical and mental health: A study of the medical records of widows. *British Medical Journal,* 1964, *2,* 274–279. (a)

Parkes, C. M. Grief as an illness. *New Society,* 1964, *80,* 11–12.

Parkes, C. M. Bereavement and mental illness: a clinical study. *British Journal of Medical Psychology,* 1965, *38,* 1–26.

Parkes, C. M. *Bereavement: Studies of grief in adult life.* New York: International Press, 1972.
Parkes, C. M. Determinants of outcome following bereavement. *Omega: Journal of Death and Dying,* 1975, *6,* 303–323.
Schoenberg, B., Gerber, I., Wiener, A., Kutscher, A., Peretz, D., & Carr, A. (Eds.). *Bereavement: Its psychosocial aspects.* New York: Columbia University Press, 1975.
Silverman, P. R. Services for the widowed during the period of bereavement. *Social work practice.* New York: Columbia University Press, 1966.
Silverman, P. R. The widow-to-widow program: An experiment in preventive intervention. *Mental Hygiene,* 1969, *53,* 333–337.
Silverman, P. R. The widow as a caregiver in a program of preventive intervention with other widows. *Mental Hygiene,* 1970, *54,* 540–547.
Silverman, P. R. Widowhood and preventive intervention. *The Family Coordinator,* 1972, *21,* 95–102.
Silverman, P. R., & Cooperband, A. On widowhood: Mutual help and the elderly widow. *Journal of Geriatric Psychiatry,* 1975, *8,* 9–27.
Silverman, P. R., & Englander, S. The widow's view of her dependent children. *Omega: Journal of Death and Dying,* 1975, *6,* 3–20.
Weiss, R. S. The fund of sociability. *Trans-ACTION,* 1969, *6,* 43–63.
Weiss, R. S. *Loneliness: The experience of emotional and social isolation.* Cambridge, Mass.: The M.I.T. Press, 1974.
Weiss, R. S. Transition states and other stressful situations: Their nature and programs for their management. In Caplan & Kililea (eds.), *Support systems and mutual help.* New York: Grune & Statton, 1976.

Changing Sex Roles and Family Structure

Janet Zollinger Giele

There is a close tie between the change in men's and women's roles and the change in family structure. But the relative status of women in family life is more difficult to measure than their status in public affairs. Political, economic, or educational activities operate in "markets" that assign the individual a formal status and pay a stated income. The family by contrast is "associational" (Weinstein and Platt, 1973: 1–19). The status of each member is enmeshed with facts of birth and death, marriage, or divorce. Participation in the family hinges on the emotional life of others as well as on individual accomplishment. Laws and public policies directed at child care, the elderly, tax rates, or public welfare affect not only one member or one sex but also the whole family unit. Consequently, examination of the relative status of women and men in the family very quickly leads to considering the structure of the family unit and the situational realities that determine its form.

Women's and men's roles will not really change unless family institutions also change, but it is not at all clear in what order and in what direction family life will be transformed. Maybe, as some economists suggest, the next steps to be taken are public measures that will support a new occupation of consumer maintenance, or allow tax deductions for household costs such as heat, light, or child care, much as corporations are allowed tax deductions for their expenses (Bell, 1975; Lekachman, 1975). Or perhaps the next steps must be personal and ideological, through commitment to the idea that the family is the responsibility of both men and women.

No matter what change comes first, it is clear now that the traditional sex-typed division of labor between women's work at home and men's work at a job is under strain in every major industrial nation. Although 40 to 60 percent of women are employed in such countries as the United States, Russia, Poland, and Japan, they pay a penalty of being overburdened by both domestic and paid work (Blake, 1974). Employed American women who have families average a total of 70 hours of work a week (Gauger, 1973: 23). Each week they have a few hours less leisure time than men for sleep or relaxation (Szalai, 1973). Thus more women have entered employment without having secured the needed adjustments in family life.

The balance of work and leisure is only one issue raised by change in sex roles. Other related problems emerge. The poverty of female-headed households is one example. If through divorce, widowhood, or desertion a woman is left alone to head a household with children, her children are about six times more likely to grow up in poverty than children living in male-headed families (Bane, 1976: 118).

In relation to changing sex roles, family issues are especially significant as the boundary between public and private life becomes more permeable. On the one hand, demographic shifts caused by the lengthening of life and the changing life cycle of women and families predate current public policy issues such as child care or homemaker allowances. On the other hand, the extension of government supports into various functions of private life such as health care and care of the elderly gives public policy potential power to influence the shape of family life and future sex roles.

The Life Cycle of Contemporary Women

Two major demographic changes have taken place that affect the family life cycle and women's role within it. The child-bearing period has been compressed, and adult women's average length of life has increased. As a result the typical American woman in this century bears fewer children and has her last child at the age of 30; that child leaves home when a woman is in her late 40s, and she can still expect to live 30 more years. As recently as the turn of the century, women were bearing their last child when they were 33, seeing their last child married when they were 56, and themselves living only 10 or 15 years more.

Each major demographic trend affecting women points to the uncertainty of following any single prescribed route over the life course. Marriage may end in divorce; a woman may have to support herself and children; a man may have to work out complicated schedules and relationships with children by a former marriage. Rather than be confined to sex-stereotyped activities or try to meet rigid timetables of accomplishment, men and women may do best to adopt a flexible time perspective that permits them to negotiate twists and turns as they appear. By this perspective the family is not so much a distraction from work as the primary social system for synchronizing the achievement and affiliative needs of both sexes.

Using the life-cycle perspective, Elder (1975) shows that the problems of the dual-career family are frequently ones of timing—handling the decision on when and where to move and whose career should take precedence, or smoothing out the periods when both members are overloaded and neither can relieve the other (Elder and Rockwell, 1976). Early in her life a woman's time at home typically coincides with childbearing and care of young children. Later a woman's employment can help the family meet periods of slowdown or unemployment. Women's work can help raise family status by raising overall income; it frequently evens out income differences of families in the same occupational or social category (Oppenheimer, 1977).

Children are affected by the activities of each parent. A mother's employment appears to provide her daughter with a less restricted view of the female role and may involve the father more in child rearing. However, if the mother is guilt ridden for being employed and has less than adequate household arrangements, or is under emotional stress, her mothering may be less adequate than that of a nonemployed mother (Hoffman and Nye, 1974; Hoffman, 1974). A couple's location in one city rather than another may offer opportunities for a wife's employment and wages that lower fertility by discouraging decisions to have more children (Havens, 1972).

The life-cycle perspective focuses on the family decisions that synchronize events such as marriage, births, education, and employment. The way these decisions are timed has implications for all the family members, not just for the husband or the wife or the children. Timing regulates the interplay of one individual's needs with those of the others. It is too soon to describe all the principles of this "family clockwork." But some evidence is available to suggest that a new set of norms is emerging to govern the interaction of paid employment, parenthood, and household work. The new normative ideal appears to be one that encourages flexibility over the life span in the tasks that one takes up at each age and in the sex-typing of these tasks. In general it appears that greater crossover between age and sex roles may be more widely institutionalized as a result of two relatively new developments. On the one hand, there is wider recognition that work patterns of men and women are becoming more similar over the life span. On the other hand, there is increasing recognition that responsibilities for parenthood and household work fall unequally on the shoulders of men and women, and there are frequent suggestions as to how the tasks might be more evenly divided. These two themes signal an emerging norm of sex equality to be achieved by flexible role allocation over the lifetime of the individual.

Paid Employment

Between 1950 and 1975, the number of families with two workers or more increased from 36 to 49 percent. Most of the increase was due to increased participation by married women in the paid labor force. Slightly less than a quarter (23.8 percent) of all wives participated in the labor-force in 1950 as compared with almost half (44.4 percent) in 1975. In 1974, of those women with children aged six to 17, one-half worked at some time during the year, and of those with children under six, one-third were employed. The median income of husband-wife families with a wife in the labor force was $14,885 as compared with $12,360 for the families where a husband only was employed and $8,225 where a wife only was employed (Hayghe, 1976). Gradual acceptance of married women's work and its positive contribution to the family now causes social scientists to examine more closely the internal dynamics of family decision-making that either enable women to work or make such a decision difficult for them.

As household size has diminished, the family enterprise has become a more limited unit requiring less total input of time in its care and maintenance. Yet is is still a demanding unit because there is less help for household work or child care. In 1790 there was an average of 2.8 children under age 16 in each household, and the average size of the private household was 5.7 persons. In 1950 there were likely to be only 1.0 persons under 16, and the average number of people living in the household had dropped to 3.4 (Grabill et al., 1958, 1973: 379; Laslett, 1973). Furthermore, among working-class families who were under economic pressure to support either young or adolescent children, as many as 20 to 35 percent once took in boarders (Modell and Hareven, 1973: 479). The practice of taking in lodgers and boarders declined markedly, however, from the nineteenth century to the present.

More married women entered the work force after 1900 as a result of the decline in the birth rate, the lengthening of women's lives, and the trend to smaller households that took place during the past century. The change is reflected in a steady rise in labor-force participation rates for women. Between 1940 and 1974 the proportion of married women in the labor-force rose from 14 to 43 percent (Kreps and Clark, 1975: 8). Moreover, the shape of the curve representing their participation at various ages also changed. Whereas the pattern through 1940 showed women entering paid employment, then leaving it at the age of marriage and childbearing, the pattern after 1940 showed a dip in participation around the age of 30, then a rise during the middle years (35 to 54) and then another fall after that as women approached the age of retirement. For men, by contrast, the years between 1953 and 1973 show falling labor-force participation rates, particularly in the later years. For married men between the ages of 55 and 64, the participation rate has fallen ten points in the last twenty years. And since the late 1960s, there has been some decline in the participation rate of married men between the ages of 45 and 54 (Taeuber and Sweet, 1976: 51–52; Kreps and Clark, 1975: 9, 14–15).

The gradual convergence of men's and women's labor force participation rates and the greater concentration of work in the middle years (caused by longer education in the early years and retirement in the later years) prompts Kreps and Clark (1975: 57–58) to suggest that work should be more evenly distributed over the life span:

> The married woman's earnings have enabled families to finance additional years of schooling for their children. Similarly, the family with two salaries over an extended portion of worklife can afford earlier retirement than the one that must rely on a single worker's income, assuming the same wage scale. Thus, the capacity to purchase an increase in free time for the male is enhanced by woman's market work. Intrafamily support of the young adults still in school and of older men in retirement offers the male greater flexibility in scheduling his work; market activity during the woman's middle years substitutes for the male's labor-force activity at each end of worklife.

But Kreps and Clark (1975: 56, 3) argue that alternative allocations of working and nonworking time could have been made over the last several decades if, instead of accumulating leisure to be used at the beginning and end of adulthood, it had been used in more piecemeal fashion through the middle years as well. "It would have been possible," they say, "to reduce work weeks, add vacation time, or even provide worker sabbaticals for education and job retraining, as productivity improved and the size of the labor force grew." Furthermore, if nonworking time were more evenly apportioned over the work life, "it would greatly enhance the male's availability for home work at critical times in the family's life cycle." Instead, as it is now, much of males' use of time freed of market work cannot easily be applied to daily performance of household chores. Leisure comes in a form that causes it to be applied to other forms of activity or to work-related pressures such as commuting time.

Parenthood

Corresponding to the growing similarity between the labor-force participation rates of men and women, there are important parallel themes in parenting trends. As families grow smaller and women's input of time to parenting diminishes, one possibility is that both parents' time with children declines. There are then smaller families as a result of the relatively higher value of both women's and men's time in the paid labor force. Economists reason that, as the price of our time increases, we substitute services we can buy, such as sending children to a day-care center or sitting them in front of a television set (Sawhill, 1977: 118). Alice Rossi (1977: 14–16, 22) finds alarming the type of similarity between men and women that deemphasizes the child bearing and child rearing functions. Among the *avant garde* advocates of new marriage forms and among the more extreme feminists concerned with women's work achievement, she notes that it is adults' satisfaction rather than the needs of children that is central.

An alternative theme, however, is also finding greater prominence. It emphasizes the role of the father in child rearing and the greater need for more sharing of parenthood responsibilities by mother and father. Beginning in the 1960s, the Scandinavian countries, particularly Sweden, engaged in a great debate over sex roles that resulted in official policies supporting the right of fathers to take leave from work or work part time during a child's early years. In the United States the Moynihan report focused attention on the positive role of the father in child development and argued for income support systems that would keep the father in the home rather than make him desert so his wife could qualify for welfare.

Now there is a positive interest in showing that fathers can be nurturant parents and adequate to the task if they need be single parents. David Lynn (1974) has marshaled an impressive array of research findings on the positive role of the father in child development and the potentially harmful effects of father absence. James Levine (1976) provides evidence from interviews with contemporary fathers that show child rearing should not be thought of so exclusively in terms of the mother-child relationship. Rather, men are capable of as much role flexibility in moving into the nurturant parent role as women are of engaging in the paid labor force. Rochelle Wortis (1971: 739), after reviewing the social science literature on mothering, concludes, "The acceptance of the concept of mothering by social scientists reflects their own satisfaction with the status quo. The inability of social scientists to explore and advocate alternatives to current child rearing practices is due to their biased concepts of what should be studied and to their unwillingness to advocate social change."

Housework and Volunteer Work

It would seem reasonable, if more women are working, that men would be helping women more with the household work. In fact, however, as recently as 1972, men did an average of only about 1.6 hours a day of work in the home, whether their wives worked or not (Hedges and Barnett, 1972). In addition women also use their base in the home to perform many needed volunteer activities in the community. When it comes to taking care of elderly parents or other older members of the community, what evidence there is suggests that these tasks fall overwhelmingly on middle-aged women, usually daughters (Blenkner, 1963: 50–51).

Some historical and sociological studies have furthermore indicated that household work has not shrunk so fast as we might have thought. Survey data show that since the 1920s there has been no homemaker's shortening of the work week, despite improvements in technology and compression of family functions. A study conducted by the Survey Research Center in Michigan in 1965–1966 showed that unemployed women spend 55 hours a week in household work, as compared with an average of 52 hours a week reported by housewives in 1925–1926, before the widespread introduction of the refrigerator or automatic washing machine (Vanek, 1974). And standards were raised: not only were the clothes washed more often and the house kept cleaner, but more time also was spent on child care, because increasing importance was accorded to the maternal function (Cochran and Strasser, 1974; Cowan, 1973; Wortis, 1971). These changes were all particularly salient for the nonemployed housewife.

By contrast employed wives spent only about half as much time on househork—26 hours. The difference could not be accounted for by their having more help either from husbands or from workers in their households (Vanek, 1974). The employed women probably had to "cut corners," accept messier houses, and perhaps eat out more.

Despite the overwhelming concentration of women in the household functions of housework, cooking, and care of clothing, and the tendency for men to take care of yard work and maintenance tasks, there is nevertheless some impressionistic and anecdotal evidence that men's involvement in female-type tasks is becoming more acceptable. Along with men taking care of children, stories on the family page of the newspaper sometimes feature men doing needlework or cooking. Retired men sometimes become involved in household tasks such as cooking and cleaning. Or they throw their energies into community volunteer activities that were once the preserve of women.

It may be in fact the possibility of experimentation with the allocation of work over the life span that will provide most leverage against the "buffers" that now prevent men from taking on household responsibilities. Joseph Pleck hypothesizes that housework within the family is like the secondary sector of the dual labor market. Men don't engage in it because their energies are reserved for their primary work outside the home. According to Pleck (1977: 420) "the most significant feature of the relation between husband and wife family role performance is the apparent bottleneck in which husbands' family time does not respond to variations in wifes' family time resulting from wives' paid employment." In addition the female work role is more vulnerable to family demands. For husbands the work-family boundary is permeable as well, but only in the other direction: to allow demands from work to impinge on family time. As I would also argue using the concept of crossover, Pleck believes that, to balance the new roles of husband and wife, each role must become symmetrically permeable to work and family demands. The question is what will make this permeability or crossover occur?

Some norms have already developed to define how couples can carry dual careers in which both are involved in family and work. For example, there is an increasing belief that a wife should get as much education as possible so that her position in the job market will be advantageous. The more work experience she has before marriage and childbearing, it is believed, the more likely her ability to reenter that world later on. She may be wise to delay marriage or childbearing until her mid- to late twenties. While she has heavy responsibilities at home, she can "keep a hand in" by taking continuing education courses, holding a part-time job, maintaining outside interests, or building up a list of credentials through volunteer work that will lead to a paid job (Loeser, 1974: 117–131).

Implied in the wife's maintenance of flexibility is that the husband will also remain open to his own inner development and perhaps after mid-career choose other directions of activity or choose more involvement in the family in order to develop his emotional side as much as his occupational side. Current interest in the male "mid-life crisis" in large part seems to reflect this emerging set of expressive concerns on the part of middle-aged males (Brim, 1976).

The new flexible life course for husband and wife is not yet fully institutionalized. Not all the public and private supports necessary in industry or education have yet been set in place. Before considering such policy changes as might be needed, we examine some of the major types of family forms that now exist and analyze what elements of each support both flexibility and symmetry in the roles of men and women.

Changes In The Family Structure

Given the changing demographic realities for women's lives—they are through raising children sooner, live longer, and are more likely to combine paid work with family life—what will be the shape of family life that will allow them a more equitable share in leisure as well as in work and family? How are family forms even now changing to show us the outlines of a more egalitarian arrangement to come? The answers are important, for they suggest not only how younger generations should be prepared to select from the available alternatives, but also how practical legislation or voluntary efforts may be undertaken that will support the forms that seem most desirable to us now.

If recent books and articles on family life can be taken as any trustworthy guide, there is remarkable convergence on a new, more egalitarian family form, which Young and Willmott (1973) term "the Symmetrical Family." Changes in the industrial and ecological order as well as limited fertility and feminism have brought about this change. The phenomenon is observable not only in the managerial and professional class but also among shift workers in the manufacturing and service trades. Yet at the same time as marriages are becoming less hierarchical, husbands being asked to share more housework, and wives working more outside the home, another development is taking place alongside. Alternative family forms are springing up here and there: communes; female-headed families that result from separation, divorce, or unwed pregnancy; or households made up of unrelated individuals living together. These new forms challenge the assumption on which the traditional nuclear family is based. Alternative styles show, for example, how child-care or cooking arrangements can be modified. But they also illustrate that any social system lives with constraints of one kind of another.

Changing patterns of participation in family life precipitate strains in the established patterns. As we have seen in the case of higher divorce rates, remarriage, and the increase in dual-worker families, now "scripts" for action are being tried out as each family experiments with its internal devision of labor and timing of decisions.

There is now a repertoire of several types of family script that may be selected to fit various economic or cultural conditions. There is considerable consensus among historians and sociologists on what these types are, though there may be differences over terminology and more refined categories. Each broad type is associated with a particular rhythm of life and a characteristic ecological niche.

Young and Willmott (1973) used the terms Stage 1, 2, and 3 families to describe the types that they observed in a broad cross-sectional study of 2,600 London families in 1970. Stage 1 roughly corresponds to what others have called the peasant or preindustrial family. The whole family participates in a family-related economic endeavor; family and occupational life are still undifferentiated, and the husband has primary authority. Stage 2 families are similar in form to the Victorian ideal of the early industrial period. In them occupation and family life are no longer joined; husbands are ideally the sole breadwinners, and wives remain at home in charge of children and other domestic responsibilities. Yet the family is not patriarchal in the way it was in the preindustrial form. Instead the two sexes have different and complementary spheres of authority. Stage 3 families have become common only recently. They differ from the Victorian ideal in that both husband and wife typically work outside the home, and ideally both share in family duties. Greater equality emerges between them because their duties are not just complementary but are nearly symmetrical.

Hayghe (1976: 16) estimates that families with both a husband and wife in the labor force now make up 41 percent of all U.S. husband-wife families, a larger single block than any other form; families with husbands only in the labor force account for 34 percent and families with wives only in the labor force account for three percent. Although it has been edged out of first place by the dual-worker form, the Victorian or early industrial type of family still constitutes a major alternative in America today, perhaps especially during that period in the family life cycle when children are young. Variant forms may occur among young adults who have not yet launched their childbearing, or among persons who have experienced marital disruption and are between families. The dual-worker family may be most common among people in the middle years when wives are reentered the labor force.

Although there now appears to be a greater range of family forms available from which people can choose depending on their point in life, the development of these alternatives seems to have been linked to the historical process of modernization. Several historical and sociological reviews of family change have questioned whether any such connection exists. Rosabeth Kanter (1977) notes that the company town, the family store, and the two-person career of the clergyman or doctor have all traditionally blurred the boundary between family and work. Elizabeth Pleck (1976) points out that poor agricultural workers frequently had to hire themselves out as laborers and the work of men and women was separate even in preindustrial times. Tamara Hareven (1975) shows the connections between family time and the actual flow of work in the factory. Nevertheless, in my opinion, the overall process of differentiation between family life and productive work that Smelser (1959) described in the cotton-manufacturing towns of early industrial England still largely describes the main trends in change of family life over the last century. The preindustrial family was both a family unit and a unit of production. The early industrial family separated child rearing and consumption tasks from the productive and instrumental tasks performed in the paid labor force. The modern symmetrical family is open to greater permeability between work and family as a result of further differentation of tasks, which makes much of the work of males and females potentially interchangeable.

One sign of ferment in the family division of labor comes from American opinion surveys conducted between 1964 and 1974. Over that decade women's attitudes toward the traditional division of labor between husbands and wives showed a consistent trend. In every major segment of the population, the proportion of women supporting the traditional pattern declined. At the same time the proportion supporting women's rights in the labor market and their options for a life without marriage or motherhood increased (Mason et al., 1976: 585).

Symmetrical families are a phenomenon of modern society not just in the United States but in Europe as well. Househusbands are not common in Sweden, but they do exist there and their roles are accepted. Dual-career families in Great Britain are the subject of a major study by Rhona and Robert Rapoport (1976). Other countries of Eastern and Western Europe where high numbers of women are in the labor force have for the time being put women under a heavy overload if they have both families and careers. The way out of this stressful situation has not yet resulted in full institutionalization of the symmetrical family. But a rising divorce rate and growing insistence by women on revising the roles within marriage point in that direction (Fogarty et al., 1971: 96; Sokolowska, 1977; Silver, 1977).

Why is the symmetrical family the likely wave of the future? The answer comes from an analysis of modern society and the kind of capacity for role flexibility that a highly differentiated structure requires. Moreover, when society is changing rapidly and circumstances are uncertain, a high degree of flexibility is more adaptive than rigid adherence to one pattern of activity or another. This is true not only of individuals, but of the family itself as well. The family performs its function best when it handles nonuniform tasks that are not easily farmed out to bureaucratic institutions, which can perform them more efficiently. But as Litwak (1970: 354–359) has pointed out, what are defined as nonuniform functions change as fast as technology and the social environment change. For the family to perform at its best, it must therefore be able to take on functions that are at the moment defined as nonuniform and to drop them when they become routine.

For example, early in the century laundry was a routine menial task, and there were outside laundry establishments prepared to provide the service; even working-class women sent out their wash. When, however, the home washing machine appeared and new fabrics and automatic washers were introduced, laundry returned to the home. The household could then meet the special requirements of each individual's laundry needs and care for each fabric type better than could the commercial establishment. Litwak (1970: 358–359) concludes analysis of the laundry example with a general rule that gives a clue to the type of family that may be best adapted to our rapidly changing society:

> [The] one key structural need of the family—given a rapidly changing technology—is the capacity to deal with changing functions, the capacity to rapidly change what are legitimate and what are nonlegitimate activities, or most generally the capacity to be flexible.

One of the main sociological consequences of flexibility in the family is role substitutability between husband and wife rather than fixed sex-typed roles. The wife cannot just be an expressive leader in the family and let the husband be the instrumental leader in the world of work outside. She may be the instrumental leader in bringing up the children of managing household affairs, but she needs the husband's expressive help to handle the tensions that may result, just as he needs her expressive help with anxieties about work. Furthermore, by Litwak's reasoning, the family has major commitments in all areas of life, not just to the care of young children. It is the most effective agent for handling other types of nonuniform problems, such as peculiar circumstances of health or emotional depression, sudden loss of income by some member, some failure in school or work, or some threat to the local neighborhood. To meet such unexpected needs, the "family clockwork" must be able to respond appropriately.

As each family experiments to produce a workable formula of interaction, certain common themes emerge. One is that couples are still more likely to put primary emphasis on the husband's job as a basis for choosing a residential location or timing major family events. The wife's role more often contains the compromises that keep the family flexible. Yet even this pattern may be caught at only one point in time, when the children and couple are relatively young. Later on, the wife's career may in fact take precedence. Families move in and out of different forms, and one must keep remembering that their very flexibility makes it difficult to capture a snapshot of them that is true for more than a moment. It is therefore important to examine some of the forms that families may take over a period of time.

Szalai's survey extended into Belgium, Bulgaria, Czechoslovakia, France, East and West Germany, Hungary, Peru, Poland, the United States, the U.S.S.R., and Yugoslavia, and it collected data from 30,000 respondents. Nowhere had the modern family structure actually been achieved. Husbands helped with household care and important peripheral activities such as maintenance and repair to a degree that almost equaled wives' hours spent in cooking and primary housework. But the two sexes still rarely crossed over to help in each other's domain. Perhaps most telling was the consistent finding that employed men after their contributions to the household still had 50 percent more leisure than the employed women (Szalai, 1973: 28–30).

Where fairness and equity had proceeded farthest, however, was in those societies that were at a high level of socioeconomic development and in those families that had a more comfortable standard of living. Among marriage partners that were better educated and in those couples where the wife was more involved outside the home as a breadwinner or otherwise, the symmetrical ideal was also closer to being realized (Szalai, 1973: 31).

Numerous studies of professional couples where the wife also has a career have shown consistently that even in this type of marriage, the husband's career is accorded somewhat greater priority than that of the wife. Yet Holmstrom (1972: 40), who interviewed 22 career couples, notes:

> The wives accommodated to their husbands' careers more than vice-versa, when deciding where to live. But the more surprising finding is how much the husbands' decisions were affected by the career interests of their wives. In quite a departure from middle-class norms, many husbands went out of their way to live in places where their wives could also obtain desirable employment.

It would be a mistake to support that the ideal patterns of role symmetry and sharing that are occasionally realized in a few dual-career families are yet in fact a reality for the great majority of two-worker families. With respect to sharing of household work, data reported in 1969 and 1970 by Kathryn Walker are sobering: Women at that time still performed considerably more housework than men—4.8 hours a day for the married women employed 30 hours a week or more as compared with 1.6 hours for the employed men who were married to working wives. Child-care routines still assume that the mother is the parent primarily responsible for coming to school conferences, delivering the child to weekday extracurricular activities, and being at home when the child is sick. Joseph Pleck (1977) perceives the differential permeability of men's and women's careers to the demands of family as patterned in such a way as to reinforce the priority of husband's commitment to work and wife's commitment to family.

Working-Class Families

New efforts to understand working-class families in the United States closely parallel the findings of Young and Willmott in London. Working-class people in some ways give more devotion to family than middle-class people, presumably because their work lives are less stimulating and all-consuming. The 1974 Virginia Slims Poll, found for example that, when women were asked what they wanted most for a son, a happy marriage or an interesting career, far more of the less educated women gave priority to family than to work.

Of course, it is also true that the older respondents gave more priority to family than to work, and, to the extent that age and lower education are associated, differential responses by education may not be related just to social class but to age as well. Yet such results seem to make sense out of what some have found to be the puzzling rejection by working-class women of women's liberation. College women and their husbands have the education that would open interesting careers to them. Educated women thus feel frustrated when doing housework, because they compare it with the work that they might do for pay. But working-class women, whose alternatives are repetitive factory work or menial service occupations, find their liberation through independence in home life, cooking, and household work. To them being a good wife and mother is one of the few routes to significant satisfaction, and the middle-class women's liberation rhetoric seems to them to be devaluing a world they consider to be of primary importance (Seifer, 1975; Levison, 1974; Meade, 1975; Coles, 1973: 106).

Nevertheless, there may soon perhaps be a convergence between the working class and the middle class in their attitudes toward family life and the roles of husbands and wives. In reviewing what is known about blue-collar women, Victoria Samuels (1975) finds signs that there has been some change since Rainwater and Komarovsky surveyed working men's wives in 1959. At that time working-class women lived a routine life segregated from much companionship with men. One day was pretty much the same as another. Husbands resisted wives' working, and wives seemed to lack self-confidence (Rainwater et al., 1959; Komarovsky, 1964). In the 1970s more working-class women view themselves as being competent in the role of housewife than the number reporting such competency in 1959. They show more interest in work and freedom to work. And they seem to feel that they can be more assertive in the home (Samuels, 1975). Even in the drabness and frustration that Rubin finds in the lives of working-class women, there is an underlying theme that more egalitarian relationships within the family are desired. The implicit ideal is more talking, more understanding, and more sharing of emotional life between wives and husbands. Ann Oakley (1975) contends that housework is also boring to working-class women. And among the working class Lein et al. (1974) finds that a significant number of husbands share in housework and child care when their wives are working.

In her studies of working-class women, Nancy Seifer (1975) got to know a few women in various parts of the United States—for example, the wife of a coal miner in Alabama and a secretary in a steel mill in Gary, Indiana. Each of these women became an activist for women's rights through some catalyzing experience that touched her own job or her family's interests. They all had been turned off by middle-class feminist rhetoric that devalued the wife and mother role, but when they perceived their common interests with other women over issues such as equal pay, opportunities for promotion, or the family health insurance plans of their unions, they became involved.

Just why such changes have occurred is still hidden. Many have speculated that a wife's working actually changes the power relationship in any couple. The husband has less opportunity to dominate when the wife also brings in a paycheck (Bahr, 1974: 184–185). In the past a wife's employment might have threatened a husband's self-esteem. But rising participation of women in the work force is now apparently changing that norm. Short-term unemployment or a cutback in working hours or overtime is such a common threat to the working class that a wife's work is unquestionably an asset for tiding the family over lean times. Seifer (1975: 14) has recently estimated that the majority of women in working-class families are now employed for at least some part of the year. Dougherty et al. (1977) found in a study of fourteen Boston area dual-worker blue-collar families that every family had experienced at least one layoff of either husband or wife in the recession period since 1972–1973. Husbands tremendously valued a wife's contribution when her wages helped keep the family income up to the standard they desired.

Emerging Family Forms

High rates of marital breakdown have put large numbers of women "at risk" of forming single-parent households. Divorce has also given rise to remarriage and reconstituted nuclear families. In addition, communal experiments and individuals in transition between single or married states have created intimate networks and other variant forms. Of these we shall give most attention to the single-parent households, reconstituted marriages, and experiments with communal and modified extended families because they have the most far-reaching implications for women's status. Each of these variant forms can provide information on the structural conditions that are conducive to equality in household and work roles, legal provisions, child-care arrangements and leisure.

From the point of view of women, the significant feature of single-parent families, particularly where a woman is head of the household, is that resources may be less than in the nuclear or extended form, and as a result the female head may be unusually burdened with responsibility. Much effort has been devoted to lowering the number of such women on the welfare rolls by means tests or by getting them into the labor force. But not even the majority of single heads of family are on welfare. Those not on welfare also have needs that should be met for the sake of the family and the children.

The proportion of white families headed by women has not changed in 40 years, although it has doubled for Blacks. What has changed markedly is the proportion of these families in younger age groups with children. It is the presence of children that makes the difference between poverty and an adequate standard of living for the families with a single head. In 1972 the Michigan Panel Study of Income Dynamics studied 5,000 families over a period of several years and found that 65 percent of all families with mother heads had no income from welfare and no more than a fifth of all mother heads received as much as half of their income from welfare. Only 47 percent received any alimony or child support from fathers, and the median amount of such support was only $1,350 (Heclo et al., 1973: 12–13). But a relatively high percentage of even college-educated female heads of families are poor, 18 percent as compared with three percent of college-educated male heads. Lack of male support coupled with women's frequent lack of marketable skills and much lower earning power, even if they are fully employed, makes it more likely that a female-headed family will be poorer than either the male-supported nuclear family or the reconstituted family.

How do these women and their families survive? More than half (56 percent) derive at least $500 or more from their own earnings and receive no welfare income. Furthermore, many of these female-headed families (10.2 percent of all families with children) reconstitute themselves into nuclear families with a husband and wife within five years. The single-parent state thus seems definitely transitional.

But the possibility that a single-parent family is a transitional state should not make us forget that, in the difficult years, parents without partners need emotional support, help with household chores, flexible working hours so that they can meet their dual-family and work responsibilities, and publicly available provision for child care so that they can meet emergencies, get away on occasion, and see that their children get proper attention while the parent attends to other responsibilities. Cogswell and Sussman (1972) note the prevailing assumption that a mother will be available to come to school during the day for a parent-child conference, take time off to get children to the doctor or dentist, chauffeur children to recreational areas, or be available to fix lunch and supper. For some working women, heading a household and meeting these expectations can prove a loss to working hours and needed income. Rather than impose on such persons the system designed for the nonemployed wife in the husband-wife family, Cogswell and Sussman suggest that mobile health-care units come to school yards, recreational facilities be in walking distance for young children, round-the-clock child care be available for emergencies, and eating facilities be present in the neighborhood where children can take morning and evening meals either accompanied or unaccompanied by parents. While there might not be sufficient demand for such services in suburban middle-class areas to be feasible, one can easily imagine what a boon such facilities would offer to poor working-class or middle-class single-parent families in large urban areas.

While the income outlook for reconstituted families is definitely better than for single-parent families, other problems remain in legal impediments and psychological drain. Established legal routines have generally given custody to the mother, thereby causing fathers a sense of loss of their children. If custody is not awarded to the mother, there is a common tendency to assume that something must be wrong with her. Visitation rights for either parent may provoke inconvenience and further conflict.

Division of property between the former spouses is likely to be a further bone of contention, particularly where a couple entered the marriage arrangement unprepared for any possible termination and merged their assets in a way that makes an equitable reckoning at the end difficult.

Finally, continuing provision for support of children or a dependent wife of a former marriage may constitute an almost intolerable burden for the husband who has also to contribute support to a second marriage. Undoubtedly in a few cases fathers do not support their legitimate offspring by a former marriage because of such a dual burden. However, this reason should not be exaggerated. One study done in 1970 in five California counties found that nonsupporting fathers were similar in their occupational distribution to the entire male population, neither predominant in low-income occupations nor more heavily represented among the unemployed: ten percent were professional or managerial and eight percent were craftsmen or foremen. Usually these fathers were living in the same county as their children. And they were not supporting any other children; 92 percent of the nonsupporting fathers had a total of three or fewer children, and only 13 percent were married to other women. Furthermore, the amount of child support awarded was not unreasonable, typically on the order of $50 per month (Winston and Forsher, 1971: 15–16). Heclo (1973: 33–36), however, explains nonsupport largely as the inability of fathers to pay. He notes that four-fifths of the fathers involved receive less than $10,000 a year. Many administrative and legal factors also contribute to nonsupport—the attitudes of the judges who make the awards, the lack of incentive for officials to enforce the order, and the lack of legal interest in the problem.

Aside from these economic complexities, which may underlie reconstituted marriages, there are also knotty interpersonal issues that may arise. The kinship terms are lacking for referring to one's spouse's children by another marriage or to the second wife whom one's father married. Household avoidance patterns and the incest taboos have to be redefined (Bohannan, 1970). As with the communes and extended family experiments that we consider next, the structural problems have just begun to be identified. Satisfactory solutions will have to be found.

In the last decade a number of variant family forms have arisen. Their sheer variety and the amount of popular attention they have aroused suggest that their significance is larger than the mere curiosity factor. Some students of the phenomenon in fact contend that these experiments are a sign of strains in the traditional nuclear family and a clue to the mutations that it must undergo if it is to be adapted to contemporary society (Cogswell, 1975: 391).

A great deal of interest has centered upon the unconventional sexual arrangements that are found in the new family forms. Some people have tried "swinging," intimate networks, and multilateral marriage as alternatives to the sexual exclusivity of the nuclear family. However, it turns out that sexual activities have lower priority than obligations of work, child care, and home duties even in the new intimate networks (Ramey, 1975). It is with respect to these daily household obligations that the new family experiments offer the most innovative alternatives for the changing domestic roles of women and men.

Betty Cogswell (1975: 401) makes the insightful observation that traditional family forms emphasize constraints, while the participants in the experimental forms speak primarily of freedom and opportunity. Yet any viable social system sets constraints as well as offers opportunities. Both age-old limits and new possibilities have been discovered by experimentation. The main innovations revolve around

(1) flexible work opportunities for female and male alike,
(2) ways of sharing cooking, cleaning, shopping, and other household duties, and
(3) new approaches to maternity, pregnancy, and child care.

Shared living arrangements among a group of adults or couples can result, for example, in rotation of responsibility for meal preparation and home maintenance, thus particularly freeing women for job responsibilities. Such experiments have been tried most notably in the kibbutzim, the Chinese collective enterprises, and the contemporary urban communes in the United States.

There is a tendency, however, toward a more traditional assignment of women to the home and kitchen tasks when children arrive. This happened when the Israeli kibbutzim were transformed from revolutionary frontier communities to more settled establishments that began to have families with young children. Women were more and more assigned to the kitchens and nurseries as part of their communal work (Talmon, 1972). Contemporary rural communes in the United States have generally had a more traditional division of labor from the beginning (Schlesinger, 1972; Berger et al., 1972). When the contemporary urban communal households begin to have children, there is some tendency for men to desert, leaving women to handle the responsibility (Bernard, 1974: 309–310). Or people do not choose to have children and are ambivalent about their care. Kanter found that there were remarkably few (only ten "full-time children" in 58 Boston area communes that she studied (Kanter, 1972: 27). It may also be that, viewed in terms of the life cycle, the experimental marriage or commune is primarily a transitional state and that people will leave when they decide to set up their own households or marry and have children (Giele, 1976). Nevertheless, recent feminist interest in public child-care facilities has drawn considerable impetus from foreign communal experiments in child care, particularly in China, Israel, and the U.S.S.R. (Sidel, 1972; Bettelheim, 1969; Bronfenbrenner, 1970).

Curiously, the idea of communal eating facilities has never caught on to the same degree among the noncommunal family population. One of the leading theorists of feminism, Charlotte Perkins Gilman (1898: 1966), in the last century, visualized a day when there would be neighborhood kitchens that would save each family's making its meals separately. Perhaps the hamburger chains, the frozen dinner, prepared mixes, and other convenience foods, together with advanced household appliances such as the gas or electric stove and the refrigerator, have obviated this alternative. By contrast, no such comparable shortcut for child care has yet appeared or, for that matter, is likely to.

Although communes have received considerable attention, there is one family form to which perhaps more examination is due than it has yet received, what Litwak (1970) has called "modified extended families." If we picture that many of the needs families are called to fill are personal, emotional, and physical, and that the individuals who fulfill them are at best in a trusting and intimate relationship to those receiving help, it is usually a relative or group of relatives who turn out to have the deepest and longest-lasting loyalties that will sustain these demands. One possibility for modifying the nuclear family, therefore, is to extend it in ways that activate and maintain these ties with a larger group of relatives. This would not be the traditional extended family of patriarchal legend, but a more flexible and egalitarian group, able to help its kin with crises of child care, illness, or financial distress. It would probably be maintained by geographical proximity, impromptu visiting, and perhaps even common economic of ethnic ties that prevail in certain farming, mining, manufacturing, or professional milieux. The nineteenth-century pattern of taking in roomers and boarders may have helped to sustain such an extended network in a tight economy. Communes in the Canadian West (which are similar to those in the United States) apparently even now take in former members on a temporary basis, much as a kinship group would operate in the past (Gagné, 1975). There may be other networks sustained through church, lodge, or colleague relationships that operate in similar fashion and of which social scientists as yet have little formal knowledge.

Affluence may allow people to buy services and support separate living arrangements in a way that diminishes the human ties based on noneconomic exchange. Or geographical mobility may be so great that even relatives who wish to maintain helping ties are prevented from doing so by their distance from each other. If this is so, we will have to decide whether such a trend is to be allowed or encouraged or whether it in the end promotes an antifamilial policy.

References

Bahr, Stephen J. 1974. "Effects on Power and Division of Labor in Family." In *Working Mothers.* Editied by L. W. Hoffman and F. I. Nye. San Francisco: Jossey-Bass.

Bane, Mary Jo. 1976. *Here to Stay: American Families in the Twentieth Century.* New York: Basic Books.

Bell, Carolyn Shaw. 1975. "The Next Revolution." *Social Policy* 6 (September-October): 5–11.

Berger, Bennett M.; Hackett, Bruce M.; and Millar, R. Mervyn. 1972. "Child-Rearing Practices in the Communal Family." In *Family, Marriage, and the Struggle of the Sexes.* Edited by H. P. Dreitzel, New York: Macmillan.

Bernard, Jessie. 1974. *The Future of Motherhood.* New York: Dial Press.

Bettelheim, Bruno. 1969 *The Children of the Dream.* New York: Macmillan.

Blake, Judith. 1974. "The Changing Status of Women in Developed Countries." *Scientific American* (September), pp. 137–147.

Blenkner, Margaret. 1968. "Social Work and Family Relationships In Later Life." In *Social Structure and the Family: Generational Relationships.* Edited by E. Shanas and G. Streib. Englewood Cliffs, N.J.: Prentice-Hall.

Bohannan, Paul (ed.), 1970 *Divorce and After.* Garden City, N.Y.; Doubleday-Anchor.

Brim, Orville G., Jr. 1976 "Theories of the Male Mid-life Crisis." *Counseling Psychologist* 6, no. 1:2–9.

Bronfenbrenner, Urie. 1970. *Two Worlds of Childhood: U.S. and U.S.S.R.* New York: Russell Sage Foundation.

———. 1975. "The Next Generation of Americans." Paper presented at the Annual Meeting of the American Association of Advertising Agencies, March 20, Dorado, Puerto Rico.

Cochran, Heidi, and Strasser, Susan. 1974. "The Efficient Home: The Technology and Ideology of Housework in the Early Twentieth Century." Paper presented at the Second Annual Conference on Marxist Approaches to History, New Haven, Ct., February 23–24.

Cogswell, Betty E. 1975. "Variant Family Forms and Life Styles: Rejection of the Traditional Nuclear Family." *Family Coordinator* 24 (October): 391–406.

Cogswell, Betty E., and Sussman, Marvin B. 1972. "Changing Family and Marriage Forms: Complications for Human Service Systems." *Family Coordinator* 21 (October): 505–516.

Coles, Robert C. 1973 "Statement." In *American Families: Trends and Pressures, 1973: Hearings Before the Subcommittee on Children and Youth, U.S. Senate.* Washington, D.C.: U.S. Government Printing Office.

Cowan, Ruth Schwartz. 1973. "A Case Study of Technology and Social Change: The Washing Machine and the Working Wife." Paper presented at the Berkshire Conference of Women Historians, Douglass College, New Brunswick, N.J.

Davis, Kingsley. 1972. "The American Family in Relation to Demographic Change." In *Research Reports, Demographic and Social Aspects of Population Growth,* Vol. 1. Commission on Population Growth and the American Future. Edited by C. F. Westoff and R. Parke, Jr. Washington, D.C.: U.S. Government Printing Office.

Dougherty, Kevin: Howrigan, Gail; Lein, Laura; and Weiss, Heather (Working Family Project). 1977. *Work and the American Family.* Chicago: National Parent Teachers Association.

Duncan, Greg, and Morgan, James N., (eds.) 1976. *Five Thousand American Families—Patterns of Economic Progress. Vol. IV: Family Composition Change and Other Analysis of the First Seven Years of the Panel Study of Income Dynamics.* Ann Arbor, Mi.: Institute for Social Research, University of Michigan.

Elder, Glen H., Jr. 1974. *Children of the Great Depression: Social Change in Life Experience.* Chicago: University of Chicago Press.

―――. 1975. "Family History and the Life Course." Paper presented at the Family Life Course in Historical Perspective Conference, Williams College, Williamstown, Ma., July.

Elder, Glen H., Jr. and Rockwell, Richard C. 1976. "Marital Timing in Women's Life Patterns." *Journal of Family History* 1 (Autumn) 34–53.

Engels, Fredrick, 1884; 1972. *The Origin of the Family, Private Property, and the State.* Edited by E. B. Leacock. New York: International Publishers.

Fogarty, Michael P.; Rapoport, Rhona; and Rapoport, Robert N. 1971. *Sex, Career, and Family.* London: Allen and Unwin.

Gagné, Jacques. 1975. Interview with Janet Zollinger Giele at the Vanier Institute of the Family, Ottawa, Canada, February.

Gauger, William. 1973. "Household work: Can We Add It to the GNP?" *Journal of Home Economics,* October, pp. 12–23.

Giele, Janet Zollinger, 1961. "A Social Change in the Feminine Role: A Comparison of Woman's Suffrage and Women's Temperance, 1870–1920." Ph.D. dissertation, Radcliffe College.

―――. 1976. "Changing Sex Roles and the Future of Marriage." In *Contemporary Marriage: Structure, Dynamics, and Therapy.* Edited by H. Grunebaum and J. Christ. Boston: Little, Brown.

Gilman, Carlotte Perkins. 1898; 1966. *Women and Economics.* Edited by C. N. Degler. New York: Harper and Row.

Grabill, Wilson H.; Kiser, Clyde V.; and Whelpton, Pascal K. 1958. "A Long View." In *The American Family in Social-Historical Perspective.* Edited by M. Gordon. New York: St. Martin's Press.

Hareven, Tamara K. 1975. "Family Time and Industrial Time: Family and Work in a Planned Corporation Town, 1900–1924." *Journal of Urban History* 1 (May): 365–389.

Havens, Elizabeth M. 1972. "The Relation Between Female Labor-Force Participation and Fertility Rates." Paper presented at the American Sociological Association Annual Meeting, New Orleans, August.

Hayghe, Howard. 1976. "Families and the Rise of Working Wives—An Overview." *Monthly Labor Review* 99 (May): 12–19.

Heclo, Hugh; Rainwater, Lee; Rein, Martin; and Weiss, Robert. 1973. "Single-Parent Families: Issues and Policies." Prepared for the Office of Child Development, Department of Health, Education, and Welfare.

Hedges, Janice N., and Barnett, Jeanne K. 1972. "Working Women and the Division of Household Tasks." *Monthly Labor Review* 95 (April): 9–14.

Hoffman, Lois Wladis. 1974. "Effects of Maternal Employment on the Child: A Review of Research." *Developmental Psychology.* 10, no. 2: 204–228.

Hoffman, Lois W., and Nye, F. Ivan, 1974. *Working Mothers.* San Francisco; Jossey-Bass.

Holmstrom, Lynda Lytle. 1972. *The Two-Career Family,* Cambridge, Ma.: Schenkman.

Hornblower, Mary T. 1973. "Divorce Rate Still Spirals." *Boston Evening Globe,* p. 37.

Kanter, Rosabeth Moss, 1972. "Communes, the Family, and Sex Roles." Paper presented at the annual meeting of the American Sociological Association, New Orleans, August.

―――1977. *Work and Family in the United States: A Critical Review and Agenda for Research and Policy.* New York: Russell Sage Foundation.

Komarovsky, Mirra. 1964. *Blue-Collar Marriage.* New York: Random House.

Kreps, Juanita M.. and Clark, Robert. 1975. *Sex, Age, and Work: The Changing Composition of the Labor Force.* Baltimore, Md.: Johns Hopkins University Press.

Laslett, Peter. 1972. *Household and Family in Past Time.* Cambridge, Eng.: Cambridge University Press.

Lein, Laura; Durham, M.: Pratt, M.; Schudson, M.; Thomas, R.; and Weiss, H. 1974. *Final Report: Work and Family Life.* Cambridge, Ma.: Center for Study of Public Policy. National Institute of Education Project No. 3-33074.

Lekachman, Robert. 1975. "On Economic Equality." *Signs* 1 (Autumn); 93–102.

Levine, James A. 1976. *Who Will Raise the Children?: New Options for Fathers (and Mothers)* Philadelphia: Lippincott.

Levison, Andrew. 1974. "The Working-Class Majority." *New Yorker.* 2 September, pp. 36–61.

Litwak, Eugene. 1970. "Technological Innovation and Ideal Forms of Family Structure in an

Industrial Democratic Society." In *Families in East and West.* Edited by R. Hill and R. Konig. Paris: Mouton.

Loeser, Herta. 1974. *Women, Work, and Volunteering.* Boston: Beacon Press.

Lynn, David B. 1974. *The Father: His Role in Child Development.* Monterey, Ca.: Brooks/Cole.

Mason, Karen Oppenheim; Czajka, John; and Arber, Sara. 1976. "Change in U.S. Women's Sex-role Attitudes, 1964–1974." *American Sociological Review* 41 (August):573–596.

Meade, Ellen. 1975. "Role Satisfaction of Housewives." Paper presented at Annual Meeting of Eastern Sociological Association. New York City, August.

Modell, John, and Hareven, Tamara K. 1973. "Urbanization and the Malleable Household: An Examination of Boarding and Lodging in American Families." *Journal of Marriage and the Family* 35(August): 467–479.

Oakley, Ann. 1975. *The Sociology of Housework.* New York: Pantheon.

Oppenheimer, Valarie Kincade. 1974. "Women's Economic Role in the Family," *American Sociological Review* 42(June): 387–406.

Pleck, Elizabeth. 1976. "Two Worlds in One: Work and Family." *Journal of Social History.* 10:178–195.

Pleck, Hoseph H. 1977. "Work-Family Role System," *Social Problems* 24: 417–427.

Preston, Samuel, and Richards, Alan Thomas. 1975. "The Influence of Women's Work Opportunities on Marriage Rates." *Demography* 12(May): 209–222.

Rainwater, Lee; Coleman, Richard P.; and Handel, Gerald. 1959. *Workingman's Wife.* New York: Oceana.

Ramey, James W. 1975. "Intimate Groups and Networks: Frequent Consequences of Sexually Open Marriage." *Family Coordinator* 24(October): 515–530.

Rapoport, Rhona, and Rapoport, Robert N. 1976. *Dual-Career Families Re-examined.* New York: Harper and Row.

Roper Organization. 1974. *The Virginia Slims American Women's Opinion Poll Vol. 3: A Survey of the Attitudes of Women on Marriage, Divorce, the Family, and America's Changing Sexual Morality.* New York: Roper Organization.

Ross, Heather, and Sawhill, Isabel V. 1975. *Time of Transition: The Growth of Families Headed by Women.* Washington, D.C.: Urban Institute.

Rossi, Alice S. 1977. "A Biosocial Perspective on Parenting." *Daedalus* 106(Spring): 1–31.

Rubin, Lillian. 1976. *Worlds of Pain: Life in the Working-Class Family.* New York: Basic Books.

Samuels, Victoria. 1975. "Nowhere to Be Found: A Literature Review and Annotated Bibliography on White Working-Class Women." New York: Institute on Pluralism and Group Identity.

Sawhill, Isabel V. 1977. "Economic Perspectives on the Family." *Daedalus* 106(Spring): 115–125.

Scanzoni, John H. 1975. *Sex Roles, Life Styles, and Childbearing.* New York: The Free Press.

Schlesinger, Benjamin. 1972. "Family Life in the Kibbutz of Israel: Utopia Gained or Paradise Lost?" In *Family, Marriage, and the Struggle of the Sexes.* Edited by H. P. Dreitzel. New York: Macmillan.

Seifer, Nancy, 1975. "The Working Family in Crisis: Who Is Listening?" Project on Group Life and Ethnic Americans, American Jewish Committee. New York: Institute on Pluralism and Group Identity.

Sidel, Ruth. 1972. *Women and Child Care in China.* New York: Hill and Wang.

Silver, Catherine Bodard. 1977. "France: Contrasts in Familial and Societal Roles." In *Women: Roles and Status in Eight Countries.* Edited by J. Z. Giele and A. C. Smock. New York: Wiley.

Smelser, Neil J. 1959. *Social Change in the Industrial Revolution.* Chicago: University of Chicago Press.

Sokolowska, Magdalena. 1977. "Poland: Women's Experience under Socialism." in *Women: Roles and Status in Eight Countries.* Edited by J. Z. Giele and A. C. Smock. New York: Wiley.

Statistical Abstract of the United States, 1973. Washington, D.C.: U.S. Department of Commerce, Social and Economic Statistics Administration.

Sweet, James A. 1971. "The Living Arrangements of Separated, Widowed, and Divorced Mothers." Madison, Wi.: University of Wisconsin, Center for Demography and Ecology. Working Paper #71–4.

Szalai, Alexander. 1973. "The Quality of Family Life—Traditional and Modern: A Review of Sociological Findings on Contemporary Family Organization and Role Differentiation in the Family." Paper presented at the United Nations Interregional Seminar on the Family in a Changing Society: Problems and Responsibilities of Its Members, London, 18–31 July, ESA/SDHA/AC. 3/6.

Taeuber, Karl A., and Sweet, James A. 1976. "Family and Work: The Social Life Cycle of women." In *Women and the American Economy.* Edited by J. M. Kreps. Englewood Cliffs, N.J.: Prentice-Hall.

Talmon, Yonina. 1972. *Family and Community in the Kibbutz.* Cambridge, Ma.: Harvard University Press.

U.S. Senate, Subcommittee on Children and Youth. 1973. *American Families: Trends and Pressures, 1973:* Hearings. Washington, D.C.: U.S. Government Printing Office.

Vanek, Joann. 1974. "Time Spent in Housework." *Scientific American,* November, pp. 116 116–120.

Walker, Kathryn E. 1969. "Time Spent in Household Work by Homeworkers." *Family Economics Review,* September, pp. 5–6.

———. 1970. "Time Spent by Husbands in Household Work." *Family Economics Review,* June, pp. 8–11.

Weinstein, Fred, and Platt, Gerald M. 1969. *The Wish to Be Free.* Berkeley, Ca.: University of California Press.

Winston, Marian P., and Forsher, Trude. 1971. "Nonsupport of Legitimate Children by Affluent Fathers as a Cause of Poverty and Welfare Dependence." Santa Monica, Ca.: Rand Corporation.

Working Family Project. 1978. "Parenting." In *Working Couples.* Edited by R. N. Rapoport and R. Rapoport. New York: Harper and Row.

Wortis, Rochelle P. 1971. "The Acceptance of the Concept of the Maternal Role by Behavioral Scientists: Its Effects on Women." *American Journal of Orthopsychiatry* 41(October): 733–746.

Young, Michael, and Willmott, Peter. 1973. *The Symmetrical Family.* New York: Pantheon.

3

Couples

Introduction

To many people, the current state of marriage seems to provide the clearest evidence that the family is falling apart. In the past two decades marriage rates declined, divorce rates went up, and increasing numbers of couples came to live together without being married. Yet these changes do not necessarily mean that people no longer want long-term commitments or that they are psychologically incapable of forming deep attachments. Rather, they reflect the fact that in the modern world marriage is increasingly a personal relationship between two people. Over time there have come to be fewer and fewer reasons for couples to remain in unsatisfactory relationships. And as the standards for emotional fulfillment in marriage have risen, the level of discontent may have increased also.

In the preindustrial past, the emotional relationship between husband and wife was the least important aspect of marriage. A marriage was an exchange between kin groups, a unit of economic production, and a means of replenishing populations with high death rates.

In traditional societies, parents often selected their children's mates. Parents were more interested in the practical consequences of choice than in romantic considerations. By contrast, in our modern society, people are supposed to marry for "love." Love researcher Zick Rubin says that you *can* have it both ways. People may marry for practical reasons or for money; nevertheless they " . . . invariably follow their culture's dictates and decide that they are 'in love.' "

People may also decide that they are in love and want to live together but do not care to have their union licensed by the state or blessed by clergy. In her review of the literature on cohabitation reprinted in chapter 6, Eleanor Macklin finds that approximately 25 percent of all college students have already lived with a partner of the opposite sex without being married. Overall this represents a major cultural change over a quarter of a century, but more research needs to be done to see whether college students are in the vanguard or are separate from their population age-mates. A preliminary analysis of 1977 census data shows a sharp increase in such couples, but still they are only one percent of household heads. If, however, the data are reinterpreted to

276

include younger persons who could be living together, the figure rises to 4 percent, suggesting an even sharper cultural transition.

Couple relations are thus influenced by a new fluidity and openness with regard to social norms in general and sexual behavior in particular. At one time a relationship between a man and a woman could be easily categorized: It was either "honorable" or "dishonorable." An "honorable" relationship went through several distinct stages of commitment: dating, keeping company, going steady, agreeing to be married, announcing the engagement, and finally getting married, presumably for life. Divorce was regarded as a personal tragedy and social stigma. Sexual relations at any point before marriage were also shameful, especially for the woman, although the shamefulness decreased depending on the closeness to marriage.

Today the system of courtship has given way to a new pattern of couple relationships. The distinction between the different stages of courtship and marriage has broken down. Couple relationships can be intensely personal and sexually intimate very early, yet marital relationships are less stable because they are not expected to last if one of the partners becomes dissatisfied. Bernard Farber (1964) has argued that, in effect, we have a "permanent availability" system of marriage; every adult remains on the marriage market, available to every other potential partner, whether currently married or not.

The tension arising out of a relationship that is deeply intimate and yet not certain to last adds another strain to an institution that already contains many strains. Further, the new symmetry between the sexes in work and sex may increase the tensions as well as the joys in marriage. The more multifaceted the relationship, the more aspects of two lives that have to mesh, the greater the potential for friction. Ultimately the basic cause of divorce, W. J. Goode once observed, is marriage:

> All marriage systems require that at least two people, with their individual desires, needs and values, live together, and all systems create some tensions and unhappiness. (1966, p. 493)

Ordinarily, the strain does not often lead to an outcome as dramatic as the killing of one spouse by another, but we do know that there is much family violence. The article reprinted in chapter 7 on battered wives and dead husbands suggests how bad marital strain can be.

Traditional societies do not necessarily have happier marriages or even lower divorce rates—some have higher rates than ours. The moment of separation is especially painful, "a severe shock to most people in society," an experience Morton and Bernice Hunt vividly describe in the selection reprinted in chapter 7. By contrast, strong kin groups in traditional societies either keep couples together regardless of how they feel or make it easier for couples to break up without severe disruption.

Still, traditional societies were quite conservative in their view of marriage, which was regarded as a permanent, moral commitment which the church and later the state was to protect and preserve. Traditional marriage was also based on a division of labor between the sexes. The husband was to be head of the family and its chief provider; the wife was to provide services in the form of child care and housework. Divorce could be granted only through the failure of one of the spouses to live up to his or her role, or the betrayal of a spouse through adultery or cruelty.

The new divorce laws, as Weitzman and Dixon point out, abolish this notion of fault or blame; instead "irreconcilable differences" are grounds for the dissolution of marriage. Further, the new laws attempt to establish more equal rights and obligations between husband and wife, both during the marriage and at the time of divorce. While it is still too early to judge the ultimate effects the new laws will have on marriage as an institution, it is clear that they codify a very different conception of marriage and divorce than existed in the law until recently.

The distinction between tradition and modernity lies behind Andrew Cherlin's article on "Remarriage as a Total Institution." Cherlin attributes the higher divorce rate of remarried persons not to personality defects or to experience with divorce—once you've gone through the separation trauma it may not be so hard another time—but to the fact that traditional marriage does not contemplate divorce. Those who remarry are therefore in an "incomplete" institution, lacking the guidelines and supports of traditional marriage. Whether or not one finds Cherlin's thesis persuasive, it is evident that his subjects found marriage attractive. Despite all its difficulties, marriage is thus not likely to go out of style in the near future. Ultimately we agree with Jessie Bernard, who, after a devastating critique of marriage from the point of view of a sociologist who is also a feminist, has this to say:

> The future of marriage is as assured as any social form can be . . . For men and women will continue to want intimacy, they will continue to want to celebrate their mutuality, to experience the mystic unity which once led the church to consider marriage a sacrament. . . . There is hardly any probability such commitments will disappear or that all relationships between them will become merely casual or transient. The commitment may not take the form we know today, although that too has a future. (Bernard 1972, p. 301)

References

Bernard, Jessie. 1972. *The Future of Marriage.* New York: World.
Farber, B. 1964. *Family Organization and Interaction.* San Francisco: Chandler.
Goode, W. J. 1966. "Family Disorganization." In *Contemporary Social Problems,* 2nd ed., edited by R. K. Merton and R. A. Nisbet, pp. 493–552. New York: Harcourt, Brace and World.

Chapter 6

Coupling

The Love Research   *Zick Rubin*

Love has always been one thing, maybe the only thing, that seemed safely beyond the research scientist's ever-extending grasp. With an assist from Masters and Johnson, behavioral scientists have, to be sure, dug rather heavily into the topic of human sexual behavior. But whereas sex might now be explored scientifically, love remained sacrosanct.

Or so we thought.

Love was a taboo topic for researchers as recently as 1958, when the president of the American Psychological Association, Dr. Harry F. Harlow, declared in faintly mournful tones, "So far as love or affection is concerned, psychologists have failed in their mission. The little we know about love does not transcend simple observation, and the little we write about it has been written better by poets and novelists." Since the poets and novelists had always been notoriously contradictory about love, defining it as everything from "a spiritual compact of fire" to "a state of perceptual anesthesia," this was a pretty severe indictment.

But the psychologists did not take this charge lying down. Instead, they rallied to the call and started a quiet revolution. Over the past dozen years, and at a positively accelerating pace, behavioral scientists have begun to study love. They have done so on their own terms, with the help of such tools of the trade as laboratory experiments, questionnaires, interviews and systematic behavioral observation. And although the new love research is still in its early stages, it has already made substantial progress. The research has proceeded on several fronts, including explorations of the psychological origins of love, its links to social and cultural factors and the ways in which it deepens—or dies—over time.

Recent studies of falling in love have indicated that there is a sense in which love is like a Brooks Brothers suit or a Bonwit dress. For one person's feelings

From *Human Behavior* Magazine (February 1977). Copyright © 1977 *Human Behavior* Magazine. Reprinted by permission.

toward another to be experienced as "love," they must not only feel good and fit well, they must also have the appropriate label. Sometimes a sexual experience contributes to such labeling. One college student told an interviewer that she was surprised to discover that she enjoyed having sex with her boyfriend, because until that time she had not been sure that she loved him. The pleasant surprise helped to convince her that she was actually "in love."

Paradoxically, however, people sometimes label as "love" experiences that seem to be negative rather than positive. Consider the rather interesting case of fear. Ovid noted in *The Art of Love,* written in first century Rome, that an excellent time for a man to arouse passion in a woman is while watching gladiators disembowel one another in the arena. Presumably the emotions of fear and repulsion stirred up by the grisly scene would somehow be converted into romantic interest.

Ovid himself did not conduct any controlled experiments to check the validity of the fear-breeds-love principle; but two psychologists at the University of British Columbia, Drs. Donald L. Dutton and Arthur P. Aron, recently did so. They conducted their experiment on two footbridges that cross the Capilano river in North Vancouver. One of the bridges is a narrow, rickety structure that sways in the wind 230 feet above the rocky canyon; the other is a solid structure, built only 10 feet above a shallow stream. An attractive female experimenter approached men who were crossing one or the other bridge and asked if they would take part in her study of "the effects of exposure to scenic attractions on creative expression." All they had to do was to write down their associations to a picture she showed them. The researchers found that the men accosted on the fear-arousing bridge were more sexually aroused than the men on the solid bridge, as measured by the amount of sexual imagery in the stories they wrote. The men on the high-fear bridge were also much more likely to telephone the young woman afterward, ostensibly to get more information about the study.

The best available explanation for these results comes from a general theory of emotion put forth by Dr. Stanley Schachter of Columbia University. Schachter's experiments suggested that the experience of emotion has two necessary elements. The first is physiological arousal—a racing heart, heightened breathing, sweating and the like. These symptoms tend to be more or less identical for any intense emtoion, whether it be anger, fear or love. The second necessary element, therefore, is the person's subjective labeling of his or her arousal. In order to determine which emtoion he or she is experiencing, the person must look around and determine what external stimulus is causing the inner upheaval.

This labeling is a complicated process, and (as Ovid apparently knew some 2,000 years ago) mistakes can happen. In the Capilano Canyon study, subjects apparently relabeled their inner stirrings of fear, at least in part, as sexual arousal and romantic attraction. This sort of relabeling is undoubtedly encouraged by the fact that the popular stereotype of falling in love—a pounding heart, shortness of breath, trembling hands—all bear an uncanny resemblance to the physical symptoms of fear. With such traumatic expectations of what love should feel like, it is no wonder that it is sometimes confused with other emotions. As the Supremes put it in a song of the 1960s, "Love is like an itching in my heart."

In the case of the Capilano Canyon study of course, one cannot say that the subjects actually "fell in love" with the woman on the bridge. But the same sort of labeling process takes place in more enduring romantic attachments. In the process, social pressures also come crashing into the picture. Young men and women are taught repeatedly that love and marriage inevitably go together, and in the large majority of cases they proceed to act accordingly on this assumption.

Americans are more likely than ever to get married (well over 90 percent do so at least once), and all but a minuscule proportion of people applying for marriage licenses will tell you that they are in love. It is not simply that people who are in love decide to follow their hearts' dictates and get married. It also works the other way around. People who are planning to get married, perhaps for economic reasons or in order to raise a family, invariably follow their culture's dictates and decide that they are "in love."

The pressure to label a promising relationship as "love" seems especially strong for women. Sociologist William Kephart of the University of Pennsylvania asked over a thousand Philadelphia college students the following question: "If a boy (girl) had all the other qualities you desired, would you marry this person even if you were not in love with him (her)?" Very few of the respondents (4 percent of the women and 12 percent of the men) were so unromantic as to say yes. But fully 72 percent of the women (compared with only 24 percent of the men) were too practical to answer with a flat no and, instead, pleaded uncertainty.

One of Dr. Kephart's female respondents put her finger on the dilemma, and also on the resolution of it. She wrote in on her questionnaire, "If a boy had all the other qualities I desired, and I was not in love with him—well, I think I could talk myself into falling in love."

Whereas women may be more highly motivated than men to fall in love with a potential spouse, men tend to fall in love more quickly and less deliberately than women. In a study of couples who had been computer-matched for a dance at Iowa State University, men were more satisfied than women with their dates, reported feeling more "romantic attraction" toward them and even were more optimistic about the possibility of a happy marriage with their machine-matched partners. In a study of dating couples at the University of Michigan, I found that among couples who had been dating briefly—up to three months—boyfriends scored significantly higher than their girlfriends did on a self-report "love scale." These men were more likely than their partners to agree with such statements as "It would be hard for me to get along without ———," "One of my primary concerns is———'s welfare" and "I would do almost anything for———." Among couples who had been together for longer periods of time the male-female difference disappeared.

The idea of measuring love on a paper-and-pencil scale is, incidentally, not an entirely new one. When Elizabeth Barrett Browning wrote, "How do I love thee? Let me count the ways," she was, as any mathematician can tell you, referring to the most basic form of measurement. Six years ago, when I was searching for an unspoiled topic for my doctoral dissertation, I decided to take Browning's advice. ("Why do you want to measure *that?*" my dissertation committee asked me. "Why not measure something more conventional like cognitive dissonance or identity diffusion?" I looked down at the rocky canyon 230 feet below and answered, voice trembling. "Because it's there.") The items on the scale that emerged refer to elements of attachment (The desire to be near the other), caring (the concern for the other's well-being) and intimacy (the desire for close and confidential communication with the other). The ancient Greeks had a similar conception of love. Where they went wrong was in never asking the masses to put their *eros* and *agape* for one another on nine-point scales.

Skeptics may point out, of course, that a paper-and-pencil love scale does not really measure how much people love each other, but simply how much they *say* they love each other. But there is some corroborating behavioral evidence for the scale's validity. For example, scores on the scale checked out with the well-known folk wisdom that lovers spend a great deal of their time gazing into each other's eyes. Surreptitious laboratory observation through a one-way mirror confirmed that "strong lovers" (couples whose members received above-average scores on the love scale) made significantly more eye contact than "weak lovers" (couples whose scores on the love scale were below average). Or, as the popular song puts it, "I only have eyes for you."

Whereas men seem to fall in love more quickly and easily than women, women seem to fall out of love more quickly and with less difficulty than men, at least in the premarital stages. For the past several years, my coworkers and I have been conducting an extensive study of student dating couples in the Boston area. We found, to our initial surprise, that women were somewhat more likely to be "breaker-uppers" than men were, that they saw more problems in the relationship and that they were better able to disengage themselves emotionally when a breakup was coming. Men, on the other hand, tended to react to breakups with greater grief and despair.

These tendencies run counter to the popular stereotypes of women as starstruck romantics and men as aloof exploiters. In fact, women may learn to be more practical and discriminating about love than men for simple economic reasons. In most marriages, the wife's status, income and life chances are far more dependent on the husband's than vice versa. As a result, the woman must be discriminating. She cannot allow herself to fall in love too quickly, nor can she afford to stay in love too long with "the wrong person." The fact that a woman's years of marriageability tend to be more limited than a man's may also contribute to her need to be selective. Men, on the other hand, can better afford the luxury of being "romantic."

Sociologist Willard Waller put the matter most bluntly when he wrote, some 40 years ago, "There is this difference between the man and the woman in the pattern of bourgeois family life: a man, when he marries, chooses a companion and perhaps a helpmate, but a woman chooses a companion and at the same time a standard of living. It is necessary for a woman to be mercenary." As more women enter business and professional careers, and as more men make major commitments to homemaking and childrearing, it is likely that this difference will diminish.

In spite of these culturally based sex differences, the usual course of love is probably pretty much the same for human beings of both sexes. A key task for love researchers is to explore the stages and sequences through which love develops. To this end, Drs. L. Rowell Huesmann of the University of Illinois at Chicago Circle and George Levinger of the University of Massachusetts recently developed a unique computer program, called RELATE, that simulates the development of close relationships. Given information about the personalities of the two partners and following a built-in set of rules and assumptions, RELATE is able to generate a "scenario" of the likely course of their relationship. In its maiden effort along these lines, RELATE simulated the relationship of two hypothetical sweethearts, John (who was described to RELATE in the computer-language equivalent of "attractive, but shy") and Susan (introduced to RELATE as "outgoing and popular").

After a few minutes of whirring and clicking, RELATE came up with its prediction. It hypothesized that after a period of time during which they interacted at a superficial level, "John learns that Susan is willing to disclose intimacies in response to his disclosures, and he confides in her completely. This leads the pair into active striving for a deep romantic involvement." By the end of RELATE's love story, John and Susan were both oriented toward a permanent relationship, although neither had yet proposed marriage. Erich Segal, eat your heart out!

Since John and Susan are only hypothetical, it is impossible to know how accurate RELATE's scenario really is. Moreover, Drs. Huesmann and Levinger freely acknowledge that at present the simulations are greatly oversimplified, providing at best pale reflections of the events of real-life relationships. But the computer-matchmaker has already proved to be of value to researchers in refining their models of the development of love in real life.

Note, for example, that John and Susan's romance did not get very far until John learned that Susan would reciprocate his disclosures. My study of Boston couples, conducted in collaboration with Drs. Letitia Anne Peplau (now at

UCLA) and Charles T. Hill (now at the University of Washington) has confirmed RELATE's working assumption along these lines, to wit: love is most likely to flourish when the two partners are *equally involed* in their relationship. In our study of 231 dating couples, 77 percent of the couples in which both partners reported that they were equally involved in 1972 were still going together (or, in some cases married) in 1974, as compared with only 45 percent of unequally involved couples.

The importance of equal degrees of involvement makes it clear that love, like water, seeks its own level. As Columbia University sociologist Peter M. Blau explains, "If one lover is considerably more involved than the other, his greater commitment invites exploitation and provokes feelings of entrapment, both of which obliterate love. . . . Only when two lovers' affection for and commitment to one another expand at roughly the same pace do they mututally tend to reinforce their love."

Because of this mutual reinforcement, love will sometimes beget love—provided that the first person's love is communicated to the second. To help make the point, Dr. Paul Rosenblatt of the University of Minnesota sifted through anthropologists' reports of "love magic" in 23 primitive societies, from the Chaga of East Africa to the Kwoma of New Guinea. He came to the conclusion that although love magic often works, it isn't really magic. Instead, such exotic practices as giving one's "victim" a charmed coconut, flashing a mirror at her or blowing ashes in her face all serve to heighten the woman's love by indirectly communicating the man's love for her. When love magic is practiced without the victim's knowledge, it is not nearly so effective. (Other studies have made it clear, however, that expressions of love must also be well-timed. If too much affection is expressed too soon, equity is undermined and the tactic will backfire.)

Dr. Rosenblatt's study illustrates quite directly what some observers fear most about the new love research—that it will rob love of its magic and mystery. Sen. William Proxmire is one of those who takes this point of view. In a much-publicized statement last year, Sen. Proxmire indentified a study of romantic love sponsored by the National Science Foundation as "my choice for the biggest waste of the taxpayer's money for the month of March. I believe that 200 million Americans want to leave some things in life a mystery, and right at the top of the things we don't want to know is why a man falls in love with a woman and vice versa."

Dr. Ellen Berscheid, the University of Minnesota researcher whose work was singled out by the senator, responded vigorously to the attack: "I assume the senator has some knowledge of the divorce rate in this country and understands that the absence of love is the basis on which many divorces are instigated. I believe he has been divorced and recently was reconciled with his second wife (in February, 1975). He ought to realize better than most people why we should know all we can about the determinants of affection."

Writing in the *New York Times,* columnist James Reston also defended the love researchers. "Mr. Proxmire is a modern man," Reston wrote, "who believes that government should help people with their problems. He is a land-grant college man and will vote any amount of money for basic research on the dangers of natural selection in animals, and on how to get the best bulls and cows together on the farms of Wisconsin, but he is against basic research on the alarming divorce rate or breakup of the human family in America. You have to assume he was kidding."

But, of course, the senator was not kidding, and his sentiments are undoubtedly shared by a large number of Americans, even if not by the entire 200 million claimed in his statement. Even some psychologists themselves share his viewpoint. At a symposium sponsored by the American Psychological Association Convention several years ago, one panelist declared that "the scientist in even attempting to interject love into a laboratory situation is by the very nature of the proposition dehumanizing the state we call love."

My view of the matter, and that of other love researchers, is rather different. We are quite aware of the difficulties inherent in the attempt to study love, and we have no illusion that we will ever unlock all of love's mysteries. But we also believe that especially at a time when many people are terribly confused about what love is or should be, the scientific study of love can make a positive contribution to the quality of life. To shun this task is no more justified than the taboo until several centuries ago against scientific study of the human body, on the grounds that such research would somehow defile it. In the words of one of the most humane of modern psychologists, the late Dr. Abraham H. Maslow, "We *must* study love; we must be able to teach it, to understand it, to predict it, or else the world is lost to hostility and to suspicion."

Nonmarital Heterosexual Cohabitation

Eleanor D. Macklin

Nonmarital cohabitation is fast becoming a part of the dominant culture in this country and it seems likely that in time to come a majority of persons will experience this lifestyle at some point in their life cycle. The phenomenon of men and women living together unmarried is, of course, not new (Berger, 1971; Rodman, 1966); and trial marriage as a concept has been a topic of debate since the early part of this century (Lindsey & Evans, 1927/1929; Mead, 1966, 1968; Russell, 1929). However, it has only been in the past decade that it has been openly practiced by a large number of middle-class Americans.

From *Marriage and Family Review*, 1:2 (March/April 1978), pp. 1–12. Reprinted by permission of The Haworth Press, Inc.

It was in college towns that evidence of the increasing incidence of cohabitation first appeared, and it is here that most of the research has occurred. In 1968, the first graduate thesis on the topic was written (Johnson, 1968); in 1972, the first professional articles appeared (Lyness, Lipetz, & Davis, 1972; Macklin, 1972) and the initial issue of the *Cohabitation Research Newsletter* was published (Macklin, 1972*a*). Since then it has become increasingly popular to do research on cohabitation, and at this writing more that 25 graduate theses on the topic are known to have been completed and numerous others are currently in process. What have we learned from all of this research activity?

Prevalence Rates

Estimates of prevalence vary to some extent with the particular definition of cohabitation used by the researcher. There has been to date little consistency in the use of the term. Operational definitions have ranged from the ambiguous "living with someone of the opposite sex to whom one is not married"; to "sharing a bedroom and/or bed for four or more nights a week for three or more consecutive months with someone of the opposite sex to whom one is not married;" to "two adult persons of different sex living together under marriage-like conditions in the same household without having officially confirmed their relationship through marriage (Cole, 1977, p. 65).

Most of the estimates of prevalence based on probability samples have come from research using college students, with the estimates seeming to vary as a function of the nature of the particular institution and the population from which it draws. Rates of "ever having cohabited" range from near zero percent at those institutions which are single-sex, or which have rigid parietals and require that all students live on campus, to about one-third of the student population at some large state universities where housing regulations are more liberal.

Because of the tremendous variation from campus to campus, one is hesitant to give an overall estimate of prevalence. However, when one averages the "percent ever having cohabited" reported in 15 known studies involving campus surveys, including both convenience and random samples, a mean of 24 percent is obtained (Macklin, in press). This is very close to the 25 percent reported by Bower and Christopherson in their survey of convenience samples in 16 state universities in eight regions of the U.S. (Bower & Christopherson, 1977). Therefore, it seems safe to conclude that about one-quarter of present U.S. undergraduate students, taking the country as a whole, have had a cohabitation experience.

At most institutions, a higher percentage of males report having cohabited than of females, although this difference usually disappears when one considers only those who have lived together three or more months. The rate will undoubtedly be much higher by the time of graduation or marriage, for the percentages tend to increase from freshman to senior year.

Statistics from noncollege populations are much harder to obtain since survey research on these groups is negligible. Some suggestion of prevalence can be obtained from Census data. In March 1976, the U.S. Bureau of the Census found that 1.3 million persons were living in two-person households in which the household head shared the living quarters with an unrelated adult of the opposite sex. This number includes resident employees and roomers as well as nonmarital partners. Of these 660,000 two-person households, 23 percent were headed by persons between 14 and 24 years of age, 41 percent between 25 and 44 years, 23 percent between 45 and 64 years, and 13 percent were 65 years and older. An increasing trend toward "unrelated adults sharing two-person households" is indicated by the fact that only 242,000 such households were reported in the 1960 Census and 327,000 in 1970; preliminary analysis of 1977 Census data suggests a continued sharp increase in such couples. In spite of this increase, such persons still represent only about 1 percent of all household heads at any given time (U.S. Bureau of the Census, 1977; Note 1).

During the period 1974–75, interviews were held with a nationwide random sample of 2,510 20–30-year-old men who had registered with the Selective Service in 1962 through 1972. Of these men, 18 percent reported having lived non-maritally with a woman for a period of six months or more. Two-thirds of them had had only one such relationship and only five percent were currently cohabiting, suggesting that most such relationships terminate or end in marriage. Cohabitants were more likely to be men who were not attending college or with less than a high school education, supporting the Census finding that cohabitation is not only a college campus phenomenon (Clayton & Voss, 1977).

Attitudes

As was true of prevalence, most of the research on attitudes toward cohabitation has been done with college students, with available evidence suggesting that students in general approve of cohabitation outside of marriage. At City College of New York in 1973, almost 80 percent said they would live with someone of the opposite sex if given an opportunity to do so (Arafat & Yorburg, 1973). About the same time, almost 60 percent of the men who had not cohabited and 35 percent of such women at Arizona State University answered yes when asked if they would want to (Henze & Hudson, 1974). In the Bower and Christopherson survey of 16 state universities in 1975, more than 50 percent of those who had not cohabited indicated they would consider doing so (Bower & Christopherson, 1977). At the University of Delaware, only 28 percent of an undergraduate sample said they would probably or definitely not cohabit (McCauley, Note 2). At Illinois State University in 1972, only 23 percent of the females and 8 percent of the males said they would definitely no cohabit, even if in love (Huang, Note 3). At Cornell University in 1972, only

7 percent of those who had not cohabited said it was because of moral reasons. The most common reasons given for not having cohabited were: Have not yet found a partner with whom I would like to stay for four or more nights a week, or am geographically separated from partner (Macklin, 1976*b*, p. 121).

It seems reasonable to estimate that, considering the country as a whole, probably about 25 percent of the undergraduate population have cohabited, 50 percent more would if they were to find themselves in an appropriate relationship or in a situation where they could, and 25 percent, for a variety of religious, moral, and personal reasons, think they probably would not, even if it were possible, more of these being female and underclassmen.

Most students do not believe that a long-term commitment to the partner is necessary before persons live together. When asked what kind of relationship should exist before a person cohabits, most students indicate that cohabitation is acceptable as long as there is a strong, affectionate, preferably monogamous relationship between the two persons. Summarizing data from four institutions where similar questionnaires were administered, roughly 5 percent of the undergraduates indicated a couple should be married before living together; 15 percent, formally or tentatively engaged; 40 percent, strong, affectionate, monogamous relationship; 25 percent, strong affectionate, also dating others, relationship, or good friends; and 15 percent, persons who find it expedient to live together should do so, and no emotional involvement is necessary (Macklin, in press).

As of 1975, the parental generation did not share this acceptance of cohabitation. Three studies have compared attitudes of parent and student generations and each reports a large generation gap. The majority of parents consider cohabitation outside of marriage to be either immoral, emotionally unhealthy, or unwise, and say they will work to prevent or eliminate such behavior in their own offspring (Smith & Kimmel, 1970; Steiner, 1975; Macklin, Note 4).

What has caused young persons today to accept a behavior pattern which was unthinkable a generation ago? A myriad of interacting factors have served to create an atmosphere conducive to the change. The shift toward acceptance of cohabitation must be seen as part of a slow evolution in sexual values and behavior patterns that began in the early part of the century with growing urbanization and its increasing opportunities for privacy and anonymity, and with the changing attitudes regarding freedom for women. One can trace from the early 1920s the gradually increasing nonvirginity rates for women and the simultaneously increasing acceptance of sexual involvement in a love relationship. By the end of the 1960s, sexual intercourse among college students who were going steady was commonly approved practice. The late Dr. Guttmacher, a former president of Planned Parenthood-World Population, said in 1972, "It is rather generally accepted that by the senior year in many colleges seventy percent of the single students of both sexes are engaging in intercourse" (Guttmacher & Vadies, 1972, p. 145). One could argue that a natural extension of this was openly to accept spending the night together, and predict that couples who enjoyed being together would come to increase their number of nights together.

Many social forces associated with the late 1960s served to support the trend. The Women's Movement, dormant for many decades, renewed its challenge of the double standard and its demand that women be granted the same rights and privileges as men. An important by-product was the increasing equalization of parietals and housing regulations for male and female students, making is possible for the first time for large numbers of college students to live off-campus or to reside in dormitories without curfew. The phenomenon of extended adolescence, the earlier entrance into puberty, the radical tenor of the period which encouraged youth to question their continued treatment as children, and the demand by college students that they be granted the same privileges as their noncollege age-mates, led to a slow erosion of "in loco parentis" and a gradual acceptance of a policy of 24-hour visitation in the dormitory.

The change in dormitory regulations and the fact that most lived far from the parental eye made it physically feasible for large numbers of young persons to cohabit. Concurrent social changes made it likely that many would take advantage of the opportunity. The increase in divorce rates and the changing conception of the function of marriage caused many youth, and many divorcees, to move more cautiously into that state. The increased acceptance of sexuality outside of marriage and of sex as an expression of affection rather than as an act of procreation, and the increased availability of effective contraception, made it easier for nonmarried persons to engage openly and comfortably in a sexual relationship. Social Security retirement benefits, which gave an advantage to single persons, caused many older persons to question the economic wisdom of marrying. The increased emphasis on relationship and on personal growth, which came with the human growth movement, called into question the superficiality of the traditional courtship process and a too-early commitment to permanence. The result was a search for styles of relating which allowed a high degree of total intimacy as well as an opportunity for individual growth and change.

Nature of the Relationship

It is impossible to discuss "*the* cohabitation relationship," since the concept covers a wide variety of types of relationships which differ in amount of time the two individuals spend together, the nature of the living arrangement, and the degree of commitment. Several attempts have been made to develop a useful typology of cohabitation relationships (Macklin, 1974a; Petty, 1975; Storm, 1973), primarily using some continuum of dyadic commitment as the basis of classification. There are at least five types:

(1) *temporary casual convenience* (including "contract cohabitation") (Van Deusen, 1974), where two persons share the same living quarters because it is expedient to do so;

(2) the *affectionate dating-going together* type of relationship where the couple stays together because they enjoy being with one another and will continue as long as both prefer to do so;

(3) the *trial marriage* type, which includes the "engaged to be engaged" and partners who are consciously testing the relationship before making a permanent commitment;

(4) the *temporary alternative to marriage,* where the individuals are committed to staying together, but are waiting until it is more convenient to marry; and

(5) the *permanent alternative to marriage,* where couples live together in a long-term committed relationship similar to marriage, but without the traditional religious or legal sanctions.

As one might expect, there are important differences among these types, causing researchers to agree unanimously that we must no longer treat unmarried cohabitants as one homogeneous group.

When college cohabitants have been asked to identify what their relationship was like at the time they *started* living together, the majority define themselves as having been in a "strong, affectionate, monogamous" relationship. This has caused many writers to declare that cohabitation on the college campus, at least during the first year, is merely an added step in the courtship process, a kind of "living out of going steady" (Bower & Christopherson, 1977; Danziger, 1976; Henze & Hudson, 1974; Johnson, 1968; Macklin, 1974 *b*). The couple generally shares a deep emotional relationship with one another but has not yet reached the point of long-term commitment. Consistent with this is that most college couples, at least initially, maintain two separate residences and may not spend every night together, and the finding by Rubin in his 2-year follow-up of college couples that cohabiting couples were as likely to break up as dating couples (Rubin, Note 5).

We do not yet know enough to say what proportion of older cohabiting couples fall into each of the above categories. One can predict, however, that length of time together will be a key variable regardless of age. The longer the couple has been together, the more likely they are to have moved up the courtship continuum: from living together simply because they enjoy it and find it convenient to do so, to living together because they want to see if they can really "make it together" to being together because they have decided to build a permanent and committed relationship with one another.

Comparison of Cohabitors and Noncohabitors

Much research to date has been directed to answering the question: Can we predict which individuals are more likely to cohabit? The usual method has been to give a questionnaire to a sample of students and compare the answers of those who have and have not cohabited. One must remember, therefore, when interpreting the findings that it is impossible to tell to what extent the established differences were present before, or developed as a consequence of, the cohabitation.

As so often has been found in other research on sexual behavior, the most significant differentiating variable is the individual's religiosity. Those who cohabit are less likely to indicate an affiliation with some established religion and have lower rates of church attendance (Arafat & Yorburg, 1973; Henze & Hudson, 1974; Macklin, 1976b, p. 119; Peterman, Ridley, & Anderson, 1974; Huang, Note 3). There are also some apparent personality differences. Cohabiting females are likely to describe themselves as more competitive, aggressive, independent, and managerial than do noncohabiting females. Cohabiting males are likely to describe themselves as less managerial and competitive and as warmer and more emotionally supportive than do noncohabiting males (Arafat & Yorburg, 1973; Guittar & Lewis, Note 6). In other words, cohabitants tend to perceive themselves as more androgynous and more liberated from traditional sex-role characteristics than do noncohabitants. They are likely to hold more liberal attitudes; their reference groups include more persons who have also cohabited; they tend to perceive campus norms as being more sexually liberal; and they are more likely to major in the arts and the social sciences than in the physical sciences and engineering. They are *not* more likely to come from unhappy or divorced homes, do not have lower academic averages, and are not significantly less likely to want eventually to marry (Henze & Hudson, 1974; Macklin, 1976 b, pp. 118–120; McCauley, 1977, Peterman et al., 1974).

Most researchers have been more impressed by the similarities than by the differences between cohabitants and noncohabitants. On campuses where a large percentage of persons engage in cohabitation at some point in their undergraduate life, persons who cohabit do not appear to be dramatically different from those who do not. As people, cohabiting students seem representative of the general undergraduate population, with their cohabitation more a consequence of the opportunity for such a relationship than a result of any demographic characteristics, although they are likely to be persons whose personal and religious values are congruent with this lifestyle, and they must possess sufficient interpersonal skills to initiate such a relationship (Macklin, 1976b, p. 122).

As nonmarital cohabitation becomes a more common phenomenon in this country and the majority of those who experience a love relationship also cohabit at some time during the courtship process, it may no longer be relevant to ask "Who cohabits?" Instead, the crucial question may be: What are the characteristics of persons who are able to engage in a love relationship? Possession of a basic level of heterosexual attractiveness and interpersonal competence may become more predictive of cohabitation than any of the other variables researched to date.

Comparison of Cohabiting and Noncohabiting Couples

In addition to efforts to determine differences between individuals who do and do not cohabit, research has been directed toward comparing cohabiting and noncohabiting couples. In general, the comparison has been between married couples and couples who were living together unmarried, with a few studies comparing cohabiting, engaged, and going-steady couples. The three most commonly studied phenomena have been degree of commitment, division of labor, and expressed satisfaction, with some attention also given to such variables as sexual exclusivity, territoriality, sources of conflict and conflict management, and attitudes regarding children. In reviewing this research it is important to ascertain whether the investigator matched the couples on such relevant variables as age, length of time together, and level of education, and to determine to what extent the couples studied were randomly selected from a clearly defined population. In most cases, the samples have consisted of self-selected volunteers.

Commitment

Commitment as a variable has probably been discussed more fully and more often in the cohabitation literature than any other variable. The interest appears to stem from an assumption that a degree of commitment is necessary for success in any interpersonal relationship, and the popular belief that cohabitation involves insufficient commitment for such success. Researchers have generally seen commitment as having two distinct components:

(1) *personal commitment,* the extent to which one is dedicated to continuing the relationship; and
(2) *behavioral commitment,* the consequences of having lived with an individual which make it more likely that one will continue to do so (specifically, the degree to which others know of the relationship and would disapprove of its termination, and the changes one would have to make in one's life were one to cease cohabiting) (Budd, 1976; Johnson, 1973).

Using the above criteria, nonmarried cohabitants indicate significantly less commitment than do married couples, with married couples reporting a stronger dedication to continuing the relationship and more external constraints on their separation (Budd, 1976; Johnson, 1973). When compared with engaged couples, unmarried cohabitants as a group tend to be as committed to their partners and to the relationship, but are less committed to the ideas of marrying their partner (Lewis, Spanier, Storm, & Lettecka, Note 7). One interesting and perhaps important finding is the indication that there are different predictors of degree of commitment for engaged and for unmarried cohabiting couples. For the engaged couples, the best predictors were such variables as length of the couple's acquaintance and amount of mother's education, while for the cohabiting couples, the more relevant variable was degree of happiness in the relationship. This suggests that commitment between engaged persons may be built more upon quantitative measures (e.g., the couple's endurance over time), whereas degree of commitment for cohabiting couples may depend more upon the present quality of the relationship (Lewis et al., Note 7).

One of the more frequently voiced concerns is that cohabitation leads to exploitation of the female partner by the male, who is often viewed as less emotionally involved and less personally committed. The evidence on this point is mixed, although there is a tendency for cohabiting females to have higher commitment scores than their male counterparts (Budd, 1976; Johnson, 1973; Kieffer, 1972, pp. 79–83; Lyness et al., 1972; Lewis et al., Note 7). Why this is the case and what effect it has on the relationship is not clear.

Division of Labor

Because cohabitation is an innovative lifestyle and the attitudes of cohabitors tend to be relatively liberal, it has been assumed that nonmarital cohabiting relationships would be more androgynous in nature and the division of labor less traditionally sex-roled. Available data suggest that this is not the case. Most studies indicate that cohabiting couples tend to mirror the society around them and engage in sex-role behavior characteristic of other couples their age. Couples today are in general more egalitarian than previously, and cohabiting couples are no more so than married ones (Bower, 1975; Macklin 1976a, p. 38; Makepeace, 1975; Segrest, 1975; Stafford, Backman, and diBona, 1977; Stevens, 1975; Cole & Bower, Note 8; Olday, Note 9). The many years of subtle socialization and role scripting, and the fact that role adaptation requires constant negotiation and accommodation, serve to maintain more conventional modes of behavior, even in what on the surface would appear to be nontraditional relationships (Whitehurst, Note 10).

Satisfaction

A number of studies have compared the degree of satisfaction experienced by nonmarital cohabitants and other couples, and have consistently found few differences (Budd, 1976; Polansky, 1974; Stevens, 1975; Olday, Note 9; Cole & Bower, Note 11; Cole & Vincent, Note 12). The conclusion reached by Cole and Vincent, after studying the degree of overall satisfaction expressed by a matched sample of 20 married and 20 cohabiting couples, is typical: "Apparently it is not so much the legal nature of the relationship that encourages or discourages satisfaction. Instead, it is more likely a factor of how the partners behave toward each other and define their roles that is predictive of happiness within an individual relationship" (Cole & Vincent, Note 13).

Budd gave a list of 32 potential problem areas to 54 cohabiting couples, 48 married couples who had cohabited before marriage, and 49 who had not. When she asked them to indicate how upset they got about each in their present relationship, she found few significant differences among groups. Feelings of being overinvolved in the relationship was the only area rated as significantly more upsetting by cohabitors than by marrieds. The mean rating given most problems, including overinvolvement, was less than 2.0 on a 5-point scale, indicating that the couples in general experienced little problem in their relationship (Budd, 1976).

Exclusivity

Many have hypothesized that cohabitants would be less monogamous in their relationships than others their age, but again there are no data to support this notion. While philosophically cohabitants are more open to nontraditional ideas (Bower & Christopherson, 1977; Peterman et al., 1974, p. 351), in their own relationships they act much like everyone else (Bower, 1975, p. 76; Huang, Note 3; Clatworthy & Scheid, Note 14). For example, Montgomery, in a study of 31 cohabiting couples, found that the majority of the respondents believed that sexual freedom should be available within the relationship; however, most voluntarily restricted their sexual activity as evidence of their commitment to the relationship (Montgomery, Note 15).

Internal Dynamics

How are cohabitation relationships formed? How do such couples deal with conflict? What causes a cohabitation relationship to end? Are the processes involved any different from those in noncohabital intimate relationships?

Formation

As in most intimate relationships, living together is seldom the result of a considered decision, at least initially, but rather results from a gradual, often unconscious, escalation of emotional and physical involvement. Most cohabitation evolves from a drift into sleeping more and more frequently together and a gradual accumulation of possessions at one residence. If and when a decision with conscious deliberation is made, it is usually precipitated by some external force, such as the end of the term, graduation, a change of job, a need for housing, or reduced income. Until such an event occurs, there is only a mutual, often unspoken, recognition of the desire to be together, with little attention given to planning for the relationship.

Survival

Some writers have suggested that because cohabiting relationships operate with fewer external support systems, and often most endure parental displeasure and societal discrimination, they need more internal unifiers than will a more traditional relationship in order to survive. The cohabiting couple may have to work more conscientiously at maintaining their relationship than does the married couple and, in exchange theory terms, may have to see more evident personal benefit from the relationship to continue the investment. This would imply that there must be more day-to-day behavioral evidence of commitment from one's cohabiting partner than from one's marital partner if the relationship is to last (Montgomery, Note 15). There is as yet little evidence concerning this point.

Hennon, in a discussion of conflict management with the cohabiting relationship, raises the question: Will cohabiting couples, because they cannot take the relationship for granted, be more likely to work at it than married couples, and, hence, be more likely to air their areas of conflict and to work at resolving them? Or, instead, because they are less secure in their relationship, will they hesitate openly to disclose and confront areas of conflict (Hennon, Note 16)? It seems likely that conflict management is more a function of the personality, maturity, and skill of the individuals involved than of the nature of the living situation, and that one might find as much variation among unmarried as among married couples.

At present there is little information on the length of cohabiting relationships or how many result in marriage. To obtain such information would require a longitudinal study and currently there is only one in progress. Cole and Bower have been studying a sample of noncollege cohabiting couples for serveral years and as of 1976 had follow-up data on 40 such dyads. At latest report, available evidence suggests that "of those relationships able to satisfactorily work through initial adjustment problems, there is as good a chance that the relationship will continue, with the same chance of success, as found among the married population." Cole lists four reasons why a cohabiting relationship might fail: emotional immaturity; insufficient or unequal degree of commitment; external crises, such as loss of employment, external interference, or pursuit of goals which necessitate an indefinite physical separation; and different value and behavior patterns, primarily with regard to use of time and money and division of labor (Cole, Note 17, pp. 13–14).

Termination

Ganson studied a sample of persons who had terminated cohabitation relationships, in an effort to identify the sources of dissolution. While the most
common reason given was "grew apart," the majority of reasons related to
feelings of overdependency and loss of identity, with women more likely to
report this than men (Ganson, 1975). Rubin, in his study of 231 college
couples, also reported that when relationships dissolved, the women tended to
cite more problem in the relationship than did men, with need for independence a key factor (Rubin, Note 5). Women may be more emotionally involved
in their relationships than men and, hence, more sensitive to problems. Or, as
Rubin suggests, they may be more alert to the quality of the relationship
because their future status is so dependent upon finding the right husband. On
the other hand, if the relationships are as traditionally sex-roled as has been
described, and if women are more interested than men in an egalitarian relationship, as has been suggested (McCauley, Note 18), they may actually experience more frustration than their partners.

One reason given for cohabiting is that the relationship is easier to terminate
than if one were married. Is separation in fact any easier for cohabiting
couples? The only eivdence to date is anecdotal. It suggests that the interpersonal dynamics involved in the severing of a relationship are the same whether
one is married or cohabiting, with the degree of trauma dependent upon the
length of time the individuals have been together and the degree of emotional
involvement between them. Cohabitants can expect to experience the same
process of denial, depression, anger, ambivalence, and reorientation to singlehood associated with the dissolution of any serious relationship. There are
probably two important differences between cohabitants and married who
separate: the public and relatives are likely to apply less social pressure to
maintain the cohabiting relationship, and separation can be completed without
litigation. With less social stigma and reduced visibility, there is often less guilt
and sense of failure, and a faster readjustment in the postseparation period.

Effects of Cohabitation

The rationale for cohabitation has been that the experience is growth-
producing for the participant, improves the quality of later marriage, and
serves as a more effective screening device, hence, eventually reducing the
present high divorce rate. To what extent are these hopes justified?

Personal Growth

The vast majority of cohabitants in studies to date give high positive ratings
to their experience, and assert that it served to foster their personal growth and
maturity. They indicate they would elect to cohabit again if they "had their

lives to live over," and would not wish to marry without having lived with the partner first (Bower, 1975; Lautenschlager, 1975; Macklin, 1976*b*, pp. 133–134; Peterman et al., 1974; Shuttlesworth & Thorman, Note 19). Unfortunately, no investigator has attempted to develop or apply any objective measures to test what extent cohabitation does in fact lead to enhanced personal growth or whether it provides for any more growth than any of the more traditional dating relationships.

Ridley, Peterman, and Avery have hypothesized that cohabitation is most likely to provide a positive learning experience and better preparation for marriage when the participants:

(1) have as cohabitation goals, greater self-understanding within a heterosexual context and increased knowledge of the day to day aspects of intimate living;
(2) have realistic and mutually agreed upon expectations for the cohabiting experience;
(3) do not have strong deficiency needs for emotional security, or a residue of past grievances and/or unfinished business;
(4) have a high interpersonal skill level, e.g., the ability to openly and honestly express their feeling, the ability to understand and accept their partner, and the ability to mutually solve problems;
(5) have had a relationship where the present degree of involvement closely approximates that of a cohabitation relationship, for example, steadily dating rather than casual dating;
(6) have a rich dating history resulting in positive self perceptions in terms of their desirability to the opposite sex; and
(7) have a fairly extensive network of like and opposite sex relationships where important needs are being met (Ridley, Peterman, & Avery, in press).

Quality of Marriage

There has been little systematic study to determine whether cohabitation leads to a more successful or a different marriage. Four descriptive studies touch on this theme, yet none involves the necessary longitudinal design. Lyness compared 11 married couples who had cohabited before marriage with 13 who had not, on 16 variables representing concepts from open marriage, and found few differences between the groups (Lyness, Note 20). Olday studied 184 married students who had cohabited before marriage and 524 who had not, and found little significant difference between them. Cohabitation before marriage did not seem related to degree of satisfaction, conflict, egalitarianism, or emotional closeness in the later marriage (Olday, Note 9).

When Budd compared 48 married couples who had cohabited before marriage, and 49 who had not, on problems experienced, amount of self-disclosure, and degree of commitment, she found few significant differences. The one major difference was that the marrieds who had not cohabited premaritally were more likely to report loss of love as a problem area that was upsetting to them. It is not clear the extent to which this is due to differences in actual love loss, marriage expectations, or individual need levels, nor is it clear whether the differences between the groups were due to initial personality differences or to the experience of having lived together before marrying (Budd, 1976).

Clatworthy and Schied (Note 14), in another study of married couples who had and had not cohabited, report that while all the couples who had premaritally cohabited considered the experience to be beneficial to their marriage, there was no evidence that couples who live together before marriage have better marriages or less conventional marriages, or that they select better or more compatible mates. They conclude that premarital cohabitation, in and of itself, cannot be considered a cure-all for the problems of traditional marriage.

Although they found many similarities between the marrieds who had and had not cohabited premaritally, Clatworthy and Schied did note some important differences: couples who had cohabited were less likely to acquiesce in disagreements; more often disagreed on such things as finances, household duties, and recreation; were less dependent on their spouses; considered their marriage a less intrinsic part of their lives; had broken up more often; and a higher percentage had sought marriage counseling. Rather than conclude that cohabitation led to these differences, one might hypothesize that these persons would have exhibited these same marital characteristics whether or not they have cohabited premaritally. It is in fact very possible that the same factors which led them to be attracted to cohabitation before marriage would lead them to practice more independence and less acquiescence in marriage, to be more likely to question the role of marriage in their lives, and to view it as less essential to their well-being.

Related to the above is the question: Does movement from cohabitation to legal marriage with its increased sanctions, rights, and responsibilities, change the nature of the couple's relationship to one another? The issue is not settled. Berger, in a retrospective study of 21 couples who had cohabited premaritally, noted that, in general, marriage did not seem to lead to any dramatic change, and that the quality of the relationship after marriage reflected to large extent the apparent quality of the relationship before marriage (Berger, Note 21). Some couples agree, reporting that being married made no difference in their relationship and served only to make parents happy and to facilitate interaction with the larger society. Others claim that they found themselves falling into stereotyped roles, with a resulting loss of identity (Keaough, 1975).

Based on what evidence we have to date, we can hypothesize that movement into marriage will escalate commitment, increase ease with relatives and social institutions, and, because of socialization, increase the likelihood of traditional sex-role behavior, possessiveness, and reduced autonomy. However, both married and unmarried couples are likely to find themselves relating to one another in these more traditional ways unless they consciously contract against this and make a determined effort to maintain the provisions of that contract.

Marriage Rates

Some writers and social critics fear that cohabitation will lead to erosion of the family, a reduction in the rate of marriage, and an increase in children born without the security of legally committed parents. They point with alarm to Sweden with its decided decrease in marriage and increase in cohabitation rates. In Sweden in 1974, 12 percent of all couples living together under marriage-like conditions were unmarried as opposed to only 6.5 percent in 1970; by 1977, this figure had risen to 15 percent. The increased percentages, however, are partly due to the fact that more couples are living together before marriage; about 99 percent of all Swedes who marry today have cohabited premaritally. It is not yet known what percentage of cohabitors will choose nonmarital cohabitation as a permanent life style. (Trost, 1975; Note 22.)

Although there has been a decrease in marriage rates in this country over the past 15 years, and a fairly dramatic increase in the percentage of singles among women aged 20–24 (Bernard, 1975), there is as yet no evidence that large numbers are permanently substituting nonmarital relationships for marriage. Because the vast majority of young persons continues to indicate they hope someday to marry (Bower & Christopherson, 1977; Macklin, 1976b, p. 128), and because societal supports for first and remarriage are so strong in this country, it is predicted that cohabitation will remain part of the courtship phase for most persons, and that there will not be a substantial decrease in marriage rates for some time.

Childrearing

Eiduson and associates are currently involved in a longitudinal comparison of 200 children reared in cohabiting, communal, single-parent, and two-parent nuclear families. Evidence to date suggests that the needs of the infant are such strong determiners of how children are reared that, during the first year of life caretaking practices in nontraditional and traditional families do not differ significantly. At the end of 1 year, the development of the total sample generally fell within the normal range, with lifestyle not a differentiating variable (Eiduson, Note 23). It will be interesting to see to what extent lifestyle appears to affect the development of these children after the first year.

Divorce

Whether cohabitation before legal marriage will lead to more or less divorce is not clear. Some argue that more effective screening of potential marital partners occurs, while others fear that it promotes a life pattern characterized by lack of commitment.

For a number of reasons, the age of marriage is increasing, and since there is general acceptance that the older a person is before marriage the more permanent the marriage, this may have some effect on the divorce rate. On the other hand, there are many factors currently operating against the permanence of relationships. A longer life span, changing views of marriage, wider range of lifestyle options, growing emphasis on personal growth with the possibility that both partners may not grow at the same rate or in the same direction, increasing opportunity for extramarital relationships coupled with little preparation in how to integrate these successfully into ongoing marriage, and greater opportunities for women to satisfy their economic and sexual needs outside of marriage all serve to increase the likelihood of divorce. The fact that a couple had an opportunity to test their initial compatibility through living together may have little effect on whether they will succeed in spending a lifetime together. Premarital cohabitation is but one factor, and probably not a primary factor, influencing the course of relationships over time.

Implications for Practice and Research

Legal statutes and practices need to be adapted to reflect the changing social realities (Hirsch, 1976; King, 1975; Massey & Warner, 1974). As of July 1976 (Lavori, 1976), cohabitation (living together as if husband and wife) was a crime in 20 states, and fornication (sexual intercourse between an unmarried man and woman) was a crime in 16 states and Washington, D. C. Although rarely enforced, the penalties for cohabitation can be stringent, with many states setting a maximum penalty of a $500 fine and a 6-month jail sentence. It would appear that such laws are unconstitutional and violate one's right to privacy without showing compelling reason for doing so, but the U. S. Supreme Court has yet to rule that this is true.

It is difficult to describe with any certainty the present legal status of cohabitants, for laws vary from state to state, the interpretation of any law waits upon judicial review, and new laws and interpretations can appear at any time. Readers are urged to seek informed legal counsel if they require definitive information regarding the laws and precedents in their own state. With this in mind, what can be said about the legal situation facing cohabitants today?

A child born to a man and woman who are living together but not married is still considered illegitimate and as such may experience discrimination, although the rights of such children have been considerably enlarged in recent years. Depending upon the jurisdiction, the rights of the father of a child born in cohabitation will vary. The U. S. Supreme Court ruled in 1972 that it is a denial of due process and equal protection to presume an unwed father an unfit parent, and to take his children from him without providing a proper hearing on the matter *Stanley v. Illinois,* 405 U.S. 645, 1972). However, there are still states which allow the mother primary right of custody, and where the father must not only establish paternity but prove her unfit before receiving custody himself. Should a couple with children divorce and one parent begin living with someone to whom she/he is not married, a judge may on the basis of such cohabitation find that parent unfit to keep custody of the child. Much of this discrimination will undoubtedly change with ratification of the federal Equal Rights Amendment (Myricks, 1977), and with the gradual trend toward recognition of the legitimacy of nontraditional lifestyles.

Since in most states there is no law prohibiting discrimination on the basis of marital status, an owner may choose not to sell, or a landlord not to rent, to an unmarried couple. Moreover, in states where cohabitation or fornication is illegal, or depending on the terms of the lease, living together can be grounds for eviction. Depending upon locale and the biases of one's employer, it is possible to lose one's job by cohabiting out of wedlock. Although Title VII of the 1964 Civil Rights Act prohibits discrimination in employment, it does not cover discrimination on the basis of marital status or living situation. Firing due to cohabitation is theoretically unconstitutional, but, again, this has not yet been established by the courts.

Because membership in professional associations and licensing may be conditional on demonstration of moral fitness, such privileges may on occasion be denied to someone cohabiting out of wedlock. Although the Equal Credit Opportunity Act prohibits discrimination in the granting of credit on grounds of marital status, there is still some question as to whether marital status will be construed to include living together, and hence, some doubt as to whether credit unions would be violating federal law by refusing to grant credit to couples who are living together unmarried. Although there has been some development in the legal protection of cohabiting couples against discrimination in insurance, there are only a few states which prohibit insurance companies from refusing coverage or charging higher premiums.

In some states, such as New York, family court is available to help persons deal with disputes occurring in the family setting, but persons must be legally related in order to have access to this court. Most nonmarital cohabitants do not have the privilege of confidential communication and, hence, unlike married persons, may be called upon to testify against one another in court. Although a notarized power of attorney may be helpful, couples living together do not have the recognized authority to consent to medical treatment for each other, even in case of emergency.

There are numerous inequities within the present tax structure which result in permitting married couples with one income and a joint return to pay less taxes on the same income than two single persons (who, in turn, pay less than a two-income married couple). Moreover, persons who are cohabiting cannot claim each other as dependents. Should the couple remain unmarried and one partner never work outside the home, they will receive less Social Security benefits upon retirement than if they had married. If a partner is injured or dies on the job, the surviving partner will receive Workman's Compensation only if there was a legal marriage.

Although there is considerable body of law regarding the distribution of property upon the termination of a marital relationship, unmarried couples have had to rely on judicial decision. When the couple has acquired real property together, the judge has usually determined property rights strictly on the basis of who has title to the property, and in the case of personal property, on the basis of receipts showing who paid for it. If one is not married and dies without a will, one's property goes to one's blood relatives rather than to one's partner, and inheritance taxes favor the married couple, for when a married partner dies and leaves property to the spouse, all or a portion of that property is tax-exempt.

In December 1976, the California Supreme Court, building on earlier cases, established a precedent which may have important legal implications for unwed couples. Michelle Marvin, who had cohabited nonmaritally with Lee Marvin for 7 years, sued for an equal share of all property acquired during their relationship, claiming that she had given up her career to property accumulated during their time together.

Rejecting Lee's contention that the agreement was unenforceable because of the immoral nature of the relationship and because he had been legally married to another woman at the time of the agreement, the majority in *Marvin* v. *Marvin* (18 Cal. 3rd 684, 1976) stated that the courts should uphold express (oral or written) agreements between nonmarital partners to pool or share income or property, unless the agreement was explicitly dependent upon illicit sexual relations. It was suggested by way of dictum, which has no precedental value (Weisberg, Note 24), that a partner may recover for the reasonable value of household services rendered less the reasonable value of support received if it can be shown that the services were rendered with the expectation of monetary reward. The court ignored the issue of whether Michelle was entitled to support after separation.

It should be noted that the *Marvin* decision serves only to establish that prior financial agreements between Michelle and Lee are enforceable. It remains for Michelle to demonstrate what agreements were in fact made, and without written contractual evidence, this may be difficult.

Indicative of the changing legal picture is the statement by Justice Tobriner of the California Supreme Court. Speaking for the majority, he wrote, "The mores of the society have indeed changed so radically in regard to cohabitation that we cannot impose a standard based on alleged moral considerations that have apparently been so widely abandoned by so many" (*Marvin* v. *Marvin,* 18 Cal. 3rd 684, 1976).

To what extent other states will be influenced by the *Marvin* case remains to be seen. Since the *Marvin* decision rested on contract principles, which are universally applicable, there is a good possibility that it may be followed by other jurisdictions (Weisberg, Note 24). On the other hand, there are many courts which may hesitate to follow the *Marvin* precedent, arguing that the household services rendered are implicitly based on sexual services and that by reimbursing such services one is essentially validating the institution of concubinage. There are others who argue that with the *Marvin* case the court is conferring legal rights and imposing legal duties on relationships which were deliberately intended to be extralegal (Foster and Freed, 1977; *The Family Law Reporter,* Note 25).

In addition, the decision left many areas of ambiguity. For instance, the Marvin relationship had extended over a period of 7 years, and it is not clear the extent to which duration may affect later decisions. The court indicated that the "reasonable expectations" of the parties should be the basis for the distribution of property acquired during the relationship, but left undefined the criteria to be used in the determination of "reasonable."

It is obvious that by not marrying, cohabitants deny themselves some of the protections provided by the law to married couples and do not necessarily escape all legal obligations, for they may find themselves economically liable in ways they had not initially anticipated. Lavori, a member of the New York State Bar and an attorney in private practice in New York City, concludes her book, *Living Together, Married or Single: Your Legal Rights,* by saying:

> A man and a woman who are both capable of financial independence and who have the foresight to protect their mutual rights through contracts, wills and compliance with legitimation procedures, and who do not mind doing some legal battle once in a while to secure their rights to housing, credit, insurance, and employment can live together permanently or temporarily with no difficulty. But most people are not in that position. Few have the awareness or the desire to take a self-protective, preventive approach to their personal relationships. For these people, marriage is probably a good idea ultimately, although living together may well be a perfectly appropriate interim status. For them, marriage defines their rights regarding each other and anticipates contingencies that they will not or cannot forsee, prevent, or provide for. (Lavori, 1976, p. 247)

Often persons living together are hesitant to go to marriage and family counselors for fear they will be considered deviant or be pressured into marriage. Yet many of the problems facing cohabiting couples are identical to those facing any couple involved in an intimate living relationship. These include differences in spending habits, degree of sexual interest, childrearing practices, division of household labor, amount of personal freedom, appropriate relationships with parents and other relatives, and expectations and hopes for the duration of the relationship. The only problems that seem unique to cohabitation are those which grow out of the lack of general societal support for this lifestyle, and the hassles some cohabitants experience when dealing with our legal, economic, and religious institutions. Although some counselors are not comfortable dealing with cohabiting couples, and many still consider such behavior as indicative of immaturity, such attitudes no longer can be considered acceptable among professionals.

Research needs to move ahead in new directions. Those who wish to continue to deal specifically with the phenomenon of cohabitation would do well to focus on developing longitudinal research with objective behavioral measures on noncollege and older populations, for it is in these areas where knowledge gaps primarily lie. Such studies should go beyond decriptive analyses comparing cohabitation and legal marriage, and test hypotheses founded on theory.

On the other hand, there is some question about the wisdom of continuing to use cohabitation as a central variable. Knowing that an individual is living with someone to whom she/he is not married tells us little about either the relationship or the person. Rather than focus on the specific legal status of a given relationship, investigators should be concerned with how the particular individuals define their own relationship, their degree of commitment to and investment in that relationship, the quality of the interaction, and the emotional maturity and interpersonal skills of the individuals involved. If the focus of research were more on the dynamics of intimate relationships and on the skills needed to function effectively within them, and less on the structural form of such relationships, progress toward understanding and improving the quality of relationships would be more rapid.

Reference Notes

1. Glick, P. C. Personal communication, June 20, 1977.
2. McCauley, B. Personal communication, 1976.
3. Huang, L. J. *Research with unmarried cohabiting couples: Including non-exclusive sexual relations.* Paper presented at the annual meeting of the National Council on Family Relations, St. Louis, Missouri, October 1974.
4. Macklin, F. D. *Comparison of parent and student attitudes toward non-marital cohabitation.* Paper presented at the annual meeting of the National Council on Family Relations, St. Louis, Missouri, October 1974.
5. Rubin, Z. *Dating project research report.* Unpublished manuscript, Harvard University Department of Psychology and Social Relations, April 1975.
6. Guittar, E. C., & Lewis, R. A. *Self concepts among some unmarried cohabitants.* Paper presented at the annual meeting of the National Council on Family Relations, St. Louis, Missouri, October 1974.
7. Lewis, R. A., Spanier, G. B., Storm, V. L., & Lettecka, C. F. *Commitment in married and unmarried cohabitation.* Paper presented at the annual meeting of the American Sociological Association, San Francisco, August 1975.
8. Cole, C. L., & Bower, D. W. *Role disparity in the cohabitation pair-bond.* Paper presented at the meeting of the North Central Sociological Association, Windsor, Canada, May 1974.
9. Olday, D. E. Personal communication, April 1976.
10. Whitehurst, R. N. *Sex role equality and changing meanings in cohabitation.* Paper presented at the annual meeting of the North Central Sociological Association, Windsor, Canada, May 1974.
11. Cole, C. L., & Bower, D. W. *Cohabitation pair-bond intimacy requirements and love-life development differences.* Paper presented at the annual meeting of the National Council on Family Relations, St. Louis, Missouri, October 1974.
12. Cole, C. M., & Vincent, J. P. *Cognitive and behavioral patterns in cohabitive and marital dyads.* Unpublished manuscript, University of Houston, 1975.

13. Cole, C. M., & Vincent, J. P. Personal communication, 1975.
14. Clatworthy, N. M., & Scheid, L. *A comparison of married couples: Premarital cohabitants with non-premarital cohabitants.* Unpublished manuscript, Ohio State University, 1977.
15. Montgomery, J. P. *Commitment and cohabitation cohesion.* Paper presented at the annual meeting of the National Council on Family Relations, Toronto, Canada, October 1973.
16. Hennon, C. B. *Conflict management within pairing relationships: The case of non-marital cohabitation.* Unpublished manuscript, University of Utah, 1975.
17. Cole, C. L. *Living together as an alternative life style.* Unpublished manuscript, Iowa State University, 1976.
18. McCauley, B. *Sex roles in alternative life styles: Egalitarian attitudes in the cohabiting relationship.* Paper presented at the International Workshop on Changing Sex Roles in Family and Society, Dubrovnik, Yugoslavia, June 1975.
19. Shuttlesworth, G. & Thorman, G. *Living together unmarried relationships.* Unpublished manuscript, University of Texas at Austin, 1973.
20. Lyness, J. F. *Open marriage among former cohabitants: We have met the enemy: Is it us?.* Unpublished manuscript, Pennsylvania State University, 1976.
21. Berger, M. E. *Trial marriage followup.* Unpublished manuscript, 140–70 Burden Crescent, Jamaica, N. Y., 1974.
22. Trost, J. *Dissolution of cohabitation and marriage.* Unpublished manuscript, Uppsala University, 1977.
23. Eiduson, B. T. Personal communication, 1977.
24. Weisberg, D. K. *How to divide the wages of living in sin: unmarried couples, property rights and the law.* Paper presented at the annual meeting of the National Council on Family Relations, San Diego, 1977.
25. *The Family Law Reporter,* January 11, 1977, *3,* (10), Sect. 2.

References

Arafat, I., & Yorburg, B. On living together without marriage. *Journal of Sex Research,* 1973, *9,* 97–106.

Berger, M. E. Trial marriage: Harnessing the trend constructively. *The Family Coordinator,* 1971, *20,* 38–43.

Bernard, J. Note on changing life styles, 1970–1974. *Journal of Marriage and the Family,* 1975, *37,* 582–593.

Bower, D. W. *A description and analysis of a cohabiting sample in America.* Unpublished master's thesis, University of Arizona, 1975.

Bower, D. W., & Christopherson, V. A. University student cohabitation: A regional comparison of selected attitudes and behavior. *Journal of Marriage and the Family,* 1977, *39,* 447–453.

Budd, L. S. *Problems disclosure, and commitment of cohabiting and married couples.* Unpublished doctoral dissertation, University of Minnesota, 1976.

Clayton, R. R., & Voss, H. L. Shacking up: Cohabitation in the 1970s. *Journal of Marriage and the Family,* 1977, *39,* 273–283.

Cole, C. L. Cohabitation in social context. In R. W. Libby & R. N. Whitehurst (eds.), *Marriage and alternatives.* Glenview, Ill.: Scott, Foresman and Co., 1977.

Danziger, C. *Unmarried heterosexual cohabitation.* Unpublished doctoral dissertation, Rutgers University, 1976.

Foster, H. H., & Freed, D. J. Law and the family. *New York Law Journal,* February 25, April 22, 1977.

Ganson, H. C. *Cohabitation: The antecedents of dissolution of formerly cohabiting individuals.* Unpublished master's thesis, Ohio State Universtiy, 1975.

Guttmacher, A. F., & Vadies, E. E. Sex on the campus and the college health services. *Journal of the American College Health Association,* 1972, *21,* 145–148.

Henze, L. F., & Hudson, J. W. Personal and family characteristics of non-cohabiting and cohabiting college students. *Journal of Marriage and the Family,* 1974, *36,* 722–726.

Hirsch, B. B. *Living together: A guide to the law for unmarried couples.* Boston: Houghton Mifflin, 1976.

Johnson, M. P. *Courtship and commitment: A study of cohabitation on a university campus.* Unpublished master's thesis, University of Iowa, 1968.

Johnson, M. P. Commitment: A conceptual structure and empirical application. *Sociological Quarterly,* 1973, *14,* 395–406.

Keaough, D. Without knotting the tie. *The American Republic,* July 27, 1975, pp. 8–15.

Kieffer, C. M. *Consensual cohabitation: A descriptive study of the relationships and sociocultural characteristics of eighty couples in settings of two Florida universities.* Unpublished master's thesis, Florida State University, 1972.

King, M. D. *Cohabitation handbook: Living together and the law.* Berkeley, Calif.: Ten Speed Press, 1975.

Lautenschlager, S. Y. *A descriptive study of consensual union among college students.* Unpublished master's thesis, California State University at Northridge, 1972.

Lindsey, B. B., & Evans, W. *The companionate marriage.* Garden City, N. Y.: Garden City Publishing Co., 1927/1929.

Lavori, N. *Living together, married or single: Your legal rights.* New York: Harper and Row, 1976.

Lyness, J. F., Lipetz, M. E., & Davis, K. E. Living together: An alternative to marriage. *Journal of Marriage and the Family,* 1972, *34,* 305–311.

Macklin, E. D. (Ed.). *Cohabitation Research Newsletter,* Ocotober 1972, 1. (a).

Macklin, E. D. Heterosexual cohabitation among unmarried college students. *The Family Coordinator,* 1972, *21,* 463–472. (b)

Macklin, E. D. (Ed.) *Cohabitation Research Newsletter,* June 1974, 2. (a)

Macklin, E. D. Students who live together: Trial marriage or going very steady. *Psychology Today,* November 1974, pp. 53–59. (b)

Macklin, E. D. (Ed.) *Cohabitation Research Newsletter,* April 1976,5. (a)

Macklin, E. D. Unmarried heterosexual cohabitation on the university campus. In J. P. Wiseman (Ed.), *The social psychology of sex.* New York: Harper and Row, 1976. (b)

Macklin, E. D. Review of research on non-marital cohabitation in the United states. In B. I. Murstein (ed.), *Exploring intimate life styles.* New York: Springer Publishing Co., in press.

Makepeace, J. M. *The birth control revolution: Consequences for college student life styles.* Unpublished doctoral dissertation, Washington State University, 1975.

Massey, C., & Warner, R. *Sex, living together and the law: A legal guide for unmarried couples and groups.* Berkeley, Calif.: Nolo Press, 1974.

McCauley, B. *Self esteem in the cohabiting relationship.* Unpublished master's thesis, University of Delaware, 1977.

Mead, M. Marriage in two steps. *Redbook,* July 1966, *127,* 48

Mead, M. A continuing dialogue on marriage: Why just living together won't work. *Redbook,* April 1968, *130,* 44

Myricks, N. The equal rights amendment: Its potential impact on family life. *The Family Coordinator,* 1977, *26,* 321–324.

Peterman, D. J., Ridley, C. A., & Anderson, S. M. A comparison of cohabiting and non-cohabiting college students. *Journal of Marriage and the Family.* 1974, *36,* 344–354.

Petty, J. A. *An investigation of factors which differentiate between types of cohabitation.* Unpublished master's thesis, Indiana University, 1975.

Polansky, L. *A comparison of marriage and cohabitation on three interpersonal variables.* Unpublished master's thesis, Ball State University, 1974.

Ridley, C. A., Peterman, D. J. & Avery, A. W. Cohabitation: Does it make for a better marriage? *The Family Coordinator,* in press.

Rodman, H. Illegitimacy in the Caribbean social structure: A reconsideration. *American Sociological Review,* 1966, *31,* 673–683.

Russell, B. *Marriage and morals.* New York: Liveright, 1929.

Segrest, M. A. *Comparison of the role expectations of married and cohabiting students.* University of Kentucky, 1975.

Smith, P. B., & Kimmel, K. Student-parent reactions to off-campus cohabitation. *Journal of College Student Personnel,* 1970, *11,* 188–193.

Stafford, R., Backman, E., & diBona, P. The division of labor among cohabiting and married couples. *Journal of Marriage and the Family,* 1977, 39, 43–57.

Steiner, D. *Non-marital cohabitation and marriage: Questionnaire responses of college women their mothers.* Unpublished master's thesis, North Dakota State University, 1975.

Stevens, D. J. H. *Cohabitation without marriage.* Unpublished doctoral dissertation, University of Texas, 1975.

Storm, V. *Contemporary cohabitation and the dating-marital continuum.* Unpublished master's thesis, University of Georgia, 1973.

Trost, J. Married and unmarried cohabitation: the case of Sweden with some comparisons. *Journal of Marriage and the Family,* 1975, *37,* 677–682.

Van Deusen, E. L. *Contract cohabitation: An alternative to marriage.* New York: Grove Press, 1974.

U.S. Bureau of the Census. Marital status and living arrangements: March 1976. *Current Population Reports* (Series P-20, no. 306). Washington, D.C.: U.S. Government Printing Office, 1977.

Marriage and Married People

*Paul C. Glick and
Arthur J. Norton*

International Comparisons of Marriage and Divorce

The United States has had one of the highest marriage rates—and the highest divorce rate—among the world's industrialized countries during recent years. This country's marriage rate reached a peak of 11.0 per 1,000 population in 1972—well above the rate for any other large country—but has declined in each subsequent year. In 1976, when the U.S. rate was 9.9, other countries with high marriage rates included the U.S.S.R. (10.1), Egypt (10.0 in 1975), Canada (8.7 in 1975), Israel (8.5), Australia (8.1), and Japan (7.8).[1] In most of these countries the rate for 1976 was lower than in one of the recent years. Through May 1977, the U.S. marriage rate remained steady at 9.9 per 1,000 population.[2] Very likely the world economic climate has a considerable bearing on the marriage rate in industrialized countries.

One reason for the high U.S. marriage rate is the fact that the U.S. divorce rate is also high and that most divorced persons (four of every five) remarry, thus swelling the total number of marriages in any given year. Another probable contributing factor—at least until recently—is the historic expansion of the U.S. job market, which has no doubt tended to instill optimism in young adults about their ability to enter marriage and to obtain relatively secure employment at an early adult age.

The U.S. divorce rate has consistently far exceeded that of any other country, but the gap has been narrowing. Between 1965 and 1976, the country's divorce rate doubled from 2.5 to 5.0 per 1,000 population. However, as of May 1977 it had stayed at 5.0 during all but one of the 12 preceding months. Among other countries with relatively high divorce rates in 1976 were Australia (4.3),

Excerpted from "Marrying, Divorcing, and Living Together in the U.S. Today," *Population Bulletin,* 32:5 (Population Reference Bureau, Inc., October 1977), pp. 2–39. Reprinted by permission.

the U.S.S.R. (3.4), Sweden (2.7), Denmark (2.5), Canada (2.2 in 1975), Finland (2.1), and Egypt (2.0). A majority of the industralized countries registered higher divorce rates in the most recent year for which data are available than in the preceding year. An exception was Sweden, where the rate declined from a peak of 3.3 in 1974 to 2.7 in 1976. Reasons for country differences in divorce, rates vary considerably, no doubt, but a factor that appears to transcend national boundaries is that the earlier the typical age at marriage the greater the likelihood of divorce.

Longtime Trends in U.S. Marriage and Divorce

An understanding of longtime trends in U.S. marriage and divorce is provided by an examination of changes in first marriage rates and remarriage rates, as shown in Figure 1. After a low point during the Depression of the 1930s, both marriage rates rose to a peak after World War II, as did also the

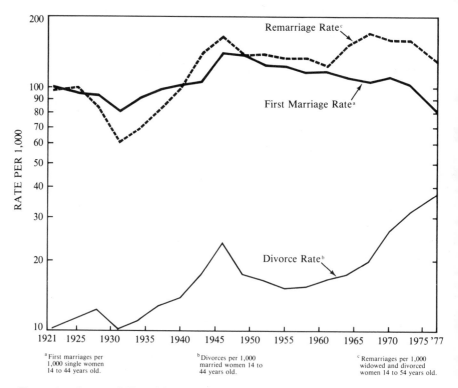

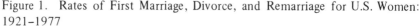

Figure 1.   Rates of First Marriage, Divorce, and Remarriage for U.S. Women: 1921–1977
    Source: Adapted with permission from Hugh Carter and Paul C. Glick, *Marriage and Divorce: A Social and Economic Study*, Rev. ed. (Cambridge, Mass: Harvard University Press, 1976) Figure 13.1, p. 394; with computations added for 1975–1977.

divorce rate. The remarriage rate was near an all-time high; many marriages that failed during the war were followed by divorce and remarriage. For a decade after these postwar peaks, the two marriage rates and the divorce rate fell in unison, but then began to take divergent paths.

Reasons for the High Divorce Rate

The divorce rate turned up again in the late 1950s and has mounted rapidly ever since.

The 1960s and early 1970s saw a prolonged war in Vietnam, followed by an often difficult readjustment to a peacetime economy and postwar family living. The upsurge in divorce has also coincided with several other rapid social changes. Along with the improvement in the status of ethnic minorities came the reinvigoration of the women's movement and more liberal attitudes toward personal behavior among most religious denominations. Along with increasing use of effective birth control methods came more delay in marriage and more years of independent living between departure from the parental home and marriage. And along with these changes came an increasing tolerance of divorce to end unsatisfactory marriages. The declining birth rate meant that young married women were having few if any children to complicate a return to "singlehood" if the decision was made to do so. Under these conditions, more and more couples were deciding to go through at least a mild crisis (divorce) in order that each partner might make another and hopefully more successful start in life through remarriage to someone else—in the light of past experience during the first marriage.[3]

Delay in First Marriage and Remarriage

The annual first marriage rate has declined almost continously for two decades. Postponement of marriage has been especially great among women in their early twenties. The proportion of women still single at ages 20 to 24 has gone up one one-half since 1960, from 28 percent to 43 percent.

The decline in first marriage rates can be explained by many of the same factors which worked to increase the divorce rate.

During the Vietnam War, increasing numbers of young men postponed marriage because of active military service while others enrolled in college as a means of delaying induction into the armed forces. Meantime, increasing numbers of young single women continued their education and obtained experience in the labor market. Thus many more women than ever before were exposed to a taste of independent self-maintenance and an attractive option to early marriage and preoccupation with child care.

For women during this period, embarking upon matrimony was further complicated by a "marriage squeeze"; the number of women reaching the usual ages at which women first marry (18 to 24) exceeded by 5 to 10 percent the number of men aged 20 to 26—the usual ages for men at first marriage. This phenomenon was a consequence of the postwar baby boom, coupled with the tendency for first-time grooms to be two or three years older than their brides. As the baby boom rose to its peak (in 1957), the number of girls born each year outstripped the number of boys born two to three years earlier.

Another legacy of the baby boom continues to have a marked effect on the first marriage rate. In the past decade, employers have found it impossible to hire the swollen number of young applicants flooding into the job market and the competition for available jobs has become increasingly stiff. Thus, undoubtedly unoptimistic about being able to establish a home and provide for a family, many young people have been postponing entry into first marriage. And yet, while delaying marriage, an increasing number of women have been bearing children out of marriage. From only 5 percent of all births in 1960, premarital births went up to 14 percent in 1975 (7 percent for white births and 49 percent for black births).

The trend in remarriage was sharply upward throughout most of the 1960s, while the divorce rate was also rising. But during the early 1970s the divorce rate continued to rise, while the remarriage rate reached a peak, leveled off, and then moved markedly downward (Figure 1). Moreover, after many years of gradual decline, the first marriage rate plunged downward after 1972. The following rates are for men, but the patterns are similar for women.

These impressive changes may be explained, to an unknown extent, by the economic recession of the mid-1970s. Obviously a very substantial number of persons who would have married under other circumstances have decided not to do so during these last few years. Some are feeling the financial pinch of having to maintain two residences while they are divorced, and others are opting for the life style of singlehood instead of marriage.

The rates presented above show that divorced men are three times as likely to remarry as never-married men are to enter first marriage. Evidently, divorced men strongly prefer being married, albeit with a different partner. As would be expected, the much older widowed men are far less likely to remarry than the much younger divorced men.

First marriage rates are far lower than remarriage rates, yet the *vast majority of marriages* still occur among those who have not been previously married (Figure 2). Back in 1960, fully 81 percent of men's marriages were their first.

| | | Remarriage Rate | |
| | First | | |
Year	Marriage Rate	After Divorce	After Widowhood
1972	70	229	41
1975	56	190	40
3-year decline	20%	17%	2.5%

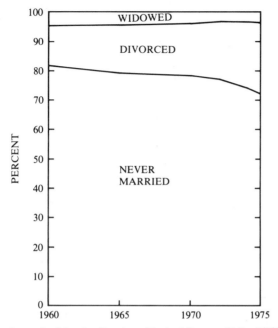

Figure 2. Marriages for Men by Previous Marital Status: U.S., 1960–1975
Sources: Various reports of the U.S. National Center for Health Statistics.

This proportion edged down gradually to 77 percent in 1972. Then in just three years, by 1975, the proportion of all marriages that were first marriages dropped 5 percentage points—more than in the preceding 12 years—to only 72 percent. Meantime, the ground lost by first marriages was made up almost entirely by remarriages after divorce; they moved up 5 percentage points from 14 percent of all marriages in 1960 to 19 percent in 1972 and then shot up another 5 points to 24 percent in 1975. As a consequence, remarriages after divorce accounted for nearly one-fourth of men's marriages in 1975 compared to less than one-seventh in 1960.

Perspective on the changing marriage patterns may be gained by relating them to the time when persons born during the baby boom of the late 1940s and the 1950s approached the customary age to marry. Persons who were born about 20 years before the 1972 peak of marriages entered life close to the middle of the high-birthrate period, which lasted from late 1945 until 1961. By the mid-1970s, the impact of the post-World War II bulge in births on the marriage market had passed its crest and was beginning to subside. Then, as single persons increasingly postponed first marriage, divorced persons followed suit and have been increasingly postponing remarriage—partly because they, like single persons, have been facing stiff competition for jobs.

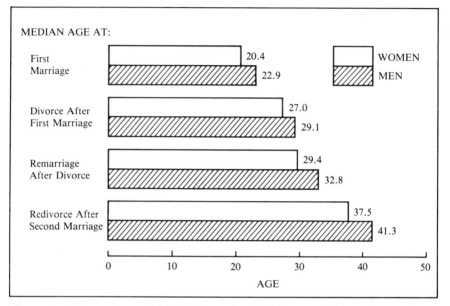

Figure 3.   Median Age at Marital Events for U.S. Men and Women Born 1900–1959
Source: U.S. Bureau of the Census, *Current Population Reports*, Series P-20, No. 297, "Number, Timing, and Duration of Marriages and Divorces in the United States, June 1975," Table H.

Time Spent In and Out of Marriage

How much time do people spend in and out of marriage? One way to estimate this is to compare the median ages at first marriage, divorce, remarriage, and redivorce. These are shown in Figure 3 (nest page), based on replies to questions asked in the Census Bureau's Current Population Survey for June 1975.*

A better way to measure the median length of time between changes in marital status is to determine the relevant interval for each person and then find the midpoint of the distribution. Results obtained in this way are presented in the following exhibit for 1967 and 1975 based on comparable Census Bureau Surveys.

Divorce after first marriage is evidently now occuring about a half year to a year sooner than a decade ago—down from close to eight to around seven years—for those who obtain a divorce. Half of those who remarry after divorce still do so within three years. Those who obtain a second divorce after they have remarried tend to do so a year and a half to two years sooner than it took

*The Current Population Survey is a monthly sample survey of approximately 47,000 households interviewed across the United States. Although the survey's primary purpose is to obtain monthly labor force statistics, supplementary questions provide current demographic data on the civilian noninstitutional population between the decennial censuses.

| Median Number | Men | | Women | |
of Years Between—	1967	1975	1967	1975
First marriage and divorce	7.7	6.7	7.9	7.3
Divorce and remarriage	3.1	3.1	3.4	3.2
Remarriage and redivorce	6.2	5.0	7.6	5.5

them to obtain their initial divorce—about 5.3 years versus 7.0 years (for men and women combined). Moreover, recent redivorces appear to be occurring about a year and a half sooner after remarriage than a decade or so ago.

The upshot is that young adults have been entering first marriage later and shortening the intervals not only between marriage and divorce but also between remarriage and redivorce. Thus, marital events are being compressed into a shorter span of years.

Although 1975 data show that four of every five divorced persons had remarried by middle age, the sharp decline (or delay) in remarriage since 1972 suggests that this proportion may decline in the near future. Even though a large majority of divorced persons remarry, many others do not. Among the consequences is an accumulation of divorced persons who have not remarried. For persons 35 to 54 years old, the proportion of persons currently divorced went up by one-third between 1970 and 1975 (from 4.6 percent to 6.2 percent). During the same period, the proportion "ever-divorced" rose about one-sixth (from 16.9 percent to 19.7 percent). Because the remarriage rate is still quite high, the proportion ever-divorced continues to be three to four times the level of the proportion currently divorced.

Marital Stability and Educational Level

Because marital status is very highly correlated with age, and because marital patterns are undergoing considerable change, the data in Table 1 on continuous first marriage by number of school years completed are limited to persons 35 to 54 years old. These persons are old enough to include most of those who will ever divorce, and yet young enough to have been affected considerably by the upsurge in divorce since 1960.

Persons who have not graduated from high school (i.e., with less than 12 years of schooling) have consistently fallen short of the overall average percentage of married persons in this age bracket who are still in their first marriage. For instance, in 1975, when 73 percent of all men of this age were still married to a first spouse, the average for men who stopped short of high school graduation was 65 percent. By contrast, in both 1960 and 1975, college graduates were above the general averages. Marital stability is greatest for men who have graduated from college or who have gone on to graduate school. Women differ in that those who have gone on to graduate school (17 or more years of completed schooling) record below-average marital stability. Thus, for

Table 1.   Percent of Persons Aged 35–54 in Intact First Marriages, by Education: U.S., 1960 and 1975

| Years of School Completed | Percent Married Once, Spouse Present | | | | Percent Change 1960–1975[a] | |
| | Men 35–54 | | Women 35–54 | | | |
	1960	1975	1960	1975	Men	Women
Total	72.8	72.5	67.4	66.0	0.2	2.3
0–11 years	67.6	64.6	62.5	57.1	–44.9	–44.3
12 years	74.6	72.2	69.8	66.4	42.6	48.7
13 or more	78.3	76.8	69.3	70.4	66.0	49.2
13–15 years	75.5	72.1	70.8	69.1	41.5	27.3
16 years	81.3	78.6	73.0	77.3	86.1	65.8
17 or more	80.2	81.8	54.8	63.4	86.4	136.1

Sources: U.S. Bureau of the Census, *Current Population Reports*, Series P-20, No. 312, "Marriage, Divorce, Widowhood, and Remarriage by Family Characteristics: June 1975," Tables F and 3; and *Census of Population: 1960*, Vol. II, 4D, *Marital Status*, Table 4.
[a] In terms of the number of married persons with spouse present.

men the relationship between socioeconomic status (whether measured by education or income) and marital stability is consistently positive. For women, however, an exception occurs among the highly educated. The reasons vary from woman to woman but probably include such factors as the many more options for career development which these women have, which often conflict with harmonious marriage, and, sometimes, personality traits that reduce their prospects for both entering and remaining in marriage.

Changes since 1960 in the number of persons aged 35 to 54 with stable first marriages have been uneven. Only about half as many such persons now as a decade and a half ago have not graduated from high school; this results from both a general increase in educational attainment and a decline in marital stability.

Despite their low marriage proportions, women with graduate school training recorded an outstanding rate of increase between 1960 and 1975 in the number who entered and remained in an initial marriage until they were in or near middle age (136 percent). This reflects both an exceptionally great increase in the number of women aged 35 to 54 who have pursued their education beyond an undergraduate degree (from 461,000 in 1960 up to twice as many, 938,000, in 1975) and the marked improvement in their marital stability (from 55 percent still in a first marriage in 1960 up to 63 percent in 1975). Evidently far more capable women are being encouraged to prepare for highly responsible positions and a growing proportion are successfully combining a professional or administrative career and marriage. It is also possible that men are more ready to accept highly educated women as wives (or vice versa), or more willing to see them add to their college credentials after marriage. The women's movement may now be beginning to affect men, too, and thus their acceptance of more egalitarian marriages.

Changes in the stability of marriage that will take place during the next decade or two among those now aged 20 to 40 cannot be predicted with much precision. But if present trends persist, the consequences for women in their forties might include: an increase from the present 4 percent single to 6 or 8 percent single; an increase from the present 8 percent ot 10 to 12 percent divorced; and a complementary decrease from about two-thirds of women with first marriages continuing into their forties as at present down closer to 60 percent. But the proportion of middle-years adults with a high educational level should continue to rise, and this will have a far-reaching impact on the nature of this age group's social, economic, and cultural acitivities.

Working Mothers

Employment rates for married women have gone up rapidly in recent years as seen in Table 2. In 1975 nearly half of all wives (44 percent), and over half of black wives (54 percent), were in the labor force. Corresponding rates for 1970 were distinctly lower—35 percent and 47 percent, respectively.

The only category of wives with above-average increases in worker rates after 1970 were mothers of preschool-age children. Wives in general had a 28 percent increase in their labor force participation rate, but wives with children under 6 years old had an increase twice as large (57 percent). In fact, the largest rate of increase in the worker rates between 1970 and 1975 for both all wives and black wives was that for mothers of children under 3 years of age (64 percent and 69 percent, respectively). by 1975, about one-third of all wives and half of the black wives with children under 3 years of age were in the labor market. Obviously, a rapidly increasing proportion of very young children are now being cared for during working hours by someone other than their own mother. Possibly, many of these caretakers are grandmothers with perhaps less education and fewer job skills than their working daughters.

Childless wives under 35 years of age still have the highest worker rates among married women. Moreover, other information available from the same source as Table 2 shows that the worker rates for *unmarried women* 20 to 35 years of age have been about the same as those for *childless married women* under 35. Taken together, these findings imply that childless wives under 35 are at least as likely as their unmarried counterparts to be members of the labor force.

Wives Who Earn More than Their Husbands

Given the lingering attitude which tends to favor the husband's dominance over the wife, the relationship between marital partners is undoubtedly still likely to be affected by the difference between their earnings levels. Usually the

Table 2. Percent of Married Women in the Labor Force, by Presence and Age of Children and Woman's Age and Race: U.S., 1960 and 1975

| Presence and Age of Children, and Age of Woman | Percent in Labor Force | | | | | |
| | All Married Women with Husband Present | | | Black Married Women with Husband Present | | |
	1960	1975	% Change 1960–1975	1960[a]	1975	% Change 1960–1975
Total	34.7	44.4	28	46.7	53.7	15
No children under age 18	38.3	43.9	15	52.6	47.5	–10
Woman aged 16–34	62.4	77.2	24	69.7	70.0	0
Woman 35 and over	34.3	35.5	3	49.2	42.5	–14
Children aged 6–17	42.7	52.3	22	56.3	61.8	10
Children under age 6	23.3	36.6	57	35.3	54.0	53
Aged 3–5 only	29.2	41.9	43	48.1	60.0	25
Under age 3	20.0	32.7	64	29.6	49.9	69

Sources: U.S. Bureau of Labor Statistics, *Special Labor Force Report No. 183*, "Marital and Family Characteristics of the Labor Force, March 1975," Tables E and F; and *Special Labor Force Report No. 64*, "Marital and Family Characteristics of the Labor Force, March 1965," Table F and I.

[a] Black and other races for 1960.

husband earns appreciably more money than the wife, but the difference shades off to the point where some wives earn appreciably more than their husbands. This can be seen in Table 3, which presents differences between their 1975 earnings for all couples where both spouses had earnings in 1975, classified by the 1975 earnings level of the husband.

In two of every three of these couples, the husband had "perceptibly higher" earnings in 1975 than the wife; "perceptibly higher" is defined as at least two intervals more in terms of the income intervals shown in Table 3. However, this also means that the wife's 1975 earnings were not perceptibly less than her husband's among one-third (32 percent) of the "both-earner couples." And in 7.3 percent of cases, the wife's earnings were perceptibly higher. But half of all wives (49 percent) had no earnings at all. Therefore, 81 percent of *all* wives had perceptibly less income than their husband, while only 19 percent were essentially on a par with their husband or earned more. Similarly, in 1970, only 21 percent of *all* wives were employed in an occupation at the same "major" level as the husband or higher, as ranked in terms of the Census Bureau's socioeconomic status scores, although the figure was 62 percent for the wives among couples with both spouses employed. Such couples made up one-third of all married couples in 1970.

Now that a substantial minority of households include an employed husband and an employed wife, and since many of these wives have a higher income or occupational level than their husbands, the Bureau of the Census

Table 3. Comparison of Husband and Wife Earnings in 1975 (Numbers in thousands)

Earnings of Husband	All Families with Both Husband and Wife Earners	Wife More Earnings than Husband by—		Wife and Husband in Same Interval	Wife Less Earnings than Husband by—	
		2 or More Intervals	1 Interval		1 Interval	2 or More Intervals
Total	22,335	1,641	800	2,171	2,625	15,098a
(Percent)	(100.0)	(7.3)	(3.6)	(9.7)	(11.8)	(67.6)
$1 to 999 or less	629	405	61	162	—	—
$1,000 to $1,199	527	285	44	83	113	—
$2,000 to $2,999	570	223	60	84	76	129
$3,000 to $3,999	636	204	62	75	77	217
$4,000 to $4,999	768	175	72	98	107	317
$5,000 to $5,999	874	143	82	93	103	453
$6,000 to $6,999	1,024	109	61	109	114	632
$7,000 to $7,999	1,276	75	81	97	139	885
$8,000 to $9,999	2,830	22	195	317	241	2,055
$10,000 to $14,999	6,917	b	82	752	809	5,276
$15,000 and over	6,283	b	b	301	846c	5,134d
Median earnings of husband	$11,370	$2,585	$6,311	$9,795	$12,117	$12,711

Source: U.S. Bureau of the Census, *Current Population Reports*, P-60, No. 105, "Money Income in 1975 of Families and Persons in the United States," Table 28.

a Besides these 15,098,000 earning wives with "perceptibly less earnings than their husbands," an additional 23,367,000 wives had no earnings. The total number of wives with perceptibly less earnings than their husbands, therefore, was 38,465,000, or 81.3 percent of all 47,318,000 husband-wife families in 1976.

b Separate information not available; included with "wife and husband in same interval."

c Wife $10,000 to $14,999.

d Wife less than $10,000.

317

has been urged in recent years to discontinue its practice of always attributing the social and economic characteristics of the husband to the entire household, with husband as the "head." Some pertinent findings on this issue come from a special survey on "Who Is the Head of Your Household?" conducted by the Census Bureau in September 1975 among a nationwide sample of 940 married couples. Of those who answered the question, 14 percent reported the wife as the head, 52 reported the husband as the head, and the other 34 percent reported both as joint heads. An equal, but small (15 percent) of the husbands and wives disagreed with the Census Bureau's procedure of always showing the husband as the head of a husband-wife household.

As a consequence of these findings, extensive discussion, and further testing, the Bureau of the Census has decided not to use the concept "head of household" in collecting data for the 1980 census; instead, household members are to be listed in terms of their relationship to the person, or one of the persons, who owns or rents the home. The Census staff is currently attempting to develop formats for publishing the data that also avoid the use of that terminology, but still will make it possible to relate the 1980 data to comparable data from past censuses. In addition, the Bureau is exploring other ways to present data on the residential unit (household or family), including new classifications by type of unit or by the income of the principal earner.

Married Women Enrolled in College

For several reasons, one might expect to discover that college enrollment rates for married women have risen especially sharply since 1970. In the first place, college enrollment regardless of marital status rose more rapidly among women than among men during the five years between the fall of 1970 and the fall of 1975. In addition, the birthrate declined by one-fifth during this period, therefore more married women should have had time to attend college classes in order to improve their employability or continue their intellectual development. Table 4 on the next page shows that this did indeed happen. Among all women aged 18 to 34, college enrollment went up half again as much for married women between 1970 and 1975 as it did for women who were not in an intact marriage (62 percent versus 41 percent).

College enrollment under age 25 has changed little in recent years as compared with the tremendous increases for persons 25 to 34 years of age. Despite the *overall* higher rate of increase among married women, the rate of increase among *older* college enrollees shown in Table 4 was twice as high among *unmarried* women (208 percent) as among *married* women (94 percent). These older (25- to 34-year-old) unmarried women attending college must have included many never-married women continuing their studies at the graduate school level as well as many separated and divorced women in transition between marriages who were preparing for meaningful employment. The college enrollment pattern for men by age has evidently also been related

Table 4.   Married and Unmarried Persons Attending College: U.S., 1970 and 1975

	Persons Attending College					
	Married, Spouse Present			Other Marital Status		
Age and Sex	1970	1975	% Change 1970–1975	1970	1975	% Change 1970–1975
	Men					
Total aged 18–34						
(In thousands)	1,202	1,433	19.2[a]	3,069	3,782	23.2[a]
Percent	100.0	100.0	—	100.0	100.0	—
Aged 18–24	41.9	26.9	−23.6	92.1	87.5	17.0
Aged 25–34	58.1	73.1	50.0	7.9	12.5	95.9
	Women					
Total aged 18–34						
(In thousands)	553	898	62.4[a]	2,330	3,293	41.3[a]
Percent	100.0	100.0	—	100.0	100.0	—
Aged 18–24	50.5	40.8	31.2	94.2	87.4	31.1
Aged 25–34	49.5	59.2	93.8	5.8	12.6	208.1

Sources: U.S. Bureau of the Census, *Current Population Reports*, Series P-20, No. 303, "School Enrollment—Social and Economic Characteristics of Students: October 1975," Table 10; and Series P-20, No. 222, "School Enrollment: October 1970," Table 11.
[a]Percent change based on the number of persons attending college.

to the increasing delay in marriage and the increasing dissolution of marriage before the age of 35. The enrollment for younger married men (under 25) actually dropped by a quarter (24 percent) between 1970 and 1975.

Wedding Anniversaries

Interest is often expressed in the proportion of couples whose marriages are likely to last for a given number of years. Of course, divorce is the main reason for attrition from marriage before middle age, whereas at successively older ages the reason becomes increasingly the death of one partner. Moreover, the duration of the marriage is related to age at marriage, and it is important to note that the average age at remarriage in the United States is about nine years older than at first marriage. These factors help to explain differences in the estimated proportions of couples who celebrate a given anniversary, shown in Table 5.

For example, one of every five couples may expect, on average, to celebrate their 50th anniversary after first marriage, but only one in every 20 *remarried* couples may expect to celebrate that anniversary. These estimates are rounded approximations based on a combination of vital statistics and census data going back to the turn of the century. The available data did not permit separate analysis of attrition through each of the main avenues—divorce and death.[4]

Table 5. Estimated Proportions of Couples Who Celebrate Selected Wedding Anniversaries

Wedding Anniversary	Proportion Who Celebrate the Anniversary After—	
	First Marriage	Remarriage
5th	5 of every 6	4 of every 5
10th	4 of every 5	3 of every 4
20th	3 of every 4	1 of every 2
30th	2 of every 3	1 of every 3
35th	1 of every 2	1 of every 5
40th	2 of every 5	1 of every 8
45th	1 of every 3	1 of every 15
50th	1 of every 5	1 of every 20
55th	1 of every 10	1 of every 50
60th	1 of every 20	1 of every 100
65th	1 of every 50	very rare
70th	1 of every 100	very rare

Sources: Various reports of the U.S. Bureau of the Census and the U.S. National Center for Health Statistics.

Thus, as expected, anniversaries after a given number of years of remarriage tend to be celebrated by an appreciably smaller proportion of couples than corresponding anniversaries after first marriage. At the longer durations of marriage, the proportions are—also as expected—about the same for anniversaries that differ by about 10 years (approximately the difference between ages at first marriage and at remarriage). For instance, one in 20 couples may expect to celebrate their 50th anniversary after remarriage, whereas for couples in a first marriage, an average one in 20 will celebrate their 60th anniversary together. Most of these couples entered either or both marriages at a relatively young age. By contrast, couples celebrating intermediate anniversaries (20th to 45th) tend to exhibit much smaller proportions for remarriages than for first marriages 10 years later. For example, only one in three celebrate their 30th anniversary after remarriage, whereas one in three celebrate their 45th anniversary after first marriage.

Footnotes

1. Marriage and divorce rates for selected foreign countries were provided by the United Nations Statistical Office.
2. Marriage and divorce rates for the United States for the year ending in May 1977 are from the U.S. National Center for Health Statistics, *Monthly Vital Statistics Report,* Vol. 26, No. 5, "Births; Marriages, Divorces, and Deaths for May 1977," p. 1.
3. For additional discussion of the factors underlying the increase in divorce, see Samuel H. Preston and John McDonald, "The Incidence of Divorce Within Cohorts of Marriages Contracted Since the Civil War," paper presented at the annual meeting of the Population Association of America, St. Louis, Missouri, April 21–23, 1977.

4. The anniversary data were based on several sources, including the U.S. National Center for Health Statistics, *Vital and Health Statistics,* Series 21, No. 24, "100 Years of Marriage and Divorce Statistics: United States, 1867–1967," Table 1; various vital statistics reports showing first marriages and remarriages; various sources from the U.S. Bureau of the Census, including *Current Population Reports,* Series P-20, No. 239, "Marriage, Divorce, and Remarriage by Year of Birth: June 1971," Table 16; and other Census Bureau reports cited in Paul C. Glick and Arthur J. Norton, "Perspectives on the Recent Upturn in Divorce and Remarriage," *Demography,* Vol. 10, No. 3 (August 1973) pp. 301–314.

Five Types of Marriage

John F. Cuber and Peggy B. Harroff

The qualitative aspects of enduring marital relationships vary enormously. The variations described to us were by no means random or clearly individualized, however. Five distinct life styles showed up repeatedly and the pairs within each of them were remarkably similar in which they lived together, found sexual expression, reared children, and made their way in the outside world.

The following classification is based on the interview materials of those people whose marriages had already lasted ten years or more and who said that they had never seriously considered divorce or separation. While 360 of the men and women had been married ten or more years to the same spouse, exclusion of those who reported that they had considered divorce reduced the number to 211. The discussion in this chapter is, then, based on 211 interviews: 107 men and 104 women.

The descriptions which our interviewees gave us took into account how they had behaved and also how they felt about their actions past and present. Examination of the important features of their lives revealed five recurring configurations of male-female life, each with a central theme—some prominent distinguishing psychological feature which gave each type its singularity. It is these preeminent characteristics which suggested the names for the relationship; the *Conflict-Habituated,* the *Devitalized,* the *Passive-Congenial,* the *Vital,* and the *Total.*

The Conflict-Habituated

We begin with the conflict-habituated not because it is the most prevalent, but because the overt behavior patterns in it are so readily observed and because it presents some arresting contradictions. In this association there is much tension and conflict—although it is largely controlled. At worst, there is some private quarreling, nagging, and "throwing up the past" of which members of the immediate family, and more rarely close friends and relatives, have some awareness. At best, the couple is discreet and polite, genteel about it in the company of others—but after a few drinks at the cocktail party the verbal barbs begin to fly. The intermittent conflict is rarely concealed from the children, though we were often assured otherwise. "Oh, they're at it again— but they always are," says the high-school son. There is private acknowledgment by both husband and wife as a rule that incompatibility is pervasive, that conflict is ever-potential, and that an atmosphere of tension permeates the togetherness.

An illustrative case concerns a physician of fifty, married for twenty-five years to the same woman, with two college-graduate children promisingly established in their own professions.

> You know, it's funny; we have fought from the time we were in high school together. As I look back at it, I can't remember specific quarrels; it's more like a running guerrilla fight with intermediate periods, sometimes quite long, of pretty good fun and some damn good sex. In fact, if it hadn't been for the sex, we wouldn't have been married so quickly. Well, anyway, this has been going on ever since. . . . It's hard to know what it is we fight about most of the time. You name it and we'll fight about it. It's sometimes something I've said that she remembers differently, sometimes a decision—like what kind of car to buy or what to give the kids for Christmas. With regard to politics, and religion, and morals—oh, boy! You know, outside of the welfare of the kids —too much and that's just abstract—we don't really agree about anything. . . . At different times we take opposite sides—not deliberately; it just comes out that way.
>
> Now these fights get pretty damned colorful. You called them arguments a little while ago—I have to correct you—they're brawls. There's never a bit of physical violence—at least not directed to each other—but the verbal gunfire gets pretty thick. Why, we've said things to each other that neither of us would think of saying in the hearing of anybody else. . . .
>
> Of course we don't settle any of the issues. It's sort of a matter of principle *not* to. Because somebody would have to give in then and lose face for the next encounter. . . .
>
> When I tell you this in this way, I feel a little foolish about it. I wouldn't tolerate such a condition in any other relationship in my life—and yet here I do and always have. . . .
>
> No—we never have considered a divorce or separation or anything so clear-cut. I realize that other people do, and I can't say that it has never occurred to either of us, but we've never considered it seriously.
>
> A number of times, there has been a crisis, like the time I was in the automobile accident, and the time she almost died in childbirth, and then I guess we really showed that we do care about each other. But as soon as the crisis is over, it's business as usual.

There is a subtle valence in these conflict-habituated relationships. It is easily missed in casual observation. So central is the necessity for channeling conflict and bridling hostility that these considerations come to preoccupy much of the interaction. Some psychiatrists have gone so far as to suggest that it is precisely the deep need to do psychological battle with one another which constitutes the cohesive factor insuring continuity of the marriage. Possibly so. But even from a surface point of view, the overt and manifest fact of habituated attention to handling tension, keeping it chained, and concealing it, is clearly seen as a dominant life force. And it can, and does for some, last for a whole lifetime.

The Devitalized

The key to the devitalized mode is the clear discrepancy between middle-aged reality and the earlier years. These people usually characterized themselves as having been "deeply in love" during the early years, as having spent a great deal of time together, having enjoyed sex, and, most importantly of all, having had a close identification with one another. The present picture, with some variation from case to case, is in clear contrast—little time is spent together, sexual relationships are far less satisfying qualitatively or quantitatively, and interests and activities are not shared, at least not in the deeper and meaningful way they once were. Most of their time together now is "duty time"—entertaining together, planning and sharing activities with children, and participating in various kinds of required community responsibilities. They do as a rule retain, in addition to a genuine and mutual interest in the welfare of their children, a shared attention to their joint property and the husband's career. But even in the latter case the interest is contrasting. Despite a common dependency on his success and the benefits which flow therefrom, there is typically very little sharing of the intrinsic aspects of career—simply an acknowledgment of their mutual dependency on the fruits.

Two rather distinct subtypes of the devitalized take shape by the middle years. The following reflections of two housewives in their late forties illustrate both the common and the distinguishing features:

> Judging by the way it was when we were first married—say the first five years or so—things are pretty matter-of-fact now—even dull. They're dull between us, I mean. The children are a lot of fun, keep us pretty busy, and there are lots of outside things—you know, like Little League and the P.T.A. and the Swim Club, and even the company parties aren't always so bad. But I mean where Bob and I are concerned—if you followed us around, you'd wonder why we ever got *married*. We take each other for granted. We laugh at the same things sometimes, but we don't really laugh together—the way we used to. But, as he said to me the other night—with one or two under the belt, I think—"You know, you're still a little fun now and then." . . .
>
> Now, I don't say this to complain, not in the least. There's a cycle to life. There are things you do in high school. And different things you do in college. Then you're a young adult. And then you're middle-aged. That's where we are now. . . . I'll admit that I do yearn for the old days when sex was a big thing and going out was fun and I hung on to everything he said about his work and his ideas as if they were coming from a genius or something. But then you get the children and other responsibilities. I have the home and Bob has a tremendous burden of responsibility at the office. . . . He's completely

responsible for setting up the new branch now. . . . You have to adjust to these things and we both try to gracefully. . . . Anniversaries though do remind you kind of hard. . . .

The other kind of hindsight from a woman in a devitalized relationship is much less accepting and quiescent:

> I know I'm fighting it. I ought to accept that it has to be like this, but I don't like it, and I'd do almost anything to bring back the exciting way of living we had at first. Most of my friends think I'm some sort of a sentimental romantic or something—they tell me to act my age—but I do know some people—not very darn many—who are our age and even older, who still have the same kind of excitement about them and each other that we had when we were all in college. I've seen some of them at parties and other places— the way they look at each other, the little touches as they go by. One couple has grandchildren and you'd think they were honeymooners. I don't think it's just sex either—I think they are just part of each other's lives—and then when I think of us and the numb way we sort of stagger through the weekly routine, I could scream. And I've even thought of doing some pretty desperate things to try to build some joy and excitement into my life. I've given up on Phil. He's too content with his balance sheets and the kids' report cards and the new house we're going to build next year. He keeps saying he has everything in life that any man could want. What do you *do?*

Regardless of the gracefulness of the acceptance, or the lack thereof, the common plight prevails: on the subjective, emotional dimension, the relationship has become a void. The original zest is gone. There is typically little overt tension or conflict, but the interplay between the pair has become apathetic, lifeless. No serious threat to the continuity of the marriage is generally acknowledged, however. It is intended, usually by both, that it continue indefinitely despite its numbness. Continuity and relative freedom from open conflict are fostered in part because of the comforts of the "habit cage." Continuity is further insured by the absence of any engaging alternative, "all things considered." It is also reinforced, sometimes rather decisively, by legal and ecclesiastical requirements and expectations. These people quickly explain that "there are other things in life" which are worthy of sustained human effort.

This kind relationship is exceedingly common. Persons in this circumstance frequently make comparisons with other pairs they know, many of whom are similar to themselves. This fosters the comforting judgment that "marriage is like this—except for a few oddballs or pretenders who claim otherwise."

While these relationships lack visible vitality, the participants assure us that there is "something there." There are occasional periods of sharing at least something—if only memory. Even formalities can have meanings. Anniversaries can be celebrated, if a little grimly, for what they once commemorated. As one man said, "Tomorrow we are celebrating the anniversary of our anniversary." Even clearly substandard sexual expression is said by some to be better than nothing, or better than a clandestine substitute. A "good man" or a "good mother for the kids" may "with a little affection and occasional attention now and then, get you by." Many believe that the devitalized mode is the appropriate mode in which a man and woman should be content to live in the middle years and later.

The Passive-Congenial

The passive-congenial mode has a great deal in common with the devitalized, the essential difference being that the passivity which pervades the association has been there from the start. The devitalized have a more exciting set of memories; the passive-congenials give little evidence that they had ever hoped for anything much different from what they are currently experiencing.

There is therefore little suggestion of disillusionment or compulsion to make believe to anyone. Existing modes of association are comfortably adequate—no stronger words fit the facts as they related them to us. There is little conflict, although some admit that they tiptoe rather gingerly over and around a residue of subtle resentments and frustrations. In their better moods they remind themselves (and each other) that "there are many common interests" which they both enjoy. "We both like classical music." "We agree completely on religious and political matters." "We both love the country and our quaint exurban neighbors." "We are both lawyers."

The wife of a prominent attorney, who has been living in the passive-congenial mode for thirty years, put her description this way:

> We have both always tried to be calm and sensible about major life decisions, to think things out thoroughly and in perspective. Len and I knew each other since high school but didn't start to date until college. When he asked me to marry him, I took a long time to decide whether he was the right man for me and I went into his family background, because I wasn't just marrying him; I was choosing a father for my children. We decided together not to get married until he was established, so that we would not have to live in dingy little apartments like some of our friends who got married right out of college. This prudence has stood us in good stead too. Life has moved ahead for us with remarkable orderliness and we are deeply grateful for the foresight we had. . . .
>
> When the children were little, we scheduled time together with them, although since they're grown, the demands of the office are getting pretty heavy. Len brings home a bulging briefcase almost every night and more often than not the light is still on in his study after I retire. But we've got a lot to show for his devoted effort. . . .
>
> I don't like all this discussion about sex—even in the better magazines. I hope your study will help to put it in its proper perspective. I expected to perform sex in marriage, but both before and since, I'm willing to admit that it's a much overrated activity. Now and then, perhaps it's better. I am fortunate, I guess, because my husband has never been demanding about it, before marriage or since. It's just not that important to either of us. . . .
>
> My time is very full these days, with the chairmanship of the Cancer Drive, and the Executive Board of the (state) P.T.A. I feel a little funny about that with my children already grown, but there are the grandchildren coming along. And besides so many of my friends are in the organizations, and it's so much like a home-coming.

People make their way into the passive-congenial mode by two quite different routes—by default and by intention. Perhaps in most instances they arrive at this way of living and feeling by drift. There is so little which they have cared about deeply in each other that a passive-congenial mode is a deliberately intended arrangement for two people whose interests and creative energies are directed elsewhere than toward the pairing—into careers, or in the case of women, into children or community activities. They say they know this and want it this way. These people simply do not wish to invest their total emotional involvement and creative effort in the male-female relationship.

The passive-congenial life style fits societal needs quite well also, and this is an important consideration. The man of practical affairs, in business, government service, or the professions—quite obviously needs "to have things peaceful at home" and to have a minimum of distraction as he pursues his important work. He may feel both love and gratitude toward the wife who fits this mode.

A strong case was made for the passive-congenial by a dedicated physician:

> I don't know why everyone seems to make so much about men and women and marriage. Of course, I'm married and if anything happened to my wife, I'd get married again. I think it's the proper way to live. It's convenient, orderly, and solves a lot of problems. But there are other things in life. I spent nearly ten years preparing for the practice of my profession. The biggest thing to me is the practice of that profession, to be of assistance to my patients and their families. I spend twelve hours a day at it. And I'll bet if you talked with my wife, you wouldn't get any of that "trapped housewife" stuff from her either. Now that the children are grown, she finds a lot of useful and necessary work to do in this community. She works as hard as I do.

The passive-congenial mode facilitates the achievement of other goals too. It enables people who desire a considerable amount of personal independence and freedom to realize it with a minimum of inconvenience from or to the spouse. And it certainly spares the participants in it from the need to give a great deal of personal attention to "adjusting to the spouse's needs." The passive-congenial menage is thus a mood as well as a mode.

Our descriptions of the devitalized and the passive-congenials have been similar because these two modes are much alike in their overt characteristics. The participants' evaluations of their *present situations* are likewise largely the same—the accent on "other things," the emphasis on civic and professional responsibilities; the importance of property, children, and reputation. The essential difference lies in their diverse histories and often in their feelings of contentment with their current lives. The passive-congenials had from the start a life pattern and a set of expectations essentially consistent with what they are now experiencing. When the devitalized reflect, however, when they juxtapose history against present reality, they often see the barren gullies in their lives left by the erosions of earlier satisfactions. Some of the devitalized are resentful and disillusioned; others, calling themselves "mature about it," have emerged with reasonable acceptance of their existing devitalized modes. Still others are clearly ambivalent, "I wish life would be more exciting, but I should have known it couldn't last. In a way, it's calm and quiet and reassuring this way, but there are times when I get very ill at ease—sometimes downright mad. Does it *have* to be like this?"

The passive-congenials do not find it necessary to speculate in this fashion. Their anticipations were realistic and perhaps even causative of their current marital situation. In any event, their passivity is not jarred when teased by memory.

The Vital

In extreme contrast to the three foregoing is the vital relationship. The vital pair can easily be overlooked as they move through their worlds of work, recreation, and family activities. They do the same things, publicly at least; and when talking for public consumption say the same things—they are proud of their homes, love their children, gripe about their jobs, while being quite proud of their career accomplishments. But when the close, intimate, confidential, empathic look is taken, the essence of the vital relationship becomes clear: the mates are intensely bound together psychologically in important life matters. Their sharing and their togetherness is genuine. It provides the life essence for both man and woman.

> The things we do together aren't fun intrinsically—the ecstasy comes from being *together in the doing.* Take her out of the picture and I wouldn't give a damn for the boat, the lake, or any of the fun that goes on out there.

The presence of the mate is indispensable to the feelings of satisfaction which the activity provides. The activities shared by the vital pairs may involve almost anything: hobbies, careers, community service. Anything—so long as it is closely shared.

It is hard to escape the word *vitality*—exciting mutuality of feelings and participation together in important life segments. The clue that the relationship is vital (rather than merely expressing the joint activity) derives from the feeling that it is important. An activity is flat and uninteresting if the spouse is not a part of it.

Other valued things are readily sacrificed in order to enhance life within the vital relationship.

> I cheerfully, and that's putting it mildly, passed up two good promotions, because one of them would have required some traveling and the other would have taken evening and weekend time—and that's when Pat and I *live*. The hours with her (after twenty-two years of marriage) are what I live for. You should meet her. . . .

People in the vital relationship for the most part know that they are a minority and that their life styles are incomprehensible to most of their associates.

Most of our friends think we moved out to the country for the kids; well —the kids *are* crazy about it, but the fact of the matter is, we moved out for ourselves—just to get away from all the annoyances and interferences of other people—our friends actually. We like this kind of life—where we can have almost all of our time together. . . . We've been married for over twenty years and the most enjoyable thing either of us does—well, outside of the intimate things—is to sit and talk by the hour. That's why we built that imposing fireplace—and the hi-fi here in the corner. . . . Now that Ed is getting older, that twenty-seven-mile drive morning and night from the office is a real burden, but he does it cheerfully so we can have our long uninterrupted hours together. . . . The children respect this too. They don't invade our privacy any more than they can help—the same as we vacate the living room when Ellen brings in a date, she tries not to intrude on us. . . . Being the specialized kind of lawyer he is, I can't share much in his work, but that doesn't bother either of us. The *big* part of our lives is completely mutual. . . .

Her husband's testimony validated hers. And we talked to dozens of other couples like them, too. They find their central satisfaction in the life they live with and through each other. It consumes their interest and dominates their thoughts and actions. All else is subordinate and secondary.

This does not mean that people in vital relationships lose their separate identities, that they may not upon occasion be rivalrous or competitive with one another or that conflict may not occur. They differ fundamentally from the conflict-habituated, however, in that when conflict does occur, it results from matters that are important to them, such as which college a daughter or son is to attend; it is devoid of the trivial "who said what first and when" and I can't forget when you. . . . " A further difference is that people to whom the relationship is vital tend to settle disagreements quickly and seek to avoid conflict, whereas the conflict-habituated look forward to conflict and appear to operate by a tacit rule that no conflict is ever to be truly terminated and that the spouse must never be considered right. The two kinds of conflict are thus radically different. To confuse them is to miss an important differentiation.

The Total

The total relationship is like the vital relationship with the important addition that it is more multifaceted. The points of vital meshing are more numerous—in some cases all of the important life foci are vitally shared. In one such marriage the husband is an internationally known scientist. For thirty years his wife has been "his friend, mistress, and partner." He still goes home at noon whenever possible, at considerable inconvenience, to have a quiet lunch and spend a conversational hour or so with his wife. They refer to these conversations as "our little seminars." They feel comfortable with each other and with their four grown children. The children (now in their late twenties) say that they enjoy visits with their parents as much as they do with friends of their own age.

There is practically no pretense between persons in the total relationship or between them and the world outside. There are few areas of tension, because the items of difference which have arisen over the years have been settled as they arose. There often *were* serious differences of opinion but they were handled, sometimes by compromise, sometimes by one or the other yielding; but these outcomes were of secondary importance because the primary consideration was not who was right or who was wrong, only how the problem could be resolved without tarnishing the relationship. When faced with differences, they can and do dispose of the difficulties without losing their feeling of unity or their sense of vitality and centrality of their relationship. This is the mainspring.

The various parts of the total relationship are reinforcing, as we learned from this consulting engineer who is frequently sent abroad by his corporation.

> She keeps my files and scrapbooks up to date. . . . I invariably take her with me to conferences around the world. Her femininity, easy charm and wit are invaluable assets to me. I know it's conventional to say that a man's wife is responsible for his success and I also know that it's often not true. But in my case I gladly acknowledge that it's not only true, but she's indispensable to me. But she'd go along with me even if there was nothing for her to do because we just enjoy each other's company—deeply. You know, the best part of a vacation is not *what* we do, but that we do it together. We plan it and reminisce about it and weave it into our work and other play all the time.

The wife's account is substantially the same except that her testimony demonstrates more clearly the genuineness of her "help."

> It seems to me that Bert exaggerates my help. It's not so much that I only want to help him; it's more that I want to do those things anyway. We do them together, even though we may not be in each other's presence at the time. I don't really know what I do for him and what I do for me.

This kind of relationship is rare, in marriage or out, but it does exist and can endure. We occasionally found relationships so total that all aspects of life were mutually shared and enthusiastically participated in. It is as if neither spouse has, or has had, a truly private existence.

The customary purpose of a classification such as this one is to facilitate understanding of similarities and differences among the cases classified. In this instance enduring marriage is the common condition. The differentiating features are the dissimilar forces which make for the integration of the pair within each of the types. It is not necessarily the purpose of a classification to make possible a clear-cut sorting of all cases into one or another of the designated categories. All cannot be so precisely pigeon-holed; there often are borderline cases. Furthermore, two observers with equal access to the facts may sometimes disagree on which side of the line an unclear case should be placed. If the classification is a useful one, however, placement should *as a rule* be clear and relatively easy. The case is only relative because making an accurate classification of a given relationship requires the possession of amounts and kinds of information which one rarely has about persons other than himself. Superficial knowledge of public or professional behavior is not enough. And even in his own case, one may, for reasons of ego, find it difficult to be totally forthright.

A further caution. The typology concerns relationships, not personalities. A clearly vital person may be living in a passive-congenial or devitalized relationship and expressing his vitality in some other aspect of his life—career being an important preoccupation for many. Or, possibly either or both of the spouses may have a vital relationship—sometimes extending over many years —with someone of the opposite sex outside of the marriage.

Nor are the five types to be interpreted as *degrees* of marital happiness or adjustment. Persons in all five are currently adjusted and most say that they are content, if not happy. Rather, the five types represent *different kinds of adjustment* and *different conceptions of marriage.* This is an important concept which must be emphasized if one is to understand the personal meanings which these people attach to the conditions of their marital experience.

Neither are the five types necessarily stages in a cycle of initial bliss and later disillusionment. Many pairings started in the passive-congenial stage; in fact, quite often people intentionally enter into a marriage for the acknowledged purpose of living this kind of relationship. To many the simple amenities of the "habit cage" are not disillusionments or even disappointments, but rather are sensible life expectations which provide an altogether comfortable and rational way of having a "home base" for their lives. And many of the conflict-habituated told of courtship histories essentially like their marriages.

While each of these types tends to persist, there *may* be movement from one type to another as circumstances and life perspectives change. This movement may go in any direction from any point, and a given couple may change categories more than once. Such changes are relatively *in*frequent however, and the important point is that relationship types tend to persist over relatively long periods.

The fundamental nature of these contexts may be illustrated by examining the impact of some common conditions on persons of each type.

Infidelity, for example, occurs in most of the five types, the total relationship being the exception. But it occurs for quite different reasons. In the conflict-habituated it seems frequently to be only another outlet for hostility. The call girl and the woman picked up in a bar are more than just available women; they are symbols of resentment of the wife. This is not always so, but reported to us often enough to be worth noting. Infidelity among the passive-congenial, on the other hand, is typically in line with the stereotype of the middle-aged man who "strays out of sheer boredom with the uneventful, deadly prose" of his private life. And the devitalized man or woman frequently is trying for an hour or a year to recapture the lost mood. But the vital are sometimes adulterous too; some are simply emancipated—almost bohemian. To some of them sexual aggrandizement is an accepted fact of life. Frequently, the infidelity is condoned by the partner and in some instances even provides an indirect (through empathy) kind of gratification. The act of infidelity in such cases is not construed as disloyalty or as a threat to continuity, but rather as a kind of basic human right which the loved one ought to be permitted to have—and which the other perhaps wants also for himself.

Divorce and separation are found in all five of the types, but the reasons, when viewed realistically and outside of the simplitudes of legalistic and ecclesiastical fiction, are highly individual and highly variable. For example, a couple may move from a vital relationship to divorce because for them the alternative of a devitalized relationship is unendurable. They can conceive of marriage only as a vital, meaningful, fulfilling, and preoccupying interaction. The "disvitality" of any other marriage form is abhorrent to them and takes on "the hypocrisy of living a public lie." We have accounts of marriages which were unquestionably vital or total for a period of years but which were dissolved. In some respects relationships of this type are more readily disrupted, because these people have become adjusted to such a rich and deep sharing that evidences of breach, which a person in another type of marriage might consider quite normal, become unbearable.

> I know a lot of close friendships occur between men and women married to someone else, and that they're not always adulterous. But I know Betty —and anyhow, I personally believe they eventually do become so, but I can't be sure about that. Anyway, when Betty found her self-expression was furthered by longer and longer meetings and conversations with Joe, and I detected little insincerities, not serious at first, you understand, creeping into the things we did together, it was like the little leak in the great dike. It didn't take very long. We weren't melodramatic about it, but it was soon clear to both of us that we were no longer the kind of pair we once were, so why pretend. The whole thing can go to hell fast—and after almost twenty years!

Husbands in other types of relationships would probably not even have detected any disloyalty on the part of his wife. And even if they had, they would tend to conclude that "you don't break up a home just because she has a passing interest in some glamorous writer."

The divorce which occurs in the passive-congenial marriage follows a different sequence. One of the couple, typically a person capable of more vitality in his or her married life than the existing relationship provides, comes into contact with a person with whom he gradually (or suddenly) unfolds a new dimension to adult living. What he had considered to be a rational and sensible and "adult" relationship can suddenly appear in contrast to be stultifying, shallow, and an altogether disheartening way to live out the remaining years. He is left with "no conceivable alternative but to move out." Typically, he does not do so impulsively or without a more or less stubborn attempt to stifle his "romanticism" and listen to well-documented advice to the effect that he should act maturely and "leave the romantic yearning to the kids for whom it is intended." Very often he is convinced and turns his back on his "new hope"—but not always.

Whether examining marriages for the satisfactions and fulfillments they have brought or for the frustrations and pain, the overriding influence of life style—or as we have here called it, relationship type—is of the essence. Such a viewpoint helps the observer, and probably the participant, to understand some of the apparent enigmas about men and women in marriage—why infidelities destroy some marriages and not others; why conflict plays so large a role for some couples and is so negligible for others; why some seemingly well-suited and harmoniously adjusted spouses seek divorce while others with provocations galore remain solidly together; why affections, sexual expression, recreation, almost everything observable about men and women is so radically different from pair to pair. All of these are not merely different objectively; they are perceived differently by the pairs, are differently reacted to, and differently attended to.

If nothing else, this chapter has demonstrated that realistic understanding of marital relationships requires use of concepts which are carefully based on perceptive factual knowledge. Unfortunately, the language by which relationships between men and women are conventionally expressed tends to lead toward serious and pervasive deceptions which in turn encourage erroneous inferences. Thus, we tend to assume that enduring marriage is somehow synonymous with happy marriage or at least with something comfortably called adjustment. The deception springs from lumping together such dissimilar modes of thought and action as the conflict-habituated, the passive-congenial, and the vital. To know that a marriage has endured, or for that matter has been dissolved, tells one close to nothing about the kinds of experiences, fulfillments, and frustrations which have made up the lives of the people involved. Even to know, for example, that infidelity has occurred, without knowledge of circumstances, feelings, and other essences, results in an illusion of knowledge which masks far more than it describes.

To understand a given marriage, let alone what is called "marriage in general," is realistically possible only in terms of particular sets of experiences, meanings, hopes, and intentions. This chapter has described in broad outline five manifest and recurring configurations among the Significant Americans.

Chapter 7

Uncoupling and Recoupling

Battered Wives, Dead Husbands

Laura Meyers

Richard J. Daley was the last of the big city bosses. For 21 years he ruled Chicago and its Democratic Party Machine. And during that time supporting The Mayor (as he was known) was never a matter of conscience for most Chicagoans, but a matter of course. In one household, though, it became a matter of life and death as well.

The story is short and sad. And Richard J. Daley brought it to a climax, even if he wasn't its cause. For the husband, the fact that his wife acted contrary to his own political opinions and signed a petition in support of The Mayor was just another excuse that evening for him to beat her—a practice for which he had been finding ample excuse for years. For the wife, however, it was the last straw. Mayor Daley made no little plans, but to hear her tell it, this bruised and desperate woman made no plans at all. "After the beating, he went to bed," recalls William Murphy of the Cook County Public Defender's Office, the man who later became her lawyer. "And then when he was asleep, she snuck up and clunked hell out of him with a Louisville Slugger."

Beating a man to death with a baseball bat is not a very pretty crime, but then neither is domestic violence. And while the short and sad story of husbands beating wives is enacted with horrid regularity in homes everywhere, cases like this are adding endings with bizarre O. Henry twists. "She was a nice lady and had a pattern of being beaten for years," says Murphy. Using a defense of mitigating circumstances he got her off. "The judge gave her probation," he smiles.

Such a decision may seem an affront to civilized values—murder is murder, after all. But the outcome is hardly surprising in light of several well-publicized trials of women accused of killing husbands who beat them, trials from which

Reprinted by permission from *Student Lawyer* Magazine, 6:7 (March 1978), pp. 46–51. © 1978 American Bar Association.

these women emerged scot-free or with light sentences, trials which seem to say that maybe murder *isn't* murder after all, but rather a justifiable action produced by a confluence of extreme circumstances.

In Lansing, Michigan, Francine Hughes poured gasoline around the double bed and sent her abusive husband up in flames while he slept; the verdict—justifiable homicide. In Rockford, Illinois, an eight-man, four-woman jury acquitted Bernestine Taylor of the stabbing death of her husband after the defense proved she had withstood nine years of serious physical abuse at his hands. And in Chicago over a single weekend, three separate women shot their husbands to death. All claimed that years of merciless beatings "forced" them to do it.

"You have to realize that most of the women who do this are not the feminist type," Murphy quietly cautions, refuting the canard that has made battered women a feminist *cause celebre.* "They're very unsophisticated women. And they're petrified that their husbands would beat them even if they did seek help." Nevertheless, some officials will not surrender their principles to the self-defense argument. Women, they reason, can now take the lethal initiative. And one attorney at Francine Hughes's trial declared the verdict of innocence signified "open season on men."

If so, then it is a goodly number of American males who are in trouble. Estimates of U.S. families harboring wife abuse range from a low of 3 million to a high of 40 million. No one knows how many batteries go unreported; no one knows in how many families violence is chronic. A recent study indicates that in one out of every six marriages, beatings become commonplace. Perhaps this is somewhat exaggerated, but Louis Harris says there may be some validity in that figure; a poll by his organization says 20 percent of all Americans, and 25 percent of those with college educations, condone the use of physical force within marriages.

Wife-beating is not only incredibly widespread, it often escalates into homicide, as the cases mentioned earlier on show. Familial spats result in one-fourth of all American murders, according to the FBI's Uniform Crime Reports, and love triangles account for another seven percent. While these statistics do not break things down by sexes—husbands-killing-wives and wives-killing-husbands—a 1971 California survey indicates that 52 percent of all women killed in that state meet their death at the hands of a husband or lover.

On the other hand, Cook County Deputy State's Attorney Kenneth Gillis claims that the majority of husband-killings by wives are "victim precipitated." That is, the abusers become eventual homicide victims by pushing their women too hard, inevitably forcing them to a homicidal conclusion. Indeed, a survey of Cook County's jail found that 40 percent of all women held for homicide at the facility were accused of killing their husbands or boyfriends after the men battered them.

One of the women held there is Billie Shropshire. Hers is a particularly traumatic case; she feared for her life and her children's. She moved three times to escape the harassment of her ex-boyfriend, but he was determined. He followed them everywhere—slashed her tires, waited for the kids after school, stood below their apartment window at night brandishing what appeared to be a shotgun to her head. Once he held a knife to the woman's throat; another time a gun. Of course, the scenario also included regular beatings.

Billie reported her tormentor to the police, took him to court, but nothing could daunt him. Finally, she took the law into her own hands and shot him.

"It was a classic case of self-defense," says one public defender, "—except for the last minute and a half." Billie Shropshire did not get off like Francine Hughes. Instead she got murder.

There are those who argue that Billie Shropshire did indeed act in self-defense, all the way up to and *through* that last moment. Despite the fact that her life was not in immediate danger, she shot her assailant because she had no alternative. Her comparative physical weakness, her inability to act during the repeated beatings and abuse, her constant terror, all these add up to a new concept of self-defense propounded by some feminist lawyers. "The perspective we have now of self-defense is a law shaped by men and it must now include the experience of women," contends Liz Schneider of New York's Center for Constitutional Rights. "More women are asserting that [killing] was necessary for their survival."

Bunk, says Thomas Tyrell, a former policeman, now a public defender. "The concept of self-defense is so basic to civilized society. It allows for a man to preserve his own life and only to take the life of another when his own life is in imminent danger. To in any way advocate, even tacitly, that someone should use deadly force at any other time than the time when his life is in immediate danger, to allow a time lag, would be to condone murder."

And more than a few female attorneys agree. Prosecutor Marcia Orr asks, "Why are women now claiming more lenient laws in self-defense, when they are claiming equality in every other area? It sets women apart as a weaker sex. If you're going to be equal, you can't take refuge in a status you don't want." Assistant State's Attorney Patricia Bobb agrees and recalls her frustration when a woman was acquitted of murdering her *third* husband. "Being a woman is much more of an advantage. I think women usually get a pass in the system. And what really gets me is women who stick around and get beaten by their husbands, for whatever reason." In Bobb's view, those women acquire "an assumption of risk" which later supersedes any claim of self-defense.

In part, their differences are an attitudinal gap. Independent women, particularly professionally trained, take-charge types like Orr and Bobb, simply cannot imagine themselves caught in an abusive, demeaning relationship. They cannot place themselves in the shoes of a woman who feels her only option is to sneak up on her unsuspecting husband and do him in with a baseball bat. It is outside their probable experience, and so it is outside their capacity for understanding.

But there are women who do feel trapped in situations like these, and worse.

And why they stay there goes beyond a question of simple economics—though not many battered women have means of supporting themselves independently. In many cases, these women have no friends or contacts outside their homes. They do not know how to improve their lot, or that the law can help them.

The sort of women who are battered beyond their limits of endurance and ultimately resort to murder are women peculiarly alone. When they succeed at killing their oppressor, their methods are often random and crude: baseball bats, immolation and the like (see sidebar). And when they fail, rarely do they even carry that off with much more finesse. Such a woman is Mary McGuire, currently serving a five-year sentence in the Oregon Women's Correctional Center for soliciting someone to kill her husband. In a way, however, she did succeed. She removed herself from her hostile environment, albeit by throwing herself into another. But most impressive is her ability now to articulate her fears, to give a voice to the mute battered woman:

"I know the horrors of beating; of being shot at and pistol-whipped; of being tied up to watch while my grave was being dug; of having my husband hold a gun to my child's head demanding obedience and threatening to pull the trigger; of trying to prevent my 12-year-old daughter from being raped by my husband, while Father laughs and states, 'I am king of this house and can do as I damn well please.' I and my children have received many beatings. I have cigarette burns on my arms, a broken nose, cracked chest and ribs, a concussion and a cracked pelvic bone. My children were terrorized by their father's attempt to run over my 4-year-old son, and by his act of beheading our pet horse.

"I tried separation but was brought back to the house at gunpoint. He has told me repeatedly that neither my children nor myself would ever be free from him and that he would stop at nothing to destroy us. . . .

"Intolerable isolation, extreme fear and a desperate need for help are the realities of my life."

McGuire notes that law enforcement officials told her that she is the cause of her own problems, and that they could not intervene in domestic conflicts. Small wonder, then, she thinks, that she took the step she did. "What is the difference then whether [a battered woman] goes to the law or takes her and her children's lives into her own hands?"

But in an indirect way, battered women may be a partial cause of their own problems, according to one psychiatrist. Severe psychological dynamics are commonly present in very abused women, says Dr. Anne Seiden of the Illinois Mental Health Department. "A woman who is grossly abused," she says, "generally develops a feeling of herself as a worthless person. The more she takes it, the more worthless she feels."

Seiden describes a pattern of pathological compliance with physical brutality—a pattern that indicates psychological problems making the women compliant to violence in the first place. "These women are pathetically oriented to 'being good.' If someone tells them what to do, they will comply. They have a very unstable sense of self, so they feel good only when they are pleasing someone else. That's partly what makes them appear as 'good girls' to the outside world, and partly why they put up with the beatings."

In Seiden's view, the women strike back finally and only after repeated abuse are the type of persons who could argue innocence under the insanity defense. In all too many cases, she has found, they understand little of their actions, but rather take on the characteristics of a borderline psychotic. (In one instance the doctor recalls, the woman testified she heard voices spurring her on, telling her to "do it, do it, do it." She emerged after the attack from an almost trance-like state, disoriented about the time, place and immediate past.) However, when the situation of stress is relieved—the attack is committed—these women's disordered and unusual behavior disappears. The women return to acting very normally, usually exceptionally agreeable and conforming. (In fact, in the case of the woman who heard voices, the attorney confided to Seiden that he felt guilty pleading the insanity defense when his client behaved so unlike "a crazy person.")

For many of these same reasons, battered women often receive the short shrift in their dealings with police officers and prosecutors. These officials complain that women in domestic-violence situations are seldom "serious" in their charges and are quick not to follow through—a complaint that is disturbingly true.

Couples in abusive relationships can easily fall into a three-stage cycle of love-tension-explosion. By the time a case comes to court, the explosion may be over and the love real. Psychologist Marlene Grossman explains, "Even a man who is abusive is not abusive 100 percent of the time. There are times when the relationship seems very warm and supportive of the woman."

Good experiences are the norm in such relationships, despite recurring violence. During the tension-building stages, the husband becomes irritable and verbally assaults the woman. Her response—harkening back to Seiden's version of these women as "good girls"—is to adopt a peacemaker stance, even at her own expense. The irritation, however, does not subside, and ultimately explodes in a beating.

At this climactic point, Grossman notes, the tension dissipates. The husband becomes tender and loving in a reconciliation effort. He sincerely believes that what he did makes no sense to him, and he doesn't plan to do it again. The woman tends to look at his loving behavior and agree that his badness isn't the "real" him.

As a result, the woman, who may have in a moment of pain reported her mate to the police, now doesn't want to press charges. She doesn't want her lover in jail, so she fails to show in court. She doesn't want to be rid of him, so she doesn't initiate divorce proceedings. "What she really wants," says

Grossman,"is to set their marriage right. It sometimes takes five or six beatings for her to be convinced that only counselling and legal remedies can make this relationship right."

Intercepting abused women when they reach this stage—and not after they have crossed the final threshold and murdered their husbands—is the goal of Chicago's Legal Center for Battered Women, the organization that Grossman is affiliated with and one of several newly created legal-service agencies designed to stem this growing problem. It is the Center's goal and that of its many volunteers, two dozen of whom have gathered on a bitterly cold winter morning inside a dreary downtown office to learn what they can do to help.

Sitting in mismatched chairs arranged in a haphazard circle, women aged 18 to 50 clutch legal pads to their breasts and take notes as the learn how to tackle the criminal courts on behalf of battered women. Hardly the least of the pains inflicted upon abused wives is the morass of a "very alienating, very dominated" court system, the Center says. And these women here today are training to help women through it, training to become "victim advocates," lay persons who can counsel and guide confused and hurt women through the courts.

"It's terribly important," Grossman tells the group, "when a woman does decide to take on the courts, that she have a lot of support; that that woman has another woman with her who understands, who doesn't think she's crazy. Women are constantly running into people who tell them it is their fault. A woman who is going to court has not only been abused by her husband; she's been abused by her encounters with the police, and she's had a hard time with some friends or family who tell her, 'You made your bed, now lie in it.' "

"We want women to be able to admit, 'I have been battered,' without shame," says Candace Wayne, director of the Center. In turning to criminal remedies, battered women attempt to put the threat of punishment or the hope of court-ordered counselling before their spouses. But all too often the police refuse to arrest, state's attorneys refuse to prosecute and judges refuse to invoke criminal sanctions. In many ways, it is a process that shames women into submission.

"The legal system has in its own way perpetuated abuse by not responding and not recognizing battered women as an issue," says Wayne. "We're talking about family violence. They're defined in police terms as 'domestic disturbances.' That's a misnomer. These are domestic *violence* cases."

One mission of the Center when it was founded by Chicago's Legal Assistance Foundation and the Chicago Community Trust was to spur recognition of domestic violence as a crime, and not merely silly threats by wives who want to scare their husbands. But since the Center's beginning in October of 1977, the lawyers have had little cooperation toward this end from judges, who, Wayne says, often make rude and stupid remarks to victims of domestic battery. One judge she cites asked a woman if she had been faithful; another queried whether a woman had been beaten by her husband before, and when she answered yes, commented, "Then you must like to get beaten up."

Despite such judicial callousness, the Center is but one example of a national trend toward encouraging enforcement of those domestic-violence laws already on the books. In Chicago specifically, police guidelines allow much less officer discretion in making battery arrests. Any use of a weapon, any intentionally inflicted serious injury, and any prior injury, court appearance or calls to the police—all require immediate arrest, according to that city's *Training Bulletin.*

And among the more creative legal solutions to the wife-beating problem is a court-ordered lawsuit in New York. The suit, which is currently awaiting trial, charges that the police department and Family Court officials violated the rights of battered women in that city by refusing to enforce wife-abuse laws. The plaintiffs represent New York and Kings counties' married women whose husbands commit crimes against them, and who seek police and/or judicial protection that is not forthcoming.

"The violence against [battered women] is not a result of isolated acts," reads the suit, "but rather reflects a societal pattern of male violence against women. As the problem is deep and widespread, so is defendants' failure to respond to it. The legal remedies provided for by the system of justice must be enforced."

A grim tale of judicial and police non-response to wife-battery unfolds in the cases cited in the New York suit. Carmen Bruno alleges that police ran into her apartment while her husband was still hitting her. The officers had to pry his hands from her neck and her face was bleeding from what have since become permanent scars, and still they refused to arrest him.

Susan Borowsky, separated from her husband for two years and paying rent on an apartment leased under her own name, was forced to leave her home after her husband broke in and police refused to arrest or evict him.

Lydia Thomas claims she was punched in the face until she blacked out. On another occasion, her husband hit her and threw her to the floor, but despite facial bruising and swelling, and despite a court order of protection, police officers would not arrest Mr. Thomas. One policeman, according to the suit, said, "You've been taking this for a long time now. You'll get over this."

Justice Abraham J. Gellicoff, the judge who ordered the trial, explained his reasoning: "For too long, Anglo-American law treated a man's physical abuse of his wife as different from any other assault, and indeed as an acceptable practice. . . . If the allegations of the complaint—buttressed by hundreds of pages of affidavits—are true, only the written law has changed; in reality, wife-beating is still condoned, if not approved, by some of those charged with protecting its victims."

Such tacit approval of wife-beating hangs over all our heads, insists Wayne of Chicago's Center. "It's not just a woman's problem, it's society's problem. We all live in a society plagued by violence." We all remember the horrifying instance of Kitty Genovese, the young New York woman killed in the early 1960s as dozens watched and none sprang to her aid. But how many remember that when bystanders were asked later why they did not help, many responded they thought her attacker was her husband?

"I don't think the legal system can change historical and societal attitudes in a short time," Wayne continues. "But if the legal system says this kind of behavior is criminal, although it does not deter every man in every case, it does set up a standard."

Right now, those values ignore women who have established a conjugal relationship with a man who beats her. Ignores them, that is, until they take matters into their own hands—something that, if matters had been handled properly from the start, they would not have had to do.

"The entire criminal-justice system regards the female victim of abuse as a second-class victim" writes James Bannon, executive deputy chief of the Detroit Police Department. "She is treated more as a 'leper' than anything else.

"She embarrasses the system and, judging from community reactions, the society as well. In fact, she is accorded the same type of treatment reserved for those with some form of social disease who have become ill due to their own vice.

"We turn our heads and close our ears to her screams."

Another World, Another Life
Morton Hunt and
Bernice Hunt

1. Crossing the Border

Emily McDowell groped for the bedside lamp and flooded the room with light. Her heart was pounding as if she'd been running, and as she sat up, sweat trickled down her sides and left wet streaks on her nightgown. She looked at the clock and saw that it was 2 A.M. Only three hours had passed.

Three hours since her husband had set down his suitcases at the door for a moment while he pulled on his gloves, then nodded silently to her, and left. They had been talking about a separation for weeks, and both of them knew it was necessary; yet, as soon as the door closed behind him she felt a sudden unreasonable sense of panic. She had taken a strong sleeping pill and gone to bed, and had slept after a while—but now the panic had broken through and she was wide awake again.

Emily got up and padded softly down the hall past the children's room, and into the kitchen. She took some grapes out of the refrigerator, ate a couple, felt slightly nauseated, hurriedly put the rest of the bunch back into the crisper. She went to the living room, and turned on the television set, but found it impossible to pay attention to the movie.

What's the matter with me, anyway? she thought. *Why am I acting like such an idiot? I wanted him to go. What am I afraid of?* Emily McDowell, thirty-five years old, registered nurse, saw frightened people every day, sick people afraid of pain, afraid of death. And she, Nurse McDowell, was strong and competent, always able to comfort and to cheer. Now who would comfort her? Who would *ever* comfort her?

She picked up a novel she'd been reading but after five minutes realized that her own obsessive thoughts crowded the story out of her mind. *This is crazy,* she thought. *I must be out of my mind. I'm acting charge nurse tomorrow, how will I ever get through the day? What will I do if I begin to cry at the hospital? Suppose the kids cry when I tell them? How will I get them off to school?*

Emily took another sleeping pill, got back into bed, and resolutely turned off the light. After a while she fell asleep and dreamed that she was all alone, lost, wandering through the dark and deserted streets of some unfamiliar city.

Ralph Lipman was planting the sixth of a dozen young fruit trees, late of a spring afternoon, when an oil-delivery truck pulled into his driveway. The driver stopped to chat for a moment on his way to the fill pipe, but he cut short his recital of neighborhood gossip and edged away as he realized that Lipman looked distinctly peculiar: there was a disturbing frenetic glitter in his eyes, he seemed unaware that his bare back and bald head had been badly sunburned on this unseasonably hot day, and he never stopped his furious digging even while talking.

Lipman had been in non-stop motion since before dawn. He and his wife had had one of their raging all-night quarrels, and at last she was screaming that she wanted him to get out and stay out. Eager to escape her voice, he began packing at 4:30, loaded the station wagon with his essential possessions, and drove to their vacation home, eighty miles away. There he unloaded and put away several cartons of books and records, a small file containing business papers, several suitcases full of clothing. He was all finished by 10:30; then he drove to the village for a great batch of groceries, beer, frozen pizza. On the way back, he stopped off at a nursery and pestered the owner into making immediate delivery of six peach trees and six apple trees. As soon as he got home, he began digging, and in between lunch and more plantings, he had a series of rambling telephone conversations with his business partner, his lawyer, and his brother. As long as Ralph kept going, he felt all right.

But by 8 o'clock, he had watered his new orchard, taken a shower, and sunk down in the living room with a cold beer. Then the anxiety attack swept over him and, with some astonishment, he watched his hands tremble as if they were motorized. *What's going on? How could I have been ordered out of my own home, my own life? Why am I sitting here, all alone in a dark room, at the age of fifty-one—on a weekday in May? What am I going to do tonight? And tomorrow, and the day after tomorrow? Will I ever be able to get up and go to work in the morning? What am I going to do with the rest of my Life?*

"So long," said Arnold Atkins to his wife, Jane. "I'll call you later, to see how you are." She looked puzzled. "Well, we *are* still friends, aren't we?" he asked. "And we do care about each other's welfare, don't we?"

"Sure," she said, smiling. "I really like you a lot—except when I can't stand you." They both laughed and then Arnold was gone.

She waited by the window until she saw him turn the corner; then she went straight to the bedroom, stripped the sheets off the king-size bed, and made it up with fresh linen. Next, she arranged the closets and drawers, expanding her things into the newly vacated spaces; finally, she put her night-time reading material on what had been his night table, the one with the better reading lamp. She chuckled at herself for marking out her new territory (just like any jungle beast, she thought), but as soon as she finished, the bad feeling began to seep in.

It was Saturday, and she had no office to go to, no idea of what to do next. For four years she had been part of something that had just ceased to exist; she'd been a—what had that sociologist called it?—a *with,* and now she was something else, a *single,* alone, disconnected, and . . . *lost* was the word that came into her mind.

Should she call her parents or friends, tell them, talk about it? Not yet; they would ask too many questions, and she wasn't ready, might become tearful and incoherent, or say things she would later regret.

Should she go shopping? She usually liked to shop, but strangely, she didn't feel like buying anything; there wasn't anything she wanted or cared about—and she felt that she looked strange, too, so strange that people in stores might stare at her, at her frozen face, tight mouth, blank eyes.

Should she go for a walk? The apartment was ominous and oppressive in its emptiness—but outside, a winter wind was driving sleet with a force that made pedestrians hold their hands in front of their smarting faces.

She seized the telephone as if it were a life preserver and she, a drowning swimmer; she dialed her mother's number, and hung up after the first ring, then dialed again, hung up again, and burst into tears of shame. *I'm acting like a frightened child, a little girl who's lost her Mommy in the crowd. I'm being ridiculous, stupid, immature. Why should I feel like a lost kid when I'm twenty-eight and a successful career woman in the big city? Damned if I know, but that's how I feel, anyway.*

Just as it was to these three people, the moment of separation is a severe shock to most people—even to those who wanted it or expected it. It stuns, disorients, and frightens, because it is a wrenching transition from the known past into an unknown future. The newly separated person has just stepped across the border from the familiar land—no matter how bad—of marriage, into the *terra incognita* of postmarital life; he or she must set foot upon what appears as a blank space on the map, ignorant of what its inhabitants are like, how newcomers are expected to behave, what dangers lie in wait, where to turn for comfort and help. No wonder the newly separated so commonly experience the nightmarish feeling of unaccountably finding themselves in a strange place with no idea of where to go or what to do to save themselves.

Yet, they will learn that the unknown territory is not a featureless void or a savage wilderness after all. It turns out to be a surprisingly "civilized" place with its own beliefs, customs, and values; it has ample opportunities for friendship, social life, sexual partnership, and love, and its own ways of indoctrinating the newcomer. Of course it isn't entirely beneficent—it has its own special dangers and deprivations, too. But, seen as a whole, it has a distinct culture —or more accurately, a *subculture* of the American culture we all share. Throughout this book we will often refer to that subculture as *the world of the formerly married,* and for convenience, to its members as the formerly married, or FMs—those who are informally separated, legally separated, divorced, or whose marriages have been annulled.

Like members of other subcultures—racial or religious minorities, homosexuals, members of high society—FMs belong to two different worlds. They are part of American society and spend most of their time living within its institutions and interacting with its people, most of whom (roughly 70 per cent of those eighteen and over) are married. But in their hearts, and in their private lives, they are separate and apart from the married, and are drawn together by their very difference and apartness. Together, a people within a people, they are no longer misfits, outsiders, but people who *belong;* to the initiates, it is the never-divorced married people who seem to be the Others, the Outsiders.

Less than a generation ago, married people knew little about the world of the formerly married; it was a semi-secret society. Its members were close-mouthed about their feelings and experiences because, in the larger society, divorce was still considered a tragedy and, in many quarters, something of a disgrace; FMs were uneasy about telling the married—whose ranks they had so recently left—that there was much that was positive and rewarding in their new world: relief, freedom, a sense of rebirth, and often, a great emotional and sexual flowering. They were quite right in thinking that none of this would have gone down too well with the married, who could sympathize wholeheartedly with the sinners—but only as long as they were suffering.[1]

But in recent years, divorce has become so common, so much more approved, and so widely discussed, that one would hardly expect separation to be as terrifying as it used to be. In the past fifteen years, for example, well over 500 books and articles about divorce have been published. Every person who can read a newspaper knows that by 1976 there was one divorce for every two marriages—an all-time high;* the divorce rate, rising since 1962, has more than doubled since then.[2] Not only were there over eleven million people in the world of the formerly married in 1976, but thirty to forty million had passed through it and rejoined the world of the married.[3] Divorce, once seen only as a failure, has come to be regarded as the creative solution to a problem. In view of these changes, how could the subculture still be so unfamiliar, so alarming? It hardly seems possible that the newly separated don't know what to expect—and yet they don't.

Even a professional social worker who should know the territory may feel terrified, unready. Mel Krantzler, a family counselor, describes in *Creative Divorce* his own early reactions to separation; they included acute loneliness, self-pity, "emotional shakes and sweats," and a view of the future as a "vortex of emptiness, fear, and uncertainty."

Strange? Not really. The explanation is cultural lag—the time needed for some elements of our culture to catch up and adjust to changes or innovations in other elements. The behavior patterns and ideals of the FM subculture have become public knowledge only within the past dozen years, and that knowledge has not yet been assimilated by the married.

To most of them, divorce is something that happens to others; few couples, at the time of marriage, accept the fact that their marriage has a one-in-two chance of breaking up either temporarily or permanently—for who would get married except in the belief that it is "forever"?[4] So not expecting it to happen, they don't bother to learn what becomes of people who separate and divorce, and if it *does* happen, they are ignorant, unprepared, and frightened. Some of our secondary schools have only just begun to give instruction in family life and marriage; it will probably be a long while before instruction in divorce becomes common. But in any case, the conditions of life for the formerly married have been changing so swiftly that even those who remarried as recently as a dozen years ago, and who now face a second separation, recognize that they are out of touch with the present realities and will have much to relearn—but they will never be as ignorant or as terrified as they were the first time.

The paradox of the increase and acceptance of divorce versus the unpreparedness of the divorcing will disappear as cultural lag is overcome. There is ample evidence that the lag is already diminishing rapidly, for divorce is no longer regarded as curious. exceptional, or deviant. Everyone knows—or at least rubs elbows with—someone who has been divorced. They can hardly

*Although the ratio of divorces to marriages is a favorite headline for journalists, a more sensitive index of the growth of divorce is the divorce rate per thousand population. This increased by 127 per cent from 1962 to 1976.

avoid it since for every nine married people there is one FM plus three FMs who have remarried.[5]

Eventually, the married will find it possible to tell their friends, families, co-workers, and neighbors of an impending divorce without shame or fear of stigma. It is already considerably easier than it was ten or fifteen years age.

That still doesn't mean that divorce will become easy. In a world that is increasingly impersonal, in a society whose people are on the move and so form few permanent bonds of friendship and community, marriage is—and will remain—emotionally more important than ever. The much-publicized decline in the marriage rate is no contradiction of this: the rate continues to be higher than it was from 1957 through 1967, and the present decline may be only a short-term phenomenon due to such factors as the recent recession, the delay of marriage by women who go to college or work, a temporary imbalance between the number of marriageable young women and marriageable young men, and so on. Indeed, in 1976, the three-year decline leveled off.[6] Because we value marriage, today and for the foreseeable future, its breakup will continue to be one of the most distressing, bewildering, and painful emotional traumas we can undergo.

2. The Elusive "Typical" FM

Who and what is this typical FM we have been speaking about? Most FMs would probably deny that they are typical, for people resent and resist being classified or categorized. We all treasure our individuality and are quick to reject any suggestion that we can easily be fathomed, *a priori,* as specimens of known types. "Yes," we say, "but my case is somewhat special," or "I'm not like most people in my category," or "I don't fit into any of the usual pigeonholes." And, in truth, every individual *is* unique: no two people, even twins, are absolutely identical, for no two people have identical life experiences.

Yet we all recognize that we do resemble certain people in various ways, or that we differ markedly from others. We categorize ourselves whenever we use that familiar kind of shorthand that helps strangers understand us: "I'm a sort of Catholic—the kind who goes to Mass on Christmas and Easter"; "At heart I'm still an upstate farmboy"; "I'm the type that wouldn't be caught dead at a costume party."

In the same way, while there is no one typical FM, there are many *categories* of FM that might be called typical because they represent the behavior of a large number of people. None of the following persons can be called a "typical" FM, and yet, each is typical of one segment of the FM population.

—Asparagus Beach, the singles' meeting ground at Amagansett, on New York's Long Island. Bob G. is busy at his favorite weekend pastime: beach-hopping. Bob is twenty-nine, a trifle too plump, but genial, curly haired, and outgoing; with his disarming affability he manages to move the length and breadth of the beach greeting and chatting with woman after woman—but deftly avoiding any commitment for the evening until he has decided which woman looks like the best of the lot. Only a year and a half ago, suffering from an ulcer, Bob began psychotherapy and discovered that he really hated being a lawyer and still mourned his original plan to become a commercial artist. He promptly quit the law, and when his status-minded young wife greeted the news with scorn and fury, he quit her, too.

After the first few bad months, Bob began to feel better than he had in years, and as his spirits rose his ulcer healed and disappeared. He has been enjoying himself ever since, even though as a beginner in the art of department an advertising agency his salary is modest and he has to live in a tiny, dingy, ground-floor apartment on a noisy Manhattan cross-street. But feeling that he might make art director some day, and that all life lies ahead of him, he has been working hard, going to parties, dating around (as far as his money will carry him), and relishing his second chance at everything. His rare moods of depression stem not from regret for the broken marriage, but from a sense of oppression and loneliness when he is alone in his bleak quarters, and from an occasional fit of concern that he might *never* care about any woman but always flit from one to another.

—Jennifer G., in a large dance studio in downtown Philadelphia, is doing pirouettes as if she were practicing for opening night at the Bolshoi. She is in a late-afternoon ballet class for people who, like herself, just want some exercise and body training. Jennifer, thirty-six, is rather plain looking, wears thick glasses, and is a bit dumpy—nobody's ideal Giselle. But ballet class does make her feel physically good and even graceful.

After class, in a fine mood, she rushes home, where the mood soon dissipates; her children, nine and eleven, are impatiently awaiting dinner, and though they help (grumbling), Jennifer has to hurry to get the cooking done, clean up the kitchen when dinner is over, and look over the homework before the children's bedtime. Afterward, thoroughly weary, she still has to put a load of laundry through the washer and dryer, pay some bills, make up a shopping list, and write to her lawyer—once again—about her vanished husband and the equally vanished child-support payments. Sometimes, it's all just a little too much, and she cries a bit; at other times, she gulps down a half a tumbler of vodka instead.

The vodka tends to blur the problems and that's a help since Jennifer has learned to keep her problems to herself. She used to take advantage of her dates to unburden herself, but while most of the men listened sympathetically, few called again. Now Jennifer knows better. She has learned to be "fun." She has also learned how to make herself look reasonably glamorous when she goes out; she wears contact lenses, chic clothes, and makeup she learned to apply in a special course. Along with the makeup, she puts on an expectant manner that is new since her divorce; it's genuine, though, for one of the surprises of her life was to discover that recently, men seem to think she's great in bed. She thinks so, too, and is tremendously excited by newfound joy in sex such as she never knew with her husband. But she has almost given up hoping or expecting that any man will be more than a pleasant date and, if she's lucky, a good lover. It seems wiser to hope for nothing than to hope, again and again, only to be disappointed each time.

—Harry T., sitting in his elegant walnut-paneled library, has been on the telephone for nearly two hours; he has called half a dozen men and women friends, including one in Mexico and one in Hawaii. This is what Harry does on those one or two evenings a week when he's alone and disheartened by his life as a divorced man. Few would understand Harry's misery: at fifty-one, he's flat of belly, has all his hair, makes $80,000 a year as a management consultant and investor, lives in a spacious duplex apartment furnished with antiques; he frequently goes to the opera or the theater, and always has an active list of two or three attractive women who are delighted to spend time with him in companionship or lovemaking—and none of whom expects anything more of him. Harry is the envy of his friends, and he doesn't tell them that their envy is misplaced because he finds it hard to explain why his life seems so barren.

The truth is that Harry hates not being married. He has been married twice, once for twenty years (there were two children), once for four years (no children). Both marriages ended in divorce, and after the second time, disillusioned, Harry told everyone who would listen, "Never again!" He made it plain to the women he dated he would flee from the first sign of involvement and, indeed, he did just that several times.

But inside himself, Harry feels incomplete in the unmarried state. Intellectually, he wants to remain single, emotionally he hungers for a woman to share his life, his thoughts and feelings, to be part of him; he longs for a wife. Harry doesn't know how to resolve his conflict—and until he does, he talks to his oldest and closest friends on the telephone so that he can feel *connected.*

—Susan M. is proud of the Swedish meatballs she made for dinner, a favorite of her two teenagers and her husband; they have all just shown their appreciation by taking second helpings. The four of them, sitting around the table in a lovely Malibu home, make a friendly, chatty family scene.

Beneath the pretty picture, however, is a curious reality. Susan's husband left her two years ago, set himself up in a bachelor apartment, and has had a string of women friends—some of them even on a live-in basis for short periods. Yet, he has consistently arrived at Susan's for dinner a couple of times a week, taking it for granted that it is his right to "visit his family."

Susan makes no protest. She is a pleasant-looking but fluttery and timid woman in her forties, who admits that she has a problem and doesn't know how to solve it. Her lawyer assures her that she can get a divorce at any time—but she doesn't want one. Her sister and friends tell her she must be crazy—and at times, Susan is sure they're right—but she knows that she secretly wants her husband to keep visiting and staying for dinner, and dreads the time when he might stop; she is both revolted and alarmed by attention from other men.

—A gay bar in San Francisco. Roger R., aggressively masculine in boots, tight jeans with studded belt, a tee-shirt that makes much of his tattooed and powerful upper arms, has turned his back on the crowd and chats with the bartender.

Roger is forty, barrel-chested, and has a bushy mustache which, like his outfit, is part of his new image. But there is far more than these externals that is new in Roger's life. Until a couple of years ago, he was a married man with two children; by day he drove a delivery truck, and during his free time he was a model husband and father—except for one or two evenings a week. These were the nights when Roger ostensibly played poker with the boys, but actually went cruising for homosexual sex—often consummated in the back of his parked truck. And then one night he was arrested in the act; when his wife found out, she was horrified and filed for divorce at once.

Roger decided to come out; he dropped all his old friends and doesn't even dare to visit his children because he doesn't know if they can understand, doesn't know how he can explain. He rents a large, dreary room and kitchenette in a rooming house, but does not feel confined since he is rarely there. He still drives a truck and now spends all his leisure time cruising in gay bars, baths, parks, and other forums; he has never had a roommate or a lover for more than a single night.

Nowadays, more and more often, he gets spells of deep depression; it seems to him that something changed with his fortieth birthday, for it is increasingly difficult to pick up the young, beautiful partners he likes best. Despite his tough confident look, Roger often thinks of suicide. One night, not long ago, the thought was so insistent that he grew frightened; he took his pistol down to the wharf and dropped it into the water.

—A walk-up cold-water apartment in a slum in the Bronx, New York. Hattie G., after a long, hot day of work in a clothing factory, labors up the steps to the fourth floor lugging a large bag of groceries. The hallways stink of urine, the paint is peeling from the walls, plaster has fallen in chunks from the ceiling, roaches scurry for cover as she approaches.

Hattie, in her early thirties, is a shapely, light-skinned black woman, still attractive though her face is set in lines of discontent and fatigue. She unlocks three locks on the door and enters her shabby, stifling apartment. There's no one home. Her sons, aged twelve and fourteen, are chronic truants who probably skipped school again today and are out somewhere with a street gang. When they come home, late, they will lie to her—skillfully and fluently—about where they've been.

Still, Hattie means to cook dinner in case they do come home in time; she tries to be a good mother although there isn't much she can do. There isn't much she can do about anything, she muses, except work, and sleep, and worry. What she really needs is a man to live with her, comfort her, love her, help her with the bills and the boys, a man who is not a drifter and a drunk like her husband. Over the years he has left her countless times for a few days or a few weeks, but the last time, he seems to have disappeared for good. Hattie wishes she knew if he were dead or alive, for even if she did find the right new man, how could she know the old one wouldn't walk back in some day? She has no idea how to protect herself from him, no idea how you get a divorce when you have no money, are scared to death of courts and judges, and can barely read and write.

Are any of these people typical FMs? They certainly aren't typical of *all* FMs, yet each is typical of one kind of FM. There are many more kinds, too. The sexually promiscuous middle-aged man-about-town, living out all the fantasies he stored up during a long, arid marriage; the attractive young woman who perceives herself as a femme fatale and gets even with her ex-husband by having one affair after the other; the woman in her sixties who has done little but drink, shop, go to doctors, ever since her husband left her to marry a woman in her thirties; the assorted habitués of singles bars, resort ships, adult camps, pick-up beaches.

The list could go on and on indefinitely, and while we would find out a great deal about the many kinds of FMs, we would never find out what a typical FM is like. To do that, we have to shift our focus away from single cases and take a broad view of the entire FM population; there, right in the center, is a composite of all the kinds of FMs we have talked about and all those we haven't mentioned—the *average* FM. To find the average, we must use numbers, and although people are more interesting than numbers, figures don't lie and people do; therefore, we resort to statistics in order, at last, to define the typical FM.

3. Truth in Numbers or: The Typical FM

The typical FM is twice as likely to be divorced as separated. Put another way, two-thirds of all FMs have been divorced—up from little more than half in 1962 when the divorce rate began its steep climb.[7] The change is a striking example of both the increased availability and acceptability of divorce. Relatively few people linger in the limbo of separation because they are afraid or unable to take the final steps; they take them quickly, too; the average lag is under one year from separation to divorce, whereas it was two years in 1960.[8]

For every five FM women there are three FM men. Divorced men marry sooner and in greater numbers than women, so that more unremarried women than men accumulate in the FM population; in 1976, the figures stood at 6,826,000 women to 4,138,000 men.*[9]

*Most of our data on the total number of divorced persons in the United States do not include those whose marriages were annulled, since the Bureau of the Census classifies these people as "single" (i.e., never married). But the figures for the number of divorces granted in any given year are compiled by the National Center for Health Statistics, which does include annulments in its totals. The discrepancies this makes for are minor, however, since annulments currently amount to well under 2 per cent of total marital dissolutions.[10]

Half of all divorces are granted within the first seven years of marriage. Contrary to popular belief, marriages do not break up much sooner than they used to: the average divorce takes place only about two-thirds of a year earlier than it did in 1962, and about a year and a half sooner than at the end of the last century. The highest rate of divorce takes place during the second year of marriage, but less than a tenth of divorces take place in that year, and though the percentage declines steadily for each succeeding year, it never drops off sharply. People continue to divorce in every year of married life; over a third of all divorces occur after ten or more years, over a tenth after twenty or more.[11]

The median age of men at the time of the final decree is a little under thirty-three, of women, thirty. (Median means that half are younger, half are older.) The median age at separation is one year less than at divorce. Though the divorce rate declines with age, a surprising number of persons divorce fairly late in life: 12 per cent of divorcing men are fifty or over, 14 per cent of divorcing women are forty-five or over, and, in 1972—the last year for which estimates can be made—some ten thousand men and five thousand women got divorced at sixty-five or over.[12]

These data shatter another popular myth: there is no divorce boom in middle age; there are more divorces at mid-life today only because there are more divorces at every age today.

The median age of a male FM is the early forties, of a woman, the late thirties. The average age of FMs is considerably higher than the average age at time of divorce, and the reason is obvious: Most FMs spend several years or more between marriages, and some (out of choice or chance) never remarry. The older people are, the longer it takes them to remarry and the less chance there is that they will ever do so; accordingly, older FMs accumulate in the population.

The typical FM is a few years younger than the typical FM of 1962, but the world of the formerly married is neither basically young nor middle-aged; the bulk of FMs are distributed throughout the years from twenty-five to sixty-five, in much the same proportion as the American population is. The following table shows the complete distribution:

Age	Separated	Divorced	Total FMs[13]
14 to 24	584,000	542,000	1,126,000
25 to 34	1,088,000	1,978,000	3,066,000
35 to 44	761,000	1,607,000	2,368,000
45 to 54	634,000	1,446,000	2,080,000
55 to 64	408,000	1,015,000	1,423,000
65 and up	296,000	601,000	897,000
	3,771,000	7,189,000	10,960,000*

*The slight discrepancy between this total and the figures on p. 13 is due to rounding.

The chance that you are currently divorced, if you are black, is about a third higher than if you were white; the chance that you are currently separated, if you are black, is nearly six times as great as if you were white. *[14] Blacks constitute about a quarter of the FM population but only about a tenth of the national population.

The lower in the socioeconomic scale you are, the greater your chance of divorce if you are a man or a non-working wife. Many people think that divorce is most common among the relatively affluent, sophisticated, discontented, spoiled darlings of our society; the families of working-class people are supposed to be noisy and brawling, but rock-solid. The truth is just the reverse, and has long been so. Studies made from the 1930's through the 1950's showed that unskilled or semi-skilled laborers were about three times as likely to get divorced as professional and business people.[15] This figure probably understated the case, for at that time (even more than now), the poor had a much higher rate of informal desertion or separation without divorce than the middle and upper classes.

But since 1960, according to Bureau of the Census demographers Arthur J. Norton and Paul C. Glick, the gap in divorce rates between the different social levels has been closing; this is due, chiefly, to a more rapid increase in the rate for upper-level men than for lower-level men.[16] One might view this as a "democratization" of divorce, with the lower-class pattern seeping upward —quite the opposite of the usual mode of cultural diffusion.

High-income women are more apt to divorce than low-income women, reversing the male pattern. If you are a woman earning $15,000 or more, you are three times as likely to be currently divorced as a woman earning under $3,000. Yet again, democratization is taking place: even though divorce rates have been increasing for all women who earn money, the rates for those at the low end of the income scale have increased more than for those at the high end, narrowing the gap between them.[17]

There is no longer any significant difference in the divorce rate among the major American religious groups. Prior to 1960, the Roman Catholic divorce rate was very low; divorce was forbidden by the Church, and Catholics obeyed the rules. Today, Catholic and Protestant divorce rates seem to be converging. There are no government data on this point, but we have reports from sociologists and public-opinion researchers. On the basis of this evidence, the Reverend James J. Young of the Paulist Fathers in Boston and the leader of a national movement to minister to divorced Catholics, wrote us, "I think one can safely say that whatever resistance to divorce existed in the Catholic community a decade or two ago has now disappeared; Catholics have become as American as apple pie, for better or for worse, and now divorce as much as everybody else."

---

*Comments in this book on black FMs and poor whites are based chiefly on government and sociological studies, not on our own survey and interviews; these, as explained on p. 272, included only an insignificant number of blacks and poverty-level whites.

There is no longer a significant difference between the divorce rates of the devout and the non-devout. The devout in every major religion used to be far less likely to divorce than those of weak or no belief. There are no recent definitive studies of this matter, but in our own survey sample, the percentage of regular churchgoers is only a little smaller than that in the American population; since regular church attendance is one indicator of devoutness, the data suggest that devoutness has little to do with willingness to divorce.

The typical FM lives in a city. It used to be thought that the typical divorced person was always a product of the wicked city—but today, we aren't so sure. Census data do show that somewhat smaller percentages of rural and village people than city people are separated or divorced,[18] but our own survey data and interviews lead us to believe that this may be because when their marriages begin to crumble, many suburban and rural people flee to the city where there are better job opportunities (particularly for women) and far greater possibilities for FM social life.

While FMs are scattered all over the nation, the West seems particularly conducive to divorce rather than to separation. Compared to the Northeast, for example, the West has lower percentages of separated persons, but double the percentage of divorced ones.[19]

The rate varies from state to state, too, and it is hard to say why. In 1975, the divorce rate in Nevada was more than six times as high as that in New Jersey, North Dakota, or Pennsylvania.[20] Some of the variation is due to differences in divorce laws, but far more complex factors must account for the variations among the counties within one state. In California, for instance, Imperial County had one divorce for every 14 marriages in 1972, while San Mateo County had one divorce for every 1.2 marriages.[21]

The typical FM is more likely to be a parent than not. And this, unlike so much else, represents no change in recent years. In 1962, close to 60 per cent of all divorcing people had children under eighteen; in 1973 (the latest year for which data are available), the figure was about the same.[22]

In the face of the facts, not many people still believe that children hold a marriage together. Yet, it is true that childless marriages, though they contribute a minority of divorces, do have a higher rate of divorce. In part, this is because couples with poor marriages avoid having children. But even after many years of marriage childless people are more apt to divorce. At Dr. Glick's suggestion, we looked at the data on women thirty-five to thirty-nine who have been, or still are, married to see what difference children make. In this group, 12 per cent of the childless are currently separated or divorced as compared with only 7 per cent of those who have children.[23] This may very well mean that in at least some cases, people stay married for the children's sake.

Although roughly 40 per cent of new FMs are childless, most of these have been married only a short time and are quite young; they are apt to rejoin single society rather than the society of FMs and most of them remarry sooner than older FMs with children. The net result is that although 60 per cent of divorcing people have children, the percentage of parents within FM society is much larger than that.

In sum, then, we can envision the typical FM in terms of the overall composition of, and averages within, the FM population. That sub-society of Americans is made up of people from all social levels, though somewhat more from the working class and lower-middle class than the higher strata. It is distributed unevenly throughout the nation, but can be found everywhere. It is concentrated in cities, their suburbs, and larger towns. Most of its members are parents who bear the special problems and worries of having disrupted the family life of their children. The society includes people of all ages from the upper teens to the nineties, but the great majority are between twenty-five and fifty-four. It is, all in all, a world not of carefree hedonists who have flung away marriage to live more freely—the "gay divorcee" of earlier times, and her male counterpart—but a world largely made up of mature, responsible adults in search of a satisfying way of life, in pursuit not just of pleasure, but of real happiness.

Notes

1. This statement, and the rest of the paragraph, are documented in Hunt, 1966, *passim*, especially Chapters III through V.
2. The 1976 ratio of divorces to marriages: National Center for Health Statistics, *Monthly Vital Statistics Report*, Vol. 25, No. 10; for the divorce rate per thousand in 1976: *ibid*; for the divorce rate in 1962: National Center for Health Statistics, 1973 (b), p. 22.
3. U.S. Bureau of the Census, 1977, Table 1; and on the larger total who have passed through: Norton and Glick, 1976, p. 13.
4. The one-in-two chance of breaking up: Weiss, 1975(a), p. 12; also, Dr. Paul C. Glick, Senior Demographer, Population Division, U.S. Bureau of the Census, personal communication.
5. Same as note 3, this chapter.
6. Marriage rate, 1957 through 1967: National Center for Health Statistics, 1973(b); for recent years, National Center for Health Statistics, *Monthly Vital Statistics Report*, Vol. 23, No. 12; Vol. 24, Nos. 5 and 12; and Vol. 25, No. 10.
7. Current ratio: U.S. Bureau of the Census, 1977, Table 1; the ratio in 1962: Hunt, 1966, p. 18.
8. Average lag between separation and divorce today: National Center for Health Statistics, unpublished worksheets for 1974; average lag in 1960: Monahan, 1962.
9. U.S. Bureau of the Census, 1977, Table 1.
10. National Center for Health Statistics, 1976, section 2, pp. 5–7.
11. Norton and Glick, 1976, p. 15; National Center for Health Statistics, 1973(b), Table 12; U.S. Bureau of the Census, 1976(a), pp. 14–15; and National Center for Health Statistics, 1976, section 2, p. 8.
12. Median age at separation: see note 8, this chapter; other data in the paragraph: National Center for Health Statistics, 1976, section 2, p. 11. Note, however, that somewhat younger median ages are given in U.S. Bureau of the Census, 1976(a); the Bureau counts persons whose divorces occurred in the past as well as those currently divorcing, hence we chose to use the National Center for Health Statistics data.
13. The figures in the table are compiled from U.S. Bureau of the Census, 1977, Table 1.
14. Same as note 13, this chapter.
15. Goode, 1956, pp. 46–53.

16. Norton and Glick, 1976, pp. 13–14; U.S. Bureau of the Census, 1972(b), Table 7.
17. Same as note 16, this chapter.
18. This is the inference one can make from data in the U.S. Bureau of the Census, 1972(b), Table 7, which deals with urbanized areas, and which can be compared with figures in same publication for all areas.
19. U.S. Bureau of the Census, 1972(b), Table 1.
20. National Center for Health Statistics: *Monthly Vital Statistics Report,* Vol. 24, No. 13.
21. National Center for Health Statistics, 1976, section 2, p. 19.
22. For 1962: National Center for Health Statistics, 1964, section 3, p. 3; for 1973: Norton and Glick, 1976, p. 15.

The Transformation Of Legal Marriage Through No-Fault Divorce

Lenore J. Weitzman*
and Ruth B. Dixon**

Introduction

Divorce and family breakdown constitute one of the major social problems in the United States today. In 1975 alone over 3 million men, women and minor children were involved in a divorce.[1] In the future it is likely that one-third to one-half of all the adults in the United States, and close to one-third of the minor children under 18 will be affected by a divorce or dissolution.[2] These data reflect not only the numerical importance of divorce, but its increased social significance as well. While divorce may have been considered a "deviant family pattern" in the past, it is rapidly becoming accepted as a possible (though not yet a probable) outcome of marriage.

Since 1970 there has been a major reform in divorce law which attempts to institutionalize fundamental social changes in family patterns. Commonly referred to as no-fault divorce, this new legislation seeks to alter the definition of marriage, the relationship between husbands and wives, and the economic and social obligations of former spouses to each other and to their children after divorce.

In 1970, California instituted the first no-fault divorce law in the United States. Since then fourteen other states have adopted "pure" no-fault divorce

Published here for the first time with permission of the authors. Copyright © 1980 by Lenore Weitzman and Ruth Dixon.

We are indebted to our co-investigator Professor Herma Hill Kay for her continued advice and collaboration on the California Divorce Law Research Project. We would also like to thank Jerome H. Skolnick and William J. Goode for their valuable comments on an earlier draft of this paper. This research was supported by NIMH grant #MH-27617-02 and National Science Foundation Grant G1-39218

*Center for the Study of Law and Society, University of California, Berkeley, CA 94720
**Department of Sociology, University of California, Davis, CA 95616

laws[3] and an additional thirteen states have added no-fault grounds to their existing grounds for divorce.[4] No-fault divorce has been praised as the embodiment of "modern" and "enlightened" law, and heralded as the forerunner of future family law in the United States. It has also been strongly attacked for "destroying the family" and for causing irreparable harm to women. This paper aims at analyzing the effects of this new legislation on both marriage and divorce.

The laws governing divorce tell us how a society defines marriage and where it sets the boundaries for appropriate marital behavior. One can generally examine the way a society defines marriage by examining its provisions for divorce, for it is at the point of divorce that a society has the opportunity to reward the marital behavior it approves of, and to punish spouses who have violated its norms.[5] In addition, in virtually all societies which allow divorce, it is assumed that people who were once married continue to have obligations to each other; and these obligations reflect the rights and duties of marriage itself.

This paper is divided into three sections. It begins with a discussion of traditional legal marriage followed by a review of traditional divorce law. The last section examines the aims of the no-fault legislation and its implications for traditional family roles.

Traditional Legal Marriage

The origins of Anglo-American family law[6] may be traced to the tenth or eleventh century, when Christianity became sufficiently influential in Britain to enable the Church to assert its rules effectively. (Clark, 1968: 281). Traditionally legal marriage was firmly grounded in the Christian conception of marriage as a holy union between a man and woman. Marriage was a sacrament, a commitment to join together for life: "to take each other to love and to cherish, in sickness and in health, for better, for worse, until death do us part."

The nature of the marital relationship, and the legal responsibilities of the spouses were specified by law—by statute, case law and common law. While a thorough analysis of legal marriage is obviously beyond the scope of this paper (but see Clark, 1968; Kay, 1974; Weitzman, 1979), five important features may be briefly summarized as follows: First, legal marriage was limited to a single man and a single woman; bigamy, polygamy and homosexual unions were prohibited. Second, legal marriage was monogamous. The spouses were to remain sexually faithful to each other and adultery was explicitly prohibited. Third, marriage was for procreation. One of the major objects of matrimony was the bearing and rearing of (legitimate) children. (Reynolds v. Reynolds, 1862)

Fourth, legal marriage established a hierarchical relationship between the spouses: the husband was the head of the family, with his wife and children subordinate to him. The husband's authority was based on the common-law doctrine of coverture which established the legal fiction that a husband and wife took a single legal identity upon marriage—the identity of the husband. At common law a married woman became a *feme covert,* a legal nonperson, under her husband's arm, protection and cover. (Blackstone, 1765)

Although most of the disabilities of coverture were removed by the Married Women's Property Acts in the nineteenth century—the common-law assumption that the husband was the head of the family remained firmly embodied in statutory and case law in the United States. The married woman's subordination was most clearly reflected in rules governing her domicile and name. In both cases the married woman assumed her husband's identity—taking his name and his domicile as her own. This basic assumption of traditional legal marriage has, of course, been challenged in recent years.

The fifth, and most important feature of traditional legal marriage, was its sex-based division of family roles and responsibilities. The woman was to devote herself to being a wife, homemaker and mother in return for her husband's promise of lifelong support. The husband was given the sole responsibility for the family's financial welfare, while he was assured that his home, his children, and his social-emotional well-being would be cared for by his wife. Professor Homer Clark, a noted authority on family law, summarizes the legal obligations of the two spouses as follows:

> Specifically, the courts say that the husband has a duty to support his wife, that she has a duty to render services in the home, and that these duties are reciprocal. . . . The husband is to provide the family with food, clothing, shelter and as many of the amenities of life as he can manage, either (in earlier days) by the management of his estates, or (more recently) by working for wages or a salary. The wife is to be mistress of the household, maintaining the home with resources furnished by the husband, and caring for children. A reading of contemporary judicial opinions leaves the impression that these roles have not changed over the last two hundred years. (Clark, 1968: 181)

All states, even those with community property systems, placed the burden of the family support on the husband; he was legally responsible for providing necessitites for his wife and his children. Similarly, all states made the wife responsible for domestic and child care services: her legal obligation was to be a companion, housewife and mother. As one court enumerated the services a man could legally expect from his wife:

> (she had a duty) to be his helpmate, to love and care for him in such a role, to afford him her society and her person, to protect and care for him in sickness, and to labor faithfully to advance his interest . . . (she must also perform) her household and domestic duties . . . A husband is entitled to the benefit of his wife's industry and economy. (Rucci v. Rucci, 1962: 127)

The wife was also assigned responsibility for child care, both during marriage and after divorce, as the law viewed her as the "natural and proper" caretaker of the young.

While no one would claim that the law was responsible for the traditional division of labor in the family, it did serve to legitimate, sanction, and reinforce these traditional family roles. For example, the law reinforced the wife's subordinate status—and her economic dependency—by defining the husband as the only person who was responsible for (and capable of) supporting the family. (Kay, 1974).

By promising the housewife lifelong support, the law provided a disincentive for women to develop their economic capacity and to work in the paid labor force. In addition, by making them legally responsible for domestic and child care services, it reinforced the primacy of these activities in their lives, leaving them with neither time nor incentive to develop careers outside of the home.

The law similarly reinforced the traditional male role by directing the husband away from domestic and childcare activities. While the law did legitimate the husband's power and authority in the family, it also encouraged a single-minded dedication to work, and to earning a living, for it made it clear that his sole responsibility was his family's economic welfare.

Traditional Divorce Law

Since marriage was regarded as an indissoluble union, it could be ended only by the death of one of the parties. (Rhinestein, 1972) "Divorce, in the modern sense of a judicial decree dissolving a valid marriage, and allowing one or both partners to remarry during the life of the other, did not exist in England until 1857." (Kay, 1970: 221)[7]

A rare exception, originating in the late 17th century, allowed divorce (on the sole ground of adultery) by special act of Parliament. As a practical matter, however, few of these divorces were granted—and they were available only to the very rich, and to men. (Clark, 1968: 281). The Church also permitted divorce *a mensa et thoro,* literally a divorce from bed and board, which allowed the parties to live apart. But this legal separation did not sever the marital bond.

The Ecclesiastical Courts retained their exclusive jurisdiction over marriage and divorce in England until 1857, when divorce jurisdiction was transferred to the Civil Court System, and divorces were authorized for adultery. But the underlying premise of divorce law remained the same: Marriage was still regarded as a permanent and cherished union which the Church—and then the state—had to protect and preserve. And it was still assumed that the holy bond of matrimony would best be protected by restricting access to divorce. As Clark observed:

> (They believed) that marital happiness is best secured by making marriage indissoluble except for very few causes. When the parties know that they are bound together for life, the argument runs, they will resolve their differences and disagreements and make an effort to get along with each other. If they

are able to separate legally upon less serious grounds, they will make no such effort, and immorality will result. (Clark, 1968: 242–43)

It should also be noted that these early divorce laws established a different standard for men and women: "wives . . . could obtain a divorce only if the husband's adultery was aggravated by bigamy, cruelty or incest, while the husband could get his divorce for adultery alone." (Clark, 1969: 282)[8]

Divorce laws in the United States were heavily influenced by the English tradition. In the middle and southern Colonies, divorces were granted by the legislature, and were rare. However, New England allowed divorce more freely. The Protestant doctrines (and the absence of any system of Ecclesiastical Courts) resulted in statutes which authorized divorce for adultery, desertion, and, in some cases, cruelty—sometimes by the courts and sometimes by acts of the Legislature.

Although some diversity in the divorce laws of the states continued, in nineteenth century most states gave the courts the jurisdiction to dissolve marriages on specified grounds (Kay, 1968: 221), and by 1900 most states had adopted what we shall refer to as the four major elements of traditional divorce laws.

First, *traditional divorce law perpetuated the sex-based division of roles and responsibilities in traditional legal marriage.* As we noted above, in legal marriage the woman presumably agreed to devote herself to being a wife, homemaker and mother in return for her husband's promise of lifelong support. Although traditional family law assumed that the husband's support would be provided in a lifelong marriage, if the marriage did not endure, and if the wife was virtuous, she was nevertheless guaranteed alimony—a means of continued support. Alimony perpetuated the husband's responsibility for economic support, and the wife's right to be supported in return for her domestic services. It thus maintained the reciprocity in the legal marriage contract.

Traditional divorce laws also perpetuated the sex-based division of roles with respect to children: the husband remained responsible for their economic support, the wife for their care. All states, by statute or by case law tradition, gave preference to the wife as the appropriate custodial parent after the divorce; and all states gave the husband the primary responsibility for their economic support.

Second, *traditional divorce law required grounds for divorce.* Divorce could be obtained only if one party committed a marital offense, giving the other a legal basis or ground for the divorce. Since marriage was supposed to be a permanent lifelong union, only serious marital offenses such as adultery, cruelty, or desertion could justify a divorce. As Professor Herma Hill Kay explains:

> The state's interest in marital stability, thus delegated to the courts, was to be guarded by the judge's diligence in requiring that evidence clearly established the ground relied on for a divorce, that the defendant had no valid defense to the plaintiff's suit, and that the parties had not conspired to put on a false case. (Kay, 1970: 221)

The standards for judging appropriate grounds also reflected the sex-typed expectations of traditional legal marriage. While the almost ritualistic "evidence" of misbehavior varied from state to state, husbands charged with cruelty were often alleged to have caused their wives bodily harm, while wives charged with cruelty, were more typically charged with neglecting their husbands (showing lack of affection, belittling him); or their homes (leaving the home in disarray, neglecting dinner), impuning their husband's self-respect or reputation (denigrating or insulting him in front of business associates or friends); or ignoring their wifely duties (what Clark calls the country club syndrome in which the wife "is entirely preoccupied with club and social life, is extravagant, drinks heavily, and wholly disregards the husband's desires for affection and comfort.") (Clark, 1968: 349).

Cruelty was the most commonly used grounds for divorce followed by desertion, which accounted for less than 18% of all divorces (Jacobson, 1959: 124). Adultery was rarely used outside of New York, where it was the only permissible ground for divorce until 1967. While the standards for desertion also varied from state to state, two sex-based standards were common to most: (1) If a wife refused to live in the domicile chosen by her husband, she was held responsible for desertion in the divorce action. In addition, if the husband moved and she refused to accompany him, *she* was considered to have deserted *him*, since he had the legal right to choose the family home. She would then be the guilty party in the divorce, and that had important economic consequences which are discussed below. Second, a spouse's withdrawal from his or her marital roles might be considered desertion, and the standards for these withdrawals were clearly sex-typed. For example, a wife who showed "lack of affection" for the husband, had a relationship with another man (but did not commit adultery), refused to do housework, and nagged the husband, would be guilty of desertion (see, for example, Anton v. Anton, 1955) but a husband who acted in a similar fashion would not—unless he also stopped supporting his wife financially.

Over time, in actual practice many divorcing couples privately agreed to an uncontested divorce where one party, usually the wife, would take the *pro forma* role of plaintiff. Supported by witnesses, she would attest to her husband's cruel conduct and he would not challenge her testimony. But even if these allegations involved collusion and perjury, as many of them did, the type of behavior reported as grounds for divorce nevertheless reflected what the courts considered "appropriate violations" of the marriage contract. The husband, supposed to support and protect his wife, was sanctioned for nonsupport and physical abuse. The wife, obligated to care for her home and husband, was sanctioned for neglecting her domestic responsibilities.

Third, traditional legal divorce *was based on adversary proceedings.* The adversary process required that one party be guilty, or responsible for the divorce, and that the other be innocent. The plaintiff's success in obtaining a divorce depended on his or her ability to prove the defendant's fault for having committed some marital offense. Divorces had to be "won" by the innocent party against the guilty party. As the Tennessee Supreme Court (Brown v. Brown, 1955: 498) stated "divorce is conceived as a remedy for the innocent against the guilty." If a spouse who was found guilty could prove the other was also at fault, or that the other had colluded in or condoned their behavior, the divorce thus might not be granted in order to punish both parties.

Finally, traditional divorce law *linked the financial terms of the divorce to the determination of fault.* Being found "guilty" or "innocent" in the divorce action had important financial consequences.

For example, alimony, or a "suitable allowance for support and maintenance" could be awarded only to the *innocent* spouse "for his or her life, or for such shorter periods as the courts may deem "just" as a judgment *against* the guilty spouse. (California Civil Code 139). Thus a wife found guilty of adultery was typically barred from receiving alimony, while a husband found guilty of adultery or cruelty could be ordered to pay for his transgressions with alimony and property. And many attorneys believed that justice was served by using alimony as a lever against a promiscuous husband, or as a reward for a virtuous wife. As Eli Bronstein, a New York matrimonial lawyer, put it: "If a woman has been a tramp, why reward her? By the same token, if the man is alley-catting around town, shouldn't his wife get all the benefits she had as a married woman?" (Wheeler, 1974: 57)

Property awards were similarly linked to fault. In most states, the court had to award more than half of the property to the "innocent" or "injured" party.[9] This standard easily led to heated accusations and counter–accusations of wrongs in order to obtain a better property settlement. (Hogoboom, 1971: 687) It also allowed a spouse who did not want a divorce to use the property award as a lever in the negotiations. In practice, since the husband was more likely to be the party who wanted the divorce, the wife was more likely to assume the role of the innocent plaintiff (Friedman and Percival, 1976: 77); and she was therefore more likely to be awarded a greater share of the property. Of course, the proportion of her share (and the extent of the inequality) was related to both the amount and type of property involved: significantly unequal awards were most likely to occur in cases in which the only family asset was the house, as the (innocent) wife was typically awarded the family home. (Weitzman, Kay & Dixon, 1979)

Custody awards could also be influenced by findings of fault. A woman found guilty of adultery or cruelty might be deprived of her preference as the custodial parent—especially if her behavior indicated that she was an "unfit" mother.[10]

By linking both the granting of the divorce and the financial settlements to findings of fault, the law gave the "aggrieved" spouse, particularly an "innocent" wife who wanted to stay married, a considerable advantage in the financial negotiations. In return for her agreement to the divorce, her husband was typically willing to be the guilty defendant (in a noncontested divorce) and to give her, as the innocent plaintiff, alimony and more than half of the property.

In summary, traditional divorce law helped sanction the spouses' roles and responsibilities in marriage—by both punishment and reward. On the negative side, if a wife was found guilty of adultery, cruelty or desertion, she would have to pay for her wrongdoings by being denied alimony (and sometimes custody and property as well). And if the husband was at fault, he would be "punished" through awards of property, alimony and child support to his ex-wife.

On the positive side, traditional divorce law promised "justice" for those who fulfilled their marital obligations. It guaranteed support for the wife who devoted herself to her family, thus reinforcing the desirability and legitimacy of the wife's role as homemaker, and the husband's role as supporter. And it assured the husband that he would not have to support a wife who betrayed or failed him. Justice in this system was the assurance that the marriage contract will be honored. If not, the "bad" spouse would be punished, the "good" spouse rewarded, and the husband's obligation to support his wife (if she was good) enforced.

No–Fault Divorce

In 1970 California instituted the first law in the Western world to abolish completely any requirement of fault as the basis for marital dissolution. (Hogoboom, 1971). The no-fault law provided for a divorce upon *one* party's assertion that "irreconcilable differences have caused the irremediable breakdown of the marriage." In establishing the new standards for marital dissolution, the California State Legislature sought to eliminate the adversarial nature of divorce and thereby to reduce the hostility, acrimony and trauma characteristic of fault-oriented divorce.

The California no-fault divorce law marked the beginning of a nationwide trend toward legal recognition of "marital breakdown" as a sufficient justification for divorce. The new law not only eliminated the need for evidence of misconduct; it eliminated the concept of fault itself. And it thereby abolished the notion of interpersonal justice in divorce. With this seemingly simple move, the California legislature dramatically altered the legal definition of the reciprocal rights of husbands and wives during marriage and after its dissolution.

Proponents of the divorce law reform had several aims. They sought to eliminate the hypocrisy, perjury and collusion "required by courtroom practice under the fault system" (Kay, 1968: 1223); to reduce the adversity, acrimony and bitterness surrounding divorce proceedings; to lessen the personal stigma attached to the divorce; and to create conditions for more rational and equitable settlements of property and spousal support. (Hogoboom, 1970; Kay, 1970; Krom, 1970) In brief, the new law attempted to bring divorce legislation into line with the social realities of marital breakdown in contemporary society. It recognized that marital conduct and misconduct no longer fit rigid categories of fault. And it eliminated the punitive element of moral condemnation that had pervaded Western thought for centuries.

The no-fault legislation changed each of the four basic elements in traditional divorce law. First, *it eliminated the fault-based grounds for divorce.* No longer did one spouse have to testify to the other's adultery, cruelty or desertion. And no longer were witnesses necessary to corroborate their testimony.

By replacing the old fault-based grounds for divorce with a single new standard of "irreconcilable differences," the legislature sought to eliminate both the artificial grounds for the breakdown of a marriage, and the artificial conception that one party was "responsible" for the breakdown. Further, the criterion of "irreconcilable differences" recognized that whatever the reasons for marital failure, they were best left out of the proceedings because they were irrelevant to an equitable settlement. Now the divorce procedure could begin with a neutral "petition for dissolution," with no specific acts or grounds needed as a justification.

Second, *the new laws eliminated the adversary process.* Divorce reformers believed that at least some of the trauma of a fault-based divorce resulted from the legal process itself, rather than from the inherent difficulties of dissolving a marriage. (See, for example, Rheinstein, 1972.) They assumed that husbands and wives who were dissolving their marriage were potentially "amicable," but that the *legal process generated hostility and trauma* by forcing them to be antagonists. The reformers assumed that if fault and the adversary process were eliminated from the legal proceedings, "human beings who are entitled to divorces could get them with the least possible amount of damage to themselves and to their families" (Proceedings from the California Assembly Committee on the Judiciary, 1964).

Each aspect of the legal process was therefore changed to reflect the new non-adversary approach to divorce: "Divorce" became "dissolution"; "plaintiffs" and "defendants" became "petitioners" and "respondents"; "alimony" became "spousal support"; and the court records read "*in re* the Marriage of Doe" instead of "Doe vs. Doe."[11] Standard printed forms written in plain English replaced the archaic legalistic pleadings. Residence requirements were reduced from one year to six months in the state before filing, and the minimum period between filing and the final decree was shortened from one year to six months. These revisions were designed in part to smooth the progress of a marital dissolution through the courts and to avoid some of the unnecessary legal wrangling and personal hostilities engendered by the adversarial model.

Third, *the financial aspects of the divorce were to be based on equity, equality, and economic need* rather than on either fault or sex-based role assignments. Proponents of no-fault divorce contended that it was outmoded to grant alimony and property as a reward for virtue, and to withhold them as punishment for wrongdoing. Instead, they advocated more realistic standards for alimony and property awards—standards based on the spouses' economic circumstances and a new principal of equality between the sexes. They argued that justice for both the wife and the husband would be better served by considering their economic situations, rather than by weighing their guilt or innocence. And they believed that men and women should no longer be shackled by the weight of traditional sex roles; new norms were necessary to bring the law into line with modern social reality.

With regard to the new economic criteria for awards, the no-fault law aimed at making the financial aspects of the divorce more equitable to facilitate the post-divorce adjustment of both men and women. Substantively, guidelines for financial settlements were changed to remove evidence of misconduct from consideration. For example, while alimony under the old law could only be awarded to the "injured party," regardless of that person's financial need, under the new law, it was to be based on the financial needs and financial resources of both spouses.

With regard to the new norm of equality between the sexes, the advocates of the divorce law reform pointed to the changing position of women in general, and to their increased participation in the labor force in particular, and urged a reformulation of alimony and property awards which recognized the growing ability of women to be self-supporting. With a reformist zeal they assumed that the employment gains of women had already eliminated the need for alimony as a means of continued support after divorce. Ignoring the fact that even full-time year-round female workers earn less than 60 percent of what men earn, some advocates went so far as to declare that "it does seem somewhat anachronistic, in an era of increasing feminine [sic] equality, that the statutes providing for alimony have remained on the books for as long as they have" (Brody, 1070:228).

The legislators also challenged the anachronistic assumption that the husband had to continue to support his wife—for life. They pointed to the difficulty that men face in supporting two households if they remarry, and argued that the old law had converted "a host of physically and mentally competent young women into an army of alimony drones who neither toil nor spin and become a drain on society and a menace to themselves." (Hofstadter and Levittan, 1967:55). Thus while the reformers were willing to consider support for the older housewife, they did not believe that the younger housewife deserved continued support; instead they saw her as a potential "alimony drone" who ought to be self-supporting.

Under the new law, California judges setting alimony are directed to consider "the circumstances of the respective parties, including the duration of the marriage, and the ability of the supported spouse to engage in gainful employment without interfering with the interests of the children of the parties in the custody of each spouse." (Civil Code 4801). California's no-fault divorce law is thus typical of new alimony legislation: It is concerned primarily with financial criteria and, while it specifically mentions the custodial spouse and the wife in a marriage of long duration, the thrust of the law is to encourage the divorced woman to become self-supporting (by engaging in gainful employ-ment.)

The implicit aim of the new alimony was to encourage (some would say force) formerly dependent wives to assume the responsibility for their own support. With the elimination of fault as the basis for alimony, the new standard explicitly excluded the granting of support awards to women just because they had been wives, or just because their husbands had left them, or just because they had spent years as homemakers. The new law recognized, in theory, the need for transitional support, support for the custodial parent, and support for the older housewife who could not become self-supporting.

Property awards under no-fault are also to be based on equity and equality and are no longer limited to findings of fault. For example, in California the community property *must be divided equally.* [12] Underlying the new law is a conception of marriage as a partnership, with each person having made an equal contribution to the community property and therefore deserving an equal share.

The standards for child custody also reflect the new equality between the spouses. The preference for the mother (for children of tender years) has been replaced by a sex-neutral standard which instructs judges to award custody in the "best interests of the child." [13] Finally, the new law makes both husbands and wives responsible for child support.

Fourth, *no-fault divorce re-defined the traditional responsibilities of husbands and wives by instituting a new norm of equality between the sexes.*

Instead of the old sex-typed division of family responsibilities the new law has attempted to institutionalize sex-neutral obligations which fall equally upon the husband and the wife. No longer is the husband the head of the family —both spouses are now presumed to be equal partners in the marriage. Nor is the husband alone responsible for support, or the wife alone obligated to care for the home and children.

Each of the provisions of the new law discussed above reflect these new assumptions about appropriate spousal roles. The new standards for alimony indicate that a woman is no longer supposed to devote herself to her home and family—rather, she now bears an equal responsibility for her own economic support. For the law has clearly established a new norm of economic self-sufficiency for the divorced woman. Similarly, the new standards indicate that men will no longer be held responsible for their wives (and ex-wives) lifelong support.

The criterion for dividing property also reflects the new norm of equality between the sexes. There is no preference or protection for the older housewife —or, even for the custodial mother (although some states do have a preference for the custodial parent to retain the family home while the children are living there). Instead, the two spouses are treated equally—each one receives an equal share of the property.

Finally, the expectations for child support are sex-neutral. Both parents are equally responsible for the financial welfare of their children after divorce.

What was previously considered the husband's responsibility is now shared equally by the wife.

In summary, traditional divorce law and no-fault reflect two contrasting visions of "justice." The traditional law sought to deliver a moral justice which rewarded the good spouse and punished the bad spouse. It was a justice based on compensation for *past* behavior, both sin and virtue. The no-fault law ignores both moral character and moral history as a basis for awards. Instead it seeks to deliver a fairness and equity based on the financial *needs* and upon equality of the two parties.

The law is based on the assumption that divorced women can be immediately self-supporting. This assumption stands in contrast to the Uniform Marriage and Divorce Act which specifies that the court should consider the time necessary to acquire sufficient education or training to enable the party seeking temporary maintenance to find appropriate employment. Under this provision, a husband whose wife has supported him during his graduate education or professional training may be required to finance her education or training in order to place her in a position more nearly akin to the one she could have achieved (Kay, 1972). The lack of such provisions in the no-fault divorce laws adopted by most states, such as California, may incur a heavier burden on the wife and make post-divorce adjustment especially difficult for women.

Thus, while the aims of the no-fault laws, i.e. equality and sex-neutrality are laudable, the laws may be instituting equality in a society in which women are not fully prepared (and/or permitted) to assume equal responsibility for their own and their children's support after divorce. Public policy then becomes a choice between temporary protection and safeguards for the transitional woman (and for the older housewife in the transitional generation) to minimize the hardships incurred by the new expectations, versus current enforcement of the new equality, with the hope of speeding the transition, despite the hardships this may cause for current divorcees.

Footnotes

1. In 1975, for the first time in U. S. history, there were over *one million* divorces in a twelve-month period (Carter and Glick, 1976: 394), and the number of divorces is expected to rise.
2. Preston estimates that 44 percent of all current marriages will end in divorce (Preston, 1974: 435), while the more conservative estimate of Carter and Glick (1976: 396) is that at least one-third of all the first marriages of couples under 30 will end in divorce.
3. As of June, 1976, the fourteen states that adopted "pure" no-fault divorce statutes (in which irretrievable breakdown is the only grounds for the dissolution of the marriage) are Arizona, California, Colorado, Delaware, Florida, Iowa, Kentucky, Michigan, Minnesota, Missouri, Montana, Nebraska, Oregon, and Washington.
4. The thirteen states that have added no-fault grounds to their existing fault-based grounds for divorce are Alabama, Connecticut, Georgia, Hawaii, Idaho, Indiana, Maine, Massachusetts, Mississippi, New Hampshire, North Dakota, Rhode Island and Texas. Most of the remaining states have recently added a provision allowing divorce for those "living separate and apart" for a specified period of time, which is an even more modified version of no-fault. Only three states, Illinois, Pennsylvania, and South Dakota, retain fault as the *only* basis for divorce (Foster and Freed, 1977, Chart B1).

5. Today more citizens come into contact with the legal system in family law cases than in any other type of litigation (with the possible exception of traffic court) as matrimonial actions now comprise over fifty percent of all civil cases at the trial court level in most cities and states. (Friedman and Percival, 1976: 281–83).
6. We are referring explicitly to divorce, or "the legal termination of a valid marriage", (Clark 1968: 280) as distinguished from an annulment, which is a declaration that a purported marriage has been invalid from its beginning.
7. Adultery remained the only grounds for divorce in England until 1937 when the Matrimonial Causes Act added desertion, cruelty and some other offences as appropriate grounds for divorce. (Clark, 1968: 282).
8. In contrast, Maxine Virtue's observations of a Chicago court (1956) indicated identical standards for cruelty among husbands and wives. As she notes (Virtue, 1956: 86–89) "The number of cruel spouses in Chicago, both male and female, who strike their marriage partners in the face exactly twice, without provocation, leaving visible marks, is remarkable."
9. Thirty-six states (twenty-eight common-law jurisdictions and eight community property states) allow the court to divide the property upon divorce. (Krause, 1976: 980). The remaining 14 states all have common law property systems which allow each person to retain the property in his or her name. However, there is a considerable impetus for reforms in these states. Legal scholars, such as Foster and Freed, have called the maintenance of the separate property system at the time of divorce obsolete, archaic and shockingly unfair. The strongest argument against it is that "in its application it ignores the contribution wives make to the family." (Foster and Freed, 1974: 170). This argument has also been the major objection of feminist groups to the common-law property system. For example, the Citizens' Advisory Council on the Status of Women (1974: 6) has advocated the importance of changing the law "to recognize explicitly the contribution of the homemaker . . . and to give courts the authority to divide property (owned by both spouses) upon divorce."
10. Of all the financial aspects of the divorce, only child support was, in theory, unaffected by fault—as it was based on the needs of the children (and the father's financial status.)
11. The new language was not always easy to adopt, however. When filmstar Linda Lovelace was divorced, the newspapers reported that she had "charged her husband with irreconcilable differences."
12. The court may make an unequal award if community property has been deliberately mis-appropriated, or if immediate equal division will incur an extreme or unnecessary hard-ship. Property may also be divided unequally in a private agreement between the two parties.
13. In California this was changed in 1972 but was part of the original recommendations from the governor's commission which initiated the no-fault legislation.

References

Anton v. Anton
  1955   49 Del. 431, 118 A.2d 605, (Supp. 1955).
Blackston, William
  1965   Commentaries on the Laws of England
Brody, Stuart
  1970   "California's Divorce Reform: Its Sociological Implication" Pacific Law Journal, 1
Brown v. Brown
  1955   198 Tenn. 600, 381 S.W. 2d 492
Carter, Hugh, and Paul C. Glick
  1970   Marriage and Divorce: A social and Economic Study. Cambridge, Mass.: Harvard.
  1976   Marriage and Divorce: A social and Economic Study, Cambridge, Mass.: Harvard (Revised Ed.).
Clark, Homer
  1968   Domestic Relations. St. Paul, Minn.: West.
Citizens' Advisory Council on the Status of Women
  1974   Recognition of Economic Contribution of Homemakers and Protection of Children in Divorce and Practice. Washington, D.C.: U.S. Government Printing Office.

Friedman, Lawrence M., and Robert V. Percival
    1976a "Who Sues for Divorce? From Fault Through Fiction to Freedom." Journal of Legal
        Studies 5 (1): 61–82.
    1976b "A Tale of Two Courts: Litigation in Alameda and San Benito Counties." Law and
        Society Review 10 (2); 267–303.
Foster, Henry H. and Doris Jonas Freed.
    1974 "Marital Property Reform in New York; Partnership of Co-Equals?" Family Law
        Quarterly, Vol. 8; pp. 169–205.
    1977 Family Law: Cases and Materials. Boston: Little, Brown (3rd ed.)
Hofstadter, Samuel H., and Shirley R. Levittan
    1967 "Alimony—A Reformulation." Journal of Family Law 7:51–60.
Hogoboom, William P.
    1971 "The California Family Law Act of 1970: 18 Months' Experience." Journal of Missouri
        Bar: 584–589.
Krause, Harry D.
    1976 Family Law: Cases and Materials. St. Paul, Minn.: West.
Kay, Herma Hill
    1970 A Family Court: The California Proposal in Paul Bohannan (ed.) Divorce and After.
        Garden City, New York: Doubleday.
    1974 "Sex-Based Discrimination in Family Law" in Kenneth M. Davidson, Ruth G. Gins-
        burg and Herma Hill Kay, Sex-Based Discrimination Text, Cases and Materials. St.
        Paul, Minn.: West.
Reynolds V. Reynolds
    1862 85 Mass. (3 Allen) 605 (1862)
Rheinstein, Max
    1972 Marriage Stability, Divorce and the Law. Chicago: University of Chicago
Rucci v. Rucci
    1962 23 Conn. Supp. 221, 181 A.2d 125.
Weitzman, Lenore
    1979 The Marriage Contract. Englewood Cliffs, N.J.: Prentice-Hall.
Weitzman, Lenore and Ruth B. Dixon
    1976 "The Alimony Myth." Paper read at the meeting of the American Sociological Associa-
        tion.
    1979 "Child Custody Standards and Awards." Journal of Social Issues, Forthcoming.
Weitzman, Lenore J., Herma Hill Kay, and Ruth B. Dixon
    1979 No Fault Divorce: The Impact of Changes in the Law and the Legal Process. California
        Divorce Law Research Project, Center for the Study of Law and Society. University
        of California, Berkeley.
Wheeler, Michael
    1974 No-Fault Divorce. Boston: Beacon Press.

Remarriage as an Incomplete Institution

Andrew Cherlin

Sociologists believe that social institutions shape people's behavior in important ways. Gerth and Mills (1953, p. 173) wrote that institutions are organizations of social roles which "imprint their stamps upon the individual, modifying his external conduct as well as his inner life." More recently, Berger and Luckmann (1966) argued that institutions define not only acceptable behavior, as Gerth and Mills believed, but also objective reality itself. Social institutions range from political and economic systems to religion and language. And displayed prominently in any sociologist's catalogue of institutions is a fundamental form of social organization, the family.

The institution of the family provides social control of reproduction and child rearing. It also provides family members with guidelines for proper behavior in everyday family life, and, presumably, these guidelines contribute to the unity and stability of families. But in recent years, sociologists have de-emphasized the institutional basis of family unity in the United States. According to many scholars, contemporary families are held together more by consensus and mutual affection than by formal, institutional controls.

The main source of this viewpoint is an influential text by Ernest Burgess and Harvey Locke which appeared in 1945. They wrote:

> The central thesis of this volume is that the family in historical times has been, and at present is, in transition from an institution to a companionship. In the past, the important factors unifying the family have been external, formal, and authoritarian, as the law, the mores, public opinion, tradition, the authority of the family head, rigid discipline, and elaborate ritual. At present, in the new emerging form of the companionship family, its unity inheres less and less in community pressures and more and more in such interpersonal relationships as the mutual affection, the sympathetic understanding, and the comradeship of its members. [P. vii]

In the institutional family, Burgess and Locke stated, unity derived from the unchallenged authority of the patriarch, was was supported by strong social pressure. But, they argued, with urbanization and the decline of patriarchal authority, a democratic family has emerged which creates its own unity from interpersonal relations.

Many subsequent studies have retained the idea of the companionship family in some form, such as the equalitarian family of Blood and Wolfe (1960) or the symmetrical family of Young and Wilmott (1973). Common to all is the notion that patriarchal authority has declined and sex roles have become less segregated. Historical studies of family life demonstrate that the authority of the husband was indeed stronger in the preindustrial West than it is now (see,

Reprinted from the *American Journal of Sociology,* 84:3 (1978), pp. 634–650, by permission of The University of Chicago Press. © 1978 by The University of Chicago. All rights reserved.

e.g., Ariès 1962; Shorter 1975). As for today, numerous studies of "family power" have attempted to show that authority and power are shared more equally between spouses (see Blood and Wolfe 1960). Although these studies have been criticized (Safilios-Rothschild 1970), no one has claimed that patriarchal authority is as strong now as the historical record indicates it once was. Even if we believe that husbands still have more authority than wives, we can nevertheless agree that patriarchal authority seems to have declined in the United States in this century.

But it does not follow that institutional sources of family unity have declined also. Burgess and Locke reached this conclusion in part because of their assumption that the patriarch was the transmitter of social norms and values to his family. With the decline of the patriarch, so they believed, a vital institutional link between family and society was broken. This argument is similar to the perspective of Gerth and Mills, who wrote that a set of social roles becomes an institution when it is stabilized by a "head" who wields authority over the members. It follows from this premise that if the head loses his authority, the institutional nature of family life will become problematic.

Yet institutionalized patterns of behavior clearly persist in family life, despite the trend away from patriarchy and segregated sex roles. As others have noted (Dyer and Urban 1958: Nye and Berardo 1973), the equalitarian pattern may be as firmly institutionalized now as the traditional pattern was in the past. In the terms of Berger and Luckmann, most family behavior today is habitualized action which is accepted as typical by all members—that is, it is institutionalized behavior. In most everyday situations, parents and children base their behavior on social norms: parents know how harshly to discipline their children, and children learn from parents and friends which parental rules are fair and which to protest. These sources of institutionalization in the contemporary American family have received little attention from students of family unity, just as family members themselves pay little attention to them.

The presence of these habitualized patterns directly affects family unity. "Habitualization," Berger and Luckmann wrote, "carries with it the important psychological gain that choices are narrowed" (1966, p. 53). With choices narrowed, family members face fewer decisions which will cause disagreements and, correspondingly, have less difficulty maintaining family unity. Thus, institutional support for family unity exists through the routinization of everyday behavior even though the husband is no longer the unchallenged agent of social control.

Nowhere in contemporary family life is the psychological gain from habitualization more evident than in the families of remarried spouses and their children, where, paradoxically, habitualized behavior is often absent. We know that the unity of families of remarriages which follow a divorce is often precarious—as evidenced by the higher divorce rate for these families than for families of first marriages (U.S. Bureau of the Census 1976). And in the last few decades, remarriage after divorce—as opposed to remarriage after widowhood—has become the predominant form of remarriage. In this paper, I will argue that the higher divorce rate for remarriages after divorce is a consequence of the incomplete institutionalization of remarriage after divorce in our society. The institution of the family in the United States has developed in response to the needs of families of first marriages and families of remarriages after widowhood. But because of the complex structure, families of remarriages after divorce that include children from previous marriages must solve problems unknown to other types of families. For many of these problems, such as proper kinship terms, authority to discipline stepchildren, and legal relationships, no institutionalized solutions have emerged. As a result, there is more opportunity for disagreements and divisions among family members and more strain in many remarriages after divorce.

The incomplete institutionalization of remarriage after divorce reveals, by way of contrast, the high degree of institutionalization still present in first marriages. Family members, especially those in first marriages, rely on a wide range of habitualized behaviors to assist them in solving the common problems of family life. We take these behavioral patterns for granted until their absence forces us to create solutions on our own. Only then do we see the continuing importance of institutionalized patterns of family behavior for maintaining family unity.

I cannot provide definitive proof of the hypothesis linking the higher divorce rate for remarriages after divorce to incomplete institutionalization. There is very little quantitative information concerning remarriages. In fact, we do not even know how many stepparents and stepchildren there are in the United States. Nor has there ever been a large, random-sample survey designed with families of remarriages in mind. (Bernard's 1956 book on remarriage, for example, was based on information supplied nonrandomly by third parties.) There are, nevertheless, several studies which do provide valuable information, and there is much indirect evidence bearing on the plausibility of this hypothesis and of alternative explanations. I will review this evidence, and I will also refer occasionally to information I collected through personal interviews with a small, nonrandom sample of remarried couples and family counselors in the northeast. Despite the lack of data, I believe that the problems of families of remarriages are worth examining, especially given the recent increases in divorce and remarriage rates. In the hope that this article will stimulate further investigations, I will also present suggestions for future research.

The Problem of Family Unity

Remarriages have been common in the United States since its beginnings, but until this century almost all remarriages followed widowhood. In the

Plymouth Colony, for instance, about one-third of all men and one-quarter of all women who lived full lifetimes remarried after the death of a spouse, but there was little divorce (Demos 1970). Even as late as the 1920s, more brides and grooms were remarrying after widowhood than after divorce, according to estimates by Jacobson (1959). Since then, however, a continued increase in divorce (Norton and Glick 1976) has altered this pattern. By 1975, 84% of all brides who were remarrying were previously divorced, and 16% were widowed. For grooms who were remarrying in 1975, 86% were previously divorced (U.S. National Center for Health Statistics 1977). Thus, it is only recently that remarriage after divorce has become the predominant form of remarriage.

And since the turn of the century, remarriages after divorce have increased as a proportion of all marriages. In 1900 only 3% of all brides—including both the single and previously married—were divorced (Jacobson 1959). In 1930, 9% of all brides were divorced (Jacobson 1959), and in 1975, 25% of all brides were divorced (U.S. National Center for Health Statistics 1977). As a result, in 7 million families in 1970 one or both spouses had remarried after a divorce (U.S. Bureau of the Census 1973). Most of this increase is due to the rise in the divorce rate, but some part is due to the greater tendency of divorced and widowed adults to remarry. The remarriage rate for divorced and widowed women was about 50% higher in the mid-1970s than in 1940 (Norton and Glick 1976).

At the same time, the percentage of divorces which involved at least one child increased from 46% in 1950 to 60% in 1974 (U.S. National Center for Health Statistics 1953, 1977). The increase in the percentage of divorces which involve children means that more families of remarriages after divorce now have stepchildren. Although it is not possible with available data to calculate the exact number of families with stepchildren, we do know that in 1970 8.9 million children lived in two-parent families where one or both parents had been previously divorced (U.S. Bureau of the Census 1973). Some of these children—who constituted 15% of all children living in two-parent families—were from previous marriages, and others were from the remarriages.

Can these families of remarriages after divorce, many of which include children from previous marriages, maintain unity as well as do families of first marriages? Not according to the divorce rate. A number of studies have shown a greater risk of separation and divorce for remarriages after divorce (Becker, Landes, and Michael 1976; Bumpass and Sweet 1972; Cherlin 1977; Monahan 1958). Remarriages after widowhood appear, in contrast, to have a lower divorce rate than first marriages (Monahan 1958). A recent Bureau of the Census report (U.S. Bureau of the Census 1976) estimated that about 33% of all first marriages among people 25–35 may end in divorce, while about 40% of remarriages after divorce among people this age may end in divorce. The estimates are based on current rates of divorce, which could, of course, change greatly in the future.[1]

Conventional wisdom, however, seems to be that remarriages are more successful than first marriages. In a small, nonrandom sample of family counselors and remarried couples, I found most to be surprised at the news that divorce was more prevalent in remarriages. There are some plausible reasons for this popular misconception. Those who remarry are older, on the average, than those marrying for the first time and are presumably more mature. They have had more time to search the marriage market and to determine their own needs and preferences. In addition, divorced men may be in a better financial position and command greater work skills than younger, never-married men. (Divorced women who are supporting children, however, are often in a worse financial position—see Hoffman [1977].)

But despite these advantages, the divorce rate is higher in remarriages after divorce. The reported differences are often modest, but they appear consistently throughout 20 years of research. And the meaning of marital dissolution for family unity is clear: when a marriage dissolves, unity ends. The converse, though, is not necessarily true: a family may have a low degree of unity but remain nominally intact. Even with this limitation, I submit that the divorce rate is the best objective indicator of differences in family unity between remarriages and first marriages.

There are indicators of family unity other than divorce, but their meaning is less clear and their measurement is more difficult. There is the survey research tradition, for example, of asking people how happy or satisfied they are with their marriages. The invariable result is that almost everyone reports that they are very happy. (See, e.g., Bradburn and Caplovitz 1965; Glenn 1975; Campbell, Converse, and Rodgers 1976). It may be that our high rate of divorce increases the general level of marital satisfaction by dissolving unsatisfactory marriages. But it is also possible that the satisfaction ratings are inflated by the reluctance of some respondents to admit that their marriages are less than fully satisfying. Marriage is an important part of life for most adults— the respondents in the Campbell et al. (1976) national sample rated it second only to health as the most important aspect of their lives—and people may be reluctant to admit publicly that their marriage is troubled.

Several recent studies, nevertheless, have shown that levels of satisfaction and happiness are lower among the remarried, although the differences typically are small. Besides the Campbell et al. study, these include Glenn and Weaver (1977), who found modest differences in marital happiness in the 1973,

[1]A study by McCarthy (1977), however, suggests that remarriages may be more stable than first marriages for blacks. Using life-table techniques on data from 10,000 women under age 45 collected in the 1973 Survey of Family Growth, McCarthy reported that the probability of separation and divorce during the first 15 years of marriage is lower for blacks in remarriages than in first marriages, but is about 50% higher for whites in remarriages than for whites in first marriages.

1974, and 1975 General Social Surveys conducted by the National Opinion Research Center. They reported that for women, the difference between those who were remarried and those who were in a first marriage was statistically significant, while for men the difference was smaller and not significant. In addition, Renne (1971) reported that remarried, previously divorced persons were less happy with their marriages than those in first marriages in a probability sample of 4,452 Alameda County, California, households. Again, the differences were modest, but they were consistent within categories of age, sex, and race. No tests of significance were reported.

The higher divorce rate suggests that maintaining family unity is more difficult for families of remarriages after divorce. And the lower levels of marital satisfaction, which must be interpreted cautiously, also support this hypothesis. It is true, nevertheless, that many remarriages work well, and that the majority of remarriages will not end in divorce. And we must remember that the divorce rate is also at an all-time high for first marriages. But there is a difference of degree between remarriages and first marriages which appears consistently in research. We must ask why families of remarriages after divorce seem to have more difficulty maintaining family unity than do families of first marriages. Several explanations have been proposed, and we will now assess the available evidence for each.

Previous Explanations

One explanation, favored until recently by many psychiatrists, is that the problems of remarried people arise from personality disorders which preceded their marriages (see Bergler 1948). People in troubled marriages, according to this view, have unresolved personal conflicts which must be treated before a successful marriage can be achieved. Their problems lead them to marry second spouses who may be superficially quite different from their first spouse but are characterologically quite similar. As a result, this theory states, remarried people repeat the problems of their first marriages.

If this explanation were correct, one would expect that people in remarriages would show higher levels of psychiatric symptomatology than people in first marriages. But there is little evidence of this. On the contrary, Overall (1971) reported that in a sample of 2,000 clients seeking help for psychiatric problems, currently remarried people showed lower levels of psychopathology on a general rating scale than persons in first marriages and currently divorced persons. These findings, of course, apply only to people who sought psychiatric help. And it may be, as Overall noted, that the differences emerged because remarried people are more likely to seek help for less serious problems. The findings, nevertheless, weaken the psychoanalytic interpretation of the problems of remarried life.

On the other hand, Monahan (1958) and Cherlin (1977) reported that the divorce rate was considerably higher for people in their third marriages who had divorced twice than for people in their second marriages. Perhaps personality disorders among some of those who marry several times prevent them from achieving a successful marriage. But even with the currently high rates of divorce and remarriage, only a small proportion of all adults marry more than twice. About 10% of all adults in 1975 had married twice, but less than 2% had married three or more times (U.S. Bureau of the Census 1976).

Most remarried people, then, are in a second marriage. And the large number of people now divorcing and entering a second marriage also undercuts the psychoanalytic interpretation. If current rates hold, about one-third of all young married people will become divorced, and about four-fifths of these will remarry. It is hard to believe that the recent increases in divorce and remarriage are due to the sudden spread of marriage-threatening personality disorders to a large part of the young adult population. I conclude, instead, that the psychoanalytic explanation for the rise in divorce and the difficulties of remarried spouses and their children is at best incomplete.[2]

A second possible explanation is that once a person has divorced he or she is less hesitant to do so again. Having divorced once, a person knows how to get divorced and what to expect from family members, friends, and the courts. This explanation is plausible and probably accounts for some of the difference in divorce rates. But it does not account for all of the research findings on remarriage, such as the finding of Becker et al. (1976) that the presence of children from a previous marriage increased the probability of divorce for women in remarriages, while the presence of children from the new marriage reduced the probability of divorce. I will discuss the implications of this study below, but let me note here that a general decrease in the reluctance of remarried persons to divorce would not explain this finding. Moreover, the previously divorced may be more hesitant to divorce again because of the stigma attached to divorcing twice. Several remarried people I interviewed expressed great reluctance to divorce a second time. They reasoned that friends and relatives excused one divorce but would judge them incompetent at marriage after two divorces.

Yet another explanation for the higher divorce rate is the belief that many remarried men are deficient at fulfilling their economic responsibilities. We know that divorce is more likely in families where the husband has low earnings (Goode 1956). Some remarried men, therefore, may be unable to earn a sufficient amount of money to support a family. It is conceivable that this inability to be a successful breadwinner could account for all of the divorce rate differential, but statistical studies of divorce suggest otherwise. Three

---

[2]Despite the lack of convincing evidence, I am reluctant to discount this explanation completely. Clinical psychologists and psychiatrists with whom I have talked insist that many troubled married persons they have treated had made the same mistakes twice and were in need of therapy to resolve long-standing problems. Their clinical experience should not be ignored, but this "divorce-proneness" syndrome seems inadequate as a complete explanation for the greater problems of remarried people.

recent multivariate analyses of survey data on divorce have shown that remarried persons still had a higher probability of divorce or separation, independent of controls for such socioeconomic variables as husband's earnings (Becker et al. 1976), husband's educational attainment (Bumpass and Sweet 1972), and husband's and wife's earnings, employment status, and savings (Cherlin 1977). These analyses show that controlling for low earnings can reduce the difference in divorce probabilities, but they also show that low earnings cannot fully explain the difference. It is possible, nevertheless, that a given amount of income must be spread thinner in many remarriages, because of child-support or alimony payments (although the remarried couple also may be receiving these payments). But this type of financial strain must be distinguished from the questionable notion that many remarried husbands are inherently unable to provide for a wife and children.

Institutional Support

The unsatisfactory nature of all these explanations leads us to consider one more interpretation. I hypothesize that the difficulties of couples in remarriages after divorce stem from a lack of institutionalized guidelines for solving many common problems of their remarried life. The lack of institutional support is less serious when neither spouse has a child from a previous marriage. In this case, the family of remarriage closely resembles families of first marriages, and most of the norms for first marriages apply. But when at least one spouse has children from a previous marriage, family life often differs sharply from first marriages. Frequently, as I will show, family members face problems quite unlike those in first marriages—problems for which institutionalized solutions do not exist. And without accepted solutions to their problems, families of remarriages must resolve difficult issues by themselves. As a result, solving everyday problems is sometimes impossible without engendering conflict and confusion among family members.

The complex structure of families of remarriages after divorce which include children from a previous marriage has been noted by others (Bernard 1956; Bohannan 1970; Duberman 1975). These families are expanded in the number of social roles and relationships they possess and also are expanded in space over more than one household. The additional social roles include stepparents, stepchildren, stepsiblings, and the new spouses of noncustodial parents, among others. And the links between the households are the children of previous marriages. These children are commonly in the custody of one parent—usually the mother—but they normally visit the noncustodial parent regularly. Thus they promote communication among the divorced parents, the new stepparent, and the noncustodial parent's new spouse.

Family relationships can be quite complex, because the new kin in a remarriage after divorce do not, in general, replace the kin from the first marriage as they do in a remarriage after widowhood. Rather, they add to the existing kin (Fast and Cain 1966). But this complexity alone does not necessarily imply that problems of family unity will develop. While families of remarriages may appear complicated to Americans, there are many societies in which complicated kinship rules and family patterns coexist with a functioning, stable family system (Bohannan 1963, Fox 1967).

In most of these societies, however, familial roles and relationships are well defined. Family life may seem complex to Westerners, but activity is regulated by established patterns of behavior. The central difference, then, between families of remarriages in the United States and complicated family situations in other societies is the lack of institutionalized social regulation of remarried life in this country. Our society, oriented toward first marriages, provides little guidance on problems peculiar to remarriages, especially remarriages after divorce.

In order to illustrate the incomplete institutionalization of remarriage and its consequences for family life, let us examine two of the major institutions in society: language and the law. "Language," Gerth and Mills (1953, p. 305) wrote, "is necessary to the operations of institutions. For the symbols used in institutions coordinate the roles that compose them, and justify the enactment of these roles by the members of the institution." Where no adequate terms exist for an important social role, the institutional support for this role is deficient, and general acceptance of the role as a legitimate pattern of activity is questionable.

Consider English terms for the roles peculiar to remarriage after divorce. The term "stepparent," as Bohannan (1970) has observed, originally meant a person who replaced a dead parent, not a person who was an additional parent. And the negative connotations of the "stepparent," especially the "stepmother," are well known (Bernard 1956; Smith 1953). Yet there are no other terms in use. In some situations, no term exists for a child to use in addressing a stepparent. If the child calls her mother "mom," for example, what should she call her stepmother? This lack of appropriate terms for parents in remarriages after divorce can have negative consequences for family functioning. In one family I interviewed, the wife's children wanted to call their stepfather "dad," but the stepfather's own children, who also lived in the household, refused to allow this usage. To them, sharing the term "dad" represented a threat to their claim on their father's attention and affection. The dispute caused bad feelings, and it impaired the father's ability to act as a parent to all the children in the household.

For more extended relationships, the lack of appropriate terms is even more acute. At least the word "stepparent," however inadequte, has a widely accepted meaning. But there is no term a child living with his mother can use to describe his relationship to the woman his father remarried after he divorced the child's mother. And, not surprisingly, the rights and duties of the child and this woman toward each other are unclear. Nor is the problem limited to kinship terms. Suppose a child's parents both remarry and he alternates between their households under a joint custody arrangement. Where, then, is his "home"? And who are the members of his "family"? These linguistic inadequacies correspond to the absence of widely accepted definitions for many of the roles and relationships in families of remarriage. The absence of proper terms is both a symptom and a cause of some of the problems of remarried life.

As for the law, it is both a means of social control and an indicator of accepted patterns of behavior. It was to the law, for instance, that Durkheim turned for evidence on the forms of social solidarity. When we examine family law, we find a set of traditional guidelines, based on precedent, which define the rights and duties of family members. But as Weitzman (1974) has shown, implicit in the precedents is the assumption that the marriage in question is a first marriage. For example, Weitzman found no provisions for several problems of remarriage, such as balancing the financial obligations of husbands to their spouses and children from current and previous marriages, defining the wife's obligations to husbands and children from the new and the old marriages, and reconciling the competing claims of current and ex-spouses for shares of the estate of a deceased spouse.

Legal regulations concerning incest and consanguineal marriage are also inadequate for families of remarriages. In all states marriage and sexual relations are prohibited between persons closely related by blood, but in many states these restrictions do not cover sexual relations or marriage between other family members in a remarriage—between a stepmother and a stepson, for example, or between two stepchildren (Goldstein and Katz 1965). Mead (1970), among others, has argued that incest taboos serve the important function of allowing children to develop affection for and identification with other family members without the risk of sexual exploitation. She suggested that current beliefs about incest—as embodied in law and social norms—fail to provide adequate security and protection for children in households of remarriage.[3]

The law, then, ignores the special problems of families of remarriages after divorce. It assumes, for the most part, that remarriages are similar to first marriages. Families of remarriages after divorce, consequently, often must deal with problems such as financial obligations or sexual relations without legal regulations or clear legal precedent. The law, like the language, offers incomplete institutional support to families of remarriages.

In addition, other customs and conventions of family life are deficient when applied to remarriages after divorce. Stepparents, for example, have difficulty determining their proper disciplinary relationship to stepchildren. One woman I interviewed, determined not to show favoritism toward her own children, disciplined them more harshly than her stepchildren. Other couples who had

---

[3]Bernard (1956) noted this problem in the preface to the reprinted edition of her book on remarriage. "Institutional patterns," she wrote, "are needed to help remarried parents establish relationships with one another conducive to the protection of their children."

children from the wife's previous marriage reported that the stepfather had difficulty establishing himself as a disciplinarian in the household. Fast and Cain (1966), in a study of about 50 case records from child-guidance settings, noted many uncertainties among stepparents about appropriate role behavior. They theorized that the uncertainties derived from the sharing of the role of parent between the stepparent and the noncustodial, biological parent. Years ago, when most remarriages took place after widowhood, this sharing did not exist. Now, even though most remarriages follow divorce, generally accepted guidelines for sharing parenthood still have not emerged.

There is other evidence consistent with the idea that the incomplete institutionalization of remarriage after divorce may underlie the difficulties of families of remarriages. Becker et al. (1976) analyzed the Survey of Economic Opportunity, a nationwide study of approximately 30,000 households. As I mentioned above, they found that the presence of children from a previous marriage increased the probability of divorce for women in remarriages, while the presence of children from the new marriage reduced the probability of divorce. This is as we would expect, since children from a previous marriage expand the family across households and complicate the structure of family roles and relationships. But children born into the new marriage bring none of these complications. Consequently, only children from a previous marriage should add to the special problems of families of remarriages.[4]

In addition, Goetting (1978a, 1978b) studies the attitudes of remarried people toward relationships among adults who are associated by broken marital ties, such as ex-spouses and the people ex-spouses remarry. Bohannan (1970) has called these people "quasi-kin." Goetting presented hypothetical situations involving the behavior of quasi-kin to 90 remarried men and 90 remarried women who were white, previously divorced, and who had children from previous marriages. The subjects were asked to approve, disapprove, or express indifference about the behavior in each situation. Goetting then arbitrarily decided that the respondents reached "consensus" on a given situation if any of the three possible response categories received more than half of all responses. But even by this lenient definition, consensus was not reached on the proper behavior in most of the hypothetical situations. For example, in situations involving conversations between a person's present spouse and his or her ex-spouse, the only consensus of the respondents was that the pair should say "hello." Beyond that, there was no consensus on whether they should engage in polite conversation in public places or on the telephone or

---

[4]In an earlier paper (Cherlin 1977), I found that children affected the probability that a woman in a first marriage or remarriage would divorce only when the children were of preschool age. But the National Longitudinal Surveys of Mature Women, from which this analysis was drawn, contained no information about whether the children of remarried wives were from the woman's previous or current marriage. Since the Becker et al. (1976) results showed that this distinction is crucial, we cannot draw any relevant inferences about children and remarriage from my earlier study.

whether the ex-spouse should be invited into the new spouse's home while waiting to pick up his or her children. Since meetings of various quasi-kin must occur regularly in the lives of most respondents, their disagreement is indicative of their own confusion about how to act in common family situations.

Still, there are many aspects of remarried life which are similar to life in first marriages, and these are subject to established rules of behavior. Even some of the unique aspects of remarriage may be regulated by social norms—such as the norms concerning the size and nature of wedding ceremonies in remarriages (Hollingshead 1952). Furthermore, as Goode (1956) noted, remarriage is itself an institutional solution to the ambiguous status of the divorced (and not remarried) parent. But the day-to-day life of remarried adults and their children also includes many problems for which there are no institutionalized solutions. And since members of a household of remarriage often have competing or conflicting interests (Bernard 1956), the lack of consensual solutions can make these problems more serious than they otherwise would be. One anthropologist, noting the lack of relevant social norms, wrote, "the present situation approaches chaos, with each individual set of families having to work out its own destiny without any realistic guidelines" (Bohannan 1970, p. 137).

Discussion and Suggestions for Research

The lack of institutionalized support for remarriage after divorce from language, the law, and custom is apparent. But when institutional support for family life exists, we take it for granted. People in first marriages rarely stop to notice that a full set of kinship terms exists, that the law regulates their relationships, or that custom dictates much of their behavior toward spouses and children. Because they pay little attention to it, the institutional nature of everyday life in first marriages can be easily underestimated. But such support contributes to the unity of first marriages despite the decline of the patriarch, who was the agent of social control in past time. Institutional guidelines become manifest not only through the transmission of social pressure by a family head but also through the general acceptance of certain habitual behavior patterns as typical of family life. Since this latter process is an ongoing characteristic of social life, the pure "companionship" family—which, in fairness, Burgess and Locke defined only as an ideal type—will never emerge. We have seen this by examining the contrasting case of remarriage after divorce. In this type of marriage, institutional support is noticeably lacking in several respects, and this deficiency has direct consequences for proper family functioning. I have tried to show how the incomplete institutionalization of remarriage after divorce makes the maintenance of family unity more difficult.

One of the first tasks for future research on remarriage is to establish some basic social demographic facts: what proportion of remarried couples have children present from a previous marriage, what proportion have children present from the remarriage, how many children visit noncustodial parents, how frequent these visits are, and so on. As I mentioned, there is no reliable information on these questions now. The U. S. Bureau of the Census, for example, has not discriminiated in most of its surveys between parents and stepparents or between children and stepchildren. Yet until figures are available, we can only guess at the number of families which face potential difficulties because of complex living arrangements.

And if we reinterviewed families of remarriage some time after obtaining this information from them, we could begin to test the importance of institutional support for family unity. It follows from the argument advanced here that the more complex the family's situation—the more quasi-kin who live nearby, the more frequently adults and children interact with quasi-kin, the more likely each remarried spouse is to have children from a previous marriage —the more serious becomes the lack of institutional guidelines. Thus, adults in remarriages with a more complex structure should be more likely to divorce or separate in the future, other things being equal. Also, a more complex structure might increase the financial strain on family members, so their earnings and financial obligations should be carefully assessed.

But beyond collecting this fundamental information, we need to discover, by a variety of means, what norms are emerging concerning remarriage and how they emerge. Content analyses of literature, for example, or close study of changes in the language and the law may be illuminating. Just in the past few years, discussion groups, adult education courses, newsletters, and self-help books for remarried parents have proliferated. Whether these developments are central to the instutionalization of remarriage remains to be seen, but they represent possible sources of information about institutionalization which should be monitored. In addition, detailed ethnographic studies could allow us to uncover emerging patterns of institutionalization among families of remarriages.

And in all these investigations of the institutionalization of remarried life, we must develop a perspective different from that of traditional family research. In much past research—starting with the work of Burgess and others —family sociologists have been concerned primarily with the interpersonal relations of family members, especially of husbands and wives (Lasch 1977). But sociologists' theories—and their research strategies—have assumed, for the most part, that interpersonal relations in families can be accounted for without many references to social institutions. Thus, Burgess and Locke (1945) popularized the notion of the companionship family, whose stability depended largely on what went on within the household. And Locke (1951) measured marital adjustment through a questionnaire which focused largely on such personal characteristics as adaptability and sociability. Yet in order to understand family life—whether in first marriages or remarriages—we must explicitly consider the influences of social institutions on husbands and wives and on parents and children.

We need to know what the institutional links are between family and society which transmit social norms about everyday behavior. That is, we need to know exactly how patterns of family behavior come to be accepted and how proper solutions for family problems come to be taken for granted. And the recent rise in the number of remarriages after divorce may provide us with a natural laboratory for observing this process of institutionalization. As remarriage after divorce becomes more common, remarried parents and their children probably will generate standards of conduct in conjunction with the larger society. By observing these developments, we can improve our understanding of the sources of unity in married—and remarried—life.

References

Ariès, Philippe. 1962. *Centuries of Childhood.* New York: Knopf.

Becker, G., E. Landes, and R. Michael. 1976 "Economics of Marital Instability." Working Paper no. 153. Stanford, Calif.: National Bureau of Economic Research.

Berger, Peter L., and Thomas Luckmann. 1966. *The Social Construction of Reality.* New York: Doubleday.

Bergler, Edmund. 1948. *Divorce Won't Help.* New York: Harper & Bros.

Bernard, Jessie. 1956. *Remarriage.* New York: Dryden.

Blood, Robert O., and Donald M. Wolfe. 1960. *Husbands and Wives.* New York: Free Press.

Bohannan, Paul. 1963 *Social Anthropology.* New York: Holt, Rinehart & Winston.

———. 1970. "Divorce Chains, Households of Remarriage, and Multiple Divorces." Pp. 127–39 in *Divorce and After,* edited by Paul Bohannan. New York: Doubleday.

Bradburn, Norman, and David Caplovitz. 1965 *Reports on Happiness.* Chicago: Aldine.

Bumpass, L. L., and A. Sweet. 1972. "Differentials in Marital Instability: 1970." *American Sociological Review* 37 (December): 754–66.

Burgess, Ernest W., and Harvey J. Locke. 1945 *The Family: From Institution to Companionship.* New York: American.

Campbell, Angus, Philip E. Converse, and Willard L. Rodgers. 1976 *The Quality of American Life.* New York: Russell Sage.

Cherlin, A. 1977. "The Effects of Children on Marital Dissolution." *Demography* 14 (August): 265–72.

Demos, John. 1970. *A Little Commonwealth: Family Life in Plymouth Colony.* New York: Oxford University Press.

Duberman, Lucile. 1975 *The Reconstructed Family.* Chicago: Nelson-Hall.

Dyer, W. G., and D. Urban. 1958. "The Institutionalization of Equalitarian Family Norms." *Journal of Marriage and Family Living* 20 (February): 53–58.

Fast, I., and A. C. Cain. 1966. "The Stepparent Role: Potential for Disturbances in Family Functioning." *American Journal of Orthopsychiatry* 36 (April): 485–91.

Fox, Robin. 1967. *Kinship and Marriage.* Baltimore: Penguin.

Gerth, Hans, and C. Wright Mills. 1953. *Character and Social Structure.* New York: Harcourt, Brace & Co.

Glenn, N. 1975. "The Contribution of Marriage to the Psychological Well-Being of Males and Females." *Journal of Marriage and the Family* 37 (August): 594–601.

Glenn, N., and C. Weaver. 1977. "The Marital Happiness of Remarried Divorced Persons." *Journal of Marriage and the Family* 39 (May): 331–37.

Goetting, Ann. 1978a. "The Normative Integration of the Former Spouse Relationship." Paper presented at the annual meeting of the American Sociological Association, San Francisco, September 4–8.

———.1978b. "The Normative Integration of Two Divorce Chain Relationships." Paper presented at the annual meeting of the Southwestern Sociological Association, Houston, April 12–15.

Goldstein, Joseph, and Jay Katz. 1965. *The Family and the Law.* New York: Free Press.

Goode, William J. 1956. *Women in Divorce.* New York: Free Press.

Hoffman, S. 1977. "Marital Instability and the Economic Status of Women." *Demography* 14 (February): 67–76.

Hollingshead, A. B. 1952. "Marital Status and Wedding Behavior." *Marriage and Family Living* (November), pp. 308–11.

Jacobson, Paul H. 1959. *American Marriage and Divorce.* New York: Rinehart.

Lasch, Christopher. 1977. *Haven in a Heartless World: The Family Besieged.* New York: Basic.

Locke, Harvey J. 1951 *Predicting Adjustment in Marriage: A comparison of a Divorced and a Happily Married Group.* New York: Holt.

McCarthy, J. F. 1977. "A Comparison of Dissolution of First and Second Marriages." Paper presented at the 1977 annual meeting of the Population Association of America, St. Louis, April 21–23.

Mead, M. 1970. "Anomalies in American Postdivorce Relationships." P. 107–25 in *Divorce and After,* edited by Paul Bohannan. New York: Doubleday.

Monahan, T. P. 1958. "The Changing Nature and Instability of Remarriages." *Eugenics Quarterly* 5:73–85.

Norton, A. J., and P. C. Glick. 1976. "Marital Instability: Past, Present, and Future." *Journal of Social Issues* 32 (Winter): 5–20.

Nye, F. Ivan, and Felix M. Berardo. 1973. *The Family: Its Structure and Interaction.* New York: Macmillan.

Overall, J. E. 1971. "Associations between Marital History and the Nature of Manifest Psychopathology." *Journal of Abnormal Psychology* 78 (2): 213–21.

Renne, K. S. 1971. "Health and Marital Experience in an Urban Population." *Journal of Marriage and the Family* 33 (May): 338–50.

Safilios-Rothschild, Constantina. 1970. "The Study of Family Power Structure: A Review 1960–1969." *Journal of Marriage and the Family* 32 (November): 539–52.

Shorter, Edward. 1975. *The Making of the Modern Family.* New York: Basic.

Smith, William C. 1953. *The Stepchild.* Chicago: University of Chicago Press.

U.S. Bureau of the Census. 1973 *U.S. Census of the Population: 1970. Persons by Family Characteristics.* Final Report PC(2)-4B. Washington, D.C.: Government Printing Office.

———. 1976. *Number, Timing, and Duration of Marriages and Divorces in the United States: June 1975.* Current Population Reports, Series P-20, No. 297. Washington, D.C.: Government Printing Office.

U.S. National Center for Health Statistics. 1953. *Vital Statistics of the United States, 1950.* Vol 2. *Marriage, Divorce, Natality, Fetal Mortality, and Infant Mortality Data.* Washington, D.C.: Government Printing Office.

———. 1977. *Vital Statistic Report. Advance Report. Final Marriage Statistics, 1975.* Washington, D.C.: Government Printing Office.

Weitzman, L. J. 1974. "Legal Regulation of Marriage: Tradition and Change." *California Law Review* 62:1169–1288.

Young, Michael, and Peter Wilmott. 1973. *The Symmetrical Family.* New York: Pantheon.

4

Parents and Children

Introduction

No aspect of childhood seems more natural, universal, and changeless than the relations between parents and children. Social scientists have traditionally looked at parent-child relations under the heading of *socialization,* a process by which new generations replace their elders. Children are born, socialized, and take their place in the social order until they die; new children are born, and the process is repeated. The obedient child, in this conception, is the forerunner of the good citizen. The parents are cast in the role of upholders of social order and civilization itself.

A few observers have seen the fallacy in this idealization of parenthood. In 1858 Herbert Spencer noted:

> Judging by educational theories, men and women are entirely transfigured in their relations to offspring. The citizens we do business with, the people we meet in the world, we know to be very imperfect creatures. In the daily scandals, in the quarrels of friends, in bankruptcy disclosures, in lawsuits, in police reports, we have constantly thrust before us the pervading selfishness, dishonesty, brutality. Yet when we criticize nursery management and canvass the misbehavior of juveniles, we habitually take for granted that these culpable persons are free from moral delinquency in the treatment of boys and girls. (p. 87)

Concepts of socialization also imply images of what children are like. Two images of the child have prevailed in Western culture. One is the child as angel, all sweetness and innocence, to be protected from the sexuality and workaday concerns of the adult world. This image has always coexisted with actual conditions of great brutality and neglect of children. The opposing image is found in both Calvinistic Protestantism and early psychoanalysis: It is the child as devil, imp of darkness, seething cauldron of murderous and sexual impulses, a beast who must be tamed. This image has been forcefully portrayed in fiction and films such as *Lord of the Flies* and *The Omen.*

Both images of the child share the assumption that socialization is something done to children, that they learn to be reasonable, moral, and competent from the outside as a result of adult guidance. As Jerome Kagan points out in his selection in chapter 9 these traditional views of child development contain several myths or, as Kagan puts it, prejudices. One of these is the assumption that "each day the child is being seriously influenced by the actions of others, and that the relationship between these social experiences (say, being spanked for stealing money) and his future behavior, motivational, and moral development is absolute, fixed, and knowable." Another questionable assumption is that there is an ideal, best adult, as well as a set of parental practices that will produce this ideal adult.

Such assumptions not only overlook the lack of social consensus concerning what the ideal adult is—business executive, artist, politician, teacher, revolutionary—they also overlook the child's role in his or her own development. The creative side of human growth has been most forcefully stated and experimentally documented in the work of Jean Piaget. According to his view the child is an active participant in the attainment of logical and moral competence rather than the passive recipient of rules and rewards from the outside. The infant banging his cup, throwing toys out of his crib, or fitting objects into each other is actually performing experiments in physics, learning about the nature of matter. Later, when he learns to communicate in words, he will also learn the rules of logic and morality. As Roger Brown writes:

> The mature persons with whom a child interacts behave in accordance with such systems of norms or rules as are called logic, mathematics, language, morality, aesthetics . . . and so on. For the most part these systems have not been explicitly formulated by the adults whose behavior is governed by them and they will not be explicitly formulated by the child who acquires them. This process is not a simple "passing over" of the systems from one generation to another. What each child extracts at a given age is a function of his idiosyncratic experience and of his present intellectual capabilities. The systems governing the child change as he grows older and they need not, in the end, simply reproduce the rules that prevail in his society. The outcome can be unique and sometimes revolutionary. (1965, p. 193)

Child Abuse

Another central theme in the traditional view was harmony between needs of children, parents, and society. The child's need for love and care were assumed to be matched by complementary needs of parents—especially mothers—to nurture them. Society, for its part, supported parental roles because of required further population. But parental love is not a social universal. Neither families nor societies always require or want the children born to them. Indeed, as noted earlier, infanticide has been a traditional means of controlling population, not only in "primitive" societies but in our own Western culture until the invention of reliable contraception. Recent historical studies show that in the allocation of scarce resources, European society preferred adults to children.

Recent findings by sociologists and psychiatrists have revealed a greater amount of physical and psychological conflict in families than had been recognized. For example, many researchers in the field of child abuse point out that such incidents are a potential for many parents, given a sufficient degree of environmental strain. Most child abusers are not pathological monsters, and the line between normal punishment and child abuse is sometimes hard to draw. In sum then, the traditional social science view of parenthood has accepted parents too often as nurturers and socializers of children and too rarely as adults whose own needs may come into conflict with those of their children.

In one of the leading studies on the battered child syndrome (Steele and Pollack 1968, p. 104), the sample consisted of parents of infants and children under three who had been significantly abused by their parents, short of direct murder. Although these children had come to the attention of hospitals, doctors, or the police, their parents seemed a cross section of the population. Such attributes as social class, occupation, IQ, or urban-rural residence did not set them apart. Nor did the researchers find any particular psychopathology or character type. What they did find was a pattern of child rearing that exaggerated the normal. They conclude:

> There seems to be an unbroken spectrum of parental action towards children ranging from the breaking of bones and the fracturing of skulls through severe bruising, through severe spanking and on to mild "reminder" pats on the bottom. To be aware of this, one has only to look at the families of one's friends and neighbors, to look and listen to the parent-child interactions at the playground and the supermarket, or even to recall how one raised one's own children or how one was raised oneself. The amount of yelling, scolding, slapping, punching, hitting, and yanking acted out by parents on very small children is almost shocking. (Steele and Pollack 1968, p. 104)

Although the idea of the battered child thus suggests a physical phenomenon, child abuse is, as Newberger and Bourne point out in chapter 8, a social phenomenon created and shaped through the definitions applied by clinicians and other professionals—often more to the advantage of their own interests than to the benefit of the clients they are supposed to serve. Children are frequently battered in our society. Reprehensible battering or "abuse" is a label, perhaps well deserved, but one that varies with such factors as social class, ethnicity, and professional intervention.

The problem is not simply that parents are sadistic. The modern family, especially in its more isolated version, gives parents nearly absolute power over children at the same time that it makes parenthood more burdensome. Jules Henry states the problem succinctly as follows:

> Pinched off alone in one's own house, shielded from critical eyes, one can be as irrational as one pleases with one's children as long as severe damage does not attract the attention of the police.

The realities of modern parenthood, especially motherhood, are considerably less idyllic than the myth portrays them. The woman who has invested the most in the culturally prescribed maternal role is most likely to be devastated by the natural course of the maternal role: the adulthood of her children. As

Alice Rossi points out in her selection in chapter 8, the transition to the role of parent is usually experienced as a life crisis. Even "good" mothers may be overwhelmed at times by the relentless demands of young children and be horrified by the rage their children are capable of stirring up in them. For battering parents, the myth that children are supposed to be fulfilling and gratifying has dangerous effects; these parents blame their own children for not living up to the mythical standards they suppose other children meet.

Maternal Deprivation

If the sentimental model of the family tends to place child beaters out in the moral limbo reserved for sex fiends and other "degenerates," while denying the danger to children from ordinary parents, it also exaggerates in an opposite but perhaps equal direction another threat to children, that of maternal deprivation.

The first studies of children placed in institutions early in life revealed many cases of irreparable emotional, intellectual, and, in some cases, physical damage. The concept of maternal deprivation passed into the popular lore on child rearing to mean that any separation from the mother must have devastating effects on the child. All separations, regardless of how long they lasted and for what reasons and without regard to what happened to the child in the interim, tended to be lumped together. One of the consequences has been large-scale inattention to the possibilities of enriching children's lives through day-care centers, supervised playgrounds, and similar institutions that relieve the strain of both parenthood and childhood.

Another consequence has been inattention to exploring the notion that men, as well as women, enjoy the capacity to be effective nurturers of their children. Robert A. Fein argues, in his article reprinted in chapter 8, that social science has been lagging in its understanding of the nurturant possibilities of fatherhood and therefore has failed to make some potentially positive contributions to social policies affecting families in the United States.

In the long run, however, we must understand that the power of parents to influence their children's lives is limited in at least two fundamental ways. The first involves interactional limitations. Jane Loevinger (1959) argues, for example, that in spite of the physical power of the parent over the child, no parent can ensure that the child will learn precisely what the parent wants him or her to learn. Even the professional knowledge of the psychiatrist or the child-development expert does not help; the parent-child relationship inevitably involves a conflict of interest and impulse.

Indeed, the vast literature advising parents how to rear their children has generated untold guilt and anxiety. It suggests that the normal state of family life is quiet and harmonious, and any tensions between parents and children or unhappiness in a child are the parents' fault.

Kenneth Keniston and the Carnegie Council on Children, in the selection reprinted in chapter 9, stress the second limitation on parental power over children. They argue that families are not the self-sufficient building blocks of society they have often been portrayed as being. On the contrary, they see the family not as the independent movers and shapers of the society but as *society's outcome,* "deeply influenced by broad social and economic forces over which they have little control."

Keniston's view is surely justified by broad historical evidence. There is a tendency to think that the concept of childhood and the relations between parents and children are universal and unchanging. Yet the historical evidence suggests that there have been profound changes in the conceptions of childhood and adulthood, in the psychological relations between children and parents, and in the stages of the life span. Thus, as society changes, so will the quality of relations between parents and children who live in that society.

Chapter 8

Parenthood

Transition to Parenthood

Alice S. Rossi

From Child to Parent: An Example

What is unique about this perspective on parenthood is the focus on the adult parent rather than the child. Until quite recent years, concern in the behavioral sciences with the parent-child relationship has been confined almost exclusively to the child. . . .

The very different order of questions which emerge when the parent replaces the child as the primary focus of analytic attention can best be shown with an illustration. Let us take, for our example, the point Benedek makes that the child's need for mothering is *absolute* while the need of an adult woman to mother is *relative*. From a concern for the child, this discrepancy in need leads to an analysis of the impact on the child of separation from the mother or inadequacy of mothering. Family systems that provide numerous adults to care for the young child can make up for this discrepancy in need between mother and child, which may be why ethnographic accounts give little evidence of postpartum depression following childbirth in simpler societies. Yet our family system of isolated households, increasingly distant from kinswomen to assist in mothering, requires that new mothers shoulder total responsibility for the infant precisely for that stage of the child's life when his need for mothering is far in excess of the mother's need for the child.

From the perspective of the mother, the question has therefore become: what does maternity deprive her of? Are the intrinsic gratifications of maternity sufficient to compensate for shelving or reducing a woman's involvement in nonfamily interests and social roles? The literature on maternal deprivation cannot answer such questions, because the concept, even in the careful specification Yarrow has given it, has never meant anything but the effect on the child of various kinds of insufficient mothering. Yet what has been seen as a failure

From the *Journal of Marriage and the Family,* 30 (February 1968), pp. 26–39. Copyrighted 1968 by the National Council on Family Relations. Reprinted by permission.

or inadequacy of individual women may in fact be a failure of the society to provide institutionalized substitutes for the extended kin to assist in the care of infants and young children. It may be that the role requirements of maternity in the American family system extract diversified interests and social expectations concerning adult life. Here, as at several points in the course of this paper, familiar problems take on a new and suggestive research dimension when the focus is on the parent rather than the child. . . .

Parsons' analysis of the experience of parenthood as a step in maturation and personality growth does not allow for negative outcome. In this view either parents show little or no positive impact upon themselves of their parental-role experiences, or they show a new level of maturity. Yet many women, whose interests and values made a congenial combination of wifehood and work role, may find that the addition of maternal responsibilities has the consequence of a fundamental and undesired change in both their relationships to their husbands and their involvements outside the family. Still other women, who might have kept a precarious hold on adequate functioning as adults had they *not* become parents, suffer severe retrogression with pregnancy and childbearing, because the reactivation of older unresolved conflicts with their own mothers is not favorably resolved but in fact leads to personality deterioration and the transmission of pathology to their children.

Where cultural pressure is very great to assume a particular adult role, as it is for American women to bear and rear children, latent desire and psychological readiness for parenthood may often be at odds with manifest desire and actual ability to perform adequately as parents. Clinicians and therapists are aware, as perhaps many sociologists are not, that failure, hostility, and destructiveness are as much a part of the family system and the relationships among family members as success, love, and solidarity are. . . .

Role-Cycle Stages

A discussion of the impact of parenthood upon the parent will be assisted by two analytic devices. One is to follow a comparative approach, by asking in what basic structural ways the parental role differs from other primary adult roles. The marital and occupational roles will be used for this comparison. A second device is to specify the phases in the development of a social role. If the total life span may be said to have a cycle, each stage with its unique tasks, then by analogy a role may be said to have a cycle and each stage in that role cycle to have its unique tasks and problems of adjustment. Four broad stages of a role cycle may be specified:

1. Anticipatory Stage

All major adult roles have a long history of anticipatory training for them, since parental and school socialization of children is dedicated precisely to this task of producing the kind of competent adult valued by the culture. For our present purposes, however, a narrower conception of the marital role, pregnancy in the case of the parental role, and the last stages of highly vocationally oriented schooling or on-the-job apprenticeship in the case of an occupational role.

2. Honeymoon Stage

This is the time period immediately following the full assumption of the adult role. The inception of this stage is more easily defined than its termination. In the case of the marital role, the honeymoon stage extends from the marriage ceremony itself through the literal honeymoon and on through an unspecified and individually varying period of time. Raush has caught this stage of the marital role in his description of the "psychic honeymoon": that extended postmarital period when, through close intimacy and joint activity, the couple can explore each other's capacities and limitations. I shall arbitrarily consider the onset of pregnancy as marking the end of the honeymoon stage of the marital role. This stage of the parental role may involve an equivalent psychic honeymoon, that post-childbirth period during which, through intimacy and prolonged contact, an attachment between parent and child is laid down. There is a crucial difference, however, from the marital role in this stage. A woman knows her husband as a unique real person when she enters the honeymoon stage of marriage. A good deal of preparatory adjustment on a firm reality base is possible during the engagement period which is not possible in the equivalent pregnancy period. Fantasy is not corrected by the reality of a specific individual child until the birth of the child. The "quickening" is psychologically of special significance to women precisely because it marks the first evidence of a real baby rather than a purely fantasized one. On this basis alone there is greater interpersonal adjustment and learning during the honeymoon stage of the parental role than of the marital role.

3. Plateau Stage

This is the protracted middle period of a role cycle during which the role is fully exercised. Depending on the specific problem under analysis, one would obviously subdivide this large plateau stage further. For my present purposes it is not necessary to do so, since my focus is on the earlier anticipatory and honeymoon stages of the parental role and the overall impact of parenthood on adults.

4. Disengagement-Termination Stage

This period immediately precedes and includes the actual termination of the role. Marriage ends with the death of the spouse or, just as definitively, with separation and divorce. A unique characteristic of parental-role termination is the fact that it is not closely marked by any specific act but is an attenuated process of termination with little cultural prescription about when the authority and obligations of a parent end. Many parents, however, experience the marriage of the child as a psychological termination of the active parental role.

Unique Features of Parental Role

With this role-cycle suggestion as a broader framework, we can narrow our focus to what are the unique and most salient features of the parental role. In doing so, special attention will be given to two further questions: (1) the impact of social changes over the past few decades in facilitating or complicating the transition to and experience of parenthood and (2) the new interpretations or new research suggested by the focus on the parent rather than the child.

1. Cultural Pressure to Assume the Role

On the level of cultural values, men have no freedom of choice where work is concerned: They must work to secure their status as adult men.

The equivalent for women has been maternity. There is considerable pressure upon the growing girl and young woman to consider maternity necessary for a woman's fulfillment as an individual and to secure her status an an adult.*

This is not to say there are no fluctuations over time in the intensity of the cultural pressure to parenthood. During the depression years of the 1930s, there was more widespread awareness of the economic hardships parenthood can entail, and many demographic experts believe there was a great increase in illegal abortions during those years. Bird has discussed the dread with which a suspected pregnancy was viewed by many American women in the 1930s. Quite a different set of pressures were at work during the 1950s, when the general societal tendency was toward withdrawal from active engagement with the issues of the larger society and a turning in to the gratifications of the private sphere of home and family life. Important in the background were the general affluence of the period and the expanded room and ease of child rearing that go with suburban living. For the past five years, there has been a drop in the birth rate in general, fourth and higher-order births in particular. During this same period there has been increased concern and debate about women's participation in politics and work, with more women now returning to work rather than conceiving the third or fourth child.**

---

*The greater the cultural pressure to assume a given adult social role, the greater will be the tendency for individual negative feelings toward that role to be expressed covertly. Men may complain about a given job, not about working per se, and hence their work dissatisfactions are often displaced to the nonwork sphere, as psychosomatic complaints or irritation and dominance at home. An equivalent displacement for women of the ambivalence many may feel toward maternity is to dissatisfactions with the homemaker role.

**When it is realized that a mean family size of 3.5 would double the population in 40 years, while a mean of 2.5 would yield a stable population in the same period, the social importance of withholding praise for procreative prowess is clear. At the same time, a drop in the birth rate may reduce the number of unwanted babies born, for such a drop would mean more efficient contraceptive usage and a closer correspondence between desired and attained family size.

2. Inception of the Parental Role

The decision to marry and the choice of a mate are voluntary acts of individuals in our family system. Engagements are therefore consciously considered, freely entered, and freely terminated if increased familiarity decreases, rather than increases, intimacy and commitment to the choice. The inception of a pregnancy, unlike the engagement, is not always a voluntary decision, for it may be the unintended consequence of a sexual act that was recreative in intent rather than procreative. Secondly, and again unlike the engagement, the termination of a pregnancy is not socially sanctioned, as shown by current resistance to abortion-law reform.

The implication of this difference is a much higher probability of unwanted pregnancies than of unwanted marriages in our family system. Coupled with the ample clinical evidence of parental rejection and sometimes cruelty to children, it is all the more surprising that there has not been more consistent research attention to the problem of *parental satisfaction,* as there has for long been on *marital satisfaction or work satisfaction.* Only the extreme iceberg tip of the parental satisfaction continuum is clearly demarcated and researched, as in the growing concern with "battered babies." Cultural and psychological resistance to the image of a nonnurturant woman may afflict social scientists as well as the American public.

The timing of a first pregnancy is critical to the manner in which parental responsibilities are joined to the marital relationship. The single most important change over the past few decades is extensive and efficient contraceptive usage, since this has meant for a growing proportion of new marriages, the possibility of and increasing preference for some postponement of childbearing after marriage. When pregnancy was likely to follow shortly after marriage, the major transition point in a woman's life was marriage itself. *This transition point is increasingly the first pregnancy rather than marriage.* It is accepted and increasingly expected that women will work after marriage, while household furnishings are acquired and spouses complete their advanced training or gain a foothold in their work. This provides an early marriage period in which the fact of a wife's employment presses for a greater egalitarian relationship between husband and wife in decision-making, commonality of experience, and sharing of household responsibilities.

The balance between individual autonomy and couple mutuality that develops during the honeymoon stage of such a marriage may be important in establishing a pattern that will later affect the quality of the parent-child relationship and the extent of sex-role segregation of duties between the parents. It is only in the context of a growing egalitarian base to the marital relationship that one could find, as Gavron has, a tendency for parents to establish some barriers between themselves and their children, a marital defense against the institution of parenthood as she describes it. This may eventually replace the typical coalition in more traditional families of mother and children against husband-father. . . .

There is one further significant social change that has important implications for the changed relationship between husband and wife: the increasing departure from an old pattern of role-inception phasing in which the young person first completed his schooling, then established himself in the world of work, then married and began his family. Marriage and parenthood are increasingly taking place *before* the schooling of the husband, and often of the wife, has been completed. An important reason for this trend lies in the fact that, during the same decades in which the average age of physical-sexual maturation has dropped, the average amount of education which young people obtain has been on the increase. Particularly for the college and graduate or professional school population, family roles are often assumed before the degrees needed to enter careers have been obtained. . . .

The major implication of this change is that more men and women are achieving full status in family roles while they are still less than fully adult in status terms in the occupational system. Graduate students are, increasingly, men and women with full family responsibilities. Within the family many more husbands and fathers are still students, often quite dependent on the earnings of their wives to see them through their advanced training. No matter what the couple's desires and preferences are, this fact alone presses for more egalitarian relations between husband and wife, just as the adult family status of graduate students presses for more egalitarian relations between students and faculty.

3. Irrevocability

If marriages do not work out, there is now widespread acceptance of divorce and remarriage as a solution. The same point applies to the work world: we are free to leave an unsatisfactory job and seek another. But once a pregnancy occurs, there is little possibility of undoing the commitment to parenthood implicit in conception except in the rare instance of placing children for adoption. We can have ex-spouses and ex-jobs but not ex-children. This being so, it is scarcely surprising to find marked differences between the relationship of a parent and one child and the relationship of the same parent with another child. If the culture does not permit pregnancy termination, the equivalent to giving up a child is psychological withdrawal on the part of the parent.

This taps an important area in which a focus on the parent rather than the child may contribute a new interpretive dimension to an old problem: the long history of interest, in the social sciences, in differences among children associated with their sex-birth-order position in their sibling set. . . .

Some birth-order research stresses the influence of sibs upon other sibs, as in Koch's finding that second-born boys with an older sister are more feminine than second-born boys with an older brother. A similar sib-influence interpretation is offered in the major common finding of birth-order correlates, that sociability is greater among last-borns and achievement among first-borns. It has been suggested that last-borns use social skills to increase acceptance by their older sibs or are more peer-oriented because they receive less adult stimulation from parents. The tendency of first-borns to greater achievement has been interpreted in a corollary way, as a reflection of early assumption of responsibility for younger sibs, greater adult stimulation during the time the oldest was the only child in the family, and the greater significance of the first-born for the larger kinship network of the family.

Sociologists have shown increasing interest in structural family variables in recent years, a primary variable being family size. . . . The question posed is: what is the effect of growing up in a small family, compared with a large family, that is attributable to this group-size variable? Unfortunately, the theoretical point of departure for sociologists' expectations of the effect of the family-size variables is the Durkheim-Simmel tradition of the differential effect of group size or population density upon members or inhabitants. In the case of the family, however, this overlooks the very important fact that family size is determined by the key figures *within* the group, i.e., the parents. To find that children in small families differ from children in large families is not simply due to the impact of group size upon individual members but to the very different involvement of the parent with the children and to relations between the parents themselves in small versus large families.

An important clue to a new interpretation can be gained by examining family size from the perspective of parental motivation toward having children. A small family is small for one of two primary reasons: either the parents wanted a small family and achieved their desired size, or they wanted a large family but were not able to attain it. In either case, there is a low probability of unwanted children. Indeed, in the latter eventuality they may take particularly great interest in the children they do have. Small families are therefore most likely to contain parents with a strong and positive orientation to each of the children they have. A large family, by contrast, is large either because the parents achieved the size they desired or because they have more children than they in fact wanted. Large families therefore have a higher probability than small families of including unwanted unloved children. Consistent with this are Nye's finding that adolescents in small families have better relations with their parents than those in large families, and Sears and Maccoby's finding that mothers of large families are more restrictive toward their children than mothers of small families.

This also means that last-born children are more likely to be unwanted than first- or middle-born children, particularly in large families. This is consistent with what is known of abortion patterns among married women, who typically resort to abortion only when they have achieved the number of children they want or feel they can afford to have. Only a small proportion of women faced with such unwanted pregnancies actually resort to abortion. *This suggests the possibility that the last-born child's reliance on social skills may be his device for securing the attention and loving involvement of a parent less positively predisposed to him than to his older siblings.*

In developing this interpretation, rather extreme cases have been stressed. Closer to the normal range, of families in which even the last-born child was desired and planned for, there is still another element which may contribute to the greater sociability of the last-born child. Most parents are themselves aware of the greater ease with which they face the care of a third fragile newborn than the first; clearly parental skills and confidence are greater with last-born children than with first-born children. But this does not mean that the attitude of the parent is more positive toward the care of the third child than the first. There is no necessary correlation between skills in an area and enjoyment of that area. Searls found that older homemakers are *more* skillful in domestic tasks but experience *less* enjoyment of them than younger home- makers, pointing to a declining euphoria for a particular role with the passage of time. In the same way, older people rate their marriages as "very happy" less often than younger people do. It is perhaps culturally and psychologically more difficult to face the possibility that women may find less enjoyment of the maternal role with the passage of time, though women themselves know the difference between the romantic expectation concerning child care and the incorporation of the first baby into the household and the more realistic expectation and sharper assessment of their own abilities to do an adequate job of mothering as they face a third confinement. Last-born children may experi- ence not only less verbal stimulation from the parents than first-born children but also less prompt and enthusiastic response to their demands—from feeding and diaper change as infants to requests for stories read at three or a college education at eighteen—simply because the parents experience less intense gratification from the parent role with the third child than they did with the first. The child's response to this might well be to cultivate winning, pleasing manners in early childhood that blossom as charm and sociability in later life, showing both a greater need to be loved and greater pressure to seek approval.

One last point may be appropriately developed at this juncture. Mention was made earlier that for many women the personal outcome of experience in the parent role is not a higher level of maturation but the negative outcome of a depressed sense of self-worth, if not actual personality deterioration. There is considerable evidence that this is more prevalent than we recognize. On a qualitative level, a close reading of the portrait of the working-class wife in Rainwater, Newsom, Komarovsky, Gavron, or Zweig gives little suggestion that maternity has provided these women with opportunities for personal growth and development. So, too, Cohen notes with some surprise that in her sample of middle-class educated couples, as in Pavenstadt's study of lower- income women in Boston, there were more emotional difficulties and lower levels of maturation among multiparous women than primiparous women. On a more extensive sample basis, in Gurin's survey of Americans viewing their mental health, as in Bradburn's reports on happiness, single men are less happy and less active than single women, but among the married respondents the women are unhappier, have more problems, feel inadequate as parents, have a more negative and passive outlook on life, and show a more negative self-image. All of these characteristics increase with age among men. While it may be true, as Gurin argues, that women are more introspective and hence more attuned to the psychological facets of experience than men are, this point does not account for the fact that the things which the women report are all on the negative side; few are on the positive side, indicative of euphoric sensitivity and pleasure. The possibility must be faced, and at some point researched, that women lose ground in personal development and self-esteem during the early and middle years of adulthood, whereas men gain ground in these respects during the same years. The retention of a high level of self-esteem may depend upon the adequacy of earlier preparation for major adult roles: men's training adequately prepares them for their primary adult roles in the occupational system, as it does for those women who opt to participate significantly in the work world. Training in the qualities and skills needed for family roles in contemporary society may be inadequate for both sexes, but the lowering of self-esteem occurs only among women because their primary adult roles are within the family system.

4. Preparation for Parenthood

Four factors may be given special attention on the question of what preparation American couples bring to parenthood.

(a) Paucity of preparation. Our educational system is dedicated to the cognitive development of the young, and our primary teaching approach is the pragmatic one of learning by doing. How much one knows and how well he can apply what he knows are the standards by which the child is judged in school, as the employee is judged at work. The child can learn by doing in such subjects as science, mathematics, art work, or shop, but not in the subjects most relevant to successful family life: sex, home maintenance, child care, interpersonal competence, and empathy. If the home is deficient in training in these areas, the child is left with no preparation for a major segment of his adult life. A doctor facing his first patient in private practice has treated numerous patients under close supervision during his internship, but probably a majority of American mothers approach maternity with no previous child-care experience beyond sporadic baby-sitting, perhaps a course in child psychology, or occasional care of younger siblings.

(b) Limited learning during pregnancy. A second important point makes adjustment to parenthood potentially more stressful than marital adjustment. This is the lack of any realistic training for parenthood during the anticipatory stage of pregnancy. By contrast, during the engagement period preceding marriage, an individual has opportunities to develop the skillls and make the adjustments which ease the transition to marriage. Through discussions of

values and life goals, through sexual experimentation, shared social experiences as an engaged couple with friends and relatives, and planning and furnishing an apartment, the engaged couple can make considerable progress in developing mutuality in advance of the marriage itself. No such headstart is possible in the case of pregnancy. What preparation exists is confined to reading, consultation with friends and parents, discussions between husband and wife, and a minor nesting phase in which a place and the equipment for a baby are prepared in the household.*

(c) Abruptness of transition. Thirdly, the birth of a child is not followed by any gradual taking on of responsibility, as in the case of a professional work role. It is as if the woman shifted from a graduate student to a full professor with little intervening apprenticeship experience of slowly increasing responsibility. The new mother starts out immediately on 24-hour duty, with responsibility for a fragile and mysterious infant totally dependent on her care.

If marital adjustment is more difficult for very young brides than more mature ones, adjustment to motherhood may be even more difficult. A woman can adapt a passive dependence on a husband and still have a successful marriage, but a young mother with strong dependency needs is in for difficulty in maternal adjustment, because the role precludes such dependency. This situation was well described in Cohen's study in a case of a young wife with a background of coed popularity and a passive dependent relationship to her admired and admiring husband, who collapsed into restricted incapacity when faced with the responsibilities of maintaining a home and caring for a child.

(d) Lack of guidelines to successful parenthood. If the central task of parenthood is the rearing of children to become the kind of competent adults valued by the society, then an important question facing any parent is what he or she specifically can do to create such a competent adult. This is where the parent is left with few or no guidelines from the expert. Parents can readily inform themselves concerning the young infant's nutritional, clothing, and medical needs and follow the general prescription that a child needs loving physical contact and emotional support. Such advice may be sufficient to produce a healthy, happy, and well-adjusted preschooler, but adult competency is quite another matter.

In fact, the adults who do "succeed" in American society show a complex of characteristics as children that current experts in child-care would evaluate as "poor" to "bad." Biographies of leading authors and artists, as well as the more rigorous research inquiries of creativity among architects or scientists, do not portray childhoods with characteristics currently endorsed by mental-

---

*During the period when marriage was the critical transition in the adult woman's life rather than pregnancy, a good deal of anticipatory "nesting" behavior took place from the time of conception. Now more women work through a considerable portion of the first pregnancy, and such nesting behavior as exists may be confined to a few shopping expeditions or baby showers, thus adding to the abruptness of the transition and the difficulty of adjustment following the birth of a first child.

health and child-care authorities. Indeed, there is often a predominance of tension in childhood family relations and traumatic loss rather than loving parental support, intense channeling of energy in one area of interest rather than an all-round profile of diverse interests, and social withdrawal and preference for loner activities rather than gregarious sociability. Thus, the stress in current child-rearing advice on a high level of loving support but a low level of discipline or restriction on the behavior of the child—the "developmental" family type as Duvall calls it—is a profile consistent with the focus on mental health, sociability, and adjustment. Yet, the combination of both high support and high authority on the part of parents is most strongly related to the child's sense of responsibility, leadership quality, and achievement level, as found in Bronfenbrenner's studies and that of Mussen and Distler.

Brim points out that we are a long way from being able to say just what parent-role prescriptions have what effect on the adult characteristics of the child. We know even less about how such parental prescriptions should be changed to adapt to changed conceptions of competency in adulthood. In such an ambiguous context, the great interest parents take in school reports on their children or the pediatrician's assessment of the child's developmental progress should be seen as among the few indices parents have of how well *they* are doing as parents.

Research on Fathering: Social Policy and an Emergent Perspective

Robert A. Fein

Discussion of fathering is becoming fashionable. Social scientists, family life educators, clinicians, and parents have begun a long-overdue assessment of the problems and possibilities of relationships between fathers and children. Increasingly, dogmas and conventional wisdoms that have guided and defined those relationships are being scrutinized—and found wanting. Rather than sit by the sidelines or serve as mothers' helpers, men are being urged to participate in the lives of their children, from conception on. And apparently increasing numbers of men are reaching out for more sustaining relationships with the young in their lives.

From the *Journal of Social Issues,* Vol. 34, No. 1 (1978), pp. 122–135. Copyright © 1978 by the Society for the Psychological Study of Social Issues. Reprinted by permission.

Changes in social norms which foster re-evaluation of fathering and relationships between men and children deserve support. But to affect relations between fathers and children (and family lives in general), examination of fathering should occur within the context of social policy, with an appreciation of the multitude of social forces that impinge on the daily behaviors of children and parents. As Kamerman and Kahn (1976) note, American social policies concerning families, which have been implicit and unexamined for years, are being made explicit, with attention given to government and business programs which affect the lives of men, women, and children.

Research concerning fathers has occurred within the context of social stereotypes and norms of American society. This paper begins with a description of the two major perspectives on fathering of the past 25 years, a *traditional* view and a *modern* view, then charts some recent developments in research on fathering which may be seen as constituting an *emergent* perspective. The paper concludes by suggesting that the time is ripe for social scientists to contribute to the development of policies that support family life.

The Traditional Perspective

The major image of the father role in the traditional perspective is the aloof and distant father. English's (1954) description exemplified how the father role was viewed.

> Traditionally, Father has been looked on as the breadwinner. In times past, so much of his time and energy was used in this role that at home he was thought of as taciturn and stern, albeit kind. He was respected but feared by his children who never learned to know him very well. He accepted the fact that he earned the money and Mother cared for the home and raised the children. (p. 323)

In the traditional perspective, a father cares for his children primarily by succeeding in the occupational arena. At home, father's job is to provide for his family so that mother can devote herself to the care of the children (Bowlby, 1951). In this view, men offer companionship and emotional support to their spouses and have relatively little direct involvement with the children. It is worth observing that Bowlby (and others in the psychoanalytic tradition) saw no direct caring role for fathers with infants and young children. Men, while symbolically important to children as close-to-home models of power and authority, were supposed to have little to do with the actual parenting of the young.

In sociology, Parsons and Bales (1955) presented the traditional perspective on men in the family: the instrumental/expressive dichotomy. Men were seen as responsible for the family's relationships with the outside world (primarily the world of work), whereas women were the primary "givers of love" at home.

The traditional perspective on fathering generally conformed to social ideals and realities of the late 1940s and 1950s. Relatively few women were in the paid labor force more than temporarily, and of these women only a small percentage were mothers with young children. Mothers stayed home and fathers went out to work. The husband-breadwinner/wife-homemaker nuclear family was the norm, both in a statistical sense and in the social values of the time.

But there were occasional commentators in the 1950s who noted that norms of American society might change to permit different patterns of childrearing. One such observer was psychiatrist Irene Josselyn:

> As long as men are seen as animated toys, mothers' little helpers, or powerful ogres who alone mete out rewards and punishment, the role of men in the family structure will be boring and/or depreciating. Being frustrated in their attempt to find gratification of their fatherliness, and dissatisfied with the watered-down expression of themselves in the home, they will continue to seek release by diverting their available free energy into channels in which they feel more adequate, with a resultant overinvestment in the gratification they attain from activities away from the home. . . .For the sake of the child and the father we should learn a great deal more of the deeper, subtler meanings of the potentialities in the father-child relationship. (1956, p. 270)

The Modern Perspective

The 1960s saw a major increase in the attention given to fathers by social scientists. Whereas the traditional view of fathering assumed that if men successfully fulfilled head of household, provider roles and mothers carried out their expressive responsibilities, children would be socialized successfully into adult roles, the modern perspective on fathering assumed that children (especially boys) were vulnerable in their psychosocial development (Biller, 1971).

Some 1950s researchers (such as Aberle & Naegele, 1956) had pointed toward the modern perspective by suggesting that fathers inculcated attitudes and behaviors that their children needed for educational and vocational attainment. In the 1960s, spurred by a concern for child development, a number of researchers turned to fathering. For example, John Nash (1965) published "The Father in Contemporary Culture and Current Psychological Literature," in which he concluded that most psychologists had mistakenly assumed that fathers were unimportant in childrearing. Apparently, questioning dominant assumptions about childrearing was risky, for Nash concluded his paper with a "disclaimer":

> This paper is not to be interpreted as an attack on motherhood, but merely as a suggestion that there are other aspects to parent-child relationships than those included in the widely discussed interaction between mother and child. (p. 292)

It is important to note that research within the modern perspective on fathering saw successful child development as a goal of fathering. Three child development outcomes were emphasized: (a) achievement of socially appropriate sex-role identity (masculinity and femininity), (b) academic performance, and (c) moral development (often measured as the absence of delinquency). Researchers attempted to study these outcomes by attending to families without fathers, so-called "father-absent" families. Studies of father-absent children, particularly boys, (reviewed, for example, in Biller, 1974) suggested that children without fathers had significantly more difficulty in the development of sex-role identity, in academic achievement, and in moral development and behavior. Since achievement in these areas was viewed as essential for interpersonal adjustment and life success, boys in father-absent families were considered to be at risk.

Whereas the traditional perspective was supportive of social policies designed to maintain the instrumental/expressive dichotomy, the modern perspective on fathering paralleled attention to policies that appeared to decrease the opportunities for children to interact with their fathers. For example, the Aid to Families with Dependent Children (AFDC) program in most circumstances provided lower benefits for families with an adult male in the household compared to those without an adult male. Concern about the development of children in fatherless families gradually became coupled with concern that AFDC appeared to provide incentives for families to exclude fathers. Such concern was highlighted in debates over the "Moynihan Report" (Rainwater & Yancy, 1967), which argued that black family structure was predominantly matriarchal and was a significant factor in maintaining high levels of black male unemployment. The implication of this debate was that young black males suffered from the absence of male role models (fathers) which contributed to their having higher unemployment levels than other segments of the population.

Concerned about claims of researchers who compared father-absent and father-present families (researchers who suggested that boys from father-absent families were more prone to fail in sex-role identity and academic attainments and were more likely to engage in antisocial behaviors), Herzog and Sudia (1968, 1972, 1974) reviewed the father-absence literature and argued that researchers had not demonstrated that boys in father-absent families were consistently different from boys in father-present families.

Herzog and Sudia's review of the research suggested:

(a) that father absence in itself is not likely to depress school performance;
(b) that there might be a slightly greater likelihood of a boy in a father-absent family engaging in delinquent behavior, but even if statistically more likely, the difference would be so small that it would not be practically important; and
(c) that there is no solid research support for the thesis that a resident father is the only source of masculine identification or that the absence of a father from the home necessarily affects a boy's masculine identity.

They noted that many studies which had reported differences between boys in father-absent and father-present families had failed to account for the power of social class, which when statistically controlled removed the differences.

To account for possible differences in some areas between father-absent and father-present families, Herzog and Sudia suggested that key factors might be the additional stresses on families attendant on the loss of a father rather than the absence of the father per se. Writing about the use of masculinity-femininity scales, the authors noted that these scales "add up to dubious definitions of adequate masculinity and femininity," and that a study of the items suggested that Stalin or Al Capone would look better on the scales than Abraham Lincoln or Martin Luther King (Herzog & Sudia, 1972, pp. 177–178).

While most researchers in the modern perspective dwelt on father-absent families, some attempted to study families with fathers present. Mussen and his colleagues conducted a number of studies which suggested that father's nurturance as perceived by the child was a key factor in the development of sex-role identity (reviewed in Mussen, 1969). However, Mussen and his colleagues did not actually observe fathers. Radin (1972, 1973) suggested that paternal nurturance is an antecedent of intellectual functioning in 4- and 5-year-old boys. While her research dealt only with child outcomes, the attention to cognitive development and her effort to observe father-child interaction were significant advances over previous studies.

While from the point of view of contemporary values the modern perspective on fathering represented an improvement on the traditional (in that the modern view focused attention on child development and on the idea that fathers' behaviors influenced their children), some of the assumptions of the modern perspective have been criticized recently. For example, the nature and desirability of sex-role identity, as measured by masculinity scales, has come under question and attack (Pleck, 1975). Researchers like Kotelchuck (1976) and Pederson (1976) highlight the fact that there were relatively few studies of actual fathering behavior by researchers in the modern perspective.

The Emergent Perspective

What I am calling the *emergent* perspective on fathering proceeds from the notion that men are psychologically able to participate in a full range of parenting behaviors, and furthermore that it may be good both for parents and children if men take active roles in childcare and childrearing. While some research in the emergent perspective focuses on effects on the child, analysis has begun to examine the impact of father-children relationships on all members of the family. Researchers are exploring the idea that children's lives are enhanced by the opportunity to develop and sustain relationships with adults of both sexes. Issues of adult development are under consideration, including the idea that opportunity to care for others, including and especially children, can be a major factor in adult well-being.

The emergent perspective on fathering is androgynous in assuming that the only parenting behaviors from which men are necessarily excluded by virtue of gender are gestation and lactation. Arguments suggesting that men are inherently limited in child-rearing capacity have drawn on studies of infrahuman animal species which suggested that parenting behaviors by males are rare. Howells (1971), reviewing these data, suggests that "the main lesson to be found from the study of the care given to young animals is that nature is flexible" (p. 128). There are examples of male animal behavior which can be seen as parental and nurturant. For one, the male stickleback builds a nest, receives eggs from females, fertilizes them, cares for them, and brings up the young. The males of some catfish carry eggs in their mouths until they hatch; "when danger threatens, *he* holds his mouth open so that the frightened youngsters can dash into it to safety" (Howells, 1971, p. 130). Data from infrahuman animal species can refute biologically-based arguments of major inherent limitations in human male parenting capabilities.

In psychology, innovative research on fathering is developing in five areas:

(a) fathers' experience before, during, and after the birth of children;
(b) fathers' ties with newborns and infants;
(c) the development and nature of bonds between young children and fathers;
(d) fathers in nontraditional childcare arrangements; and
(e) effects of parenting experiences on fathers.

While there are overlaps in these categories, each contributes an important focus to the development of the emergent perspective.

Entering Parenthood

Several studies in the 1970s have employed models of male parenting that assume that men are able to participate in pregnancy and childbirth. Influenced by media accounts of men who participated in delivery and by the popularity of childbirth education programs (Wapner, 1976), researchers have compared experiences of men who participated in childbirth education courses with men who did not and have described experiences of men who shared labor and delivery experiences with their wives. Cronenwett and Newmark (1974) gave a questionnaire to 152 fathers and found that fathers who attended childbirth preparation classes and/or the birth rated their overall experience during childbirth and the experience of their wives significantly higher than other men. Interestingly, there were no differences on infant-related items reported between fathers who attended classes and/or the birth and men who did not. Fein (1976) found that effective postpartum adjustment in men was related to development of a coherent fathering role. Interviews with 30 middle-income couples suggested that neither the women nor the men were particularly well prepared for the practical realities of parenting, with men's lack of experience in part a result of social attitudes that have assumed that boys and young men have little interest or aptitude to learn about children and childcare. Reiber (1976) studied nine couples before and after the birth of a child and noted that the fathers were interested in being nurturers and the men appeared to be involved in caring for their babies to the extent that their wives allowed them to be. Manion (1977), in a correlational study of 45 first-time fathers several weeks after the birth of their children, found that although fathers were seldom included in postpartum hospital instruction about child-care, men did become involved in providing care for their infants. Men who remembered their parents as nurturant tended to be more active in childcare than other men. Fathers who had a higher degree of involvement in the birth had a higher degree of involvement in childcare activities.

Ties with Newborns and Infants

Parke and Savin (1976) recently summarized the traditional view of fathers' roles in infancy:

1. Fathers are uninterested in and uninvolved with newborn infants.
2. Fathers are less nurturant toward infants than mothers.
3. Fathers prefer noncaretaking roles and leave the caretaking up to mothers.
4. Fathers are less competent than mothers to care for newborn infants. (p. 365)

Research about father-infant relationships is questioning the credibility of these assumptions. Greenberg and Morris (1974) gave a written questionnaire to 30 first-time fathers who had either attended the births of their babies or who had been shown their babies shortly after birth. In addition, a series of interviews was conducted with half the sample. The researchers noted that fathers enjoyed looking at their babies, reported a desire for and pleasure in physical contact with the newborns, and were aware of unique features and characteristics of their babies. Many fathers were surprised at the impact their contact with the baby had on them. Greenberg and Morris suggested that fathers begin developing a bond to their newborns within three days after birth and called this phenomenon "engrossment."

Parke and O'Leary (1976) observed men interacting with their newborns. Fathers were seen to be active with their infants, being more likely to touch and rock their infants when alone than with the mother. In one of their studies, the researchers compared fathers of different social classes and found that "high interaction fathering" occurred across socioeconomic class lines. Parke and O'Leary suggested that early contact with infants may be important for the development of father-child bonds, raising questions about the thresholds of paternal responsivity to infants.

Bonds Between Young Children and Fathers

Given the power and primacy of cultural assumptions about mother-child bonds, only in the last decade have researchers begun to look carefully at the relationships men establish with their young children. Yogman, Dixon, Tronick, Adamson, Als, and Brazelton (Note 1) found that infants responded differentially to their fathers compared to strangers by four weeks of age, even when the fathers were not their primary caretakers. Kotelchuck (Note 2, 1976), in an observational study of 144 children, found that children responded to both fathers and mothers more than to strangers. While the child's parental preferences at 18 months of age were strongly related to parental involvement in the home, Kotelchuck concluded that the overall lack of mother-father differences in terms of children's observed behaviors suggested that neither the quality of parent-child interaction nor specific caretaking practices are critical issues in formation of a relationship. His study strongly suggested that young children form significant relationships with their fathers.

Cohen and Campos (1974), attempting to measure both attachment behaviors of young children and distress indicators, concluded that fathers were more powerful elicitors of attachment behaviors than strangers, but that mothers were superior to fathers as elicitors of these behaviors. There were no differences between fathers and mothers in eliciting distress vocalization. Lamb and Lamb (1976), reviewing the literature on the development of father-child bonds, concluded that fathers are salient figures in the lives of their children from infancy on. These researchers suggested that the family should be seen as a complex system in which all persons (including infants) influence and are affected by all.

Nontraditional Childcare Arrangements

Responding to changes in family and marital patterns in the United States, a number of social scientists have begun to study fathers who parent outside of the context of the husband-provider/wife-homemaker nuclear family. Separated fathers, widowed fathers, divorced fathers, unmarried fathers, adopting fathers, and stepfathers are recent subjects of study.

Hetherington, Cox, and Cox (1976) studied 96 families, comparing relationships in divorced families with those in intact families. Two years after their divorces, fathers in this group were seen as influencing their children significantly less than the fathers in intact families. Noting that divorced fathers in their sample generally left the home, the children remaining with the mother, Hetherington et al. report that divorced men complained of being rootless, with separation inducing great feelings of loss, particularly with regard to feelings about their children.

Finkelstein-Keshet (1977), studying the coping strategies of fathers following marital separation, found that for some men the opportunity to care for their children became the basis of a major life reorganization. Levine (1976), in a book about varieties of fathering, reported on single men who adopt children, men who share childcare on an equal basis with their wives, and men who become primary parents of their children. His study suggested that a wide variety of fathering roles is practiced in the United States. Rallings (1976), noting that step-fathering has been an understudied phenomenon, suggested that since 15% of all children under age 18 were living with a divorced parent (in 1970), and since courts were more likely to give custody to a mother than to a father, and since remarriage rates have been high, it is likely that there are several million children now living with stepfathers.

Effects of Parenting on Fathers

How men respond to and are affected by the children in their lives is a key area of the emergent perspective on fathering. While novels and popular magazines have presented personal accounts, there has been little systematic exploration of the fathering experience. The clinical literature that exists in this area (see Fein, 1976, and Earls, 1976, for reviews) highlights pathological experiences, with titles such as "Pregnancy as a Precipitant of Mental Illness in Men" (Freeman, 1951), "Fatherhood as a Precipitant of Mental Illness" (Wainwright, 1966), and "Paranoid Psychoses Associated with Impending or Newly Established Fatherhood" (Retterstoll, 1968). Researchers in the four other areas discussed above occasionally touch on aspects of male parenting development—noting, for example, that men may be profoundly affected by participating in childbirth, by holding their newborns, by caring regularly for their toddlers, by becoming primary parents for adolescent children—but there is a need for systematic research. These questions gain importance when placed next to survey data that suggest that a large number of men feel that the trait "able to love" is not highly characteristic of themselves (Tavris, 1977).

The Emergent Perspective and Social Policy

The emergent perspective on fathering both proceeds from and leads to different social policy considerations than either traditional or modern ideologies of fathering. For one thing, the emergent perspective seeks to deal with the reality that increasing numbers of women are entering the paid labor force. A perspective on fathering that accepts the possibility that significant numbers of men can be effective nurturers of children may provide some relief from burdensome debates of the "should mothers mother or should mothers work?" variety (Rowe, 1976). If fathers are seen as able to care for their young, from a social policy perspective the question of childcare becomes one of family support: How can families be aided to carry out their childrearing and paid employment responsibilities? For example, an emergent perspective on fathering suggests attention to parental leave rather than maternity leave, to examination of the ways in which personnel and employment practices and policies affect the options of women and men both to care for their children and to provide economically for their families (Levine, 1977).

The idea of equal parenting, consistent with an emergent perspective on fathering, is receiving attention in discussions of family support. Sweden, several years ahead of the United States in these debates, embarked in the 1960s on a policy to support women to have a full range of options in paid employment. Premised on the ideal of equality, the Swedish program to support women in paid employment was concerned also with developing men's opportunities to participate in home life (Palme, 1972). To these ends, Sweden has enacted programs which allow men and women to care for children at home in the months after their birth and to be compensated at 90% of pre-birth salaries. Furthermore, men and women have the same right to stay home from work if the children are sick. Data from Sweden indicate that only one to two percent of fathers of newborn children took advantage of the new policy during the first year after it was enacted into law, but the figure rose to six percent the second year (Liljestrom, 1977).

It would be naive to suggest that the emergent perspective on fathering will provide full answers to complicated questions concerning the relationship between family life and work life in the United States. Liljestrom suggests that, for Swedish society, it would be foolhardy to imagine that fathers should seek to emulate the role of yesterday's mothers and points to the need to think about the implications of equal parenting:

> The time is ripe for retesting our notions about the meaning of parenthood. Perhaps future parents will live in more open families, where it is easier for the adults to coordinate parenthood with work and public affairs interests and where the children are surrounded by a network of adult contacts. Otherwise, how will we be able to solve the conflicts between the roles of parents and other adult life roles? (1977, p. 77)

The new perspective calls attention to issues of equal parenting. That there may indeed be a need for such discussion in the United States is highlighted by a front-page *New York Times Book Review* article on Selma Fraiberg's 1977 book, *Every Child's Birthright: In Defense of Mothering.* Describing the debate about family policy in the United States, the reviewer, Kenneth Keniston, comments on widespread concerns that maternal employment has resulted in inadequate care for many children. While noting that research has not supported a linkage between maternal employment and negative child outcomes (such as failure to thrive in infancy or criminality in adulthood), and arguing that children have a right to be nurtured, Keniston, amazingly, does not once mention fathers as a part of the solution to these problems (Keniston, 1977). In ignoring almost one-half of potential childcarers (men), Keniston may be seen as writing from the traditional perspective on fathering. The exclusion of fathers in a consideration of the needs of children and families would appear to underscore the need for a new perspective.

It seems increasingly clear that the next several years will witness considerable discussion and debate about parenting, family life, and work in the United States. I have tried to suggest that social scientists have tended to lag behind or at best run parallel to debates about social values and policies concerning parenting and fathering. Both the traditional and the modern perspectives of fathering have limited usefulness in a society marked by increasing levels of female paid employment and growing concerns about the care of children. Forthcoming debates on family life will provide opportunities for social scientists to contribute to the formation of policies that will affect millions of American parents and children. Given the importance of these issues, attention to an emergent perspective of fathering appears timely and prudent.

Reference Notes

1. Yogman, M. W., Dixon, S., Tronick, E., Adamson, L., Als, H., & Brazelton, T. B. *Development of infant social interaction with fathers.* Paper presented at the meeting of the Eastern Psychological Association, New York, April 1976.
2. Kotelchuck, M. *The nature of the infant's tie to his father.* Paper presented at the meeting of the Society for Research in Child Development, Philadelphia, 1973.

References

Aberle, D., & Naegele, K. Father's occupational role and attitudes toward children. *American Journal of Orthopsychiatry.* 1956. *22,* 366–378.
Biller, H. B. *Father, child, and sex role.* Lexington, MA.: D. C. Heath, 1971.
Biller, H. B. *Paternal deprivation.* Lexington, MA: D. C. Heath, 1974.
Bowlby, J. *Maternal care and mental health.* Geneva: World Health Organization, 1951.
Cohen, J. J., & Campos, J. J. Father, mother, and stranger as elicitors of attachment behaviors in infancy. *Developmental Psychology,* 1974, *10,* 146–154.
Cronenwett, L. R., & Newmark, L. L. Father's responses to childbirth. *Nursing Research,* 1974, *23,* 210–217.
Earls, F. The fathers (not the mothers): Their importance and influence with infants and young children. *Psychiatry,* 1076, *39,* 209–226.
English, O. S. The psychological role of the father in the family. *Social Casework,* 1954, pp. 323–329.
Fein, R. A. Men's entrance to parenthood. *The Family Coordinator,* 1976, *25,* 341–350.
Finkelstein-Keshet, H. *Marital separation and fathering.* Unpublished doctoral dissertation, University of Michigan, 1977.
Freeman, T. Pregnancy as a precipitant of mental illness in men. *British Journal of Medical Psychology,* 1951, *24,* 49–54.
Greenberg, M., & Morris, N. Engrossment: The newborn's impact upon the father. *American Journal of Orthopsychiatry,* 1974, *44,* 520–531.
Herzog, E., & Sudia, C. Fatherless homes. *Children,* 1968, pp. 177–182.
Herzog, E., & Sudia, C. Families without fathers. *Childhood Education,* 1972, pp. 175–181.
Herzog, E., & Sudia, C. Children in fatherless families. In E. M. Hetherington & P. Ricciuti (Eds.), *Review of child development research* (Vol. 3). Chicago: University of Chicago, 1974.
Hetherington, E. M., Cox, M., & Cox, R. Divorced fathers. *The Family Coordinator,* 1976, *25,* 417–428.
Howells, J. G. Fathering. In J. G. Howells (Eds.), *Modern perspectives in child psychiatry.* New York: Bruner-Mazel, 1971.
Josselyn, I. M. Cultural forces, motherliness and fatherliness. *American Journal of Orthopsychiatry,* 1956, *26,* 264–271.
Kamerman, S. B., & Kahn, A. J. Explorations in family policy. *Social Work,* 1976. *21.* 181–186.
Keniston, K. First attachments. (Review of *Every child's birthright: In defense of mothering* by S. Fraiberg.) *The New York Times Book Review,* December 11, 1977, pp. 1; 40–41.
Kotelchuck, M. The infant's relationship to the father: Experimental evidence. In M. E. Lamb (Ed.), *The role of the father in child development.* New York: Wiley, 1976.
Lamb, M. E., & Lamb, J. E. The nature and importance of the father-infant relationship. *The Family Coordinator,* 1976, *25,* 379–386.

Levine, J. *Who will raise the children? New options for fathers (and mothers).* New York: Lippincott, 1976.

Levine, J. Redefining the child care "problem"—Men as child nurturers. *Childhood Education,* November/December 1977, pp. 55–61.

Liljestrom, R. The parent's role in production and reproduction. *Sweden Now,* 1977, *11,* 73–77.

Manion, J. A study of fathers and infant caretaking. *Birth and the Family Journal,* 1977, *4,* 174–179.

Mussen, P. Early sex-role development. In D. Goslin (Ed.), *Handbook of socialization theory and research.* New York: Rand McNally, 1969.

Nash, J. The father in contemporary culture and current psychological literature. *Child Development,* 1965, *36,* 261–297.

Palme, O. The emancipation of man. *Journal of Social Issues,* 1972, *28*(2), 237–246.

Parke, R. D., & O'Leary, S. E. Father-mother-infant interaction in the newborn period. In K. Riegel & J. Meacham (Eds.), *The developing individual in a changing world.* The Hague: Mouton, 1976.

Parke, R. D., Savin, D. B. The father's role in infancy: A re-evaluation. *The Family Coordinator,* 1976, *25,* 365–372.

Parsons, T., & Bales, R. F. *Family, socialization, and interaction process,* Glencoe, IL: The Free Press, 1955.

Pederson, F. Does research on children reared in father-absent families yield information on father influences? *The Family Coordinator,* 1976, *25,* 459–464.

Pleck, J. H. Masculinity-femininity: Current and alternate paradigms. *Sex Roles,* 1975, *1,* 161–178.

Radin, N. Father-child interaction and the intellectual functioning of four-year-old boys. *Developmental Psychology,* 1972, *6,* 353–361.

Radin, N. Observed paternal behaviors as antecedents of intellectual functioning in young boys. *Developmental Psychology,* 1973, *8,* 369–376.

Rainwater, L., & Yancy, W. L. *The Moynihan report and the politics of controversy.* Cambridge, MA: MIT Press, 1967.

Rallings, E. M. The special role of stepfather. *The Family Coordinator,* 1976, *25,* 445–450.

Reiber, V. D. Is the nurturing role natural to fathers? *American Journal of Maternal Child Nursing,* 1976, *1,* 366–371.

Retterstol, N. Paranoid psychoses associated with impending or newly established fatherhood. *Acta Psychiatrica Scandinavica,* 1968, *44,* 51–61.

Rowe, M. O. That parents may work and love and children may thrive. In N. B. Talbot (Ed.), *Raising children in modern America.* Boston: Little, Brown, 1976.

Tavris, C. Men and women report their views on masculinity. *Psychology Today,* 1977, *10,* 34–43.

Wainwright, W. Fatherhood as a precipitant of mental illness. *American Journal of Psychiatry,* 1966, *123,* 40–44.

Wapner, J. The attitudes, feelings and behaviors of expectant fathers attending Lamaze classes. *Birth and the Family Journal,* 1976, *3,* 5–14.

The Medicalization and Legalization of Child Abuse

Eli H. Newberger and Richard Bourne

. Child abuse has emerged in the last fifteen years as a visible and important social problem. Although a humane approach to "help" for both victims of child abuse and their families has developed (and is prominently expressed in the title of one of the more influential books on the subject[29]), a theoretical framework to integrate the diverse origins and expressions of violence toward children and to inform a rational clinical practice does not exist. Furthermore, so inadequate are the "helping" services in most communities, so low the standard of professional action, and so distressing the consequences of incompetent intervention for the family that we and others have speculated that punishment is being inflicted in the guise of help.[3, 28]

What factors encourage theoretical confusion and clinical inadequacy? We propose that these consequences result, in part, from medical and legal ambiguity concerning child abuse and from two fundamental, and in some ways irreconcilable, dilemmas about social policy and the human and technical response toward families in crisis. We call these dilemmas *family autonomy versus coercive intervention* and *compassion versus control.*

This paper will consider these dilemmas in the context of a critical sociologic perspective on child abuse management. Through the cognitive lens of social labeling theory, we see symptoms of family crisis, and certain manifestations of childhood injury, "medicalized" and "legalized" and called "child abuse," to be diagnosed, reported, treated, and adjudicated by doctors and lawyers, their constituent institutions, and the professionals who depend on them for their social legitimacy and support.

We are mindful, as practitioners, of the need for prompt, effective, and creative professional responses to child abuse. Our critical analysis of the relationship of professional work to the societal context in which it is embedded is meant to stimulate attention to issues that professionals ignore to their and their clients' ultimate disadvantage. We mean not to disparage necessary efforts to help and protect children and their families.

How children's rights—as opposed to parents' rights—may be defined and protected is currently the subject of vigorous, and occasionally rancorous, debate.

The *family autonomy* vs. *coercive intervention* dilemma defines the conflict central to our ambiguity about *whether* society should intervene in situations of risk to children. The traditional autonomy of the family in rearing its offspring was cited by the majority of the U.S. Supreme Court in its ruling against the severely beaten appellants in the controversial "corporal punish-

From the *American Journal of Orthopsychiatry,* Vol. 48, No. 4 (October 1978), pp. 593–607.

ment" case (*Ingraham* vs. *Wright et al*).[25] The schools, serving *in loco parentis,* are not, in effect, constrained constitutionally from any punishment, however cruel.

Yet in California, a physician seeing buttock bruises of the kind legally inflicted by the teacher in the Miami public schools risks malpractice action if he fails to report his observations as symptoms of child abuse *(Landeros* vs. *Flood).*[32] He and his hospital are potentially liable for the cost of the child's subsequent injury and handicap if they do not initiate protective measures.[7]

This dilemma is highlighted by the recently promulgated draft statute of the American Bar Association's Juvenile Justice Standards Project, which, citing the low prevailing quality of protective child welfare services in the U.S., would sharply *restrict* access to such services.[28] The Commission would, for example, make the reporting of child neglect discretionary rather than mandatory, and would narrowly define the bases for court jurisdiction to situations where there is clear harm to a child.

Our interpretation of this standard is that it would make matters worse, not better, for children and their families.[3] So long as we are deeply conflicted about the relation of children to the state as well as to the family, and whether children have rights independent of their parents', we shall never be able to articulate with clarity *how* to enforce them.

The *compassion vs. control* dilemma has been postulated and reviewed in a previous paper,[47] which discussed the conceptual and practical problems implicit in the expansion of the clinical and legal definitions of child abuse to include practically every physical and emotional risk to children. The dilemma addresses a conflict central to the present ambiguity about *how* to protect children from their parents.

Parental behavior that might be characterized as destructive or criminal were it directed towards an adult has come to be seen and interpreted by those involved in its identification and treatment in terms of the psychosocial economy of the family. Embracive definitions reflect a change in the orientation of professional practice. To the extent to which we understand abusing parents as sad, deprived, needy human beings (rather than as cold, cruel murderers) we can sympathize with their plight and compassionately proffer supports and services to aid them in their struggle. Only with dread may we contemplate strong intervention (such as court action) on the child's behalf, for want of alienating our clients.

Notwithstanding the humane philosophy of treatment, society cannot, or will not, commit resources nearly commensurate with the exponentially increasing number of case reports that have followed the promulgation of the expanded definitions. The helping language betrays a deep conflict, and even ill will, toward children and parents in trouble, whom society and professionals might sooner punish and control.

We are forced frequently in practice to identify and choose the "least detrimental alternative" for the child[21] because the family supports that make it safe to keep children in their homes (homemakers, child care, psychiatric and medical services) are never available in sufficient amounts and quality.

That we should guide our work by a management concept named "least detrimental alternative" for children suggests at least a skepticism about the utility of these supports, just as the rational foundation for child welfare work is called into question by the title of the influential book from which the concept comes, *Beyond the Best Interests of the Child.*[21] More profoundly, the concept taps a vein of emotional confusion about our progeny, to whom we express both kindness and love with hurt.

Mounting attention to the developmental sequelae of child abuse[16, 33] stimulates an extra urgency not only to insure the physical safety of the identified victims but also to enable their adequate psychological development. The dangers of child abuse, according to Schmitt and Kempe in the latest edition of the Nelson Textbook of Pediatrics,[53] extend beyond harm to the victim:

> If the child who has been physically abused is returned to his parents without intervention, 5 per cent are killed and 35 per cent are seriously reinjured. Moreover, the untreated families tend to produce children who grow up to be juvenile delinquents and murderers, as well as the batterers of the next generation.

Despite the speculative nature of such conclusions about the developmental sequelae of child abuse,[6, 10, 11] such warnings support a practice of separating children from their natural homes in the interest of their and society's protection. They focus professional concern and public wrath on "the untreated families" and may justify punitive action to save us from their children.

This professional response of control rather than of compassion furthermore generalizes mainly to poor and socially marginal families, for it is they who seem preferentially to attract the labels "abuse" and "neglect" to their problems in the public settings where they go for most health and social services.[36] Affluent families' childhood injuries appear more likely to be termed "accidents" by the private practitioners who offer them their services. The conceptual model of cause and effect implicit in the name "accident" is benign: an isolated, random event rather than a consequence of parental commission or omission.[37, 38]

Table 1 presents a graphic display of the two dilemmas of social policy *(family autonomy* vs. *coercive intervention)* and professional response *(compassion* vs. *control).* The four-fold table illustrates possible action responses. For purposes of this discussion, it is well to think of "compassion" as signifying responses of support, such as provision of voluntary counseling and child care services, and "control" as signifying such punitive responses as "blaming the victim" for his or her reaction to social realities[49] and as the criminal prosecution of abusing parents.

Table 1. Dilemmas of Social Policy and Professional Response

Response	*Family Autonomy* *Versus*	*Coercive Intervention*
Compassion ("support") _____Versus_____	1 Voluntary child development services 2 Guaranteed family supports: e.g. income, housing, health services	1 Case reporting of family crisis and mandated family intervention 2 Court-ordered delivery of services
Control ("punishment")	1 "Laissez-faire": No assured services or supports 2 Retributive response to family crisis	1 Court action to separate child from family 2 Criminal prosecution of parents

Child Abuse and the Medical and Legal Professions

The importance of a technical discipline's conceptual structure in defining how it approaches a problem has been clearly stated by Mercer:[34]

> Each discipline is organized around a core of basic concepts and assumptions which form the frame of reference from which persons trained in that discipline view the world and set about solving problems in their field. The concepts and assumptions which make up the perspective of each discipline give each its distinctive character and are the intellectual tools used by its practitioners. These tools are incorporated in action and problem solving and appear self-evident to persons socialized in the discipline. As a result, little consideration is likely to be given to the social consequence of applying a particular conceptual work to problem solving.

> When the issues to be resolved are clearly in the area of competence of a single discipline, the automatic application of its conceptual tools is likely to go unchallenged. However, when the problems under consideration lie in the interstices between disciplines, the disciplines concerned are likely to define the situation differently and may arrive at differing conclusions which have dissimilar implications for social action.

What we do when children are injured in family crises is shaped also by how our professions respond to the interstitial area called "child abuse."

"Medicalization"

Though cruelty to children has occurred since documentary records of mankind have been kept,[9] it became a salient social problem in the United States only after the publication by Kempe and his colleagues describing the "battered child syndrome."[30] In the four-year period after this medical article appeared, the legislatures of all 50 states, stimulated partly by a model law developed under the aegis of the Children's Bureau of the U.S. Department of Health, Education, and Welfare, passed statutes mandating the identification and reporting of suspected victims of abuse.

Once the specific diagnostic category "battered child syndrome" was applied to integrate a set of medical symptoms, and laws were passed making the syndrome reportable, the problem was made a proper and legitimate concern for the medical profession. Conrad has discussed cogently how "hyperactivity" came officially to be known and how it became "medicalized."[5] Medicalization is defined in this paper as the perception of behavior as a medical problem or illness and the mandating or licensing of the medical profession to provide some type of treatment for it.

Pfohl[41] associated the publicity surrounding the battered child syndrome report with a phenomenon of "discovery" of child abuse. For radiologists, the potential for increased prestige, role expansion, and coalition formation (with psychodynamic psychiatry and pediatrics) may have encouraged identification and intervention in child abuse. Furthermore,

> . . . the discovery of abuse as a new "illness" reduced drastically the intraorganizational constraints on doctors' "seeing" abuse . . . Problems associated with perceiving parents as patients whose confidentiality must be protected were reconstructed by typifying them as patients who needed help . . . The maintenance of professional autonomy was assured by pairing deviance with sickness . . .

In some ways, medicine's "discovery" of abuse has benefited individual physicians and the profession.

> One of the greatest ambitions of the physician is to discover or describe a "new" disease or syndrome.[24]

By such involvement the doctor becomes a moral entrepreneur defining what is normal, proper, or desirable: he becomes charged "with inquisitorial powers to discover certain wrongs to be righted."[24] New opportunities for the application of traditional methods are also found—for example, the systematic screening of suspected victims with a skeletal X-ray survey to detect previous fractures, and the recent report in the neurology literature suggesting the utility of diphenylhydantoin* treatment for child abusing parents.[46]

Pfohl's provocative analysis also took note of some of the normative and structural elements within the medical profession that appear to have reinforced a *reluctance* on the part of some physicians to become involved: the norm of confidentiality between doctor and patient and the goal of professional autonomy.[41] For many physicians, child abuse is a subject to avoid.[50]

First, it is difficult to distinguish, on a theoretical level, corporal punishment that is "acceptable" from that which is "illegitimate." Abuse may be defined variably even by specialists, the definitions ranging from serious physical injury to nonfulfillment of a child's developmental needs.[13, 19, 30]

---

*Dilantin, a commonly-used seizure suppressant.

Second, it is frequently hard to diagnose child abuse clinically. What appears on casual physical examination as bruising, for example, may turn out to be a skin manifestation of an organic blood dysfunction, or what appear to be cigarette burns may in reality be infected mosquito bites. A diagnosis of abuse may require social and psychological information about the family, the acquisition and interpretation of which may be beyond the average clinician's expertise. It may be easier to characterize the clinical complaint in terms of the child's medical symptom rather than in terms of the social, familial, and psychological forces associated with its etiology. We see daily situations where the exclusive choice of medical taxonomy actively obscures the causes of the child's symptom and restricts the range of possible interventions: examples are "subdural hematoma," which frequently occurs with severe trauma to babies' heads (the medical name means collection of blood under the *dura mater* of the brain), and "enuresis" or "encopresis" in child victims of sexual assault (medical names mean incontinence of urine or feces).

Third, child abuse arouses strong emotions. To concentrate on the narrow medical issue (the broken bone) instead of the larger familial problem (the etiology of the injury) not only allows one to avoid facing the limits of one's technical adequacy, but to shield oneself from painful feelings of sadness and anger. One can thus maintain professional detachment and avert unpleasant confrontations. The potentially alienating nature of the physician-patient interaction when the diagnosis of child abuse is made may also have a negative economic impact on the doctor, especially the physician in private practice.

"Legalization"

The legal response to child abuse was triggered by its medicalization. Child abuse reporting statutes codified a medical diagnosis into a legal framework which in many states defined official functions for courts. Immunity from civil liability was given to mandated reporters so long as reports were made in good faith; monetary penalties for failure to report were established; and familial and professional-client confidentiality privileges, except those involving attorneys, were abrogated.

Professional autonomy for lawyers was established, and status and power accrued to legal institutions. For example, the growth in the number of Care and Protection cases* before the Boston Juvenile Court "has been phenomenal in recent years . . . four cases in 1968 and 99 in 1974, involving 175 different children."[44] Though these cases have burdened court dockets and personnel, they have also led to acknowledgement of the important work of the court. The need for this institution is enhanced because of its recognized expertise in handling special matters. Care and Protection cases are cited in response to

*Care and Protection cases are those juvenile or family court actions which potentially transfer, on a temporary or permanent basis, legal and/or physical custody of a child from his biological parents to the state.

recommendations by a prestigious commission charged with proposing reform and consolidation of the courts in Massachusetts. Child protection work in our own institution would proceed only with difficulty if access to the court were legally or procedurally constrained. Just as for the medical profession, however, there were normative and structural elements within law which urged restraint. Most important among them were the traditional presumptions and practices favoring family autonomy.

If individual lawyers might financially benefit from representing clients in matters pertaining to child abuse, they—like their physician counterparts—were personally uncertain whether or how to become involved.

> Public concern over the scope and significance of the problem of the battered child is a comparatively new phenomenon. Participation by counsel in any significant numbers in child abuse cases in juvenile or family courts is of even more recent origin. It is small wonder that the lawyer approaches participation in these cases with trepidation.[26]

Lawyers, too, feel handicapped by a need to rely on concepts from social work and psychiatry and on data from outside the traditional domain of legal knowledge and expertise. As counsel to parents, lawyers can be torn between advocacy of their clients' positions and that which advances the "best interest" of their clients' children. As counsel to the petitioner, a lawyer may have to present a case buttressed by little tangible evidence. Risk to a child is often difficult to characterize and impossible to prove.

Further problems for lawyers concerned with child abuse involve the context of intervention: whether courts or legislatures should play the major role in shaping practice and allocating resources; how much formality is desirable in legal proceedings; and the propriety of negotiation as opposed to adversary confrontation when cases come to court.

Conflicts Between Medical and Legal Perspectives

Despite the common reasons for the "medicalization" and the "legalization" of child abuse, there are several areas where the two orientations conflict:

1. *The seriousness of the risk.* To lawyers, intervention might be warranted only when abuse results in serious harm to a child. To clinicians, however, *any* inflicted injury might justify a protective legal response, especially if the child is very young. "The trick is to prevent the abusive case from becoming the terminal case."[14] Early intervention may prevent the abuse from being repeated or from becoming more serious.
2. *The definition of the abuser.* To lawyers, the abuser might be defined as a wrongdoer who has injured a child. To clinicians, both the abuser and child might be perceived as victims influenced by sociological and psychological factors beyond their control.[17, 35]

3. *The importance of the abuser's mental state.* To lawyers, whether the abuser intentionally or accidentally inflicted injury on a child is a necessary condition of reporting or judicial action. So-called "accidents" are less likely to trigger intervention. To clinicians, however, mental state may be less relevant, for it requires a diagnostic formulation frequently difficult or impossible to make on the basis of available data. The family dynamics associated with "accidents" in some children (*e.g.,* stress, marital conflict, and parental inattention) often resemble those linked with inflicted injury in others. They are addressed with variable clinical sensitivity and precision.

4. *The role of law.* Attorneys are proudly unwilling to accept conclusions or impressions lacking empirical corroboration. To lawyers, the law and legal institutions become involved in child abuse when certain facts fit a standard of review. To clinicians, the law may be seen as an instrument to achieve a particular therapeutic or dispositional objective (*e.g.,* the triggering of services or of social welfare involvement) even if, as is very often the case, the data to support such objectives legally are missing or ambiguous. The clinician's approach to the abuse issue is frequently subjective or intuitive (*e.g.,* a *feeling) that a family is under stress or needs help, or that a child is "at risk"),* while the lawyer demands evidence.

Doctoring and Lawyering the Disease

These potential or actual differences in orientation notwithstanding, both medicine and law have accepted in principle the therapeutic approach to child abuse.

To physicians, defining abuse as a disease or medical syndrome makes natural the treatment alternative, since both injured child and abuser are viewed as "sick"—the one, physically, the other psychologically or socially. Therapy may, however, have retributive aspects, as pointed out with characteristic pungency by Illich:[24]

> The medical label may protect the patient from punishment only to submit him to interminable instruction, treatment, and discrimination, which are inflicted on him for his professionally presumed benefit.

Lawyers adopt a therapeutic perspective for several reasons. First, the rehabilitative ideal remains in ascendance in criminal law, especially in the juvenile and family courts which handle most child abuse cases.[1]

Second, the criminal or punitive model may not protect the child. Parents may hesitate to seek help if they are fearful of prosecution. Evidence of abuse is often insufficient to satisfy the standard of conviction "beyond all reasonable doubt" in criminal proceedings. An alleged abuser threatened with punishment and then found not guilty may feel vindicated, reinforcing the pattern of abuse. The abuser may well be legally freed from any scrutiny, and badly needed social services will not be able to be provided. Even if found guilty, the perpetrator of abuse is usually given only mild punishment, such as a short jail term or probation. If the abuser is incarcerated, the other family members may equally suffer as, for example, the relationship between spouses is undercut and child-rearing falls on one parent, or children are placed in foster home care or with relatives. Upon release from jail, the abuser may be no less violent and even more aggressive and vindictive toward the objects of abuse.

Third, the fact that child abuse was "discovered" by physicians influenced the model adopted by other professionals. As Freidson[15] noted:

> Medical definitions of deviance have come to be adopted even where there is no reliable evidence that biophysical variables "cause" the deviance or that medical treatment is any more efficacious than any other kind of management.

Weber, in addition, contended that "status" groups (e.g., physicians) generally determine the content of law.[45]

The Selective Implementation of Treatment

Medical intervention is generally encouraged by the Hippocratic ideology of treatment (the ethic that help, not harm, is given by practitioners), and by what Scheff[52] called the medical decision rule: it is better to wrongly diagnose illness and "miss" health than it is to wrongly diagnose health and "miss" illness.

Physicians, in defining aberrant behavior as a medical problem and in providing treatment, become what sociologists call agents of social control. Though the technical enterprise of the physician claims value-free power, socially marginal individuals are more likely to be defined as deviant than are others.

Characteristics frequently identified with the "battered child syndrome," such as social isolation, alcoholism, unemployment, childhood handicap, large family size, low level of parental educational achievement, and acceptance of severe physical punishment as a childhood socializing technique, are associated with social marginality and poverty.

Physicians in public settings seem, from child abuse reporting statistics, to be more likely to see and report child abuse than are those in private practice. As poor people are more likely to frequent hospital emergency wards and clinics,[36] they have much greater social visibility where child abuse is concerned than do people of means.

The fact that child abuse is neither theoretically nor clinically well defined increases the likelihood of subjective professional evaluation. In labeling theory, it is axiomatic that the greater the social distance between the typer and the person singled out for typing, the broader the type and the more quickly it may be applied.[48]

In the doctor-patient relationship, the physician is always in a superordinate position because of his or her expertise; social distance is inherent to the relationship. This distance necessarily increases once the label of abuser has been applied. Importantly, the label is less likely to be fixed if the diagnostician and possible abuser share similar characteristics, especially socioeconomic status, particularly where the injury is not serious or manifestly a consequence of maltreatment.

Once the label "abuser" is attached, it is very difficult to remove; even innocent behavior of a custodian may then be viewed with suspicion. The tenacity of a label increases in proportion to the official processing. At our own institution, until quite recently, a red star was stamped on the permanent medical record of any child who might have been abused, a process which encouraged professionals to suspect child abuse (and to act on that assumption) at any future time that the child would present with a medical problem.

Professionals thus engage in an intricate process of selection, finding facts that fit the label which has been applied, responding to a few deviant details set within a panoply of entirely acceptable conduct. Schur[55] called this phenomenon "retrospective reinterpretation." In any pathological model, "persons are likely to be studied in terms of what is 'wrong' with them," there being a "decided emphasis on identifying the characteristics of abnormality;" in child abuse, it may be administratively impossible to return to health, as is shown by the extraordinary durability of case reports in state central registers.[58]

The response of the patient to the agent of social control affects the perceptions and behavior of the controller. If, for example, a child has been injured and the alleged perpetrator is repentant, a consensus can develop between abuser and labeler that a norm has been violated. In this situation, the label of "abuser" may be less firmly applied than if the abuser defends the behavior as proper. Support for this formulation is found in studies by Gusfield,[22] who noted different reactions to repentant, sick, and enemy deviants, and by Piliavin and Briar,[42] who showed that juveniles apprehended by the police receive more lenient treatment if they appear contrite and remorseful about their violations.

Consequences of Treatment for the Abuser

Once abuse is defined as a sickness, it becomes a condition construed to be beyond the actor's control.[39] Though treatment, not punishment, is warranted, the *type* of treatment depends on whether or not the abuser is "curable," "improvable," or "incurable," and on the speed with which such a state can be achieved.

To help the abuser is generally seen as a less important goal than is the need to protect the child. If the abusive behavior cannot quickly be altered, and the child remains "at risk," the type of intervention will differ accordingly (*e.g.,* the child may be more likely to be placed in a foster home). The less "curable" is the abuser, the less treatment will be offered and the more punitive will society's response appear. Ironically, even the removal of a child from his parents, a move nearly always perceived as punitive by parents, is often portrayed as helpful by the professionals doing the removing ("It will give you a chance to resolve your own problems," etc.).

Whatever the treatment, there are predictable consequences for those labeled "abusers." Prior to diagnosis, parents may be afraid of "getting caught" because of punishment and social stigma. On being told of clinicians' concerns, they may express hostility because of implicit or explicit criticism made of them and their child-rearing practices yet feel relief because they love their children and want help in stopping their destructive behavior. The fact that they see themselves as "sick" may increase their willingness to seek help. This attitude is due at least in part to the lesser social stigma attached to the "sick," as opposed to the "criminal," label.

Socially marginal individuals are likely to accept whatever definition more powerful labelers apply. This definition, of course, has already been accepted by much of the larger community because of the definers' power. As Davis[8] noted:

> The chance that a group will get community support for its definition of unacceptable deviance depends on its relative power position. The greater the group's size, resources, efficiency, unity, articulateness, prestige, coordination with other groups, and access to the mass media and to decision-makers, the more likely it is to get its preferred norms legitimated.

Acceptance of definition by child abusers, however, is not based solely on the power of the labelers. Though some might consider the process "political castration,"[43] so long as they are defined as "ill" and take on the sick role, abusers are achieving a more satisfactory label. Though afflicted with a stigmatized illness (and thus "gaining few if any privileges and taking on some especially handicapping new obligations"[15]) at least they are merely sick rather than sinful or criminal.

Effective social typing flows down rather than up the social structure. For example, when both parents induct one of their children into the family scapegoat role, this is an effective social typing because the child is forced to take their definition of him into account.[48] Sometimes it is difficult to know whether an abusive parent has actually accepted the definition or is merely "role playing" in order to please the definer. If a person receives conflicting messages from the same control agent (*e.g.* "you are sick and criminal") or from different control agents in the treatment network (from doctors who use the sick label, and lawyers who use the criminal), confusion and upset predictably result.[56]

As an example of how social definitions are accepted by the group being defined, it is interesting to examine the basic tenets of Parents Anonymous, which began as a self-help group for abusive mothers:

> A destructive, *disturbed* mother can, and often does, produce through her actions a physically or emotionally abused, or battered child. Present avail-

able *help* is limited and/or expensive, usually with a long waiting list before the person requesting help can actually receive *treatment* . . . We must understand that a problem as involved as this cannot be *cured* immediately . . . the problem is *within us* as a parent . . . [29] [emphases added]

To Parents Anonymous, child abuse appears to be a medical problem, and abusers are sick persons who must be treated.

Consequences of Treatment for the Social System

The individual and the social system are interrelated; each influences the other. Thus, if society defines abusive parents as sick, there will be few criminal prosecutions for abuse; reports will generally be sent to welfare, as opposed to police, departments.

Since victims of child abuse are frequently treated in hospitals, medical personnel become brokers for adult services and definers of children's rights. Once abuse is defined, that is, people may get services (such as counseling, child care, and homemaker services) that would be otherwise unavailable to them, and children may get care and protection impossible without institutional intervention.

If, as is customary, however, resources are in short supply, the preferred treatment of a case may not be feasible. Under this condition, less adequate treatment stratagems, or even clearly punitive alternatives, may be implemented. If day care and competent counseling are unavailable, court action and foster placement can become the only options. As Stoll[56] observed,

> . . . the best therapeutic intentions may be led astray when opportunities to implement theoretical guidelines are not available.

Treating child abuse as a sickness has, ironically, made it more difficult to "cure." There are not enough therapists to handle all of the diagnosed cases. Nor do most abusive parents have the time, money, or disposition for long-term therapeutic involvement. Many, moreover, lack the introspective and conceptual abilities required for successful psychological therapy.

As Parents Anonymous emphasizes, abuse is the *abuser's* problem. Its causes and solutions are widely understood to reside in individuals rather than in the social system.[5, 17] Indeed, the strong emphasis on child abuse as an individual problem means that other equally severe problems of childhood can be ignored, and the unequal distribution of social and economic resources in society can be masked.[20] The child abuse phenomenon itself may also increase as parents and professionals are obliged to "package" their problems and diagnoses in a competitive market where services are in short supply. As Tannenbaum[57] observed in 1938:

> Societal reactions to deviance can be characterized as a kind of "dramatization of evil" such that a person's deviance is made a public issue. The stronger the reaction to the evil, the more it seems to grow. The reaction itself seems to generate the very thing it sought to eliminate.

Conclusion

Dispelling the Myth of Child Abuse

As clinicians, we are convinced that with intelligence, humanity, and the application of appropriate interventions, we can help families in crisis.

We believe, however, that short of coming to terms with—and changing—certain social, political, and economic aspects of our society, we will never be able adequately to understand and address the origins of child abuse and neglect. Nor will the issues of labeling be adequately resolved unless we deal straightforwardly with the potentially abusive power of the helping professions. If we can bring ourselves to ask such questions as, "Can we legislate child abuse out of existence?" and, "Who benefits from child abuse?", then perhaps we can more rationally choose among the action alternatives displayed in the conceptual model (Table 1).

Although we would prefer to avoid coercion and punishment, and to keep families autonomous and services voluntary, we must acknowledge the realities of family life and posit some state role to assure the well-being of children. In making explicit the assumptions and values underpinning our professional actions, perhaps we can promote a more informed and humane practice.

Because it is likely that clinical interventions will continue to be class and culture-based, we propose the following five guidelines to minimize the abuse of power of the definer.

1. *Give physicians, social workers, lawyers, and other intervention agents social science perspectives and skills.* Critical intellectual tools should help clinicians to understand the implications of their work, and, especially, the functional meaning of the labels they apply in their practices.

   Physicians need to be more aware of the complexity of human life, especially its social and psychological dimensions. The "medical model" is not of itself inappropriate; rather, the conceptual bases of medical practice need to be broadened, and the intellectual and scientific repertory of the practitioner expanded.[12] Diagnostic formulation is an active process that carries implicitly an anticipation of intervention and outcome. The simple elegance of concepts such as "child abuse" and "child neglect" militate for simple and radical treatments.

   Lawyers might be helped to learn that, in child custody cases, they are not merely advocates of a particular position. Only the child should "win" a custody case, where, for example, allegations of "abuse" or "neglect," skillfully marshalled, may support the position of the more effectively represented parent, guardian, or social worker.

2. *Acknowledge and change the prestige hierarchy of helping professions.* The workers who seem best able to conceptualize the familial and social context of problems of violence are social workers and nurses. They are least paid,

most overworked, and as a rule have minimal access to the decision prerogatives of medicine and law. We would add that social work and nursing are professions largely of and by women, and we believe we must come to terms with the many realities—including sexual dominance and subservience—that keep members of these professions from functioning with appropriate respect and support. (We have made a modest effort in this direction at our own institution, where our interdisciplinary child abuse consultation program is organized under the aegis of the administration rather than of a medical clinical department. This is to foster, to the extent possible, peer status and communication on a coequal footing among the disciplines involved—social work, nursing, law, medicine, and psychiatry.)

3. *Build theory.* We need urgently a commonly understandable dictionary of concepts that will guide and inform a rational practice. A more adequate theory base would include a more etiologic (or causal) classification scheme for children's injuries, which would acknowledge and integrate diverse origins and expressions of social, familial, child developmental, and environmental phenomena. It would conceptualize strength in families and children, as well as pathology. It would orient intervenors to the promotion of health rather than to the treatment of disease.

A unified theory would permit coming to terms with the universe of need. At present, socially marginal and poor children are virtually the only ones susceptible to being diagnosed as victims of abuse and neglect. More affluent families' offspring, whose injuries are called "accidents" and who are often unprotected, are not included in "risk" populations. We have seen examples of court defense where it was argued (successfully) that because the family was not poor, it did not fit the classic archetypes of abuse or neglect.

The needs and rights of all children need to be spelled out legally in relation to the responsibilities of parents and the state. This is easier said than done. It shall require not only a formidable effort at communication across disciplinary lines but a serious coming to terms with social and political values and realities.

4. *Change social inequality.* We share Gil's[20] view that inequality is the basic problem underlying the labeling of "abusive families" and its consequences. Just as children without defined rights are *ipso facto* vulnerable, so too does unequal access to the resources and goods of society shape a class hierarchy that leads to the individualization of social problems. Broadly-focused efforts for social change should accompany a critical review of the ethical foundations of professional practice. As part of the individual's formation as doctor, lawyer, social worker, or police officer, there could be developed for the professional a notion of public service and responsibility. This would better enable individuals to see themselves as participants in a social process and to perceive the problems addressed in their work at the social as well as the individual level of action.

5. *Assure adequate representation of class and ethnic groups in decision-making forums.* Since judgments about family competency can be affected by class and ethnic biases, they should be made in settings where prejudices can be checked and controlled. Culture-bound value judgments in child protection work are not infrequent, and a sufficient participation in case management conferences of professionals of equal rank and status and diverse ethnicity can assure both a more appropriate context for decision making and better decisions for children and their families.

References

1. Allen, F. 1964. The Borderland of Criminal Justice. University of Chicago Press, Chicago.
2. Becker, H. 1963. Outsiders: Studies in the Sociology of Deviance. Free Press, New York.
3. Bourne, R. and Newberger, E. 1977. 'Family autonomy' or 'coercive intervention?' ambiguity and conflict in a proposed juvenile justice standard on child protection. Boston Univ. Law Rev. 57(4):670–706.
5. Conrad, P. 1975. The discovery of hyperkinesis: notes on the medicalization of deviant behavior. Soc. Prob. 23(10):12–21.
6. Cupoli, J. and Newberger, E. 1977. Optimism or pessimism for the victim of child abuse? Pediatrics 59(2):311–314.
7. Curran, W. 1977. Failure to diagnose battered child syndrome. New England J. Med., 296(14):795–796.
8. Davis, F. 1975. Beliefs, values, power and public definitions of deviance. *In* The Collective Definition of Deviance, F. Davis and R. Stivers, eds. Free Press, New York.
9. Demause, L., ed. 1974. The History of Childhood. Free Press, New York.
10. Elmer, E. 1977. A follow-up study of traumatized children. Pediatrics 59(2):273–279.
11. Elmer, E. 1977. Fragile Families, Troubled Children. University of Pittsburgh Press, Pittsburgh.
12. Engel, G. 1977. The need for a new medical model: a challenge for biomedicine. Science 196(14): 129–136.
13. Fontana, V. 1964. The Maltreated Child: The Maltreatment Syndrome in Children. Charles C. Thomas, Springfield, Ill.
14. Fraser, B. 1977. Legislative status of child abuse legislation. *In* Child Abuse and Neglect: the Family and the Community, C. Kempe and R. Helfer, eds. Ballinger, Cambridge, Mass.
15. Freidson, E. 1970. Profession of Medicine: A Study of the Sociology of Applied Knowledge. Dodd, Mead, New York.
16. Galdston, R. 1971. Violence begins at home. J. Amer. Acad. Child Psychiat. 10(2):336–350.
17. Gelles, R. 1973. Child abuse as psychopathology: a sociological critique and reformulation. Amer. J. Orthopsychiat. 43(4):611–621.
18. Gelles, R. 1978. Violence toward children in the United States. Amer. J. Orthopsychiat. 48(4):580–592.
19. Gil, D. 1975. Unraveling child abuse. Amer. J. Orthopsychiat. 45(4): 346–356.
20. Gil, D. 1970. Violence Against Children. Harvard University Press, Cambridge, Mass.
21. Goldstein, J., Freud, A. and Solnit, A. 1973. Beyond the Best Interests of the Child. Free Press, New York.
22. Gusfield, J. 1967. Moral passage: the symbolic process in public designations of deviance. Soc. Prob. 15(2):175–188.
23. Hyde, J. 1974. Uses and abuses of information in protective services contexts. *In* Fifth National Symposium on Child Abuse and Neglect. American Humane Association, Denver.
24. Illich, I. 1976. Medical Nemesis: The Expropriation of Health. Random House, New York.
25. *Ingraham v. Wright.* 1977. 45 LW 4364 U.S. Supreme Court.
26. Isaacs, J. 1972. The role of the lawyer in child abuse cases. *In* Helping the Battered Child and His Family, R. Helfer and C. Kempe, eds. Lippincott, Philadelphia.
27. Joint Commission on the Mental Health of Children. 1970. Crisis in Child Mental Health. Harper and Row, New York.

28. Juvenile Justice Standards Project. 1977. Standards Relating to Abuse and Neglect. Ballinger, Cambridge, Mass.
29. Kempe, C. and Helfer, R., eds. 1972. Helping the Battered Child and His Family. Lippincott, Philadelphia.
30. Kempe, C. et al. 1962. The battered child symdrome. JAMA 181(1):17–24.
31. Kittrie, N. 1971. The Right To Be Different. Johns Hopkins University Press, Baltimore.
32. *Landeros v. Flood.* 1976. 131 Calif. Rptr 69.
33. Martin, H., ed. 1976. The Abused Child: A Multidisciplinary Approach to Developmental Issues and Treatment. Ballinger, Cambridge, Mass.
34. Mercer, J. 1972. Who is normal? two perspectives on mild mental retardation. *In* Patients, Physicians and Illness (2nd ed.), E. Jaco, ed. Free Press, New York.
35. Newberger, E. 1975. The myth of the battered child syndrome. *In* Annual Progress in Child Psychiatry and Child Development 1974, S. Chess and A. Thomas, eds. Brunner Mazel, New York.
36. Newberger, E., Newberger, C. and Richmond, J. 1976. Child health in America: toward a rational public policy. Milbank Memorial Fund Quart./Hlth. and Society 54(3): 249–298.
37. Newberger, E. and Daniel, J. 1976. Knowledge and epidemiology of child abuse: a critical review of concepts. Pediat. Annuals 5(3):15–26.
38. Newberger, E. et al. 1977. Pediatric social illness: toward an etiologic classification. Pediatrics 60(1): 178–185.
39. Parsons, T. 1951. The Social System. Free Press, Glencoe, Ill.
40. Paulsen, M. 1966. Juvenile courts, family courts, and the poor man. Calif. Law Rev. 54(2): 694–716.
41. Pfohl, S. 1977. The 'discovery' of child abuse. Soc. Prob. 24(3):310–323.
42. Piliavin, I. and Briar, S. 1964. Police encounters with juveniles. Amer. J. Sociol. 70(2): 206–214.
43. Pitts, J. 1968. Social control: the concept. *In* The International Encyclopedia of the Social Sciences 14:391. Macmillan, New York.
44. Poitrast, F. 1976. The judicial dilemma in child abuse cases. Psychiat. Opinion 13(1):22–28.
45. Rheinstein, M. 1954. Max Weber on Law in Economy and Society. Harvard University Press, Cambridge, Mass.
46. Rosenblatt, S., Schaeffer, D. and Rosenthal, J. 1976. Effects of diphenylhydantoin on child abusing parents: a preliminary report. Curr. Therapeut. Res. 19(3):332–336.
47. Rosenfeld, A. and Newberger, E. 1977. Compassion versus control: conceptual and practical pitfalls in the broadened definition of child abuse. JAMA 237 (19): 2086–2088.
48. Rubington, E. and Weinberg, M. 1973. Deviance: The Interactionist Perspective (2nd ed.). Macmillan, New York.
49. Ryan, W. 1971. Blaming the Victim. Random House, New York.
50. Sanders, R. 1972. Resistance to dealing with parents of battered children. Pediatrics 50(6): 853–857.
51. Scheff, T. 1966. Being Mentally Ill: A Sociological Theory. Aldine, Chicago.
52. Scheff, T. 1972. Decision rules, types of error, and their consequences in medical diagnosis. *In* Medical Men and Their Work, E. Freidson and J. Lorber, eds. Aldine, Chicago.
53. Schmitt, B. and Kempe, C. 1975. Neglect and abuse of children. *In* Nelson Textbook of Pediatrics (10th ed.), V. Vaughan and R. McKay, eds. W. B. Saunders, Philadelphia.
54. Schrag, P. 1975. The Myth of the Hyperactive Child. Random House, New York.
55. Schur, E. 1971. Labeling Deviant Behavior. Harper and Row, New York.
56. Stoll, C. 1968. Images of man and social control. Soc. Forces 47(2):119–127.
57. Tannenbaum, F. 1938. Crime and the Community. Ginn and Co., Boston.
58. Whiting, L. 1977. The central registry for child abuse cases: rethinking basic assumptions. Child Welfare 56(2):761–767.

Chapter 9

Childhood

The Psychological Requirements for Human Development

Jerome Kagan

> *Our society needs to restore its belief in the honesty, sincerity, and humanity of its members. It has lost its optimism, temporarily, we hope, and this lacuna is as serious as the absence of engineers at the turn of the century.*
>
> Jerome Kagan

The Western mind is friendly to four prejudices regarding the development of the child. The first premise is that each day the child is being seriously influenced by the actions of others, and that the relationship between those social experiences (say, being spanked for stealing money) and his future behavioral, motivational and moral development is absolute, fixed and knowable. The second assumption is that development consists of a series of discrete stages, each with its own unique pattern of characteristics, catalyzed by a special alchemy between maturation and experience. "Now you see it, now you don't" captures this metaphor for growth. The third notion, a corollary of the second, is that successful passage through one developmental stage makes passage through the next easier. Contrariwise, failure to master all the necessary tasks of one stage impedes movement to the next higher one, as if development were like rising through successive Boy Scout ranks rather than an intercontinental sea journey. The final premise, which is at once the most profound and most controversial, is that there is an ideal, best adult and, correspondingly, a best collection of experiences that maximizes the probability that the ideal adult will emerge from the cacophony of childhood encounters. In simpler terms, most American parents believe in the existence of a small set of psychological traits that are necessarily correlated with a maximally happy adulthood. If parents and teachers praise, punish and posture at the right time and with the proper enthusiasm—like the conducting of a major symphony—they would create the perfect adult. This essay questions this last idea by suggesting that there are several reasonable answers to the query, "What are a child's psychological requirements?" The substance of each of the answers depends, first, on one's views concerning the nature of the human child and the mechanisms that mediate his growth and, second, on the subtle messages the larger society communicates to parents regarding the kinds of adult that are needed for the succeeding generation.

The most popular contemporary American conception of the young child is that he is an inherently helpless, dependent organism prepared by nature to establish a strong emotional bond with the adults who care for him. If these adults attend to his drives and desires with consistency and affection, it is assumed that he will gradually learn to trust them, be motivated to adopt their values and develop such a sturdy concept of self that he will possess a vital capacity for love and will be able to deal with conflict, anxiety and frustration effectively. The traditional Japanese mother, prior to the Western acculturation of her attitudes, viewed her young infant through different lenses. He was neither helpless nor dependent, but a willful, asocial creature destined to move away from people unless she could tame him and deflect his natural instincts. Hence, she usually soothed and quieted her infant, suppressing the excitement that the American mother tried to arouse. The Indian mother in the highlands of Guatemala believes that infants are born with different dispositions depending upon the day of their birth. She is convinced there is little she can do to change these fixed developmental directions, and her fatalism leads her to stand aside so that her child can grow as nature intended.[1] Most children in all three communities grow up equally well adapted to their societies. Moreover, there is such a remarkable similarity among the ten-year-olds in each of these settings that one is forced to question the validity of these local theories.

Most parents are absolutistic in their view of psychological growth, assuming that all children should be headed for the same ideal telos and should require a best combination of psychological nourishment to complete the long and difficult journey. Contrast this view of the infant, which is predominant in the United States, with the more relativistic notion that a child's psychological requirements not only change with his stage of development, but also become, with age, increasingly dependent upon the local culture. Lest this statement sound too general, consider a concrete illustration. In contemporary America, a willingness to defend intrusions into one's space and property and acceptance of the effect of anger and the motive of hostility are regarded as necessary for taming each day. Hence, it is generally acknowledged that the family should not always punish mild displays of anger or aggression in or out of the home. A parent who never permitted the child any expression of hostility would be called bad names by the majority of American psychologists, psychiatrists, pediatricians and social workers.

Among the Utku of Hudson Bay, who are restricted for nine months a year to a tight three hundred feet of living space, it is necessary that any sign of anger, hostility and aggression be consistently suppressed. A good mother conscientiously starts to train this inhibition as early as twenty-four months of her child's age by ignoring acts of defiance and, by the time he is nine, the behavioral indexes of anger, so common in American children, are not in evidence.[2] An Eskimo mother who allowed her child easy displays of aggression would be called the same bad names we apply to the American mother who did not permit this behavior. The Eskimo ten-year-old is as well adjusted to his community as his American counterpart. But if the Eskimo and American children exchanged locales, each would quickly develop the symptoms psychiatrists call neurotic. Each would have brought to his new home a set of dispositions inappropriate to the standards of that residential space.

Freda Rebelsky has noted that during the first ten months of life infants in the eastern part of Holland are held only when they are being fed.[3] At other times, they lie tightly bound in bassinets that are placed in small rooms isolated from the more dynamic parts of the house. They have no toys, no mobiles, and minimal stimulation, and the amount and variety of adult contact is far less than that encountered by the average American infant. Yet, by age five, these Dutch children do not seem to be different from five-year-old Americans. Indian infants living in the isolated highlands of Guatemala are held by adults over six hours a day, in contrast to the sixty minutes of maternal carrying characteristic of American Homes. Yet, at age ten, there is no evidence of major differences in fundamental intellectual competence or affective vitality between Indian and American children.

Since these are not uniquely exotic examples of relativism in child development, it is reasonable to repeat the question contained in the title of this paper: namely, "What do children need?" when food and protection from excessive disease and physical discomfort are guaranteed. We wish to take a strong stand on this issue by suggesting that *children do not require any specific actions from adults in order to develop optimally.* There is no good evidence to indicate that children must have a certain amount or schedule of cuddling, kissing, spanking, holding or deprivation of privileges in order to become gratified and productive adults. The child does have some psychological needs, but there is no fixed list of parental behaviors that can be counted on to fill these critical requirements.

Psychologists must develop an appreciation for the message it took biologists so long to learn: namely, that environmental niches are neither good nor bad in any absolute sense. Rather, they are appropriate or inappropriate for a specific species; hence, an organism's requirements can never be separated from the environment in which it grows. Frogs are best situated in a New England forest pond, not in the Mojave Desert; lizards have the opposite profile of ecological requirements. To ask what a child needs is to pose half a question. We must always specify the demands the community will make upon the adolescent and young adult. Since we are primarily concerned with the problems of psychological growth in this society, the remainder of the discussion will take America as the context of development, although it is hoped that some of the presumptious statements to be made have some application beyond North America.

An American child must believe, first of all, that he is valued by his parents and a few special people in his community (usually a teacher or two, but often older peers, uncles, aunts and coaches). Since our society makes personal competence synonymous with virtue, the sculpting of a particular talent, or better yet, talents, is usually necessary but not sufficient requirement for the development of a sense of worth. Obviously it is possible to list the appropriate set of competences to be attained only if one knows the domains of mastery that the community values. In the remote Indian village in western Guatemala in which I worked last year, the ability to care for young children with efficiency and skill produced this feeling of worth in preadolescent girls. In the United States, it is more closely tied to quality of performance in junior high school. Hence, competence in academic subjects is a *sine qua non* for the American child. It is difficult, if not impossible, to fail this requirement completely and still retain a sense of dignity and worth in adulthood.

The American child must also develop autonomy, the belief that he or she is able to and desires to make decisions regarding his conduct and his future, independent of coercive pressures from parents, teachers, and friends. The recent increase in drug use among American youth threatens older Americans not because of an automatic revulsion toward pills or smoking, but because it is believed that marijuana and heroin destroy the desire to be independent and autonomous. In a culture in which the majority of twenty-five-year-olds do not live within visiting distance of the family and friends with whom intense childhood intimacies were shared, it can be argued that it is adaptive for autonomy to be promoted so conscientiously. There is another reason why autonomy has become such a precious characterstic. A society's typical mode of livelihood always exerts some influence on the psychological characteristics it extols. There is greater independence, autonomy and permissiveness toward aggression among African tribes in which pastoralism dominates the economy than among tribal groups in the same country where agriculture is the main source of income.[4] The reasonableness of this correlation derives from the fact that a twelve-year-old boy who is given daily responsibility for fifty head of cattle must make a series of independent decisions that do not arise for a twelve-year-old who helps his father plow a field or plant maize. Moreover, personal disputes are less disruptive in a pastoral setting, where the disputants can easily put miles between them, than in a fixed agricultural village, where actors are totally captive in a small area, and feuds, therefore, must be suppressed.

Most Americans earn and increase their livelihood by perfecting talents that an institution wants. We have an economy in which services and skills are offered for payment. Unlike the situation in modern Japan, where each worker has a primary lifetime loyalty to the company for which he works,[5] the unwritten understanding in the United States is that primary loyalty is not awarded to the institution (be it company, university or governmental agency) but to the self. (I assume it is understood that the writer is not condoning this arrangement, but merely describing it.) If financial gain is to be maximized, young adults must be socialized to make decisions that are best for them. Hence, most parents unconsciously encourage their children to decide conflicts for themselves. The parental admonition to a fifteen-year-old, "You will have to decide whether you want to go to the movies or save your allowance," which is so rare outside the Western community, is part of the daily preparation for adulthood. Parents are probably unaware of the hidden message in these communications, but their effect is measurable, nonetheless.

Finally, and here we are more similar to other cultures, America requires the young adult to be heterosexually successful; to be able to love and be loved and to take pleasure from sexual experience. As a result we promote a permissive attitude toward sexuality.

These attributes comprise the core of America's current ego ideal. There is much to celebrate in this list, but also much to mourn. There is, in our opinion, insufficient emphasis on intimacy and too much on self-interest; insufficient emphasis on cooperation and too much on competitiveness; insufficient emphasis on altruism and too much on narcissism. But we cannot alter this catechism by shaking our heads and pulling at our chins. These values derive, in part, from the form of our economy, our densely crowded, impersonal cities and the fact that our educational institutions function as twelve-to-sixteen-year selection sites for tomorrow's doctors, teachers, laywers, administrators, scientists and business executives. These basic structures will have to change a little if we want our values to reflect more humanism. Put succinctly, the fact that Bobby Fischer's flagrant narcissism was excusable because he beat Boris Spassky for the chess championship last year suggests that the only thing more important to Americans than character is individual success.

Since it is not likely that our economy, our cities and our institutions will change dramatically during the next decade—perhaps they will over a longer period—American parents will probably not alter their tendency to encourage the values and associated competences listed above: namely, academic success, autonomy, independence, and a permissive emotional attitude toward hostility and sexuality. However, at another time, they might easily be persuaded to promote a different creed.

The ego ideal we have been considering is appropriate to the adolescent and adult. There is merit in considering the more specific accomplishments appropriate to each of the developmental stages—infancy, the preschool years, preadolescence, and adolescence—and it is these to which we now turn our attention. Again, these suggestions are to be taken as speculations for discussion and hypotheses for testing in the harsh empirical arena, rather than firm inferences from reliable empirical information.

Infancy

During the first year and a half to two years, the infant needs at least four classes of experience. He must have environmental variety that can be assimilated with moderate effort. An excessively homogeneous environment with little discrepant experience temporarily retards psychological growth and turns the child away from the world around him. My observations in the Indian village in Guatemala suggest that infants who received an abundance of physical contact—they were on their mother's bodies a large part of the day—but insufficient experiential variety were intellectually retarded and affectively depressed in comparison with American children during the first two years of life. These infants, who were nursed on demand and held for hours but rarely spoken to or played with, resembled the marasmic infants Spitz saw in the South American orphanages he visited almost thirty years ago.[6] These Indian infants had sufficient physical affection and love, but insufficient stimulus variety. Most American homes have enough assimilable variety for proper psychological growth. For the few that do not, existing information suggests a mild retardation in cognitive and affective processes.

Experiences that are too discrepant to be understood often frighten the child and provoke withdrawal and inhibition; excessive homogeneity promotes a listless, nonalert attitude. The first task of development is to understand unusual happenings in the outside world.

The infant also needs regularity of experience. Regularity is, of course, a relativistic concept. It does not mean that the mother must put the child on a two-, four- or eight-hour schedule, only on a regular one. The child needs some predictability, for by the time he is six months old he is making predictions and altering his sleeping, activity and eating cycles as a function of the regularities in his day. When his expectations are not realized, anxiety grows and can disturb major aspects of functioning. The child needs caretaking by adults rather than machines because our culture requires the older child to relate to people rather than objects. Finally, the infant needs the opportunity to practice his emerging motor skills. There is cognitive and affective gain derived from banging mobiles, shaking rattles, knocking down block towers and crawling.

Preschool Child, Age Two to Five Years

The child continues to need opportunities to master body and object problems. Additionally, when he has begun to master the symbolic language of his community—anywhere from eighteen to thirty months of age—he needs exposure to language. If he does not live in a sea of speech he will remain mute, even though he possesses the biological competence for talking and understanding. Existing evidence suggests that all the child needs is exposure—no special tutoring, books, television programs or radios. The simple experience of hearing people talking—especially to him—seems sufficient.

Third, the child must encounter actions, gestures and communications that affirm his virtue, value and worth. Families will communicate this message in different ways. Hence, the concept of parental (later on, peer) rejection should not be biased toward an absolute definition. There is no definable set of behaviors that always means rejection and leads inevitably to a particular form of the child's self-concept. There has been a tendency for American psychologists to assume that there are specific parental actions that signify rejection, for there is an enormous degree of commonality in the definition of this concept among investigators who have studied a mother's behavior with her child.[7] These and others decided that harsh physical punishment and absence of social play and affection are the signs of maternal rejection. It would be impossible for an American psychologist to categorize a mother as high on both aloofness and a loving attitude. But that view may be provincial. Alfred Baldwin reports that in rural areas of northern Norway where homes are five to ten miles apart, one sees maternal behavior which an American observer would regard as pathognomonically rejecting in an American mother.[8] The Norwegian mother sees her four-year-old sitting in a doorway blocking the passage to the next room. She does not ask him to move, but bends down, picks him up, and silently moves him away before she passes to the next room. A middle-class observer would be tempted to view this indifference as a sign of dislike. However, most mothers in this Arctic outpost behave this way; and the children do not behave the way rejected children should by our theoretical propositions.

An uneducated black mother from North Carolina slaps her four-year-old across the face when he does not come to the table on time. The intensity of the act tempts our observer to conclude that the mother resents her child. However, during a half-hour conservation, the mother indicates her warm feelings for the boy. She hit him because she does not want him to become a "bad boy," and she believes physical punishment is the most effective socialization procedure. Now her behavior seems to be issued in the service of affection rather than hostility. Evaluation of a parent as rejecting or accepting cannot be answered by noting the parent's behavior, for rejection is not a fixed quality of behavior. Like pleasure, pain or beauty, rejection is in the mind of the rejectee. It is a belief held by the child, not an action by a parent.

We must acknowledge an important discontinuity in the meaning of acceptance-rejection for the child prior to eighteen months of age, before he symbolically evaluates the actions of others, in contrast to the symbolic child of three of four years. We require a concept to deal with the child's belief in his value in the eyes of others. The five-year-old is conceptually mature enough to recognize that certain resources parents possess are difficult for him to obtain. He views these resources as sacrifices and interprets receiving them as signs that the parents value him. The child constructs a tote board of the differential value of parental gifts, be they psychological or material. The value of the gift depends on its scarcity. A ten-dollar toy from an executive father is not a valued resource; the same toy from a father out of work is prized. The value depends on the child's personal weighting. This position would lead to solipsism were it not for the fact that most parents are narcissistic and do not readily give the child long periods of uninterrupted companionship. Hence most children place a high premium on this act. Parents are also reluctant to donate unusually expensive gifts, and such a prize acquires value for many youngsters. Finally, the American child learns through the public media that physical affection means a positive evaluation, and he is persuaded to assign premium worth to this experience. There is, therefore, some uniformity across children in our culture with respect to the evaluation of parental acts of acceptance or rejection. But the anchor point lies within the child, not with particular parental behaviors. It is suggested, therefore, that different concepts are necessary for the following phenomena:

- an attitude on the part of the parent,

- the quality and frequency of acts of parental care and stimulation, and, finally,

- the child's assessment of his values in the eyes of another.

All three categories are currently viewed as of the same cloth.

Fourth, the preschool child needs models to whom he feels similar and who he believes possess competence, power and virtue in the group he takes as his primary reference. This phenomenon of vicarious sharing in the strength and positive emotional states of another to whom one feels similar is called identification. A young man recalls his childhood feelings for his father: "My admiration for him transcended everything. I always wanted to work with my hands on machinery, to drive big trucks, to fix things like he did. I didn't really like spinach, but I never lost the image of his bathtub filled with it, and up until a few years ago I always ate it—it was good for me and would make me strong like him."[9]

The child's self-concept and values derive, in part, from his pattern of identifications with those models with whom he shares basic psychological and physical similarities. Although parents are the primary identification figures for most children, each teacher is a potential model, and the teacher's power to sculpt values and self-esteem is usually underestimated.

Since school success is so important in American society, we should not forget that the teacher has the power to persuade the child of the joy, beauty and potential utility of knowledge, even though the typical second-grader initially rejects that idea. The teacher's most potent weapon of persuasion is herself, for if she is seen as kind, competent and just, the child will award to the school tasks she encourages the same reverence he assigns to her.

Finally, the preschool child needs to experience consistency with respect to the standards being socialized. The content of those standards is less critical than the fact of knowing that what is wrong and what is right remain constant from day to day. A child cannot deal with the dissonance that is produced by being punished for fighting on Monday but jokingly teased for the same violation on Wednesday. It was suggested that during the first two years, the infant was trying to understand unusual experiences in the world. The primary task during the preschool years is to understand the self, and the child needs information that will help him solve that problem.

The School-Age and Preadolescent Years

During preadolescence, the child must successfully master the school's basic requirements, which happen to be at the moment reading, writing and mathematics. These competences are not as central in many parts of the world as they are in our community. Second, the child has to be successful in some minimal number of peer-valued talents. Third, the preadolescent continues to require desirable models for identification. These heroes can be older siblings or friends who seem to have access to resources the ten-year-old values. These resources have a universal quality and usually include strength, power over others, competence at culturally valued skills and a belief in the moral goodness of the model. The ten-year-old needs exposure to one or two of these figures, as well as information that indicates that he shares some similarity with them so that he can confidently expect eventually to become like them. The preadolescent also needs the opportunity to match his attributes to the standards that society has declared to be the sex role ideal. A Kyoto girl is taught that gentleness is the central feminine quality, a Kipsigis girls believes that bearing many children is central, a Los Angeles girl is told that physical beauty has priority. Each of these adolescents wants to know how feminine she is and each tries to elaborate the attributes that define the ideal female identity.

The Needs of the Adolescent

In most peasant societies, it is not necessary that the adolescent be particularly talented at some special aptitude. But America so finely differentiates its children that they cannot carve identities of their own unless they possess beliefs and proficiencies that are, in some way, unique. The adolescent also has to believe that he is attractive to his peers, members of the opposite as well as of the same sex. Many American upper-middle-class adolescents who have developed strong group bonds that are partly asexual promote the value of being attractive to all of one's peers.

The adolescent continues to need exposure to and interaction with models whom he perceives to be heroic, for they make the difficult task of becoming an adult attractive. Moreover, the adolescent must have the opportunity to practice roles and actions that define adulthood, for he must develop an expectation that he can attain that status. Finally, because possession of an ideology is so critical to the modern American adolescent, he needs freedom from excessive dissonance. The adolescent is generating a consistent set of rules to which he wishes to be loyal, and he requires some peer and family support for the tenets he hopes to use in adult life. While the adolescent is trying to give roots to these ideals—as one would a fragile plant—he must believe that this personal ideology is, in some way, better than other dogmas he might have selected. The daily experience of encountering rival beliefs that are inconsistent with one's own premises and displayed by persons whom one cannot easily disenfranchise often leads to chronic anxiety, which erodes the confidence in principles that comes from believing there is something special about the ideology one has established.

Adolescents of all societies must build a sense of self, and the ingredients used in this construction will vary with time and community. Each society posts the rules by which the adolescent can diagnose the rate at which he is progressing toward maturity. In many locales, the simple roles of wife, father, mother and husband are the only requirements for admission into adult circles. Our own community has placed a special obstacle in the path of the adolescent by requiring that he display an autonomously built belief system—a distinct set of values—in order to gain admission into that identity we call adulthood. Since the fourteen-year-old realizes that his values are borrowed from his family, he experiences a deep conflict between what he must attain and his current state. He strives to alter his beliefs in order to persuade himself that the resulting arrangement is his own personal creation and not a warmed-over version borrowed from his family. The ideational rebellion that has become characteristic of middle-class adolescents in our society does not primarily serve hostility, but rather is a product of the more pressing need to persuade the self that its configuration of wishes, values and behaviors derives from a personally constructed philosophy. If "what one believes" were less central to the integrity of the American adolescent than it is at the present time, the clash of values between child and parent might not occur with such ferocity. The task for the adolescent is to know what he believes.

These are tentative suggestions for the needs of American children. It is a much more difficult task to suggest strategies for gratifying these needs. Since we have argued that development of talent is central, we must make serious changes in our educational systems in order to maximize the child's sense of competence. We must, for example, expand the number of talents that we applaud. The Spartans valued physical fitness, the Athenians music, the Puritans knowledge of the Bible, and we, reading and mathematics. Perhaps we should include all of these areas of expertise in our curriculum. The honest award of praise for art, music, oratory, and physical fitness in the primary school would help many children, who, by reason of historical circumstance, enter the first grade less well prepared than others for reading and mathematics instruction.

Although the school cannot, without cooperation from the larger society, singlehandedly change the community's value system, it can at least begin the work. This is not just a sentimental plea for a softer view of education. The industrial revolution following the Civil War created a strong need for managers and technicians, and our educational institutions responded efficiently and met that need. Historical events during the last decade, the war being only one, have created a new, but equally vital, requirement. Our society temporarily needs to restore its belief in the honesty, sincerity and humanity of its members. It has lost its optimism, temporarily, we hope, and this lacuna is as serious as the absence of engineers at the turn of the century. The school and the family, two of our most central institutions, must arrange conditions so that these qualities are awarded greater value until the psychological repair process has been accomplished.

Summary

Let me try to weave the themes of this essay into a closer fabric so that the design is less hazy. The needs of children vary with their age and their context of growth. In our society, they include varieties of manageable experiences during infancy, the opportunity to practice maturing capacities and to attain locally valued talents, to believe one is valued and to identify with role models who are regarded as powerful, talented and virtuous and, finally, protection from excessive irregularity and dissonance of values. I am assuming that the child is not exposed to regular and severe physical pain, hunger, cold and disease.

The psychological differences between a young Boston lawyer and a young Guatemalan Indian farmer do not depend so much on the specific actions their parents displayed toward them during childhood, but rather on their ability to carry out the messages their reference groups sent them regarding the missions to be accomplished on the journey to adulthood. A healthy society is one that both selects missions that need to be assigned to solve future problems and provides the largest number of its youth with opportunities to carry out the requisite assignments.

References

1. Jerome Kagan, "Cross Cultural Perspectives in Early Development" (paper delivered to the American Association for the Advancement of Science, Washington, D.C., December 26, 1972).
2. Jean Briggs, *Never in Anger* (Cambridge: Harvard University Press, 1970).
3. Freda Rebelsky, "Infancy in Two Cultures," *Nederlands Tijdschrift voor de Psychologie* 22 (1967):379–385.
4. Robert B. Edgerton, *Individual in Cultural Adaptation: A Study of Four East African Peoples* (Berkeley: University of California Press, 1971).
5. Chie Nakane, *Japanese Society* (Berkeley: University of California Press, 1972).
6. René A. Spitz and Katherine M. Wolf, "Anaclitic Depression: An Inquiry into the Genesis of Psychiatric Conditions in Early Childhood," in Anna Freud et al., eds., *The Psychoanalytic Study of the Child* (New York: International Universities, 1946), II, 313–342.

7. Alfred L. Baldwin, Joan Kalhorn, and Faye H. Breese, "Patterns of Parent Behavior," *Psychological Monographs* 58, no. 3 (1945); Wesley Becker, "Consequences of Different Kinds of Parental Discipline," in Martin L. Hoffman and Lois W. Hoffman, eds., *Review of Child Development and Research* (New York: Russell Sage Foundation, 1964), I, 169–208; Jerome Kagan and Howard A. Moss, *Birth to Maturity* (New York: Wiley, 1962); Earl S. Schaefer, "A Circumplex Model for Material Behavior." *Journal of Abnormal and Social Psychology* 59 (1959): 226–235; Earl S. Schaefer and Nancy Bayley, "Maternal Behavior, Child Behavior, and Their Intercorrelations from Infancy through Adolescence," *Monographs of the Society for Research in Child Development.* no. 87 (1963), p. 28; and Robert R. Sears, Eleanor E. Maccoby, and Harry Levin, *Patterns of Child Rearing* (Evanston, Ill: Rowe, Peterson, 1957).
8. Alfred L. Baldwin, personal communication.
9. George W. Goethals and Dennis S. Klos, *Experiencing Youth* (Boston: Little, Brown & Co., 1970), p. 44.

The Effects of Parental Divorce: Experiences of the Child in Later Latency

Judith S. Wallerstein and Joan B. Kelly

The child of latency age* has somehow managed to escape the intensive psychological scrutiny with which his younger and older siblings have been regarded. Although no one has disputed the central significance of latency, which Erickson[3] has characterized as "socially, a most decisive stage," much less is known or conceptualized regarding parent-child relationships during these middle years than of those developmental years which immediately precede or follow them. Moreover, relatively little attention has been devoted to the varying effects of disrupted or fixated development during latency. Although many school-age children come into therapy, the central focus is usually on failure to resolve conflicts that stem from earlier developmental periods. Nor do we tend to learn much about latency from the treatment of adults; there is a relative unavailability of transferences and reconstructions pertaining to these years in most adult analyses. Bornstein[2] attributed the fact that "One learns relatively little about latency from the analysis of adults" to the distorted and idealized memories of adult patients who recall "the ideal of latency," namely, the successful warding-off of instinctual impulses during this time.

It is commonly agreed that the confluence of developmental and social forces propel the school-age child outward and away from the family towards

From the *American Journal of Orthopsychiatry,* Vol. 46, No. 2 (April 1976), pp. 257–269. Copyright © 1976 the American Orthopsychiatric Association, Inc. Reproduced by permission.
*[Latency is a psychoanalytic concept referring to school age, around 6–12, when sexuality is considered "latent" compared to the developmental stages immediately preceding or following.]

peer relationships and new adult figures. Clinicians have stressed[1,2,5,6,8] the special importance of assuring developmental continuity during these years. Bornstein[2] specifically cautioned against environmental interruptions, referring to the importance of "free energies needed for character development," and observing that the latency child "fears nothing more than the upsetting of his precarious equilibrium." Erikson,[3,4] in addressing the fundamental tasks of this period, called attention to the lasting consequences of partial or total failure to successfully master these at their appropriate times. And Sarnoff,[8] more recently, referring to the fragility of the newly-consolidated latency defenses, warned that the drives in latency "may be stirred into activity at any time by seduction or sympathetic stimulation."

It is within this context, stressing the overriding importance of developmental continuity during his life phase, that our understanding of the impact of parental divorce upon the child must be set. For divorce necessarily affects the freedom of the child to keep major attention riveted outside the family circle. Moreover, the decision of divorce frequently ushers in an extended several year period marked by uncertainty and sharp discontinuity which has the potential to move the psychological and social functioning of the latency child into profound disequilibrium and painfully altered parent-child relationships. Alternatively, these changes can bear the potential for promoting development and maturation, as well as the possibility of more gratifying relationships within the post-divorce family structure.

Our data for this paper are drawn from the sample already described,[7] of 57 latency aged children from 47 families, here focused on the experiences of the 31 children from 28 families who were between nine and ten years old at the time that they were initially seen by us. As elaborated elsewhere,[7,9,10] these 31 children from 28 families represent part of a cohort of 131 children from 60 divorcing families referred for anticipatory guidance and planning for their children around the separation, and then seen by us again approximately a year later for the first of two planned follow-up studies.

The Initial Responses

How They Looked When They Came

Many of these children had presence, poise, and courage when they came to their initial interviews. They perceived the realities of their families' disruption and the parental turbulence with a soberness and clarity which we at first found startling, particularly when compared with the younger children who so frequently appeared disorganized and immobilized by their worry and grief. These youngsters were, by contrast, actively struggling to master a host of intense conflicting feelings and fears and trying to give coherence and continuity to the baffling disorder which they now experienced in their lives.

Robert said, "I have to calm myself down. Everything is happening too fast."

Katherine told us that a long time ago, when she was little, she thought everything was fine, that her parents really loved each other, and that, "Nothing would happen to them until they got real, real old." She added with the fine perceptions of a latency age child, "Mom and Dad married 12½ years ago. They met 17½ years ago. I always thought love would last if they stayed together that long."

Some children came prepared with an agenda.

Anna, after a few general comments from the interviewer, designed to put her at ease, interrupted with a brisk, "Down to business," and went on immediately to describe the diffuse feelings of anxiety with which she suffered these days and which made her feel "sick to her stomach."

Mary volunteered that she was "so glad" her mother brought her to talk about the divorce because, "If I don't talk about it soon I'll fall apart."

For others the opportunity to be with a concerned adult had considerable significance seemingly unrelated to specific content. Some of these children tried in many ways to continue the relationship.

Janet begged to return the following week. She offered, "I like to talk about my troubles," and drew a heart on the blackboard, writing under it, "I like Miss X."

Mary tried to extend her interview time, saying that her mother had not yet returned to fetch her, and then confessing that she had just lied.

Still others among these children found these interviews threatening and painful, and barely kept their anxiety controlled by keeping themselves or their extremities in continual motion, the rhythm of which motion correlated with the subject discussed.

Thus, legs moved much faster when Daddy was mentioned to Jim, who was bravely trying to maintain his calm and referred with some disdain to "Mother's divorce problem," adding, "I wonder who she's got now?"

Others maintained their composure by denial and distancing.

Jack stated, "I keep my cool. It's difficult to know what I'm thinking."

David said darkly, "I don't try to think about it."

The Layering of Response

These various efforts to manage—by seeking coherence, by denial, by courage, by bravado, by seeking support from others, by keeping in motion, by conscious avoidance—all emerged as age-available ways of coping with the profound underlying feelings of loss and rejection, of helplessness and loneliness that pervaded these children and that, in most of them, only gradually became visible within the context of the several successive interviews. Actually, testament to the resourcefulness of so many of these children is just this capacity to function simultaneously on these two widely discrepant levels, not always discernible to the outside observer. At times, only information from collateral sources revealed their simultaneous involvement in the mastery efforts of the coping stance and the succumbing to the anguish of their psychic pain. This at times conscious layering of psychological functioning is a specific finding in this age group. It is profoundly useful in muting and encapsulating the suffering, making it tolerable and enabling the child to move developmentally. But it does not overcome the hurt, which is still there and takes its toll.

> After his father left the home, Bob sat for many hours sobbing in his darkened room. The father visited infrequently. When seen by our project, Bob offered smilingly, "I have a grand time on his visits," and added unsolicited and cheerily, "I see him enough." Only later would he shamefacedly admit that he missed his father intensely and longed to see him daily.

A few children were able to express their suffering more directly to their parents, as well as to us. This is the more poignant if one bears in mind Bornstein's[2] admonition that the latency child is *normally* engaged developmentally in a powerful battle against painful feelings.

> Jane's father left his wife angrily after discovering her infidelity, and ceased visiting the children. He moved in with a woman who had children approximately the age of his own children. Jane cried on the telephone in speaking with her father "I want to see you. I want to see you. I miss you. Alice (referring to the child of the other woman) sees you every day. We only see you once a month. That's not enough."

A very few children succumbed more totally and regressively.

> Paul responded to his father's departure by lying curled up sobbing inside a closet. He alternated this behavior, which lasted intermittently for several weeks, with telephone calls to his father, imploring him to return.

The suffering of these children was governed not only by the immediate pain of the family rupture, but expressed as well their grief over the loss of the family structure they had until then known, as well as their fears for the uncertain future that lay ahead for their newly diminished family. In a sense, as compared with younger children, their more sophisticated and mature grasp of time and reality and history increased their comprehension of the meanings and consequences of divorce—which enabled some of them better to temper the impact.

> Jim, when told by his parents of the plan to divorce, cried, "Why did you have to wait until we were so old?"

Finally, efforts to master inner distress were conjoined at times with efforts to conceal from the outside observer because of an acute sense of shame.

Feelings of shame did not appear in the younger children in our study, but emerged specifically with this age group. These children were ashamed of the divorce and disruption in their family, despite their awareness of the commonness of divorce; they were ashamed of their parents and their behaviors, and they lied loyally to cover these up; and they were ashamed of the implied rejection of themselves in the father's departure, marking them, in their own eyes, as unlovable. . . .

Attempted Mastery by Activity and by Play

Unlike the younger latency children, so many of whom were immobilized by the family disruption, the pain which the children in this age group suffered often galvanized them into organized activity. This was usually a multidetermined response geared to overcome their sense of powerlessness in the face of the divorce, to overcome their humiliation at the rejection which they experienced, and to actively—and as energetically as possible—reverse the passively suffered family disruption. In some, this was a direct effort to undo the parental separation.

> Marian, with considerable encouragement at long distance from the paternal grandfather, embarked on a frenzied sequence of activities designed to intimidate her mother and force her to return to the marriage. Marian scolded, yelled, demanded, and berated her mother, often making to impossible for her mother to have dates, and indeed almost succeeding in reversing the divorce decision by mobilizing all her mother's guilt in relation to herself and the other children. In one such episode, the child screamed in anger for several hours and then came quietly and tearfully to her mother, saying softly, "Mom, I'm so unhappy," confessing that she felt "all alone in the world." Following this, the harassment ceased.

Several children in this older latency group energetically developed a variety of new, exciting, and intrinsically pleasurable mastery activities which combined play action with reality adaptation. Many of these activities required not only fantasy production but the enterprise, organization, and skill of the later latency child.

> Ann, whose father was a successful advertising and public relations man, designed and issued a magazine with articles and drawings, announcing the impending divorce of her parents, together with other interesting happenings, which she distributed and sold in her school and community.

In her role identification with her public media father, Ann not only overcame the loss of his ongoing presence, at the very same time, through her newspaper publication, she proclaimed her acceptance of the reality of this loss. But central to this maneuver is the psychic gratification in it—Ann transformed pain into the pleasure of achievement, and recaptured the center stage of interest. . . .

Anger

The single feeling that most clearly distinguished this group from all the younger children was their conscious intense anger. It had many sources, but clearly a major determinant was its role in temporarily obliterating or at least obscuring the other even more painful affective responses we have described. Although we have reported elsewhere[10] a rise in aggression and irritability in the pre-school child following parental separation, the anger experienced by these older latency children was different in being both well organized and clearly object-directed; indeed, their capacity directly to articulate this anger was striking.

> John volunteered that most of the families of the kids on his block were getting a divorce. When asked how the children felt, he said, "They're so angry they're almost going crazy."

Approximately half of the children in this group were angry at their mothers, the other half at their fathers, and a goodly number were angry at both. Many of the children were angry at the parent whom they thought initiated the divorce, and their perception of this was usually accurate.

> Amy said she was angry at Mom for kicking Dad out and ruining their lives. "She's acting just like a college student, at age 31—dancing and dating and having to be with her friends."

> Ben accused his mother, saying, "You told me it would be better after the divorce, and it isn't."

> One adopted child screamed at his mother, "If you knew you were going to divorce, why did you adopt us?"

Interestingly, despite detailed and often very personal knowledge of the serious causes underlying the divorce decision, including repeated scenes of violence between the parents, most of these children were unable at the time of the initial counseling to see any justification for the parental decision to divorce. (By follow-up, many had come more soberly to terms with this.) Although one father had held his wife on the floor and put bobbie pins in her nose while their two children cried and begged him to stop, both children initially strongly opposed the mother's decision to divorce.

For some, anger against the parents was wedded to a sense of moral indignation and outrage that the parent who had been correcting their conduct was behaving in what they considered to be an immoral and irresponsible fashion.

> Mark said that "three days before my dad left he was telling me all these things about 'be good.' That hurt the most," he said, to think that his father did that and knew he was going to leave all the time.

This kind of moral stance in judgment upon parents is reminiscent of the attitudes we found frequently in the adolescent group,[9] but not in the younger groups.

The intense anger of these children was variously expressed. Parents reported a rise in temper tantrums, in scolding, in diffuse demandingness, and in dictatorial attitudes. Sometimes the anger was expressed in organized crescendos to provide a calculated nuisance when the mother's dates arrived.

> Shortly after the divorce, Joe's abusive, erratic, and rejecting father disappeared, leaving no address. The mother reported that now she had to ask the boy for permission to go out on dates, was reproached by him if she drank, and had her telephone calls monitored by him; when she bought something for herself, he screamingly demanded that the same amount of money be spent on him. Joe used his sessions with us primarily to express his anger at his mother for not purchasing a gun for him.

Adding to the dictatorial posturing and swaggering expressions that these children enjoyed playing out following the departure of their fathers was the fact that, in many of these households, the father had carried responsibility for a harsh and frightening discipline. His departure thus signaled a new freedom to express impulses that had been carefully held in check during his presence, a freedom to do so with impunity and with pleasure.

> Mary said that she was scared of her father. He had always required that things be spic and span around the house. "In that way I'm glad he's gone," she said.

Many mothers were immoblized by their own conflicts, as well as by their unfamiliarity with the role of disciplinarian. Others indicated in covert ways that they fully expected that one of the children would assume the father's role within the family. For some of these children the taking on of such an aggressive stance clearly reflected an identification with the attributes of the departed father, and thus an undoing of the pain of his departure.

> Anne congratulated her mother warmly on her decision to divorce her tyrannical husband. Shortly thereafter, however, Anne herself began to act out a commanding and screaming role vis-a-vis her mother and the younger children. This culminated in a dramatic episode of screaming for many hours when an uncle attempted to curb her wild behavior. She became very frightened after this, offering that all men were untrustworthy and that nobody would ever love her again.

Other children showed the obverse of all this—namely, an increased compliance and decreased assertiveness following the divorce.

> Janet's behavior shifted in the direction of becoming mother's helper and shadow, and showing unquestioning obedience to her mother's orders. She became known throughout the neighborhood as an excellent and reliable baby-sitter despite her very young age (nine years). She was, however, not able to say anything even mildly critical of her rejecting father, and was one of the few children who openly blamed herself for the divorce. When initially seen by us, she was preoccupied with her feelings of inadequacy and her low self-esteem.

Fears and Phobias

Unlike the pre-school children and the younger latency group, the children of this sample were not worried about actual starvation, and references to hunger in response to the parental separation were rare. Their fears, however, were nonetheless pervasive. Some, while not entirely realistic, were still tied to reality considerations; others approached phobic proportions. In fact, among this group it was often difficult for us to separate out the reality bases, including their sensitivity to the unspoken wishes of their parents, from the phobic elaboration. Thus, approximately one-quarter of these children were worried about being forgotten or abandoned by both parents.

> John, in tears, said that his mother had left him at the doctor's office and didn't return on time. He cried, "She said that she was doing errands, but I know she was with her boyfriend."

> Martha said to her mother, "If you don't love Daddy, maybe I'm next."

Some of their responses related to their accurate perception of parental feelings that children represent an unwelcome burden at this time in their lives.

> Peggy reported that her mother had said to her, "If you're not good I'm going to leave." Although Peggy knew that her mother had said this in anger, she still worried about it.

> Ann opined, "If Daddy marries Mrs. S., she has two daughters of her own, and I'll be Cinderella."

Some expressed the not wholly unrealistic concern that reliance on one rather than two parents was considerably less secure, and therefore the child's position in the world had become more vulnerable.

> Katherine told us, "If my mother smokes and gets cancer, where would I live?" She repeatedly begged her mother to stop smoking, and worried intensely whenever her mother was late in arriving home.

Some worried, not unrealistically, about emotionally ill parents.

> Ann stated about her mother, "I love her very much, but I have feelings. I'm afraid when Mom takes a long time to come home. She once tried to commit suicide. One day she ate a whole bottle of pills. I think of someone dying . . . how I'll be when I'm alone. Mom tried to commit suicide because of my father. It wasn't until after the divorce that she stopped crying. I think of her jumping over the Golden Gate Bridge. Mom thinks no one worries about her, but I do."

Many of these children experienced the additional concern that their specific needs were likely to be overlooked or forgotten.

> Wendy referred several times through her interviews to the fact that her mother insisted on buying Fig Newtons, when she perfectly well knew that Wendy hated them.

Responsibility for the Divorce

Only a few children expressed concern about having caused the divorce, although we endeavored in a variety of ways, including direct observations, play, and drawings, to elicit such material. We may, perhaps, cautiously infer from the fact that their occasional stealing occurred in situations where the child was assured of being caught, that there may exist some need for punishment relating to guilty fantasies. However, our direct evidence on this issue was limited to a few children in this later latency group, and appeared only in those children who showed a variety of other symptomatic behaviors in addition to the guilty thinking.

> Lorraine, whose petty pilfering and lying and school difficulties were greater exacerabated with the parental separation, said, "Whenever I think something is going to happen, it goes and happens. Like the time I thought my great-aunt was going to die, and then she died. And like the time I thought there was going to be a divorce." She wished that she could grow up and become a good witch, like Samantha.

Shaken Sense of Identity

Many of these children experienced a sense of a shaken world in which the usual indicators had changed place or disappeared. For several children, these changed markers were particularly related to their sense of who they were and who they would become in the future. Critical to this new sense of stress is that during latency years the child's normal conception of his own identity is closely tied to the external family structure and developmentally dependent on the physical presence of parental figures—not only for nurture, protection, and control, but also for the consolidation of age appropriate identifications.[3,7] Specifically, the self image and identity which in latency is still organized around, "I am the son of John and Mary Smith," is profoundly shaken by the severance of the parental relationship. Some children expressed this confusion and sense of ruptured identity with anxious questions, comparing physical characteristics of their parents and themselves, as if trying in this manner to reassemble the broken pieces into a whole.

> Jack, unsolicited, volunteered a long discussion of his physical features. "My eyes change colors, just like my Mom's. My hair is going to change to light brown, just like my Dad's. Other people say I'm like my Dad. My Dad says I'm like my Mom. I say I'm like a combination."

Another aspect of this threat to the integrity of self which occurs at the time of divorce is posed more specifically to the socialization process and superego formation. The child feels that his conscience controls have been weakened by the family disruption, as the external supports give way and his anger at the parents moves strongly into consciousness. One manifestation of this may be new behaviors of petty stealing and lying which make their appearance in this age group around the time of family disruption. The threat the child perceives to his sense of being socialized is related, as well, to his concern of having to take care of himself; it was conveyed to us by Bob's moving story of his two rabbits.

> Bob volunteered, "I think I want to talk to you today." He told about the two little rabbits he had bought several years ago and cared for in an elaborate high-rise hutch he had carefully constructed. One day, despite his protective watchfulness, vicious neighborhood dogs ripped the cage apart, and the rabbits disappeared or were dragged off. The two rabbits, whom he had named Ragged Ear and Grey Face, may have escaped, he thinks, because recently he came upon two rabbits playing in the woods. They were wild rabbits now, but they resembled the two he had lost.

The two rabbits of this rich fantasy may well have referred to the child and his brother, and his story may reflect his fear of the primitive angers (the vicious dogs) let loose at the time of divorce, his fear that he would be destroyed, and the projected rescue solution—via return to a pre-socialized wild state in which the child-equals-rabbit takes responsibility for his own care. Clearly, the little wild rabbits who survived had a different identity and a different superego formation than the rabbits who were cared for so lovingly in the elaborately built hutch.

Loneliness and Loyalty Conflicts

Children in this older latency group described their loneliness, their sense of having been left outside, and their sad recognition of their powerlessness and peripheral role in major family decisions.

> Betty said,"We were sitting in the dark with candles. Then they (her parents) told us suddenly about the divorce. We didn't have anything to say, and so then we watched TV."

These feelings of loneliness, not observed in this way in the younger age groups, reflect not only the greater maturational achievement of these children but also their more grown-up expectation of mutuality, as well as reciprocal support, in their relationships with parents and other adults. They thus felt more hurt, humiliated, and pushed aside by the events visited upon them, over which they had so little leverage.

It should be noted that these children, in their wrestling with this loneliness, realistically perceived the very real parental withdrawal of interest in children which so often occurs at the time of divorce. In addition to the departure of one parent, both parents understandably at such times become preoccupied with their own needs; their emotional availability, their attention span, and even the time spent with the children are often sharply reduced. Moreover, the families in our study were, by and large, nuclear families, unconnected to wider extended families or support systems of any enduring significance to the children. In this sense the children's feelings of loneliness and of loss reflected their realization that the central connecting structures they had known were dissolving.

Perhaps, however, the central ingredient in the loneliness and sense of isolation these children reported was related to their perception of the divorce as a battle between the parents, in which the child is called upon to take sides.[7] By this logic, a step in the direction of the one parent was experienced by the child (and, of course, sometimes by the parent) as a betrayal of the other parent, likely to evoke real anger and further rejection, in addition to the intrapsychic conflicts mobilized. Thus, paralyzed by their own conflicting loyalties and the severe psychic or real penalties which attach to choice, many children refrained from choice and felt alone and desolate, with no place to turn for comfort or parenting. In a true sense, their conflict placed them in a solitary position at midpoint in the marital struggle. . . .

Changes in Parent-Child Relationships

We turn now to a necessarily abbreviated discussion of some of the new parent-child configurations that emerged as a response to the marital strife and parental separation. These changed relationships constitute a significant component of the total response of children in this age group. The divorce-triggered changes in the parent-child relationship may propel the child forward into a variety of precocious, adolescent, or, more accurately, pseudoadolescent behaviors. They can, on the other hand, catalyze the development of true empathic responsiveness and increased responsibility in the child. And they can also result, as in the case of alignment with one parent against the other, in a lessening of the age-appropriate distance between parent and child and a retreat by the child along the individuation-separation axis of development.

Alignment

One of the attributes of the parent-child relationship at this particular age is the peculiar interdependence of parent and child, which can become enhanced at the time of the divorce, and which accords the child a significant role in restoring of further diminishing the self-esteem of the parent. Thus the child in late latency, by his attitude, his stance, and his behavior has independent power to hurt, to reject, to confront, to forgive, to comfort, and to affirm. He also has the capacity to be an unswervingly loyal friend, ally, and "team member," exceeding in reliability his sometimes more fickle and capricious adolescent sibling.

Among the 31 children in this cohort, eight (or 26%) formed a relationship with one parent following the separation which was specifically aimed at the exclusion or active rejection of the other. These alignments were usually initiated and always fueled by the embattled parent, most often by the parent who felt aggrieved, deserted, exploited, or betrayed by the divorcing spouse. The angers which the parent and the child shared soon became the basis for complexly organized strategies aimed at hurting and harassing the former spouse, sometimes with the intent of shaming him or her into returning to the marriage. More often the aim was vengeance. For many of these parents, these anger-driven campaigns served additionally to ward off depressions, and their intensity remained undiminished for a long time following parental separation. It should be noted that none of these children who participated, many of them as ingenious and mischievous allies, had previously rejected the parent who, subsequent to the alignment, became the target of their angers. Therefore, their provocative behavior was extremely painful and their rejection bewildering and humiliating to the excluded parent.

Our data indicate that, although the fight for allegiance may be initiated by the embattled parent, these alignments strike a responsive chord in the children within this specific age group. In fact, it is our suggestion that for children in late latency, the alignment with one parent against the other represents a highly complexly organized, over-determined, ego-syntonic coping behavior, which serves a diversity of psychological needs and keeps at bay a number of significant intrapsychic conflicts and their attendant anxieties. A central part of the dynamic of this behavior is the splitting of the ambivalent relationship to the parents into that with the good parent and the bad parent. Moreover, in our findings, these alignments have the hurtful potential for consolidation and perpetuation long past the initial post-separation period, especially in those families where the child is aligned with the custodial parent.

> Paul's father was referred to us informally by the court to which the father had gone to complain of his wife's vindictive blocking of his visits with his three children. The father, a successful chemical engineer, expressed sadness and longing for his children, and concern that his children were being systematically turned against him by their mother's unremitting attacks and falsehoods. For example, the children were told by the mother that they had to give up their dog because the father was refusing to purchase food for it, although at that time the family was receiving well over $16,000 a year in support. Paul's mother expressed astonishment and bitterness at his father for the unilateral divorce decision, describing her many years of devoted love and hard work to support the father's graduate education. She coldly insisted that, as a devout Christian woman, she would never harbor anger. Yet she was convinced that, since the father had rejected both her and their three children, Paul would "never forgive his father, nor forget."
>
> Paul's initial response to the parental separation was his regression to sobbing in a dark closet, which we have earlier described, alternating with telephone pleas to his father to return. Later, in recalling this time, the child said to us, "I felt that I was being torn into two pieces." By the time we saw Paul, several months following the separation, he had consolidated an unshakable alignment with his mother. He extolled her as small and powerful, possessed of ESP, and knowledgeable in six languages. Of his father, he stated, "He'll never find another family like us." He volunteered that he never wanted to visit his father—ever. In response to our efforts to elicit fantasy

material, he said that he would like best to live on a desert island with his mother and siblings and have a very, very long telephone cord for speaking with his father, and maybe a speedboat for visiting him.

Among Paul's activities during the year following our initial contact was his continuing reporting to his mother, and eventually to her attorney, about his father's "lurid" social life and presumed delinquencies, and his continued rejections of his father's increasingly desperate overtures, including gifts and wishes to maintain visitation. Paul also maintained a coercive control over his younger sisters, who were eager to see their father, and he made sure by his monitoring of them that they would not respond with affection in his presence. At follow-up he told us, "We are a team now. We used to have an extra guy, and he broke us up into little pieces." His anger and his mother's anger seemed undiminished at this time.

Empathy

Heightened empathic response to one or both distressed parents—and siblings—was catalyzed in several children as a specific consequence of the separation and the ensuing divorce.

> With unusual insight, Anne described this process in *status nascendi*. She said, "I know that my mother isn't ready for the divorce, because I can put myself in her place. I can think just like I think my mother thinks."

Some youngsters were able to perceive their parent's needs with great sensitivity, and to respond with compassion and caring.

> Mary told us, "My mom cried. She was so tired of being so strong for the children, and she asked us to sleep with her." Mary and her brother complied. "It made Mom feel better. Then we got up in the morning and made her breakfast in bed. Sometimes we just tell her, 'we are here, it's going to be all right.' "

We were interested to find that parents were often profoundly appreciative of this sensitivity and consideration.

> Jane's mother told us that Jane was a wonderful child who wordlessly responded to the mother's needs and feelings. "Whenever I feel alone in the evening she cuddles me," her mother said.

Some of these children, especially the little girls, worried about their fathers and were concerned about the particulars of where they were sleeping and eating.

> Jane told us how much she worries about her father, that he works late, that he only has a couch to sleep on, and that he seems so "extra tired."

Sometimes the children took on responsibility for the younger children, as well as for themselves, and for important routines in the household. Many parents had no adult relationships to lean on, and they relied heavily on these children for emotional support and advice, as well as for practical help.

> Sometimes empathic feelings were stimulated by unequal treatment of siblings by the departing parent.

> Jack suddenly began to wheeze as he told us that his father had invited him, but not his sister, to live with him. He added that his father had sent him a Christmas card, signing it, "With all my love," but had only sent his sister a signed card. "I guess it made her feel pretty bad," he added sadly.

A few children were particularly sensitive to the changing moods and needs of their emotionally ill parent, and learned early to dissemble and protect what they understood to be the fragility of the parent's adjustment.

> Jane stated as one of her problems that it was hard for her to be honest with her mother. Her mother kept asking questions about the father's relationship with his new girlfriends. She, Jane, could not tell her mother that her father and his girlfriend didn't fight, because "I'm scared that it will make her sad and cry." At follow-up, Jane solemnly told us, "Mom will probably marry, but she is not ready. She just got the divorce and wants to be settled. I think she has gone through a lot of trouble and sadness and needs more time."

Follow-up at One Year

A first follow-up on these youngsters took place a year after the initial consultation. By and large, as with the younger latency children, the turbulent responses to the divorce itself had mostly become muted with the passage of the intervening year. In about half the children (15 of the 29 available at follow-up) the disequilibrium created by the family disruption—the suffering, the sense of shame; the fears of being forgotten, lost, or actively abandoned, and the many intense worries associated with their new sense of vulnerability and dependence on a more fragile family structure—had almost entirely subsided. But even these children with apparent better outcomes, who seemed relatively content with their new family life and circle of friends, including step-parents, were not without backward glances of bitterness and nostalgia. In fact, the anger and hostility aroused around the divorce events lingered longer and more tenaciously than did any of the other affective responses. Of the total group, ten (or one-third) of the children maintained an unremitted anger directed at the non-custodial parent; of these, four did so in alignment with the custodial mother, the other six on their own.

> Edward, who was doing splendidly in school and in new friendship relationships with his mother and with an admired male teacher, nonetheless said bitterly of his father, "I'm not going to speak to him any more. My dad is off my list now." (This was a father who, prior to the divorce, had had a very warm relationship with his son.)

Although some of these children who were doing well continued to harbor reconciliation wishes, most had come to accept the divorce with sad finality. Some seemed to be unconsciously extrapolating from these reconciliation wishes to plan future careers as repairmen, as bridge builders, as architects, as lawyers. Others, like Jane, were perhaps extending their protective attitudes towards their disturbed parents.

Asked what she might like to do when she grows up, Jane responded, "You might laugh. A child psychiatrist. You're one, aren't you?" She talked movingly of working someday "with blind children, or mentally retarded children, or children who cannot speak."

By contrast, the other half (14 of the 29 seen at follow-up) gave evidence of consolidation into troubled and conflicted depressive behavior patterns, with, in half of these, *more* open distress and disturbance than at the initial visit. A significant component in this now chronic maladjustment was a continuing depression and low self-esteem, combined with frequent school and peer difficulties. One such child was described by his teacher at follow-up as, "A little old man who worries all the time and rarely laughs." In this group, symptoms that had emerged had generally persisted and even worsened. For instance, phobic reactions had in one instance worsened and spread; delinquent behavior such as truancy and petty thievery remained relatively unchanged; and some who had become isolated and withdrawn were even more so. One new behavior configuration that emerged during the first post-divorce year in these nine-and ten-year-olds was a precocious thrust into adolescent preoccupation with sexuality and assertiveness, with all the detrimental potential of such phase-inappropriate unfoldings. And amongst all the children, both in the groups with better and with poorer outcomes, relatively few were able to maintain good relationships with both parents.

In a future report we shall present a fuller discussion of the many variables which seem to relate to this bimodal spread of outcomes for the post-divorce course of these children. Here we would like to close with the remarks of a ten-year-old sage from our study, whose words capture the salient mood of these children at the first follow-up—their clear-eyed perception of reality, their pragmatism, their courage, and their muted disappointment and sadness. In summarizing the entire scene, she said, "Knowing my parents, no one is going to change his mind. We'll just all have to get used to the situation and to them."

References

1. Becker, T. 1974. On latency, Psychoanal. Study of Child 29:3–11.
2. Bornstein, B. 1951. On latency. Psychoanal. Study of Child, 6:279–285.
3. Erickson, E. 1959. Identity and the life cycle. Psychological Issues vol. 1.
4. Erickson, E. 1963. Childhood and Society. Norton, New York.
5. Harris, I. 1959. Normal Children and Mothers. Free Press, Glencoe, Ill.
6. Kaplan, S. (Reporter). 1957. Panel: the latency period. JAPA 5:525–538.
7. Kelly, J. and Wallerstein, J. 1976. The effects of parental divorce: experiences of the child in early latency. Amer. J. Orthopsychiat. 46(1):20–32.
8. Sarnoff, C. 1971. Ego structure in latency. Psychoanal. Quart. 40:387–414.
9. Wallerstein, J. and Kelly, J. 1974. The effects of parental divorce: the adolescent experience. *In* the Child in His Family: Children at Psychiatric Risk, J. Anthony and C. Koupernik, eds. John Wiley, New York.
10. Wallerstein, J. and Kelly, J. 1975. The effects of parental divorce: experiences of the preschool child. J. Amer. Acad. Child Psychiat. 14(4).

"Children and Families"   *Kenneth Keniston*

American parents today are worried and uncertain about how to bring up their children. They feel unclear about the proper balance between permissiveness and firmness. They fear they are neglecting their children, yet sometimes resent the demands their children make. Americans wonder whether they are doing a good job as parents, yet are unable to define just what a good job is. In droves, they seek expert advice. And many prospective parents wonder whether they ought to have children at all. None of this is altogether new or uniquely American. Within forty years of their arrival in the Plymouth colony, the first white settlers were afraid their children had lost the dedication and religious conviction of the founding generation. Ever since, Americans have looked to the next generation not only with love and solicitude but with a good measure of anxiety, worrying whether they themselves were good parents, fearful that their children would not turn out well. Today, parents and other adults all over the world are concerned about the effects on the next generation of changing family values and new institutions.

What *is* new and very American is the intensity of the malaise, the sense of having no guidelines or supports for raising children, the feeling of not being in control as parents, and the widespread sense of personal guilt for what seems to be going awry. For when the right way to be a parent is not clear, almost any action can seem capricious or wrong, and every little trouble or minor storm in one's children's lives can become the cause for added self-blame.

The sense that it no longer is possible to raise their children the way they were raised is underscored for many parents by statistics documenting dramatic changes in family life and in the lives of the forty-nine out of every fifty American children who live in families. In 1948, for example, only 26 percent of married women with schoool-age children worked at anything but the job of keeping house and raising children.[1]* Now that figure has more than doubled: in March, 1976, 54 percent worked outside the home, a majority of them full time.[2] The increase in labor-force participation is even more dramatic for married women who have preschool children once considered too young to be without a parent during the day: the proportion of such mothers who work rose from 13 percent in 1948 to 37 percent in 1976.[3] In 1975, in only 34 out of 100 husband-wife families was the husband the sole breadwinner, compared with 56 out of 100 such families a quarter century ago.[4]

To be sure, changes in American family structure have been fairly continuous since the first European settlements, but today these changes seem to be occurring so rapidly that the shift is no longer a simple extension of long-term trends. We have passed a genuine watershed: this is the first time in our history that the *typical* school-age child has a mother who works outside the home.

Consider the number of children affected by divorce, a 700 percent increase since the turn of the century.[5] Today about one out of every three marriages ends in divorce, and more and more of them involve children. Although divorced people remarry at rates that are even higher—age for age, the marriage rate is higher among divorced people than among single people—it is now estimated that four out of every ten children born in the 1970's will spend a part of their childhood in a one-parent family, usually with their mother as head of the household.[6]

Accompanying rising divorce rates and the attendant splitting up of nuclear family groups are other significant changes in familial groupings. The proportion of first births to women who have no legal marriage partners has more than doubled—from 5 percent in the late 1950's to 11 percent in 1971—and almost one million of these mothers are setting up their own households with their babies every year. There has been an eightfold increase in the number of single persons of opposite sex living together in single households.[8] Communes are more common than they used to be. Each of these new forms demonstrates the flux in our cultural habits. But each one certainly deserves to be called a family as much as does the by now atypical family form, with husband as breadwinner and wife as homemaker.

Statistics only hint at the personal stresses that accompany these shifts. Whatever their reasons for working, mothers who go off to a job every day are likely to worry about harming their children by neglecting them. For many generations in this country, the ideal (though less often the reality) has been the stay-at-home mother, involved full time with her children until they enter school and, once they children are in the first grade, at home after school waiting for them. The evidence from social science suggests that a mother working does not necessarily produce disadvantages for a child.* But the worries persist, partly because of the practical problems in making good child-care arrangements during the working hours, partly because of the traditional view than an "adequate" mother is on tap for her children twenty-four hours a day, while an "adequate" father is one who earns so much money that his wife's earnings are not necessary to maintain a desirable standard of living.**

When mothers work outside the home, subtle changes take place in the relationships between the parents as well as between the parents and their children. Complete financial dependence of the wife on the husband becomes

---

*For a review of the research, see a background report to this Council, Alison Clarke-Stewart, *Child Care in the Family: A Review of Research and Some Propositions for Policy.* New York: Academic Press, 1977.

**The worries can be exactly reversed, of course, in a social circle where everyone believes strongly that women should work. There the widespread belief is that a woman who is *only* a mother is inadequate; she gets paid nothing for her full-time job and has trouble defining herself except in terms of her children and her husband's career.

a thing of the past; new pressures are put on men to share in housework and child care; traditional marriage roles begin to shift and at times to collapse. Another part of the anxiety of parents springs from these shifts. Are fathers who vacuum the house "real men"? Do they provide "adequate" role models for their sons? And how can it be good for children when their parents return home at the end of the day exhausted from demanding or draining work? In the absence of widely accepted answers, the response is likely to be worry and discomfort in the parents themselves and a fear of the "breakdown of the family" in those who observe these trends nationwide.

Rising divorce rates both reflect and lead to similarly complicated tensions. Divorce usually produces anger and a sense of failure for parents, issues of conflicting loyalty for children, and questions for everyone involved about whether the children will be harmed. What scientific evidence there is suggests that divorce is often better (or at least less harmful) for children than an unhappy, conflict-ridden marriage.* But this is scant consolation for parents and children who have to navigate the emotional transition from a two-parent to a one-parent family at the same time the split-up is spreading financial resources as thin as the self-confidence of family members.

When both parents work, or a single parent is not around regularly, who *is* raising the children? Not siblings, for one thing. As parents have fewer children, the days are over when young children in large families could be raised by older brothers and sisters still living at home. Although aunts and uncles, cousins and grandparents still do a surprising amount of child rearing and baby-sitting for working parents, they rarely live in the same house.[9]

Partly as a result, children now enter group settings outside their families earlier and earlier in their lives. These settings range from the daily group set up by a neighbor who takes in the children of three or four working mothers to the "developmental" day-care center with the latest curriculum and equipment, from nursery schools to Head Start programs.

Are these settings really good for children? If they are publicly sponsored, should parents worry that their children are being raised by the state—"collectivized" and "Sovietized," as critics have charged? If the settings are private and profit-making, are the children being shortchanged in the interest of a fast dollar? And in any case, do the children really get the kind of individual attention and concern that a loving parent could provide?

Television also plays a new role in the development of American children. By the age of eighteen, the average American child has spent more time watching television than in school or with his or her parents. The difference between television and a human companion is striking. One can reprimand or even fire a baby sitter who constantly talks of murder, mayhem, and violence,

---

*It is probably true, as Paul Bohannan and others[10] have arugued, that amicable divorces where the parents become attached to new partners can provide children with positive new versions of family life, enriching their lives with multiple adult models. No one knows how common this outcome really is.

or how wonderful the latest toys, cereals, and candies are, but it is impossible for an individual parent to influence programs and advertisements that do the same thing. If what is broadcast consistently conflicts with the parents' values, they have virtually no recourse short of smashing or locking up the set—and if parents did that, what would *they* watch? The result, again, is a sense of uneasiness about the handy but uncontrollable electronic baby sitter that seems to play so large a role in raising children.

Some children in this country have no contact with adults for extended periods every day. They are either locked up alone in empty apartments or left for hours out on the streets, more prone than other children to getting into trouble. No one knows how many "latchkey" children there are, but the fact that they exist at all contributes to the general feeling that American families are in real difficulty.

The discomforts and anxieties of today's parents are not nightmares dreamed up from nothing: they refelct deep changes in family life and in society. Americans have not had an easy time comprehending these changes —or imagining how to deal with them—in large part because our reactions are shaped by an outmoded set of views about how families work.

The Myth of the Self-Sufficient Family

When we Americans perceive unsettling changes in social patterns, such as the tremendous shifts in family life, we commonly blame them on the individuals involved. One current reaction to changes in families, for example, is the proposal for more "education for parenthood," on the theory that this training will not only teach specific skills such as how to change diapers or how to play responsively with toddlers, but will raise parents' self-confidence at the same time. The proposed cure, in short, is to reform and educate the people with the problem. One kind of education for parenthood takes the form of programs such as high school courses on "parenting" or lectures and demonstrations in hospitals for expectant mothers and fathers. In addition, a growing number of agencies and companies offer workshops, often at high fees, on "effective" parenting, or on how to stimulate children's development, or on how to increase their IQ's. A parallel for families defined as "disadvantaged" are federally funded "Home Start" courses that try to teach parents to play, "interact," and talk "more responsively" with their children. And of course by far the largest movement in parent education is the informal instruction American parents seek from newspapers, books, and magazines. No newspaper or family magazine is complete without one or more regular columns of advice on child rearing; drugstores have volumes of paperback counsel about every aspect of raising children.

Not that the experts agree. Burton White, a psychologist at Harvard, argues in a recent book[11] that the first three years are crucial in determining the rest of a child's life. His Harvard colleague, psychologist Jerome Kagan, says that the importance of the first three years has been overrated[12]—that late starts are not lost starts. Traditional child psychoanalysts advise parents to attend to their children's inner fantasies, fears, and dreams, while behaviorists counsel ignoring these and simply rewarding desired behavior.

Although the experts differ, they share one basic assumption: that parents alone are responsible for what becomes of their children. Of course, many parents can use information, advice, and counseling on everything from how to deal with illness to what can be expected of a moody teen-ager. But the columns and courses rarely mention the external pressures on parents' and children's lives—for example, the possibility that a harassed working parent who does not "interact responsively" with a child may not have much time or energy to do so after a long and exhausting day. It is not surprising that research on parent education in past decades[13] does not provide grounds for much optimism about the power of this approach to make significant changes in the family life of large numbers of people.

Naturally, if parents are considered solely responsible for what becomes of their children, they must be held at fault if things go awry. It is easy to leap from here to the conclusion that children's problems are caused entirely by the irresponsibility, selfishness, and hedonism of their parents. "Parents today are selfish and self-centered," one angry parent wrote us. "They aren't willing to make sacrifices for their children. But that's what being a parent is all about, so is it any wonder that the children grow up on drugs?" By this logic, everything from working mothers to the rising divorce rate can be blamed on the moral failing of those involved. Families on welfare are lazy, sponging chiselers. Parents who divorce are indulging themselves at the expense of their children. Working mothers neglect their children for a few dollars a day which they waste on clothes and vacations. If children get the outlandish idea from television advertising that there is a box or bottle with a cure for every problem, their parents must not be talking enough, guiding them enough, or supervising them enough. *Parents* are to blame; and if there is a solution, it must lie in reforming them.

Blaming parents and giving them advice both spring from the assumption that the problems of individuals can be solved by changing the individuals who have the problems. This implies a second assumption as well: that families are free-standing, independent, and autonomous units, relatively free from social pressures. If a family proves less than independent, if it is visibly needy, if its members ask for help, then it is by definition not an "adequate" family. Adequate families, the assumption runs, are self-sufficient and insulated from outside pressures.

These two assumptions form the core of the American myth of personal self-sufficiency. This myth has deep roots in American history, although it did not emerge in its full form until the early 1800's.

The notion of society as a voluntary assembly of independent and self-sufficient indviduals who freely contract with each other to form a community or nation was at the heart of the Enlightenment-Age thinking that flourished in the American colonies 200 years ago. The revolution that freed Americans from British rule has a psychological impact that was particularly important in establishing the myth of family independence and self-sufficiency. The American colonies had never provided fertile soil for feudal ideas of hierarchy, interdependence, and mutal obligation—ideas that bound peasants, vassals, and serfs to lords, squires, and landowners in return for benevolent protection and support in times of crisis. After the Revolution, free from British rule and isolated from Europe by an ocean that took weeks to traverse, Americans felt truly independent. The expulsion of the Indians to the area west of the Mississippi under Jackson opened vast tracts of forests and prairie for farming and land speculation and helped confirm the view that any American possessed of a minimum of ingenuity and industriousness could become self-sufficient in short order.

There were moral, political, and economic lessons in the ideal of the self-made man who knew no master, depended on no one, and lived by his wits. First, this ideal assigned special virtue to personal independence. To depend on others was not merely a misfortune but virtually a sin. Being independent attested to the possession of *moral* qualities: industriousness, enterprise, self-control, ingenuity, and rectitude. The dependent were suspected above all of idleness (the cause, most Americans came to think, of "pauperism") and sensuality (manifest in such sins as intemperance with alcohol, sexual immorality, and general self-indulgence).

Politically, the ideal of self-sufficiency helped define the qualities of the new democratic man in America. He would be free to make up his own mind and beholden to no man and no superstition—above all, to no foreign allegiance, Pope, or prince. He was not to rely on the state, nor was the state to interfere in civil society except when absolutely necessary to protect his basic rights. In the triumph of democratic ideas in the early 1800's, the active exercise of state power came to be seen not only as tyrannical but, perhaps even worse, as potentially weakening American independence and free spirit. Americans contrasted their democracy of free men to the allegedly decadent societies of Europe, where the political freedom, independence, and initiative of ordinary citizens supposedly was sapped by an overactive and authoritarian state. The ideal society—and most Americans believed that it was being realized in America—was like an assembly of free atoms: men who came together occasionally to vote and who expected the state to protect their freedoms, but who were otherwise on their own.

As an economic doctrine, the myth of self-sufficiency was built on images of the independent farmer and entrepreneur. The economic facts of life in seventeenth- and eighteenth-century America encouraged Americans to think of themselves as especially self-sufficient. The nation's economy was primarily agricultural. Before the development of large agricultural markets and specialized farm production, most farmers in the northern states were indeed largely able to provide for themselves, raising their own food and bartering their surplus or their labor for the necessities (few by today's standards) that they could not produce themselves. The myth was, in turn, closely connected to the work ethic, with its glorification of work not as a means to an end but as a good in itself. For children in particular, "industry"—industriousness—was a moral quality as well as a useful one. It showed good character; it established a presumption that the child was neither idle nor sensual, the two great vices to be avoided. But children's industriousness, in addition to establishing their virtue, was a prerequisite to adult economic self-sufficiency, which was thought possible for all those willing to work hard. The emerging capitalism of the early nineteenth century provided enough examples of success apparently achieved through industriousness to make this aspect of the myth believable.

In the early nineteenth century, the doctrine of self-sufficiency came to apply to families as well as individuals. Until then, families had been seen as fundamentally similar to the wider society, as "little commonwealths," in the Puritan phrase, governed by the same principles of piety and respect as the community at large. In the early 1800's, however, the more prosperous, urban classes pioneered a redefinition of the family. In their thinking—soon widely accepted as the ideal—the family became a special protected place, the repository of tender, pure, and generous feelings (embodied by the mother) and a bulwark and bastion against the raw, competitive, aggressive, and selfish world of commerce (embodied by the father) that was then beginning to emerge as the nation industrialized. A contemporary essay title was typical: "The Wife, Source of Comfort and Spring of Joy."[14] The family's task—and especially the mother's—was to protect the children's innocence against the temptations and moral corruptions of the treatening outside world. No longer simply a microcosm of the rest of society, the ideal family became a womblike "inside" to be defended against a corrupting "outside."

In performing this protective task, the good family was to be as self-sufficient as the good man. Ideally, it needed no outside help to armor its inhabitants against the vices of the streets. To be sure, an urban father had to venture into those streets to earn the family's living, and at times had to dirty his hands. But the pure wife-and-mother stayed at home, in part as a sign of the father's success, but also to protect her children from sin and temptation.

As the nineteenth century passed, Americans came to define the ideal family as one that was not only independent and self-sustaining but almost barricaded, as if the only way to guard against incursions from the outside was to reduce all contact with the rest of the world to a minimum.

If anything, this pristine portrait represented upper middle-class life in the cities, but only a privileged few American families could afford the insulation of women and children that the myth decreed. Most families lived a very different kind of life. Indians, slaves, Mexicans, poor people, immigrants, and growing numbers of factory workers were rarely as self-sufficient and independent as the myth said they should be. The ideal merely defined them as groups

to be changed, pitied, condemned, educated, uplifted, reformed, or American-
ized.

Nonetheless this ideal, like many other ideals, became a myth—the myth
of the self-sufficient individual and of the self-sufficient, protected, and protective family. And the myth prevailed. Even those who could not make it real
in their own lives often subscribed to it and felt guilty about not meeting its
standards. The myth determined who was seen as virtuous and who was
wanting; it provided, and still provides, the rationale for defining familial
adequacy and morality. This moralizing quality is one of its most important
features. For this myth tells us that those who need help are ultimately inadequate. And it tells us that for a family to need help—or at least to admit it
publicly—is to confess failure. Similarly, to give help, however generously, is
to acknowledge the inadequacy of the recipients and indirectly to condemn
them, to stigmatize them, and even to weaken what impulse they have toward
self-sufficiency.

The myth of self-sufficiency blinds us to the workings of other forces in
family life. For families are not now, nor were they ever, the self-sufficient
building blocks of society, exclusively responsible, praiseworthy, and blamable
for their own destiny. They are deeply influenced by broad social and economic
forces over which they have little control.

Notes

1. *Toward a National Policy for Children and Families,* the report of the Advisory Committee
   on Child Development of the National Academy of Sciences, Washington, D.C.: National
   Academy of Sciences, 1976.
2. U.S. Department of Labor, "Married Persons' Share of the Labor Force Declining, BLS Study
   Shows," *Department of Labor News,* No. 77191, March 8, 1977.
3. National Academy of Sciences, *op. cit.,* for 1948 figure; U.S. Department of Labor, *op.cit.,*
   for 1976 figure.
4. Howard Hayghe, "Families and the Rise of Working Wives—An Overview," *Monthly Labor
   Review,* May, 1976, U.S. Department of Labor, Bureau of Labor Statistics. During the year
   1975, about two-fifths of all children under age 18 were in families where both husband and
   wife worked, i.e., 22 million children (p. 16).
5. Kingsley Davis, "The American Family in Relation to Demographic Change," in *Demographic and Social Aspects of Population Growth,* Vol. 1, Charles R. Westoff and Robert Parke,
   Jr., eds., Commission on Population Growth and the American Future. Washington, D.C.:
   Government Printing Office, 1972.
6. Mary Jo Bane, "Marital Disruption and the Lives of Children," *Journal of Social Issues,* Vol.
   32, No. 1, 1976, pp. 109–110. Bane estimated that in the 1970's, between 20 percent and 30
   percent of all children under 18 will experience the divorce of their parents; an additional 3
   percent to 5 percent can be expected to be affected by an annulment or long-term separation;
   and about 9 percent will lose one or both parents by death. Thus, between 32 percent and
   44 percent will be involved in marital disruption. Another 2 percent will spend a substantial
   period of time in a single-parent home with a never married mother, bringing the total to
   between 34 percent and 46 percent.
       Americans marry at earlier ages than people in any other Western industrialized country;
   they marry more often and at any given time; more of them over the age of 14 are counted
   as married than their counterparts in other countries. Today 4 out of 5 divorced Americans
   eventually remarry; the average time between divorce and remarriage is 3 years. As noted,

age for age, the marriage rate is higher among the divorced population than it is among the single population. In 1970, about three-fifths of all children of a divorced parent were living in husband-wife families in which one was a stepparent.

For a discussion of the American habit of changing marital partners and its impact on children, see Davis, *op. cit.;* Paul Glick, "Some Recent Changes in American Families," *Current Population Reports,* Sepcial Studies, Series P-23, No. 52, U.S. Department of Commerce, Bureau of the Census, Washington, D.C.: Government Printing Office, 1976; and Alexander Plateris, "100 Years of Marriage and Divorce Statistics, United States 1867–1967," Department of Vital and Health Statistics, Series 21, No. 24, National Center for Health Statistics, U.S. Department of Health, Education and Welfare, December, 1973.

7. Glick, *op. cit.,* p. 3.

8. *Ibid.,* p. 13

9. Even when other adults are living with husband-wife families, they are more than likely to be found in the labor force. In 1975, of the 23 million families in which both husband and wife worked, 17.4 percent (almost a fifth) had a third worker in the family (*Monthly Labor Review,* May, 1976, U.S. Department of Labor, Bureau of Labor Statistics, p. 14, Table 3). That this trend will continue is evidenced by the numbers of young people aged 16–19 seeking work. But many are unable to find jobs. Unemployment rates for this group grew from 13 percent in 1973 to 20.5 percent in 1975. Of these 2 million young people, 89 percent were living at home or with a relative who was head of the household (*Monthly Labor Review,* January, 1976, U.S. Department of Labor, Bureau of Labor Statistics, p. 14, Table 3; p. 50, Table 1; p. 54, Table 7).

10. Paul Bohannan, ed., *Divorce and After.* New York: Doubleday, 1971.

11. Burton, L. White, *The First Three Years of Life,* Englewood Cliffs, N.J.: Prentice-Hall, 1975.

12. Jerome Kagan and R. E. Klein, "Cross-Cultural Perspectives on Human Development," *American Psychologist,* Vol. 28, 1973, pp. 947–961.

13. Orville G. Brimm, Jr., *Education for Child Rearing,* New York: Russell Sage Foundation, 1959.

14. John P. Demos, "The American Family in Past Time," *Contemporary Marriage: Structure, Dynamics and Therapy,* Henry Grunebaum and Jacob Christ, eds., Boston: Little, Brown & Co., 1976, p. 434.

5

Variations in Household and Life Style

Introduction

Introduction

During the 1950s and 1960s, family scholars and the mass media presented an image of the typical, normal, or model American family. It included a father, a mother, and two or three children, who lived a middle-class existence in a single-family home in an area neither rural nor urban. Father was the breadwinner, and mother was a full-time homemaker. Both were, by implication, white.

No one denied that many families and individuals fell outside the standard nuclear model. Single persons, one-parent families, two-parent families in which both parents worked, three-generation families, and childless couples abounded. Three- or four-parent families were not uncommon, as one or both divorced spouses often remarried. Moreover, many families, neither white nor well-off, varied from the dominant image. White and seemingly middle-class families of particular ethnic, cultural, or sexual styles also differed from the model. The image scarcely reflected the increasing ratio of older people in the postfamily part of the life cycle. But like poverty before its "rediscovery" in the middle 1960s, family complexity and variety existed on some dim fringe of semiawareness.

When noticed, individuals or families departing from the nuclear model were analyzed in a context of pathology. Studies of one-parent families or working mothers, for example, focused on the harmful effects to children of such situations. Couples childless by choice were assumed to possess some basic personality inadequacy. Single persons were similarly interpreted, or else thought to be homosexual. Homosexuals symbolized evil, depravity, and degradation.

As Marvin Sussman has noted, "This preoccupation with the model nuclear family pattern and efforts to preserve it at all costs prevented sociologists from describing what was becoming obvious to non-sociological observers of the American scene: a pluralism in family forms existing side by side with members in each form having different problems to solve and issues to face" (Sussman 1971, p. 42). Curiously, although social scientists have always emphasized the pluralism of American society in terms of ethnic groups, religion, and geographic region, the concept of pluralism had never been applied to the family.

464

Changing the Image

What we are actually witnessing today is not so much new forms of family living as a new way of looking at alternative family patterns that have been around for a long time. Even the flowering of communal living experiments in America during the late 1960s was not something new under the sun but rather the revival of an old American tradition. But while communes were being developed, nuclear family ideology was challenged on other grounds. Blacks challenged the validity of the white middle-class family as a model for all groups in society; the population explosion made singleness, childlessness, and even homosexuality seem to be adaptive responses to a pressing social problem; the women's movement challenged the traditional roles of wife and mother and argued for the validity of singleness, childlessness, unwed motherhood, homosexuality, and even celibacy.

Our selections here are intended to reflect this diversity and the controversies surrounding it. Elmer and Joanne Martin's article is actually an appendix to their book on the black extended family. We chose it because it illuminates two major social science views of black family life in America. One is the "pathology-disorganization perspective," represented in works of such authors as E. Franklin Frazier and Daniel Patrick Moynihan. The other, the "strength-resiliency perspective," is represented by such authors as Andrew Billingsley, Joyce Ladner, and Robert Hill. The article not only presents these perspectives but constructively and often appreciatively criticizes each in light of the other.

There has been far more written about the black family than about the Mexican-American. The article in chapter 10 by Alfredo Mirandé examines the literature on the Chicano family and analyzes the dialectic between positive and unsympathetic views of the Chicano family. Mirandé concludes that "probably the most significant characteristic of the Chicano family is its strong emphasis on familism."

The Italian family, particularly the Sicilian family described by Richard Gambino, bears some striking resemblances to the Chicano family. The strong familistic orientation of the Chicano and Italian family is similar to, although not exactly the same as, the peasant family everywhere. Families rooted in a peasant culture traditionally place a high value on blood ties. They also stress the domination of men over women, the older generation over the younger, and the kin group over the individual. When a peasant family system is strongly influenced by a modern urban culture, in which compatibility rather than consanguinity dominates familial values, some of the older practices remain, while others are gradually phased out.

Many believe that the aged might benefit by returning to traditional values, assuming that the three-generational family would solve the problem of the aged. But, as Hess and Waring point out, "some parents with large families, often the foreign-born with 'extended expectations,' will be disappointed at the unwillingness or inability of children to meet such claims." In reality, the problems of the aging result from the triumph of modernization, which implies the development of new values, plus a major extension of the life span. During the past 100 years the proportion of the population over sixty-five has tripled, and expectations that might have worked for a much smaller population of the aged will not work for a much larger.

Besides, it would be a mistake to assume that the extended family or the three-generational household was ever the norm in American or western European society. The myth of the large kin group living happily on the grandparents' farm has repeatedly been laid to rest by sociologists and historians. Still, it lives on in the minds of many. Confronted with the different problems raised by a modern aging population, it is easy to yearn for some golden time of the past when the old lived happily in the bosom of the family. Yet there is little evidence that such a golden time ever existed. Even when old people and young people lived together, their lives were not necessarily idyllic (Kent, 1965).

Can There Be an Ideal?

Is there some ideal form of family—or nonfamily organization—that will unfailingly provide love, security, and personality fulfillment throughout the life cycle? The answer seems to be no. We now have evidence concerning a variety of family forms: the traditional extended family; the nuclear or conjugal family; the mother-child or matrifocal family; and many varieties of communal family. Each offers benefits as well as liabilities. For example, traditional family systems may provide lifelong security, but they are often experienced as oppressive by the family members locked into them, especially women and young people.

In part, family life falls short of the ideals ascribed to it because families are not isolated havens set off from the surrounding society. In societies marked by scarcity, insecurity, inequalities of goods and power, anxiety over status, fear, and hatred, family life will bear the impact of these qualities. The family, in a malfunctioning society, is usually part of the problem.

Chances are family life will still be problematic, even in a relatively untroubled society, because of the special psychology of close relationships. The family, as one writer put it, is where you are dealing with life and death voltages. No matter what form the family takes, the distinctive intimacy and commitment of family life provide the source of both the joy and torment to be found there.

As we move toward the future, public policy requires that full recognition be given to the complexity and variety of forms and life styles the family and other intimate environments can take. This is not to suggest that the nuclear family is going to disappear, nor should it. But as Schorr and Moen point out in their selection in chapter 11, the traditional family of husband, wife, and children of the first marriage of the spouses now accounts for only 45 percent of American families. Even in the suburbs, where the traditional nuclear family still reigns, changes in the ecology and organization of domestic work could ease the strain on that venerable institution as well as on the single person. The trick, of course, is to maintain a philosophy of public policy that seeks to provide facilitative communal arrangements while avoiding the temptation to intrude on private lives. In any case, public policy should be based on the reality of variation, rather than on unrealistic visions of an outmoded orthodoxy.

References

Kent, Donald, P. "Aging—Fact or Fancy," *The Gerontologist,* Vol. 5, No. 2. (June 1965), pp. 51–56.

Sussman, Marvin B. 1971. "Family Systems in the 1970s: Analysis, Policies, and Programs." *The Annals of the American Academy of Political and Social Science,* Vol. 396. The American Academy of Political and Social Science.

Chapter 10

Varieties of Family and Kinship Experience

The Black Family: An Overview

Elmer P. Martin and Joanne M. Martin

In our review of major social science literature on the black family, we discovered two major views of black family life in America:

(1) the "pathology-disorganization perspective," which is presented in the works of such authors as E. Franklin Frazier, Horace Cayton, St. Clair Drake, Gunnar Myrdal, and Daniel Patrick Moynihan; and
(2) the "strength-resiliency perspective," which is presented in the works of such authors as Andrew Billingsley, Joyce Ladner, and Robert Hill.

Proponents of the first view emphasize black family instability and deviant, maladaptive characteristics which they consider to be inherent in or acquired by black families. Proponents of the second emphasize the ability of black families to adapt to cultural demands and to show indications of growth in spite of persistent social, political, and economic hardships in America.

The pathology-disorganization view goes far back into the social thought of America. Both the pro- and anti-slavery literature was permeated with it. Early sociologists such as Henry Hughes and George Fitzhugh took the pathology-disorganization perspective in their defense of slavery.[1] The general line of argument for pro-slavery advocates was that black people were incapable of developing a stable family life without the guidance of the slave master. Anti-slavery advocates, on the other hand, often presented lurid descriptions of the licentiousness and degradation of the slaves. They thought that anything in slavery had to be as debased as slavery itself. To present slaves in the worst

Reprinted from *The Black Extended Family* by Elmer P. Martin and Joanne M. Martin by permission of The University of Chicago Press. © 1978 by The University of Chicago. All rights reserved.

468

possible light was a means of arousing sympathy for the anti-slavery cause.[2] W. E. B. DuBois in 1908 complained that "it is difficult to get a clear picture of the family relations of slaves, between the Southern apologist and his picture of cabin life, with idyllic devotion and careless toil, and that of the abolitionist, with his tales of family disruption and cruelty, adultery and illegitimate mulattoes. Between these pictures, the student must steer clear to find a reasonable statement of the average truth."[3]

After emancipation, the literature did not change concerning the black family. The main debate then was whether or not the Negro was intelligent and responsible enough to carry the burden of his newly won political rights. Philip Bruce did not think so. This is how he described the black man in 1889: "Illiterate, credulous, feeble in judgment, weak in discriminiation, a child in his traits of dependence and self-indulgence, accessible to every temptation and with little ability to resist, without a hope of aspiration beyond his physical pleasures, he was raised on the instant from the level of a beast of burden to the full employment of the noblest preogative of freedom—the right to vote. It was actually the admission to the franchise of a man who, from the degradation of his previous condition, was incapable as a savage out of the bush of understanding the duties of the new situation."[4]

In 1908, DuBois wrote what is considered to be the first social science study of the black family, *The Negro American Family.* DuBois was concerned with how far the Negro had progressed in the twentieth century with respect to family life and other conditions. Though he concluded that there was statistical evidence of a trend toward an integrated family life among black people, he maintained that "without a doubt the point where the Negro American is furthest behind modern civilization is in his sexual mores."[5] However, he was quick to point out that the "sexual irregularities" of black people "go to prove not the disintegration of the Negro family but the distance which integration has gone and has yet to go."[6]

DuBois attempted to avoid both the prevalent pathology-disorganization perspective and the budding strength-resiliency perspective. He argued: "It is begging and obscuring the question to harp on ignorance and crime among Negroes as though these were unexpected; or to laud exceptional accomplishments as though they were typical. The real, crucial question is: what point has the mass of race reached which can justly be looked upon as the average accomplishment of the group?"[7] DuBois, however, was too preoccupied with the older perspective to escape it; yet his defensive stance brought him close to adopting the newer view himself.

DuBois's study made much less impact on social scientists than did the work of E. Franklin Frazier. Producing several books on the black family between 1930 and 1940, Frazier became the leading scholar in this area.[8] He too was concerned with the assimilation of blacks in America. According to his thinking, it was the moral disorganization of black families, especially lower-class black families, which impeded full assimilation. One of the controlling theses of Frazier was that the failure of lower-class blacks to bring their sexual urges under the constraints of conventional morality and community control resulted in pervasive "social disorganization" of black families.[9]

Showing a preference for upper-class Negroes and mulattoes, Frazier often spoke of lower-class Negro families in a condemning manner. His moralizing and his emphasis on what he repeatedly described as the "loose" and "impulsive" sexual behavior of the lower-class Negro sound like the standard racist propaganda of his time. Charles S. Valentine has charged Frazier with establishing the "pejorative tradition" of studying the black family.[10] We question this charge, for the Negro family had been treated in a pejorative manner in all phases of American cultural and intellectual life long before Frazier was born. A quick thumbing through Bruce's *Plantation Negro as Freeman* demonstrates a vilification of the Negro family beyond compare. We do think, however, that it was through Frazier's work that the pathology-disorganization perspective was firmly established in the social sciences. So influential was Frazier's thinking that many authors writing after him would merely parrot themes and issues he dealt with years before.

Two works considered classic sociological studies, Gunnar Myrdal's *An American Dilemma* and Horace Cayton's and St. Clair Drake's *Black Metropolis,* both published in 1945, reveal the prominence of Frazier's thinking.

Myrdal's entire study is held together by a negative view of black people. He saw Negro American culture as "a distorted development, or a pathological condition of the general American culture."[11] His central "vicious circle" thesis propounded that, "on the one hand, the Negro's plane of living is kept down by discrimination from the side of the whites while, on the other hand, the whites' reason for discrimination is partly dependent upon the Negro's poverty, ignorance, superstition, slum dwelling, health deficiencies, dirty appearance, disorderly conduct, bad odor and criminality which stimulate and feed the antipathy of the whites for them."[12]

Though Myrdal, as the previous quotation indicates, could well hold his own in discovering black pathologies, he looked to Frazier for his ideas on the Negro family. He called Frazier's *Negro Family in the United States* "such an excellent description and analysis of the American Negro family that it is practically necessary only to relate its conclusions to our context and to refer to its details."[13]

Horace Cayton and St. Clair Drake, on the other hand, seemingly attempted to outdo Frazier. They saw the black lower-class family through the mirror of broken families, junkies, pimps, prostitutes, and what they termed "wild children," "forceful women," and "dependent men."[14] They classified "the world of the lower-class" into three groups: "the disorganized," "the church folk," and "the sinners".[15]

There were other works on the black family before and after Frazier's work which escaped to a large degree both the pathology-disorganization and the strength-resiliency perspectives. We have in mind particularly Charles S. Johnson's *Shadow of the Plantation* (1929) and Hylan Lewis's *Blackways of Kent* (1955). Johnson followed his own precept of pointing out "first what seems to be a conformity of the conventions of the group itself without reference to outside standards,"[16] and thus avoided viewing the black family from the standpoint of conventional morality. Though Lewis was unable to escape the pathology-disorganization perspective altogether—he tended to divide the black community into "respectable" and "nonrespectable" categories[17]—he, like Johnson, presented a "balanced perspective." However, neither Johnson nor Lewis exerted noticeable influence on the prevailing pathology-disorganization perspective, which by the 1960s was an established tradition in the social sciences.

That perspective reached its apex with Daniel Patrick Moynihan's *The Negro Family: A Case for National Action* (1965), also known as the "Moynihan report." Moynihan presented a massive amount of statistical data, which, he held, indicated widespread disorganization of black family life. In line with Philip Bruce, who in 1889 found the black family "pregnant with innumerable calamities,"[18] Moynihan in 1965 found it characterized by a "tangle of pathologies."[19] He concluded that the Negro family was "at the heart of the deterioration of Negro society"[20] and therefore called for large-scale government intervention for the rehabilitation and restructuring of lower-class black family life.

Though the Moynihan report aroused great controversy, it did not view the black family in any worse light than many other studies exposing black family defects. Abram Kardiner and Lionel Ovesey, for example, in their *Mark of Oppression* (1951), contended that blacks were so psychologically maladjusted that they identified their black skin with feces;[21] Kenneth Clark's *Dark Ghetto* (1965) presented a devastating portrayal of black self-hatred and other psychological pathologies of "ghetto" life; Oscar Lewis in 1968 drew up a long list of "culture of poverty" traits which were popularized throughout the social sciences;[22] and Lee Rainwater's *Behind Ghetto Walls* (1970) went to great length to show how "ghetto" people are socially and psychologically different from normal, healthy, middle-class people. Even Moynihan could scarcely have outdone the following paragraph from Rainwater:

> Lower class people perceive the world as dangerous and chaotic. This perception carries with it a tendency also to see the body as immediately or potentially dangerous. Many lower class people seem to think of their bodies as in some way likely to injure or incapacitate them, and they relate to their bodies in magical rather than instrumental ways. When they talk about illness, they communicate a sense of distance from the processes going on in their bodies. Unlike middle class people, they do not identify themselves with their bodies and work toward cure of physical difficulties the same way they work toward solutions to other kinds of problems. This tendency to see the body as mysterious and potentially dangerous carries with it a rather poor differentiation of bodily parts and functions. For example, in a study of how lower class men and women think about the process of reproduction, there appeared a low differentiation of the sexual parts among both men and women, and the

majority of the respondents had poor notions of the process of conception. This was closely related to their inability to understand or trust chemical methods of contraception or feminine methods such as the diaphragm. The low self-evaluation that is generally characteristic of lower class people means that they do not uphold the sacredness of their persons in the same ways as middle class people, and their tendency to think of themselves as of little account is, of course, readily generalized to their bodies.[23]

The Moynihan report came at a wrong time in history. Had it appeared at the time E. Franklin Frazier was publishing, it might well have been overshadowed by Frazier's pathology-disorganization perspective. Moynihan certainly was no more negative in his treatment of the black family than was E. Franklin Frazier. The major difference between Frazier's and Moynihan's thinking is that Frazier believed that the advancement of lower-class Negroes depended largely on what they could do in cleaning themselves up and becoming morally ready to assimilate fully into white society; whereas Moynihan, seeking to check the impact of the black protest-black consciousness movement, thought the government should step in and take control over the lower-class Negro family.[24]

The Moynihan report aroused consternation among blacks because it came during a time when the black consciousness mood was sweeping the nation, when blacks were taking a positive view of themselves and were actively seeking liberation from racial oppression. The Moynihan report (to summarize Albert Murray)[25] told blacks that their lives were filled with pathologies, absolved the government and the dominant society of major responsibility for the oppression of blacks, provided white racists with fresh ideological ammunition to use against blacks, and implied that blacks were inferior and not ready for freedom.

Paradoxically, the Moynihan report gave rise to a more positive view of black family life in the social sciences. Three of the chief exponents of the strength-resiliency perspective—Billingsley, Ladner, and Hill—opened their studies with a critique of the Moynihan report in particular and of the pathology-disorganization perspective in general.

Andrew Billingsley's *Black Families in White America* (1968) signaled the emergence of the strength-resiliency focus. "Unlike Moynihan and others," he wrote, "we do not view the Negro as a causal nexus in a 'tangle of pathologies,' which feeds on itself. Rather, we view the Negro family in the theoretical perspective of a subsystem of the larger society. It is, in our view, an absorbing, adaptive, and amazingly resilient mechanism for the socialization of its children and the civilization of its society."[26] Billingsley concentrated on the black family's "instrumental" and "expressive" functions. Discussing various types of black families, he concluded that the "range and variety does not suggest, as some commentaries hold, that the Negro family is falling apart, but rather that these families are fully capable of surviving by adapting to the historical and contemporary social and economic conditions facing the Negro people."[27]

Billingsley pointed out that black families historically have adapted to cultural demands and have survived against great odds. He focused on middle- and upper-class blacks to illustrate how some black families, despite economic barriers, were able to take advantage of scarce opportunities and "to move beyond survival to stability and social achievement."[28] Billingsley saw racism, "the illusion of white superiority," as the barrier which kept many Negro families from "reaching the level of achievement of which they were capable" and as a "barrier against freedom, opportunity, and manhood of the Negro people."[29] How does a people survive in the face of oppression and sharply restricted economic and social support? There are, of course, numerous ways, but surely one of them is to adapt the most basic of its institutions, the family, to meet the conflicting demands placed on it. In this context, then, the Negro family has proved to be an amazingly resilient institution."[30]

Joyce Ladner, acknowledging her indebtedness to Billingsley, was concerned in *Tomorrow's Tomorrow* (1971) "with depicting the strength of black families and black girls within the family structure."[31] Like Billingsley, Ladner critiqued the pathology-disorganization perspective. She maintained that "the preoccupation with deviancy, as opposed to normalcy, encourages the researcher to limit his scope and to ignore some of the most vital elements of the lives of the people he is studying."[32] The power of blacks "to cope and adapt to a set of unhealthy conditions—not as stereotyped sick people, but as normal ones—is a factor few people seem to accept, or even realize."[33] White Americans, she held, should commend "the way blacks have adapted to poverty and racism, and yet emerge relatively unscarred."[34]

Ladner attributed the strength of black family life to "African survivalisms" in black culture. "African survivalisms have shaped black family life, and particularly black womanhood in America. Africanisms (the strong semi-independent economic function and close relationship between mother and children) have been perpetuated, reinforced by contemporary atttiudes and behaviors."[35]

Ladner's thesis is opposed to E. Franklin Frazier's view that African culture did not survive the impact of slavery in America;[36] but it is consistent with Melville Herskovits's thinking that significant features of African culture were carried over into the New World. Among the African survivalisms which Herskovits recognized in his *Myth of the Negro Past* (1958) were patterns of the black extended family.[37]

Robert Hill's *Strengths of Black Families* marks the rapidly increasing acceptability of the strength-resiliency perspective. Hill isolated and discussed what he considered major black family strengths: strong kinship bonds, strong work orientation, adaptability of family roles, high achievement orientation, high religious orientation.

Just a few years after the Moynihan report Ladner was so jubilant over the establishment of the strength-resiliency perspective of the black family that she led a group of scholars declaring "the death of white sociology."[38] The announcement may have been a little premature, for the pathology-disorganization perspective, after many years of dominance, was merely in a state of decline.

The black extended family is touched on but seldom examined at length in the literature of either perspective. Not only is the nuclear family usually taken as the norm, but the white nuclear family has often been used as the standard by which to judge black family behavior.

Several of the families DuBois observed had extended family characteristics such as multigenerational households. Frazier's studies indicate some awareness of extended family ties among Negroes. His discussion of the role of the grandparent in the black family is clearly an examination of extended family relationships.[39] We found Frazier's brilliant discussion of the secularization of black family life in the city[40] and his accurate predictions[41] relevant to our observations of the black extended family. In spite of some serious drawbacks in his studies, Frazier has been by far the leading contributor to the study and understanding of black family life.

Billingsley recognized, but barely discussed, various types of black extended families.[42] Joyce Ladner viewed the extended family as an important part of the socialization of urban black girls.[43] Robert Hill described crucial elements of the extended family, for example, kinship bonds and the informal adoption process among black families.[44]

Though the black extended family did not come fully into view in either Charles S. Johnson's or Hylan Lewis's work, the work of these authors or kinship ties, survival mechanisms, and the black family's view of itself generated questions which guided some of our own research.

Both Lewis and Johnson, however, like other students of the black family, discussed the extended family mainly in relation to poverty or race relations or some other primary topic. Their focus was mainly on the nuclear family, and their information was not complete enough to influence other scholars to consider the extended family as a crucial part of black family life. Two books of readings on the black family, Charles V. Willie's *The Family Life of Black People* (1970) and Robert Staples's *The Black Family: Essays and Studies* (1971) did not include one article dealing exclusively with the extended family.

The mid-seventies brought in three new books which were greatly concerned with kinship ties among black people: Carol B. Stack's *All Our Kin* (1974), Herbert G. Gutman's *Black Family in Slavery and Freedom, 1750–1925* (1975), and Alex Haley's *Roots: The Saga of an American Family* (1976).

Carol B. Stack's book is devoted to the strategies black kinship networks have developed in surviving in an impoverished environment. Her chief focus is on the exchange systems which link kin and non-kin in a domestic circle of reciprocal sharing and mutual help. "My purpose in this book," she writes, "is to illustrate the collective adaptations to poverty of men, women, and children within the social-cultural network of the urban black family. I became poignantly aware of the alliances of individuals trading and exchanging goods, resources, and the care of children, the intensity of their acts of domestic cooperation, and the exchange of goods and services of these persons, both kin and non-kin."[45] Stack's observation that "the nuclear family, or the matrifocal family, blocks the way to understanding how people in the flats describe and order the world in which they live"[46] is consistent with our theme that black family life cannot be understood without some grasp of extended family ties.

However, our observations have shown that, given the economic deprivation of urban black families, the impersonality of the urban environment, the cultural push toward individualism, the preference shown by urban institutions for the nuclear family structure, and the difficulty of maintaining strong kinship ties in the urban environment, the reciprocal exchange system is not as effective as Stack suggests. We have also found that including non-kin in the mutual aid process is virtually impossible in the urban environment. Eager to show how well poor blacks have adapted to poverty, Stack fails to discuss the strains, setbacks, and contradictions within urban kinship networks. To survive urban culture is far different, we believe, from participating in it.

Herbert G. Gutman describes his study as "an examination of the Afro-American family prior to and after the general emancipation, but it is also a study of the cultural beliefs and behaviors of a distinctive lower-class population. It examines its adaptive capacities at critical moments in history. Slavery is viewed as an oppressive circumstance that tested adaptive capacities of several generations of men and women."[47]

Gutman provides some very fresh documentation on the black family and its kinship ties during slavery and shortly after emancipation. But we believe his study is weakened by having been "stimulated by the bitter public and academic controversy surrounding Daniel P. Moynihan's *The Negro Family in America.*"[48] Gutman sought to provide historical proof that slavery did not make for black family instability, disorganization, or pathology. He gathered copious data on marital and family records, focused on slave kinship arrangements, and examined naming practices of slaves to demonstrate that black people developed stable family networks and made positive adaptations to historical circumstances.

Just as Stack set out to show how well black kinship units have adapted to poverty, Gutman set out to show how well the black family has adapted to certain "critical moments in its history." Both writers give a somewhat distorted account of the extended family because their primary motive is to win an ideological argument, to prove a point. Their studies are a little overzealous.

We are puzzled that social scientists find so remarkable that ability of black families to adapt to poverty, to develop strong families even in slavery. After all, black historians such as J. A. Rogers, Carter G. Woodson, and Benjamin Quarles, sociologists such as W. E. B. DeBois, theologians such as Alexander Crummel and Howard Thurman, and almost all the Harlem Renaissance writers talked decades ago not only about black strengths but about black contributions to America. Why is it that, more than a hundred years after slavery, some social scientists feel it necessary to validate blacks' capacities to adapt, remain strong, and survive? Ralph Ellison said that "men have made a way of life in caves and upon cliffs, why cannot Negroes have made a life upon the horns of the white man's dilemma?"[49]

Studies such as Gutman's and Stack's are primarily aimed at the social scientists who have not been convinced that black families could be strong or healthy, given the oppressive situation for which these scholars either blame society or "blame the victim."[50] Black people, at least the ones we know, have always known, even if social scientists have not, that there were strong black families and terribly disorganized ones too, but never a consistent pattern of either-or. The black people we have talked to are also aware that, though many blacks developed a stable family life in slavery, slavery and poverty have put black families generally at a great disadvantage in becoming economically stable units in the American society.

Alex Haleys *Roots: The Saga of an American Family,* part fact and part fiction, written partly as a serious portrayal and partly to shock and to entertain, is an important piece of literature which illustrates the influence of black kinship ties. Haley traces his family tree back to Africa and carries his family history through the slavery period on up to his own adulthood. Though the book has created a great deal of interest, the saga of Alex Haley's family must not be construed to be the saga of every black family in America.

Haley's family lineage, as he traces it through the maternal side of his family tree, with one noticeable exception was pure black.[51] However, J. A. Rogers, who wrote extensively on race-mixing, particularly among blacks and whites, pointed out that "everyone has two parents, four grandparents, and eight great-grandparents. How many know all of the eight? How many three of them? How many even one? In ten generations the number of one's ancestors runs into the millions. After we go back a few generations, our ancestors increase so prodigiously that it is practically impossible to determine exactly the various elements which constitute our being."[52]

Haley's historic family, as presented in *Roots,* consisted mainly of morally upright, intelligent, freedom-loving people. But anyone looking back into his family history, Rogers reminds us, would find kings, priests, scholars, murderers, cutthroats, morons, and people of all colors.[53]

Haley's family uprooted itself from slavery and branched out into mainstream America, with Haley eventually becoming a wealthy man—a Horatio Alger success story despite the fact that it took over three hundred years to pull off such a feat. In short, the exploits of Haley's family form the plot out of which good novels are made.

We believe that a full and realistic portrayal of the black extended family requires a perspective broader than either the strength-resiliency or pathology-disorganization perspective will allow. The black family defies both formulas. For example, each of Robert Hill's black family "strengths" from another viewpoint can be seen as weaknesses. One could say that it is the inability of nuclear black families to survive which forces them to develop strong kinship bonds. One could say that a person who works at just any job or who works just for the sake of working or who works without receiving fair benefits is a fool. One could say that the high degree of family role adaptability is based on weaknesses in the black family, which makes it difficult for family members to carry out normal societal roles. One could say that high achievement orientation is bound to end in frustration, since family members seldom have the opportunity to succeed. One could say that a person with a strong religious orientation in a secular society which believes that the "good guys always come in last" will never achieve anything.

In other words, Hill was no more successful in placing the black family in a straitjacket of strengths than St. Clair Drake and Horace Cayton were years ago in attempting to lump black experience into "staying alive," "praising God," "getting ahead," "advancing the race," and "having a good time."[54]

1. See Wish, *George Fitzhugh: Propagandist of the Old South;* Fitzhugh, *Sociology of the South* and *Cannibals All;* Hughes, *A Treatise on Sociology.* For a discussion of Hughes and his work, see Bernard, "Henry Hughes, First American Sociologist," *Social Forces* 15:154–74.
2. See Quarles's discussion of abolitionist literature in his *Black Abolitionists,* pp. 65–66.
3. DuBois, *The Negro American Family.* p. 9.
4. Bruce, *The Plantation Negro as Freeman,* pp. 61–62.
5. DuBois, *The Negro American Family,* p. 37.
6. Ibid., p. 31.
7. Ibid., p. 128.
8. Frazier, *The Negro Family in Chicago; The Free Negro Family;* and *The Negro Family in the United States* (his major work).
9. This theme runs throughout Frazier's *The Negro Family in the United States.*
10. Valentine, *Culture and Poverty,* pp. 20–25.
11. Myrdal, *An American Dilemma,* p. 928.
12. Ibid., p. 1066.
13. Ibid., pp. 930–31.
14. Drake and Cayton, *Black Metropolis.* For these authors' pejorative analysis of lower-class black family life, see ibid., chaps. 20–21 (pp. 564–658).
15. Ibid., p. 385.
16. Johnson, *Shadow of the Plantation,* p. 210.
17. For Lewis's discussion of "respectable" and "nonrespectable" Negroes, see his *Blackways of Kent,* pp. 233–56.
18. Bruce, *The Plantation Negro as Freeman,* p. 26.
19. Quoted in Rainwater and Yancey, eds., *The Moynihan Report and the Politics of Controversy,* p. 75.
20. Quoted in ibid., p. 51.
21. Kardiner and Ovesey, *Mark of Oppression,* p. 316.
22. See particularly Lewis, *A Study of Slum Culture.*
23. Rainwater, *Behind Ghetto Walls,* pp. 106–7.
24. Throughout his report, Moynihan shows a concern for the impact of the black consciousness movement. "It was not a matter of chance that the Negro movement caught fire in America at just that moment when the nations of Africa were gaining their freedom. Nor is it merely incidental that the world should have fastened its attention on events in the United States at a time when the possibility that the nations of the world will divide along color lines seems suddenly not only possible, but even imminent . . . Since racist views (Black Nationalism and Third Worldism) have made progress within the Negro community itself—which can hardly

be expected to be immune to a virus that is endemic in the white community, the Black Muslim doctrines, based on total alienation from the white world, exert a powerful influence. On the far left, the attraction of Chinese communism can no longer be ignored . . . It is clear that what happens in America is being taken as a sign of what can, or must, happen in the world at large." Quoted in Rainwater and Yancy, *The Moynihan Report and the Politics of Controversy,* p. 1.

25. Murray, *The Omni-Americans,* pp. 46–61.
26. Billingsley, *Black Families in White America,* p. 33.
27. Ibid., p. 21.
28. Ibid., p. 97.
29. Ibid., p. 155.
30. Ibid., p. 21.
31. Ladner, *Tomorrow's Tomorrow,* p. 10.
32. Ibid., p. 2.
33. Ibid., p. 5.
34. Ibid., p. 5.
35. Ibid., pp. 4–5.
36. See Frazier's chapter 1, "Forgotten Memories," in his *The Negro Family in the United States,* pp. 2–17.
37. Herskovits, *The Myth of the Negro Past,* pp. 171–72.
38. Ladner, ed., *The Death of White Sociology.*
39. Frazier, *The Negro Family in the United States,* pp. 114–27.
40. Frazier, *The Negro Family in Chicago,* pp. 223–45.
41. Frazier, *The Negro Family in the United States,* pp. 367–68.
42. Billingsley, *Black Families in White America,* pp. 19–21.
43. Ladner, *Tomorrow's Tomorrow.*
44. Hill, *The Strengths of Black Families,* pp. 1–10.
45. Stack, *All Our Kin,* p. 28.
46. Ibid., p. 31.
47. Gutman, *The Black Family in Slavery and Freedom, 1750–1925,* pp. xx–xxi.
48. Ibid., p. xvii.
49. Ellison, *Shawdow and Act,* pp. 315–16.
50. See Ryan, *Blaming the Victim.*
51. Haley, *Roots: The Saga of an American Family.* One of Haley's relatives, Kizzie, had a child by a white man who raped her.
52. Rogers, *Sex and Race,* vol. 2., p. 11. Also see vols. 1 and 2 for an interesting account of race mixing.
53. *Sex and Race,* vol. 3. pp. 11–12.
54. See Drake and Cayton, *Black Metropolis,* vol. 1.

The Chicano Family: A Reanalysis of Conflicting Views

Alfredo Mirandé

While there has been a proliferation of research and writing on the American family, studies have tended to focus on the dominant family type and little is known about family forms that vary from the modal middle-class, white Protestant ideal (Mindel and Habenstein, 1976:vii). In their quest to generalize about "the family," researchers have tended to neglect or minimize internal social class and ethnic variations. When ethnic variations have been considered, the dominant family system typically has served as a yardstick against which to measure such deviations. Analyses of ethnic families thus tend to be pathological and pejorative evaluations conducted by researchers who are insensitive to the nuances of the sociocultural systems they are studying. In recent years, minority scholars have begun to question such generalizations. Many of the widely held beliefs and stereotypes surrounding black culture and the black family, for example, are coming under the scrutiny of critical black scholars (Ladner, 1973). While social scientists have shown an inordinate concern for the black family, historically this interest has been problem-oriented (Staples, 1976: 221). Under the guise of objectivity and the value-free ethic, one finds that social scientists are frequently asking "what is wrong with the black family and why is it different from the white middle-class norm?" As the largest ethnic minority, blacks have made significant inroads and they have been able not only to set aside many erroneous beliefs about the black family but to present a more objective view of the organization and functions of the family in the black community.

Behavioral scientists have similarly shown great interest in the Mexican-American family.[1] Despite the absence of hard data, generalizations concerning the Mexican-American family abound. However, such generalizations tend to be based on meager, if not nonexistent, empirical evidence. A number of Chicano writers have sought to counter the mythical and stereotypical social science characterization of the Mexican-American family (Montiel, 1970; Murillo, 1971), but Chicanos lack power and influence and their protests have typically been either muted or ignored. Also, while Chicano perspectives on *la familia* have served as a badly needed corrective for the negative and stultifying social science view, they have not been without their own pitfalls. In their eagerness to counter the pejorative social science view, some research-

From the *Journal of Marriage and the Family* (November 1977), pp. 747–756. Copyrighted 1977 by the National Council on Family Relations. Reprinted by permission.

[1]The terms Mexican-American and Chicano are used interchangeably to denote persons of Mexican descent residing permanently in the United States. The terms, however, have very different connotative meanings. Mexican-American connotes greater integration into American society and is, not surprisingly, the preferred term of social scientists. Chicano connotes greater ethnic identification and politicization and is more commonly used by Chicanos themselves.

ers have tended to overcompensate and present an idealized and romanticized image of the family.

Thus, two polar and contradictory views of the family have emerged. Detractors of the family see it as a "tangle of pathology" which impedes the advancement and acculturation of Chicanos, whereas supporters see it as a warm and nurturing institution that provides succorance in an otherwise hostile and unrewarding environment. This paper seeks to present an overview and evaluation of these polar perspectives and to offer a new, more balanced and objective framework for studying the Chicano family. It will attempt, more specifically, to:

(1) discuss and evaluate both traditionally pejorative social science depictions of the family and more sympathetic views of the family; and
(2) reassess the structure, functions, and values of the Chicano family in light of these earlier perspectives.

It is hoped that this revised and more complete perspective will supersede both the traditional, pejorative, social science view and the newer, romanticized and idealized internal view of the family, thereby enhancing our understanding of the contemporary Mexican-American family.

The Social Science Myth of the Mexican-American Family

An examination of social science literature on the Mexican-American family reveals a consistently pathological and pejorative view. These negative depictions have resulted from the tendency of social scientists to see the Mexican-American family as a radical departure or deviation from the dominant, egalitarian, Anglo-American family; Mexican and Mexican-American families appear rigid and authoritarian by comparison.

A prevailing feature of these studies is that they uncritically accept the concept of *machismo* as an explanation for all that is wrong with the Mexican and the Mexican-American family (Montiel, 1970). Infused with psychoanalytic concepts and paradigms, they attempt to establish a modal Mexican personality type which is characterized by a pervasive feeling of inferiority and a rejection of authority. An added assumption is that the Mexican family and the Mexican-American family are isomorphic so that one can extrapolate findings from one setting to another. Despite the obvious hazards involved in applying psychoanalytically based Mexican national character studies to the United States, these explorations "have been accepted as the 'true' description of the Mexican character, the Mexican male, and ultimately, the Mexican and Mexican American family" (Montiel, 1970:58).

Among the most influential studies of Mexican national character and the Mexican family are Maria Bermúdez' *La Vida Familiar del Mexicano,* Díaz-Guerrero's *Psychology of the Mexican,* and G. M. Gilbert's (1959) study of mental health in a Mexican village. Bermudez (1955:101) argues that Mexicans are locked into rigid conceptions of masculinity and femininity which make it difficult for men to be "candid and humane" and for women to be "dignified and independent." Díaz-Guerrero (1975:10) similarly concludes from 11 structured questions that the male and the female are unable to fulfill their rigid role expectations and consequently tend toward neurosis. Despite the careful use of psychoanalytic jargon and pseudoscientific disclaimers, these studies inevitably conclude that *machismo* produces maladaptive pathological responses. They adopt a simple psychoanalytic model in which *machismo* becomes a malady and Mexican cultural traits are symptomatic of illness or disease. This pathological view is then used to perpetuate deeply ingrained though unsupported assumptions about Mexican culture. G. M. Gilbert (1959:212), for example, asserts on the basis of interviews with nine older males that there was:

> a pronounced tendency to either severely constricted affect or to morbid-depressed-hypochondriacal types of responses among the older males . . . this may be indicative of increasing impotence and "castration anxiety" as the males fail in the lifelong struggle to live up to the demands of *machismo*.

The pathological model of the family has in turn been applied by American social scientists to Chicanos. Researcher after researcher, without the benefit of empirical evidence, depicts a *macho*-dominated, authoritarian Mexican-American family (cf. Humphrey, 1944; Jones, 1948; and Peñalosa,1968). Marriage, according to this view, does not encumber the freedom of the male as he is allowed to pursue the same pattern of social life after marriage that he did as a bachelor. He comes and goes as he pleases, stays out all night (engages in *parrandas*), drinks, fights, and may even establish a second household (*casa chica*). Life for the male is characterized by an incessant preoccupation with sex. Although all women are sexual objects to be pursued and conquered, an important distinction is made between good and bad women. Bad women are considered fair game, while good women are to be respected and revered. Mothers, wives, and daughters are saintly, virginal creatures who do not enjoy sex and who are to be shielded and protected from male predators. Good women are not only virtuous but self-sacrificing and enduring figures as well. Whereas the man retains much of his autonomy after marriage, women are completely circumscribed by marital and familial roles (Peñalosa, 1968:683). Women who do not accept their subordinate position or who question the authority of the male typically are subjected to physical punishment or abuse (Hayden, 1966:20). Wives, moreover, "should accept this punishment as deserved" and they may even be "grateful for punishment at the hands of their husbands for such concern with shortcomings indicates profound love" (Madsen, 1973:22).

The *macho* male demands complete deference, respect, and obedience not only from the wife but from the children as well. In fact, social scientists maintain that this rigid, male-dominated family structure has negative consequences for the personality development of Mexican-American children. It fails to engender achievement, independence, self-reliance, or self-worth—values which are highly esteemed in American society. Celia Heller (1966:34–35) observes:

> The kind of socialization that Mexican-American children generally receive at home is not conducive to the development of the capacities needed for advancement . . . by stressing values that hinder mobility—family ties, honor, masculinity, and living in the present—and by neglecting the values that are conducive to it—achievement, independence, and deferred gratification.

The authoritarian Mexican-American family constellation then produces dependence and subordination and reinforces a present-time orientation which impedes advancement. Chicanos live in a perpetual "mañana land." The resulting conclusion is that Anglo culture stresses achievement and control of the environment, while Chicano culture stresses fatalism and resignation (Samora and Lamanna, 1967:135). Alvin Rudoff's (1971:236–237) categorical condemnation of the family and culture is also illustrative of this view of Mexican-Americans:

> The family constellation is an unstable one as the father is seen as withdrawn and the mother as a self-sacrificing and saintly figure. The Mexican-American has little concern for the future, perceives himself as predestined to be poor and subordinate, is still influenced by magic, is gang-minded, distrusts women, sees authority as arbitrary, tends to be passive and dependent, and is alienated from the Anglo culture.

In comparison to the Anglo-American family, the Mexican-American family is perceived as a tangle of pathology for many social scientists. It propagates the subordination of women, impedes individual achievement, engenders passivity and dependence, stifles normal personality development, and on occasion can even give rise to incestuous feelings among siblings. The following comment demonstrates this point of view.

> It may very well be that this type of family structure also increases the incestuous attraction between brothers and sisters. In middle-class families this attraction may become accentuated by the family being partly closed off from the outside world and in poor families by the cramped living quarters. This theme of incestuous feelings between brothers and sisters is significantly a fairly common one in Mexican novels, movies, and plays (Peñalosa, 1968:688).

The stereotypical view of the family is so deeply ingrained that social scientists are reluctant to abandon it even in the fact of evidence to the contrary. When research findings indicate that the Chicano family is less rigid than was previously assumed, there is a tendency either to dismiss them or suggest that they reflect greater acculturation and assimilation to the dominant pattern. Hawkes and Taylor (1975:807), for example, were struck by the finding that the prevailing pattern of decision-making and action-taking among husbands and wives in Chicano migrant farm families was egalitarian rather than male-dominated as hypothesized. Faced with these unexpected results, they turned to factors that might explain them, such as increasing acculturation, urbanization, and "the decreasing dependence of women upon their husbands in *this country*" (Hawkes and Taylor, 1975:810; emphasis added). Only after unsuccessful attempts to account for these results do the authors reluctantly suggest that:

> many of the traditional stereotypes of groups such as ethnic minorities noted in the literature and in public assumptions need more adequate verification. It is possible that more sophisticated methods of research may negate many of our previous assumptions (Hawkes and Taylor, 1975:811).

Sympathetic Views of *La Familia*

Some Chicano social scientists have sought to reexamine social science depictions of the Mexican-American family and in the process they try to dispel the many myths and stereotypes that surround it. Miguel Montiel (1970), as was noted earlier, has written an incisive critique of Mexican-American family studies. He argues that such studies have perpetuated erroneous stereotypes as a result of their unquestioned reliance on a pathological psychoanalytic model that sees *machismo* as the root of all the problems encountered by Mexican-Americans. According to Montiel (1970:62), "this formulation is inherently incapable of defining normal behavior and thus automatically labels all Mexican and Mexican American people as sick—*only in degree of sickness do they vary.*" Despite the cogency of his remarks, Montiel presents neither a revised view of the family nor an alternative framework for future studies to follow. In other words, while Montiel clearly refutes prevailing stereotypes about the family, he fails to offer new insights into the dynamics of Chicano family life.

Octavio Romano (1973) has similarly criticized social science accounts of Mexican-American culture and family life. After reviewing the works of Tuck, Heller, and Samora and Lamanna, he concludes that these works constitute an exercise in social science fiction which present a distorted picture of Mexican-Americans as passive, masochistic vegetables, controlled by a traditional culture. With respect to the family, Romano (1973:52) notes that social scientists would have us believe that Mexican-American parents "are their children's own worst enemies" and that they potentially threaten the American way of life. Romano uses Madsen as an example of this view. According to Madsen (Romano, 1973:50), ' "Anglos believe that equality in the home and self-advancement are necessary to maintain the American ideals of freedom, democracy, and progress. Mexican-Americans believe that putting family above self is necessary to fulfill the will of God.' " The emphasis on familism not only impedes advancement and acculturation but threatens the very foundations of our democratic form of government. The work of Romano is an important corrective for mythical social science depictions but, like that of Montiel, it does not offer a substitute view of the family.

A number of Chicano writers have offered an alternative view of the family. They argue that *la familia* is not the cold and unstable constellation social scientists depict, but a warm and nurturing institution. Parents are not their children's own worst enemies: "only a person who has never experienced the warmth of the Mexican-American family would tend to see it primarily from a negative perspective" (Alvirez and Bean, 1976:277). The family, according to this new perspective, is the most important unit in life and the individual is likely to place the needs of the family above his own (Murillo, 1971:102). Thus, if there is a conflict between the family and school or work, the individual will usually be more sensitive to familial demands. The concept of *machismo* is important but it is defined more in terms of family pride and respect than in terms of male dominance. As the ultimate authority in the family, the father is responsible to the outside world for the behavior of family members. "An important part of his concept of machismo or maleness, however, is that of using his authority within the family in a just and fair manner. Should he misuse his authority, he will lose respect" (Murillo, 1971:103), not only within the family but in the community at large. *Machismo* is not a pathological force or a tool for protecting male perogatives but a mechanism for upholding family pride and honor.

What was previously described as a rigid and authoritarian family is now redefined as a stable structure in which the individual's place is more clearly established and secure. The family "seems to provide more emotional security and sense of belonging to its members" (Murillo, 1971:99). Roles and expectations are largely determined by a member's age and gender. The father is granted deference and respect as head of the household but other adults such as grandparents (*abuelitos* and *abuelitas*) are also accorded respect.

The family is thus seen as a warm and nurturing unit that provides support throughout the lifetime of the individual. In times of stress or when problems arise one typically turns to the family for help rather than to outside agencies. Sharing and cooperation are encouraged and valued not only among children but among adult family members. Anglo-controlled agencies find it difficult to understand why Chicanos are leary of outside help (Ramos, 1973) or why badly needed resources are distributed to more needy family members. Help patterns are clearly established and it is not uncommon for family members to pool resources to purchase large or expensive items such as a house or a car (Alvirez and Bean, 1976:277).

A Reassessment of the Chicano Family

Thus, we have two views of the Chicano family that are at variance with one another—the traditional social science view of the Chicano family as rigid, cold, and unstable, and a more sympathetic view of it as warm, nurturing and cohesive. Although these two views would appear at first glance to be polar and irreconcilable, they are not totally dissimilar. They are in agreement concerning a number of characteristics of the Chicano family. Both views hold that the Chicano family is characterized by:

(1) male dominance;
(2) rigid sex-age grading so that the older order the younger, and the men order the women;
(3) clearly established patterns of help and mutual aid among family members; and
(4) a strong familistic orientation whereby individual needs are subordinated to collective needs.

The basic difference between the two views then, is not to be found in their substantive characterization of the family, since there is much overlap between them, but in their interpretation and evaluation of these characteristics. While the familistic orientation of Chicanos is universally recognized, critics see it as undemocratic, un-American, and impeding individual achievement and advancement; supporters see it as a source of emotional and material support in a hostile and unrewarding world. These polar depictions of the family are important not so much for what they reveal about the family, but for what they reveal about those who study the family.

Although the more positive view of the Chicano family emerged as a response to stereotypical characterizations, it too has demonstrated a strong tendency to make sweeping generalizations about the family that neglect or minimize its internal diversity. In their quest to negate pejorative depictions, defenders of the family have substituted a series of positive and idealized stereotypes which, ironically, incorporate many of the same beliefs they sought to supplant. Thus, negative stereotypes have been discarded in favor of positive and romanticized characterizations that result in polar caricatures of the Chicano family.

The task at hand now is to present a more balanced and objective view that captures the reality of Chicano family life without exaggerating or distorting that reality. It is therefore important to note that the family system as it is depicted is an ideal type that may not correspond to any real family. Just as there is no one uniform Anglo-American family, there is no one Chicano family but a number of family types that vary according to region, recentness of migration to the United States, education, social class, age, and urban-rural locale. Given this internal diversity it is necessary to extrapolate key features found among Chicano families across various settings and situations. The traits attributed to the Chicano family are not true of all families, but they are more likely to characterize the Chicano than the Anglo family.

Probably the most significant characteristic of the Chicano family is its strong emphasis on familism. While the impact of the family may have been eroded somewhat by urbanization and acculturation, it is still a central institution for the individual. The family is a basic source of emotional support for the child as he develops close bonds not only with members of the immediate family but with grandparents, aunts and uncles, cousins and family friends. A study of young children, age seven to thirteen, in a Houston *barrio* concluded that "in the child's-eye-view the central feature is home, and the people at home" (Goodman and Beman, 1971:111). Significantly, in response to the question, "Who do you love?" none of the *barrio* children included anyone but relatives in their responses, whereas Anglo children and black children included many nonfamily members, and friends also played a prominent part in their listing of persons loved (Goodman and Beman, 1971:112). Grandparents are also important in the lives of children but they are likely to be seen as warm and affectionate rather than as authority figures. "Grandparents appear to be highly influential, as distinguished from being powerful" (Goodman and Beman, 1971:111). Similar to parents in the kibbutz, they are free of the responsibilities of parenthood and their relationships with grandchildren can be warm and nurturing (Talmon, 1961). In addition to being loved, however, grandparents are respected because they are considered to be older and wiser.

The familistic orientation of Chicanos is such that relatives are frequently included as friends. There is no sharp distinction made between relatives and friends as they are often one and the same. Not only are relatives included as friends, but friends are symbolically incorporated into the family. The institution of *compadrazgo* dates back to the early post-Conquest period in Mexico. This Spanish custom was apparently adopted by the Indians during the Colonial Period (1550–1650) as widespread epidemics led to massive native depopulation leaving many orphaned children (Gibson, 1966:142). Godparents thus originally functioned as parent substitutes. Over the centuries the original meaning of *compadrazgo* has been modified so that *compadres* have more of a social function that one as parent substitutes. Nonetheless, the custom remains intact. A recent study found that nearly all of the adult respondents reported at least one such relationship and, in many instances, two, three, or more (Goodman and Beman, 1971:111).

Both pejorative and positive accounts of the Chicano family see the male as the ultimate and unquestioned authority in the family. Such characterizations have focused on the formal aspects of Chicano culture, neglecting its more subtle and informal nuances. The father is formally accorded much deference and respect but he is not the all-powerful lord and master of the household, as has been suggested. There is, in fact, an implicit contradiction in the stereotypical view of the *macho* who comes and goes as he pleases and the view of him as the all-powerful authority and arbitrator in the family. The male may officially be the ultimate authority but he is frequently aloof or uninvolved in family matters. The father tends to be warm and affectionate when children are little, but as they enter puberty, relations between him and children become more tenuous (Rubel, 1966:66). The expectation of women, on the other hand, is one of almost total devotion to the family (Murillo, 1971:104). A woman should be warm, nurturing, and minister to the needs of her husband and children. Ministering mothers are respected, revered, and recognized as important figures, despite their alleged low status in the family. Indeed, for children, their importance appears to take precedence over the father. A study of Chicano children found that the father is seen as a somewhat distant authority figure, and is frequently slighted, especially by boys. "Few say they go to him with questions, either for information or for permission to do something" (Goodman and Beman, 1971:112). Significantly, few children want to be "like father when they grow up" or to have a job like his. This remoteness may result from his frequent absence from home. He may leave home before the children are awake and not return until late in the evening (Goodman and Beman, 1971:112). Mothers, however, play a critical part in the lives of children. They perform many domestic tasks such as preparing breakfast, fixing lunches, cooking dinner, doing dishes, and various other household chores. Mothers are also responsible for setting parameters on the children's behavior. They determine when one gets up or goes to bed and when one comes in from playing (Goodman and Beman, 1971:112). "She scolds, she sometimes slaps or spanks for disobeying small rules, and she stops sibling squabbles" (Goodman and Beman 1971:112). Thus, while the woman does not have the formal prestige or status of the man, she has great informal influence in the home.

The strong familistic orientation of the Chicano family has led some observers to conclude that it is an extended family system much like the traditional Chinese family system. While Chicanos are familistic, the Chicano family is not a functioning extended system identical to that of the Chinese.[2] The father is formally head of the household but, as has been noted, much of his authority is more apparent than real. The concept that the oldest surviving male should be recognized as the patriarchal head of the household is also not found in Chicano culture. Grandparents are more important as sources of warmth and support than as authority figures. While patterns of mutual aid and support are clearly established, nuclear families should ideally function as relatively autonomous and independent units. One may choose to live near parents and other relatives, or perhaps even with them, out of economic necessity, but the norm is that the nuclear family remains autonomous and in a separate residence.

Although the mother has been depicted as a lowly and insignificant figure, she is extremely important in intrafamily relationships. Her relationships with children are characterized by warmth and affection. Whereas the father-son relationship is somewhat distance, the mother's relation with her daughter is more intimate. Early participation in the domestic realm produces identifica-

---

[2]For a discussion of the traditional Chinese family see Levy (1968), Leslie (1973:80–122), Ho (1965), Lee (1953), and Huang (1976).

tion with the mother and her maternal role. "Little girls learn early to assume responsibilities and tasks, especially those that are particularly maternal in character, such as taking care of smaller siblings" (Peñalosa, 1968:687). In addition, "the confinement of females within the home gives rise to a closely knit group of a mother and her daughters, a relationship which endures throughout the lifetime of the individuals" (Rubel, 1966:100). The same close environment gives rise to enduring relationships between sisters.

Although the mother-son relationship does not appear to be as strong as the mother-daughter relationship, it is nonetheless a close bond. During childhood the mother is more likely to be pampering and indulgent with her son than with her daughter. During adolescence especially, mothers are permissive with their sons. These socialization practices are indicative of a dualistic conception of appropriate behavior for males and females. The boy is a fledging *macho* who must be allowed to venture out of the home so he may "test his wings" and establish a masculine identity. Peers contribute significantly to the process of socialization into manhood. He begins to hang out with other boys, or *la palomilla,* and peer relations may begin to rival family ties in importance. These associations are prominent for the man and are retained even after marriage.

Adolescent girls are much more restricted and sheltered than adolescent boys. Throughout her life, a female is prepared for her role as a virtuous mother of *la raza:*

> The girl has been brought up in such a manner that she represents herself as a paragon of virtue, a woman fit to mother the children of a respectable male of *la raza.* Early in her life she was made aware that she represented her household group fully as much as she represented herself, an individual. In all instances her claims to enjoyment were made secondary to the claim of propriety. In other words, hers was a road carefully planned from girlhood to womanhood within the tight restraint of family discipline (Rubel, 1966:77).

Premarital chastity is the culmination of feminine virtue. The norm of premarital virginity prevails, although its enforcement may prove more difficult today than in the past. Thus, the behavior and character of the contemporary Chicana, like that of her ancient forebears, is severely circumscribed by rigid role expectations which limit her activities to the domestic sphere. The ancient exhortation an Aztec mother gave her daughter when the latter became of marrying age spelling out her wifely, submissive role might just as easily be invoked today:

> When God decides that you should take a husband . . . don't condemn him . . . don't defy him; God, who is everywhere, will see you; he will be angry with you; he will avenge himself as he wishes; or, you will befoul yourself at his command, or be blinded, or your body will rot, or you will be stricken by poverty because you dared hurl yourself into defiance of your husband; for which fortune will kill you, or hold you beneath her feet and cast you into hell (translation of Sahagún, 1946, Tomo I:541–542).

Despite the persistence of social roles which severely circumscribe the behavior of the female, there is evidence that these roles are undergoing change and modification. Many women, especially the younger generation, are challenging their traditional roles. In urban areas *Chicanitas* are venturing beyond the protective confines of the home and joining social clubs or gangs. Thus, the *palomilla* is no longer the exclusive domain of the male. "There are fewer and fewer women who are willing to accept the traditional role assigned to them according to traditional values. Chicanas are struggling for greater equality not only in the Anglo society but also in comparison to the Mexican American male" (Murillo, 1971:106). Traditional male-female relations are undergoing change, particularly among younger and better-educated urban Chicanos. Many Chicanas are advocating changes that incorporate positive cultural values and permit "more flexibility in carrying out a greater variety of activities that traditionally have been denied her" (Murillo, 1971:106).

The Chicano family has thus been subjected to many of the same forces of change as the Anglo-American family. It has had to adapt to changes resulting from increasing urbanization, industrialization, and acculturation. Middle-class urban Chicano families appear to be more equalitarian and to have discarded some of the more traditional features of the family. Similarly, as the influence of the Church declines, so has the importance of the institution of *compadrazgo*. These changes however, are Americanization for many Chicanos are self-consciously seeking to modify sexual and familial roles without rejecting their cultural heritage or assimilating into mainstream Anglo-American society.

The Chicano Family in a Colonial Context. Social scientists have approached the study of ethnic families with a melting-pot, immigrant group, model of American society. According to this model, American society is composed of diverse ethnic groups who migrate freely to the United States. New arrivals may bring in different cultural values, but they inevitably are integrated into the melting-pot. Recent immigrants also tend to be economically disadvantaged but their position improves with time. Ultimately, then ethnic minorities are incorporated into the dominant culture and society.

Armed as they were with this assimilationist paradigm, it is not surprising that social scientists would see Chicanos as a curious anomaly. Chicanos did not join the melting pot but clung to their traditional culture and familiar values. The Chicano family structure was thus seen as rigid and authoritarian in comparison to the egalitarian Anglo ideal and parents were considered their children's worst enemies because they were obstacles to assimilation and acculturation.

These social scientists have failed to recognize that Chicanos are native to the Southwest. They are not recent immigrants; their arrival in this region predates not only the founding of the United States as a nation but the landing of the Pilgrims at Plymouth Rock. The entrance of Chicanos into the society, moreover, unlike other immigrant groups, was not voluntary but forced. Chicanos are a colonized people that were conquered militarily, were forcefully incorporated into the United States, and had a foreign culture and language imposed upon them. Although Chicanos are not colonized in the classic sense of the word, they are an "internal colony."[3] Internal colonialism differs from the classic variety in that it does not entail the subordination of a distant land but the acquisition of contiguous territory. Another difference is that classic colonialism allows for more continuity between pre- and postconquest society. Native leadership and elites come under foreign control but remain largely intact, while native institutions are modified and retained (Moore, 1970:466). In internal colonialism, however, local elites are deposed from power and indigenous institutions are completely destroyed. Finally, the "classic" colony is recognized formally and legally, while the "internal" colony has only an informal existence.

This informality can make internal colonization more insidious and oppressive, however. The effects are more devastating, precisely because the existence and legitimacy of native institutions or culture are not recognized. One of the most effective mechanisms of destruction is benign neglect. The culture, values, and language of Chicanos thus have no formal or legitimate standing within American society. Chicanos are oftentimes punished in school, for example, for speaking their native tongue or for expressing familial or cultural values that run counter to dominant Anglo values.

Chicanos, however, have actively opposed the insidious oppressive conditions of internal colonialism and the family has been a critical force in this opposition. In an environment where Chicano institutions have been rendered subordinate and dependent, the family has been the only institution to escape colonial intrusion. Whereas the black family was controlled and manipulated by slavery, the Chicano family has been relatively free of direct manipulation and control. The *macho* as titular head of the family is usually seen as actively combating acculturation and assimilation, but the women resists equally via her own traditional role. As the center of the family and the mainstay of the culture and its traditions, the Chicana has helped to counter the encroachment of colonialism. She perpetuates the language and values of Chicanos.

Another factor that has helped to stem the tide of colonialism is the proximity of Mexico to the United States. Chicano patterns of migration are not random or arbitrary. People tend to migrate to areas where they anticipate work or where relatives, friends, or acquaintances reside. This continual influx of new arrivals maintains and reinforces cultural bonds that resist the push toward integration and Americanization. Unlike European immigrants who found themselves isolated from a distant homeland, Chicanos are not far from

---

[3]The concept of internal colonialism has been discussed by a number of writers. See, for example, Moore (1970), Acuña (1972:3), Barrera *et al.* (1972:483), Blauner (1969, 1972), and Almaguer (1971).

their native roots. The influence of Mexican culture and the Spanish language are therefore ongoing.

In closing, it appears that the Chicano family has been viewed as in impediment to democratic ideals and counter to the "American way of life" because it has resisted acculturation and assimilation. Attacks on the family by social scientists and the public at large indicate that it has not been a "tangle of pathology," as we have been led to believe, but an institution that has worked only too well.

References

Acuña, Rodolfo
  1972   Occupied America: The Chicano's Struggle Toward Liberation. San Francisco: Canfield Press.
Almaguer, Tomás
  1971   "Toward the study of Chicano colonialism." Chicano Journal of The Social Sciences and the Arts 2 (Spring): 7–21.
Alvirez, David, and Frank D. Bean
  1976   "The Mexican American family." Pp. 271–292 in Charles H. Mindel and Robert W. Habenstein (Eds.), Ethnic Families in America. New York: Elsevier.
Barrera, Mario, Carlos Muñoz, and Charles Ornelas
  1972   "The barrio as an internal colony." Pp. 465–498 in Harlan H. Hahn (Ed.), Urban Affairs Annual Reviews (Vol. 6). Beverly Hills, California: Sage Publications.
Bermúdez, Maria Elvira
  1955   La Vida Familiar del Mexicano. Mexico, D. F.: Antigua Librería Robredo.
Blauner, Robert
  1969   "Internal colonialism and ghetto revolt." Social Problems 16 (Spring): 393–408.
  1972   "Colonized and immigrant minorities." Pp. 51–81 in R. Blauner (Ed.), Racial Oppression in America, New York: Harper and Row.
Díaz-Guerrero, Rogelio
  1975   Psychology of the Mexican: Culture and Personality. Austin: University of Texas Press.
Gibson, Charles
  1966   Spain in America. New York: Harper and Row.
Gilbert, G. M.
  1959   "Sex differences in mental health in a Mexican village." The International Journal of Social Psychiatry 3 (Winter): 208–213.
Goodman, Mary Ellen, and Alma Beman
  1971   "Child's-eye-views of life in an urban barrio." Pp. 109–122 in Nathaniel N. Wagner and Marsha J. Haug (Eds.), Chicanos: Social and Psychological Perspectives. Saint Louis: C. V. Mosby
Hawkes, Glenn R., and Minna Taylor
  1975   "Power structure in Mexican and Mexican-American farm labor families." Journal of Marriage and the Family 37 (November): 807–811.
Hayden, Robert G.
  1966   "Spanish-Americans of the southwest: Life style patterns and their implications." Welfare in Review 4 (April): 14–25.
Heller, Celia S.
  1966   Mexican American Youth: Forgotten Youth at the Crossroads. New York: Random House.
Ho, Ping-ti
  1965   "An historian's view of the Chinese family system." Pp. 15–30 in Seymour M. Farber, Piero Mustacchi, and Roger H. L. Wilson (Eds.), The Family's Search for Survival. New York: McGraw-Hill.

Huang, Lucy Jen
  1976   "The Chinese American family." Pp. 124–147 in Charles H. Mindel and Robert W.
          Habenstein (Eds.), Ethnic Families in America. New York: Elsevier.
Humphrey, Norman Daymond
  1944   "The changing structure of the Detroit Mexican family: An index of acculturation."
          American Sociological Review 9 (December): 622–626.
Jones, Robert C.
  1948   "Ethnic family patterns: The Mexican family in the United States." American Journal
          of Sociology 53 (May): 450–452.
Ladner, Joyce A.
  1973   The Death of White Sociology. New York: Random House.
Lee, Shu-Ching
  1953   "China's traditional family, its characteristics and disintegration." American Sociologi-
          cal Review 18 (June): 272–280.
Leslie, Gerald R.
  1973   The Family in Social Context (2nd ed.). New York: Oxford University Press.
Levy, Marion J., Jr.
  1968   The Family Revolution in Modern China. New York: Atheneum.
Madsen, William
  1973   The Mexican-Americans of South Texas (2nd ed.). New York: Holt, Rinehart and
          Winston.
Mindel, Charles H., and Robert W. Habenstein
  1976   Ethnic Families in America. New York: Elsevier.
Montiel, Miguel
  1970   "The social science myth of the Mexican American family." El Grito: A Journal of
          Contemporary Mexican American Thought 3 (Summer): 56–63.
Moore, Joan W.
  1970   "Colonialism: The case of the Mexican Americans." Social Problems 17 (Spring):
          463–472.
Murillo, Nathan
  1971   "The Mexican American family." Pp. 97–108 in Nathaniel N. Wagner and Marsha J.
          Haug (Eds.), Chicanos: Social and Psychological Perspectives. Saint Louis: C. V.
          Mosby.
Peñalosa, Fernando
  1968   "Mexican Family Roles." Journal of Marriage and the Family 30 (November): 680–
          689.
Ramos, Reyes
  1973   "A case in point: An ethnomethodological study of a poor Mexican American family."
          Social Science Quarterly 53 (March): 905–919.
Romano, Octavio Ignacio V
  1973   "The anthropology and sociology of the Mexican-Americans: The distortion of Mexi-
          can-American history." Pp. 43–56 in O. Romano (Ed.), Voices: Readings from El
          Grito, A Journal of Contemporary Mexican American Thought. Berkeley, California:
          Quinto Sol Publications.
Rubel, Arthur J.
  1966   Across the Tracks: Mexican Americans in a Texas City. Austin: University of Texas
          Press.
Rudoff, Alvin
  1971   "The incarcerated Mexican-American delinquent." Journal of Criminal Law,
          Criminology and Police Science 62 (June): 224–238.
Sahagún, Fray Bernardino de
  1946   Historia General de las Cosas de Nueva España. Tomos I–III. Mexico, D. F.: Editorial
          Nuéva España.
Samora, Julian, and Richard A. Lamanna
  1967   Mexican-Americans in a Midwest Metropolis: A Study of East Chicago. Advanced
          Report 8, Mexican-American Study Project. Los Angeles: Division of Research, Grad-
          uate School of Business Administration, University of California.

Staples, Robert
1976   "The Black American family." Pp. 221–247 in Charles H. Mindel and Robert W.
       Habenstein (Eds.), Ethnic Families in America. New York: Elsevier.
Talmon, Yonina
1961   "Aging in Israel, a planned society." American Journal of Sociology 67 (November):
       284–295.

The Italian-American Family System

Richard Gambino

During the first sixteen years of my life I lived in Red Hook, Brooklyn. Still largely Italian today, the area then was almost exclusively composed of Italian-American families, many of whose men were longshoremen on Brooklyn's large waterfront. It was typical of the many "Little Italies" in America, and, incidentally, is the area where Arthur Miller chose to set his forceful play about the Italian-American longshore family, *A View from the Bridge*. Also typical of many families in the Little Italies, I lived with my parents (my father emigrated from Palermo, Sicily, at age thirteen; my mother was born in Red Hook shortly after her parents came from Palermo), and my maternal grandparents.

One of my early memories is of an event that happened when I was perhaps seven years old. One of my closest friends was an Italian immigrant boy named Tony. One winter day, I forget why, Tony and I fought. We tumbled on the ground and hit at each other. Somehow, Tony's nose began to bleed. The sight of the blood on the dirty snow terrified both of us, and we each ran home. Because both my parents worked during the day, I went to my grandparents' basement flat rather than to my own, immediately above it. Of course I kept silent about the fight and the blood, preferring to shiver in fear next to the hot coal stove. In a few minutes, the inevitable happened. The doorbell rang, and I watched with a sense of doom as my grandmother walked the long corridor to the outside "gate" of the old brownstone. I though my fate was sealed a minute later when I heard her call to me in the uniquely sharp, decisive Sicilian dialect, *Veni icca!* (come here!). My second-generation mother had taught me that fighting was wrong, that hurting someone was wrong, and sometimes reinforced these and other lessons of American morality by spankings. I was thus totally unprepared for the scene I found at the gate. There was my grandmother, a big woman, standing in the doorway facing Tony's mother, blocking the latter's view. My grandmother stood squarely on both feet, hands resting on hips, palms turned *outward* from the body—the reverse of the American manner. In the body language of Southern Italy, the stance's meaning was unmistakable—"Don't tread on me or mine!" The two women were engaged in delivering ritual insults to each other, in hissing voices, almost spitting as they spoke. Southern Italians have a name for a game of ritualized oratory—*passatella.* The gist of my grandmother's part of this serious passatella was that Tony was a worthless son of worthless blood and it was a *vergogna* (outrage) to allow him to walk the streets with her *nipotino* (fine little grandson). This was news to me—my grandmother often saw me play with Tony and previously had spoken to his mother with courtesy, hence as a peer. After the confrontation, back inside the house, my grandmother asked me what had happened. Her only comment upon my explanation was that since I shed Tony's blood, *he* must have committed some *infamia* (infamy)!

I was astonished. My mother, when informed by my teacher of some misbehavior on my part in school, had automatically taken the teacher's side and promised me a beating when I came home—a promise kept. But my grandmother's only punishment to me was a one-sentence lecture on choosing my companions more carefully. She did not even mention the incident to my "American" parents.

My parents were embarked on the *via nuova* (new way), and I suppose my grandmother, in accordance with a Sicilian proverb, considered them too far down the road to recognize what was demanded in such a family confrontation. The proverb is, *Chi lascia la via vecchia per la nuova, sa quel che perde e non sa quel che trova*—"Whoever forsakes the old way for the new knows what he is losing but not what he will find."

At least 85 per cent of the total of Italians who immigrated to the United States, and perhaps 90 per cent of those who came in the great flood of immigration from 1875 to 1920, were from areas south and east of Rome. Italians call this area the Meridone or Midi or Mezzogiorno. It is composed of the six provinces of Abruzzi, Campania, Apulia, Lucania (also known as Basilicata), Calabria, and Sicily. The name Mezzogiorno is rich in connotations. One of the most significant is, "the land that time forgot." About 25 per cent of the immigrants from the land forgotton by time came from Sicily.

Italian immigrants were overwhelmingly of the *contadino* class—peasant farmers—but also fishermen, artisans, and unskilled urban poor whose ways of life were contadino from such cities as Naples, Palermo, Bari, Messina, Catania, Reggio di Calabria, Foggia, Salerno, Cosenza, Catanzaro, Enna, Ragusa, and Agrigento. In the contadino tradition shared by these people, there was one and only one social reality, the peculiar mores of family life. *La famiglia* and the personality it nurtured were very different from the American nuclear family and the personalities that are its typical products. The famiglia was composed of all of one's blood relatives, including those relatives Americans would consider very distant cousins, aunts and uncles, an extended clan whose genealogy was traced through paternity. The clan was supplemented through an important custom known as *comparatico* or *comparaggio* (godparenthood), through which carefully selected outsiders became to an important (but incomplete) extent members of the family.

The only system to which the contadino paid attention was *l'ordine della famiglia,* the unwritten but all-demanding and complex system of rules governing one's relations within, and responsibilities to, his own family, and his posture toward those outside the family. All other social institutions were seen within a spectrum of attitudes ranging from indifference to scorn and contempt.

One had absolute responsibilities to family superiors and absolute rights to be demanded from subordinates in the hierarchy. All ambiguous situations were arbitrated by the *capo di famiglia* (head of the family), a position held within each household by the father until it was given to—or, in the case of the father's senility, taken away by—one of the sons, and in the larger clan, by a male "elder" (*anziano*). The contadino showed calculated respect (*rispetto*) to members of other families which were powerful, and *pietà,* a mixture of pity, charity, and haughtiness or indifference toward families less powerful than his own. He depised as a *scomunicato* (pariah) anyone in any family who broke the ordine della famiglia or otherwise violated the *onore* (honor, solidarity, tradition, "face") of the family.

Thus the people of the Mezzogiorno survived a harsh history of invasions, conquests, colonizations, and foreign rule by a procession of tribes and nations (including Phoenicians, Carthaginians, Greeks, Romans, Vandals, Goths, Austrians, Byzantines, Arabs, Normans, French, Spanish, and various Northern Italian powers) and centuries of exploitation by landowners of great estates. Although they rose in violent rebellion many times, these insurrections were always crushed, betrayed, or both. What enabled the contadini to endure and develop their own culture was a system of rules based solely on a phrase I heard uttered many times by my grandparents and their contemporaries in Brooklyn's Little Italy: *sangu du me sangu,* Sicilian dialect for "blood of my blood." (As is typical of Sicilian women, my grandmother's favorite and most earnest term of endearment when addressing her children and grandchildren, and when speaking of them to others, was *sangu miu*—literally "my blood.")

It was a norm simple and demanding, protective and isolating, humanistic and cynical. The unique family pattern of Southern Italy constituted the real sovereignty of that land, regardless of which governments nominally ruled it. Governments and aliens came and went over the centuries. If they brought any customs that might strengthen the family system, these were gradually absorbed. Indeed, in an important sense, all who are derived from this land are descendants of these many cultures, "indigenuous" and "alien," of thousands of years. But those customs that were hostile to the family were resisted.

Although much was absorbed from many cultures, the famous Sicilian collector of his island's folklore, Dr. Giuseppe Pitre, was essentially correct when before his death in 1913 he wrote, *"Noi siamo in mezzo a un popolino che non conosce altro galateo di la dal suo, altri usi se non i suoi"*—"We are in the midst of a people who know no other life pattern than their own, no other customs than those of their ancestors."

I was once again reminded of Pitre's words when I visited my sole surviving relatives in Palermo, one great aunt, age seventy-six, and one great aunt by marriage, age eighty-five. They could not understand why my "distant" relatives in America—cousins, great-uncle, etc.—and I do not often see each other. I tried to explain the busy pace of the United States, but they kept returning to the puzzle, at one point asking me if Manhattan (where I live) is very far from Brooklyn and Long Island (where my relatives live). At the end of many attempts at explanation on my part, one of them closed the conversation by saying in a resigned voice, without a trace of irony, "You must all live far from each other."

Among those raised in it, and this to various degrees includes all Italian-Americans, it is impossible to be untouched, if not determined, by *la via vecchia.* An understanding of this pattern of family life is critical to any understanding of Italian-Americans of any generation, the most "assimilated" third-and fourth-generation young people as well as wizened old immigrants. La via vecchia, cultivated for centuries, does not die quickly and certainly not easily. Even in the life of an urbane man like Luigi Pirandello, it had remarkable stamina. The great writer, whose works probe the philosophical implications of the subtle line between illusion and reality and are among the most sophisticated of our time, lived much of his life away from his homeland. Yet when he decided to marry, he chose to return to his native Agrigento in southwest Sicily to marry a young woman selected for him by his father, *a woman whom the writer had never seen before!*

An example analogous to Pirandello's occurred in my own family about ten years ago. It began with a tragic loss for a cousin of mine, then a woman twenty-four years old. Her Italian-born husband, age twenty-eight, drowned in a boating accident, leaving with her two very young children. Following the morality of la via vecchia, after the proper interval of time for mourning, the dead man's parents took it upon themselves to send word back to their relatives in the homeland to find a suitable new husband for their widowed daughter-in-law and father for their grandchildren. But here the parallel with Pirandello ends. For my cousin is of the third generation of Italian-Americans and would not accept a "match." Several other American-born members of my family had to meet with her parents-in-law to explain that she wished to choose her own spouse in her own time. Although they acceded to the *via nuova,* the immigrant parents regarded it with disbelief and alarm. I doubt that they were really resigned to it until sometime later when my cousin married again—to a man of her own choice.

The role played in my cousin's dilemma is typical of the second generation, a generation that forged a great compromise between la via vecchia and la via nuova. Thus, in this example, they interceded between the two ways. Interceding on behalf of the third-generation preference for the via nuova to be sure, but interceding in a manner typical of la via vecchia, *the family interceded.* This pattern of relations between second generation (now mostly middle-aged people) and the third and fourth generations, mostly young adults, teen-agers, and children, is common. In my opinion, it will prove to be one of the decisive determinants in the just beginning quest for identity on the part of the younger generations of Italian-Americans. The strengths of this pattern will be a boon to them. The weaknesses in the pattern will define some of the chief problems they will have to overcome.

There is an illuminating saying among Southern Italians that the father is the head of the family, and the mother the center. The father, as the ultimate retainer of la via vecchia, made all important decisions concerning the family. A living for the family and good marriages for its children were the primary goals toward which decisions were aimed. In this culture, young people had to re-establish in each generation the only social reality of the land, the family, by marriage. Therefore a good marriage was more than just a question of social status. It was tantamount to survival and was treated as a basic bread-and-butter necessity.

In the first aim, a living, the father played an active key role. He labored and maneuvered to gain the most produce and money. In this he acted according to true Machiavellian principles, guarding and guiding the welfare of his family in a dangerous, even treacherous world where *la miseria,* desperate poverty, was a constant plague. He acted as a true monarch for the good of his endangered kingdom, according to the severe rules of *Realpolitik.* Family security, power, status, and necessities of life were goals pursued in this microcosm of the world of sovereign states. And as in the system of nations, they were goals pursued without regard to sentimentality or other moralities that were disastrous in the amoral social world. The father exercised this responsibility without confiding its problems or details to his wife. They were simply *fatti suoi,* his business. He would discuss them only when necessary, and then only with close male relatives, most often the clan's elder. To a more guarded degree, he might consult his *padrino* (older godparent) or his *compare* (a close friend, a peer godparent).

In a tradition that continues to puzzle foreigners who have a simplistic stereotyped notion of the Italian man's ideal of manliness, which they mislabel with the Spanish word *machismo,* the father turned over his earnings to his wife for complete management, keeping only a small allowance for his daily needs. Except for reserving the right to intercede in the case of mismanagement or other crisis, the father did not further concern himself with the family budget. Similarly, although he retained the right of veto over any proposed match, often the father was not the one who initiated arrangements for the marriages of his children. Often he did not enter into the picture until the way for the match had been carefully and quietly arranged by the mothers, aunts, and godmothers of the prospective bride and groom. Usually it was only when a match was virtually assured that the fathers of the respective families would enter into negotiations of which the public was aware. Similarly, the father played a subdued, background role in the raising of young children, stepping in only when he thought it necessary to preserve the over-all aim of the process —to turn out children who were *ben educati,* or, in the dialect, *buon educati.* As we shall see, this notion of being well educated had nothing to do with schooling. Rather it meant being brought up to value la via vecchia in thought and feeling, and to honor it in practice.

The family was the major transmitter of its own culture, and other institutions were welcomed only if they aided this goal. Those that were perceived as neither aiding l'ordine della famiglia nor endangering it were tolerated. Hence one source of the Italian's legendary attitude of "live and let live." To be more precise, institutions not affecting la via vecchia were regarded with simple indifference as *cose senza significato,* things of no consequence. But any person or event, idea or institution that was perceived as a threat to la via vecchia or to the members of the family served by the old way was stubbornly, fiercely, and if necessary violently resisted. Not only the father, but every member of the family down to the limit of the *bambini* (roughly the age of seven) was expected to protect the established code of behavior, the onore della famiglia. For example, the sons of the family above the age of puberty were expected to defend any undermining of the welfare of the females of the family, or, worse, any insult to their reputation or status, this being synonymous with an insult to the family's onore.

Individual rights, wishes and feelings were defined by one's membership in the family. One treated a person according not so much to his individual characteristics as to the status of his family and his particular place in it. In fact, it was difficult to conceive of a "person" in any realistic sense apart from his place and role in a family. The famous book *Christ Stopped at Eboli* offers an excellent proof of this. Its author, Carlo Levi, an artist, physician, and writer from Turin, in Northern Italy, was a vociferous opponent of the Fascist regime of Mussolini. Because of this, he was exiled in 1935 to a small village in the southern province of Lucania (the "anklebone" of the Italian boot).

His book describes the life of the people there. In one passage, Levi tells of a visit to him by his sister, Luisa, and the dramatic difference it created in his status as a person among the contadini. As he tells us, until then he might just as well have been a creature from Mars in the eyes of the people of the Mezzogiorno.

> Hitherto they had thought of me as a sort of man from Mars, the only one of my species, and the discovery that I had blood connections here on earth seemed somehow to fill in their picture of me in a manner that pleased them.

The sight of me with my sister tapped one of their deepest feelings: that of blood relationship, which was all the more intense since they had so little attachment to either religion or the State. It was not that they venerated family relationship as a social, legal or sentimental tie, but rather that they cherished an occult and sacred sense of communality. A unifying web not only of family ties (a first cousin was often as close as a brother), but of the acquired and symbolic kinship called *comparaggio* [godparenthood], ran throughout the village . . .

Toward evening, when my sister and I walked arm in arm along the main street, the peasants beamed at us from their houses; "Blessed is the womb that bore you!" they called out to us from the doorways; "Blessed the breasts that suckled you!" Toothless old creatures looked up from their knitting to mumble proverbs: "A wife is one thing, but a sister's something more!" "Sister and brother, all to one another." Luisa, with her rational, city [Turin]-bred way of looking at things, never got over their strange enthusiasm for the simple fact that I had a sister.*

All obligations, feelings, or rights of radical individuality were repressed by any good father or mother, daughter or son. For example, if a married daughter claimed she or her children were being abused by her husband—which could mean only that he was not conforming to la via vecchia—it was her brothers and, if necessary, other young male relatives who were expected to confront the culprit. Upon confirmation of the charge, the offending husband would be privately warned to mend his ways. In the Mezzogiorno, such a warning of offended onore, like everything else that touched upon the maintenance of la via vecchia, was never taken (or given) lightly.

In their tenacious will to survive inbred over centuries, the contadini paradoxically valued la via vecchia more than their very lives. For survival and the old way had been synonymous for ages.

Changing Patterns of Aging and Family Bonds in Later Life

Beth B. Hess and Joan M. Waring

Family sociology has gained in sophistication from developments in related disciplines. For example, research by historians of the family has put to rest, at last, the "classical family of Western nostalgia" (Goode, 1963). Unfortunately, this mythical family does not rest in peace, but inhabits the consciousness of the general public with a wondrous tenacity.

The use of the cohort analysis in the study of social change or continutiy directs attention to the changing characteristics of specific age cohorts or generations not only as they move through their life course but also among successive cohorts in a particular society. Both foci warn us against generalizations regarding parent-child relations as fixed. Intergenerational relationships must be studied in historical context, especially in terms of the linkages between family and other institutional spheres as these undergo continual change.

While we may never disabuse the general public of the notion that there once was a time in which the extended family reigned supreme—and, more importantly, that mutual respect and satisfaction governed adult child/aged parent interaction—we must, as family sociologists and practitioners, take an unromanticized view of intergenerational relations at the distal end of the life course. The question usually asked of this topic is "how can such bonds be strengthened?" The one we propose here is "why have any such bonds persisted?"

The modern family is characterized by choice: whom to marry, where to live, how to earn a living, how many children to bear, and, increasingly, how to conduct interpersonal relations and allocate tasks within the nuclear family. As we move from the family of obligatory ties to one of voluntary bonds, relationships outside the nuclear unit similarly lose whatever normative certainty or consistency governed them at earlier times. For example, sibling relationships today are almost completely voluntary, subject to disruption through occupational and geographic mobility, as, indeed, it might be said of marriage itself. Is this also to be the fate of parent-offspring ties in later life? There are many indicators of growing distance between generations, especially so in later life. Thre are also clues to enduring qualities of the parent/child bond. We shall examine the most important of these forces—centripetal and centrifugal—at both the societal and familial levels.

From *Family Coordinator* (October 1978), pp. 304–314. Copyrighted 1978 by the National Council on Family Relations. Reprinted by permission.

Societal Level Processes

Social-Historical Change

Family studies often have concentrated exclusively on the effects of world-wide social trends for young people. Goode's (1963) influential analysis of the "world revolution" in family systems is, for example, basically concerned with the freedom of younger generations, although he does make note of the potential dysfunctions for older family members. But a change in one part of a system has ramifications for other parts; thus, if respect for parents and the obligation to care for elders once was based upon their control of resources, reinforced by religious tradition and normative sanction, then the increasing ability of younger members to determine their own fates in marriage and in work must necessarily reduce the power of elders to demand filial piety. Nonetheless, filial responsibility is often mandated in the law, if not fully realized in practice (Schorr, Note 1; Brody, 1970, for a decade comparison).

The choices which we consider our birthright and that of our children, today, are at the expense of claims on care from our offspring many decades later. Recognition of this dilemma may be one of the compelling forces behind another trend in modern nation states—toward the public assumption of responsibility for income maintenance and primary health care of the aged. In many developed countries, transportation, housing and recreation have also been provided through allocation of societal rather than familial resources. The trade-off is evident: removing claims from the interpersonal system achieves the same aims which Weber (1958) suggests for bureaucracy over nepotism.

Considerations of kinship give way to impersonal but theoretically fairer mechanisms of allocation, "without fear or favor." Although the politically conservative might perceive a usurpation of family obligations, these trends in no way preclude high levels of kin caring for those families willing and able to do so. Yet public programs do ensure that all old people will be taken care of, albeit minimally in many cases, thus removing a financial (and often emotional) burden from both generations. Intergenerational hostility will most likely be muted by transposing this issue to the societal level, so that family ties are strengthened rather than attenuated: an extremely difficult concept to convey to members of a society which idealizes family life. To the extent that practitioners and educators share the public value orientation that families should take care of their own, the myth of the extended family will continue to generate unnecessary levels of guilt among middle-aged children, and resentment among their parent(s).

Cohort Differences

The model for cohort analysis follows the life course of successive birth aggregates, thus allowing us to distinguish (though never perfectly) historical from biographical from aging effects. Several points are immediately apparent: at any one historical moment, cohorts are of different ages. At the same ages, each is in a different historical epoch. And closer analysis will indicate that cohorts vary in their original composition, in fertility and mortality, in life course experiences such as educational and occupational opportunities, and ultimately in the needs and resources they bring to old age.

Before comparing today's oldest cohorts (those 65 with those of their off-spring, we should note the overriding significance of one *similarity*: aged parents and their children are both adults. This means, first, that they are to be considered status equals; and, second, that each is the product of decades of living outside the daily orbit of the other. Moreover, in our society, primary loyalties in adulthood are to the conjugal rather than the consanguine bond. Parent-child relationships in later life are, for the most part, negotiated from positions of independence vis-á-vis the other, and may, during adulthood, actually resemble those of friendship formation and maintenance, what Goode (1963) refers to as "ascriptive friendships," more than the family model of earlier stages with its imbalance in power and emotional dependencies. In extreme old age or illness, of course, the parent may be placed in a position of dependence upon a caretaking offspring, a "role reversal" often difficult for both parties to accept or enact appropriately (Blau, 1973; Simos, 1970). In this respect, Arling (1976) found that friendships are even more important than contacts with grown children for high morale in old age, and for precisely the reasons we suggest: cohort and life stage differences between generations, and intra-cohort similarities.

Age and Life Stage Differences

Differences in age mean differences in life stage concerns and exigencies, which, for example, are reflected in considerations of *life space*. The middle-aged male in our society is often portrayed as overburdened with commitments to family, work and community. Many are caught in a "life cycle squeeze" when earnings have peaked while expenses continue to rise, especially if there are college-age children to be educated (Oppenheimer, 1974).

Goode (1960) has analyzed the "role strain" arising from simultaneous demands placed on status-incumbents by role partners, and Brim (1976) speaks of a male "mid-life crisis" as social, economic and biological stresses accumulate. At this point, to deal also with the needs of an aging parent for time, energy, care or financial assistance can only exacerbate the strain. Typically, the beleaguered male could delegate kinkeeping tasks to his wife, freed of her own child-rearing responsibilities, and considered to be the family specialist in interpersonal relations. But no more may she be thus taken for granted. College enrollment (U.S. Dept. of Labor, Note 2) and labor force participation rates of middle-aged women have risen dramatically in the past decade (U.S. Dept. of Labor, Note 3). It is possible that her plans remain somewhat tentative, however, inhibited by the knowledge that an ailing parent or adult child experiencing some setback may require her attention.

Conversely, the aged parents experience a constriction of life space—a spouse or friends die, work-place contacts are given up, neighborhoods are less hospitable than before, energies flag, the body becomes recalcitrant. Needs increase as resources decline. Schooled in independence and self-sufficiency, it is difficult for many old people to place demands upon adult children, especially if they are aware that such needs will conflict with those of grandchildren. Once again, intergenerational tensions are reduced by shifting the offspring's responsibility from the filial to the citizen role. By the same token, with the state rather than the family as caretaker, the recipient of retirement income and health care can define such entitlements as a right of citizenship. However, as one anonymous referee of this paper noted, we are assuming continuing expansion of the economy. Under conditions of contraction and scarcity, the maintenance of nucleated households becomes problematic, with what we would predict to be very stressful outcomes in many cases (including increased incidence of "parent abuse" [Steinmetz, Note 4]).

Differences in Cohorts as Populations

The two age groups of interest here also vary greatly in original composition. Among those who are older Americans today are large numbers of foreign-born, or individuals who grew up on farms and villages here as well as abroad, with less than high school education and a high probability of relatively low-skill employment. Many may have lingering expectations of intrafamily caretaking (Seelbach & Sauer, Note 5), while others are ill adapted to coping with urban life (Lopata, 1973). But most will have internalized the great American virtues of independence and self-reliance, and consider making a home with an adult child only as last resort (Riley & Foner, 1968; National Council on Aging, Note 6; Sussman, Vanderwyst & Williams, Note 7) yet would call for assistance upon a child rather than a friend or neighbor (Berghorn, Schaefer, Steer & Wisemen, 1977).

Their children, on the other hand, are primarily native-born, at least high school educated, beneficiaries of an expanding economy in the post-war era, and examplars of urban or suburban family life. Where the older generation had experienced uprootedness, the Great Depression and other social instabilities of the 1930's, with a consequent low fertility rate, their offspring knew the Depression only as youngsters, and came to adulthood in time to participate in the Second World War, to enjoy the benefits of the GI Bill for further education, to marry and proceed to produce a bumper crop of infants, and to take advantage of the opportunities for geographic and occupational mobility which characterized their young adulthood.

When these mature adults reach old age in the coming decades they will have greater resources—personal and economic—than do their parents for coping with social change, the bureaucracy, and their own physical decrements. Further, they will have more children for whatever benefits can be derived from intergenerational contact. It would seem from the foregoing that a very large "generation gap" could exist between these cohorts today, potentially wider than that between these middle-aged parents and their own young adult children.

As demographic aggregates, birth cohorts not only vary in the characteristics just noted, but also in terms of original size, fertility and differential mortality. The size of any cohort is determined by three processes: fertility, mortality and migration, and all three of these have changed dramatically throughout this century. The experience of cohort members will vary accordingly—family size, dependency ratios, mobility opportunities, life expectancy and probability of institutionalization in old age are contingencies which ultimately affect individual lives (Waring, 1975).

The relative size of age cohorts exerts one of its most obvious effects on the ratios of wage earners to "dependents," namely children and the aged. As already mentioned, today's middle aged are small in number with many children and surviving parents. Cohorts differ in life expectancy at various ages, and in the sex ratio of these survivors, with female life expectancy continuing to diverge from that of males even as life styles are converging. The probability today is that the "dependent" older population as a whole will remain a constant 10–11% through the remainder of this century. But when the "baby boom" contingent reaches old age in the next century, proportions of old people will rise to 15–17% in the 2020's and 2030's (Seigel, Note 8). These shifting percentages place differential burdens on family members and on the society as a whole, but they also translate into political influence as well as the possibility of intergenerational conflict.

And lastly, the process of aging itself has changed over time—the ages at which roles are assumed or relinquished, health and income status, and self definitions. When is one "old," what is it to be old, how does one behave as an older person? Members of different cohorts will answer these questions differently, largely as a consequence of the cohort's experience and current situation. With respect to family interaction in later life, the primary question is "what are the appropriate modes of relating across generations?" Once the query is posed, the lack of a simple ready answer is striking. It is in this sense that we speak of a shift from obligatory to voluntary bonds, to a set of relationships which depend upon mutual initiative and persistence. The contact must be rewarding in some fashion for both parties to agree to its maintenance over time. Not only is the family context changed, but so are aging and old people. One might well reverse the theme of this volume and discuss "The Family in a Changing Context of Aging."

Family Level Processes

Factors Which Inhibit Generational Contacts

While residential and social mobility have not staunched the flow of help between generations, they have contributed to generating "distance" between adult children and their aged parents (Adams, 1970; but cf. Glasser & Glasser, 1962). It is noteworthy that four-fifths of all old parents live within easy visiting range of one child, but these researchers seldom tell us how many children live near their parents. Opportunities for helping may also decline because there is no need to call upon kin for *basic maintenance* (although socioemotional needs remain). That is, Social Security, Medicare and other programs free the older generation from potential dependency or even intimations of material need. Moreover, large numbers of old people value greatly their independence, preferring to live alone until they can no longer do so. There are no more grounds for assuming that older parents wish to live with their adult children than for believing that the middle aged regularly "dump" unwanted parents into institutions.

If parent-child interaction in later life resembles more the process of friendship than that of earlier intrafamily relations, relying upon similarities of values and attitudes leading to liking and the wish for more contact, i.e., homophily (Lazarsfeld & Merton, 1954; Hess, 1972), then the kinds of age and cohort differences discussed above should operate to reduce agreement and attraction between generations. Nonetheless, many similarities result from family socialization and stability of socio-economic status within the lineage. Extent of value agreement might differentiate those children who maintain contact from those who do not, but much of our data is biased by not having measures from all family members.

Another source of intergenerational tension, rarely mentioned in the gerontological literature, are the residues of those earlier conflicts which dominate studies of childhood and adolescence. Can relationships originally founded on disparities of power easily evolve into those based upon mutual respect? What of the rivalries and hostilities engendered during the oedipal phase? And, as the aged parent experiences the inevitable decrements of old age, how graciously can the adult child assume the "parental" role of caretaking? Injunctions to "filial maturity" (Blenkner, 1965; Troll, 1971) notwithstanding, the barriers are considerable (Simos, 1970; Kent & Matson, 1972; Miller, Bernstein & Sharkey, 1975; Clark & Anderson, 1967). Contrary to public perception, most adult offspring make every effort to maintain a declining parent in the community (and often in the child's home) before seeking institutionalization (Riley & Foner, 1968). Such efforts are at the expense of alternative investments of time and energy and finances, which cannot be entirely void of resentment, although ameliorated by a sense of sacrifice in having "honored thy father and mother,"[1] and, in many cases, thy mother-in-law as well.

These various sources of intergenerational distance probably "explain" the trend toward independent residence and the repeated assertions of old people that they prefer it that way. The percentage of aged parents making a home with an adult offspring has steadily declined, while the proportions living as one-person households has risen commensurately (Kobrin, 1976; Siegel, Note 8). Thus, when an old person does move in with the child, she or he is apt to be quite ancient, frail or disoriented. There is, understandably, some ambivalence on the part of the adult offspring to undertake such a responsibility (Wake & Sporakowski, 1972; Fendetti & Gelfand, 1976; Sussman, Vanderwyst & Williams, Note 7).

A final consideration in this section has to do with transitions. Later life is characterized by a number of status passages, most of a decremental nature: post-parenthood, retirement, widowhood. While presenting opportunities for personal growth, these are also periods of difficult adjustment. Those undergoing transition often look to other family members for support in managing the strains of relinquishing an old role and learning a new one. But often family members are disappointing sources of support, absorbed as they are in their own problems. For example, both generations may be undergoing difficult transitions simultaneously, as when a parent reaches retirement at the same time the offspring faces an empty nest. Or both could be responding to the same loss in different ways, as when the death of a spouse for the parent is also the death of a parent for the child. In addition, an event may require of role partners a "counterpart transition," whereby family members must learn to relate to the other in terms of the new role, not always an easy task (Riley & Waring, 1976). Such complex demands may prevent meeting the needs of the other; but, on the other hand, becoming a source of strength to one another should help both in dealing with personal loss. This is illustrative of Erikson's (1959) discussion of "self-absorption" vs. "generativity," in which reaching out to help the other is defined as the "positive" outcome. It is characteristic of the later years that there are many such challenges and that some of these will strain the bonds between family members (Waring, Note 9). For example, remarriage of the parent often leads to generational strain—from fears of losing an inheritance, inability to perceive the parent as sexually active, or beliefs that he or she is being exploited. Once the remarriage has taken place, however, the offspring typically appreciate its positive aspects (McKain, 1972; Treas & Van Hilst, Note 10).

We have discussed some of the more obvious elements tending to inhibit intergenerational contacts: mobility, declining opportunities for helping, age

---

[1]We are indebted to Mildred Seltzer for pointing out that this injunction itself suggests that people needed to be reminded, under extreme sanction, of their duties—an ideal rather than a reflection of intergenerational relations in the earliest historical societies as well as contemporary ones.

and cohort differences in attitudes and values, psychological barriers to closeness, desires for independence, and difficulties in coping with life-course transitions. In the absence of any pressing need to maintain the relationship, how
are these impediments overcome by so many—and why?

Factors Which Enhance Intergenerational Bonds

It has been argued by anthropologists that the giving of a gift or favor
obligates the recipient to return something of equal value, generating social ties
among individuals and groups (Levi-Strauss, 1964). Gouldner (1960) speaks
of the Norm of Reciprocity, and Sussman (1976) of an implicit bargain struck
with parents during the years of the infant's dependency. The parental investment in the child's survival does create, at some level, a sense of obligation on
the part of the child when grown to care for an ailing parent. Guilt and anxiety
over one's performance as a dutiful offspring operate as a form of social control
(Simos, 1970). The reactions of others—siblings, social work and medical
personnel, neighbors, friends—reinforce the norms of filial piety.

Solidarity within lineages is supported by many aspects of socialization: the
transmission of values across the generations, moral and religious upbringing,
role modeling, and the continued flow of information among members of
different age groups. There are powerful forces toward congruence, if not
complete agreement, in value orientation within familes (Troll, 1971; Bengtson, 1975; Jacobsen, Berry & Olsen, 1975; Hill, 1970; Kalish & Johnson, 1972;
Bengtson & Acock, Note 11). However, some of this apparent harmony may
be an artifact of selective perception or lack of data from offspring not in
contact with parents. Bengtson and Kuypers (1971) suggest that some distortion arises from the "developmental stake" which old people have in minimiz-
ing value disagreement but which junior members of the family will emphasize
in order to preserve their self-image as unique. Yet despite the many real and
apparent potentials for value dissonance, most families appear to have developed a "tent of values" (Jacobsen, Berry & Olsen, 1975) under which members
can meet, enjoy one another's company, share a consciousness of sameness and
sense of responsibility for one another.

Socialization involves both direct transmission of expectations for behavior
and the indirect learning which is conveyed through role modeling. For example, middle-aged parents caring for an aged relative can hope their own children will observe, record and repeat this behavior in due time, as protection
against abandonment in their old age. As a socializing force, role modeling in
later life cuts both ways. The aged parent is often coping with situations which
will one day be the lot of the adult child, and the latter is attempting to
demonstrate ways of gracious aging for the older parent to emulate (e.g.,
staying youthful). The role modeling efforts of both are complicated by the fact
that there are few appropriate role models from previous generations regarding
how to grow old or be old.

The exchange of visits and gifts across generations also serves to connect and reaffirm the viability of a lineage. The two- and three-way transfer of gifts, advice, help in emergencies, goods and services is amply documented (Sussman, 1976; Riley & Foner, 1968; Hill, 1970; Cantor, 1975; National Council on Aging, Note 6; Jackson, 1972). There is a "family network" if not precisely a "modified extended family," and it is based upon *voluntary* exchanges, with the amount and direction of flow affected by the relative resources at the disposal of generations. Among the inner city poor, for example, aged parents receive material support from adult children in return for services such as baby sitting or advice (Cantor, Note 12). In more affluent lineages, money and goods are distributed from the oldest generation downward through gifts and inheritance, while the younger members reciprocate with visits and services (Sussman, Cates & Smith, 1970). Two caveats are in order: (a) most adult children (a majority in a recent Social Security Administration survey [Murray, Note 13] provide no material support to parents, and (b) there is no *necessary* relationship between these expressions of solidarity and positive affect (Arling, 1976; Brown, 1969; Berghorn et al., 1977), although some have found such a link (e.g., Adams, 1975; Medley, 1976). A respect for privacy and tactful assessment of the relationship may well govern visiting patterns (Aldous, 1967; Stinnett, Collins & Montgomery, 1970).

Nor can we assume that those who voluntarily establish multi-generation households do so without strain. To the contrary, when independent households are preferred by old and young (see above), sharing a home is a "last resort"—literally—and those who do so may not be in the best of health or spirits. On the other hand, when undertaken out of genuine affection as a freely chosen and well though-out alternative, multi-generation living can be mutually beneficial (e.g., Lynn, 1976). We would expect that such arrangements in the future will be of this nature, given the characteristics of incoming cohorts of old people already noted. For this cohort, however, practitioners should be aware of the peculiar historical circumstances which have shaped the needs and resources of members of both adult generations.

While some of the tasks which traditionally linked generations have become attenuated or obsolete, Kreps (1977) and others in the volume by Shanas and Sussman (1977) have noted the development of a new set of functions for family members: negotiating the bureaucracy and supervising the terminal phases of life. The adult offspring become the guides and interpreters of the administratively arcane, interceding on behalf of the aged parent, securing entitlements, and ultimately making judgments regarding institutionalization and heroic efforts at preserving life. The impersonal must ultimately be made personal. How ironic if this should be the source of a new-found closeness between parent and child in later life. Yet this may be precisely where educators and practitioners could also intercede effectively, offering support and proffering understanding.

Intergenerational Relations and Later Life Satisfaction

Given these varied sources of strain and solidarity at both the societal and interpersonal levels, our frank conclusion is that few conclusive statements can be made at this time. Not that we lack research but that there are no clear-cut patterns readily discernable yet. There are simply (or not so simply) too many vicissitudes to take into account. It would appear logical to state that elderly parents with many offspring should have greater resources for later life satisfaction than do those with a limited supply of family, but the data are equivocal. Some parents with large families, often the foreign-born with "extended expectations," will be disappointed at the unwillingness or inability of children to meet such claims (Lopata, 1973, 1976). Even when such expectations are met some will remain resentful at having to feel like "guests" in the child's home (Cosneck, 1970).

What, then, do adult children contribute to parental well-being in later life? This whole question is clouded by methodological considerations: studies vary greatly in their sampling techniques, the questions asked, and the measurements utilized. Above all, the problem of selective survival intrudes (Spanier, Lewis & Cole, 1975); the only people able and willing to answer such questions are the survivors of a birth cohort whose poorer, less educated, less healthy and perhaps less happy members have already died off. Studies of life satisfaction among the aged may simply be measuring the qualities which have allowed certain subgroups to survive to answer the questionnaire.

Thus, we find Medley (1976, p. 448) declaring that "satisfaction with family was found to make the greatest single impact on life satisfaction" of old people, while finances had no direct impact. Edwards and Klemmack (1973), on the other hand, found that SES washed out other effects; similarly, Spreitzer and Snyder (1974) pinpoint perceived health status (as well as financial position). Sears and Barbee (1977), studying Terman's sample of gifted women in their middle years, find that children are related to one measure of life satisfaction for some women, but that childfree career women do very well on a variety of aspects of life satisfaction (see also Campbell, Converse & Rodgers, 1976). With incoming cohorts of older women being higher than those now old on *both* fertility and work experience, we might predict that life satisfaction of older females will be enhanced. Since males still typically define themselves in terms of occupation rather than family roles, their life satisfaction in old age should be minimally affected by intergenerational resources, which is the finding of Watson and Kivett (1976).

Whether or not children add much more to life satisfaction than does health or financial status, we do know that the absence of family can often have deleterious effects. Old men without family ties are prime candidates for suicide, accidental death, alcoholism and other socially generated diseases (Gove, 1973; Bock & Webber, 1972). There is evidence that older females are somewhat preserved by their ability to seek out and maintain close friends when family ties have disintegrated (Hess, Note 14).

Regarding the relationship between non-family networks—neighborhood, friendship and voluntary association participation—and family integration the evidence is conflicting and complex (Hess, 1972). Some find integration into community life more related to friendship than to family networks (Spakes, Note 15), and others note that respondents living alone, without strong family ties or opportunity to play traditional family roles, tend to compensate through community activity (Trela & Jackson, Note 16; see also Rutzen, Note 17). This pattern of dependency on family vs. friends or neighbors was also found among old people in Kansas City: where relatives were nearby, especially children, one depended upon these when necessary, but where no children lived in the area, old people were likely to depend upon friends and neighbors when in need (Berghorn et al., 1977). The researchers relate these patterns to a cultural level aversion to dependency of any sort in our society, but when it does become necessary, dependency on children carries the least stigma, and may even be justified by invoking the norms of reciprocity and filial piety which are also part of the value system.

Still other studies show that persons with high levels of kin interaction are also high interactors with non-kin, and those with low rates of contact with relatives have similarly depressed investments in other social networks (Booth, 1972; Biesty, DiComo & Hess, Note 18; Croog, Lipson & Levine, 1972). Clearly, there is no simple relationship between family and other social networks: some people will be high or low interactors with anybody; others compensate for losses in one area with enhanced involvement in different groups. Such substitutability, however, may be governed by considerations of functional alternatives; that is, various networks operate to meet certain kinds of needs, so that there are limits to how these can be mixed and matched (Weiss, 1969; Litwak & Szelenyi, 1969). In some cases, moreover, integration into non-family social systems—friendships, voluntary associations, neighborhood, even senior centers—is preferable to total dependence upon a spouse, for if that one person should die the survivor is, indeed, bereft (Bock & Webber, 1972; Rutzen, Note 17).

Much as children and non-family associations add to the life satisfaction of some old people, there is considerable evidence that for those elderly with surviving spouses the martal relationship not only remains paramount but is enhanced by the children's leaving after adolescence. Possibly, there was nowhere for scores of marital satisfaction to go except up since families with adolescent children do show signs of stress (Burr, 1970; Rollins & Feldman, 1970; Renne, 1970; Smart & Smart, 1975; Gilford & Bengtson, Note 19; Miller, 1976). If the presence of teen-age children strains the resources and emotional energies of mid-life parents, postparenthood offers relief which is reflected in satisfaction scores (e.g., Neugarten, 1976). But an additional benefit of the absence of children is the potential for an increase in couple-companionate activities (Miller, 1976; Rollins & Cannon, 1974). The literature on postparental marriages indicates a turning again toward one another for companionship and psychic satisfaction often described as comparable to that of the honeymoon period. However, it must be noted that selective processes have been operating. These are not static relationships—the marriage and the partners themselves have changed over time; efforts at enrichment have been made, experiences shared, tolerance deepened. Couples unable to adapt or develop in these directions drop out of the data base via divorce, desertion or separation. The very poor, whose marital satisfaction is highly problematic, have lower life expectancy as well, further reducing the probability of their experiencing long-term intact marriages (Spanier, Lewis & Cole, 1975).

Not only will selective survival of certain marriages bias the findings on later life satisfaction, perceptual processes may further distort the data. Spanier, Lewis and Cole (1975) note that the longer a couple has remained together, the greater their investment in believing that the commitment has been worthwhile, the less likely to acknowledge threats, and the more apt to reduce dissonance by denying unhappiness. Whatever the forces at work, the end result seems to be that many marriages are strengthened by the departure of offspring and that the conjugal relationship is enhanced and deepened at this time. For the couples who jointly survive, through middle age and later, there is also evidence of a "coming together" of personality traits among postparental spouses (Livson, Note 20): i.e., a relaxing of rigid sex role expectations and behaviors, and a growing acceptance of previously inappropriate tendencies such as nurturance for men and dominance by women (see also Lowenthal, Thurnher & Chiriboga, 1975; Brim, 1976; Neugarten, 1968; Clausen, 1972). A "mellowing"—in every sense of the word—seems to infuse these relationships as the spouses relax from the rigors of rearing children and striving for occupational success. Of course, many couples grow further apart at this stage if a shared interest in the children has been the only bond, but there is no clear evidence of a surge of divorces (Schoen, 1975).

Unfortunately, the facts of later life are that many older women will not be members of a conjugal unit. While widows seem to cope with loss of a spouse less lethally than do widowers, they do not share the high morale of still marrieds. As with measures of life satisfaction and morale applied to postparental couples, the widowed are also affected by non-family variables such as health, education and income (Lopata, 1973; Chevan & Korson, 1972; Morgan, 1976; Cosneck, 1970; Adams, 1968). The role of children in the life space of a widowed parent can be minimal or all-embracing as in the case of sharing a home, and there will be happy and unhappy old people in both categories. However, the existence of adult children with whom one could make a home *is* a hedge against institutionalization (Soldo & Myers, Note 21). We might speculate, however, that in the future, women who limit fertility or choose to remain childfree will also have high educational attainment, retirement incomes from life-time work, and out-going relationships in a variety of non-family systems, and thus reduce the differences in old-age resources between women with many children and those with few or none. In other words, the preservative value of children may become less marked as the life course of women changes.

Conclusion

We began our exploration of intergenerational relations in later life by asking a basic, if impertinent, question, "why do they persist?" We think that the evidence suggests that the maintenance and sustenance of the parent/child bond will be increasingly based upon the willingness of both parties to engage in supportive behaviors, and that this willingness, in turn, hinges on the quality of the relationship over many preceding decades. While guilt and shame will remain powerful motivators of filial performance, and the injunction to "honor thy father and mother" continues to shape our socialization to obligations toward aged parents, the actual course of contacts and the satisfactions derived from them will be subject to the same type of role negotiation characterizing other interpersonal relationships. As a consequence, such variables as basic trust, respect, shared values and beliefs, and genuine affection—the foundations of homophily—will increasingly determine parent/child relations in later life.

The foundation of such a relationship can, of course, be laid in the early years of infancy and childhood dependency, or fostered by the skill with which the generations negotiate an ultimate release from these dependencies. But it is also possible that parents and offspring who were never deeply affectionate at earlier life stages can develop a mutual respect and liking when both are freed from relations of superordination/subordination. Although much of the literature deals with a "special relationship" between older women and their adult daughters (Neugarten, 1968), we would guess that the adult male child might also find his father easier to talk to and get along with after leaving the parental home and becoming a "man" in his own right, free of the need to compete with the father on the latter's own ground.

Trends at both the societal and familial level support our contention that parent and child relations in later life are moving toward the voluntaristic model. Demographically, compared with those now old, incoming cohorts of old people will be more independent financially, better educated, with higher probabilities of joint survival after completion of parental tasks. In terms of attitudes toward family responsibilities, there is evidence that extended expectations of care from one's children (Espenshade, Note 22; Yankelovich, Skelly & White, 1977).

Family life educators and practitioners, looking ahead, might speculate on what such changes portend. Our guesses are that older women, especially, will be affected by the trends noted above, and although widowhood will remain the fate of most, those qualities that enhance independent living and adaptation to loss will increasingly characterize their lives: education, work experience, financial security and lifelong involvement in non-family associations. As for older men, there is some evidence that family roles and leisure activities are encroaching on the time and energies previously expended in the occupational sphere. In old age, these men will have alternative sources of satisfaction, and, possibly, more companionate relationships with their wives than do men currently retired. Aging parents will not have to make demands upon the material or social resources of offspring, although many may do so. Adult children will be spared excruciating choices between the needs of their own children, themselves, and their parents. And those bonds which do persist will do so because they have been willingly sought and nurtured by adults who are authentically concerned with the well-being of one another. Far from disintegrating, the future of parent-child relations in later life may be characterized by the strongest ties of all: mutual respect.

Reference Notes

1 Schorr, A. Filial responsibility in the modern American family. Social Security Administration, DHEW, USGPO, Washington, D.C. 20402, 1960.
2. U.S. Department of Labor. *Marital and family characteristics of the labor force,* March, 1975. Special Labor Force Report 183, Bureau of Labor Statistics, Washington, D.C., 1975.
3. U.S. Department of Labor. *Going back to school at 35 and over.* Special Labor Force Report 184, Bureau of Labor Statistics, Washington, D.C., 1975.
4. Steinmetz, S. *The politics of selective inattention: The case of parent abuse.* Unpublished working paper, University of Delaware, 1978.
5. Seelbach, W., & Sauer, W. *Filial responsibility expectations and morale among aged parents.* Paper presented at the annual meeting of the Gerontological Society, New York City, October, 1976.
6. National Council on the Aging. *The myth and reality of aging in America.* 1974.
7. Sussman, M. B., Vanderwyst, D., & Williams, G. K. *Will you still need me, will you still feed me when I'm 64?* Paper presented at the annual meeting of the Gerontological Society, New York City, October, 1976.
8. Siegel, J. S. *Demographic aspects of aging and the older population in the United States.* Current Population Reports, Special Studies, Series P-23, No. 59, USGPO, Washington, D.C. 20402: U.S. Department of Commerce, Bureau of the Census, May, 1976.
9. Waring, J. M. *Conflict between the middle aged and old: Why not?* Paper presented at the annual meeting of the American Sociological Association, San Francisco, August, 1975.
10. Treas, J., & Van Hilst, A. *Marriage and remarriage among the older population.* Paper presented at the annual meeting of the Gerontological Society, Louisville, 1975.
11. Bengtson, V. L., & Vcock, A. G. *On the influence of mothers and fathers: A covariance analysis of political and religious socialization.* Paper presented at the annual meeting of the American Sociological Society, New York, August, 1976.
12. Cantor, M. *The configuration and intensity of the informal support system in a New York City elderly population.* Paper presented at the annual meeting of the Gerontological Society, New York, October, 1976.
13. Murray, J. *Family structure in the pre-retirement years.* (Retirement History Study Report #4.) U.S. Dept. HEW, Social Security Administration, Publication No. (SSA) 74-11700 USGPO, Washington, D.C. 20402, 1973.
14. Hess, B. B. *Age, gender role and friendship.* Paper presented at annual meeting of the Gerontological Society, New York, October, 1976.
15. Spakes, P. *Social integration, age, and family participation.* Paper presented at the annual meeting of the Gerontological Society, New York, October, 1976.

16. Trela, J. E., & Jackson, D. *Family life and substitutes in old age.* Paper presented at the annual meeting of the Gerontological Society, New York, 1976.
17. Rutzen, R. *Varieties of social disengagement among the aged: A research report on correlates of primary socialization.* Paper presented at the annual meeting of the Eastern Sociological Society, New York City, March, 1977.
18. Biesty, P., DiComo, W., & Hess, B. B. *The elderly of Morris County, New Jersey: Findings of a senior citizens assessment of needs (SCAN) survey.* Mimeo. Morristown, N.J., Area Agency on Aging, 1977.
19. Gilford, R., & Bengtson, V. L. *Measuring marital satisfaction in three generations: Positive and negative dimensions.* Paper presented at the Gerontological Society, New York, October, 1976.
20. Livson, F. B. *Coming together in the middle years: A longitudinal study of sex role convergence.* Paper presented at the annual meeting of the Gerontological Society, New York, October, 1976.
21. Soldo, B. J., & Myers, G. C. *The effects of total fertility on living arrangements among elderly women.* Paper presented at the annual meeting of the Gerontological Society, New York, October, 1976.
22. Espanshade, T. J. *The value and cost of children.* Bulletin of the Population Reference Bureau, Inc. Washington, D.C., 32, 1977.

References

Adams, B. N. The middle-class adult and his widowed or still-married mother. *Social Problems,* 1968, 16, 50–59.
Adams, B. N. *The family: A sociological interpretation* (2nd ed.). Chicago: Rand McNally, 197
Adams, B. N. Isolation, function and beyond: American kinship in the 1960's. *Journal of Marriage and the Family,* 1970, 32, 575–597.
Aldous, J. Intergenerational visiting patterns: Variations in boundary maintenance as an explanation. *Family Process,* 1967, 6, 235–251.
Arling, G. The elderly widow and her family, neighbors and friends. *Journal of Marriage and the Family,* 1976, 38, 757–768.
Bengtson, V. L., & Kuypers, J. A. Generational differences and the developmental stake. *Aging and Human Development,* 1971, 2, 249–260.
Bergtson, V. L. Generation and family effects in value socialization. *American Sociological Review,* 1975, 40, 358–371.
Berghorn, F. L., Schafer, D. E., Steere, G. H., & Wiseman, R. F. *The urban elderly: A study of life satisfaction.* Montclair, N.J.: Allenheld Osman, 1977.
Blau, Z. S. *Old age in a changing society.* New York: New Viewpoints, 1973.
Blenkner, M. Social work and family relationships in later life, with some thoughts on filial maturity. In E. Shanas & G. Streib (Eds.), *Social structure and the family: Generational relations.* Englewood Cliffs, N.J.: Prentice-Hall, 1965.
Bock, E. W., & Webber, I. L. Suicide among the elderly: Isolating widowhood and mitigating alternatives. *Journal of Marriage and the Family,* 1972, 34, 24–31.
Booth, A. Sex and social participation. *American Sociological Review,* 1972, 37, 183–192.
Brim, O. G., Jr. Mate mid-life crisis: A comparative analysis. In B. B. Hess (Ed.), *Growing old in America.* New Brunswick, N.J.: Transaction, 1976.
Brody, E. M. Congregate care facilities and mental health of the elderly. *Aging and Human Development,* 1970, 1, 279–321.
Brown, R. Family structure and social isolation of older persons. *Journal of Gerontology,* 1969, 15, 170–174.
Burr, W. R. Satisfaction with various aspects of marriage over the life cycle: A random middle class sample. *Journal of Marriage and the Family,* 1970, 32, 29–37.
Campbell, A., Converse, P. E., & Rodgers, W. L. *The quality of American life: Perceptions, evaluations and satisfactions.* New York: Russell Sage, 1976.
Cantor, M. Life space and the social support system of the inner city elderly of New York. *The Gerontologist,* 1975, 15, 23–27.
Chevan, A., & Korson, J. H. The widowed who live alone: An examination of social and demographic factors. *Social Forces,* 1972, 51, 45–52.

Clark, M., & Anderson, B. G. *Culture and aging.* Springfield, Ill.: Thomas, 1967.

Clausen, J. The life course of individuals. In M. W. Riley, M. Johnson, & A. Foner (Eds.), *Aging and society* (Vol. 3): *A sociology of age stratification.* New York: Russell Sage, 1972

Cosneck, B. J. Family patterns of older widowed Jewish people. *The Family Coordinator,* 1970, 19, 368–373.

Croog, S. H., Lipson, A., & Levine, S. Help patterns in severe illness: The roles of kin network, non-family resources and institutions. *Journal of Marriage and the Family,* 1972, 34, 32–41.

Edwards, J. N., & Klemmack, D. L. Correlates of life satisfaction: A re-examination. *Journal of Gerontology,* 1973, 28, 497–502.

Erikson, E. Identity and the life cycle. In G. Klein (Ed.), *Psychological issues.* New York: International, 1959.

Fendetti, D. V., & Gelfand, D. E. Care of the aged: Attitudes of white ethnic families. *The Gerontologist,* 1976, 16, 545–549.

Glasser, P. H., & Glasser, L. N. Role reversal and conflict between aged parents and their children. *Marriage and Family Living,* 1962, 24, 46–51.

Goode, W. J. A theory of role strain. *American Sociological Review,* 1960, 25, 483–496.

Goode, W. J. *World revolution and family patterns.* New York: Free Press, 1963.

Gouldner, A. The norm of reciprocity: A preliminary statement. *American Sociological Review,* 1960, 25, 161–178.

Gove, W. Sex, marital status and mortality. *American Journal of Sociology,* 1973, 79, 45–67.

Hess, B. B. Friendship. In M. W. Riley, M. Johnson, & A. Foner (Eds.), *Aging and society* (Vol. 3): *A sociology of age stratification.* New York: Russell Sage, 1972.

Hill, R. *Family development in three generations.* Cambridge, Mass.: Schenkman, 1970.

Jackson, J. J. Marital life among aging blacks. *The Family Coordinator,* 1972, 21, 21–27.

Jacobson, R. B., Berry, K. J., & Olsen, K. F. An empirical test of the generation gap: A comparative intrafamily study. *Journal of Marriage and the Family,* 1975, 37, 841–852.

Kalish, R. A., & Johnson, A. I. Value similarities and differences in three generations of women. *Journal of Marriage and the Family,* 1972, 34, 49–53.

Kent, D. P., & Matson, M. B. The impact of health on the aged family. *The Family Coordinator,* 1972, 21, 29–36.

Kobrin, F. E. The primary individual and the family: Changes in living arrangements in the United States since 1940. *Journal of Marriage and the Family,* 1976, 38, 233–239.

kreps, J. M. Intergenerational transfers and the bureaucracy. In E. Shanas & M. B. Sussman (Eds.), *Family, bureaucracy and the elderly.* Durham, N.C.: Duke, 1977.

Lazarsfeld, P. F., & Merton, R. K. Friendship as social process: A substantive and methodological inquiry. In M. Berger, T. Abel, & C. H. Page (Eds.), *Freedom and control in modern society.* Princeton, N.J. : Van Nostrand, 1954.

Levi-Strauss, C. Reciprocity, the essence of social life. In R. L. Coser (Ed.), *The family: Its structure and functions.* New York: St. Martin's, 1964.

Litwak, E., & Szelenyi, I. Primary group structures and their functions: Kin, neighbors and friends. *American Sociological Review,* 1969, 34, 64–78.

Lopata, H. Z. *Widowhood in an American city.* Cambridge, Mass.: Schenkman, 1973.

Lopata, H. Z. *Polish Americans.* Englewood Cliffs, N.J.: Prentice-Hill, 1976.

Lowenthal, M. F., Thumher, M., & Chiriboga, D. *Four stages of life.* San Francisco: Jossey-Bass, 1975.

Lynn, I. Three-generation household In the middle-class. In B. B. Hess (Ed.), *Growing old in America.* New Brunswick, N.J.: Transaction, 1976.

McKain, W. C. A new look at older marriages. *The Family Coordinator,* 1972, 21, 61–69.

Medley, M. L. Satisfaction with life among persons sixty-five and over. *Journal of Gerontology,* 1976, 31, 448–455.

Miller, B. C. A multivariate developmental model of marital satisfaction. *Journal of Marriage and the Family,* 1976.

Miller, M. B., Bernstein, H., & Sharkey, H. Family extrusion of the aged patient. *The Gerontologist,* 1975, 15, 291–296.

Morgan, L. A. A re-examination of widowhood and morale. *Journal of Gerontology,* 1976, 31, 687–695.

Neugarten, B. L. The awareness of middle age. In B. L. Neugarten (Ed.), *Middle age and aging.* Chicago, Ill.: University of Chicago, 1968.

Neugarten, B. L. Middle age and aging. In B. B. Hess (Ed.), *Growing Old in America.* New Brunswick, N.J.: Transaction, 1976.

Oppenheimer, V. K. Life cycle squeeze: The interaction of men's occupational and family life cycles. *Demography,* 1974, 11, 227–245.

Renne, K. S. Correlates of dissatisfaction In marriage. *Journal of Marriage and the Family,* 1970, 32, 54–67.

Riley, M. W., & Foner, A. *Aging and society* (Vol. 1): *An inventory of research findings.* New York: Russell Sage, 1968.

Riley, M. W., Johnson, M., & Foner, A. *Aging and society* (Vol. 3): *A sociology of age stratification.* New York: Russell Sage, 1972.

Riley, M. W., & Waring, J. J. Age and aging. In R. K. Merton & R. Nisbet (Eds.), *Contemporary social problems* (4th ed.). New York: Harcourt, 1976.

Rollins, B. C., & Feldman, H. Marital satisfaction over the family life cycle. *Journal of Marriage and the Family,* 1970, 32, 20–28.

Schoen, R. California divorce rates by age at first marriage and duration of first marriage. *Journal of Marriage and the Family,* 1975, 37, 548–555.

Sears, P., & Barbee, A. H. Career and life satisfaction among Terman's gifted women. In J. Stanley, W. George & C. Solano (Eds.), *The gifted and the creative: Fifty year perspective.* Baltimore: Johns-Hopkins, 1977.

Shanas, E., & Sussman, M. B. (Eds.) *Family, bureaucracy and the elderly.* Durham, N.C.: Duke, 1977.

Simos, B. G. Relations of adults with aging parents. *The Gerontologist,* 1970, 10, 135–139.

Smart, M. S., & Smart, R. C. Recalled, present and predicted satisfaction in stages of the family life cycle in New Zealand. *Journal of Marriage and the Family,* 1975, 37, 408–415.

Spanier, G. B., Lewis, R. A., & Cole, C. L. Marital adjustment over the family life cycle: The issue of curvilinearity. *Journal of Marriage and the Family,* 1975, 37, 263–275.

Spreitzer, E., & Snyder, E. Correlates of life satisfaction among the aged. *The Gerontologist,* 1974, 29, 454–458.

Stinnett, N., Collins, J., & Montgomery, J. E. Marital need satisfaction of husbands and wives. *Journal of Marriage and the Family,* 1970, 32, 428–434.

Sussman, M. B., Cates, J. N., & Smith, D. T. *The family and inheritance.* New York: Russell Sage, 1970.

Sussman, M. B. The family life of old people. In R. Binstock & E. Shanas (Eds.), *Handbook of aging and the social sciences.* New York: Van Nostrand, 1976.

Troll, L. E. The family of later life: A decade review. *Journal of Marriage and the Family,* 1971, 33, 263–290.

Wake, S. B., & Sporakowski, M, J. An intergenerational comparison of attitudes toward supporting aged parents. *Journal of Marriage and the Family,* 1972, 34, 42–48.

Waring, J. M. Social replenishment and social change: The problem of disordered cohort flow. *American Behavioral Scientist,* 1975, 19, 237–256.

Watson, J. A., & Kivett, V. R. Influences on the life satisfaction of older fathers. *The Family Coordinator,* 1976, 25, 482–488.

Weber, M. Bureaucracy. In H. H. Gerth & C. W. Mills, *From Max Weber.* New York: Oxford, 1958.

Weiss, R. S. The fund of sociability. *Transaction,* 1969, 6, 36–43.

Yankelovich, Skelly, & White, Inc. *Raising children in a changing society.* Minneapolis, Minn. General Mills, 1977.

Chapter 11

Variations in Life Style

Singlehood: An Alternative   *Peter J. Stein*
to Marriage

> Well, today I think I'll stay single forever. It's a hell of a lot more freedom
> than it would be either in a marriage or an exclusive relationship. . . . This
> affords the opportunity of getting to know well and be friends with a lot of
> different people. No restrictions except the restrictions that I happen to
> choose.
>
> —Joan M., 31, college instructor

Serious research about singlehood is notably missing from the field of family
sociology. "To date there has been very little empirical research on the state
of singleness, and virtually none on single men. Sociologists are as human and
as culture-bound as anyone else and thus tend to ignore those elements of
society that do not conform to our cultural norms . . . the neglect reflects our
adherence to the ideal that everyone should marry . . . " (Duberman, 1974).
There are a few valuable studies of those previously married, such as Helena
Lopata's study of widowhood (1973), William Goode's study of divorced
women (1956), Jessie Bernard's study of second marriages (1956), and Lucile
Duberman's study of reconstituted families (Duberman, 1975). However, an
examination of twelve leading texts in family sociology revealed that only three
dealt with singles, and, even then, rather briefly. When not completely ignored
by most of the writers on the family, single people are defined in terms of their
relationship to marriage. In our society, adulthood has been synonymous with
marriage and parenthood, to the extent that "the good life is defined as marriage . . . any living arrangement is wrong that may make any marriageable
individual forego marriage" (Mead, 1967). Hence, the prevailing attitude that
those who remain single are seen as deviant or in some way inadequate for
normal adult roles.

From *Family Coordinator* (October 1975), pp. 489–503. Copyrighted 1975 by the National
Council on Family Relations. Reprinted by permission.

Emerging Styles of Singlehood

There is, however, an emergent new style of singlehood that opposes the generally held view that single people are not single by right or by choice; rather, that single people do indeed have a choice and a growing number of them are exercising that choice consciously and voluntarily, in order to pursue life styles that will meet their needs for human growth and supportive interpersonal relationships. The emergence of singlehood as a life style is seen as a developmental phenomenon in response to the dissatisfaction with traditional marriage. As such, it represents a significant change in the cultural expectations underlying many of our social values.

An inquiry to determine the extent to which singlehood provides a viable alternative to marriage and family life is particularly urgent in view of the increasing number of single persons in American society. Paul C. Glick, a prominent demographer who has studied the fluctuation in marriage patterns since the Depression, notes the movement away from conformity to the marriage and family norm, "especially as such conformity comes in conflict with the development of the full potentiality of each member of the family" (1975). The demographic trends are most striking in the recent delay in marriage among the young and growing divorce rates.

Summarizing 1960 census data Glick (1969) predicted that "of all the young in 1960, probably all but 3 or 4 percent will eventually marry." Recent demographic data, however, indicates a dramatic shift in patterns that suggest the percentage of persons opting against marriage is rising rapidly. In March 1974 there were 16,817,300 single men eighteen years and older in the United States and 16,476,000 single women. Thus there was a total of 33,293,300 never married, separated, and divorced men and women eighteen years and older. Of the never married, 12.7 million were between the ages of 20 and 34; this represents a 50 percent increase for that age group since 1960. The rate of marriage among single persons under 45 is as low now as it had been at the end of the Depression in the mid-1930's. "For the first time since soon after World War II the marriage total for a 12 month period was significantly smaller (by 68,000) than it had been in the preceding year. However, the divorce total for the 12 months ending in August 1974 had continued to rise (by 56,000) above the level for the preceding 12 months" (Glick, 1975). This amounts to a divorce rate of 4.5 per 1000, the highest in the world. The 1.3 million persons under 34 years of age who are divorced but have not remarried is more than double the 1960 figure. Thus, the growing divorce rate has also increased the number of singles, most of whom now stay unmarried for a longer period of time than did their counterparts a decade earlier.

Some supporting evidence for the decreasing attraction of marriage comes from attitudinal studies. In a 1962 study of unmarried college women, Bell found that "only 2 percent of them had little or no interest in future marriage" (Bell, 1971). In a panel study conducted a decade later, in which unmarried college women were queried in their freshman and senior years, Stein found significant shifts in attitudes. As first-year students, only 2.7 percent of the sample did not expect to marry, while as seniors 7.7 percent did not expect to marry. In 1973, as seniors, a startling 40 percent of the women said they did not know whether or not they would marry (Stein, 1973).

The panel study by Stein also showed that 39 percent of seniors felt that traditional marriage is becoming obsolete, and 25 percent agreed with the statement that the traditional family structure of mother, father, and children living under one roof no longer works. This parallels national trends in student values as cited in the Yankelovitch survey of *The Changing Values on Campus* (1972), which reports that the number of students who believe that the present institution of marriage is becoming obsolete has increased from 24 percent in 1969 to 28 percent in 1970, to 34 percent in 1971. In 1971 (these questions were not asked earlier), 32 percent of students did not look forward to being married, or were not sure about it, and 29 percent either agreed or were not sure that traditional family structure works.

These attitude changes are also reflected in the nation-wide data collected by the Census Bureau. The median age at first marraige for women increased from 20.3 in 1960 to 21.0 in 1973. The corresponding increase for men was from 22.8 in 1960 to 23.2 in 1973. The proportion of singles in the 20–24 age group increased by ten percent for women and four percent for men. Within this age group, 57 percent of men and 38 percent of women are single. While in Glick's words, "it is too early to predict with confidence that the increase in singleness among the young will lead to an eventual decline in lifetime marriage . . . just as cohorts of young women who have postponed childbearing for an unusually long time seldom make up for the child deficit as they grow older, so also young people who are delaying marriage may never make up for the marriage deficit later on. They may try alternatives to marriage and they may like them" (Glick, 1975, 18).

The trend toward the erosion of the ideological and economic bases for traditional marriage is such that "men no longer (have) to marry to get sex and women no longer (have) to marry to get financial support" (Bird, 1972), and given the development of the women's liberation movement and its stress upon self-fulfillment through means other than wifehood and motherhood, as well as the impact of other social movements such as communal living, open marriage, and gay liberation, there is clear evidence that "conventional marriage is no longer inevitable or even necessarily desirable. People can choose relationships that emphasize companionship, rather than children and family, and their relations need not be heterosexual, exclusive or permanent" (Passin, 1973). More and more people are postponing or rejecting marriage in favor of independence.

In an attempt to identify the major aspects of the emerging life styles of singlehood the author conducted 20 in-depth interviews with single persons who have intentionally made the choice to stay single. The focus here is an exploration of the reasons people choose to remain single and some of their experiences in being single.[1] For the purposes of the following analysis we included only those men and women who responded negatively to the following three questions:

(1) Is there one person of the opposite sex or the same sex you now see exclusively?
(2) Do you plan to marry in the near future?
(3) Do you hope to live with one person in a sexually exclusive relationship in the near future?

When asked how long they plan to stay single, respondents' answers ranged from a minimum of five years to the rest of their lives. Although most did not categorically discount marriage, it was a low priority concern for all of them.

This exploratory study represents 20 adults, ten men and ten women. The median age for men is 34.6 and their ages range from a low of 27 to a high of 45. The median age for women is 28.7 and their ages range from 22 to 33 years of age. Women respondents included two psychiatric social workers, an interior designer, a grammar school teacher, a college instructor, an educational test designer, a statistician, a programmer, an editorial assistant for a major publishing firm, and a high school teacher. The men included a lawyer, two writers, a furniture salesman, two college professors, a systems analyst, a programmer, a health administrator, and a legal secretary.

Four of the women have been married, one of them twice. Six of the women have lived with men in sexually exclusive relationships for periods ranging from six months to three years. Seven of the men have been married and six, including four of those who have also been married, have lived in sexually exclusive relationships with women. None are currently involved in a sexually exclusive relationship.

The selection of respondents deliberately favored persons who at some time in their lives have been involved in exclusive relationships, in or out of mar-

---

[1]Some of the problems faced by singles are paralleled in the experiences of married women who decide to be childless. Veevers shows how the voluntarily childless constitute a deviant category: statistically, socially, ethically, and psychologically. For example, Veevers reports that "all of the wives interviewed reported that virtually everyone disapproved of their rejection of motherhood . . . everyone except their husbands." Her article examines four mechanisms employed by childless wives to justify their deviant life style: selective perception of the experience of parenthood, association with advocates of childlessness (and psychological isolation from detractors), structuring of social situations to reinforce the variant view (as in "borrowing" children under adverse circumstances), and reinterpretation of societal ambivalence toward parenthood as envy of a superior life style. Similar mechanisms are no doubt used by singles, whose way of life also runs counter to the norm. While the present study focuses on reasons given by respondents for their choice, our data reveals a reliance on support structures parallel to those described by Veevers. Further study of the psychological mechanisms of singles will be presented in Stein's book *Single in America* (Prentice-Hall, forthcoming). J.E. Veevers, the Moral Careers of Voluntarily Childless Wives, Forthcoming in *Marriage and the Family in Canada: A Reader* (Toronto, 1975).

riage. (Only one woman and one man have never been). For the purpose of this study we are combining those who have been legally married with those who have cohabited without the legal sanction since their experiences were very similar.[2] Such respondents, it was felt, would be able to assess their preference for singlehood on the basis of comparative experience. Having tried both singlehood and non-singlehood, they are in a better position to make decisions than the less experienced singles, particularly those who are just leaving their families. The men and women we interviewed have clearly chosen, at least for the foreseeable future, the single state as the more viable life style for the fulfillment of their needs.

The Decision to Remain Single

> Marriage is a purposeless institution. Everything that marriage provides—
> tenderness, love, sex, warmth—you don't have to sign a lifetime contract for.
> —Garry M., 35, hospital administrator

Of the men and women who are members of our sample, nine have never been married, eleven have been married, and twelve have lived with a member of the opposite sex in a mutually exclusive monogamous relationship. None are currently seeking mates, and though some may well marry eventually, most feel they will not.

The positive choice of singlehood over marriage contrasts our respondents with those interviewed by Kuhn in the fifties. Kuhn, in his analysis of those who fail to marry, concluded that failure to marry reflected a high rate of personal and social problems; there is little suggestion in his findings that such people might be making a conscious, positive decision not to marry. Kuhn cites a number of reasons why individuals never marry:

(1) hostility toward marriage or toward members of the opposite sex;
(2) homosexuality;
(3) emotional fixation on one or both parents causing an inability to love someone else;
(4) poor health or deviant physical characteristics;
(5) unattractiveness;
(6) unwillingness to assume responsibility;
(7) inability to find "the one," the true love based on romantic expectations;
(8) social inadequacy in the dating-mating game;
(9) marriage perceived as a threat to career goals;

[2]The interviews, although not focused primarily on the interaction between partners, did not reveal any important differences in the mode of interaction or the experiences of married and cohabiting couples. Marriages did last longer on the average: cohabiting couples stayed together from six months to three years; marriages lasted from a low of three years to a high of eleven years. The average cohabiting couple stayed together for sixteen months; the average married couple stayed together for six years and three months.

(10) economic factors precluding the financial responsibilities of marriage;
(11) geographical, educational, or occupational isolation such that the chance
of meeting an eligible mate is drastically limited.

The main thrust of Kuhn's findings is that never to marry is a failure which
reflects an individual's shortcomings and inadequacies. Singles are expected to
adapt to a social context that rewards marriage and wherein "almost all major
roles and related values are based on the assumption of marital experience"
(Kuhn, 1955). Bell (1975), in a discussion of Kuhn's work, suggests that
certain characteristics, such as unattractiveness, are "a factor in *not being
selected,* whereas hostile marriage attitudes refer to *not actively selecting.*"

Bell further states that "a person who is not actively seeking a mate has . . .
withdrawn from the mate selection process." This description also applies to
our respondents, who are not actively selecting a mate. They have exercised
the choice not to do so. However, in contrast to Kuhn's findings, most of our
respondents offered positive reasons for remaining single. Such factors as
homosexuality, parent fixation, physical or health problems, unattractiveness,
unrealistic romantic expectations, economic problems, conflict between marriage and career desires, and isolation from the dating market did not characterize any of our respondents. There did not appear to be a lack of proficiency
in dealing with the dating-mating game, but rather a rejection of it as competitive, outmoded, and exploitative.

Negative attitudes toward marriage and its implied roles and responsibilities
may be termed "pushes" away from marriage toward singlehood insofar as
dissatisfaction motivates the search for an alternative. Our respondents reflected a spectrum of negative attitudes, mostly based on their own experience
in a marriage or coresidential exclusive relationship. While most did not
question the validity of marriage as an institution, the majority were quite
certain that they would not choose to marry in the future. Several persons
indicated that although they felt some guilt about not being married because
of pressures from family or married friends, they rejected marriage as a personal choice. The idea of a non-marital exclusive relationship elicited more
ambivalent feelings. A number of the respondents stated that they were open
about this as an option for some future time, on a strictly tentative and
experimental basis, however. All respondents emphasized that exclusivity at
this time in their lives would constitute a critical limitation on their freedom
and growth.

Indeed, the theme of marriage as a restriction and obstacle to human growth
showed up as the strongest push in our study. It was often based on the attitude
that one central relationship as an exclusive source of emotional support and
social identity was both unrealistic and confining. In response to the question
of why he chose to remain single, Tom said:

> When I was in an unofficial marriage with a woman, I would see only her and
> would be totally focused on her as the deciding factor of how my mood would

be. It was a way of keeping myself out of having anything for myself and depriving myself of friends.

With the nuclear family marriage has come to mean a closed, often mechanical interaction of two. Respondents emphasized that such dependency on one's mate cannot satisfy the multiple demands of self-development. Garry, divorced three years ago after a ten year marriage, stated:

> It's simplistic to think that one person is always going to fill all my needs and that I'm not going to change and she's not going to change.

Correlative with the lack of self-development is the sense of isolation often felt in an exclusive relationship. This was cited as a second major push. A number of respondents pointed out that marriage, rather than singlehood, paradoxically creates conditions of loneliness they did not want to experience. Marilyn, discussing her marriage, exemplifies this problem:

> The marriage lasted about five years . . . I didn't know what I was missing, but I knew I was missing something. I felt a tremendous isolation . . .

Loneliness may occur because of inability to share experience meaningfully with one's mate. Many respondents described a feeling of disconnectedness and resultant frustration, both psychological and sexual, within the marital relationship that we may identify as a push. Steve noted how the failure to communicate with his wife, while he was involved in graduate school and she with their infant, drew him apart, creating anger and temporary impotence. Driven to seek relationships with other women, he experienced guilt and further estrangement which subsequently led to his divorce.

Several respondents mentioned the tendency in marriage to associate only with mutually satisfying friends as a push toward the single state. Joan remarked that "While I was married I was really upset at how limited the ability to have other friends was." In fact, Tom suggested, it is the fear of involvement with people that brings about the overinvolvement with a mate:

> I find that it is easier for single people to have friends than married people because I think the reason why people get married is to cut down on the amount of friends they have. Marriage is a protective thing . . .

As Pearce and Newton (1969) have observed, "the early marriage can constitute a flight from experience," and friendships normally make up an important part of one's experience. An individual may recognize this pattern, however, and come to desire more interpersonal involvement. Since for many of our interviewees marriage has functioned to avoid friendships, loneliness tends to be associated with marriage and accordingly serves as a push away from it.

A final push brought out by a majority of the men and women we interviewed was the idea that marriage restricts opportunities. The dominant view was that marriage is an entrapment, requiring constant accommodation and compromise and cutting off variety of experience. In stating his reasons for singlehood, Sven implied these objections to marriage:

> There aren't any conditions under which I would consider getting married . . .
> I want freedom of choice, freedom to do what I want instead of being tied
> to living with just one person and doing the same, mutually satisfying, things
> over and over.

Most respondents concluded that the security and interdependence of marriage inhibits independence, experimentation, and learning. They rejected what they saw as a stalemated, boring situation.

Members of our study offered many positive reasons for remaining single. They spoke of freedom, enjoyment, opportunities to meet people and develop friendships, economic independence, more and better sexual experiences, and personal development. These values may be termed "pulls" toward singlehood insofar as they are positive inducements. Margaret Adams (1971), in a discussion of some of the problems faced by single women, suggests three factors that can make being single pleasurable: economic independence, social and psychological autonomy, and a clear intent to remain single by preference. Adams notes that "the unmarried women has greater freedom to take advantage of the exceptional opportunities for new experiences offered by today's rapidly changing world." These women who remain unmarried past thirty "are beginning to build up economic independence, an investment in work, and a viable value system that allows them to identify and exploit major sources of personal and social satisfaction in other areas than marriage and family."

Adams' observations are reflected in the responses of the women in our study. Lilith spoke of the abundant opportunities she has available to her with the attainment of economic self-sufficiency:

> There are so many things I want to do. Now that I've completed school and
> am making a good living, there is fun to be had. I've started a dance class,
> learned pottery, and joined a women's group.

The satisfaction of economic independence and the options it presents constitutes a strong pull toward singlehood. Most of the other female respondents corroborated Lilith's experience of finding her time and energies fully taken up in a meaningful life style. The consensus was that marriage or an exclusive relationship would only impinge on the freedom to pursue their personal development.

The pull of psychological autonomy was emphatically brought out by most women respondents, who stated that while theoretically women can be both married and active in a career or involved in stimulating relationships, this is very hard to realize. Most testified to a feeling of being secondary to the male in an exclusive relationship and a tendency to put his needs ahead of their own. Susan, for example, who had lived with a man for about a year, found herself focusing on her partner's activities and discounting hers. With singlehood came greater self-assurance and motivation. A psychiatric social worker, Susan has become involved in several professional activities, particularly in helping to organize a regional conference dealing with health care issues. She reported enjoying her newly felt freedom and feeling better about her professional development.

Alice's experiences underscored the pull of social autonomy in particular. Her three year monogamous relationship, in which she tried to be all things to her mate—"friend, lover, mother, shrink"—culminated in her feeling like a "victim," isolated from her own needs. Through a women's group

> I started to feel like I really could have other people available to me and . . . it was really possible to get together with other people.

Alice's single life style today emphasizes growth through multiple friendships and sexual freedom. Instead of modelling her life on a mate, she is moving outward, enjoying a diversity of human contacts that she is convinced have helped her attain a stronger and clearer sense of selfhood.

Male respondents often cited the pull of a loosely structured life. Rather than being bound into the roles of husband, father, and breadwinner, they felt free as singles to try out a plurality of roles, through which they could seek elements of their own identity. Roger mused on some of the options:

> clown, promoter, radical, friend, playboy, priest . . . you name it, the possiblities are there. I'm in a situation to discover my potentials and act on them. It's an exciting process, sometimes frightening, but I like having alternatives to choose from.

Married six years, Roger, a writer, prefers the "more existential" situation of a single. He enjoys making day-to-day decisions, decisions that are individual instead of joint, and often spontaneous, based on a changing assessment of his needs. Flexibility in schedule and greater mobility have helped him create a free-flowing, integrated life, as opposed to the "disjunctive" pattern of his marriage. He writes, studies, travels, and relaxes without the guilt and constraints associated with his former life.

Singlehood can create the conditions through which an individual attains self-respect and confidence. This emerged as a major pull, related closely to the psychological autonomy already discussed in relation to women. Although marriage is associated with responsibility, many of the single men interviewed believed that being on their own gave them a stronger sense of their capacities by eliminating both pressures and excuses. Jim, who has been married twice, but has lived as a single for five years, noted:

> I am having an experience I never had before since I was always answerable to someone—my family or wife. I never had the experience of being completely self-motivated, having to consider someone else's reaction to what I do—approval, disapproval, does the job pay enough. It makes me feel potent . . . and very responsible for what I do. Productive, capable of dealing with life's exigencies, and capable even of seeking friendly help when I need it. Whether you are self-realized or not cannot be blamed or credited to someone else.

Both men and women mentioned sexual availability as an important motivation, or pull, for remaining single. They enjoyed the stimulation and variety of an open dating pattern and tended to see their cross-sex relationships in terms of friendship rather than romance. Many respondents testified to the difficulty of achieving a fully open and relaxed accommodation to people of the opposite sex, however. They felt a measure of distance due to their social conditioning, specifically the norms of the double standard, the attitude that sexual intercourse must be condoned by marriage, and the learning of stereo-typed sex roles. Monogamy as a social ideal further perpetuates the distancing of the sexes since it requires guarding against extra-marital liaisons. "I think," Marion commented:

> my upbringing, everybody's upbringing, tended to dichotomize sexual rela-tionships and friendships. With a person of the opposite sex you are either in a sexual relationship or you are not . . . but it is the sexual nature of the relationship that determines the relationship and not the friendly nature of it. That has tended to make enemies out of us.

Still, respondents emphatically chose to work at overcoming their acquired fears and reserves rather than accent the lack of human interaction seemingly imposed by society. Furthermore, many respondents had discovered that the attempt to develop friendly cross-sex relationships was linked to the process of growing closer to members of their own sex. Steve observed that

> my wife would be threatened by having another woman over to talk about a project or work together, whereas being single I can have multiple non-sexual relationships with men and women as well as sexual relationships.

Others spoke of the increase in same-sex friendships they had experienced once they left a sexually exclusive situation and removed much of the motivation for possessiveness and jealousy.

Our respondents, then, indicate that singlehood provides a situation condu-cive to human growth and self-fulfillment, and that the framework of marriage is no longer necessary in order to find emotional support, sex, and an active social life. Unencumbered by the constraints of marriage, there is, among the members of our sample, a redirection of social energies and social interaction through which singlehood by choice may be seen as a positive alternative to marriage.

The Social Context of Being Single

> This society has not yet learned to accept singles. Marriage is still being sold to us, but the sales pitch is breaking down. Most of my friends are pretty skeptical about it. Yet if you look at the tax structures, the banks, the mass media, the churches—they all want us to marry.
>
> —Dan, 36, systems analyst

The dominant value system in American society upholds the importance of marriage in such a way that singlehood is devalued and derogated by an array of social sanctions. Adams (1971) speaks of "the severe psychological and social devaluation that has settled like an accretion around the concept of singleness . . . this attitude is a societal product capable of being changed once its destructive potential is understood." This social bias results in overt and subtle pressures to conform to the marital norm, in discrimination by certain institutions, and in commercial exploitation. The social context is weighted against singlehood despite the growing numbers of singles and their emergent ideology. That the case for singlehood has not been presented to society is underscored by the stereotyping of singles, when, in fact, "the diversity of single life . . . contradicts both the old fashioned image of unmarried people as lonely losers and the current media picture of 'swingles' who cavort through an endless round of bars, parties, and no strings attached sexual adventures" (Jacoby, 1974).

The prevailing attitudes which maintain that the most desirable and acceptable adult life condition lies within marriage generate pushes in the socialization process. For many, the pushes have been so well internalized that they appear as pulls in the outlook and behavior of young men and women. Marriage seems to them not only a desirable state, but also the only natural one. All of our interviewees, indeed most Americans, have been socialized according to the values of previous generations, where in one's social status, sex-role, and self-image are embedded in marital status. Among the respondents, five have been married once, one twice, seven have lived in an exclusive relationship, and five have done both. Thus for eighteen of the 20 we spoke to, the pushes and pulls toward marriage or marriage-like living arrangements were strong enough to have convinced them at an earlier time in their lives that this was desirable. It was only after the marital situation was in effect that its underlying assumptions were questioned and largely rejected. Because of the social context, however, single persons continue to experience the contradictions stemming from a clash between the older values stressing marriage and parenthood, and the newer values stressing the choice to marry or remain single, the modification of traditional sex-roles, equalitarianism, individual freedom, and self-actualization.

This often creates for singles an uncertainty about their own social identity. This is heightened by a continuing push towards marriage in the form of pressure from parents, relatives, colleagues, and married friends. Such pressures were felt by many of our respondents. Jim, a writer, said that he felt

> a non-specific pressure, a sort of wonderment that at 35 I can be alone. I sometimes feel pressure from my own confusion of how come I don't conform to the patterns of people who are in the same situation as I am in terms of career and age.

Brenda, who at 28 has never been married, sometimes feels that she should be. She feels her parents pressuring her to marry, and, although she does not plan to marry in the near future, she is concerned about what others think of her:

> When I tell people I'm 28 and not married, they look at me like there's something wrong with me—they think I'm a lesbian. Some just feel sorry for me. What a drag.

A more subtle form of social pressure is illustrated by Phil, an assistant professor at a major university:

> It was hard being the only single person in the department. I would be invited to social gatherings and would get pretty nervous about who my date should be. The men would get into shop talk and the women, in some other part of the house, would talk about their families, the school system, and summer vacations. My date and I would usually feel uneasy, not quite fitting in and yet feeling a bit guilty about not fitting in.

Lucille Duberman (1974) states that "unattached people, especially women, are considered a threat to married people." Most of our respondents corroborated this by indicating flatly that they "were not friendly with" or "avoided" married couples. Joan, one of the few who elaborated, speaking of her relationship with married couples whom she knows, said:

> They're looking for a nice doctor for me to marry. I also found that when I'm friends with married people, I have to be very careful in how I act around husbands. Either one or both might think I'm coming on to the husband, when I'm really not.

A further example of the confusion and emotional frustration generated by singles' lower status may be seen in Ellen's statement:

> What does it mean for me to be single? There is a whole part of me that sees as freedom the possibilities of meeting different people and having different kinds or relationships, which is the exciting part. And then, there is the part of me that looks at where I'm not doing what I'm supposed to be doing, where I'll ultimately end up lonely, where something is the matter with me because I'm not in love with somebody, whatever that means.

Respondents in this study testified to the strength of the pushes brought to bear in a marriage-oriented society. For some this amounts to an assault on their identity. "Not being married seemed abnormal," commented Mike, a 45-year-old lawyer. While they may find some recourse in associating with others who share their life style, they must contend with misunderstanding and condemnation from the society at large. Natalie, who, as a programmer, works in a predominantly male occupation, reported a "depressing" conversation she'd had with several of her male colleagues, all of whom are married:

> My boss couldn't, or didn't want to, understand why I was not married. He imagines all sorts of orgies going on. Two of the younger guys said they felt sorry for me, that I was missing out on a lot of fun. When I told them I was happy and that I neither wanted to marry nor be a mother, they looked upset . . . they couldn't understand my position and I think they didn't believe me. I was pretty upset by it.

As Natalie reflected further, she began to feel that her own certainty about remaining single had threatened her colleagues. Instead of dealing with and accepting her values, they challenged her perception of her needs and tried to convince her that she was wrong.

Lack of tolerance and perpetuation of stereotypes extends from attempts to dissuade singles to outright discrimination, as seen, for instance, in the job market. In a survey of fifty major corporations, it was found that 80 percent of the responding companies asserted that marriage was not essential to upward mobility; however, a majority indicated that only 2 percent of their executives, including junior management, were single. Over 60 percent reported that single executives tend to make snap judgments, and 25 percent believed singles to be "less stable" than married people (Jacoby, 1974).

Without cultural support structures for remaining single, those who are not married are highly susceptible to commercial exploitation and mass misrepresentation. Singles are subjected to commercialized approaches and appeals that play up the ways and means of finding a mate. Whether the item being sold is an alluring cologne or a "singles weekend," the approach is essentially the same. Entrepreneurs have become skilled in exploiting the needs of single people for self-worth and meaningful relationships through the merchandising of images of glamour and adventure.[3]

Singles bars serve as a prominent example. In an interesting ethnographic study, Allon and Fischel (1973) examine the social motivations of patrons. They report that men and women frequent singles bars in search of companionship, affection, excitement, and social acceptance. Using Seeman's discussion of alienation, they identify the singles' attempted moves from various degrees of powerlessness, isolation, normlessness, and self-estrangement in the direction of intimacy, social integration, opportunity for nurturant behavior, and reassurance of worth. Though some are successful in their search and make contact with others who can meet some of their needs, for most the singles bar scene is a disappointment. The amount of role-playing required severely limits the quality of interaction.

A number of respondents in our sample had experienced the exploitation of the "singles scene."

One of the men, who used to frequent various singles clubs on the east side of Manhattan, talked about his degrading and depressing experience:

[3]The increased number of single people has spurred various business enterprises to supply the services singles are willing to buy and consume. *Newsweek* estimates that the unmarried population spends some $40 billion annually. Chateau D'Vie, a year-round country club designed for single people, recently opened in a New York City suburb and promptly signed up one thousand members at an annual cost of $550 per person. In July of 1973, a new monthly magazine called *Single* had its initial press run of 750,000 copies.

The large cities, like New York, San Francisco, Chicago, etc., have always catered to single people. Clubs for single people—there are more than 40 such clubs in New York City alone—are only one index of such commercial interest in singles. Bars, resort areas, special tours, summer communities, dances, etc., all reflect commercial interest in single persons. Housing units for single people are booming: in 1972, about 100,000 singles-only units were built throughout the United States.

> I went into one place and I was ready to check the women over, but when they started checking me back, I panicked. Those questions about what I did, which meant like how much money I make and what I would be worth ten years from now, really threw me. I felt like I should carry a vita around and just hand it over.

Paul, corroborating the finding of Allon and Fischel, related one episode with a real sense of sadness:

> She was standing next to me . . . and I asked her if she'd ever been to this place before. Of course, we'd both been here before. We had a drink, exchanged lots of small talk bullshit, and eventually split to her place. She kept saying that she didn't like New York and the scene, and I kept thinking about her large breasts and how much longer it would be before we got into bed . . . The next morning I lied about having an early appointment somewhere . . . When I got home, my stomach started hurting and I had a bad headache. It's not what I wanted.

As Allon and Fischel report, "the goal of all these establishments is not to provide an adequate alternative to marriage, but to provide places where . . . singles can meet, have fun, and contemplate marriage." Certainly, the social settings provided by singles bars are not conducive to the development of meaningful relationships between men and women. They epitomize the commercial exploitation to which singles are subject in their search for "eligible" single members of the opposite sex. In the absence of places designed to meet the human needs of single people, in the absence of an ideology that makes singlehood a viable alternative, and in the absence of control by singles over their own lives and environments, the conditions of exploitation thus continue to flourish.

The consequence of exploitation, discrimination, and the misrepresented stereotypical image of singles is to be seen in a recent study of single men (Gilder, 1974). Statistics indicate that single men, as opposed to married counterparts, are more prone to mental and physical problems, suicide, crime, and lower income status. In some cases the existence of such problems undoubtedly predates and accounts for the individuals' failure to marry. The probability, however, given the disproportion in statistics, is that the experience of the two groups are sharply differentiated: it is harder to be single in American society. Although Gilder uses this data to support the necessity of traditional marriage, it is here suggested that these statistics result not from failure to marry, in itself, but rather may represent in part the high cost of rigid social attitudes in a society that regards singles as deviants and as categorically unstable and incomplete.[4]

This data reflects the "destructive potential" inherent in the "severe psycho-

---

[4]The major methodological problem with Gilder's data is his indiscriminate use of correlational techniques. He relies on cross-sectional studies and does not search out longitudinal or panel studies, nor has he conducted any original research of his own. As we suggest in the last section of this paper there is a need for longitudinal data supplemented by the life history method. For a more extensive analysis and comparison of cross-sectional and longitudinal data see Peter Stein, "The Impact of the Family, Education and the Social-Historical Context of the Values of College Students," unpublished Ph.D. dissertation, Princeton University, 1969.

logical and social devaluation ... of singleness," to reiterate the words of Margaret Adams. These negative social forces reflect the lack of a positive ideology of singlehood and a lack of supportive values.

Toward an Ideology of Singlehood

> Why shouldn't I stay single? I'm enjoying it and not feeling guilty about it any more.
> —Frank, 37, writer

We have examined some of the dynamics in the choice of singlehood by 20 respondents and viewed their situation in a marriage-oriented society. The material collected in this exploratory study provides a tentative profile of an emerging group. Women and men who remain single by choice are subject to self-doubt and to economic and social discrimination, but they are developing an ideology which enables them to articulate and support their alternative life style. The growing number of singles in America implies that the values represented by this challenge to traditional marriage hold validity for many people at the present time.

It is instructive to chart the movement from marriage to singlehood suggested by the respondents' experiences as a series of pushes and pulls. Typically, they were propelled by the factors cited into a marriage or marriage-like situation; subsequently their motivations for marriage were overcome by their dissatisfactions and the attractions of singlehood were found more compelling.

The strength of these pushes and pulls is highly relative. There is, for example, considerable difference between the experience of a person legally married for ten years and that of a person involved in an exclusive relationship for six months. Since the research on singles is just beginning, there are currently more questions to be asked than there are available answers. More data is required for identification on the points in people's lives when the decisions to remain single or to marry, cohabit, or separate are made. We need to differentiate segments of the singles population in terms of their life histories and commitments. What sorts of men and women choose singlehood from the start? How many people are pushed to become single as a reaction against marriage? Which singles regard their situation as temporary and which as permanent? What are the social correlates of various sorts of decisions?

The life history may be the best source for such data. Kimball Young (1952) has devised a comprehensive guideline for this approach, which will be utilized in a further study planned by the author. The life history provides data on all members of the family, on the individual's developmental history and subjective experiences, sense of self, power operations, satisfactions and frustrations, dating and sexual experiences. Viewed in light of the social and economic background, including demographic, ethnic, religious, educational, and occupational patterns, life histories could reveal specific causal factors linked to the choice of singlehood. Panel studies, which yield data from a sample of respon-

Table 1. Toward Marriage

Pushes	Pulls
Economic security	Influence of parents
Influence from mass media	Desire for family
Pressure from parents	Example of peers
Need to leave home	Romanticization of marriage
Interpersonal and personal reasons	Love
Fear of independence	Physical attraction
Loneliness	Emotional attachment
Alternatives did not seem feasible	Security, Social Status, Prestige
Cultural expectations, Socialization	
Regular sex	
Guilt over singlehood	

Toward Singlehood

Pushes	Pulls
Restrictions	Career opportunities
Suffocating one-to-one relationships, feeling trapped	Variety of experiences
	Self-sufficiency
Obstacles to self-development	Sexual availability
Boredom and unhappiness and anger	Exciting life-style
Role playing and conformity to expectations	Freedom to change and experiment
	Mobility
Poor communication with mate	Sustaining friendships
Sexual frustration	Supportive groups
Lack of friends, isolation, loneliness	Men's and women's groups
Limitations on mobility and available experience	Group living arrangements
Influence of and participation in Women's Movement	Specialized groups

dents questioned at different intervals, may also prove a fruitful approach to the study of singlehood, since they allow a close charting and comparison of individuals' developments.

National studies to date reveal a pattern of discontent with traditional marriage. Longitudinal studies systematically report that disenchantment, disengagement, and corrosion mark the developmental course of marriage. Skolnick summarizes a number of them, including a national study in which researchers interviewed couples during their engagement period, again after five years of marriage, and a third time after they had been married eighteen to 20 years. "They found a decline over time in the following areas: companionship, demonstration of affection including both kissing and intercourse, common interests, common beliefs and values, beliefs in the permanence of marriage, and marital adjustment. Feelings of loneliness increased." She concludes that "The pushes and pulls generated by contemporary social life strain the best of marriages and, at the same time, hold together couples whose marriages are only 'empty shells.' " Hicks and Platt concur. There is an increasing realization on the part of counselors and social scientists that, contrary to conventional wisdom, marital stability does not necessarily indicate marital satisfaction.[5]

Active experimentation with alternatives to the nuclear family underscores the discontent with marriage as a norm. There has been a growth in the number and types of nontraditional family forms in the late 1960's and 1970's. Cogswell and Sussman (1972) discuss these variant family forms, including open marriage, group and multilateral marriages, communal families, cohabiting couples, one-part families, "swinging," and other experimental forms. Singehood represents one of the most significant alternatives in terms of the numbers of people who have chosen to stay single and the shift in public opinion from a negative to a more positive image of the single state. Our contention is that the visibility of singlehood will increase with the development of a positive ideology that in turn will attract more adherents.

Evidence exists that singlehood is emerging as a social movement, overlapping with other liberation movements, but in the process of establishing a distinctive body of ideas. Lewis Killian (1973) identifies three elements of a social movement; it begins in response to sources of discontent; it has a set of goals and subsequently evolves a program to implement the goals. The ideas supporting the goals and program constitute the ideology of the movement. Using Killian's criteria, singlehood may be considered at present a potential social movement. As evidenced by our respondents' comments, many people choose to be single in part because they are pushed by the restrictions of marriage. Their goals are variously cited as self-development, change, interaction, freedom of choice, and more varied opportunities. Their program, so far tentative, centers on the development of social and personal support structures, and additionally, the elimination of social biases and discrimination.

The heterogeneity of the singles population makes the development of a cohesive ideology, with its body of shared meanings, somewhat difficult. However, the ideology and goals of the women's, men's, and gay liberation movements are helping to lay the groundwork. Their common critique of conventional marriage and sex-role stereotyping has served to articulate and direct the general discontent of people who have felt "trapped" in marriage. The format of rap sessions, or consciousness raising, provides in itself a model of people relating intimately outside the context of a one-to-one relationship. This example of a supportive group conveys the implicit message that dependence on a marital partner may be both limiting and unnecessary for the satisfaction of interpersonal needs. The extensive publicity given these movements by the mass media, furthermore, has added coherence to their major

[5]Arlene Skolnick, *The Intimate Environment* (1973, 218, 230–31). She cites Mary W. Hicks and Marilyn Platt, Marital Happiness and Stability, *Journal of Marriage and the Family,* 1970, 32, 533–74.

shared concepts of self-actualization, freedom in life style, and the importance of open-ended human relationships.

Other groups and organizations have also emerged as social support structures for the development of a singles ideology, particularly in regard to the decision about parenthood. Zero Population Growth provides a rationale for persons wishing to limit or avoid having children. The National Organization of Non-Parents, additionally, in Veevers' words (1973) functions as a "truly supportive social movement" for married and nonmarried people who seek adult status without having children. Parents-Without-Partners, designed to help single parents, also heightens awareness that there are viable options outside marriage.

The greatest need single people feel, in their departure from traditional family structure, is for substitute networks of human relationships that provide the basic satisfactions of intimacy, sharing, and continuity. This theme emerged in all the interviews through the emphasis respondents placed on their friendships and interpersonal (bonding) activities. The feeling of support from like-minded people appears to be an essential psychological condition for the choice of singlehood. While individuals may be driven into singlehood through a negative reaction to marriage, they cannot sustain it for long without validation from people they respect. The single people we spoke to are very much rooted in a web of social interactions which they have joined by their own volition. This context of friendly relationships, as reported by our respondents, differs from the family environment in being more open, more subject to change, and based more on a sense of choice and free exchange than on an accident of birth, blood ties, conventionality, and reciprocal role-obligations. However, although respondents emphasized the importance of variety and change, they were virtually unanimous in upholding the value of close, caring friendships that last over a period of time.

Certain more formal structures are emerging to provide intimacy and continuity among adults. They frequently take the form of group living arrangements, illustrating one type of what Cogswell and Sussman call the experimental family. While communal homes might include the socialization of children, they "focus on the needs for identity, intimacy, and interaction of adult members." Other structures include women's and men's groups, therapy and encounter groups, and organizations centered around specialized interests. Although not restricted to singles, they are particularly well adapted to meet the needs of single people, and they were cited by respondents as illustrations of the positive content of their lives. Such group interactions foster friendship and spur growth by providing a supportive content. The interactions may be painful, as in the feedback given in a group living situation or therapy session, for example, but the sense of mutual concern was felt to be dominant. Respondents spoke about the relief they had found in discovering other people shared similar feelings and experiences. Through day-to-day living or in regular rap sessions they reported achieving close peer relationships that enabled them to overcome the role-playing, competitiveness, and reserve that had characterized their interactions in the past.

As Caroline Bird has written, the satisfactions of caring and daily involvement are being provided by a variety of groups in ways that are frequently more successful than traditional marriage:

> not the least of these is the frankly experimental and informal character of the group which encourages exploration of the psyche of the other and dispenses with sanctions that shrivel mutuality.
>
> (Bird, 1972, 348).

Singlehood for our respondents would clearly not be a desirable choice without the existence of sometimes frightening yet basically joyful human involvement.

The collective portrait that emerges is one of single persons who are trying to forge a meaningful life in a society that, though changing, continues to uphold marriages and the family as the model for interpersonal bonding. While the experience of being single is beset by problems and pressures created by restrictive social attitudes, singlehood as an alternative life style is in the process of cultural emergence.

As it has with other minority groups, the social credence of singlehood will grow as its supportive ideology develops, and, as our interviews suggest, it will then be recognized as an acceptable and viable choice.

References

Adams, Margaret, The Single Women in Today's Society. *The American Journal of Orthopsychiatry*, 1971, 41, 776–786.

Allon, Natalie and Diane Fishel. Urban Courting Patterns: Singles' Bars. Paper presented at the annual meeting of the American Sociological Association in New York City, August 1973.

Bell, Robert. *Marriage and Family Interaction.* Homewood, IL: Dorsey, 1971.

Bernard, Jessie. *Remarriage.* New York: Dryden Press, 1956.

Bird, Caroline. The Case Against Marriage. In Louise Kapp Howe (Ed.), *The Future of the Family.* New York: Simon and Schuster, 1972.

Cogswell, Betty E. and Marvin B. Sussman. Changing Family and Marriage Forms: Complications for Human Service Systems. *The Family Coordinator,* 1972, 21, 505–516.

Duberman, Lucile. *Marriage and Its Alternatives.* New York: Praeger, 1974.

Duberman, Lucile. *The Reconstituted Family.* Chicago: Nelson-Hall, 1975.

Gilder, George. *Naked Nomads.* New York: Quadrangle, 1974.

Glick, Paul C. Bachelors and Spinsters. In Jeffrey Hadden and Marie Borgatta (Eds.), *Marriage and the Family.* Itasca, IL: Peacock, 1969.

Glick, Paul C. A Demographer Looks at American Families. *Journal of Marriage and the Family.* 1975, 37, 15–26.

Goode, William. *Women in Divorce.* New York: Free Press, 1965.

Hicks, Mary W. and Marilyn Platt. Marital Happiness and Stability. *Journal of Marriage and the Family.* 1970, 32, 553–574.

Jacoby, Susan, 49 Million Singles Can't Be All Right. *The New York Times Magazine,* February 17, 1974.

Killian, Lewis. Social Movements. In *Society Today* (2nd Ed.). Del Mar, CA: CRM Books, 1973.

Kuhn, Manfred. How Mates Are Sorted. In Howard Becker and Rueben Hill (Eds.), *Family, Marriage and Parenthood.* Boston: Health, 1955.

Lopata, Helena Znaniecki. *Widowhood in an American City.* Cambridge: Schenkman, 1973.

Mead, Margaret. *Male and Female.* New York: W. Morrow, 1967.

Passin, Herbert. The Single Past Imperfect. *Single,* 1, August, 1973.

Pearce, Jane and Saul Newton. *The Conditions of Human Growth.* New York: Citadel, 1969.

Skolnick, Arlene. *The Intimate Environment.* Boston: Little, Brown, 1973.

Stein, Peter. *Single in America.* Englewood Cliffs: Unpublished manuscript, Rutgers University, 1973.

Stein, Peter. *Single in America.* Englewood Cliffs: Prentice-Hall, 1976, (forthcoming).

Veevers, J. E. The Moral Careers of Voluntarily Childless Wives: Notes on the Defence of a Variant World View. *Marriage and the Family in Canada: A Reader.* Toronto: Copp-Clark, 1975, (forthcoming).

Veevers, J. E. Voluntary Childless Wives: An Exploratory Study. *Sociology and Social Research.* 1973, 57, 356–365.

Yankelovich, Daniel. *The Changing Values on Campus.* New York: Washington Square Press, 1972.

Young, Kimball. *Personality and Problems of Adjustment.* New York: Appleton-Century-Crofts, 1952.

Homosexualities: A Study of Diversity Among Men and Women

Alan P. Bell and Martin S. Weinberg

In what follows we present composite pictures of the types of homosexual men and women that emerged from our samples, involving their standings on the various measures of sexual experience and social and psychological adjustment. Each composite picture will include descriptions of some of the actual respondents assigned to the particular type. These descriptions are excerpts of "thumbnail sketches" prepared for each respondent by his or her interviewer, who, of course, did not know we would by "typing" the homosexual respondents.

Close-Coupleds

We resisted the temptation to call this group "happily married," although some of its members described themselves that way, because we did not want to imply that heterosexual relationships and marriage in particular are standards by which to judge people's adjustment. Instead, we use the word "close" in two senses. First, the partners in this kind of relationships are closely bound together. Second, the partnership is closed in that the Close-Coupleds tend to look to each other rather than to outsiders for sexual and interpersonal satisfactions.

The ways in which the Close-Coupleds differ from respondents in other homosexual groups bear out this description. They were the least likely to seek partners outside their special relationship, had the smallest amount of sexual problems, and were unlikely to regret being homosexual. They tended to spend more evenings at home and less leisure time by themselves, and the men in this group seldom went to such popular cruising spots as bars or baths. Although the Close-Coupleds did not have the highest level of sexual activity, they reported more than most respondents, and their sexual lives were evidently gratifying to them. They were likely to have engaged in a wide variety of sexual techniques and tended not to report the kinds of problems that might arise from a lack of communication between partners.

The Close-Coupleds' superior adjustment is demonstrated in other aspects of their lives. The men in this group had rarely experienced difficulties related to their sexual orientation such as being arrested, trouble at work, or assault and robbery. They were less tense or paranoid and more exuberant than the average respondent. The Close-Coupled lesbians were the least likely of all the groups ever to have been concerned enough about a personal problem to have sought professional help for it. Both the men and the women were more self-accepting and less depressed or lonely than any of the others, and they were the happiest of all.

Our interviewers described some of the Close-Coupled respondents as follows:

> There was an obvious warmth and caring between him and his roommate. Altogether I felt that he had his life in better order than the vast majority of people I've met.

> Although he and his roommate do not think of themselves as husband and wife, there seemed to be some consistent division of roles. For example, his roommate does most of the cooking and serving, while he does more about keeping their finances in order. They seem to have a very good relationship. Although they did not display physical affection in my presence, they clearly like each other.

> She was very friendly, interested, talkative, and open. I felt like I was a friend whom she was inviting in to share part of her life. I liked her paintings, her roommate's photographs of the Bay Area, and the warm togetherness of their home. She and her roommate were obviously very much in love. Like most people who have a good, stable, five-year relationship, they seemed comfortable together, sort of part of one another, able to joke, obviously fulfilled in their relationship. They work together, have the same times off from work, do most of their leisure activities together. She is helping her roommate to learn to paint, while her roommate is teaching her about photography. They sent me home with a plateful of cookies, a good symbolic gesture of the kind of welcome and warmth I felt in their home.

> The apartment which he shares with his lover is very clearly "their" home. A lot of love went into fixing it up. Interestingly, when I asked him questions about his own siblings, he called in his roommate to help him out with the answers!

> The room was filled with *their* things—paintings her roommate had done, their books and records, etc. The relationship seemed quite stable and satisfying to them both.

> She lives in a nice modern home with her girlfriend, who is in real estate. They really have a loving, happy thing going together. Although she's had previous relationships, she says she's really happy for the first time.

> I got the feeling that both were warm and loving people and had their heads together as to what they were doing and wanted.

The salience of a viable "coupled" relationship among our homosexual respondents is evident in comparisons between the Close-Coupleds and the next group to be described, the Open-Coupleds. The latter are not as fully committed to their special partner, placing more reliance on a large circle of homosexual friends and less stress on the importance of their relationship with their partner. They are also less happy, self-accepting, and relaxed than the Close-Coupleds. These differences seem to suggest that the Open-Coupled relationship reflects a conflict between the ideal of fulfilled monogamy and dissatisfactions within the partnership.

Open-Coupleds

Like their Close-Coupled counterparts, the men and women in this group were living with a special sexual partner. They were not happy with their circumstances, however, and tended (despite spending a fair amount of time at home) to seek satisfactions with people outside their partnership. For example, the Open-Coupled men did more cruising than average, and the lesbians in this group cruised more than any of the other female respondents. Concomitantly, the Open-Coupleds worried about their cruising, especially about the possibility of being arrested or otherwise publicly exposed—perhaps because of their partner's ignorance of their cruising activities. In addition, the Open-Coupleds reported more sexual activity than the typical homosexual respondent and broader sexual repertoires, but the men tended to have trouble getting their partner to meet their sexual requests, and the women had the greatest worry about their partner wanting to do unwelcome sexual things or about being unable to carry on a conversation with her.

In most respects of their social and psychological adjustment, the Open-Coupleds could not be distinguished from the homosexual respondents as a whole. For example, they were not notable in how they spent their leisure time, how often they had experienced various social difficulties connected with homosexuality, or how many other people knew about their sexual orientation. Psychologically, they were about as happy, exuberant, depressed, tense, paranoid, or worrisome as the average homosexual respondent. However, the Open-Coupled lesbians were less self-accepting than any of the other groups.

> He tries to give the appearance of happiness with his roommate but cruises continually, feels grave guilt about this, and says that it contributes to his

domestic travail. He stopped me from introducing myself to his roommate, as if I were a pickup he wanted to keep secret.

At first he wanted his roommate to sit in on the interview but later acknowledged that he was glad I hadn't allowed this, since his roommate doesn't know he cruises.

He indicated that he has never had moral qualms about his homosexuality, but he is upset about his promiscuity.

As she talked, I discovered that her lover is very jealous and that she (the respondent) would like to date men and explore her own sexual orientation further, but that her lover was demanding a long-term commitment and she was not free to try out other relationships.

He is having a serious problem with his lover right now. The latter jumped off a third-floor porch on Christmas Day in an alcoholic stupor.

His partner is eleven years older than he and has begun slowing down sexually, which is a problem for them both. He has another friend with whom he's sexually compatible, but he doesn't want to end his present relationship. He appears troubled by this dilemma.

In discussing her current affair, she said that they had had sex twice and that she doesn't care to again and that she is not involved emotionally with her partner.

He was disappointed that he and his lover do not have sex anymore.

He said that he could not say whether he was in love with his roomate because he did not know what love really is.

It should be noted that the Open-Coupleds were the modal type among the males but relatively rare among the females, many more of whom were Close-Coupled. Whether lesbians find it easier than do homosexual males to achieve a stable and satisfying relationship with just one person, or whether they are more strongly motivated by romantic feelings than the men are, is not clear. However, our analysis of variance did show that the Open-Coupled males expressed more self-acceptance and less loneliness than the females did. This kind of relationship, then, is apparently more trying for the lesbian than for her male counterpart.

Compared with members of the other groups, the Open-Coupleds are intermediate in their adjustment. They went out more often and also spent more time alone than the Close-Coupleds did, and among the males, felt more lonely. On the other hand, the Open-Coupled males appear much better off than the Dysfunctional males do. The latter were less likely to have many homosexual friends or to value having a special partner, and the Open-Coupleds were significantly better adjusted psychologically, reporting more happiness and self-acceptance and less worry, paranoia, tension, or depression. Since the Open-Coupled lesbians did not differ from their Dysfunctional counterparts in these ways, it seems possible that managing a less than exclusive homosexual relationship is more difficult for women than for men.

Functionals

If Close- and Open-Coupled respondents are in some respects like married heterosexuals, the Functionals come closest to the notion of "swinging singles." These men and women seem to organize their lives around their sexual experiences. They reported more sexual activity with a greater number of partners than did any of the other groups, and the Functional lesbians had been married more times than the rest of the female respondents. The Functional men and women were least likely to regret being homosexual, cruised frequently, and generally displayed a great deal of involvement in the gay world. They were not particularly interested in finding a special partner to settle down with, engaged in a wide variety of sexual activities, considered their sex appeal very high, and had few if any sexual problems. They were particularly unlikely to complain about not getting enough sex or difficulties in their sexual performance. Of all the groups, they were the most interested in sex, the most exuberant, and the most involved with their many friends. In addition, the Functional men had the fewest psychosomatic symptoms. They were also the most likely ever to have been arrested, booked, or convicted for a "homosexual" offense; this may be related to their greater overtness, their high attendance at gay bars, and perhaps as well their relative lack of worry or suspicion of others—or even a certain degree of recklessness.

> He lived in a very neat apartment. A music lover, he must have had close to a thousand blues and jazz records on the shelf. He also had three motorcycle trophies.

> He seemed very self-assured, and it was enjoyable interviewing him.

> He was a very energetic and open kid, looking much younger than twenty-seven. He seemed to be feeling very happy, likes his job in the Merchant Marine, and enjoys being back for just short stays. Although this militates against long-term relationships, he really enjoys his feelings of independence.

> Just a warm, lovely lady.

> She was friendly and completely comfortable during the interview. She had a very pleasant, lively personality.

> A very calm, well-adjusted "man's man" type. His social skills were most evident.

> He is a crusty but likable old Yankee from Maine, a warm, friendly person who lives in a renovated Victorian house full of gay roomers. He has plenty of money and seems beautifully adjusted.

> He is a well-adjusted, confident, relaxed homosexual male: obvious but not flamboyant.

The Functionals' good adjustment seems to be a function of their particular personalities. They are energetic and self-reliant, cheerful and optimistic, and comfortable with their highly emphasized sexuality. One should not conclude, however, that Functionals are an ideal type as regards coping with a homosexual orientation. It is rather the Close-Coupled men and women who have made the best adjustment. For example, while the Functionals had few sexual problems and were not very depressed or unhappy, the Close-Coupleds surpass them in these respects. When the two groups are compared directly, we see that the Functionals understandably spend less time at home and see their friends more often, but the males are more tense, unhappy, and lonely than their Close-Coupled counterparts.

Dysfunctionals

The Dysfunctionals are the group in our sample which most closely accords with the stereotype of the tormented homosexual. They are troubled people whose lives offer them little gratification, and in fact they seem to have a great deal of difficulty managing their existence. Sexually, socially, and psychologically, wherever they could be distinguished from the homosexual respondents as a whole, the Dysfunctionals displayed poorer adjustment.

In terms of their sexual lives, the Dysfunctionals were the most regretful about their homosexuality. They reported more sexual problems than any other group, and they were especially prone to worry about their sexual adequacy, how they could maintain affection for their partner, and whether they or their partner would attain orgasm. Despite fairly frequent cruising (among the males) and a relatively high number of partners, they tended to complain about not having sex often enough and were most likely of all the groups to report that they and their partner could not agree on what kind of sexual activity should take place. In addition, the men had trouble finding a suitable partner and were the most likely ever to have experienced impotence and premature ejaculation. Not surprisingly, with all these difficulties, the Dysfunctionals tended to think they were sexually unappealing.

Other aspects of the Dysfunctionals' lives were similarly problematic for them. Among the men in this group, there were more reports of robbery, assault, extortion, or job difficulties due to their being homosexual; they were also more likely ever to have been arrested, booked, or convicted regardless of the reason. The Dysfunctional lesbians were the least exuberant and the most likely to have needed long-term professional help for an emotional problem, and their male counterparts were more lonely, worrisome, paranoid, depressed, tense, and unhappy than any of the other men.

> He is a bookkeeper type, prim and a little stuffy, not a warm person. He lives alone with his ledgers.

> He has a languid, apathetic manner.

> He seems to have an adolescent religious hang-up. I see his admission to being a "chicken queen" as a way for him to relive or act out his lost youth. He drives to the Tenderloin "meat rack," picks up young hustlers, drives them to Redwood City, and then pays them for sex.

He tends to project his own inadequacies onto others. For example, he claims that others are shallow and not desirous of lasting relationships, and yet he's had more than a thousand partners in the past two years.

He lives in an ugly, bleak two-room apartment, where he seems to devote most of his time to watching TV. He has no close friends, and those he has he seldom sees. All relationships seem casual and unimportant to him.

He wanted very much to be an Episcopal priest, but his moral conflict over his homosexuality stood in his way. He seemed very depressed and low in self-esteem.

I felt a horrible sense of resignation about him, of surrender to a dead-end fate.

She seemed quiet, somewhat stiff, almost cold.

He says he enjoys drinking more than sex. He kept referring to his drinking when I asked a question about sex.

She seemed very well put together for someone with two psychotic breaks to her record.

Direct comparisons of the Dysfunctionals with other groups strengthen the impression of their general distress. The Dysfunctional men differ significantly from both the Functionals and the Open-Coupleds on virtually every measure of psychological adjustment. If we had numbered only Dysfunctionals among our respondents, we very likely would have had to conclude that homosexuals in general are conflict-ridden social misfits.

Asexuals

The most prominent characteristic of the Asexual men and women in our samples is their lack of involvement with others. They scored the lowest of all the groups in the level of their sexual activity, reported few partners, had narrow sexual repertoires, rated their sex appeal very low, and tended to have a fair number of sexual problems. In this regard, the Asexual males tended to mention trouble finding a partner and not having sex often enough, but they were also less interested in sex than the other men. The Asexuals were the least likely of all the groups to describe themselves as exclusively homosexual, and among the males, they were less overt about their homosexuality and had fewer same-sex homosexual friends. Both the men and the women in this group tended to spend their leisure time alone and to have infrequent contact with their friends. They described themselves as lonely and (among the men) unhappy; the Asexual lesbians were most apt to have sought professional help concerning their sexual orientation but also to have given up counseling quickly, and they had the highest incidence of suicidal thoughts (not necessarily related to their homosexuality).

This woman now lives alone, has had no sexual experience with a partner in the past year, and seems never to have had any deep commitments to anyone. I can't imagine her really responding with warmth to any person or any need.

Quite subdued and reticent, he lives alone in his apartment with five cats. There are five different cat food bowls on the floor in the kitchen. One for each cat.

When the interview came to an end, he asked me why he had difficulty relating to people and why people didn't like him, exclaiming, "I'm always clean, neat, polite, proper . . . " He seems very lonely to me.

He seemed like a totally ineffectual, frightened, withdrawn sort of person. He was desperately shy and seemed very afraid of me for the first part of the interview. The house was a fantastic state of rubble, full of boxes of junk, files, and furniture. He explained them by saying simply, "I collect things."

He has to be one of the saddest, most forlorn human beings I've ever met. He said to me, "Here I've made it financially and professionally. I could travel anywhere or do anything, but why bother? I'm more lonesome away than I am at home, and I'm desperately lonesome at home." He has a big dog named Chipper who is very important in his life.

She says no one has ever loved her. Indubitable!

She was a bit cool and businesslike. Her difficulties with interpersonal relations were hinted at when she said she tends to be suspicious of people who are "too nice." When the interview was over she was pleasant, but it felt superficial.

He lives alone in a run-down Nob Hill apartment. He's over fifty years old and engages only in solitary masturbation with male fantasies. This has been the case for over four years.

He was a very soft-spoken and shy person. I couldn't imagine this short, timid little guy driving a big bus around the city.

The Asexual life-style is a solitary one. Despite their complaints of loneliness, Asexuals are not very interested in establishing a relationship with a special partner or in any of the rewards the gay world might offer them. For example, in addition to their lack of involvement with friends, the Asexual men seldom went to gay bars and did less cruising than any of the other groups except the Close-Coupleds. When compared directly with the Dysfunctionals, the Asexuals differed from them chiefly in terms of their disengagements from others. Nevertheless, since the Asexuals of either sex did not differ from the sample as a whole in many respects of psychological adjustment or in the extent to which being homosexual had caused them difficulty, it seems reasonable to infer that these people's quiet, withdrawn lives are the inevitable product of an underlying apathy toward the panoply of human experience.

Epilogue

It would be unfortuante to conclude this study of homosexual men and women without making its meaning more explicit and urging serious attention by those for whom our findings have special import. Such persons include state legislators involved in debates over the decriminalization of homosexual conduct, community leaders addressing themselves to the matter of civil rights for gays, governmental and business executives charged with the responsibility of hiring and firing personnel, educators and lay people dealing with sex education, religious leaders who are reexamining their churches' sexual beliefs and values, counselors with homosexual clients, and, finally, homosexual men and women themselves.

Until now, almost without exception, people in general, as well as those above, have been outraged, fearful, or despairing toward homosexuality because of the stereotypes they hold. Not only have they believed that homosexuals are pretty much alike, but that this similarity necessarily involves irresponsible sexual conduct, a contribution to social decay, and, of course, psychological pain and maladjustment. Given such a stereotype, it is little wonder that the heterosexual majority has seen fit to discourage the acceptance of homosexuality by criminalizing homosexual behaviors and ferreting out people who engage in them, refusing to employ homosexuals, withholding from homosexual men and women the civil rights enjoyed by the majority and by a growing number of other minority groups, trying to cure homosexuals of their "aberration," and feeling grief or shame at the discovery that a loved one is "afflicted" by homosexual propensities. Reactions such as these to the millions of homosexual men and women in America and elsewhere are understandable in the light of common notions about what it means to be homosexual.

The present investigation, however, amply demonstrates that relatively few homosexual men and women conform to the hideous stereotype most people have of them. In addition, it is reasonable to suppose that objectionable sexual advances are far more apt to be made by a heterosexual (usually, by a man toward a woman) than a homosexual. In the same vein, seduction of an adolescent girl by a male teacher is probably more frequent than the seduction of young people by homosexual teachers, who are more apt to regard the class as a surrogate family than as a target for their sexual interests. And outside the classroom, the seduction of "innocents" far more likely involves an older male, often a relative, and a pre- or postpubescent female. Moreover, rape and sexual violence more frequently occur in a heterosexual than a homosexual context. Rape (outside of prisons) generally involves sexual attacks made by men upon women, while the relatively rare violence occurring in a homosexual context is usually the result of male youths "hunting queers" or a man's guilt and disgust over a sexual episode just concluded. Finally, with respect to homosexuals' sexual activity itself, as our study notes, it commonly begins with highly cautious pursuits in places not normally frequented by heterosexuals or in more public surroundings where heterosexuals are not aware of what is taking place. Most often it is consummated with the full consent of the persons involved and in the privacy of one of the partners' homes. Even this description, however, disregards the numerous instances in which homosexual contact occurs solely between persons whose commitment to each other includes sharing a household.

As for homosexuals' social and psychological adjustment, we have found that much depends upon the type of homosexual being considered. Many could very well serve as models of social comportment and psychological maturity. Most are indistinguishable from the heterosexual majority with respect to most of the nonsexual aspects of their lives, and whatever differences there are between homosexuals' and heterosexuals' social adjustment certainly do not reflect any malevolent influence on society on the part of the homosexuals concerned. Close-Coupleds and Open-Coupleds behave much like married heterosexuals. Functionals draw on a host of support systems and display joy and exuberance in their particular life-style. To be sure, Dysfunctionals and Asexuals have a difficult time of it, but there are certainly equivalent groups among heterosexuals. Clearly, a deviation from the sexual norms of our society does not inevitably entail a course of life with disastrous consequences. The homosexual who is afraid that he might end up a "dirty old man," desperately lonely, should be assured that such a plight is not inevitable and that, given our society's failure to meet the needs of aging people, heterosexuality hardly guarantees well-being in old age. Between the time of their "coming out" and whatever years remain, homosexual men and women must become increasingly aware of the array of options they have in their lives.

Perhaps the least ambiguous finding of our investigation is that homosexuality is not necessarily related to pathology. Thus, decisions about homosexual men and women, whether they have to do with employment or child custody or counseling, should never be made on the basis of sexual orientation alone. Moreover, it should be recognized that what has survival value in a heterosexual context may be destructive in a homosexual context, and vice versa. Life-enhancing mechanisms used by heterosexual men or women should not necessarily be used as the standard by which to judge the degree of homosexuals' adjustment. Even their personality characteristics must be appraised in the light of how functional they are in a setting that may be quite different from the dominant cultural milieu. It must also be remembered that even a particular type of homosexual is never entirely like others categorized in the same way, much less like those whose life-styles barely resemble his or her own. And while the present study has taken a step forward in its delineation of types of homosexuals, it too fails to capture the full diversity that must be understood if society is ever to fully respect, and ever to appreciate, the way in which individual homosexual men and women live their lives.

Voluntarily Childless Wives: An Exploratory Study

J. E. Veevers

Students of the family have generally tended to accept the dominant cultural values that married couples should have children, and should want to have them. As a result of this value bias, although parenthood (especially voluntary parenthood) has been extensively studied, the phenomenon of childlessness has been virtually ignored (Veevers, 1972a). This selective inattention is unfortunate, for to a large extent the social meanings of parenthood can be comprehensively described and analyzed only in terms of the parallel set of meanings which are assigned to non-parenthood (Veevers, forthcoming). Although sociologists have occasionally discussed the theoretical relevance of voluntary childlessness, and have speculated regarding some empirical aspects of it (Pohlman, 1970), virtually no direct research has been conducted. As a preliminary step towards filling this gap in the sociological study of the family, an exploratory study of voluntarily childless wives was conducted. The present article will not attempt to describe this research in its entirety, but rather will be concerned with brief discussions of four aspects of it: first, the career paths whereby women come to be voluntarily childless; second, the social pressures associated with that decision; third, the symbolic importance attributed to the possibility of adoption; and fourth, the relevance of supportive ideologies relating to concern with feminism, and with population problems.

Selection and Nature of the Sample

Conventional sampling techniques cannot readily be applied to obtain large and representative samples of voluntarily childless couples (Gustavus and Henly, 1971). Only about five percent of all couples voluntarily forego parenthood (Veevers, 1972b), and this small deviant minority is characterized by attitudes and behaviors which are both socially unacceptable and not readily visible. The present research, which is exploratory in nature, is based on depth interviews with a purposive sample of 52 voluntarily childless wives. Although the utilization of non-random samples without control groups is obviously not the ideal approach, and can yield only suggestive rather than definitive conclusions, in examining some kinds of social behaviors it is often the only alternative to abandoning the inquiry.

In the present study, respondents were solicited by three separate articles appearing in newspapers in Toronto and in London, followed up by advertisements explicitly asking for volunteers. Of the 86 individuals who replied, 52 wives were selected. Three criteria were evoked in these selections. First, the

From *Sociology and Social Research* (April 1973), pp. 356–365. Reprinted by permission.

wife must have stated clearly that her childlessness was due to choice rather than to biological accident. Second, she must either have been married for a minimum of five years, or have been of post-menopausal age, or have reported that either she or her husband had been voluntarily sterilized for contraceptive purposes. Third, she must have affirmed that she had never borne a child, and had never assumed the social role of mother.

The interviews, which were unstructured, averaged about four hours in length, and included discussion of the woman's life history, considerable detail concerning her marriage and her husband, and attitudinal and evaluative aspects of her responses to the maternal role. Data are thus available on the characteristics of 104 voluntarily childless husbands and wives, whose demographic and social characteristics may be briefly summarized as follows. The average age of the sample is 29, with a range from 23 to 71 years. All are Caucasian and living in urban areas, most are middle class, and many are upwardly mobile. Although educational experience ranges from grade school to the post doctoral level, most have at least some university experience. With the exception of one housewife, all are either employed full-time or attending univeristy. Most individuals are either atheists or agnostics from Protestant backgrounds, and of the minority who do express some religious preference, almost all are inactive. Most individuals come from stable homes where the mother has been a full-time housewife since her first child was born. The incidence of first born and only children is much higher than would ordinarily be expected.

With the exception of two widowers, all of the subjects in the present research are involved in their first marriage. The average marriage duration is seven years, with a range from three to twenty-five years. Most couples have relatively egalitarian relationships, but still maintain conventional marriages and follow the traditional division of labor. Configurations of marital adjustment cover the entire continuum described by Cuber and Harroff (1966), ranging from conflict-habituated to total relationships, with many wives reporting vital or total relationships with their husbands.

All of the couples agree on the desirability of preventing pregnancy, at least at the present time. Most of the wives had never been pregnant, but about a fifth had had at least one induced abortion, and most indicate they would seek an abortion if pregnant. More than half of the wives are presently on the pill. About a quarter of the husbands have obtained a vasectomy, and another quarter are seriously considering doing so. Many of the women express positive interest in tubal ligation, but only one, a girl of 23, has actually been sterilized.

The Nature of Childless Careers

In reviewing the processes whereby couples come to define themselves as voluntarily childless, two characteristic career paths are apparent. One route to childlessness involves the formulation by the couple, before they are even married, of a definite and explicitly stated intention never to become involved in parental roles; a second and more common route is less obvious, and involves the prolonged postponement of childbearing until such time as it was no longer considered desirable at all. These two alternatives will be elaborated.

Nearly a third of the wives interviewed entered into their marriages with a childlessness clause clearly stated in their marriage "contract." Although none of these women had a formal written contract in the legal sense of the work, the husband and wife explicitly agreed upon childlessness as a firm condition of marriage. The woman deliberately sought a future mate who, regardless of his other desirable qualities, would agree on this one dimension. Generally the negative decisions regarding the value of children were made during early adolescence, before the possibility of marriage had ever been seriously considered. In contrast, a few of the wives had different or even vaguely positive attitudes towards childbearing until they met their future husbands. During their courtship and engagement, they gradually allowed themselves to be converted to the world view of voluntary childlessness, and by the time of their marriage were quite content to agree to never have children.

More than two thirds of the wives studied remained childless as a result of a series of decisions to postpone having children until some future time, a future which never came. Rather than explicitly rejecting motherhood prior to marriage, they repeatedly deferred procreation until a more convenient time. These temporary postponements provided time during which the evaluations of parenthood were gradually reassessed relative to other goals and possibilities. At the time of their marriages, most wives involved in the postponement model had devoted little serious thought to the question of having children, and had no strong feelings either for or against motherhood. Like conventional couples, they simply assumed that they would have one or two children eventually; unlike conventional couples, they practiced birth control conscientiously and continuously during the early years of marriage.*

Most couples involved in the postponement pattern move through four separate stages in their progression from wanting to not wanting children. The first stage involves postponement for a definite period of time. In this stage, the voluntarily childless are indistinguishable from conventional and conforming couples who will eventually become parents. In most groups, it is not necessarily desirable for the bride to conceive during her honeymoon. It is considered understandable that before starting a family a couple might want to achieve certain goals, such as graduating from school, travelling, buying a house, saving a nest egg, or simply getting adjusted to one another. The degree of specificity varies, but there is a clear commitment to have children as soon as conditions are right.

---

*Whelpton, Campbell, and Patterson report in one study that nearly two out of three newly-weds do not start using contraception before the first conception. See Whelpton, Campbell, and Patterson (1966).

The second stage of this career involves a shift from postponement for a definite period of time to indefinite postponement. The couple remains committed to the idea of parenthood, but becomes increasingly vague about when the blessed event is going to take place. It may be when they can "afford it," or when "things are going better" or when they "feel more ready."

The third stage in the cycle involves another qualitative change in thinking, in that for the first time there is an open acknowledgment of the possibility that in the end the couple may remain permanently childless. The third stage is a critical one, in that the very fact of openly considering the pros and cons of having children may increase the probability of deciding not to. During this time, they have an opportunity to experience directly the many social, personal, and economic advantages associated with being childless, and at the same time to compare their life styles with those of their peers who are raising children. It seems probable that the social-psychological factors involved in the initial decision to postpone having children may be quite disparate from the social-psychological factors involved in the inclination to remain childless, and to continue with the advantages of a life style to which one has become accustomed. At this stage in the career, the only definite decision is to postpone deciding until some vague and usually unspecified time in the future.

Finally, a fourth stage involves the definite conclusion that the couple are never going to have children, and that childlessness is a permanent rather than a transitory state. Occasionally this involves an explicit decision, usually precipitated by some crisis or change in the environment that focuses attention on the question of parenthood. However, for most couples, there is never a direct decision made to have or to avoid children. Rather, after a number of years of postponing pregnancy until some future date, they gradually become aware that an implicit decision has been made to forego parenthood. The process involved is one of recognizing an event which has already occurred, rather than of posing a question and then searching or negotiating for an answer. At first, it was "obvious" that "of course" they would eventually have children; now, it is equally "obvious" that they will not. The couple are at a loss to explain exactly how or when the transition came about, but they both agree on their new implicit decision, and they are both contented with its implications.

Childlessness and Informal Sanctions

All of the wives interviewed feel that they are to some extent stigmatized by their unpopular decision to avoid having children, and that there exists a ubiquitous negative stereotype concerning the characteristics of a voluntarily childless woman, including such unfavorable traits as being abnormal, selfish, immoral, irresponsible, immature, unhappy, unfulfilled, and non-feminine (Veevers, 1972c). In addition, these devaluating opinions are perceived to have behavioral consequences for their interaction with others, and to result in considerable social pressure to become mothers. Some of the sanctions reported are direct and obvious, including explicit and unsolicited comments advocating childbirth and presenting arguments relating to the importance of motherhood. Other pressures are more subtle, and in many cases are perceived to be unintentional. For example, the childless frequently complain that, whereas parents are never required to explain why they chose to have children, they are frequently required to account for their failure to do so.

Childlessness is of course not always a disapproved state. Couples are rewarded, not punished, for remaining childless for the first several months of marriage, and thereby negating the possibility that they were "forced" to get married. After the minimum of nine months has passed, there is a short period of time when the young couple is excused from not assuming all of their responsibilties, or are perceived as having been having intercourse for too short a period of time to guarantee conception. The definition of how long a period of time childbearing may be postponed and still meet with conventional expectations is difficult to determine, and apparently varies considerably from one group to another. In most groups, the first twelve months constitutes an acceptable period of time. After the first year, the pressure gradually but continually increases, reaching a peak during the third and fourth years of marriage. However, once a couple have been married for five or six years there appears to be some diminution of negative responses to them. Several factors are involved in this change: part may be attributable to the increased ability of the childless to avoid those who consistently sanction them; part may be attributable to the increased ability of the childless to cope with negative and hostile responses, making the early years only seem more difficult in restrospect; and part may reflect an actual change in the behavior of others. After five or six years, one's family and friends may give up the possibility of persuading the reluctant couple to procreate or to adopt, and resign themselves to the fact that intervention, at least in this case, is ineffective.

It is noteworthy that although all wives report considerable direct and indirect social pressures to become mothers, most are remarkably well defended against such sanctions. Although on specific occasions they may be either indignant or amused, in most instances they are indifferent to negative responses, and remain inner-directed, drawing constant support and reaffirmation from the consensual validation offered by their husbands. Many strategies are employed which "discredit the discreditors" (Veevers, 1973) and which enable the voluntarily childless to remain relatively impervious to the comments of critics and the wishes of reformers. One such strategy concerns the possibility of adoption.

The Symbolic Importance of Adoption

A recurrent theme in discussions with childless wives is that of adoption. Most wives mention that they have in the past considered adopting a child, and many indicate that they are still considering the possibility at some future date. However, in spite of such positive verbalizations, it is apparent that adoption is not seriously contemplated as a viable alternative, and that their considerations are not likely to result in actually assuming maternal roles. The lack of serious thought about adoption as a real possibility is reflected in the fact that generally they have not considered even such elementary questions as whether they would prefer a boy or girl, or whether they would prefer an infant or an older child. With few exceptions, none of the couples have made even preliminary inquiries regarding the legal processes involved in adoption. Those few that had made some effort to at least contact a child placement agency had failed to follow through on their initial contact. None had investigated the issue thoroughly enough to have considered the possibility that, should they decide to adopt, a suitable child might not be immediately available to them.

For the voluntarily childless, the importance of the recurrent theme of adoption appears to lie in its symbolic value, rather than in the real possiblity of procuring a child by this means and thereby altering one's life style. This symbolic importance is twofold: the reaffirmation of normalcy, and the avoidance of irreversible decisions. A willingness to consider adoption as a possiblity communicates to one's self and to others that in spite of being voluntarily childless, one is still a "normal" and "well-adjusted" person who does like children, and who is willing to assume the responsibilities of parenthood. It is an effective mechanism for denying the possibility of considerable psychological differences between parents and non-parents (Veevers, forthcoming), and legitimates the claim of the childless to be just like parents in a number of important respects.

The possibility of adoption at a later date is of symbolic value, in that it prevents the voluntarily childless from being committed to an irreversible state. One of the problems of opting for a postponement model is that eventually one must confront the fact that childbirth cannot be postponed indefinitely. The solution to this dilemma is to include possibility of adoption as a satisfactory "out" should one be needed. The same strategy is employed by many couples who choose sterilization as a means of birth control, but who are not entirely comfortable with the absolute and irreversible solution. The theoretical possibility of adoption is also comforting when faced with the important but unanswerable question of how one will feel about being childless in one's old age.

The Relevance of Supportive Ideologies

The voluntarily childless appear to be in a state of pluralistic ignorance, in that they are unaware of the numbers of other individuals who share their world view. Although the deliberate decision to avoid parenthood is a relatively rare phenomenon, it is not nearly as rare as the childless themselves perceive it to be, especially among urban and well-educated middle class couples. A large proportion of wives indicated that until they read the article and/or advertisement asking for subjects for the present study, they had never seen the topic of voluntary childlessness discussed in the mass media. Many reported that they did not know any other couple who felt as they did about the prospect of parenthood, and many others reported having met only one or two like-minded people during the course of their marriage.

Feelings of uniqueness and of isolation are somewhat mitigated by the explicit agreement of husbands on the appropriateness of foregoing parental roles. However, regardless of how supportive the husband is in his reaffirmation of the legitimacy of childlessness, and how committed he is personally to avoiding fatherhood, because of cultural differences in sex roles he does not share an entirely comparable situation. He may be totally sympathetic, but he has a limited ability to empathize. The childless wife may be generally comfortable with her decision not to have children, and still express the wish that she could discuss her situation with other like-minded women who might have shared similar experiences within the female subculture, and who migth provide a model for identification.

It is noteworthy that within the psychological world of the voluntarily childless, existing social movements concerned with population or with feminism have surprisingly little relevance, and provide relatively little intellectual or emotional support. The concern with population problems, especially as manifest in the Zero Population Growth movement, does provide a supportive rationale indicating that one is not necessarily being socially irresponsible and neglectful of one's civic obligations if one does not reproduce. However, although there is a clear statement that procreation is not necessary for all, most ZPG advocates are careful to indicate that it is not procreation *per se* they are opposed to, but rather excessive procreation. The slogan "Stop at Two" asserts that one should have no more than two children, but also implies that one perhaps should have at least one or two. Some of the childless wives are superficially involved in ZPG and sympathetic with its goals, but in all cases this identification is an *ex post facto* consideration, rather than a motivating force, and their satisfaction with being childless is related to concerns other than their contributions to the population crisis.

It is sometimes suggested than an inclination to avoid motherhood is a logical extension of the new feminism. It is difficult to generalize about a social phenomenon as amorphous as the women's liberation movement, a rubric which incorporates many diverse and even contradictory attitudes. However, "A significant feature of the women's liberation movement is that, although its demands have been made on the basis of equity for women, it has not usually been anti-marriage or anti-children (Commission on Population Growth, 1972, p. 68).

In many instances, the ideological statements endorsed by the women's liberation movement are implicitly or explicitly pro-natalist. Motherhood is not perceived as an unfulfilling and unrewarding experience; rather, it is perceived as a positive experience which, although desirable, is not sufficient in and of itself for maximum self-actualization. Considerable concern is expressed with the problems involved in combining successful motherhood with comparable success in other careers. Rather than advising women to give up having children, the new feminist literature advised them to consider other careers in addition to motherhood, and advocates changes in society which would make the motherhood role easier. For example, there is considerable stress on the provision of maternity leaves, on increased involvement of fathers in childcare, on accessibility to adequate day care facilities. Although advocates of the new feminism may provide some support for the idea that motherhood is neither necessary nor sufficient for fulfillment, they do still advocate that normally it will be an important part of that fulfillment. Only a few of the voluntarily childless are at all concerned with women's liberation, and these few apparently came into the movement after their decision was made and their life style was established.

Although none of the voluntarily childless are actively seeking group support for their life style, many would welcome the opportunity to become involved in a truly supportive social movement. The first example of such an association is the National Organization for Nonparenthood (NON) which was formed in California in 1971. Because of the state of pluralistic ignorance which surrounds voluntary childlessness, and because of the inadequacy of demographic and feminist movements in expressing the world view of the childless, such attempts to formulate a counter culture might be expected to be very successful.

Summary

The present research on a purposive sample of 52 voluntarily childless wives is exploratory in nature. Although it is not possible to make definitive statements regarding the nature of childless couples, several tentative conclusions are offered. It is suggested that couples come to be voluntarily childless by a number of diverse paths beginning both before and after marriage, and that considerable diversity might be expected between those who enter marriage only on the condition of a clear childlessness clause in the marriage contract, and those who remain childless after a series of postponements of parenthood. Although considerable social pressures are directed towards the childless, most of the individuals involved appear to be very well defended against such sanctions, and the mechanisms of redefining situations and of protecting themselves are worthy of further study. One such mechanism appears to be the use of the possibility of adoption to deny the status of voluntary childlessness while not seriously threatening the accompanying life style. Finally, it is suggested that existing social movements do not provide much relevant support for the voluntarily childless, and that an explicit counter culture, such as the National Organization for Nonparenthood, might be expected to meet with considerable success.

References

Commission on Population Growth and the American Future, *Report.* Washington, D.C.: Commission on Population Growth and the American Future, 1972.

Cuber, John F., and Peggy B. Harroff. *Sex and the Significant Americans: A Study of Sexual Behavior among the Affluent.* Baltimore: Penguin, 1966.

Gustavus, Susan O., and James R. Henly, Jr. "Correlates of Voluntary Childlessness in a Select Population." *Social Biology,* 18 (September 1971): 277–284.

Pohlman, Edward. "Childlessness: Intentional and Unintentional." *The Journal of Nervous and Mental Disease,* 151 (1970), no. 1: 2–12.

Veevers, J. E. "Voluntary Childlessness: A Neglected Area of Family Study." *The Family Coordinator,* 21 (April 1972).

Veevers, J. E. "Factors in the Incidence of Childlessness in Canada: An Analysis of Census Data." *Social Biology.* 19 (December 1972).

Veevers, J. E. "The Violation of Fertility Mores: Voluntary Childlessness as Deviant Behavior." In *Deviant Behavior and Societal Reaction,* edited by Craig L. Boydell, Carl F. Grindstaff, and Paul C. Whitehead, pp. 571–592. Toronto: Holt, Rinehart and Winston, 1972.

Veevers, J. E. "The Moral Career of Voluntarily Childless Wives: Notes on the Construction and Defense of a Deviant World View." In *Marriage and the Family in Canada,* edited by S. Parvez Wakil. Toronto: Longmans Green, 1973.

Veevers, J. E. "The Social Meanings of Parenthood." *Psychiatry: Journal for the Study of Interpersonal Processes,* forthcoming.

Whelpton, Pascal K., Arthur A. Campbell, and J. E. Patterson. *Fertility and Family Planning in the United States.* Princeton: Princeton University Press, 1966.

The Single Parent and Public Policy

Alvin L. Schorr and Phyllis Moen

The divorce rate in the United States is at an all time high; we are commonly said to have the highest divorce rate in the world. One result of this has been a striking increase in female-headed families; the number of divorced women heading families nearly tripled between 1960 and 1975 alone.[1] As a result, the number of children living in one-parent families increased by 60 percent in the last decade.[2] A number of quite different forces have contributed to these changes—the increased propensity of mothers without husbands to form separate families, women's increased labor force participation, and the spread of no-fault divorce.

From *Social Policy,* 9:5 (March/April 1979), pp. 15–21. Copyright 1979 by Social Policy Corporation. Reprinted by permission of the publisher, Social Policy Corporation, New York, N.Y. 10036.

Despite these changes, somewhere in their minds Americans still tend to hold a conventional view of the family as having two parents and two or three children. This conventional version of the family is so powerful that scholars, like citizens, label other family forms pejoratively—as "deviant," "broken," or "unstable."[3] Indeed, single parents label themselves as unique and "abnormal."[4] Nor are conventional views quite repudiated by minorities and the poor. On the contrary, while in some neighborhoods or subcultures half or more of all children live in single-parent families, their parents regard their single status as demonstrably normal on one hand and as evidence of failure and delinquency on the other.

Meanwhile, the traditional family—husband, wife, and children from the first marriage of the spouses—accounts for only 45 percent of American families.[5] The next most frequent types are the single-parent family (15 percent) and the nuclear-dyad—husband and wife alone without children (15 percent).

By the age of eighteen, nearly one out of two children will have lived a period of time with a single parent.[6] Meanwhile, the number of husband-wife families has begun to decline. At any moment in time, 25 to 30 percent of all children are in one-parent families.[7] The gap between the public image of the single-parent family and reality cannot be laid to a new situation we have not had time to recognize. It may be stipulated that conditions are changing, but they have been changing for a long time, and there was extensive foreshadowing of current patterns. There have, for hundreds of years, been single-parent families and considerable variation in family form, including the three-generation family, the commune, and the nuclear family. Early death of the father combined with an extended span of child-bearing has made the single-parent family fairly common in the twentieth century.[8]

The view that the single-parent family is unique and deviant has other elements bound up in it. Single parenthood is seen as a transitional state. For example, four out of five divorced and widowed persons remarry. Nevertheless, past the age of 30, a greater proportion remain single,[9] and the tendency to remarry appears now to be declining.[10] A recent longitudinal study of unmarried women who headed households found that fewer than one-fifth had married in a five-year period.[11] Single-parent families may live "as if" in a permanent state, whatever their futures may hold, though policy-makers may see their status as transitional.

Pathology is a prominent element of the public view of single parenthood. Although the term has come to be associated with the "Moynihan controversy" of 1965, in truth professionals and social agencies have long regarded single parenthood as pathological for reasons arising from their own backgrounds.[12] "Trained in the clinical model, [they] are conditioned to recognize pathology. While some attention in professional education may be given to preventive care and normal growth and development, the overriding emphasis is on the successful treatment and reversal of problems."[13] Against the background of this public image of single parenthood, policy has been couched in terms of improving the stability of existing intact families and services have been designed to facilitate the reconstitution of families.

Public discussion of the single-parent family in the last decade or two has come to overlap considerably with a discussion of Black family life and welfare. Consequently, the mainstream reality of single-parent families is hidden. A larger proportion of Black families than white families have single parents, 35 percent compared with 11 percent. For reasons that are all but obvious— single-parent families are usually headed by one wage-earner who is usually a woman and likely to earn less than a man—single-parent families are likely to rely on welfare. Still, a third of the women-headed, single-parent families never receive welfare.[14] The stereotype that recipients have simply resigned themselves to welfare has no relation to fact. Of seven million mothers who received welfare over a ten-year period, the typical woman was assisted for two years, left welfare, and eventually received it for two years more. Only 770,000 received welfare for nine or ten years.[15]

Generalizing inevitably leaves an impression of uniformity but the situation of single-parent families varies considerably. For example, single fathers may be in a markedly different position from single mothers. Though still a small minority, single fatherhood is increasing at a faster rate than families headed by women.[16] In part, this reflects changes in courtroom attitude toward custody, but also changing conceptions of the roles of men and women. As women have sought to define identities apart from that of wife and mother, so too have more men seen themselves in roles other than wage-earner.[17]

The most prominent difference is that single fathers command higher incomes. The average income of single mothers in 1973 was $6,000, compared to $12,000 for single fathers.[18] Though a single father's income may more easily permit him to buy housekeeping services, recent studies show that he too usually performs housekeeping duties—helped by his children.[19] Still, many of the stereotypes that constrain women also confine men. Since child care is not seen as their role, it is difficult for fathers to adjust their working hours to meet the needs of their children.[20] Although they report a need for services— child care in the evening, transportation to day care, and so forth —single fathers express feelings of success and satisfaction about parenting; in this they are like single mothers.[21]

Widows with children are a significantly different group from the divorced and separated. Less than a fifth are under 35 (compared with 55 percent of divorced and separated women with children). Possibly for that reason and because they usually receive Social Security benefits, their total income is substantially higher.[22] On the average, Black single-parent families are different from white. Black single mothers are twice as likely to have three children or more—30 out of 100 compared with 15 out of 100 for white single mothers. Black single parents are less likely than white to be working; they have higher unemployment rates, lower educational levels, and higher rates of poverty.[23]

One may attempt to classify single parents logically—as widowed, divorced, separated, and unmarried.[24] Such a distinction directs attention to the rather different causes and feelings that may be at play for the families. For example, death may be a more sudden and final blow. Separation may be a stage on the road to divorce. The unmarried mother faces more stigma, though possibly this is changing a little. She is likely to be younger than the others, and her financial difficulties even more serious. Unmarried mothers are becoming increasingly consequential, as one birth in seven in the United States is now illegitimate.[25]

In whatever ways they differ, however, all single parents suffer from public images of the ideal family.

Parenthood, Work, and Income

Closely linked to the image of the traditional two-parent family is an ideological stance concerning the proper division of labor within the family. Specifically, the male is thought of as the head of the household—the "breadwinner" of the family. Weitzman speaks of the "hidden contract" of marriage: 1) that the husband is the head of the household and responsible for economic support and 2) that the wife is responsible for child care.[26] Consequences of this role differentiation by sex are profound for women in general and especially painful for single mothers. Because women are viewed as marginal workers, they are given marginal jobs—low paying, low status, and insecure.[27]

Most of the wage differentials between men and women arise either from the smaller amount of labor market experience attained by women or from discrimination against women. The former arises directly from the hidden contract or the sexist assignment of roles. Discrimination arises indirectly and directly from the image of the male as provider.[28]

Because women earn 40 percent less than men, on the average, in every occupational category,[29] it is not surprising that in general the most important single determinant of a change in family economic well-being appears to be a change in family composition.[30] With divorce, the economic status of women relative to need goes down while that of men apparently goes up.[31] Three out of five poor children are in single-parent families.

One cannot explore single parenthood and work for women without becoming aware that work affects marital status and vice versa. More divorced than married women work and more work full time at every educational level.[32] Most divorced and separated mothers work a full year; others work less than a full year only because they have been laid off.[33] Conversely, the better a husband provides, the less likely is divorce.[34] Separation rates are twice as high among families where the husband experiences serious unemployment, suggesting that it is not the amount of income alone but its stability that is part of a decision to remain married or separate.[35] Studies of women's earnings produce quite consistent findings. As more women work, some postpone marriage and fewer get married in total.[36] Other things being equal, the higher a wife's earnings, the more likely that a couple will separate.[37] In short, a man's income tends to cement a marriage and a woman's tends to make dissolution possible.

It is important to remember that the amount of income alone does not equal financial security. For example, a study of women who had been divorced for up to two years found every woman saying that despite reduced income the family was better off financially. The researcher suggests that stability and control may have been more important than amount. Respondents said such things as, "I don't have much money to spend, but at least it's regular," and "Now I can buy things for the children."[38]

In any event, the problems concerning work for women are general and rooted in social arrangements broader than single parenthood. They have special impact for single parents but cannot be dealt with within that framework, nor avoided simply if single parenthood could be avoided.

Structured for time and commitment, jobs leave no more time for domestic activities to the mother than to the father. Hours are inflexible and long; few part-time jobs pay enough to support a family. Unless informal care is at hand, adequate, reliable, and inexpensive child care is rarely available. And institutions and businesses operate on the assumption that there are two parents, one of them free to carry on transactions during the day. As we noted the combined effect of working and mothering at once upon the income of single mothers, we now note the strain working creates for housekeeping and parenting. (The problem is felt by married mothers as well; half of them are employed.) If the parenting of single parents may suffer, part of the reason is that, like many mothers with husbands, they work outside the home.

A critical aspect for single parent and dual-worker families is that children are likely to be cared for by persons other than their parents. Implicit in the public image of poor parenting is the belief that small children spend their time in over-crowded institutional settings.[39] The fact is otherwise: Nine out of ten preschool children with working mothers spend their time in informal settings —with relatives, neighbors, or friends. Nor is that because congregate care is scarce, though to be sure it is. Single parents, poor parents, and welfare parents, like middle-class parents who live together, prefer informal care both because it appears to be better and is more practical.[40] As to congregate care, research reveals no effect on intellectual development but possible difficulty in emotional and social development. Studies have generally failed to distinguish between good and poor congregate care though and it is possible that studies of good care would produce different findings.[41] There is no body of research on the effects of informal care.

A modern view regards substitute care as a supplement to maternal care rather than as a substitute for it.[42] A considerable argument can be made for such a development as moderating the "hothouse" aspect of the mother and child bond and "shifting back towards a more natural *i.e., less confined and intense* way of life for both women and children"[43] Seen in this light, conflict is no longer so sharply drawn between maternal and substitute care. The questions about substitute care are no longer categorical: Is substitute care intrinsically a good or bad idea? What qualities are required in substitute care? What duration optimum? And so forth.

Single parents do, of course, face special circumstances. An asset in the two-parent home is the presence of another adult to provide consultation and support with respect to children.[44] "Parents . . . need to have other voices joined with theirs in transmitting values and maturity demands to their children."[45]Single parents may have no one to provide emotional support. The sense of failure which separation may have provoked may readily lead—without adult company and support—to feelings of isolation.[46] A British study reports these feelings as the main personal problem of single parents.[47] Conversely, children with single parents have access to fewer adults and tend to emphasize peer relationships.[48]

The presence or absence of both parents *per se* makes little difference in the adequacy of child-rearing[49] or the socialization of children.[50]There is no evidence that the absence of a father from the home has an effect on the child's sense of sex identity.[51] Single mothers hold the same values for their children as mothers with husbands.[52] A series of studies over the years has found more delinquency in unhappy intact homes than in single-parent ones.[53] In their famous study, Glueck and Glueck found the quality of maternal supervision more important for delinquency than the presence or absence of a man.[54] "What scientific evidence there is suggests that divorce is often better (or at least less harmful) for children than an unhappy conflict-ridden marriage."[55]

What can one make of all this? Do strain and the absence of one parent or another not alter child-rearing noticeably and adversely? Perhaps the key point with respect to parenting is that the choice of the parents and children does not lie between a sound marriage and single parenthood. Happy couples rarely separate. The choice for many children lies between an unhappy home and a single parent. Parents themselves—though they commonly worry about the effects of a divorce on their children[56]—with experience come to think they have done well by them.[57]

To be sure, some children from single-parent homes pay a penalty, and curiously they may suffer more from maternal than paternal absence, since a single mother without family, friends or the money to purchase help often must deprive a child of her [58] company and attention; that is the deprivation the child feels most keenly.[58] This is consistent with the British finding that damage to school attainment and social adjustment, when they are observed, result from poverty rather than single parenthood itself.[59]

One final effect of single parenthood is relevant. Today, a higher proportion of children under five are living with only their mothers than ever before.[60] The number of children in institutions and in substitute families is declining.

One reason is that children are remaining with single parents.[61] For children, single parenthood is an alternative not only to a two-parent family but to no family at all.

Of a sample of single mothers with preschool children, 72 percent had "a moderate or severe distress problem compared to 46 percent of 'married' mothers."[62] While this study shows the disadvantage of single-parent families, it is surely more important that half of the intact families have the same problem. If one starts with that as the basic issue, one can understand the reason why young mothers may feel exhaustion and depression and how single parenthood may add to the problem.[63] But the problem becomes general and not solely one of single parenthood. It is within that context that one must ask how society is to help single-parent families.

Public Image and Public Policy

The core of the argument here is that single-parent families are misrepresented to the public and to themselves. They have special problems and they may benefit from special institutional supports, but that is true of any number of groups otherwise regarded as normal and acceptable. The unemployed, veterans, and widows are examples at one end of the alphabet while single-parent families are statistically and historically in the American mainstream.

Yet the image is itself a powerful policy. The most moving effect of misrepresentation is that many single parents believe what is said of them and add that belief to the problems they face. Separation and divorce are a troubled if not stormy period and so the people involved are vulnerable. While separation is part of every married person's at least occasional speculation, and the actual event a crystal around which fantasies cling, the people involved usually blame themselves, adding normality to their worries about financial responsibility, judgment, concern about children, sexual responsibility, and self-worth. The stereotypes involved are about as legitimate as most that are involved in discriminatory behavior—and as destructive.

It is apparent that changing the image would imply broad changes in government, employment, and other policies. Conversely, such policies are potent in maintaining or altering the image. Each set of policy issues requires extensive exploration not possible here. An examination of these issues indicates the powerful and pervasive influence of the current image in our social arrangements.

If one sees women as normal and regular wage-earners, issues of sex discrimination in wages and occupational opportunity must be faced. Both work at home with children and at outside occupations must permit more flexibility. On one hand are questions of aids for child-care and homemaking, and also the operating assumption that shopping and transactions with physicians and utilities can be carried on in the middle of the day. The spread of single parenthood creates a demand that has moved some businesses to expanded hours, but professions and public utilities seem less sensitive. On the other hand are questions of the structuring of work and careers, the scheduling of employment, the feasibility of shared work, and the growth of part-time work.

Issues in income maintenance policy are similarly complex. The financial problem of the working poor, much debated in the last few years, is from another perspective an issue of single parenthood and minimum wages. That is, a single year-round minimum wage does not provide enough income to keep four people (a couple and two children, a single parent and three children, a grandmother, her daughter, and two children) out of poverty. Most industrial countries have tried to meet this problem by relatively small payments for all children. Americans have preferred to regard the issue as a welfare policy problem, seeing low-paid working people pitted against separated or unmarried women—though often enough they are the same people. If we see these two groups as sharing a problem rather than competing, the solution of a small subsidy for children to which other Western countries have come may seem appealing. The Earned Income Credit, recently introduced into the federal income tax, would, if improved in level and expanded to all children, serve quite well.

In implementation, policies that favor two-parent families are likely to operate to the disadvantage of single-parent families. For example, a woman with children might receive a higher payment from welfare compared with the family's entitlement if the husband were present. Obviously, the family needs more if the husband is not there. On the other hand, making equivalent payments to two-parent families would present costs that are impossible in the real world of limited resources. The result is commonly a smaller payment to the single-parent family than even the amount thought minimally necessary. Regarding this issue, Isabel Sawhill has proposed an attempt to "define a neutral policy—that is one which would neither encourage [nor] discourage various kinds of family behavior such as marriage or child-bearing." She concludes that considerations such as equity and need make a quite neutral system unlikely.[64] Nevertheless, seeking a system that neither rewards nor penalizes family structure would open negotiation about program design in a way that might portend progress.* But it would be difficult to work at designing neutral programs while talking the language of a policy partisan to intact families.

Another direction to go in income maintenance, more special to single parenthood, is to recognize separation and divorce as social risks similar to the risk of being widowed. There have been proposals to establish a program of "fatherless child insurance"—or "single-parent insurance"—along lines well

*As an example of recent confusion, in pressing their welfare reforms Presidents Nixon and Carter both said that welfare encourages family breakup. If the observation is accurate, which is doubtful despite the chorus to the contrary, both sets of proposals would still have provided an incentive to separation. That is, they would have allowed more income in total to a separated husband and mother with children than to the intact family.

understood in Social Security. As single parenthood is voluntary, when compared with being widowed, careful design is required but appears to be feasible.[65] In one conception, such programs may be taken as supplementing income that would otherwise be inadequate. In another conception, one may argue that it is sound and constructive for one of the single parents to remain in the traditional role of homemaker, and not to work. The same programs providing "income by right," with possibly larger payments, would enable them to do this.[66] More conservatively and more limited, it has been argued that even if income is not provided, at least the government should provide credit towards Social Security for the work implicit in homemaking.[67]

The issue of parental support of children when there is marital separation is not, by any means, simply a welfare issue. "The primary purpose of child support laws is the protection of the public purse,"[68] but with respect to non-welfare families, the primary issue is one of family law. Courts and administrative agencies are likely to be more lenient in securing support than the law might seem to require. Each state has a welfare standard, a non-welfare standard or understanding, the understanding that will really be enforced, and the agreements that result from the pressures and evasive tactics that husband and wife can bring to bear. There is no general social contract to which courts, agencies, or couples (if they wish to avoid dispute or exploitation of one another) can refer. In this absence of public agreement, as always, the weakest and poorest suffer most.

A Change in Outlook

In this field, the development of a reasonable set of ideas that might lead to consensus would be a giant step for single "mankind." It is a difficult problem, for it involves reconciling concepts as old as common law with twentieth century reality; and balancing the rights and needs of a wage earner and, chances are, the wage earner's new family against those of the family that is being left; all in a context in which everyone's standard of living is at risk of declining.

The delivery of social services contains its own complex set of issues. Counsellors, for example, need to approach giving help in terms of managing the transition from a marital to a post-marital way of life.[69] Underlying this is professional acceptance that marital separation is a normal transition, a statement that may sound disarmingly simple but requires a profound change in professional point of view. Similarly, if single parenthood is regarded as a normal way of life, practical aids and supports must assume a degree of importance they have possibly not been accorded by social agencies. Day care for children has received a good deal of public attention; we have noted that the single-parent family seems to prefer and have good practical reason for using informal and neighborhood arrangements rather than the congregate care that has been extensively discussed. Beyond this, service organizations attentive to their clients should help them to secure reasonable aid or arrangements from employers, public schools, hospitals, and other institutions. Once again, a more profound change in posture is implied than may have been indicated at first.

With or without the aid of established organizations, it would be constructive to see self-generated groups of single parents organize. In the nature of single parenthood, individuals tend to move in and out of such groups. Nevertheless, they provide a means for sharing experience, moderating the sense of loneliness from which single parents may suffer, and reinforcing their sense of self-esteem. Under certain circumstances such groups can exercise broad influence in securing the social changes that may be important.[70]

Employment, income maintenance, child support, and social services present relatively self-evident issues, but when we grasp the broad changes that have swept over us, other issues will also appear. For example, it seems possible that single parents are living in housing designed for other times. That is, the basic design of apartments and houses was long since established for large families and other two-parent families. While the basic design has been modified to suit smaller families and new construction methods and to meet exigencies of cost and financing, those modifications have been mechanical, not functional—that is, fewer bedrooms, room sizes scaled down, and rooms devoted to certain functions (the dining room, the kitchen) in some cases made rudimentary. However, housing is not designed for one-parent family living. Preparing food and dining may be a unitary activity and more significant for single parents than for others; it may be that a single larger room would serve them better than the conventional kitchen and dining room. Again, it may be that two combination bedroom-work (or play) rooms would serve a parent and child better than the conventional two bedrooms and a living room.[71] Such issues will not be raised until we think of single parenthood as normal rather than marginal. Then designs may be worked out, money ventured, and the judgment of the market cast.

A good deal more thought is required about the issues related to single parents. This discussion is simply intended to indicate how issues change focus if one views single parenthood as a normal and permanent feature of our social landscape.

Notes

1. Allyson Sherman Grossman, "The Labor Force Patterns of Divorced and Separated Women," *Monthly Labor Review* 16 (1977) p. 50.
2. Isabel Sawhill, Gerald E. Peabody, Carol Jones, and Steven Caldwell, *Income Transfers and Family Structure* (Washington, D.C.: The Urban Institute, 1975).
3. Ruth Brandwein, Carol Brown, and Elizabeth Maury Fox, "Women and Children Last: The Social Situation of Divorced Mothers and Their Families," *Journal of Marriage and the Family* 36 (1974), pp. 488–489.
4. William J. Goode, "Economic Factors and Marital Stability," *American Sociological Review* 16 (1951); Robert S. Weiss, *Marital Separation* (New York: Basic Books, 1975).

5. Marvin B. Sussman, "Family Systems in the 1970s: Analysis, Policies and Programs," *The Annals of the American Academy* 396 (July 1971), p. 38.
6. Martin Rein and Lee Rainwater, *The Welfare Class and Welfare* (Cambridge, Mass.: Joint Center for Urban Studies, 1977); Mary Jo Bane, "Marital Disruption and the lives of Children," *Journal of Social Issues* 32, no. 1 (1976), pp. 103–109.
7. Bane, *ibid.*
8. Tamara Hareven, "Family Time and Historical Time," *Daedalus* (Spring 1977), pp. 57–70.
9. Hugh Carter and Paul C. Glick, *Marriage and Divorce: A Social and Economic Study* (Cambridge: Harvard University Press, 1970); Paul C. Glick, "A Demographer Looks at American Families," *Journal of Marriage and the Family* 15 (1975), p. 26.
10. A. J. Norton and P. C. Glick, "Marital Instability: Past, Present and Future," *Journal of Social Issues* 32, no. 1 (1976), pp. 5–19.
11. Greg J. Duncan, "Unmarried Heads of Households and Marriage," in Greg J. Duncan and James N. Morgan (eds.) *Five Thousand American Families—Patterns of Economic Progress* (Ann Arbor, Mich.: Institute for Social Research, 1977).
12. Daniel P. Moynihan, *The Negro Family: The Case for National Action* (Washington, D.C.: U.S. Department of Labor, 1965).
13. Robert Moroney, *The Family and the State: Considerations for Social Play* (London: Longman, 1976).
14. Lee Rainwater, *Welfare and Working Mothers* (Cambridge, Mass.: Joint Center for Urban Studies, 1977).
15. Rein and Rainwater, *op. cit.*
16. Dennis K. Orthner, Terry Brown, and Dennis Ferguson, "Single-Parent Fatherhood: An Emerging Family Life Style," *The Family Coordinator* (October 1976), pp. 429–437.
17. Danile D. Molinoff, "Life With Father," *New York Times Magazine* (May 22, 1977), p. 13.
18. Isabel V. Sawhill, "Discrimination and Poverty Among Women Who Head Families," *Signs* no. 1–3 (1976), pp. 201–221.
19. Brandwein, *op. cit.*; Orthner et al., *op. cit.*; Gassner and Taylor, *op. cit.*
20. James Levine, *Who Will Raise the Children? New Options for Fathers (and Mothers)* (Philadelphia: J.B. Lippincott, 1976).
21. Orthner, *op. cit.*; Gasser and Taylor, *op. cit.*
22. Lucy B. Mallan, "Young Widows and Their Children: A Comparative Report," *Social Security Bulletin* (May 1975).
23. J. Brubacher and W. Rudy, *Higher Education in Transition: A History of American Colleges and Universities,* 1636–1968 (New York: Harper and Row, 1968), pp. 13–14.
24. Benjamin Schlesinger, *The One-Parent Family: Perspectives and Annotated Bibliography* (Toronto: University of Toronto, 1975).
25. Reynolds Farley and Suzanne Bianchi, "Demographic Aspects of Family Structure Among Blacks: A Look at Data a Decade After the Moynihan Report." Paper presented at the American Sociological Association; Chicago, Illinois; 1971.
26. L. J. Weitzman, "To Love, Honor, and Obey: Traditional Legal Marriage and Alternative Family Forms," *The Family Coordinator* 24 (1975).
27. Edward Gross, "Plus ça Change?: The Sexual Structure of Occupations Over Time," *Social Problems* 16 (1968), pp. 198–208.
28. Erik Gronseth, "The Breadwinner Trap," in *The Future of the Family* (New York: Simon and Schuster, 1972), pp. 175–191; Erik Gronseth, "The Husband-Provider Role: A Critical Appraisal," in Andree Michel (ed.), *Family Issues of Employed Women in Europe and America* (Leiden: E.J. Brill, 1971).
29. U.S. Department of Labor, *The Earnings Gap Between Women and Men* (Washington, D.C.: U.S. Government Printing Office, 1976).
30. Greg J. Duncan and James W. Morgan, *Five Thousand American Families—Patterns of Economic Progress,* vol. V (Ann Arbor: Institute of Social Research, 1977).
31. Saul Hoffman and John Holmes, "Husbands, Wives and Divorce," in Greg J. Duncan and James N. Morgan (eds.), *Five Thousand American Families—Patterns of Economic Progress,* vol. IV (Ann Arbor: Institute for Social Research, 1976).
32. Grossman, *op. cit.*
33. *Ibid* and Beverly Johnson McEaddy, "Women Who Head Families: A Socioeconomic Analysis," *Monthly Labor Review* (June 1976).
34. Carter and Glick, *op. cit.*; Goode, *op. cit.*

35. Heather Ross and Isabel Sawhill, *Time of Transition: The Growth of Families Headed by Women* (Washington, D.C.: The Urban Institute, 1975).
36. S. G. Johnson, "The Impact of Women's Liberation on Marriage, Divorce, and Family Life-Style," In C. B. Lloyd (ed.), *Sex Discrimination and the Division of Labor* (New York: Columbia University Press); F. B. Santos, "The Economics of Marital Status," in C. Lloyd (ed.), *Sex Discrimination and Division of Labor* (New York: Columbia University Press).
37. Sawhill, *op. cit.*
38. Goode, *op. cit.*
39. Alice S. Rossi, "A Biosocial Perspective on Parenting," *Daedalus* (Spring 1977).
40. Suzanne H. Woolsey, "Pied Piper Politics and the Child Care Debate." *Daedalus* (Spring 1977), pp. 127–146; Arthur C. Emlen and Joseph B. Perry, "Child-Care Arrangements," in Hoffman and Nye (eds.), *Working Mothers* (San Francisco: Jossey-Bass, 1974).
41. Urie Bronfenbrenner, "Research on the Effects of Daycare on Child Development," in *Toward a National Policy for Children and Families* (Washington, D.C.: National Academy of Sciences, 1976).
42. B. Caldwell, "Infant Day Care—The Outcasts Gain Respectability," in P. Roby (ed.), *Child Care—Who Cares? Foreign and Domestic Infant and Early Childhood Development Policies* (New York: Basic Books, 1973).
43. Alice S. Rossi, "A Biosocial Perspective on Parenting," *Daedalus* (Spring 1977).
44. Ruth Brandwein, Carol Brown, and Elizabeth Maury Fox "Women and Children Last: The Social Situation of Divorced Mothers and Their Families," *Journal of Marriage and the Family* 36 (1974), pp. 488–489.
45. Eleanor E. Maccoby, "Current Changes in the Family and Their Impact Upon the Socialization of Children." Paper presented at the American Sociological Association Meeting, 1977.
46. Maccoby, *op. cit.*; Weiss, *op. cit.*
47. Benjamin Schlesinger, "One-Parent Families in Great Britain," *The Family Coordinator* 26 (1977), pp. 139–141.
48. John C. Condry and M. A. Simon, "Characteristics of Peer and Adult-Oriented Children," *Journal of Marriage and the Family* 36 (1974), pp. 543–554.
49. Reuben Hill, "Social Stress on the Family," in Marvin Sussman (ed.), *Sourcebook in Marriage and the Family* (Boston: Houghton Mifflin, 1968).
50. Jane K. Burgess. "The Single-Parent Family: A Social and Sociological Problem," *The Family Coordinator* 9 (1970), pp. 137–144.
51. Maccoby, *op. cit.*
52. Louis Kriesberg, *Mothers in Poverty* (Chicago: Aldine, 1970).
53. Lee Burchinal, "Characteristics of Adolescents from Unbroken Homes and Reconstituted Families," *Journal of Marriage and the Family* 26 (1964), pp. 44–51; Judson Landis, "The Trauma of Children When Parents Divorce," *Marriage and Family Living* 22 (1960), pp. 7–13; F. Ivan Nye, "Child Adjustment in Broken and in Unhappy Unbroken Homes," *Marriage and Family Living* 19 (1957), pp. 356–361.
54. Sheldon Glueck and Eleanor Glueck, *Family Environment and Delinquency* (Boston: Houghton Mifflin, 1962).
55. Kenneth Kenniston, *All Our Children* (Carnegie Council on Children, 1977); and *Toward a National Policy for Children and Families* (Washington, D.C.: National Academy of Sciences, 1976).
56. William J. Goode, *Women in Divorce* (New York: Free Press, 1956); Dennis Marsden, *Mothers Alone: Poverty and the Fatherless Family* (London: Penguin, 1969).
57. C. A. Brown, R. Feldberg, E. M. Fox, and J. Kohen, "Divorce: Chance of a New Lifetime," *Journal of Social Issues* 32 (1976), pp. 119–132.
58. Brandwein et al., *op. cit.*
59. Elsa Ferri, "Growing-Up in a One-Parent Family," *Concern* 20 (1976), pp. 7–10; Schlesinger, *op. cit.*
60. Farley and Bianchi, *op. cit.*
61. Ross and Sawhill, *op. cit.*
62. Peter Moss and Ian Plewis, "Mental Distress in Mothers of Pre-School Children in Inner London." Undated paper from the Tomas Coram Research Unit, University of London.
63. Alison Clarke-Stewart, *Child Care in the Family: A Review of Research and Some Propositions for Policy* (New York: Academic Press, 1977); J. A. Clausen and S. R. Clausen, "The Effect of Family Size on Parents and Children," in J. T. Fawcett (ed.), *Psychological Perspectives on*

Population (New York: Key Book Services, 1972); N. Richman, "Depression in Mothers of Pre-School Children," *Journal of Child Psychology and Psychiatry* 17 (1976); Rossi, *op. cit.*

64. Sawhill, 1977, *op. cit.*

65. Irvin Garfinkel, "Testimony on Welfare Reform to State Senate Human Services Committee," in Madison, Wisconsin; August 15 and 16, 1978.

66. Heather Ross, "Poverty: Women and Children Last," in Jane Roberts Chapman and Margaret Gates (eds.), *Economic Independence for Women: The Foundation for Equal Rights* (Beverly Hills: Russell Sage, 1976).

67. "Working America." A report of a special task force to the Secretary of Health, Education, and Welfare (Cambridge: MIT Press, 1973).

68. James Kent, *Commentaries on American Law,* vol. 2 (New York: Da Capo, 1826).

69. Weiss, *op. cit.*

70. Michael J. Smith and Beth Moses, "Social Welfare Agencies and Social Reform Movements: The Case of the Single-Parent Family" (Community Service Society of New York, 1976).

71. Thelma Stackhouse, "Housing for One-Parent Families—Faddism or Favorable Options" (Community Service Society of New York, August 1975).

Accommodation of Work to Family

Lotte Bailyn

Every employed person is faced with the task of defining the relationship between work and family in his or her life. If one is single, without children or dependent parents to care for, this task seems relatively easy. But even in this situation the seeming ease is somewhat deceptive. Single people are very dependent on non-institutionalized relations with friends and community, and employers have sometimes found, contrary to what one might expect, that they are *less* likely than those who are married to accept geographical relocation. The complications are generally greater, however, for working couples, where each partner must resolve this issue in a way that is congruent with the other's commitments. This joint resolution is a crucial life-task for working couples, and it is the ways in which this task is accomplished that forms the focus for this chapter.

Let us define accommodation as the degree to which work demands are fitted into family requirements. Then the way each person integrates work and family in his or her life may be described by the extent to which this integration is accommodative. The extreme points of this dimension are represented by individuals who integrate family and work requirements by focusing primarily on one or the other of these areas. The highly career-committed male executive, for instance, who follows the demands of his job wherever they take him, is an example of an almost exclusive focus on work. In contrast, the wife and

From pp. 159–174 in *Working Couples,* edited by Robert and Rhona Rapoport with Janice Bumstead. Harper Colophon Books. Copyright © 1978 by Robert and Rhona Rapoport. Reprinted by permission of Harper & Row, Publishers, Inc.

mother in a relatively traditional family situation, who, even when she works, is guided by family needs rather than by job requirements, is typical of someone whose primary focus is on family. The male executive is the most non-accommodative, the traditionally minded female who makes her outside interests secondary, the most accommodative. Both entail potential difficulties: the executive may find himself totally detached from his family and unable to communicate with them; the accommodative mother may not be able to give enough commitment to her work to perform effectively and get satisfaction from it. Both may be deprived of a fair and optimal chance at self-realization.

Traditional patterns have tended to approximate these extremes. The husband in our society has traditionally been minimally accommodative to family needs: his primary commitment has been to his work. And though the fruits of his labor provide for the physical needs of his family, his decisions about how best to link the family to the economy have characteristically been based solely on the requirements of his work, and have ignored the more subtle, psychological needs of his wife and children. Organizational policies have reinforced this non-accommodative stance by selectively rewarding those employees who demonstrate such a primary commitment to their work. Traditional wives' roles have been necessarily complementary: they have had to be fully accommodative, placing primary emphasis on the family. Any outside work they might do has had to be adjusted to fit this primary commitment.

But times are changing. Most of us now accept the legitimacy of women's participation in the world of work and their less accommodative orientation. And women themselves, even if their outside work was initially motivated solely by financial need, have discovered that some expression of personal competence and mastery outside the family setting often enhances their sense of well being (Barnett and Baruch, 1976). For some, of course, having to work is an indication of failure in their family situations. But when the conditions at work are right, many find that employment gives them a better opportunity to get out of themselves and to feel that they have some autonomy than the family, which may be too demanding to allow for the satisfaction of this need.

Analogously, one can find accommodative men, particularly in the middle years. These are men who resolve any potential conflict between their work and family links by re-evaluating work requirements and strengthening ties to family and community. But here, too, there are different bases for such accommodation. For some it represents the expression of a basic value: a commitment to a multi-dimensional approach to life. There are *successful* managers, for example, who at mid-career choose to reject career advancement open to them because the additional work responsibilities would entail sacrifices of family and personal involvements to which they are committed (Rapoport, 1970; Beckhard, 1972). For others, in contrast, accommodation is a response to unfulfilled expectations at work: to positions not attained and achievements not realized (Evans, 1974; Faulkner, 1974). In this case, accommodation carries with it some of the negative consequences associated with failure (cf. Bailyn, 1977).

In general, there are forces today that are decreasing the likelihood that deviation from traditional roles will be associated with a sense of failure (Albrecht and Gift, 1975). The hazards of excessive career involvement ('work-aholism') are being documented; concern about equal opportunity for women in the work force is putting pressure on organizational policies that only reward non-accommodation; and more young couples are starting out their adult lives committed to an equitable relationship between them, where each has equal opportunity for occupational and family involvements (Van Maanen *et al.*, 1977; Tarnowieski, 1973; *Work in America,* 1973).

But even in a world in which options are opening up, the working couple is faced with the difficult task of managing a system based on three links, which each respond to different external and internal pressures: the *wife's work link,* the *husband's work link* and the *family link.* Each link, further, consists of a complex of elements. Work links include, at a minimum, one's orientation to the content of what one is doing, one's reaction to the organization where one is employed, and one's relations with the people with whom one works: peers, supervisors and subordinates. The family link, similarly, encompasses many different relations, including those with one's spouse, one's children and parents, and with the community in which one lives. Somehow these complex links must all be simultaneously joined in a consistent pattern. In considering accommodation in some detail, I hope to throw light on the patterns that can be forged from these three links, and on the consequences they have for the lives of working couples.

Patterns of Accommodation

Each individual couple will, of course, find its own unique interrelation of these three links. But certain principles underlying these various patterns can be abstracted for analysis.[1]

A basic distinction relates to the way in which responsibilities are allocated. Some patterns are based on the principle that *responsibility for work and family is differentially distributed* between the partners. Such patterns are based on a specialization of function: though both partners maintain both family and work links, each person has primary responsibility for only one area; one is more accommodative, the other more non-accommodative. Another set of patterns, in contrast, is based on a principle of *equal sharing of responsibilities* for work and family. In such patterns, both partners have equal commitment to and responsibility for each area. Some couples who follow the principle of equal sharing of responsibilities may be quite accommodative, others may be more non-accommodative. But wherever they fall on the dimension of accom-modation, the essence of such patterns is that husband and wife have the same orientation to the relation between work and family in their lives.

This distinction should not be confused with ways of describing conjugal relations according to the division of labor in performing family tasks or in making family decisions. Differentiation and equal sharing as used here refer to the relation between paid work outside the home and care and maintenance tasks within it, and the emphasis is on taking responsibility for an area, not only on task performance. Even a 'companionship' marriage, in which 'husband and wife shared both power and tasks' (Gold and Slater, 1958, p. 67) is not necessarily based on equal sharing of responsibility for both work and family.

Patterns Based on Differentiated Responsibility

The essence of differentiated patterns is that one partner has primary responsibility for the family link and the other for his or her work link. They differ, however, from the traditional family in two important ways: first, they refer to working couples, in which both partners are in fact involved in both work and family and thus exclude the traditional situation where the wife's work link does not exist at all. Second, the decision as to which partner takes primary responsibility for which area is assumed to be based on individual negotiation and not made automatically on the basis of traditional expectations. Many of us can today point to examples of couples in which the wife's career is dominant and the husband is the more accommodative partner. And though this is not likely soon to become the modal pattern for working couples, it is differentiated in the same way as the more common case in which the wife, though committed to her work, retains a primary responsibility for the family.

The advantages of differentiation are clear. By building into the lives of working couples a hierarchy of commitments and responsibilities for each partner, the intensity of potential conflict is reduced. The process of decision-making is eased by having such built-in guidelines. Decisions ranging from the everyday (such as who stays home when a child has a cold) to the more far-reaching (where to live, for instance, and what jobs to accept) are easier to handle.

Such clarity in everyday life is very appealing. The trouble is that consequences of decisions guided by such differentiation are often irreversible. And since neither work nor family situations are static, a pattern that has worked for many years may, as one gets past mid-life, produce a sense of loss and deprivation in one or the other partner. The work-oriented or non-accommodative partner may wonder whether it was all worth while and may feel alienated from the family at a time when meaningful personal ties take on great importance. Or, the family-oriented partner may suffer from the greater work success or satisfactions of other people (particularly, perhaps, the spouse) resulting not from any differences in ability and interest, but based merely on a forced reduction in total commitment to work (see, e.g., Bailyn, 1964). Though such consequences are less likely to be disturbing if real differences guide the initial allocation—differences in age, or in abilities, or in temperament—differentiated patterns, which are one-sided by definition, entail these risks.

Patterns Based On Equally Shared Responsibilities

In patterns based on the principle of equal sharing, both partners have the same commitment to each area and share equally the responsibilities of each. This situation represents the ideal lifestyle for many young couples, who embark on their adult lives in a more equalitarian atmosphere than was true even a decade or so ago. Such 'symmetrical' patterns, where there are 'no monopolies for either sex in any sphere,' are increasingly visible (Young and Willmott, 1973, p. 275) and have been shown to be associated with an increased enjoyment of activities by both husband and wife, particularly the latter (Rapoport et al., 1974). They are supported also by analysts who feel that a meaningful and satisfactory life in a complicated world necessitates fully androgynous sex-roles (Rossi, 1964; Rowe, 1974). But the principle of equal sharing, because it does not provide the guidelines implicit in differentiation, requires more attention, more energy to make it work. In general, it confronts the working couple with a more complex situation. Its potential rewards are high, but the difficulties of implementation cannot be ignored.

Without some way of reducing complexity, patterns based on equal sharing may produce, particularly at certain stages of life, a serious condition of overload (cf. Rapoport and Rapoport, 1976).[2] Such a stage is likely to be reached in the late 20s or early 30s—often near the seven-year 'danger' point in a marriage (Chilman, 1968). Both families and work careers go through identifiable stages, which vary according to the degree of involvement they require. The difficulty at this vulnerable point in life stems from the fact that stresses in both cycles characteristically peak then: both seem to require maximum attention (Wilensky, 1961; Troll, 1975). Sociologically and biologically this is the optimal time to have young children, hence family demands are maximal. It is also the time in their employees' lives when employing organizations tend to make decisions about future placement, decisions at least partially based on the degree of involvement and commitment to work demonstrated by the employee. 'I live two lives,' one male teacher in his early 30s explained; 'one is professional and one is as a family man. The two lives are neither mutually exclusive nor fully compatible. . . . The main problem . . . is to establish a healthy balance between the two lives in order not to sacrifice my family life *now* to build for a better family life in the future. The other half of the conflict is, of course, not to sacrifice my career opportunities *now*. . . .' And if the wife is also working, the task of establishing a 'healthy balance' is even more complicated.

How can a working couple reduce the complexity of a pattern based on the principle of equal sharing, particularly at such a vulnerable stage? Three general strategies are available. The first is perhaps the most obvious: *limitation* of both partners' involvement in one or the other area. Which area is chosen will depend, primarily, on how accommodative the couple is. Couples who believe in the principle of equal sharing and tend to be non-accommodative find it useful to lessen the family demands on them by having no children, or only one child. In contrast, if the couple tends to be accommodative, they lower their career aspirations and intentionally step off the fastest promotion tracks. Both decisions, of course, may have irreversible, lifetime consequences, but by being taken jointly and shared equally, they are less likely to become sources of deep regret or acrimony. Certain environmental supports, more-over, which are increasingly seen, also help limit the demands of each area. Day-care centers and housing developments with shared central facilities in-troduce in a new context some of the advantages of the extended family. And on the work side, there are flexible time schedules, reduced time requirements and shared jobs.

A second approach to reducing complexity might be called *recycling:* a shift in the staging of work and family events (Rapoport and Rapoport, 1976; Strober, 1975). This too is a strategy that combines individual decisions and external forces. Its main effect is to reduce the likelihood that periods of maximum demands in the family and work areas overlap. Medical advances in diagnosing and treating prenatal abnormalities and wide use of adoptions —both of which allow families to have children at a later stage than is now deemed optimal—help couples shift the periods of peak demands in the family cycle. Analogously, the increasing incidence of successful 'seconds careers' (Sheppard, 1971; Sarason *et al.,* 1975) shows that periods of maximum work involvement can fruitfully be postponed to later stages in one's life. Organiza-tions, of course, will have to stop considering age a legitimate ground for employment discrimination if such recycling options are to be widely available. But age stereotypes that constrain flexibility in employment patterns are al-ready being challenged: by the necessity to retrain employees of all ages because of technological change; by the entrance of older women into the labor market. Ideally, the strategy of recycling allows one to make up at a later stage in life the limitations one imposed earlier. And though limitations once im-posed can never be fully recovered, by balancing the consequences for the two areas, this strategy is particularly useful for couples whose orientation is near the middle of the accommodation scale.

A final strategy to reduce complexity introduces *segmentation* into each partner's life by strengthening the boundaries between family and work: by compartmentalizing each area so that one does not have to deal with family and work issues at the same time. This strategy seems, at first, counter-intuitive, as it has been seen as a shortcoming of our comtemporary society to have such a degree of segregation between work and family life. However, by allowing one to express one's commitment to each area sequentially instead of simultaneously, it eases the strain of equal-sharing patterns. Leaving one's work at the office is the day-to-day expression of this strategy. Work concerns are attended to in one place during one period of time; at home, in contrast, during the rest of the day, family needs take absolute priority. Geographical separations, including long-distance commuting, which have been described in other chapters in this book (chapters 7 and 10), often emerge, unexpectedly, as mechanisms for allowing one of the partners to concentrate completely on work for one period of time, for instance during the week, and revert to total immersion in the family the rest of the time, as on weekends. Another innovative expression of this strategy is to apply it to a lifetime. This is not new to women, of course; indeed, sequential involvements were for many years deemed optimal for working wives and mothers. What is new is to apply this strategy to *both* partners of a working couple. Paternity leaves are a social innovation that begins to make such life planning possible.

Whatever the time frame, however, the essence of this strategy is to reduce complexity by strictly segmenting work concerns from family concerns.[3] A comparison of two occupations—the college teacher and the engineer in industry—will emphasize the point. College teaching is often assumed to be an ideal occupation for one or both partners in an 'equal-sharing' family. Formal responsibilities are minimal: daily time schedules have great flexibility, the location of work is often immaterial, there are long periods with no formal duties at all. How much easier to mesh such a work schedule with a working spouse than that of the engineer who has to be away from home every day from at least nine to five, 50 weeks of the year. Of course there is truth in this, but an important fact is often overlooked. The engineer, despite the rigid time schedule, can segment work and family concerns, whereas the college teacher finds this much more difficult. Academic norms put heavy pressure on a professor to keep up with a field, to do research, to write, often to consult—activities that are much harder to segment than the formal requirements of a job. And, indeed, research in America has shown that the permeable boundary between work and family that exists in the academic profession tends to outweigh the advantage of flexible schedules: male professors in the USA are considerably less accommodative than male engineers (Bailyn and Schein, 1976).

The above strategies indicate some of the ways working couples can reduce the complexity of patterns based on equal sharing of responsibilities. But there is still another issue, that goes beyond complexity: such patterns maximize the potential conflict between the work links of the two partners because they are based on the principle that these two links are given equal weight. This kind of conflict is much less likely to occur in differentiated patterns, where the two work links are ordered into a hierarchy of importance.

One way of dealing with this potential conflict is for the couple to participate in a *joint venture,* thus reducing the two work links to one.[4] Obviously such an approach is only possible if both partners do the same or highly complementary kinds of work, though some joint ventures—such as small family businesses—require such general input that a wide variety of couples can participate. This is an intriguing way of eliminating potential conflict between the work links because it is the only one where achievements at work are truly additive, where both partners can limit their aspirations and involvements with work and yet both reap the benefits of career success. Despite this appealing quality, however, there are also drawbacks. Most obvious is the fact that the two partners' skills and interests may not mesh in the requisite way. Moreover, joint ventures require a degree of intimacy and lack of personal competitiveness that is beyond the capacity of some people. Finally, it is more difficult, in a joint venture, to reduce complexity by segmenting work and family concerns. When Bertrand Russell and his wife started a school, for instance, it was a most successful venture for everyone except their own children, who evidently suffered from the lack of segmentation in their parents' lives (Tait, 1975). But even here inventive solutions are possible. I know one couple who in remodeling their home to house a business, specifically did not build an inner door to connect the two halves of the house. There were two entrances and one had to go outside and re-enter when moving between family residence and place of work.

Joint ventures, where feasible, can meet the needs of 'equal-sharing' couples, whether accommodative or non-accommodative. Other ways of dealing with the potential conflict between the two work links are more suited to either an accommodative or a non-accommodative orientation. Indeed, for very accommodative couples the whole issue of potential conflict between work links may never arise since all work decisions are made on the basis of the requirements of family. And though such couples may find it more difficult to meet their needs for accomplishment in the external world, the simplification of the issues involved in obvious.

An entirely different way of responding to the potential conflict between the partners' work links in patterns based on equal sharing is particularly suited to the needs of more non-accommodative or career-oriented couples. It is almost the exact opposite of the joint venture and rests on an *independent* relation by each partner to his or her work. In this approach, a favorite of young ambitious couples starting their joint lives at the same stages in their work careers, the decision is initially made not to resolve any conflicts between the work links, but to adapt to them. In other words, each partner follows his or her optimal career path and the couple adapts to the consequences that ensue. Full-time nannies, whether they come in the form of grandmothers, au pair girls or day-care supervisors, and long-distance commuting are examples of such adaptive mechanisms. Such a strategy capitalizes on the autonomy of each partner and is not likely to work well with people who are more dependent on others. Quite the contrary, it probably is most successful when used by those who have some difficulty in forming intimate relations. Indeed, from the findings on commuting couples (Ngai, 1974 and ch. 10), it seems that some of these marriages survive only because of the separation imposed by the commuting. Such marriages obviously are different from those that succeed on the basis of a full sharing of lives. But for the people involved they may represent a very satisfactory alternative to complete separation.

Thus, patterns based on equal sharing of responsibilities confront couples with a number of issues to be resolved. Two have been discussed here—level of complexity and potential conflict between the two work links—along with some of the strategies that can be used in dealing with them. Any of these patterns, whether based on differentiated or equally shared responsibilities, may be successful in providing each partner in a working couple with satisfactory family relations and with rewarding work. But the probability of success will be different for each depending on the personal characteristics of the partners (temperament, needs and abilities), the way in which these mesh with each other, and such other factors as family structure and the circumstances of work. The success of an 'equal-sharing' pattern, for example, depends on similarity of personal characteristics in the partners—at least on the major issue of how they balance the relation between work and family in their lives —whereas a differentiated pattern is likely to be more successful if these orientations are different, though complementary. Similarly, some patterns will fit better with some family structures than others. A couple pursuing an independent pattern based on equal sharing, for instance, will probably find life difficult if they try to have many children. Indeed, unless there is at least one fairly accommodative partner, the decision to have children at all, or more than one child, can lead to a serious condition of overload.

As to the constraints imposed by the requirements of work, we have already alluded to the fact that different occupations will fit better with certain patterns than with others. There is one general point, however, that must be made. The path to most higher positions in organizations—whether technical, professional or managerial—is premised on a career progression that primarily fits the life of a non-accommodative person—indeed, in some cases it actually requires the services of an accommodative spouse (Papanck, 1973). Though we now question the assumed 'naturalness' of this situation and some beginning has been made in loosening the organizational policies that propagate this assumption, it is a 'fact' of organizational life, as we know it today, that working couples cannot ignore. It is unlikely, for instance, that any of the highest occupational positions in our society will soon be held by an accommodative person. For anyone aspiring to such a position, therefore, the appropriate differentiated pattern is more likely to be successful than one based on equal sharing of responsibilities. Indeed, research has shown that even professionally trained wives of highly career-oriented husbands find it difficult to work in their professions (Bailyn, 1973), and if they do, the couple's marital satisfaction is likely to be low (Bailyn, 1970; Rapoport and Rapoport, 1976).

What this means is that though working couples have many options in organizing their lives, these options all involve costs. It is the understanding of what these costs are that may allow us to set in motion processes that will reduce or modify them in the future, and help us minimize the toll taken by uninformed life choices.

The Dynamics of Accommodation

All of this has so far been described in a fairly static way, as though the task of fitting the demands of work to family requirements were resolved once and for all at a single point in time. But accommodation is not, in fact, a static state. On the contrary, it reflects a continuing process of response to the changing demands of work and family and to the successes and failures experienced in each area.

Each adult, upon embarking on the twin tasks of starting a family and entering the world of work, has some idea of what he or she assumes the relation between work and family will be. This initial set of assumptions is based on the culture in which the person lives, on the example of the parents' pattern, and on some sense by each individual of important needs and abilities. Such an initial orientation may be more or less accommodative. When it is based on the assumption that life will revolve around family concerns, the person's career and family decisions, expectations and reactions to experience are guided by a highly accommodative orientation. At the other extreme, if one assumes that work will be the focus of one's life, one's orientation is very non-accommodative and one will make different decisions and have different expectations and different reactions to experiences. As long as these experiences are relatively congruent with the initial orientation, it is unlikely to be much modified. If, however, results turn out to be unsatisfactory or not to fit initial expectations, then a process of re-evaluation may be set in motion which will change the initial orientation.

Sometimes this initial orientation is primarily shaped by external pressure: by society or parental models. If a person's own capacities, needs and interests are not accurately reflected in such a 'stereotyped' orientation, dissatisfaction is likely to result. A woman who remains a housewife because she assumes that that is what she ought to do, even though her talents go in very different directions, is likely sooner or later to suffer from this discrepancy between her initial orientation and her talents. She may find that a re-evaluation toward a more non-accommodative orientation will lead her to seek employment outside of the house and result in a more satisfactory life for her and her family. Or, a man who works very hard to become president of his company because his father is a successful business man and expects it of him, may discover that successive promotions do not bring the satisfactions he anticipated. He may realize that his needs are not met by rising in an organization's hierarchy and may find that a redirection toward a more family-centered lifestyle provides more meaningful rewards for him. In both these examples, a re-evaluation is set in motion because of a discrepancy between an initial orientation based on externally imposed role expectations and what might be called a person's 'real' self.

But even if an initial orientation is consonant in essential aspects with a person's 'real' self, discrepancies may arise. The most general pressure toward re-evaluation stems from the failure of primary expectations. Frequently these are 'disconfirmed' expectations, but re-evaluations can also be stimulated when initial expectations are exceeded. A middle manager, for instance, who receives an unexpected series of new job challenges is likely to become very work-oriented; one who fails to receive a desired promotion is likely to become more oriented to his family (Evans, 1974). Similarly, a symphony player who fails to achieve a desired seat in a top orchestra learns to value the slower-paced life provided by the community orchestra in which he is employed (Faulkner, 1974).

Whenever there is a discrepancy between primary expectations and actual experiences, a pressure for change is built up. New orientations that respond to this pressure are likely to be based on a more realistic understanding of the circumstances in which one lives, and hence more likely to lead to satisfaction with one's life. Sometimes, of course, circumstances can be overwhelming. But occasionally even such traumatic events as the loss of a job or the death of a spouse can force a re-evaluation which in the long run will lead to a more satisfactory fit between one's orientation and the circumstances of one's life.

At other times, however, a change in life circumstances or in basic values may transform a good fit between orientation and experience into a discrepancy. In fact, any major discontinuities in one's life may make a re-evaluation of initial orientations necessary. Thus, a group of happy, family-centered, 30-year-old women were found to be maladjusted at 70 when their children had left home and were inaccessible; in contrast, a group of unsatisfied 30-year-old housewives who changed their basic orientation and became 'work centered' were found, at 70, to be very contented (Maas and Kuypers, 1974).

Personalities vary, of course, in their capacity to react constructively, and sometimes no re-evaluation occurs despite very great discrepancies between orientations and life experiences. This may happen when a person's investment in the initial orientation is so strong—for reasons probably related to the early development of the personality—that change is seen as impossible. An example might be the man who continues to work hard and long, ignoring most other aspects of life, despite the fact that he no longer gets any enjoyment or sense of accomplishment from his work; or the woman who finds life empty after her children are gone, but is unable to reorient herself to activities outside the home. Such unresolved discrepancies between orientations and experiences may on occasion lead to depression or to other symptoms of distress such as alcoholism (cf. McClelland et al., 1972; Wilsnack, 1972).[5]

There are also external constraints to change. Most organizations, for instance, put pressure on their employees to stay highly involved in their work, and feel that something is wrong if they become very accommodative. But as long as not all the work that must be done is intrinsically challenging, and as long as organizations must find a place for their 'plateaued' employees (Goode, 1967), such secondary accommodation may actually be more beneficial than disruptive to the enterprise as a whole (Bailyn, 1977). Indeed, we know that it cuts down on employee turnover (Getchell, 1975).

More important to the concerns of this paper, however, is the impact of a change in orientation on a *couple's* pattern of adaptation. What happens when one partner changes and the other doesn't, or when both change but in opposite directions? Although we do not know very much about this yet, it seems that some of the satisfactions of the later years stem from the fact that reduced demands from work and family permit couples to share their lives more equally (Deutscher, 1964). Thus a change by one partner of a differentiated couple in a direction of the other one is likely to be adaptive. Sometimes, though, there is a criss-crossing of previous orientations (Gutmann, 1973; Lowenthal *et al.,* 1975): the accommodative partner becomes so non-accommodative and the non-accommodative one so accommodative, that a reversed differentiated pattern may result.

There is also, of course, the possibility of radical change. The second career, for instance, may require relocation and certainly requires re-establishment. Though sometimes this takes the form of a joint venture and therefore does not lead to direct conflict with the spouse's work link, some re-adaptation between the partners will always be necessary. Even more disruptive to established couple patterns are the re-evaluations that sever the family link entirely. Divorce at all stages—even after decades of living together—is becoming more prevalent (Glick and Norton, 1973), and we are only beginning to understand how men and women in different circumstances adapt to it (see, e.g., Weiss, 1975). It is interesting, however, that some analysts see divorce as the 'chance of a new lifetime' for mothers (Brown *et al.*, 1976), and others suggest that divorce (severing the *family link*), as a response to an unmanageable situation, is no more extreme than the severance of the *wife's work link,* which happens when a competent and committed professional wife resumes the traditional family role when she has a child (Holmstrom, 1972).

Obviously, there is much still to be learned about these dynamics. Some couples' patterns will change during the course of life-development, others not, depending on the experiences encountered and the capacity of the partners to adapt to new circumstances. Clearly the goal is neither change nor stability for its own sake, but change or stability in order to achieve a workable resolution of family and work demands for each partner that meshes well with the needs of the other.

All indications point to an increase in the number of working couples in the future. As more people attempt to work out the problems of such double careers they will exert pressure on employing organizations to reconsider some of the policies that now restrain available options. But the complications introduced by superimposing two work links on the family link will remain. And though innovative resolutions will emerge in dealing with different degrees of accommodation in the partners, the potentially successful combinations are not limitless. It is not possible for both partners in a working couple to do everything. Some choices will always be necessary: regarding work, perhaps; or family; or both. Let us hope that the continuing study of the situation faced by working couples will enable them to make these life choices more rationally. The more accurately the reality of their situation is perceived, the more likely it is that their chosen lifestyle will be successful.

Notes

1. Detailed accounts of the lives of working couples are available in Rapoport and Rapoport (1976), Holmstrom (1972), Lein *et al.* (1974).
2. Bebbington (1973) points out that the stress involved in these patterns may replace, and be preferable to, stress stemming from an unsatisfactory resolution of conflict between desired and actual roles by one of the partners of a dual-working couple.
3. Pleck (1975) points out that the boundary between work and family is 'differentially permeable' for men and women. Segmentation, therefore, requires that men stop the spillover of work into familiy areas, and women and the spillover from family to work.
4. Some of the issues involved in such joint ventures are examined by Epstein (1971) in her investigation of husband-wife law partnerships and by Rapoport and Rapoport (1976, pp. 95–150) in their discussion of a husband-wife partnership in architecture.
5. Turner (1971) offers the intriguing hypothesis that since external constraints to divorce are decreased in dual-career households (particularly those patterned on a principle of equal sharing), personal and individual compatibilities are more determining of marital stability or dissolution in these cases. This hypothesis gets support from an analysis of couples in communal households, where external constraints to divorce are even less (Jaffe and Kanter, 1976).

Bibliography

Albrecht, G. L., and Gift, H. C. (1975), 'Adult socialization: ambiguity and adult life crises,' in N. Datan and L. H. Ginsberg (eds), *Life-span Developmental Psychology: Normative Life Crises,* New York: Academic Press.

Bailyn, L. (1964), 'Notes on the role of choice in the psychology of professional women,' *Daedalus,* 93, pp. 700–10.

Bailyn, L. (1970), 'Career and family orientations of husbands and wives in relation to marital happiness,' *Human Relations,* 23, pp. 97–113.

Bailyn, L. (1973), 'Family constraints on women's work,' *Annals of the New York Academy of Sciences,* 208, pp. 82–90.

Bailyn, L. (1977), 'Involvement and accommodation in technical careers: An inquiry into the relation to work at mid-career,' in J. Van Maanen (ed.), *Organizational Careers: Some New Perspectives,* London: Wiley.

Bailyn, L. and Schein, E. H. (1976), 'Life/career considerations as indicators of quality of employment,' in A. D. Biderman and T. F. Drury (eds), *Measuring Work Quality for Social Reporting,* New York: Halsted.

Barnett, R. C., and Baruch, G. K. (1976), 'Women in the middle years: A critique of research and theory,' Radcliffe Institute.

Bebbington, A. C. (1973), 'The function of stress in the establishment of the dual-career family,' *Journal of Marriage and Family,* 35, pp. 530–37.

Beckhard, R. (1972), 'The executive you're counting on may be ready to mutiny,' *Innovation,* May, pp. 3–10.

Brown, C. A., Feldberg, R., Fox, E. M., and Kohen, J. (1976), 'Divorce: Chance of a new lifetime,' *Journal of Social Issues,* 32, pp. 119–33.

Chilman, C. S. (1968), 'Families in development at mid-stage of the family life cycle,' *Family Coordinator,* 172, pp. 297–310.

Deutscher, I. (1964), 'The quality of postparental life: Definitions of the situation,' *Journal of Marriage and Family,* 26, pp. 52–9.

Epstein, C. F. (1971), 'Law partners and marital partners,' *Human Relations,* 24, pp. 549–64.

Evans, P. A. L. (1974), 'The price of success: Accommodation to conflicting needs in managerial careers,' unpublished Doctoral Thesis, Sloan School of Management, M. I. T.

Faulkner, R.R. (1974), 'Coming of age in organizations: A comparative study of career contingencies and adult socialization,' *Sociology of Work and Occupations,* 1, pp. 131–73.

Getchell, E. (1975), 'Factors affecting employee loyalty,' unpublished Master's Thesis, Sloan School of Management, M.I.T.

Glick, P.C., and Norton, A.J. (1973), 'Perspectives on the recent upturn in divorce and remarriage,' *Demography,* 10, pp. 301–14.

Gold, M., and Slater, C. (1958), 'Office, factory, store—and family: A study of integration setting,' *American Sociological Review,* 23, pp. 64–74.

Goode, W.J. (1967), 'The protection of the inept,' *American Sociological Review,* 32, pp. 5–19.

Gutmann, D. (1973), 'Men, women, and the parental imperative,' *Commentary,* December, pp. 59–64.

Holmstrom, L.L. (1972), *The Two-Career Family,* Cambridge, Mass,: Schenkman.

Jaffe, D.T., and Kanter, R.M. (1976), 'Couple strains in communal households: A four-factor model of the separation process,' *Journal of Social Issues,* 32, pp. 169–91.

Lein, L., et al. (1974), *Final Report: Work and Family Life,* Cambridge, Mass.: Center for the study of Public Policy.

Lowenthal, M.F., Thurnher, M.P., and Chiriboga, D. (1975), *Four Stages of Life,* San Francisco: Jossey-Bass.

Maas, H.S., and Kuypers, J.A. (1974), *From Thirty to Seventy,* San Francisco: Jossey-Bass.

McClelland, D.C., Davis, W.N., Kalin, R., and Wanner, E. (1972), *The Drinking Man,* New York: Free Press.

Ngai, S.Y.A. (1974), 'Commuting as a solution to geographical long-distance limitation to career choices of two-career families,' unpublished Master's Thesis, Sloan School of Management, M.I.T.

Papanek, H. (1973), 'Men, women, and work: Reflections on the two-person career,' *American Journal of Sociology,* 78, pp. 852–72.

Pleck, J.H. (1975), 'Work and family roles: From sex-patterned segregation to integration,' paper presented at the meetings of the American Sociological Association, San Francisco, August.

Rapoport, R., and Rapoport, R.N. (1976), *Dual-Career Families Re-Examined,* London: Martin Robertson; New York: Harper & Row.

Rapoport, R., Rapoport, R.N., and Thiessen, V. (1974), 'Couple symmetry and enjoyment,' *Journal of Marriage and Family,* 36, pp. 588–91.

Rapoport, R.N. (1970), *Mid-Career Development: Research Perspectives on a Developmental Community for Senior Administrators,* London: Tavistock.

Rossi, A.S. (1964), 'Equality between the sexes: An immodest proposal,' *Daedalus,* 93, pp. 607–52.

Rowe, M.P. (1974), 'Prospects and patterns for men and women at work,' *Child Care Reprints IV,* Washington: Day Care and Child Development Council of America, pp. 91–118.

Sarason, S.B., Sarason, E.K., and Cowden, P. (1975), 'Aging and the nature of work,' *American Psychologist,* 30, pp. 584–92.

Sheppard, H.L. (1971), 'The emerging pattern of second careers,' *Vocational Guidance Quarterly,* 20, pp. 89–95.

Strober, M.H. (1975), 'Women and men in the world of work: Present and future,' paper presented at the Aspen Workshop on Women and Men: Changing Roles, Relationships and Perceptions, August.

Tait, K. (1975), *My Father Bertrand Russell,* New York: Harcourt Brace.

Tarnowieski, D. (1973), *The Changing Success Ethic,* New York: Amacom.

Troll, L.E. (1975), *Early and Middle Adulthood,* Monterey: Brooks/Cole.

Turner, C. (1971), 'Dual work households and marital dissolution,' *Human Relations,* 24, pp. 535–48.

Van Maanen, J., Schein, E.H. and Bailyn, L. (1977), 'The shape of things to come: A new perspective on organizational careers,' in L.W. Porter, E.E. Lawler and J.R. Hackman (eds), *Perspectives on Behavior in Organizations.* New York: McGraw-Hill.

Weiss, R.S. (1975), *Marital Separation,* New York: Basic Books.

Wilensky, H.L. (1961), 'Life Cycle, work situation, and participation in formal associations,' in R.W. Kleemeier (ed.), *Aging and Leisure,* New York: Oxford.

Wilsnack, S.C. (1972), 'Psychological factors in female drinking,' unpublished Doctoral Thesis, Department of Social Relations, Harvard.

Work in America (1973), Report of a Special Task Force to the Secretary of Health, Education, and Welfare, Cambridge, Mass.: M.I.T. Press.

Young, M., and Willmott, P. (1973), *The Symmetrical Family,* London: Routledge & Kegan Paul.